USERS' GUIDES
——TO THE——
MEDICAL
LITERATURE

Notice

Medicine is an ever-changing science. As new research and clinical experience broaden our knowledge, changes in treatment and drug therapy are required. The authors and the publisher of this work have checked with sources believed to be reliable in their efforts to provide information that is complete and generally in accord with the standards accepted at the time of publication. However, in view of the possibility of human error or changes in medical sciences, neither the authors nor the publisher nor any other party who has been involved in the preparation or publication of this work warrants that the information contained herein is in every respect accurate or complete, and they disclaim all responsibility for any errors or omissions or for the results obtained from use of the information contained in this work. Readers are encouraged to confirm the information contained herein with other sources. For example and in particular, readers are advised to check the product information sheet included in the package of each drug they plan to administer to be certain that the information contained in this work is accurate and that changes have not been made in the recommended dose or in the contraindications for administration. This recommendation is of particular importance in connection with new or infrequently used drugs.

USERS' GUIDES
—— TO THE ——
MEDICAL
LITERATURE

A MANUAL FOR
EVIDENCE-BASED CLINICAL PRACTICE

SECOND EDITION

The Evidence-Based Medicine Working Group

Editors

Gordon Guyatt, MD, MSc
Departments of Clinical Epidemiology
and Biostatistics and Medicine
Faculty of Health Sciences
McMaster University
Hamilton, Ontario, Canada

Drummond Rennie, MD
JAMA
Chicago, Illinois
Philip R. Lee Institute for Health Policy
Studies
University of California, San Francisco
San Francisco, California, USA

Maureen O. Meade, MD, FRCPC, MSc
Departments of Medicine and Clinical
Epidemiology and Biostatistics
Faculty of Health Sciences
McMaster University
Hamilton, Ontario, Canada

Deborah J. Cook, MD, MSc
Departments of Medicine and Clinical
Epidemiology and Biostatistics
Faculty of Health Sciences
McMaster University
Hamilton, Ontario, Canada

New York Chicago San Francisco Lisbon
London Madrid Mexico City Milan
New Delhi San Juan Seoul Singapore
Sydney Toronto

JAMAevidence

5 6 7 8 9 0 DOC/DOC 14 13 12 11

Set: ISBN 978-0-07-159034-1; MHID 0-07-159034-X
Book: ISBN 978-0-07-159036-5; MHID 0-07-159036-6
Pocket Cards: ISBN 978-0-07-160850-3; MHID 0-07-160850-8

JAMA and *Archives* Journals:
Editor in Chief: Catherine D. DeAngelis, MD, MPH
Executive Deputy Editor: Phil B. Fontanarosa, MD, MBA
Managing Deputy Editor: Annette Flanagin, RN, MA
Manuscript Editor: Cara Wallace

McGraw-Hill Professional:
This book was set in Minion and Zurich by Silverchair Science + Communications, Inc.
The editors were James F. Shanahan and Robert Pancotti.
The production supervisor was Philip Galea.
The illustration manager was Armen Ovsepyan.
Project management was provided by Peter Compitello, The Egerton Group, Ltd.
The cover designer was The Gazillion Group.
Cover photograph by Brand X Photography.
RR Donnelley was printer and binder.
This book is printed on acid-free paper.

Library of Congress Cataloging-in-Publication Data

Users' guides to the medical literature : a manual for evidence-based clinical practice / edited by Gordon Guyatt, Drummond Rennie, Maureen O. Meade, Deborah J. Cook—2nd ed.
    p. ; cm.
  Rev. ed. of: Users' guides to the medical literature : a manual for evidence-based clinical practice / edited by Gordon Guyatt, Drummond Rennie. c2002.
  Includes bibliographical references and index.
  ISBN-13: 978-0-07-159034-1 (pbk. : alk. paper)
  ISBN-10: 0-07-159034-X (pbk. : alk. paper)
  1. Evidence-based medicine–Handbooks, manuals, etc. 2. Clinical medicine–Handbooks, manuals, etc.
I. Guyatt, Gordon. II. Rennie, Drummond. III. Meade, Maureen O. IV. Cook, Deborah J.
  [DNLM: 1. Resource Guides. 2. Evidence-Based Medicine. 3. Decision Making. 4. Review Literature as Topic. WB 39 U845 2008]
  R723.7.U84 2008
  515—dc22   2007047778

To our students, in many countries, whose interest, passion, and probing questions made possible the development of the methods we use to communicate the concepts of evidence-based medicine.

GG, MOM, and DJC

To Deb, who has watched over and tended me while I have watched over and tended this wonderful group of authors, with gratitude for her love and her good humor.

DR

CONTENTS

Part A

The Foundations

Part B

Therapy

Part C

Harm (Observational Studies)

Part D

Diagnosis

Part E

Prognosis

Part F

Summarizing the Evidence

Part G

Moving From Evidence to Action

JAMAevidence

JAMAevidence: Using Evidence to Improve Care

Founded around the *Users' Guides to the Medical Literature* and *The Rational Clinical Examination: Evidence-Based Clinical Diagnosis*, JAMAevidence offers an invaluable online resource for learning, teaching, and practicing evidence-based medicine. Updated regularly, the site includes fully searchable content of the *Users' Guides to the Medical Literature* and *The Rational Clinical Examination* and features podcasts from the leading minds in EBM, interactive worksheets, question wizards, functional calculators, and a comprehensive collection of PowerPoint slides for educators and students.

www.JAMAevidence.com

Please visit the following Web site for information on subscription rates: www.mhprofessional.com/jama

Contributors

Elie A. Akl, MD, MPH
Department of Medicine
School of Medicine and Biomedical
  Sciences
University of Buffalo
Buffalo, New York, USA

Alexandra Barratt, MBBS, FAFPHM,
MPH, PhD
Department of Epidemiology
School of Public Health
University of Sydney
Sydney, New South Wales, Australia

Mohit Bhandari, MD, MSc, FRCSC
Departments of Surgery and Clinical
  Epidemiology and Biostatistics
McMaster University
Hamilton, Ontario, Canada

Jan Brozek, MA, PhD
Department of Medicine
Jagiellonian University School of
  Medicine
Krakow, Poland

Heiner C. Bucher, MD
Clinical Epidemiology
Basel Institute for Clinical Epidemiology
University Hospital Basel
Basel, Switzerland

Jason W. Busse, HBSc, MSc, DC
Department of Clinical Epidemiology
  and Biostatistics
McMaster University
Hamilton, Ontario, Canada

Daniel Capurro, MD
General Internal Medicine
Departamento de Medicina Interna
Pontificia Universidad Católica de
  Chile
Santiago, Chile

Deborah J. Cook, MD, MSc
Departments of Medicine and Clinical
  Epidemiology and Biostatistics
Faculty of Health Sciences
McMaster University
Hamilton, Ontario, Canada

Richard Cook, BSc, MMath, PhD
Department of Statistics and Actuarial
  Science
University of Waterloo
Waterloo, Ontario, Canada

Robert Cumming, MB BS, MPH, PhD,
FAFPHM
School of Public Health
Centre for Education and Research on
  Ageing
The University of Sydney
Sydney, New South Wales, Australia

J. Randall Curtis, MD, MPH
Department of Medicine
University of Washington School of
  Medicine
Seattle, Washington, USA

Antonio L. Dans, MD, MSc
College of Medicine
University of the Philippines
Manila, Philippines

Leonila F. Dans, MD, MSc
Departments of Pediatrics and Clinical
  Epidemiology
College of Medicine
University of the Philippines
Manila, Philippines

P. J. Devereaux, BSc, MD, PhD
Departments of Medicine and Clinical
  Epidemiology and Biostatistics
McMaster University
Hamilton, Ontario, Canada

Michael Drummond, MCom, DPhil
Centre for Health Economics
University of York
Heslington, York, UK

Pierre H. Durieux, MD, MPH
Santé Publique et Informatique
    Médicale
Université Paris Descartes—Ecole de
    Médecine
Paris, France
Hôpital Européen Georges Pompidou
Paris, France

**Mahmoud El Barbary, MD, MSc, PhD,
EDIC**
Critical Care Medicine
College of Medicine
King Saud Bin Abdulaziz University of
    Health Sciences
Riyadh, Saudi Arabia

Ignacio Ferreira-Gonzalez, MD
Cardiology Department
Vall d'Hebron Hospital
Barcelona, Spain

**Robbie Foy, MBChB, MSc, PhD,
MRCGP, MFPHM, DCH**
Centre for Health Services Research
Institute for Health and Society
Newcastle University
Newcastle upon Tyne, England, UK

Toshi A. Furukawa, MD, PhD
Department of Psychiatry and Cognitive-
    Behavioral Medicine
Nagoya City University Graduate
    School of Medical Sciences
Nagoya, Japan

**Amit Garg, MD, MA, PhD, FRCPC,
FACP**
Department of Clinical Epidemiology
    and Biostatistics
McMaster University
Hamilton, Ontario, Canada
Department of Medicine and
    Epidemiology
University of Western Ontario
London, Ontario, Canada
Division of Nephrology
London Health Sciences Centre
London, Ontario, Canada

Mita Giacomini, PhD
Department of Clinical Epidemiology
    and Biostatistics
McMaster University
Hamilton, Ontario, Canada

Paul Glasziou, MBBS, PhD
Department of Primary Care
University of Oxford
Old Road Campus
Oxford, England, UK

Ron Goeree, MA
Departments of Pathology and
    Clinical Epidemiology and
    Biostatistics
St. Joseph's Healthcare
McMaster University
Hamilton, Ontario, Canada

**Sir J. A. Muir Gray, CBE, DSc, MD,
FRCP, FRCPS(Glas)**
Institute of Health Sciences
UK National Screening Committee
University of Oxford
Oxford, England, UK

Lee Green, MD, MPH
Department of Family Medicine
University of Michigan Medical
    Center
Ann Arbor, Michigan, USA

Gordon Guyatt, MD, MSc
Departments of Clinical Epidemiology
and Biostatistics and Medicine
Faculty of Health Sciences
McMaster University
Hamilton, Ontario, Canada

Ted Haines, MD, MSc
Departments of Clinical Epidemiology
and Biostatistics and Occupational
Health Program
McMaster University
Hamilton, Ontario, Canada

Rose Hatala, MD, MSc, FRCPC
Department of Internal Medicine
University of British Columbia
Vancouver, British Columbia, Canada

Brian Haynes, MD, MSc, PhD
Department of Clinical Epidemiology
and Biostatistics
McMaster University
Hamilton, Ontario, Canada

**Nicholas Hicks, MA, BMBCh, FRCP,
FPH, MRCGP**
Public Health
Milton Keynes NHS Primary Care
Trust
Milton Keynes, England, UK

**Anne Holbrook, MD, PharmD, MSc,
FRCPC**
Department of Medicine
Division of Clinical Pharmacology and
Therapeutics
McMaster University
Hamilton, Ontario, Canada

Dereck Hunt, MD, MSc, FRCPC
Health Information Research Unit
Henderson General Hospital
Hamilton, Ontario, Canada

John P. A. Ioannidis, MD, PhD
Department of Hygiene and
Epidemiology
University of Ioannina School of
Medicine
Ioannina, Greece
Department of Medicine
Tufts University School of Medicine
Boston, Massachusetts, USA

Les Irwig, MBBCh, PhD
Screening and Test Evaluation Program
School of Public Health
University of Sydney
Sydney, New South Wales, Australia

Roman Jaeschke, MD, MSc
Department of Medicine
McMaster University
Hamilton, Ontario, Canada

Sheri A. Keitz, MD, PhD
Associate Dean for Faculty Diversity
and Development
Miller School of Medicine
University of Miami
Chief, Medical Service
Miami Veterans Administration
Healthcare System
Miami, Florida, USA

Deborah Korenstein, MD
Division of General Internal
Medicine
Department of Medicine
Mount Sinai School of Medicine
New York, New York, USA

Regina Kunz, MD, PhD
Basel Institute of Clinical
Epidemiology
University Hospital Basel
Basel, Switzerland

Christina Lacchetti, MHSc
Cancer Care Ontario
Program in Evidence-Based Care
McMaster University
Hamilton, Ontario, Canada

Luz Maria Letelier, MD
General Internal Medicine
Hospital Sótero del Río and School of
   Medicine
Pontificia Universidad Católica de
   Chile
Santiago, Chile

Mitchell Levine, MD, MSc
Centre for Evaluation of Medicines
St. Joseph's Healthcare
Hamilton, Ontario, Canada

Finlay A. McAlister, MD, MSc, FRCPC
Department of Medicine
University of Alberta
Edmonton, Alberta, Canada

Thomas G. McGinn, MD, MPH
Department of General Internal
   Medicine
Mount Sinai School of Medicine
New York, New York, USA

Ann McKibbon, MLS, PhD
Department of Clinical Epidemiology
   and Biostatistics
Health Information Research Unit
McMaster University
Hamilton, Ontario, Canada

Maureen O. Meade, MD, FRCPC, MSc
Departments of Medicine and Clinical
   Epidemiology and Biostatistics
Faculty of Health Sciences
McMaster University
Hamilton, Ontario, Canada

Solange Rivera Mercado, MD
Family Medicine Department
Universidad Católica de Chile
Santiago, Chile

**Paul Moayyedi, BSc, MB ChB, PhD,
MPH, FRCP, FRCPC, FACG, AGAF**
Department of Medicine
McMaster University
Hamilton, Ontario, Canada

Victor Montori, MD
Department of Medicine
Knowledge and Encounter Research
   Unit
Mayo Clinic and Foundation
Rochester, Minnesota, USA

Thomas Newman, MD, MPH
Departments of Epidemiology and
   Biostatistics, Pediatrics, and
   Laboratory Medicine
University of California, San Francisco
San Francisco, California, USA

Gaieta Permanyer-Miralda, MD
Research on Sanitary Services
Foundation Research Institute
Vall d'Hebron Hospital
Barcelona, Spain

Kameshwar Prasad, MD, DM, MMSc
Clinical Epidemiology Unit
All India Institute of Medical Sciences
New Delhi, India

Gabriel Rada, MD
Department of Internal Medicine
Hospital Sótero del Río
Pontificia Universidad Católica de Chile
Santiago, Chile

Angela Raffle, FFPH
Public Health
Bristol Primary Care Trust
Bristol, England, UK

Adrienne Randolph, MD, MSc
Department of Anesthesia, Perioperative and Pain Medicine
Children's Hospital Boston
Harvard Medical School
Boston, Massachusetts, USA

Drummond Rennie, MD
JAMA
Chicago, Illinois
Philip R. Lee Institute for Health Policy Studies
University of California, San Francisco
San Francisco, California, USA

Scott Richardson, MD
Department of Internal Medicine
Wright State University
Dayton, Ohio, USA

Holger J. Schünemann, MD
Department of Epidemiology
Italian National Cancer Institute Regina Elena
Rome, Italy
Departments of Medicine and Social and Preventive Medicine
State University of New York at Buffalo
Buffalo, New York, USA

Ian Stiell, MD, MSc, FRCPC
Department of Emergency Medicine
University of Ottawa
Ottawa, Ontario, Canada

Sharon Straus, MD
Department of Medicine
University of Calgary
Calgary, Alberta, Canada
Department of Medicine
University of Toronto
Toronto, Ontario, Canada

Gunn E. Vist, PhD
Section for Prevention and International Health
Norwegian Knowledge Centre for the Health Services
Oslo, Norway

Richard J. Wall, MD, MPH
Pulmonary and Critical Care Medicine
Valley Medical Center
Renton, Washington, USA

Stephen Walter, PhD
Department of Clinical Epidemiology and Biostatistics
McMaster University
Hamilton, Ontario, Canada

Mark C. Wilson, MD, MPH
Department of Internal Medicine
University of Iowa Hospitals and Clinics
Iowa City, Iowa, USA

Juan Wisnivesky, MD, MPH
Department of Medicine
Mount Sinai School of Medicine
New York, New York, USA

Peter Wyer, MD
Department of Medicine
Columbia University College of Physicians and Surgeons
New York, New York, USA

FOREWORD

When I was attending school in wartime Britain, staples of the curriculum, along with cold baths, mathematics, boiled cabbage, and long cross-country runs, were Latin and French. It was obvious that Latin was a theoretical exercise—the Romans were dead, after all. However, although France was clearly visible just across the Channel, for years it was either occupied or inaccessible, so learning the French language seemed just as impractical and theoretical an exercise. It was unthinkable to me and my teachers that I would ever put it to practical use—that French was a language to be spoken.

This is the relationship too many practitioners have with the medical literature—clearly visible but utterly inaccessible. We recognize that practice should be based on discoveries announced in the medical journals. But we also recognize that every few years the literature doubles in size, and every year we seem to have less time to weigh it,[1] so every day the task of taming the literature becomes more hopeless. The translation of those hundreds of thousands of articles into everyday practice appears to be an obscure task left to others. And as the literature becomes more inaccessible, so does the idea that the literature has any utility for a particular patient become more fanciful.

This book, now in its second edition, is designed to change all that. It's designed to make the clinician fluent in the language of the medical literature in all its forms. To free the clinician from practicing medicine by rote, by guesswork, and by their variably-integrated experience. To put a stop to clinicians being ambushed by drug company representatives, or by their patients, telling them of new therapies the clinicians are unable to evaluate. To end their dependence on out-of-date authority. To enable the practitioner to work from the patient and use the literature as a tool to solve the patient's problems. To provide the clinician access to what is relevant and the ability to assess its validity and whether it applies to a specific patient. In other words, to put the clinician in charge of the single most powerful resource in medicine.

The Users' Guides Series in *JAMA*

I have left it to Gordon Guyatt, MD, MSc, the moving force, principal editor, and most prolific coauthor of the "Users' Guides to the Medical Literature" series in *JAMA*, to describe the history of this series and of this book in the accompanying preface. But where did *JAMA* come into this story?

In the late 1980s, at the invitation of my friend David Sackett, MD, I visited his department at McMaster University to discuss a venture with *JAMA*—a series examining the evidence behind the clinical history and examination. After these discussions, a series of articles and systematic reviews was developed and, with the enthusiastic support of then *JAMA* editor in chief George Lundberg, MD, *JAMA* began publishing the Rational Clinical Examination series in 1992.[2] By that time, I had formed an excellent working relationship with the brilliant group at McMaster. Like their leader, Sackett, they tended to be iconoclastic, expert at working together and forming alliances with new and talented workers, and intellectually exacting. Like their leader, they delivered on their promises.

So, when I heard that they were thinking of updating the wonderful little series of Readers' Guides published in 1981 in the *Canadian Medical Association Journal*, I took advantage of this working relationship to urge them to update and expand the series for *JAMA*. Together with Sackett, and first with Andy Oxman, MD, and then with Gordon Guyatt taking the lead (when Oxman left to take a position in Oslo), the Users' Guides to the Medical Literature series was born. We began publishing articles in the series in *JAMA* in 1993.[3]

At the start, we thought we might have 8 or 10 articles, but the response from readers was so enthusiastic, and the variety of types of article in the literature so great, that 7 years later I still found myself receiving, sending for review, and editing new articles for the series. Just before the first edition of this book was published, Gordon Guyatt and I closed this series at 25, appearing as 33 separate journal articles.

The passage of years during the preparation of the original *JAMA* series and the publication of the first edition of this book had a particularly useful result. Some subjects that were scarcely discussed in the major medical journals in the early 1990s, but that had burgeoned years later, could receive the attention that had become their due. For instance, in 2000, *JAMA* published 2 users' guides[4,5] on how readers should approach reports of qualitative research in health care. To take another example, systematic reviews and meta-analyses, given a huge boost by the activities of the Cochrane Collaboration, had become prominent features of the literature. An article in the series,[6] first published in 1994, discusses how to use such studies. Another example would be the guide on electronic health information resources,[7] first published in 2000. Each of these users' guides has been reviewed and thoroughly updated for this second edition.

The Book

From the start, readers kept urging us to put the series together as a book. That had been our intention right from the start, but each new article delayed its implementation. How fortunate! When the original Readers' Guides appeared in the *CMAJ* in 1981, Gordon Guyatt's phrase "evidence-based medicine" had never been coined, and only a tiny proportion of health care workers possessed computers. The Internet did not exist and electronic publication was only a dream. In 1992, the Web—for practical purposes—had scarcely been invented, the dot-com bubble had not appeared, let alone burst, and the health professions were only beginning to become computer literate. But at the end of the 1990s, when Guyatt and I approached my colleagues at *JAMA* with the idea of publishing not merely the standard printed book but also Web-based and CD-ROM formats of the book, they were immediately receptive. Putting the latter part into practice has been the notable achievement of Rob Hayward, MD, of the Centre for Health Evidence of the University of Alberta.

The science and art of evidence-based medicine, which this book does so much to reinforce, has developed remarkably during the past 2 decades, and this is reflected in every page of this book. Encouraged by the immediate success of the first edition of the *Users' Guides*, Gordon Guyatt and the Evidence-Based Medicine Working Group have once again brought each chapter up to date for this second edition. They have also added 7 entirely new chapters: Randomized Trials Stopped Early for Benefit, Making Sense of Variability in Study Results, Composite

Endpoints, Dealing With Misleading Presentations of Clinical Trial Results, Spectrum Bias, Changing Behavior to Apply Best Evidence in Practice, and finally Teachers' Guides to the *Users' Guides.*

An updated Web version of the *Users' Guides to the Medical Literature* will accompany the new edition, building upon the excellent work completed by Rob Hayward and his colleagues at the Centre for Health Evidence, University of Alberta, Edmonton. As part of a new online educational resource entitled JAMAevidence, the second edition of the *Users' Guides* online will be intertwined online with the first edition of the *Rational Clinical Examination: Evidence-Based Clinical Diagnosis.* Together they will serve as the cornerstones of a comprehensive online educational resource for teaching and learning evidence-based medicine. Interactive calculators and worksheets will provide practical complements to the content, while downloadable PowerPoint presentations will serve as invaluable resources for instructors. Finally, podcast presentations will bring the foremost minds behind evidence-based medicine to medical students, residents, and faculty around the world.

Once again, I thank Gordon Guyatt for being an inspired author, a master organizer, and a wonderful teacher, colleague, and friend. I know personally and greatly admire a good number of his colleagues in the Evidence-Based Medicine Working Group, but it would be invidious to name them, given the huge collective effort this has entailed. This is an enterprise that came about only because of the strenuous efforts of many individuals. On the *JAMA* side, I must thank Annette Flanagin, RN, MA, a wonderfully efficient, creative, and diplomatic colleague at *JAMA.* I also wish to thank Barry Bowlus, Joanne Spatz, Margaret Winker, MD, and Richard Newman of the *JAMA* and *Archives* Journals, who have made important contributions. In addition, I acknowledge the efforts of our partners at McGraw-Hill Medical—James Shanahan, Robert Pancotti, Scott Grillo, and Helen Parr.

Finally, I thank Cathy DeAngelis, MD, MPH, editor in chief of the *JAMA* and *Archives* Journals, for her strong backing of me, my colleagues, and this project; for her tolerance; and for keeping up everyone's spirits with her dreadful jokes. Throughout, Cathy has guided the project forward with wisdom, humor, and understanding, and we are all grateful.

Drummond Rennie, MD

JAMA

University of California, San Francisco

References

1. Durack DT. The weight of medical knowledge. *N Engl J Med.* 1978;298(14):773-775.

2. Sackett DL, Rennie D. The science of the art of the clinical examination. *JAMA.* 1992;267(19):2650-2652.

3. Guyatt GH, Rennie D. Users' guides to the medical literature. *JAMA.* 1993;270 (17):2096-2097.

4. Giacomini MK, Cook DJ; Evidence-Based Medicine Working Group. Users' guides to the medical literature, XXIII: qualitative research in health care A: are the results of the study valid? *JAMA*. 2000;284(3):357-362.

5. Giacomini MK, Cook DJ; Evidence-Based Medicine Working Group. Users' guides to the medical literature, XXIII: qualitative research in health care B: what are the results and how do they help me care for my patients? *JAMA*. 2000;284(4):478-482.

6. Oxman AD, Cook DJ, Guyatt GH; Evidence-Based Medicine Working Group. Users' guides to the medical literature, VI: how to use an overview. *JAMA*. 1994;272(17):1367-1371.

7. Hunt DL, Jaeschke R, McKibbon KA; Evidence-Based Medicine Working Group. Users' guides to the medical literature, XXI: using electronic health information resources in evidence-based practice. *JAMA*. 2000;283(14):1875-1879.

PREFACE

In fewer than 20 years, evidence-based medicine (EBM) has gone from a tentative name of a fledgling concept to the fundamental basis for clinical practice that is used worldwide. The first history of the movement has already appeared in the form of an authoritative book.[1] This second edition of *Users' Guides to the Medical Literature* reflects that history and the evolving conceptual and pedagogic basis of the EBM movement.

In 1981, a group of clinical epidemiologists at McMaster University, led by Dave Sackett, published the first of a series of articles advising clinicians how to read clinical journals.[2] Although a huge step forward, the series had its limitations. After teaching what they then called "critical appraisal" for a number of years, the group became increasingly aware of both the necessity and the challenges of going beyond reading the literature in a browsing mode and using research studies to solve patient management problems on a day-to-day basis.

In 1990, I assumed the position of residency director of the Internal Medicine Program at McMaster. Through Dave Sackett's leadership, critical appraisal had evolved into a philosophy of medical practice based on knowledge and understanding of the medical literature (or lack of such knowledge and understanding) supporting each clinical decision. We believed that this represented a fundamentally different style of practice and required a term that would capture this difference.

My mission as residency director was to train physicians who would practice this new approach to medical practice. In the spring of 1990, I presented our plans for changing the program to the members of the Department of Medicine, many of whom were not sympathetic. The term suggested to describe the new approach was *scientific medicine*. Those already hostile were incensed and disturbed at the implication that they had previously been "unscientific." My second try at a name for our philosophy of medical practice, *evidence-based medicine*, turned out to be a catchy one.

EBM first appeared in the autumn of 1990 in an information document for residents entering, or considering application to, the residency program. The relevant passage follows:

> Residents are taught to develop an attitude of "enlightened scepticism" towards the application of diagnostic, therapeutic, and prognostic technologies in their day-to-day management of patients. This approach.. has been called "evidence-based medicine"....
> The goal is to be aware of the evidence on which one's practice is based, the soundness of the evidence, and the strength of inference the evidence permits. The strategy employed requires a clear delineation of the relevant question(s); a thorough search of the literature relating to the questions; a critical appraisal of the evidence and its applicability to the clinical situation; a balanced application of the conclusions to the clinical problem.

The first published appearance of the term was in the American College of Physicians' Journal Club in 1991.[3] Meanwhile, our group of enthusiastic evidence-based medical educators at McMaster, including Brian Haynes, Deborah J. Cook, and Roman Jaeschke, were refining our practice and teaching of EBM. Believing that we were on to something big, the McMaster folks linked up with a larger group of academic physicians, largely from the United States, to form the first Evidence-Based Medicine Working Group and published an article that expanded greatly on the description of EBM, labeling it as a "paradigm shift."[4]

This working group then addressed the task of producing a new set of articles, the successor to the readers' guides, to present a more practical approach to applying the medical literature to clinical practice. Although a large number of people made important contributions, the non-McMaster folks who provided the greatest input to the intensive development of educational strategies included Scott Richardson, Mark Wilson, Rob Hayward, and Virginia Moyer. With the unflagging support and wise counsel of *JAMA* deputy editor Drummond Rennie, the Evidence-Based Medicine Working Group created a 25-part series called the Users' Guides to the Medical Literature, published in *JAMA* between 1993 and 2000.[5] The first edition of the *Users' Guides* was a direct descendant of the *JAMA* series and this second edition represents its latest incarnation.

It didn't take long for people to realize that the principles of EBM were equally applicable for other health care workers including nurses, dentists, orthodontists, physiotherapists, occupational therapists, chiropractors, and podiatrists. Thus, terms such as *evidence-based health care* or *evidence-based practice* are appropriate to cover the full range of clinical applications of the evidence-based approach to patient care. Because this book is directed primarily to physicians, we have stayed with the term EBM.

This edition of *Users' Guides to the Medical Literature* presents what we have learned from our students in 25 years of teaching the concepts of EBM. Thanks to the interest, enthusiasm, and diversity of our students, we are able to present the material with increasing clarity and identify more compelling examples. For more than 10 years, our group has hosted a workshop called How to Teach Evidence-Based Practice at McMaster. At the workshop, more than 100 EBM teachers from around the world, at various stages of their careers as educators, engage in a week of mutual education. They share their experiences, communicating EBM concepts to undergraduate and graduate students, residents and fellows, and colleagues. Invariably, even the most senior of us come away with new and better ways of helping students to actively learn EBM's underlying principles.

We are also blessed with the opportunity to travel the world, helping to teach at other people's EBM workshops. Participating in workshops in Thailand, Saudi Arabia, Egypt, Pakistan, Oman, Singapore, the Philippines, Japan, Peru, Chile, Brazil, Germany, Spain, France, Belgium, Norway, and Switzerland—the list goes on—provides us with an opportunity to try out and refine our teaching approaches with students who have a tremendous heterogeneity of backgrounds and perspectives. At each of these workshops, the local EBM teachers share their own experiences, struggles, accomplishments, and EBM teaching tips that we can add to our repertoire.

We are grateful for the extraordinary privilege of sharing, in the form of the second edition of *Users' Guides to the Medical Literature*, what we have learned.

Gordon Guyatt, MD, MSc
McMaster University

References

1. Daly J. *Evidence-Based Medicine and the Search for a Science of Clinical Care*. Berkeley, CA: Milbank Memorial Fund and University of California Press; 2005.

2. How to read clinical journals, I: why to read them and how to start reading them critically. *CMAJ*. 1981;124(5):555-558.

3. Guyatt G. Evidence-based medicine. *ACP J Club (Ann Intern Med)*. 1991;114 (suppl 2):A-16.

4. Evidence-Based Medicine Working Group. Evidence-based medicine: a new approach to teaching the practice of medicine. *JAMA*. 1992;268(17):2420-2425.

5. Guyatt GH, Rennie D. Users' guides to the medical literature. *JAMA*. 1993;270 (17):2096-2097.

Part A

The Foundations

How to Use the Medical Literature— and This Book—to Improve Your Patient Care

Gordon Guyatt and Maureen O. Meade

IN THIS CHAPTER:

The Structure of the *Users' Guides*: The Foundations, Essential Skills, and Advanced Topics

The Approach of the *Users' Guides to the Medical Literature*

The objective of this book is to help you make efficient use of the published literature in guiding your patient care. What does the published literature comprise? Our definition is broad. You may find *evidence** in a wide variety of sources, including original journal articles, *reviews* and *synopses* of *primary studies*, *practice guidelines*, and traditional and innovative medical textbooks. Increasingly, clinicians can most easily access many of these sources through the World Wide Web. In the future, the Internet may be the only route of access for some resources.

THE STRUCTURE OF THE *USERS' GUIDES*: THE FOUNDATIONS, ESSENTIAL SKILLS, AND ADVANCED TOPICS

The first part (Part A) of this book introduces the foundations of *evidence-based practice*. Chapter 2, The Philosophy of Evidence-Based Medicine, presents the 2 guiding principles of *evidence-based medicine* (*EBM*), places EBM in the context of a humanistic approach to medical practice, and reminds us of some of the current challenges to *evidence-based health care*. The subsequent chapters in Part A deal with defining your clinical question, locating the best evidence to address that question, and a key principle of critical appraisal: distinguishing *bias* and *random error*.

Clinicians are primarily interested in making accurate diagnoses and selecting optimal treatments for their patients. They must also avoid harmful *exposures* and offer patients prognostic information. Parts B through E begin by outlining what every medical student, every intern and resident, and every practicing physician will need to know to address these 4 principal issues in providing patient care. The initial core chapters in Parts B through E provide clinicians the skills necessary to use the medical literature for these aspects of patient care.

When someone has gone to the trouble of systematically summarizing *primary studies* addressing a specific clinical question, clinicians should take advantage of that summary. Indeed, efficient *evidence-based practice* dictates bypassing the critical assessment of primary studies and, if they are available, moving straight to the evaluation of rigorous *systematic reviews*. Even more efficient than using a systematic review is moving directly to an evidence-based recommendation. Ideally, management recommendations—summarized in practice guidelines or *decision analyses*—will incorporate the best evidence and make explicit the *value judgments* used in moving from evidence to recommendations for action. Parts F and G provide clinicians with guides for using literature reviews and recommendations to optimize their patient care.

We have kept the initial chapters of each part simple and succinct. From an instructor's point of view, these core chapters constitute a curriculum for a short

---

*The italicization, here and in every other chapter, represents the first occurrence in the chapter of a word that you will find defined in the glossary.

course in using the literature for medical students or house staff; they are also appropriate for a continuing education program for practicing physicians.

Moving beyond the Essentials, the advanced topics in this book will interest clinicians who want to practice EBM at a more sophisticated level. Advanced topics are collated into a single chapter at the end of each part, and many of the core chapters provide alerts to specific advanced topics. Thus, if you would like to gain a deeper understanding of a topic raised in a core chapter, an alert will direct you to the relevant part, chapter, and discussion.

The presentations of advanced topics will deepen your understanding of study methodology, of statistical issues, and of how to use the numbers that emerge from medical research. We wrote the advanced chapters mindful of an additional audience: those who teach evidence-based practice. Many advanced entries read like guidelines for an interactive discussion with a group of learners in a tutorial or on the ward. That is natural enough because the material originated in just such small-group settings. Indeed, the Evidence-Based Medicine Working Group has produced materials that specifically discuss the challenges that arise when these concepts are presented in small-group settings.[1-3]

This book is not like a novel that you read through from beginning to end. Indeed, the *Users' Guides* are so designed that each part is largely self-contained. Thus, we anticipate that clinicians may be selective in their reading of the core content chapters and will certainly be selective when they move beyond the essentials. On the first reading, you may choose only a few advanced areas that interest you. If, as you use the medical literature, you find the need to expand your understanding of studies of *screening tests* or of the use of *surrogate outcomes*, you can consult the relevant chapters to familiarize or reacquaint yourself with the issues. You may also find the glossary of terms (all items in the glossary appear in italics in the text of the chapters) a useful reminder of the formal definitions of terms used in the book. We rely heavily on examples to make our points: you will find examples identified by their blue background.

The Approach of the *Users' Guides* to the *Medical Literature*

The structure of this book reflects how we believe you should go about using the literature to provide optimal patient care. Our approach to addressing diagnosis, treatment, *harm*, and *prognosis* begins when the clinician faces a clinical dilemma (Figure 1-1). Having identified the problem, the clinician then formulates a structured clinical question (see Chapter 3, What Is the Question?), and continues with finding the best relevant evidence (see Chapter 4, Finding the Evidence) (Figure 1-1).

Most chapters include an example search for the best evidence. These searches were accurate when they were done, but it is unlikely that you will get exactly the

FIGURE 1-1

Using the Medical Literature to Provide Optimal Patient Care

Identify your problem.

↓

Define a structured question.

↓

Find the best evidence.

(original primary study or evidence summary)

↓

How valid is the evidence?

↓

What are the results?

↓

How should I apply the results to patient care?

same results if you replicate the searches now. Reasons include additions to the literature and occasional structural changes in databases. Thus, you should view the searches as illustrations of searching principles, rather than as currently definitive searches addressing the clinical question.

Having identified the best *evidence*, the clinician proceeds through 3 steps in evaluating that *evidence* (Figure 1-1). The first step is asking the question, are the results of the study valid? This question has to do with the believability of the results. Another way to state this question is, do these results represent an unbiased estimate of the truth, or have they been influenced in some systematic fashion to lead to a false conclusion?

In the second step—What are the results?—we consider the size and precision of the *treatment effect* (therapy) (see Chapter 6, Therapy; Chapter 7, Does Treatment Lower Risk? Understanding the Results; and Chapter 8, Confidence Intervals), the evidence that helps us generate *pretest probabilities* and move to *posttest probabilities* according to test results (diagnosis) (see Chapter 14, The Process of Diagnosis; Chapter 15, Differential Diagnosis; and Chapter 16, Diagnostic Tests), the size and precision of our estimate of a harmful effect (harm) (see Chapter 12, Harm [Observational Studies]), and our best estimate of a patient's fate (prognosis) (see Chapter 18, Prognosis).

Once we understand the results, we can ask ourselves the third question, how can I apply these results to patient care? This question has 2 parts. First, can you *generalize* (or, to put it another way, particularize) the results to your patient? For instance, you should hesitate to institute a treatment if your patient is too dissimilar from those who participated in the trial or trials. Second, if the results are generalizable to your patient, what is the significance for your patient? Have the investigators measured all *outcomes* of importance to patients? The impact of an intervention depends on both benefits and *risks* of alternative management strategies.

To help demonstrate the clinical relevance of this approach, we begin each core chapter with a clinical scenario, demonstrate a search for relevant literature, and present a table that summarizes criteria for assessing the validity, results, and applicability of the article of interest. We then address the clinical scenario by applying the validity, results, and applicability criteria to an article from the medical literature.

Experience on the wards and outpatient clinics, and with the first edition of the *Users' Guides*, has taught us that this approach is well suited to the needs of any clinician who is eager to achieve an evidence-based practice.

References

1. Barratt A, Wyer P, Hatala R, et al. Tips for learners of evidence-based medicine, 1: relative risk reduction, absolute risk reduction and number needed to treat. *CMAJ.* 2004;171(4):Online-1 to Online-8.

2. Wyer P, Hatala R, Guyatt G. Challenges of teaching EBM. *CMAJ.* 2005;172(11):1424-1425.

3. Wyer P, Keitz S, Hatala R, et al. Tips for learning and teaching evidence-based medicine: introduction to the series. *CMAJ.* 2004;171(4):347-348.

2

THE PHILOSOPHY OF EVIDENCE-BASED MEDICINE

Gordon Guyatt, Brian Haynes, Roman Jaeschke, Maureen O. Meade, Mark Wilson, Victor Montori, and Scott Richardson

IN THIS CHAPTER:

Evidence-based medicine (*EBM*) is about solving clinical problems. In 1992, we described EBM as a shift in medical paradigms.[1] In contrast to the traditional paradigm of medical practice, EBM places lower value on unsystematic clinical experience and pathophysiologic rationale, stresses the examination of *evidence* from clinical research, suggests that interpreting the results of clinical research requires a formal set of rules, and places a lower value on authority than the traditional medical paradigm. Although we continue to find this paradigm shift a valid way of conceptualizing EBM, the world is often complex enough to invite more than 1 useful way of thinking about an idea or a phenomenon. In this chapter, we describe another conceptualization that emphasizes how EBM complements and enhances the traditional skills of clinical practice.

TWO FUNDAMENTAL PRINCIPLES OF EBM

As a distinctive approach to patient care, EBM involves 2 fundamental principles. First, EBM posits a *hierarchy of evidence* to guide clinical decision making. Second, evidence alone is never sufficient to make a clinical decision. Decision makers must always trade off the benefits and *risks*, inconvenience, and costs associated with alternative management strategies and, in doing so, consider their patients' values and preferences.[1]

A Hierarchy of Evidence

What is the nature of the *evidence* in EBM? We suggest a broad definition: any empirical observation constitutes potential evidence, whether systematically collected or not. Thus, the unsystematic observations of the individual clinician constitute one source of evidence; physiologic experiments constitute another source. Unsystematic observations can lead to profound insights, and wise clinicians develop a healthy respect for the insights of their senior colleagues in issues of clinical observation, diagnosis, and relations with patients and colleagues.

At the same time, our personal clinical observations are often limited by small sample size and by deficiencies in human processes of making inferences.[3] Predictions about *intervention effects* on patient-important outcomes based on physiologic experiments usually are right but occasionally are disastrously wrong. Numerous factors can lead clinicians astray as they try to interpret the results of conventional open trials of therapy. These include *natural history, placebo effects,* patient and health worker expectations, and the patient's desire to please. We provide a number of examples of just how wrong predictions based on physiologic rationale can be in Chapter 9.2, Surprising Results of Randomized Trials.

Given the limitations of unsystematic clinical observations and physiologic rationale, EBM suggests a number of hierarchies of evidence, one of which relates to issues of *prevention* and treatment (Table 2-1).

TABLE 2-1

Hierarchy of Strength of Evidence for Prevention and Treatment Decisions

- N-of-1 randomized trial
- Systematic reviews of randomized trials
- Single randomized trial
- Systematic review of observational studies addressing patient-important outcomes
- Single observational study addressing patient-important outcomes
- Physiologic studies (studies of blood pressure, cardiac output, exercise capacity, bone density, and so forth)
- Unsystematic clinical observations

Issues of diagnosis or *prognosis* require different hierarchies. For instance, *randomization* is not relevant to sorting out how well a test is able to distinguish individuals with a *target condition* or disease from those who are healthy or have a competing condition or disease. For diagnosis, the top of the hierarchy would include studies that enrolled patients about whom clinicians had diagnostic uncertainty and that undertook a *blind* comparison between the candidate test and a *criterion standard* (see Chapter 16, Diagnostic Tests).

Clinical research goes beyond unsystematic clinical observation in providing strategies that avoid or attenuate spurious results. The same strategies that minimize *bias* in conventional therapeutic trials involving multiple patients can guard against misleading results in studies involving single patients.[4] In the *n of 1 randomized controlled trial (n-of-1 RCT)*, a patient and clinician are *blind* to whether that patient is receiving active or placebo medication. The patient makes quantitative ratings of troublesome symptoms during each period, and the n-of-1 RCT continues until both the patient and the clinician conclude that the patient is or is not obtaining benefit from the target intervention. N-of-1 RCTs can provide definitive evidence of treatment effectiveness in individual patients[5,6] and may lead to long-term differences in treatment administration (see Chapter 9.5, N-of-1 Randomized Controlled Trials).[7] Unfortunately, n-of-1 RCTs are restricted to chronic conditions with treatments that act and cease acting quickly and are subject to considerable logistic challenges. We must therefore usually rely on studies of other patients to make inferences regarding the patient before us.

The requirement that clinicians generalize from results in other people to their patients inevitably weakens inferences about treatment impact and introduces complex issues of how trial results apply to individual patients. Inferences may nevertheless be strong if results come from a *systematic review* of methodologically strong RCTs with consistent results. Inferences generally will be somewhat weaker if only a single RCT is being considered, unless it is large and has enrolled patients much like the patient under consideration (Table 2-1). Because *observational studies* may underestimate or, more typically, overestimate *treatment effects* in an unpredictable fashion,[8,9] their results are far less trustworthy than those of RCTs.

Physiologic studies and unsystematic clinical observations provide the weakest inferences about treatment effects.

This hierarchy is not absolute. If treatment effects are sufficiently large and consistent, carefully conducted observational studies may provide more compelling evidence than poorly conducted RCTs. For example, observational studies have allowed extremely strong inferences about the efficacy of penicillin in pneumococcal pneumonia or that of hip replacement in patients with debilitating hip osteoarthritis. Defining the extent to which clinicians should temper the strength of their inferences when only observational studies are available remains one of the important challenges in EBM.

The hierarchy implies a clear course of action for physicians addressing patient problems. They should look for the highest quality available evidence from the hierarchy. The hierarchy makes it clear that any claim that there is no evidence for the effect of a particular treatment is a non sequitur. The evidence may be extremely weak—it may be the unsystematic observation of a single clinician or physiologic studies that point to mechanisms of action that are only indirectly related—but there is always evidence.

Clinical Decision Making: Evidence Is Never Enough

Picture a woman with chronic pain resulting from terminal cancer. She has come to terms with her condition, resolved her affairs, and said her good-byes, and she wishes to receive only palliative care. She develops severe pneumococcal pneumonia. Evidence that antibiotic therapy reduces morbidity and mortality from pneumococcal pneumonia is strong. Even evidence this convincing does not, however, dictate that this particular patient should receive antibiotics. Her *values* are such that she would prefer to forgo treatment.

Now picture a second patient, an 85-year-old man with severe dementia who is mute and incontinent, is without family or friends, and spends his days in apparent discomfort. This man develops pneumococcal pneumonia. Although many clinicians would argue that those responsible for his care should not administer antibiotic therapy, others would suggest that they should. Again, evidence of treatment effectiveness does not automatically imply that treatment should be administered.

Finally, picture a third patient, a healthy 30-year-old mother of 2 children who develops pneumococcal pneumonia. No clinician would doubt the wisdom of administering antibiotic therapy to this patient. This does not mean, however, that an underlying value judgment has been unnecessary. Rather, our values are sufficiently concordant, and the benefits so overwhelm the risks of treatment, that the underlying value judgment is unapparent.

By values and preferences, we mean the collection of goals, expectations, predispositions, and beliefs that individuals have for certain decisions and their potential outcomes. The explicit enumeration and balancing of benefits and risks that is central to EBM brings the underlying value judgments involved in making management decisions into bold relief.

Acknowledging that values play a role in every important patient care decision highlights our limited understanding of how to ensure that decisions are consistent with individual and, where appropriate, societal values. Health economists have played a major role in developing the science of measuring patient preferences.[10,11] Some decision aids incorporate patient values indirectly. If patients truly understand the potential risks and benefits, their decisions will reflect their preferences.[12] These developments constitute a promising start. Nevertheless, many unanswered questions remain concerning how to elicit preferences and how to incorporate them in clinical encounters already subject to crushing time pressures. We discuss these issues in more detail in Part G, Moving From Evidence to Action.

Next, we briefly comment on additional skills that clinicians must master for optimal patient care and the relation of those skills to EBM.

CLINICAL SKILLS, HUMANISM, AND EBM

In summarizing the skills and attributes necessary for evidence-based practice, Table 2-2 highlights how EBM complements traditional aspects of clinical expertise. One of us, a secondary-care internist, developed a lesion on his lip shortly before an important presentation. He was concerned and, wondering whether he should take acyclovir, proceeded to spend the next 30 minutes searching for and evaluating the highest-quality evidence. When he began to discuss his remaining uncertainty with his partner, an experienced dentist, she cut short the discussion by exclaiming, "But, my dear, that isn't herpes!"

This story illustrates the necessity of obtaining the correct diagnosis before seeking and applying research evidence regarding optimal treatment. After making the diagnosis, the clinician relies on experience and background knowledge to define the relevant management options. Having identified those options, the clinician can search for, evaluate, and apply the best evidence regarding treatment.

TABLE 2-2

Knowledge and Skills Necessary for Optimal Evidence-Based Practice

- Diagnostic expertise
- In-depth background knowledge
- Effective searching skills
- Effective critical appraisal skills
- Ability to define and understand benefits and risks of alternatives
- In-depth physiologic understanding allowing application of evidence to the individual
- Sensitivity and communication skills required for full understanding of patient context
- Ability to elicit and understand patient values and preferences and apply them to management decisions

In applying evidence, clinicians rely on their expertise to define features that affect the applicability of the results to the individual patient. The clinician must judge the extent to which differences in treatment (local surgical expertise or the possibility of patient *nonadherence*, for instance), the availability of monitoring, or patient characteristics (such as age, comorbidity, or the patient's personal circumstances) may affect estimates of benefit and *risk* that come from the published literature.

Understanding the patient's personal circumstances is of particular importance[12] and requires compassion, sensitive listening skills, and broad perspectives from the humanities and social sciences. For some patients, incorporation of patient values for major decisions will mean a full enumeration of the possible benefits, risks, and inconvenience associated with alternative management strategies that are relevant to the particular patient. For some patients and problems, this discussion should involve the patient's family. For other problems—the discussion of *screening* with prostate-specific antigen with older male patients, for instance—attempts to involve other family members might violate strong cultural norms.

Some patients are uncomfortable with an explicit discussion of benefits and risks and object to clinicians placing what they perceive as excessive responsibility for decision making on their shoulders.[13] In such cases, it is the physician's responsibility to develop insight to ensure that choices will be consistent with the patient's values and preferences. Understanding and implementing the sort of decision-making process that patients desire and effectively communicating the information they need require skills in understanding the patient's narrative and the person behind that narrative.[14,15]

ADDITIONAL CHALLENGES FOR EBM

Clinicians will find that time limitations present the biggest challenge to evidence-based practice. Fortunately, new resources to assist clinicians are available and the pace of innovation is rapid. One can consider a classification of information sources that comes with a mnemonic device, 4S: the individual study, the *systematic review* of all the available studies on a given problem, a *synopsis* of both individual studies and summaries, and *systems* of information.[16] By *systems*, we mean summaries that link a number of synopses related to the care of a particular patient problem (acute upper gastrointestinal bleeding) or type of patient (the diabetic outpatient) (Table 2-3). Evidence-based selection and summarization is becoming increasingly available at each level (see Chapter 4, Finding the Evidence).

A second enormous challenge for evidence-based practice is ensuring that management strategies are consistent with the patient's values and preferences. In a time-constrained environment, how can we ensure that patients' involvement in decision making has the form and extent that they desire and that the outcome reflects their needs and desires? Progress in addressing this daunting question will require a major expenditure of time and intellectual energy from clinician researchers.

TABLE 2-3

A Hierarchy of Preprocessed Evidence[16]

Studies	Preprocessing involves selecting only those studies that are both highly relevant and characterized by study designs that minimize bias and thus permit a high strength of inference
Systematic reviews	Reviews involving the identification, selection, appraisal, and summary of primary studies addressing a focused clinical question using methods to reduce the likelihood of bias
Synopses	Brief summaries that encapsulate the key methodologic details and results of a single study or systematic review
Systems	Practice guidelines, clinical pathways, or evidence-based textbook summaries that integrate evidence-based information about specific clinical problems and provide regular updates to guide the care of individual patients

This book deals primarily with decision making at the level of the individual patient. Evidence-based approaches can also inform health policy making,[17] day-to-day decisions in public health, and systems-level decisions such as those facing hospital managers. In each of these areas, EBM can support the appropriate goal of gaining the greatest health benefit from limited resources.

In the policy arena, dealing with differing values poses even more challenges than in the arena of individual patient care. Should we restrict ourselves to alternative resource allocation within a fixed pool of health care resources, or should we be trading off health care services against, for instance, lower tax rates for individuals or corporations? How should we deal with the large body of observational studies suggesting that social and economic factors may have a larger influence on the health of populations than health care delivery? How should we deal with the tension between what may be best for a person and what may be optimal for the society of which that person is a member? The debate about such issues is at the heart of evidence-based health policy making, but, inevitably, it has implications for decision making at the individual patient level.

References

1. Evidence-Based Medicine Working Group. Evidence-based medicine: a new approach to the teaching of medicine. *JAMA*. 1992;268(17):2420-2425.

2. Napodano R. *Values in Medical Practice.* New York, NY: Humana Sciences Press; 1986.

3. Nisbett R, Ross L. *Human Inference.* Englewood Cliffs, NJ: Prentice-Hall; 1980.

4. Guyatt G, Sackett D, Taylor D, Chong J, Roberts R, Pugsley S. Determining optimal therapy—randomized trials in individual patients. *N Engl J Med.* 1986;314(14):889-892.

5. Guyatt G, Keller J, Jaeschke R, Rosenbloom D, Adachi J, Newhouse M. The n-of-1 randomized controlled trial: clinical usefulness: our three-year experience. *Ann Intern Med.* 1990;112(4):293-299.

6. Larson E, Ellsworth A, Oas J. Randomized clinical trials in single patients during a 2-year period. *JAMA.* 1993;270(22):2708-2712.

7. Mahon J, Laupacis A, Donner A, Wood T. Randomised study of n of 1 trials versus standard practice. *BMJ.* 1996;312(7038):1069-1074.

8. Guyatt G, DiCenso A, Farewell V, Willan A, Griffith L. Randomized trials versus observational studies in adolescent pregnancy prevention. *J Clin Epidemiol.* 2000;53(2):167-174.

9. Kunz R, Oxman A. The unpredictability paradox: review of empirical comparisons of randomised and non-randomised clinical trials. *BMJ.* 1998;317(7167):1185-1190.

10. Drummond M, Richardson W, O'Brien B, Levine M, Heyland D. Users' Guide to the Medical Literature XIII: how to use an article on economic analysis of clinical practice, A: are the results of the study valid? *JAMA.* 1997;277(19):1552-1557.

11. Feeny D, Furlong W, Boyle M, Torrance G. Multi-attribute health status classification systems: health utilities index. *Pharmacoeconomics.* 1995;7(6):490-502.

12. O'Connor A, Rostom A, Fiset V, et al. Decision aids for patients facing health treatment or screening decisions: systematic review. *BMJ.* 1999;319(7212):731-734.

13. Sutherland H, Llewellyn-Thomas H, Lockwood G, Tritchler D, Till J. Cancer patients: their desire for information and participation in treatment decisions. *J R Soc Med.* 1989;82(5):260-263.

14. Greenhalgh T. Narrative based medicine: narrative based medicine in an evidence based world. *BMJ.* 1999;318(7179):323-325.

15. Greenhalgh T, Hurwitz B. Narrative based medicine: why study narrative? *BMJ.* 1999;318(7175):48-50.

16. Haynes R. Of studies, syntheses, synopses, and systems: the "4S" evolution of services for finding current best evidence. *ACP J Club.* 2001;134(2):A11-A13.

17. Muir Gray F, Haynes R, Sackett D, Cook D, Guyatt G. Transferring evidence from research into practice, III: developing evidence-based clinical policy. *ACP J Club.* 1997;126(2):A14-A16.

3

WHAT IS THE QUESTION?

Gordon Guyatt, Maureen O. Meade,
Scott Richardson, and Roman Jaeschke

IN THIS CHAPTER:

THREE WAYS TO USE THE MEDICAL LITERATURE

Consider a medical student, early in her training, seeing a patient with newly diagnosed diabetes mellitus. She will ask questions such as the following: What is type 2 diabetes mellitus? Why does this patient have polyuria? Why does this patient have numbness and pain in his legs? What treatment options are available? These questions address normal human physiology and the pathophysiology associated with a medical condition.

Traditional medical textbooks that describe underlying physiology, pathology, epidemiology, and general treatment approaches provide an excellent resource for addressing these *background questions*. The sorts of questions that seasoned clinicians usually ask require different resources.

Browsing

A general internist scanning the September/October 2005 *ACP Journal Club* (http://www.acponline.org/journals/acpjc/jcmenu.htm) comes across the following articles: "Intensive Insulin-Glucose Infusion Regimens With Long-Term or Standard Glucose Control Did Not Differ for Reducing Mortality in Type 2 Diabetes Mellitus and MI,"[1] and "Review: Mixed Signals From Trials Concerning Pharmacologic Prevention of Type 2 Diabetes Mellitus."[2]

This internist is in the process of asking a general question—what important new information should I know to optimally treat my patients? Traditionally, clinicians address this question by subscribing to a number of target medical journals in which articles relevant to their practice appear. They keep up to date by skimming the table of contents and reading relevant articles. This traditional approach to what we might call the browsing mode of using the medical literature has major limitations of inefficiency and resulting frustration. *Evidence-based medicine* offers solutions to this problem.

The most efficient strategy is to restrict your browsing to *secondary journals*. For internal and general medicine, *ACP Journal Club* publishes *synopses* of articles that meet criteria of both clinical relevance and methodologic quality. We describe such secondary journals in more detail in Chapter 4, Finding the Evidence.

Some specialties (primary care, mental health) and subspecialties (cardiology, gastroenterology) already have their own devoted secondary journals; others do not. The New York Academy of Medicine keeps a current list of available secondary journals in many health care disciplines (http://www.ebmny.org/journal.html). If you are not yet fortunate enough to have your own, you can apply your own relevance and methodologic screen to articles in your target specialty or subspecialty journals. When you have learned the skills, you will be surprised at the small proportion of studies to which you need attend and at the efficiency with which you can identify them.

Problem Solving

Experienced clinicians confronting a patient with diabetes mellitus will ask questions such as, In patients with new-onset type 2 diabetes mellitus, which clinical features or test results predict the development of diabetic complications? In patients with type 2

FIGURE 3-1

Background and Foreground Questions

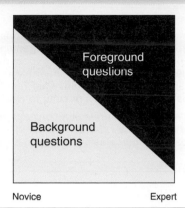

diabetes mellitus requiring drug therapy, does starting with metformin treatment yield improved diabetes control and reduce long-term complications better than other initial treatments? Here, clinicians are defining specific questions raised in caring for patients and then consulting the literature to resolve these questions.

Background and Foreground Questions

One can think of the first set of questions, those of the medical student, as *background questions* and of the browsing and problem-solving sets as *foreground questions*. In most situations, you need to understand the background thoroughly before it makes sense to address foreground issues.

A seasoned clinician may occasionally require background information, which is most likely when a new condition or medical *syndrome* appears ("What is SARS?") or when a new diagnostic test ("How does PCR work?") or treatment modality ("What are atypical antipsychotic agents?") appears in the clinical arena.

Figure 3-1 represents the evolution of the questions we ask as we progress from being novices posing background questions to experts posing foreground questions. This book explores how clinicians can use the medical literature to solve their foreground questions.

CLARIFYING YOUR QUESTION

The Structure: Patients, Exposure, Outcome

Clinical questions often spring to mind in a form that makes finding answers in the medical literature a challenge. Dissecting the question into its component parts to facilitate finding the best *evidence* is a fundamental skill.[2] One can divide most

TABLE 3-1

Framing Clinical Questions

1. *The population*. Who are the relevant patients?

2. *The interventions or exposures* (diagnostic tests, foods, drugs, surgical proce-dures, time, risk factors, etc). What are the management strategies we are inter-ested in comparing or the potentially harmful exposures about which we are concerned? For issues of therapy, prevention, or harm, there will always be both an experimental intervention or putative harmful exposure and a control, alternative, or comparison intervention or state to which it is compared.

3. *The outcome*. What are the patient-relevant consequences of the exposures in which we are interested? We may also be interested in the consequences to society, including cost or resource use. It may also be important to specify the period of interest.

questions into 3 parts: the patients, the intervention or *exposure*, and the *outcome* (Table 3-1).

Five Types of Clinical Questions

In addition to clarifying the population, intervention or exposures, and outcome, it is productive to label the nature of the question that you are asking. There are 5 fundamental types of clinical questions:

1. Therapy: determining the effect of interventions on *patient-important outcomes* (*symptoms*, function, morbidity, mortality, costs)

2. Harm: ascertaining the effects of potentially harmful agents (including therapies from the first type of question) on patient-important outcomes

3. Differential diagnosis: in patients with a particular clinical presentation, establishing the frequency of the underlying disorders

4. Diagnosis: establishing the *power* of a test to differentiate between those with and without a *target condition* or disease

5. Prognosis: estimating a patient's future course

Finding a Suitably Designed Study for Your Question Type

You need to correctly identify the category of study because, to answer your question, you must find an appropriately designed study. If you look for a *randomized trial* to inform you of the properties of a diagnostic test, you are unlikely to find the answer you seek. We will now review the study designs associated with the 5 major types of questions.

To answer questions about a therapeutic issue, we identify studies in which a process analogous to flipping a coin determines participants' receipt of an *experimental treatment* or a control or standard treatment, a *randomized controlled trial* (*RCT*) (see Chapter 6, Therapy [Randomized Trials]). Once investigators allocate participants to treatment or *control groups*, they follow them forward in time to

FIGURE 3-2

Structure of Randomized Trials

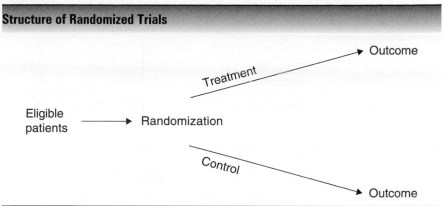

determine whether they have, for instance, a stroke or heart attack—what we call the outcome of interest (Figure 3-2).

Ideally, we would also look to randomized trials to address issues of *harm*. For many potentially harmful exposures, however, randomly allocating patients is neither practical nor ethical. For instance, one cannot suggest to potential study participants that an investigator will decide by the flip of a coin whether or not they smoke during the next 20 years. For exposures like smoking, the best one can do is identify studies in which personal choice, or happenstance, determines whether people are exposed or not exposed. These *observational studies* (often subclassified as *cohort* or *case-control studies*) provide weaker evidence than randomized trials (see Chapter 12, Harm [Observational Studies]).

Figure 3-3 depicts a common observational study design in which patients with and without the exposures of interest are followed forward in time to determine whether they experience the outcome of interest. For smoking, one important outcome would likely be the development of cancer.

FIGURE 3-3

Structure of Observational Cohort Studies

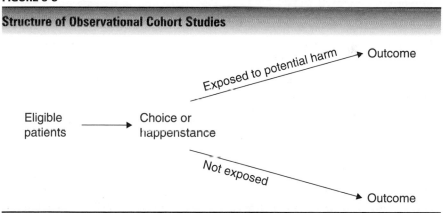

FIGURE 3-4

Structure for Studies of Differential Diagnosis

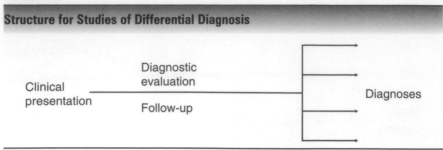

For sorting out *differential diagnosis*, we need a different study design (Figure 3-4). Here, investigators collect a group of patients with a similar presentation (painless jaundice, syncope, headache), conduct an extensive battery of tests, and, if necessary, follow patients forward in time. Ultimately, for each patient they hope to establish the underlying cause of the *symptoms* and *signs* with which the patient presented.

Establishing the value of a particular diagnostic test (what we call its properties or operating characteristics) requires a slightly different design (Figure 3-5). In diagnostic test studies, investigators identify a group of patients in whom they suspect a disease or condition of interest exists (such as tuberculosis, lung cancer, or iron-deficiency anemia), which we call the target condition. These patients undergo the new diagnostic test and a *reference standard*, *gold standard*, or *criterion standard*. Investigators evaluate the diagnostic test by comparing its classification of patients with that of the reference standard (Figure 3-5).

A final type of study examines a patient's *prognosis* and may identify factors that modify that prognosis. Here, investigators identify patients who belong to a particular group (such as pregnant women, patients undergoing surgery, or

FIGURE 3-5

Structure for Studies of Diagnostic Test Properties

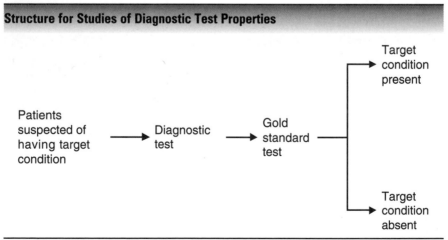

FIGURE 3-6

Structure of Studies of Prognosis

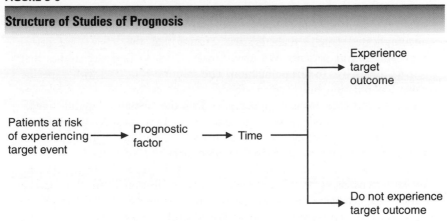

patients with cancer) with or without factors that may modify their prognosis (such as age or *comorbidity*). The exposure here is time, and investigators follow patients to determine whether they experience the *target outcome*, such as a problem birth at the end of a pregnancy, a myocardial infarction after surgery, or survival in cancer (Figure 3-6).

Three Examples of Question Clarification

We will now provide examples of the transformation of unstructured clinical questions into the structured questions that facilitate the use of the medical literature.

Example 1: Diabetes and Target Blood Pressure

A 55-year-old white woman presents with type 2 diabetes mellitus and hypertension. Her glycemic control is excellent with metformin, and she has no history of complications. To manage her hypertension, she takes a small daily dose of a thiazide diuretic. During a 6-month period, her blood pressure is near 155/88 mm Hg.

Initial Question: When treating hypertension, at what target blood pressure should we aim?

Digging Deeper: One limitation of this formulation of the question is that it fails to specify the population in adequate detail. The benefits of tight control of blood pressure may differ in diabetic patients vs nondiabetic patients, in type 1 vs type 2 diabetes, and in patients with and without diabetic complications.

The detail in which we specify the patient population is a double-edged sword. On the one hand, being very specific (middle-aged women with uncomplicated type 2 diabetes) will ensure that the answer we get is applicable to our patients. We may, however, fail to find any studies that restrict themselves to this population. The solution is to start with a specific patient population but be ready to drop specifications to find a relevant article. In this case, we may be ready to drop the "female," "middle-aged," "uncomplicated," and "type 2," in that order. If we suspect that optimal target blood pressure may be similar in diabetic and nondiabetic patients, and it proves absolutely necessary, we might drop the "diabetes."

We may wish to specify that we are interested in the addition of a specific antihypertensive agent. Alternatively, the intervention of interest may be any antihypertensive treatment. Furthermore, a key part of the intervention will be the target for blood pressure control. For instance, we might be interested in knowing whether it makes any difference if our target diastolic blood pressure is less than 80 mm Hg vs less than 90 mm Hg. Another limitation of the initial question formulation is that it fails to specify the criteria by which we will judge the appropriate target for our hypertensive treatment.

Improved (Searchable) Question: *A question of THERAPY*

- *Patients:* Hypertensive type 2 diabetic patients without diabetic complications.

- *Intervention:* Any antihypertensive agent aiming at a target diastolic blood pressure of 90 mm Hg vs a comparison target of 80 mm Hg.

- *Outcomes:* Stroke, myocardial infarction, cardiovascular death, total mortality.

Example 2: Transient Loss of Consciousness

A 55-year-old man, previously well, although a heavy drinker, presents to the emergency department with an episode of transient loss of consciousness. On the evening of presentation, he had his usual 5 beers and started to climb the stairs at bedtime. The next thing he remembers is being woken by his son, who found him lying near the bottom of the stairs. The patient took about a minute to regain consciousness and remained confused for another 2 minutes. His son did not witness any shaking, and there had not been any incontinence. Physical examination result was unremarkable; the electrocardiogram showed a sinus rhythm with a rate of 80/min and no abnormalities. Glucose, sodium, and other laboratory results were normal.

Initial Question: How extensively should I investigate this patient?

Digging Deeper: The initial question gives us little idea of where to look in the literature for an answer. As it turns out, there is a host of questions that could be helpful in choosing an optimal investigational strategy. We could, for instance, pose a question of differential diagnosis: If we knew the distribution of ultimate diagnoses in such patients, we could choose to investigate the more common and omit investigations targeted at remote possibilities.

Other information that would help us would be the properties of individual diagnostic tests. If an electroencephalogram were extremely accurate for diagnosing a seizure, or a 24-hour Holter monitor for diagnosing arrhythmia, we would be far more inclined to order the tests than if they missed patients with the underlying problems or falsely labeled patients without the problems.

Alternatively, we could ask a question of prognosis. If patients like ours had a benign prognosis, we might be much less eager to investigate extensively than if patients tended to do badly. Finally, the ultimate answer to how intensively we should investigate might come from a randomized trial in which patients similar to this man were allocated to more vs less intensive investigation.

Improved (Searchable) Questions: *A question of DIFFERENTIAL DIAGNOSIS*

- *Patients:* Middle-aged patients presenting with transient loss of consciousness.
- *Intervention/Exposure:* Thorough investigation and follow-up.
- *Outcomes:* Frequency of underlying disorders such as vasovagal syncope, seizure, arrhythmia, and transient ischemic attack.

A question of DIAGNOSIS

- *Patients:* Middle-aged patients presenting with transient loss of consciousness.
- *Intervention/Exposure:* Electroencephalogram.
- *Outcomes:* Gold standard investigation (probably long-term follow-up).

A question of PROGNOSIS

- *Patients:* Middle-aged patients presenting with transient loss of consciousness.
- *Intervention/Exposure:* Time.
- *Outcomes:* Morbidity (complicated arrhythmias or seizures, strokes, serious accidents) and mortality in the year after presentation.

A question of THERAPY

- *Patients:* Middle-aged patients presenting with loss of consciousness.

- *Intervention/Exposure:* Comprehensive investigation vs a comparator of minimal investigation.

- *Outcomes:* Morbidity and mortality in the year after presentation.

Example 3: Squamous Cell Carcinoma

A 60-year-old man with a 40-pack-year smoking history presents with hemoptysis. A chest radiograph shows a parenchymal mass with a normal mediastinum, and a fine-needle aspiration of the mass shows squamous cell carcinoma. Aside from hemoptysis, the patient is asymptomatic and physical examination result is entirely normal.

Initial Question: What investigations should we undertake before deciding whether to offer this patient surgery?

Digging Deeper: The key defining features of this patient are his non–small cell carcinoma and the fact that his medical history, physical examination, and chest radiograph show no evidence of intrathoracic or extrathoracic metastatic disease. Alternative investigational strategies address 2 separate issues: Does the patient have occult mediastinal disease, and does he have occult extrathoracic metastatic disease? For this discussion, we will focus on the former issue. Investigational strategies for addressing the possibility of occult mediastinal disease include undertaking a mediastinoscopy or performing a computed tomographic (CT) scan of the chest and proceeding according to the results of this investigation.

What outcomes are we trying to influence in our choice of investigational approach? We would like to prolong the patient's life, but the extent of his underlying tumor is likely to be the major determinant of survival, and our investigations cannot change that. We wish to detect occult mediastinal metastases if they are present because, if the cancer has spread to the mediastinum, resectional surgery is unlikely to benefit the patient. Thus, in the presence of mediastinal disease, patients will usually receive palliative approaches and avoid an unnecessary thoracotomy.

We could frame our structured clinical question in 2 ways. One would be asking about the usefulness of the CT scan for identifying mediastinal disease. More definitive would be to ask a question of therapy: what investigational strategy would yield superior clinical outcomes?

Improved (Searchable) Questions: *A question of DIAGNOSIS*

- *Patients:* Newly diagnosed non–small cell lung cancer with no evidence of extrapulmonary metastases.

- *Intervention*: CT scan of the chest.

- *Outcome:* Mediastinal spread at mediastinoscopy.

A question of THERAPY

- *Patients:* Newly diagnosed non–small cell lung cancer with no evidence of extrapulmonary metastases.

- *Intervention:* Mediastinoscopy for all or restricted to those with suspicious lesions on CT scan of the thorax.

- *Outcome:* Unnecessary thoracotomy.

DEFINING THE QUESTION: CONCLUSION

Constructing a searchable question that allows you to use the medical literature to solve problems is no simple matter. It requires a detailed understanding of the clinical issues involved in patient management. The 3 examples in this chapter illustrate that each patient encounter may trigger a number of clinical questions and that you must give careful thought to what you really want to know. Bearing the structure of the question in mind—patient, intervention or exposure and control, and outcome—is extremely helpful in arriving at an answerable question. Identifying the type of questions—therapy, harm, differential diagnosis, diagnosis, and prognosis—will further ensure that you are looking for a study with an appropriate design.

Careful definition of the question will provide another benefit: you will be less likely to be misled by a study that addresses a question related to the one in which you are interested, but with 1 or more important differences. For instance, making sure that the study compares experimental treatment to current optimal care may highlight the limitations of trials that use a *placebo* control (see Chapter 11.3, Dealing With Misleading Presentations of Clinical Trial Results). Specifying that you are interested in patient-important outcomes (such as long bone fractures) makes vivid the limitations of studies that focus on *substitute* or *surrogate endpoints* (such as bone density) (see Chapter 11.4, Surrogate Outcomes). Specifying that you are primarily interested in avoiding progression to dialysis will make you appropriately wary of a *composite endpoint* of progression to dialysis or doubling of serum creatinine level (see Chapter 10.4, Composite Endpoints). You will not reject such studies out of hand, but the careful definition of the question will help you to critically apply the results to your patient care.

A final crucial benefit from careful consideration of the question is that it sets the stage for efficient and effective literature searching to identify and retrieve the best evidence. Chapter 4, Finding the Evidence, uses the components of patient, intervention, and outcome for the questions in this chapter to provide you with the searching tools you will need for effective *evidence-based practice.*

References

1. Yusuf S. Intensive insulin-glucose infusion regimens with long-term or standard glucose control did not differ for reducing mortality in type 2 diabetes mellitus and MI. *ACP J Club.* 2005;143(2):43.

2. Kenealy TAB. Review: mixed signals from trials concerning pharmacological prevention of type 2 diabetes mellitus. *ACP J Club.* 2005;143(2):44.

4

FINDING THE EVIDENCE

Ann McKibbon, Peter Wyer, Roman Jaeschke, and Dereck Hunt

IN THIS CHAPTER:

INTRODUCTION

Assessment of knowledge gaps, question formulation, gathering and synthesis of *evidence*, and application of that evidence to the care of patients are among the foundations of informed health care. Clinicians frequently use information resources such as textbooks, MEDLINE, and consultation with respected colleagues in gathering evidence. Many information resources exist, and each discipline and subspecialty of medicine has unique information tools and resources. Not all resources, however, provide sound information that can be easily and efficiently accessed. This chapter will help you hone your information-seeking skills and guide you in choosing the best resources for your clinical use.

We begin by describing one way of categorizing resources and then review some of the most useful resources in detail, concentrating on those that are evidence based with high potential for clinical impact. We end the chapter by illustrating searching strategies in several of the databases that can be challenging to use. Our goal is not to discuss all possible choices, but rather to provide a representative sample of the most useful resources and a framework for you to explore different types and classes. Few "best buy" recommendations are in this chapter. A resource's usefulness to you is contingent on many factors, such as your institutional provision of resources, your specialty, your stage of training, and your familiarity with the specific topic of a search. In addition, little evidence exists that compares resources. The American Board of Internal Medicine is studying this issue. They will make their findings public in late 2008. We will address finding information to answer *background questions* and *foreground questions*, as well as searching related to browsing and keeping up to date.

To start our consideration of external information resources, let us quickly review the distinction between background questions and foreground questions described in the previous chapter (see Chapter 3, What Is the Question?).

Background questions can involve a single fact such as the causative microbiologic agent of Chagas disease, a recommended dose of a drug, or a list of the attributes of the CHARGE syndrome (coloboma of the eye, heart defects, atresia of the choanae, retardation of growth and/or development, genital and/or urinary abnormalities, and ear abnormalities and deafness). Often, they involve much more information such as questions of "What is Gerstmann syndrome?" or "How do I insert a jugular venous central line?"

Foreground questions—targeted questions that provide the evidentiary basis for specific clinical decisions—are best structured using the framework of patient, intervention or exposure, a possible comparison intervention, and *outcomes* of interest: the PICO format. This chapter, and the *Users' Guides* overall, focuses on efficiently finding the best answers to foreground questions.

Four Categories of Information Sources and How Clinicians Use Them

Table 4-1 summarizes 4 categories of information resources. A fuller description of each category with examples of resources follows.

1. *Systems:* Some information resources provide regularly updated clinical evidence, sometimes integrated with other types of health care information, and provide guidance or recommendations for patient management. Existing systems include PIER (http://pier.acponline.org/index.html), UpToDate (http://www.uptodate.com/), *Clinical Evidence* (http://www.clinicalevidence.com/ceweb/conditions/index.jsp), and EBM Guidelines: Evidence-Based Medicine (http://www3.interscience.wiley.com/cgi-bin/mrwhome/112605734/HOME).

2. *Synopses:* Preappraised resource journals and products such as *ACP Journal Club* (http://www.acpjc.org/) and InfoPOEMs (http://www.infopoems.com/) serve 2 functions. Initially, the articles act as an alerting service to keep physicians current on recent advances. When rigorously and systematically assembled, the content of such resources becomes, over time, a database of important articles. The New York Academy of Medicine maintains a list of preappraised resource journals for various disciplines (http://www.ebmny.org/journal.html).

3. *Summaries:* The Cochrane Collaboration (http://www.cochrane.org/index.htm) provides systematic reviews of health care interventions, whereas the Campbell Collaboration provides similar reviews in the social, behavioral, and educational arenas (http://www.campbellcollaboration.org/). You can also find systematic reviews in MEDLINE and other databases. By collecting the evidence on a topic, systematic reviews become more useful than individual or *primary studies.*

4. *Studies:* Original or primary studies (eg, those stored in MEDLINE). Many studies exist but the information they contain needs evaluation before application to clinical problems.

Clinical practice guidelines illustrate that this classification (like any other) has its limitations: guidelines have aspects of systems and summaries, and sometimes of synopses. For instance, DARE (Database of Abstracts of Reviews of Effects; http://www.york.ac.uk/inst/crd/crddatabases.htm) not only includes reviews themselves but also has elements of guidelines in that expert commentators suggest how clinicians might apply the findings of the reviews.

Clinicians use resources corresponding to all of the above categories to find the information they need during clinical care.[2] Not all resources, however, yield useful answers to clinical questions. Several studies[2-4] show that when clinicians use information resources to answer clinical questions, the resources they choose provide the best evidence only about 50% of the time. Despite this, some evidence suggests that searching for external information improves patient-care processes and may improve health outcomes.[5-8]

SEARCHING THE MEDICAL LITERATURE IS SOMETIMES FUTILE

Consider the following clinical question: In patients with pulmonary embolism, to what extent do those with pulmonary infarction have a poorer *outcome* than those without pulmonary infarction?

TABLE 4-1

Categories of Clinical Information Resources

Category	Description	Degree of Evidence Processing	How Many Exist	Ease of Use
Systems	Textbook-like resources that summarize and integrate clinical evidence with other types of information directed at clinical practice decisions/directions	Substantial processing with the integration of evidence and practice—can direct care (give answers) or provide evidence on a clinical action	Few	Very easy
Synopses	Summaries of studies and systematic reviews that include guides or advice for application by expert clinicians	Evidence is externally assessed, with strengths and weaknesses provided for each article/topic	Several thousand	Easy
Summaries	Systematic review of articles and clinical practice guidelines—you assess the information and make decisions	Systematic reviews and high-quality guidelines summarize and present evidence from primary studies; some exemplary guidelines can also be considered synopses	Fewer than 50000	Use may be time consuming and access to full text may require some searching
Studies	Individual studies (eg, MEDLINE articles)	No processing of evidence at all—individuals must assess and apply	In the millions	Requires the clinician to critically appraise; they are hard to find and may require searching large databases

Derived from Haynes.[1]

Before formulating our search strategy and beginning our literature search to answer this question, we should think about how investigators would differentiate between those with and without infarction. Because no 100% definitive method, short of autopsy, makes this differentiation, our literature search is doomed before we even begin.

This example illustrates that the medical literature will not help you when no feasible study design exists that investigators could use to resolve an issue. Your search will also be futile if no one has taken the time and effort to conduct and publish the necessary study. Before embarking on a search, carefully consider whether the yield is likely to be worth the time expended.

FOUR CRITERIA FOR CHOOSING INFORMATION RESOURCES

Efficient searching involves choosing information sources appropriate for the clinical question—in much the same way you choose diagnostic tests appropriate for your patient's symptoms. The scheme in Table 4-1 offers an initial guideline for making choices. If a fully integrated and reliable resource (a "system" type resource) is likely to address your question, you would be wise to consider it. Depending on the level of detail you need, a *practice guideline* or systematic review, or a well-done synopsis of a guideline or systematic review, could be the next best option. For some questions, you will seek individual studies.

Table 4-2 describes selection criteria that are specific to deciding on an optimal information source. Although most clinicians would like at least 1 comprehensive

TABLE 4-2

Selection Criteria for Choosing or Evaluating Resources

Criterion	Description of Criterion
Soundness of evidence-based approach	How strong is the commitment to evidence to support inference?
	How well does the resource indicate the strength of the evidence behind the recommendations or other content?
	Does the resource provide links for those who wish to view the evidence?
Comprehensiveness and specificity	Does the resource cover my discipline or content area adequately?
	Does it cover questions of the type I am asking (eg, therapy, diagnosis, prognosis, harm)?
	Does it target my specific area of practice?
Ease of use	Does it give me the kind of information I need quickly and consistently?
Availability	Is it readily available in all locations in which I would use it?
	Can I easily afford it?

source of information on which they can rely, the particularities of the question being asked may demand access to a variety of resources.

Soundness of Evidence-Based Approach

An evidence-based information resource will provide access to a representative sample of the highest quality of evidence addressing a clinical question. Evidence-based resources that summarize evidence will explicitly frame their question, conduct a comprehensive search, assess the *validity* of the individual studies, and if appropriate provide a pooled estimate of the impact of the *outcomes* of interest (see Chapter 19, Summarizing the Evidence). Evidence-based resources that provide recommendations will use existing systematic reviews, or conduct their own, to provide best estimates of benefit and *risk* of alternative management strategies for all *patient-important outcomes*. They then will use an appropriate system to grade recommendations and will make explicit underlying *values and preferences* (see Chapter 21, How to Use a Patient Management Recommendation).

Comprehensiveness and Specificity

An ideal resource will cover most of the questions relevant to your practice—and that is all. Thus, resources limited to your area of practice, such as collections of synopses designed to help you keep up on the latest developments (eg, *Evidence-Based Cardiovascular Medicine*, *Evidence-Based Mental Health*, and *Evidence-Based Oncology*), may serve your needs most efficiently.

Some resources are specific to particular types of questions. For example, Clinical Evidence and Cochrane Database of Systematic Reviews currently restrict themselves to management issues and do not include studies of diagnostic accuracy (although both plan to soon include this material). The databases of the Cochrane Library are confined to *controlled trials* and systematic reviews of such trials.

Ease of Use

Some resources are easy and quick to use. For example, the relatively small size of the *ACP Journal Club* database facilitates searching. The database contains a collection of synopses of the most relevant high-quality studies appearing in approximately 140 journals related to internal medicine. Its excellent search engine further ensures an easy search for anything from viniyoga for low back pain through *meta-analyses* on cholesterol-lowering drugs or breast cancer associated with oral contraceptive use.

MEDLINE is much more challenging to use efficiently because of its size: slightly less than 17 million articles at the start of 2008 (http://www.nlm.nih.gov/bsd/licensee/2008_stats/baseline_med_filecount.html) and growing at the rate of 700 000 articles per year. PubMed, an interface to MEDLINE, is one of the easier ways of using MEDLINE. PubMed is designed for clinicians and includes features such as "Clinical Queries" that limit retrievals to those articles with high probability of being relevant to clinical decisions.

Clinicians may also find the Cochrane reviews challenging. Although you will usually be able to find a relevant Cochrane review quickly when it exists, the reviews are so comprehensive, complex, and variable in the quality of their presentation that they often require considerable time to digest and apply.

Availability

The most trustworthy and efficient resources are frequently expensive. Academic physicians characteristically have access to the online information resources of their medical school or hospital libraries, including the full texts of many journal articles. Physicians in private practice in high–gross domestic product countries may have access to some resources through their professional associations but otherwise may be burdened by the cost of subscriptions. Health professionals in poorer countries may have institutional access through the World Health Organization Health InterNetwork Access to Research Initiative (HINARI) project (http://www.who.int/hinari/en/) or other organizations but otherwise face even greater financial obstacles. Nevertheless, some resources such as PubMed and certain journals (eg, *Canadian Medical Association Journal* and most BioMed Central journals) are free to everyone (http://www.gfmer.ch/Medical_journals/Free_medical. php). Many other journals provide free access to content 6 to 12 months after publication (eg, *BMJ*, *JAMA*, and the *Mayo Proceedings*) or a portion of their contents at the time of publication. *Merck Manual*, an often-used online textbook (http://www.merck.com/mrkshared/mmanual/home.jsp), is also free. However, it largely fails the criterion of being as evidence based in its approach as some of the fee-based resources.

INFORMATION SOURCES THAT DO WELL ON AT LEAST SOME CRITERIA

Tables 4-3 and 4-4 provide brief comparative information concerning examples of resources in each category (systems, synopses, summaries, and studies). Table 4-3 includes those information resources that synthesize data and provide summaries of existing knowledge. For these resources, we include explicit discussions of how evidence is assessed and how this is transmitted to the users of specific information.

Table 4-4 includes those resources that do not synthesize data—they provide access to individual systematic reviews and original studies. We have included some of the major players in each table while trying to include some low-cost (or free) resources for those with limited budgets. The cost of resources is variable, depending on many factors, including individual vs library subscriptions and nationality. We have used US dollars rounded to the nearest $50 and late 2007 pricing for individual subscriptions. At the end of the tables, we offer a narrative description of the individual resources, paying special attention to their purpose and how they are prepared.

TABLE 4-3

Categorization of Representative Examples of Information Resources Readily Available

Category/ Examples of Category	Soundness of Evidence- Based Approach	Comprehensiveness	Ease of Use and Availability/Cost in US Dollars Rounded to the Nearest $50
Textbook-like Resources (Systems)			
Clinical Evidence	Strong	Only therapy; mainly primary care	Easy to use; commercially available; $300 for online and print version
PIER	Strong	Mostly therapy; mainly primary care and internal medicine	Easy to use; commercially available; $100 for PDA version
UpToDate	Moderate	Most clinical areas, especially internal medicine and primary care	Easy to use, although searching somewhat lacking; $450 for individuals for their first year, then $350 per year; $10000 plus for libraries
DynaMed	Strong	More than 2000 disease summaries presented in standard formats for primary-care physicians	Easy to use; $200 but free if you help in the development
EBM Guidelines	Strong	Most areas of primary-care practice	Internet versions $100; mobile (handheld PC, palm or telephone based) + Internet version $300; print $400; libraries and groups priced individually
Merck Manual	Weak	Covers most clinical areas	Easy to use; free
Preappraised (Synopses)			
ACP Journal Club	Strong	Recently published internal medicine studies; covers all categories of studies	Easy to use; $100 for print version
InfoPOEMs	Strong	Recently published family medicine studies; covers all categories of studies	Easy to use; $250
DARE (Database of Abstracts of Reviews of Effects) York, UK	Strong	Covers all disciplines; concentrates on therapy and prevention; summaries of systematic reviews of studies of diagnostic test performance may also be found	Easy to use; free
Bandolier	Strong	Limited coverage for primary-care physicians in the UK	Easy to use; $100 for print version, online free, although a lag time of several months between the two

TABLE 4-4

Information Resources That Provide Access to Systematic Reviews and Original Studies (Weight of the Evidence Applies to Each Study or Review Rather Than to the Total Resource)

Category/Examples of Categories	Comprehensiveness	Ease of Use/Availability
Systematic Reviews and Guidelines (Syntheses)		
Systematic reviews	Reviews of use in clinical care are often limited in scope; therefore, one needs to be able to quickly identify whether a relevant article exists	Hard to find and then even harder to get in full text; also need some work to apply the information in the review for clinical care
US National Guide-lines Clearinghouse	Comprehensive coverage of US and many other nations' guidelines; often several guidelines on the same topic	Easy to search; one of the strengths of the site is being able to "compare" guidelines on the same topic; free; many full-text guidelines available
Cochrane Database of Systematic Reviews	Covers broad range of disci-plines; limited to therapy and prevention	Easy to find a Cochrane review but sometimes difficult to apply because of the depth of cover-age; $300 but abstracts free; included in many composite resources such as Ovid
Primary Studies		
MEDLINE	Lots of primary studies across all disciplines and areas of research	Hard to find a specific study and often difficult to use; free through PubMed
Cochrane Con-trolled Trials Registry (CCTR)	All specialties and all topics for which a controlled trial is relevant (therapy and preven-tion mainly)	The Cochrane Library includes DARE, Cochrane systematic reviews, and CCTR; $300 for the whole library; the fastest way to determine whether a controlled trial has been published on the topic
PubMed Clinical Queries	Limits searches to those arti-cles with some possibility of having direct clinical application	Easier to use than MEDLINE because the queries turn MED-LINE into a clinical tool; free
CINAHL	Nursing database costs are high for those not associated with a teaching facility, hospi-tal library	Similar to MEDLINE in that the size introduces problems with being able to search easily and efficiently
Others		
Google	One of the major search engines to the Web—almost everything	Easy to find something, hard to find just what you want and to know the worth and evidence behind the content; fastest way to find high-impact articles that have recently made press and media headlines

(Continued)

TABLE 4-4

Information Resources That Provide Access to Systematic Reviews and Original Studies (Weight of the Evidence Applies to Each Study or Review Rather Than to the Total Resource) (Continued)

Category/Examples of Categories	Comprehensiveness	Ease of Use/Availability
SumSearch	One search system for many of the major health databases—one-stop searching; comprehensive	Easy to use; free access
TRIP	A single search system for 150 health databases; one-stop searching; comprehensive; also has 27 specialist subsections (allergy to urology)	Easy to use; free access
MEDLINEPlus	Comprehensive, with major emphasis on patient/consumer information; some good background information for physicians	Patient information with links to Web sites; free
Individual Web sites	Broad coverage but scattered	Almost unlimited and unknowable information; free

Often, information resources are available in various packages or formats of information (eg, the Internet, on PDAs, as standalone electronic or paper-based resources, and integrated into service packages). The vendor or supplier of the product or a librarian associated with your institution or professional group can help you determine your options for access. We end the chapter by providing search hints for those resources that are potentially useful for a broad range of clinicians but may be challenging to use efficiently.

Textbook-like Resources (Systems)

Clinical Evidence from the *BMJ* Publishing Group (http://www.clinicalevidence.com/ceweb/conditions/index.jsp) covers more than 200 diseases and 2500 treatments and is regularly updated and extended with new topics. Its content draws on published systematic reviews or reviews that the staff completes for authors and is presented in question format (eg, Does regular use of mouthwashes reduce halitosis?). The resource provides the evidence for benefits and *harms* for specific treatments and tells you if the *evidence* is weak or nonexistent (eg, sugar-free gum for halitosis). *Clinical Evidence* has started to begin to address some issues of diagnosis.

PIER is the Physician Information Education and Resource from the American College of Physicians (http://pier.acponline.org/index.html). Its strengths are the direction that it provides for the clinician and the strong evidence-based approach. Authors who are clinical experts receive notification of newly published studies and systematic review articles that have importance to their chapter. Chapters are carefully built around a consistent structure, and all recommendations are tightly linked to the evidence behind the recommendation.

In contrast to *Clinical Evidence*, PIER provides explicit recommendations. Content and evidence are presented using standard methods across diseases and disciplines. The authors of each chapter explicitly state their question, are comprehensive in considering all interventions and patient-important outcomes, assess the validity of individual studies, use a high-quality grading system, and make their values and preference explicit. PIER focuses on treatment, although it does include diagnosis and legal and ethical aspects of health care issues. Its major limitation is lack of comprehensive coverage.

UpToDate is an online textbook that, at least in part because of its ease of use, comprehensiveness, and inclusion of disease-oriented information, is very popular with generalists, specialists, and particularly house staff (http://www.uptodate.com/index.asp). Like PIER, and unlike *Clinical Evidence*, UpToDate provides recommendations (guidelines) for clinicians. It is pricey for libraries, although costs for individuals are similar to those of other information products. Although there is some variation in the extent to which it currently succeeds across topics, UpToDate is committed to structured formulation of questions, identifying an unbiased selection of relevant evidence-based literature on a wide-ranging (though not comprehensive) search, and, in its latest development, using the grades of recommendation, assessment, development, and evaluation (GRADE) system (see Chapter 22.4, Grading Recommendations) to assess quality of evidence and strength of recommendations. UpToDate explicitly acknowledges the importance of values and preferences in decision making and includes value and preference statements.

DynaMed is a service for primary-care physicians with almost 2000 disease summaries that are updated with information from journal hand-searches and electronic scans of more than 500 journal titles (http://www.dynamicmedical.com/). All information has levels of evidence and grades of recommendations. Although you can obtain DynaMed by subscription or through your library, if you volunteer to help build the resource, you receive free access to the database.

EBM Guidelines is a series of recommendations covering a wide range of topics relevant to primary care. It was originally produced by the Finnish Medical Society with government funding to provide evidence-based guidelines and recommendations for national use. All guidelines are reviewed annually. Recommendations are linked to the evidence, and both the Cochrane and DARE systematic reviews are summarized to produce and maintain a comprehensive collection of treatment and diagnostic guidelines. Recommendations are linked to almost 1000 clinical guidelines and 2500 graded evidence summaries, with more than 350 clinical experts as authors. Images and audio files are also included. Specialists consulting on neighboring specialties may find it of use. It is available in several languages, including English, Finnish, German, Swedish, Russian, Estonian, and Hungarian, with more to follow. Subscription information is at http://www.ebm-guidelines.com.

Merck Manual is available on the Internet at no cost. Unlike UpToDate or *Clinical Evidence*, a systematic consideration of current research does not routinely underlie its recommendations. Strengths include its comprehensiveness, user friendliness, and zero cost (http://www.merck.com/mrkshared/mmanual/home.jsp).

Preappraised Resources (Synopses)

ACP Journal Club, *Evidence-Based Medicine*, and a number of journals modeled on *ACP Journal Club* are available by print subscription or as online publications. The research staff of *ACP Journal Club* read 140 core health care and specialty journals to identify high-quality studies and review articles that have potential for clinical application (those that have strong methods, answer a clinical question, and report data on clinically important outcomes). From this pool of articles, practicing physicians choose the most clinically important studies with the greatest potential clinical impact. These are then summarized in structured abstracts. A clinical expert comments on methods and provides advice on application of the findings. Only 1 in approximately 150 articles is deemed important enough for abstracting. The online version (current issues and a searchable database of all content) is available from the American College of Physicians or through the Ovid Technologies collection of databases. *ACP Journal Club* is aimed largely at internal medicine and its subspecialties but also includes limited entries relevant to other specialties including pediatrics.

InfoPOEMs is similar to *ACP Journal Club* in that it provides alerting to well-done and important clinical advances and a searching service of its collected articles. Its main focus is family medicine. Clinical staff read more than 100 journals for articles of direct application to common and uncommon diseases and conditions seen by family physicians. The compilation of past issues (searchable database) is called InfoRETRIEVER (http://www.infopoems.com/). Well structured and well presented, all articles have a clinical bottom line for primary-care decisions that users appreciate. Like *ACP Journal Club*, InfoPOEMs is restricted in its scope of practice and to recently published articles. Subscription includes regular e-mail notification of new evidence, as well as downloading to individual computers and ongoing Web access.

Bandolier provides a summary service for the National Health Service in the United Kingdom that is also available worldwide (http://www.jr2.ox.ac.uk/bandolier/). It covers selected clinical topics over a broad range of disciplines and combines a review of clinical evidence with clinical commentary and recommendations.

The New York Academy of Medicine Web site (http://www.ebmny.org/journal.html) provides a list of these preappraised resources (synopses) including specialty-specific journals modeled on *ACP Journal Club*. Non-English examples of preappraised resources exist. For example, Medycyna Praktyczna is published in Polish (http://www.mp.pl). *Evidence-Based Medicine*, the synoptic journal for primary-care physicians and internists, published by the BMJ Publishing Group (http://ebm.bmjjournals.com/), is also translated into French (http://www.ebm-journal.presse.fr/) and Italian (http://www.infomedica.com/ebm.htm).

Systematic Reviews and Guidelines (Summaries)

Cochrane Database of Systematic Reviews, built and maintained by the Cochrane Collaboration, contains systematic reviews that cover almost all health care interventions (therapy and prevention) (http://www3.interscience.wiley.com/cgi-bin/mrwhome/106568753/HOME). As of the 2008 Issue 1, 3385 reviews had been completed, with an additional 1786 posted protocols of reviews in progress. Each review is extremely comprehensive—to a fault. The Cochrane reviews are available in many forms and from various vendors (eg, in Ovid and PubMed, as well as standalone and Web versions from Wiley InterScience). Searching is easy, although some systems are easier to use than others. Abstracts are free, but the full reviews require a subscription or institutional source. Some countries such as the United Kingdom, Australia, New Zealand, and Iceland have country-wide access provided by government funding, and some lower-GDP countries have been granted free access (http://www3.interscience.wiley.com/cgi-bin/mrwhome/106568753/DoYouAlreadyHaveAccess.html). Most academic and large hospital libraries provide access to the full text of the Cochrane reviews.

DARE (Database of Abstracts of Reviews of Effects) is a free database of critically appraised summaries of non-Cochrane systematic reviews in a broad range of health topics and disciplines (http://www.york.ac.uk/inst/crd/crddatabases.htm#DARE). It is a stand-alone Web-based resource and is also included in the Cochrane Library. DARE includes more systematic reviews than does Cochrane, but the DARE reviews are not as comprehensive—more than 600 reviews are added annually. DARE is easy and fast to search, and the developers pay attention to the strength of the evidence of each review they summarize. The DARE summaries of others' reviews may be particularly useful to clinicians who do not have either the time to appraise or electronic access to the full text of the original reviews—this feature allows some people to suggest that DARE can be categorized as a synopses resource.

Clinical practice guidelines that are strongly evidence based provide helpful direction for decision making by health professionals. The US National Guidelines Clearinghouse database includes the full text of many US and international guidelines on almost all conceivable topics (http://www.guideline.gov/). The Web site includes thousands of guidelines and provides systematic summaries of more than 2200. Searching is easy, although initial retrievals are often relatively large. The site allows comparison of several guidelines on the computer screen at the same time by checking the guidelines you want, adding them to your collection, and comparing the checked guidelines. The resulting information includes a side-by-side comparison of the components of the guideline such as methods of searching the literature and specification of their making values and preferences explicit (see Chapter 21, How to Use a Patient Management Recommendation). Other international guidelines can be found at the UK National Library for Health (http://libraries.nelh.nhs.uk/guidelinesFinder/default.asp?page=INTER). The Ontario Medical Association goes one step further in the evaluation process. They provide a collection of preappraised guidelines that meet strict quality criteria (http://www.gacguidelines.ca/).

Many systematic reviews are included in MEDLINE and other large databases. The systematic reviews are often difficult to retrieve from these databases because of the volume of other citations.

Original/Primary Studies (Studies)

Millions of primary studies exist, and processing of the evidence takes time and effort. Because systems, synopses, and summaries conduct much of this processing, we recommend using original studies in clinical care only when you cannot find the answers to your questions elsewhere. If you do need to retrieve original studies, you will likely use the following large bibliographic databases to aid your retrieval.

MEDLINE is the premier database of health care research and practice. Many of the more traditional methods of access to the MEDLINE articles (eg, Ovid Technologies; http://www.ovid.com/site/index.jsp?top=1) are designed to facilitate complex search strategies such as those done by medical librarians. You have many options for obtaining access to MEDLINE (http://www.diabetesmonitor.com/database.htm), although most clinicians use Ovid (through their institutions) or PubMed.

PubMed Clinical Queries (http://www.ncbi.nlm.nih.gov/entrez/query/static/clinical.shtml) function so that your searching is restricted to a "virtual" database of the studies in MEDLINE that are likely to have direct clinical application. PubMed also can search the whole MEDLINE database.

CINAHL (Cumulative Index to Nursing and Allied Health Literature; http://www.cinahl.com/) database is independent of MEDLINE and is the premier nursing and allied health database. Clinicians of all backgrounds may find it useful to search for articles on *quality of care* and *quality improvement*. It is also rich in *qualitative research*. Emergency physicians may use it as a source for issues relevant to prehospital emergency care. As with other large databases, multiple access routes are available (http://www.cinahl.com/prodsvcs/prodsvcs.htm).

EMBASE (http://www.elsevier.com/wps/find/bibliographicdatabasedescription.cws_home/523328/description#description) is a large European database (more than 11 million citations) that is similar to MEDLINE in scope and content, with strengths in drugs and allied health disciplines. Clinicians are unlikely to use EMBASE because of its limited availability—major research institutions rather than hospitals or smaller organizations are the most common suppliers of access based on cost considerations. Up to 70% of citations in EMBASE are not included in MEDLINE.

Cochrane Controlled Trials Registry, part of the Cochrane Library (http://www.cochrane.org/reviews/clibintro.htm), is the largest electronic compilation of controlled trials in existence (527885 citations as of 2008, Issue 1) and is available as part of a subscription to the Cochrane Library or several Ovid Evidence-Based Medicine Review packages of databases (http://www.ovid.com/site/catalog/DataBase/904.jsp?top=2&mid=3&bottom=7&subsection=10). Their registry of original trials is a companion database to the Cochrane systematic reviews database. This registry is built from large databases, including MEDLINE and EMBASE, as well as other sources used by the review groups within the Cochrane Collaboration, including hand-searches of most major health care journals. The trials registry is the fastest, most reliable method of determining whether a controlled trial has been published on any topic.

Alerting or Updating Services

Electronic communication (ie, e-mail) is an excellent method of keeping clinicians abreast of evidence in newly published studies and systematic reviews. You can easily receive the table of contents of journals or newly published articles on a specific topic or subscribe to a service that notifies you of advances across many journals.

PubMed, through its My NCBI service (http://www.ncbi.nlm.nih.gov/books/bv.fcgi?rid=helpPubMed.section.PubMedhelp.My_NCBI), allows you to establish a search that will automatically e-mail you citations of newly published articles based on content (eg, asthma in adolescents) or journal titles. The Chinese University of Hong Kong maintains a Web site with links to sign up for e-mail alerts from all major journal publishers (http://www.lib.cuhk.edu.hk/information/publisher.htm).

Bmjupdates+ is a free alerting service to newly published studies and systematic reviews from 140 journals (http://bmjupdates.mcmaster.ca/index.asp). You choose the frequency with which you want to receive e-mail notifications, choose the disciplines in which you are interested, and set the score level on clinical relevance and newsworthiness as determined by peer raters in multiple disciplines.

InfoPOEMs (http://www.infopoems.com/) also provides e-mail alerts to new clinical evidence in studies and systematic reviews. Each alert includes a clinical bottom line on the application of the findings.

Journal Watch Online is another alerting service (http://www.jwatch.org/issues_by_date.shtml) with a broad coverage of new evidence. *The New England Journal of Medicine* produces this service with the aim of keeping clinicians up to date on the most important research in the general medical literature. Journal Watch provides nonstructured summaries and commentaries on articles it identifies but does not use a quality filter or structured critical appraisal of the sort embodied in the resources described above under synopses.

Other Resources

Many search engines exist for the Internet, of which Google (http://www.google.com/) is the most popular, followed by Ask (formerly Ask Jeeves) (http://www.ask.com/), MSN (http://www.msn.com/), and Yahoo (http://www.yahoo.com/). Search engines either send out electronic "spiders" that "crawl" the Web to index material for later retrieval or rely on human indexing of sites. Search Engine Watch maintains a list of important and heavily used services (http://searchenginewatch.com/links/article.php/2156221) and rates usefulness of each. Almost limitless amounts of information are available on the Internet. Characteristically, one finds information from unsubstantiated or nonscientifically supervised sources freely interspersed with references to articles in peer-reviewed biomedical journals.

Internet searchers should understand that they are not searching a defined database but rather are surfing the constantly shifting seas of electronic communications. The material that is supported by evidence may not float to the surface at any particular time. On the other hand, an Internet search may constitute the fastest way of tracking down an article that has attracted media attention shortly after its release and during the period in which it has not yet been indexed by MEDLINE or will not likely be indexed.

Google Scholar (http://scholar.google.com/) is a service that provides Google-like searching of scholarly information (eg, articles, dissertations, books, abstracts, and full text from publishers). MEDLINE is included (although it may be up to a year out of date). You have access to ranked material (most important and not necessarily the newest information first) and to other documents that cite an important item you have identified. Google Scholar has a complex searching system, and the Help feature is actually quite helpful (http://scholar.google.com/intl/en/scholar/help.html).

Search engines that retrieve and combine results from multiple search engines (metasearch engines) also exist (http://searchenginewatch.com/links/article.php/2156241).

- **SumSearch** is a medical metasearch engine. By using it, you can search multiple medical databases with 1 entry of search terms (http://sumsearch.uthscsa.edu/). For example, the entry of 1 word, "bedrest," provided grouped links to 27 entries in Wikipedia, 21 guidelines (US National Guidelines Clearinghouse), 18 broad or narrative reviews (good to answer background questions), 1 DARE or Cochrane systematic review, 87 other systematic reviews from PubMed, and 59 original studies covering therapy and etiology studies from PubMed Clinical Queries. In contrast, Google retrieves approximately 588 000 entries on "bedrest" and the items are not grouped by source or like items for easier access.

- **TRIP** is similar to SumSearch in that it searches multiple databases and other strongly evidence-based resources with just 1 entry of your term or terms (http://www.tripdatabase.com/). TRIP currently searches more than 150 databases and related resources. It is rich in systematic reviews, clinical practice guidelines (US, UK, Canadian, Australian, and New Zealand national collections), clinical questions and answers, and medical images. It also has a substantial collection of patient information resources, as well as critical appraisal topics (CATs). It harnesses the PubMed Clinical Queries in its searching and includes links to the bmjupdates+ to enable a more clinically relevant retrieval set of documents. TRIP was once a fee-based system but is now free. It has 27 specialist mini-TRIP systems based on health care content (allergy to urology) early in 2008.

MEDLINEPlus is the premier site for Web links to health information on the Internet. The US National Library of Medicine provides this free service, which is designed to provide high-quality and important health information to patients and families. The staff members provide access to Web sites that meet preestablished quality criteria. Some information is likely useful to clinicians, especially in areas in which they are not experts. Many clinicians feel confident sending their patients to MEDLINEPlus for consumer/patient information (http://medlineplus.gov/).

Format

Information resources are available in many formats: paper, standalone computer installations (eg, CD-ROM disks), or via the Internet. The handheld computer is becoming a major player in providing information resources quickly and at the site of care. We have not included a primer on how to choose handhelds or information resources for them. Peers, commercial sites, or the handhelds themselves are the best sources of determining if handheld devices are the vehicle for providing you with information resources.

ADDRESSING EXAMPLE QUESTIONS

The rest of this chapter provides searching tips for question types and specific information resources. We concentrate on resources that are challenging to use effectively and that are readily available.

Background Questions

Most background questions are often best answered by standard textbooks such as *Harrison's Principles of Internal Medicine, Nelson Textbook of Pediatrics, Benson's Current Obstetric and Gynecological Diagnoses and Treatments*, and *Lawrence's Essentials of General Surgery* or innovative electronic texts such as UpToDate. To provide faster searching for background questions, some companies also group collections of textbooks together to be searched in tandem. Two major collections of medical texts are MDConsult (http://www.mdconsult.com/offers/standard.html) and Stat!Ref (http://www.statref.com/). These collections often include other resources besides textbooks.

Textbooks and other resources classified as systems are often easy to search. Most of them rely on entry of a single concept such as a disease or diagnostic test that leads you to various categories or chapters. The Internet may also be very useful for background questions.

Foreground Questions

The most efficient sources of information for foreground questions are resources that are classified in the information categories of systems and synopses.

Searching in Systems and Synopses-Based Resources (Small Resources)

You can search small-sized resources using common words or phrases such as diseases or conditions and categories such as therapy or prognosis—their size makes them easy and efficient to search. For example, in *ACP Journal Club*, all of the 9 "house dust mite" articles can be found by putting in only "mites" as a searching word (Ovid MEDLINE and PubMed have approximately 10000 articles on mites). Usually, some simple experimentation with a new system or a few tips from fellow users are sufficient for getting started. Continued experience with the resource usually hones searching skills.

Searching for Synopses and Summaries (Moderately Sized Resources)

As a resource grows, it becomes more difficult to use effectively—single words or simple phrases retrieve too much information. Synopses and summary resources are usually resources that are larger than the systems (textbook-like resources) but far smaller than resources that include studies (eg, MEDLINE). Simple terms and phrases with some category choices are sufficient for smaller resources, but designing effective searching strategies with these larger information resources requires more attention.

The same or similar search strategy may perform differently, depending on the route of access to a particular database. For example, the standalone version of Cochrane systematic reviews by the electronic publisher Wiley InterScience has a search engine that often searches for all occurrences of your search terms across the full information in the database. This method can retrieve large sets of citations, many of which are not relevant but are retrieved because of single occurrences of the search terms.

The Ovid search engine for the same database performs differently. Ovid Technologies is a major resource in providing information to clinicians. Ovid provides access to a large selection of databases, including MEDLINE and the Cochrane Library. Its strength is its comprehensive collection of resources that are accessed using the same searching mechanisms. The drawback of this approach is that because of the size of some of the resources, the searching system is complex, requiring a relatively steep learning curve. Ovid searching is more complex and often more parsimonious. For example, the search of the Cochrane Database of Systematic Reviews using the Ovid interface yields 31 reviews, whereas the Wiley InterScience database yields 42 reviews, even though both systems search for the phrase "patient adherence."

Most resources beyond very small products have tutorials and searching tips, and medical librarians are often available to help you learn how to use a system individually or in a class session.

Searching for Summaries and Primary Studies Using PubMed

If (and only if) resources similar to the ones described above fail to provide an answer to your clinical questions, you then can move to one of the large databases such as MEDLINE. One of the most available systems is PubMed. The US National Library of Medicine has done substantial work to develop the PubMed search interface to the MEDLINE database so that PubMed is easy for clinicians to use effectively. PubMed is free and more than 70 million searches are done each month (http://www.nlm.nih.gov/pubs/factsheets/PubMed.html). The makers of PubMed have developed a useful and comprehensive tutorial (http://www.nlm.nih.gov/bsd/PubMed_tutorial/m2001.html) that can complement trial-and-error learning.

Because PubMed is a useful resource across disciplines and is readily available, we will show you some simple tips and techniques. Our demonstration is designed to equip the reader with a basic orientation. Many clinicians in search of relatively high-quality studies pertaining to a specific question find it expedient to bypass most of this system and to go directly to the Clinical Queries function, which we describe below. To facilitate the effectiveness of these demonstrations, we recommend that you call up PubMed on your own browser and "follow along" by performing the steps yourself as we describe them.

Simple Searching Using Phrases (Natural Language)

Like many other information resources such as Google, PubMed has a single searching box. Just type in a sentence or series of phrases that represent exactly what you are searching. The choice of terms to use will be easy if you have developed questions using the PICO format: patients, intervention, comparison, and outcome. PubMed uses Google spell checker and is programmed to do the work of finding synonyms for your terms—just put in 1 phrase or word per PICO concept. Generally, if you use 3 or more concepts, your retrieval will be limited to a reasonable-sized retrieval. No matter how effective your searching skills, however, your search retrievals will almost inevitably include some citations that are not on topic.

One often successful method to enrich your search retrieval is to click on the Related Articles button to the right of the article in which you are most interested. PubMed will then search for articles it thinks are related to yours. If your initial searching finds an article that is an exact match to your topic, the Related Articles feature is often fruitful to identify more citations.

To show you how these approaches to searching can work, see figures in the text. We started with a PICO question (Table 4-5) looking at determining the ideal gestational age for a term twin pregnancy in a 35-year-old woman who wants to know whether a planned cesarean section or planned vaginal delivery is associated with improved outcomes, specifically, mortality.

We entered the 4 sets of searching terms in January 2008 (term twin pregnancy, planned C-section, vaginal delivery, and mortality) in the PubMed searching box and only found 3 articles (Figure 4-1). The second one, by Smith et al,[9] looks like a very good match to our question. This retrieval set is small and the question of cesarean section or vaginal delivery for twins fairly common; therefore, many more studies have probably addressed this question. Rather than selecting another set of terms and trying again, you can click on the Related Articles link in Figure 4-1. This retrieval is now 1301 articles (Figure 4-2). These are too many, but the search is still useful because the articles are listed in rank order of perceived importance—you only need to scan down the list until you have the information you need or find another citation that you want to check for related articles. This Related Articles method of searching is very quick and removes the necessity of finding precise searching terms. If you do not like your results, just quickly switch to another set of searching phrases and start the cycle again.

You can also see the related articles as you go through a list of citations. For example, if you were looking for studies that used children's drawings in the

TABLE 4-5

PICO and Determination of Searching Terms

PICO	Element	Search Terms for PubMed
P(atient)	Term twin pregnancy	Term twin pregnancy
I(ntervention)	Planned cesarean section	Planned C-section
C(omparison)	Planned vaginal delivery	Vaginal delivery
O(utcome)	Infant mortality	Mortality

FIGURE 4-1

PubMed Retrieval Using a Set of Phrases

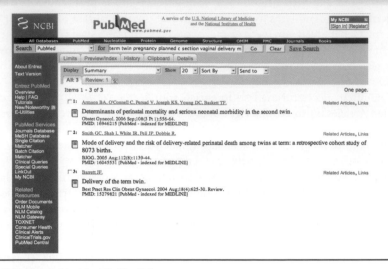

Note the Related Articles links at the right of the citations.

Reproduced with permission of the U.S. National Library of Medicine (NLM) and PubMed.

FIGURE 4-2

Retrieval Based on the Related Article Link, Going From 3 Citations to Many More Returned in "Importance" Order

Reproduced with permission of the U.S. National Library of Medicine (NLM) and PubMed.

diagnosis of migraine headache and retrieved a set of citations that looked interesting, you can ask for the display format to be "AbstractPlus" (Figure 4-3). You will obtain the view below. The main article shows that children's drawings are useful starting at 4 years of age for helping with the diagnosis of migraine. The first related article is an update of the study that shows that the same drawing mechanism can provide data that can plot the success or failure of the treatment of the children's migraines.

In PubMed, or other systems, you are not limited to phrases that could be in the title or abstract alone. The search in the screen below is one that is set to retrieve an article that we know already exists in *CMAJ*. Belanger studied the timing of infant cereal feeding and the risk for celiac disease. We used the terms "belanger cmaj timing" in Figure 4-4. Note the full-text icon—all articles in *CMAJ* are freely available in full text, and you can get to the whole article directly from a PubMed citation.

Articles that are available in full text have symbols providing this access either at the publisher's site or at PubMed Central. These full-text links are available for several hundred journal titles, and their numbers are increasing. To add to the number of full-text articles to which you have access, some hospital and university libraries have installed links from their collection of full-text journals into PubMed. To access the version of PubMed that is customized for your library and its

FIGURE 4-3

Diagnosis of Migraine in Children by Using Their Drawings

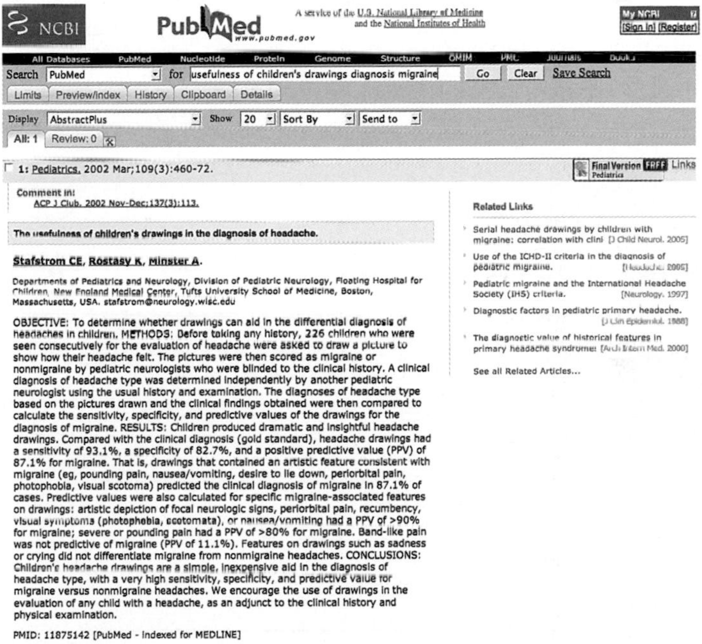

NCBI PubMed www.pubmed.gov

A service of the U.S. National Library of Medicine and the National Institutes of Health

My NCBI [Sign In] [Register]

All Databases PubMed Nucleotide Protein Genome Structure OMIM PMC Journals Books

Search PubMed for usefulness of children's drawings diagnosis migraine Go Clear Save Search

Limits Preview/Index History Clipboard Details

Display AbstractPlus Show 20 Sort By Send to

All: 1 Review: 0

1: Pediatrics. 2002 Mar;109(3):460-72.

Final Version FREE Pediatrics Links

Comment in:
ACP J Club. 2002 Nov-Dec;137(3):113.

The usefulness of children's drawings in the diagnosis of headache.

Stafstrom CE, Rostasy K, Minster A.

Departments of Pediatrics and Neurology, Division of Pediatric Neurology, Floating Hospital for Children, New England Medical Center, Tufts University School of Medicine, Boston, Massachusetts, USA. stafstrom@neurology.wisc.edu

OBJECTIVE: To determine whether drawings can aid in the differential diagnosis of headaches in children. METHODS: Before taking any history, 226 children who were seen consecutively for the evaluation of headache were asked to draw a picture to show how their headache felt. The pictures were then scored as migraine or nonmigraine by pediatric neurologists who were blinded to the clinical history. A clinical diagnosis of headache type was determined independently by another pediatric neurologist using the usual history and examination. The diagnoses of headache type based on the pictures drawn and the clinical findings obtained were then compared to calculate the sensitivity, specificity, and predictive values of the drawings for the diagnosis of migraine. RESULTS: Children produced dramatic and insightful headache drawings. Compared with the clinical diagnosis (gold standard), headache drawings had a sensitivity of 93.1%, a specificity of 82.7%, and a positive predictive value (PPV) of 87.1% for migraine. That is, drawings that contained an artistic feature consistent with migraine (eg, pounding pain, nausea/vomiting, desire to lie down, periorbital pain, photophobia, visual scotoma) predicted the clinical diagnosis of migraine in 87.1% of cases. Predictive values were also calculated for specific migraine-associated features on drawings: artistic depiction of focal neurologic signs, periorbital pain, recumbency, visual symptoms (photophobia, scotomata), or nausea/vomiting had a PPV of >90% for migraine; severe or pounding pain had a PPV of >80% for migraine. Band-like pain was not predictive of migraine (PPV of 11.1%). Features on drawings such as sadness or crying did not differentiate migraine from nonmigraine headaches. CONCLUSIONS: Children's headache drawings are a simple, inexpensive aid in the diagnosis of headache type, with a very high sensitivity, specificity, and predictive value for migraine versus nonmigraine headaches. We encourage the use of drawings in the evaluation of any child with a headache, as an adjunct to the clinical history and physical examination.

PMID: 11875142 [PubMed - indexed for MEDLINE]

Related Links

- Serial headache drawings by children with migraine: correlation with clini [J Child Neurol. 2005]
- Use of the ICHD-II criteria in the diagnosis of pediatric migraine. [Headache. 2005]
- Pediatric migraine and the International Headache Society (IHS) criteria. [Neurology. 1997]
- Diagnostic factors in pediatric primary headache. [J Clin Epidemiol. 1988]
- The diagnostic value of historical features in primary headache syndrome: [Arch Intern Med. 2000]

See all Related Articles...

Article presented with links to related articles.

Reproduced with permission of the U.S. National Library of Medicine (NLM) and PubMed.

FIGURE 4-4

Searching for a Known Article and Notice of Full-Text Availability

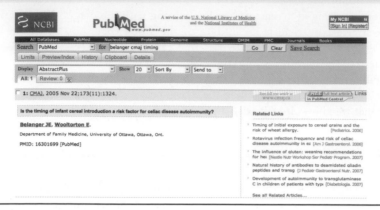

Reproduced with permission of the U.S. National Library of Medicine (NLM) and PubMed.

collection of online journals, check with your librarian to see if this feature is available to you and how best to access it.

Limits

You can limit your retrieval in PubMed by using all sorts of aspects of individual articles (eg, year of publication, sex of participants, English language, and article type such as a randomized controlled trial [RCT] or meta-analysis). We will look at the function of the limits button in Figure 4-5, as well as describe the ability of PubMed to "understand" your search terms. In the search, we wanted to identify meta-analyses of nursing clinics to reduce hospitalizations in elderly patients with congestive heart failure. The

FIGURE 4-5

PubMed Searching Showing Limits

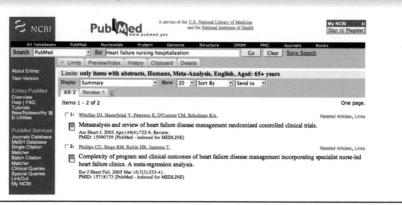

Reproduced with permission of the U.S. National Library of Medicine (NLM) and PubMed.

TABLE 4-6

PICO and Determination of Searching Terms

PICO	Element	Search Terms for PubMed
P(atient/opulation)	Elderly patients with heart failure	Limit by age to > 65 y heart failure
I(ntervention)	Nurse-led clinics	Nursing
C(omparison)	Any	[Nothing—leave concept out]
O(utcome)	Hospital admission	Hospitalization
Other concepts	Meta-analysis	Limit to meta-analysis

PICO representation of the question follows in Table 4-6. In this case, we are dealing with a patient population rather than a patient—both fit into the PICO format.

Taking advantage of PubMed's ability to recognize alternate searching terms, we limited our typing by entering "heart failure nursing hospitalization" in the search box and clicking on limits for meta-analysis, human participants, participants who are more than 65 years of age, English language, and articles with abstracts (a technique to retrieve more studies and fewer letters and editorials) (Figure 4-5). PubMed automatically translated our search into the strategy in Table 4-7. Note that the concept of hospitalization is searched using US and UK spellings. Note also that this translation of terms does not always work, because we not only got the aspect of using nurses to improve care but also got articles on breast feeding. Because we added the geriatric age limit, the breast feeding aspect will likely not complicate our retrieval.

Text word means any occurrence of the word or phrase in the title or abstract of the article; MeSH terms are medical subject headings (controlled vocabulary) that indexes apply to all MEDLINE articles.

Clinical Queries are available in PubMed, as well as Ovid, and are used by many clinicians to make their MEDLINE searching faster and more efficient for clinical topics. The "path" to Clinical Queries is on the left-hand side of the screen within

TABLE 4-7

PubMed Translation of Concepts Into Searching Terms and Strategies

Heart failure	"heart failure" [Text Word] or "heart failure" [MeSH Terms]
Hospitalization	"hospitalization" [Text Word] or "hospitalisation" [Text Word] or "hospitalization" [MeSH Terms]
Nursing	"nursing" [Subheading] or "nursing" [MeSH Terms] or ("breast feeding" [Text Word]) or "breast feeding" [MeSH Terms] or "nursing" [Text Word]
Geriatrics	"aged" [MeSH Terms]
Humans	"humans" [MeSH Terms]

FIGURE 4-6

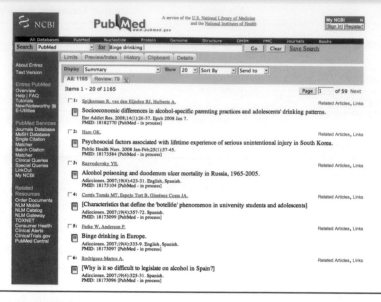

Binge Drinking Retrievals From All of MEDLINE

Reproduced with permission of the U.S. National Library of Medicine (NLM) and PubMed.

the blue bar (see Figure 4-5). The screen shots in Figures 4-6 to 4-8 show how one would progress through several screens, looking for high-quality clinical studies assessing the mortality related to binge drinking. The PICO question ("In adults, is binge drinking compared with nonbinge drinking associated with an increase in mortality?") with search terms is included in Table 4-8.

Figure 4-6 shows a search for binge drinking only: it retrieves more than 1100 articles. Adding the Clinical Queries limit for etiology with a broad search (sensitive search) brings the total down to 796—still too high (Figure 4-7). What the clinical queries do in practice is to take a set of search terms that have proven effective at retrieving high-quality clinical articles that have the potential to be important to questions related to

TABLE 4-8

PICO and Determination of Searching Terms

PICO	Element	Search Terms for PubMed
P(atient)	Adults	[Leave blank]
I(ntervention/exposure)	Binge drinking	Binge drinking
C(omparison)	No binge drinking	[Leave blank]
O(utcome)	Mortality	Mortality

FIGURE 4-7

Clinical Queries Search for Binge Drinking: Broad-Based Etiology/Harm Search

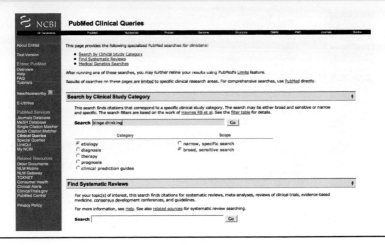

Reproduced with permission of the U.S. National Library of Medicine (NLM) and PubMed.

therapy, diagnosis, etc. You then add your content, in this case binge drinking, and PubMed adds the appropriate methods terms. For a broad etiology search, these terms are (risk *[Title/Abstract] OR risk *[MeSH:noexp] OR risk *[MeSH:noexp] OR cohort studies [MeSH Terms] OR group *[Text Word]). (The asterisk [*] denotes truncation—picking up multiple endings for the term. The noexp indicates that the system is not picking up terms related but not equivalent to the term in question.) You can see the start of this search strategy string in the searching box of Figure 4-8. Switching to the narrow clinical queries search for etiology (specific search) brings the number of retrieved studies down to approximately 100 citations. Figures 4-9 and 4-10 show you how to "take control" of the searching process and do some of your own manipulation.

By clicking on the "history" tab, you can get to a list of the search statements that you have used in your most recent search session (Figure 4-9). For our search, the statement number 9 is the search that is binge-drinking limited by using the broad clinical category search for etiology. (If you are following along, your statement number is likely different.) The retrieval for search statement 9 is substantial, and we have not added the concept of "mortality." We could do this in several ways. However, for this example, we work with our existing search statements. We want to combine our etiology search on binge drinking with mortality. In the search box at the top of the page, we type in "#9" and combine it with the term "mortality"—note that you can use "AND" or "and" (#9 AND mortality). ANDing in the term "mortality" brings retrieval down to 83 citations of mortality associated with binge drinking, using the etiology clinical queries filter.

Searching for Summaries and Primary Studies Using Other Large Information Resources

The large databases such as MEDLINE, CINAHL, PsycINFO, and EMBASE provide challenges to clinicians wanting to find information directly applicable to

FIGURE 4-8

Search Retrieval Using the Broad Etiology Hedge

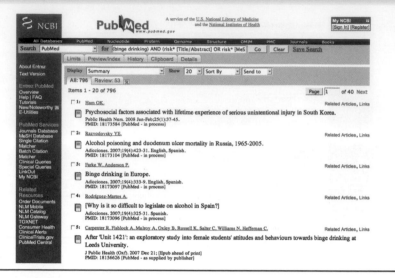

Reproduced with permission of the U.S. National Library of Medicine (NLM) and PubMed.

FIGURE 4-9

Taking Control of PubMed and Adding Terms of Your Choice to Existing Searches

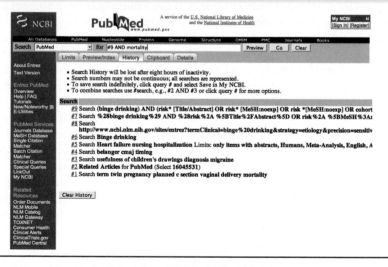

Reproduced with permission of the U.S. National Library of Medicine (NLM) and PubMed.

FIGURE 4-10

Retrieval Using ANDing a Word to Previous Searches

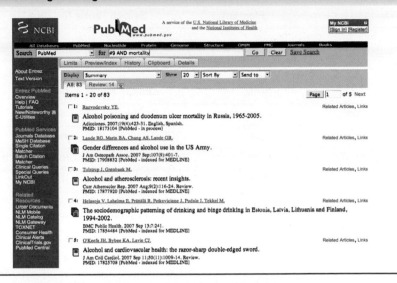

Reproduced with permission of the U.S. National Library of Medicine (NLM) and PubMed.

clinical care. The size of the database and the relatively few important and relevant studies that are buried within the large volume of literature make the searching complex. Although a few initial tips followed by trial-and-error practice should allow you to become proficient in doing simple searches, comprehensive searches aiming at high accuracy require the expertise of a research librarian.

Many libraries are equipped with a customized collection of databases and services from Ovid Technologies. Ovid provides a single front-end search and links across databases and services to full texts of articles available to that library system. To show some of the power and complexity of searching using Ovid, we have entered a search in Ovid format designed to look for studies of using either oral or intravenous antibiotics in a 28-year-old male intravenous drug user with endocarditis. The PICO format of the question is shown in Table 4-9.

In Ovid searching, one builds searches idea by idea (Figure 4-11). To start this building process, our first search concept is endocarditis—entering the term and checking it in the list of preferred terminology MeSH shows that, between 1996 and 2008, 5726 articles include information on endocarditis. We have asked the system to automatically search for all aspects of a topic—this "explode" feature allows for gathering together general aspects of endocarditis and bacterial endocarditis. Using the same approach during the same period, 5679 articles deal with some aspect of intravenous substance abuse, more than 100 000 articles on any antibiotic, almost 40 000 on oral administration of drugs, and more than 25 000 on parenteral infusions. The explosion of parenteral infusions picks up the intravenous infusions, a closer approximation of what we are looking for. We combine the sets and identify only 1 citation that includes all of our concepts. We will stop here, but for illustration purposes, we could also limit to adults, humans, and a clinical query–

TABLE 4-9

PICO and Determination of Searching Terms

PICO	Element	Search Terms for PubMed
P(atient)	IV drug user	Substance abuse; intravenous
	Endocarditis	Endocarditis
	Adult	Limit to adults (18-44 y)
I(ntervention)	Antibiotics	Antibiotics
	Oral	Administration; oral
C(omparison)	Antibiotics	[Leave blank]—already have it
	Intravenous	Infusions, parenteral
O(utcome)	Any	[Leave blank]

FIGURE 4-11

Ovid Searching in MEDLINE Showing a Complex Multistep Search

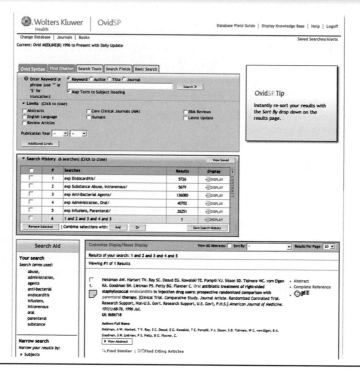

sensitive search for high-quality therapy articles. We could have also limited on other aspects of retrieval such as English language or articles with abstracts. The retrieved citation is an RCT reported in 1996.[10]

Miscellaneous Searching Issues

We did not cover many aspects of finding information such as looking for health-related statistics. The Web pages of the University of Michigan (http://www.lib.umich.edu/govdocs/stats.html), the Centers for Disease Control and Prevention, National Center for Health Statistics (http://www.cdc.gov/nchs/), and the National Library of Medicine (http://www.nlm.nih.gov/services/statistics.html) are good places to start looking for international, national, and local statistics on mortality, morbidity, utilization, education, and human resource requirements. We also did not cover searching for some areas of content (eg, *economic evaluation, clinical prediction rules*, disease *prevalence*, health services, and qualitative studies). If you want to expand your searching skills in these and other areas, check with the librarians in your organization for individual or group instruction, as well as the searching tips and examples that accompany the scenario at the start of each chapter in this book.

You may also want to develop your own customized resources in specific content areas. Many practitioners find it convenient to compile their own summaries of evidence on topics of particular interest for easy access in the course of teaching and patient care. Such resources may take advantage of institutional informatics capabilities or of options such as the Catmaker, developed by the Centre for Evidence-Based Medicine (http://www.cebm.net/catmaker.asp). The Evidence-Based Emergency Medicine Working Group at the New York Academy of Medicine offers the Journal Club Storage Bank (http://ebem.org/jcb/journalclubbank.html) to emergency teachers and practitioners as an online repository of evidence summaries. Individuals may post their own summaries for easy retrieval. It is password protected to prevent its contents from being misconstrued as electronic publications for external use.[11]

CONCLUSION

In this chapter, we looked briefly at many, but by no means all, potential information resources. We encourage you to consider updating your information tools and develop effective methods of finding the evidence you need in practice. We urge you to use strongly evidence-based resources appropriate for your discipline. Most efficient searching involves seeking information from some of the textbook-like systems first, moving to synopses and summaries of evidence (systematic reviews and clinical practice guidelines) next, and then going to the large bibliographic databases only if required.

Acknowledgments

Conflict of interest statement: Ann McKibbon, Dereck Hunt, and Roman Jaeschke have worked with *ACP Journal Club*; Ann McKibbon received salary support. Roman

Jaeschke continues this work. Roman Jaeschke has also researched the use of UpToDate and is an external consultant for this resource. Ann McKibbon and Roman Jaeschke have written Cochrane systematic reviews. Ann McKibbon helped develop PubMed Clinical Queries and bmjupdates+. Peter Wyer is part of the Evidence-Based Emergency Medicine Working Group at the New York Academy of Medicine, which offers the Journal Club Storage Bank. None of the authors will gain personally or financially from the use of any of the resources listed in this chapter.

References

1. Haynes RB. Of studies, syntheses, synopses, and systems: the "4S" evolution of services for finding current best evidence. *ACP J Club*. 2001;134(2):A11-A13.

2. McKibbon KA, Fridsma DB. Effectiveness of clinician-selected electronic information resources for answering primary care physicians' information needs. *JAMA*. 2006;13(6):653-659.

3. Hersh WR, Crabtree MK, Hickman DH, et al. Factors associated with success in searching MEDLINE and applying evidence to answer clinical questions. *J Am Med Inform Assoc*. 2002;9(3):283-293.

4. Westbrook JI, Coirea WE, Gosling AS. Do online information retrieval systems help experienced clinicians answer clinical questions? *JAMA*. 2005;12(3):315-321.

5. Schaafsma F, Verbeek J, Hulshof C, van Dijk F. Caution required when relying on a colleague's advice: a comparison between professional advice and evidence from the literature. *BMC Health Serv Res*. 2005;5:59.

6. Lindberg D, Siegel ER, Rapp BA, Wallingford KT, Wilson SR. Use of MEDLINE by physicians for clinical problem solving. *JAMA*. 1993;269(24):3124-3129.

7. Klein MS, Ross FV, Adams DL, Gilbert CM. Effect of online literature searching on length of stay and patient care costs. *Acad Med*. 1994;69(6):489-495.

8. Pluye P, Grad RM, Dunikowski LG, Stephenson R. Impact of clinical information-retrieval technology on physicians: a literature reviews of quantitative, qualitative and mixed methods studies. *Int J Med Inform*. 2005;74(9):745-768.

9. Smith CS, Pell JP, Cameron AD, Dobbie R. Mode of delivery and the risk of delivery-related perinatal death among twins at term: a retrospective cohort study of 8073 births. *BJOG*. 2005;112(8):1139-1144.

10. Heldman AW, Hartert TV, Ray SC, et al. Oral antibiotic treatment of right-sided staphylococcal endocarditis in injection drug users: prospective randomized comparison with parenteral therapy. *Am J Med*. 1996;101(1):68-76.

11. Yeh B, Wyer PC. Bringing Journal Club to the bedside: a hands-on demonstration of an on-line repository allowing electronic storage and point-of-care retrieval of journal club exercises for emergency medicine residency programs [abstract 349]. *Acad Emerg Med*. 1999;6(5):487.

Why Study Results Mislead: Bias and Random Error

Gordon Guyatt, Roman Jaeschke,
and Maureen O. Meade

IN THIS CHAPTER:

Random Error

Bias

Strategies for Reducing Bias: Therapy and Harm

Our clinical questions have a correct answer that corresponds to an underlying reality or truth. For instance, there is a true underlying magnitude of the impact of β-blockers on mortality in patients with heart failure, of the impact of inhaled steroids on exacerbations in patients with asthma, and of the impact of carotid endarterectomy on incidence of strokes in patients with transient ischemic attacks. Research studies attempt to estimate that underlying truth. Unfortunately, however, we will never know what that true impact really is (Table 5-1). Studies may be flawed in their design or conduct and introduce *systematic error (bias)*. Even if a study could be perfectly designed and executed, we would remain uncertain whether we had arrived at the underlying truth. The next section explains why.

RANDOM ERROR

Consider a perfectly balanced coin. Every time we flip the coin, the *probability* of its landing with head up or tail up is equal—50%. Assume, however, that we as investigators do not know that the coin is perfectly balanced—in fact, we have no idea how well balanced it is, and we would like to find out. We can state our question formally: What is the true underlying probability of a resulting head or tail on any given coin flip? Our first experiment addressing this question is a series of 10 coin flips; the result: 8 heads and 2 tails. What are we to conclude? Taking our result at face value, we infer that the coin is very unbalanced (that is, biased in such a way that it yields heads more often than tails) and that the probability of heads on any given flip is 80%.

Few would be happy with this conclusion. The reason for our discomfort is that we know that the world is not constructed so that a perfectly balanced coin will always yield 5 heads and 5 tails in any given set of 10 coin flips. Rather, the result is subject to the play of chance, otherwise known as *random error*. Some of the time, 10 flips of a perfectly balanced coin will yield 8 heads. On occasion, 9 of 10 flips will turn up heads. On rare occasions, we will find heads on all 10 flips. Figure 5-1 shows the actual distribution of heads and tails in repeated series of coin flips.

TABLE 5-1

Study Results and the Underlying Truth

Result from a completed study yields an apparent treatment effect

- Technical term: point estimate (of the underlying truth)
- Example: relative risk of death is 0.75 or 75%
- Possible underlying truth 1: reduction in relative risk of death really is 25%
- Possible underlying truth 2: reduction in relative risk of death is appreciably less than or greater than 25%

Possible explanations for inaccuracy of the point estimate

- Random error (synonym: chance)
- Systematic error (synonyms: bias, limitation in validity)

FIGURE 5-1

Theoretical Distribution of Results of an Infinite Number of Repetitions of 10 Flips of an Unbiased Coin

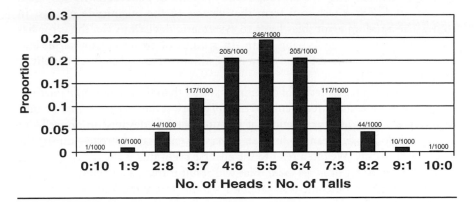

What if the 10 coin flips yield 5 heads and 5 tails? Our awareness of the play of chance leaves us uncertain that the coin is a true one: a series of 10 coin flips of a very biased coin (a true probability of heads of .8, for instance) could, by chance, yield 5 heads and 5 tails.

Let us say that a funding agency, intrigued by the results of our first small experiment, provides us with resources to conduct a larger study. This time, we increase the sample size of our experiment markedly, conducting a series of 1000 coin flips. If we end up with 500 heads and 500 tails, are we ready to conclude that we are dealing with a true coin? Not quite. We know that, were the true underlying probability of heads 51%, we would sometimes see 1000 coin flips yield the result we have just observed.

We can apply the above logic to the results of experiments addressing health care issues in humans. A *randomized controlled trial (RCT)* shows that 10 of 100 treated patients die in the course of treatment, as do 20 of 100 control patients. Does treatment really reduce the death rate by 50%? Maybe, but awareness of chance will leave us with considerable uncertainty about the magnitude of the *treatment effect*—and perhaps about whether treatment helps at all.

To use an actual example, in a study of congestive heart failure, 228 of 1320 (17%) patients with moderate to severe heart failure allocated to receive *placebo* died, as did 156 of 1327 (12%) allocated to receive bisoprolol.[1] Although the true underlying reduction in the *relative risk* of dying is likely to be in the vicinity of the 32% suggested by the study, we must acknowledge that considerable uncertainty remains about the true magnitude of the effect (see Chapter 8, Confidence Intervals).

Let us remember the question with which we started: Why is it that no matter how powerful and well designed our experiment, we will never be sure of the true treatment effect? The answer is: chance.

BIAS

What do we mean when we say that a study is valid or believable? In this book, we use *validity* as a technical term that relates to the magnitude of bias. In contrast to random error, bias leads to systematic deviations (ie, the error has direction) from the underlying truth. In studies of treatment or *harm*, bias leads to either an underestimate or an overestimate of the underlying benefit or harm (Table 5-2).

Bias may intrude as a result of differences, other than the *experimental intervention*, between patients in treatment and *control groups* at the time they enter a study. At the start of a study, each patient, if left untreated, is destined to do well—or poorly. To do poorly means to have an adverse event—say, a stroke—during the course of the study. We often refer to the adverse event that is the focus of a study as the *target outcome* or *target event*. Bias will result if treated and control patients differ in substantive outcome-associated ways at the start of the study. For instance, if control-group patients have more severe atherosclerosis or are older than their counterparts, their destiny will be to have a greater proportion of adverse events than those in the intervention or treatment group, and the results of the study will be biased in favor of the treatment group; that is, the study will yield a systematically greater estimate of the treatment effect than would be obtained were the study groups alike prognostically.

Even if patients in the intervention and control groups begin the study with the same *prognosis*, the result may still be biased. This will occur if, for instance, effective interventions are differentially administered to treatment and control groups. For instance, in a study of a novel agent for the *prevention* of complications of atherosclerosis, the intervention group might receive more intensive statin therapy than the control group.

Finally, patients may begin prognostically similar, and stay prognostically similar, but the study may end with a biased result. This could occur if the study loses patients to *follow-up* (see Chapter 6, Therapy [Randomized Trials]), or because a study is *stopped early* because of an apparent large treatment effect (see Chapter 9.3, Randomized Trials Stopped Early for Benefit).

TABLE 5-2

How Can a Study of an Intervention (Treatment) Be Biased?

Intervention and control groups may be different at the start

   Example: patients in control group are sicker or older

Intervention and control groups may, independent of the experimental treatment, become different as the study proceeds

   Example: patients in the intervention group receive effective additional medication

Intervention and control groups may differ, independent of treatment, at the end

   Example: more sick patients lost to follow-up in the intervention group

Strategies for Reducing Bias: Therapy and Harm

We have noted that bias arises from differences in *prognostic factors* in treatment and control groups at the start of a study, or from differences in prognosis that arise as a study proceeds. What can investigators do to reduce these biases? Table 5-3 summarizes the available strategies in RCTs of therapy and *observational studies* addressing issues of harm.

When studying new treatments, investigators often have a great deal of control. They can reduce the likelihood of differences in the distribution of prognostic features in treated and untreated patients at baseline by *randomly allocating* patients to the 2 groups. They can markedly reduce placebo effects by administering identical-appearing but biologically inert treatments—placebos—to control-group patients. *Blinding* clinicians to whether patients are receiving active or

TABLE 5-3

Ways of Reducing Bias in Studies of Therapy and Harm

Source of Bias	Therapy: Strategy for Reducing Bias	Harm: Strategy for Reducing Bias
Differences Observed at the Start of the Study		
Treatment and control patients differ in prognosis	Randomization	Statistical adjustment for prognostic factors in the analysis of data
	Randomization with stratification	Matching
Differences That Arise as the Study Proceeds		
Placebo effects	Blinding of patients	Choice of outcomes (such as mortality) less subject to placebo effects
Cointervention	Blinding of caregivers	Documentation of treatment differences and statistical adjustment
Bias in assessment of outcome	Blinding of assessors of outcome	Choice of outcomes (such as mortality) less subject to observer bias
Differences at the Completion of the Study		
Loss to follow-up	Ensuring complete follow-up	Ensuring complete follow-up
Stopping study early because of large effect	Completing study as initially planned	
Omitting patients who did not receive assigned treatment	Adhering to intention-to-treat principle and including all patients in the arm to which they are randomized	

placebo therapy can eliminate the risk of important *cointerventions*, and blinding outcome assessors minimizes bias in the assessment of *event rates*.

In general, investigators studying the effect of potentially harmful exposures have far less control than those investigating the effects of potentially beneficial treatments. They must be content to compare patients whose exposure is determined by their choice or circumstances, and they can address potential differences in patients' fate only by statistical adjustment for known prognostic factors. Blinding is impossible, so their best defense against placebo effects and bias in outcome assessment is to choose *endpoints*, such as death, that are less subject to these biases. Investigators addressing both sets of questions can reduce bias by minimizing loss to follow-up (see Table 5-1).

These general rules do not always apply. Sometimes, investigators studying a new treatment find it difficult or impossible to randomize patients to treatment and control groups. Under such circumstances, they choose observational study designs, and clinicians must apply the validity criteria developed for questions of harm to such studies.

Similarly, if the potentially harmful exposure is a drug with beneficial effects, investigators may be able to randomize patients to intervention and control groups. In this case, clinicians can apply the validity criteria designed for therapy questions to the study. Whether for issues of therapy or harm, the strength of inference from RCTs will almost invariably be far greater than the strength of inference from observational studies.

Reference

1. CIBIS-II Investigators and Committees. The Cardiac Insufficiency Bisoprolol Study II (CIBIS-II): a randomised trial. *Lancet*. 1999;353(9146):9-13.

Part B

Therapy

6

THERAPY (RANDOMIZED TRIALS)

Gordon Guyatt, Sharon Straus, Maureen O. Meade,
Regina Kunz, Deborah J. Cook, PJ Devereaux,
and John Ioannidis

IN THIS CHAPTER:

How Can I Apply the Results to Patient Care?

Were the Study Patients Similar to the Patient in My Practice?

Were All Patient-Important Outcomes Considered?

Are the Likely Treatment Benefits Worth the Potential Harm and Costs?

Clinical Resolution

CLINICAL SCENARIO

A Patient With Coronary Disease and a Gastrointestinal Bleed: How Can I Best Help Avoid Vascular Events and Minimize Bleeding Risk?

You are a general internist following a 62-year-old man with peptic ulcer disease and stable angina for whom you have been prescribing low-dose aspirin, a statin, an angiotensin-converting enzyme inhibitor, and as-needed nitrates. Recently, the patient developed an upper gastrointestinal bleed. Biopsy done at endoscopy was negative for *Helicobacter pylori*. In hospital, the gastroenterologist looking after your patient changed the aspirin to clopidogrel (and supported his action by citing a systematic review of thienopyridine derivatives, including clopidogrel, in high-risk vascular patients that found a decrease in the odds of a gastrointestinal bleed compared with aspirin; odds ratio, 0.71; 95% *confidence interval* [*CI*], 0.59-0.86).[1]

You use *ACP Journal Club* to browse the medical literature and, reviewing the patient's story, you recall a recent article that may be relevant. The patient is currently stable and you ask him to return in a week for further review of his medications.

FINDING THE EVIDENCE

Evidence from populations with vascular disease suggests that clopidogrel is likely to be similar, if not superior, to aspirin in its ability to prevent vascular events in patients with stable angina,[2] allowing you to focus on prevention of bleeding. You therefore formulate the relevant question: in a patient with previous aspirin-associated ulcer, is clopidogrel effective in preventing recurrent ulcer bleeding? Searching *ACP Journal Club* in your medical library's Ovid system with the terms "clopidogrel" and "gastrointestinal bleeding" identifies 3 articles, one of which turns out to be your target: "Aspirin plus esomeprazole reduced recurrent ulcer bleeding more than clopidogrel in high-risk patients."[3] You print a copy of this and the original full-text article.[4]

This article describes a *randomized, placebo*-controlled trial including 320 patients with endoscopically confirmed ulcer bleeding, either negative test results for *H pylori* or successful eradication of *H pylori*, and anticipated regular use of antiplatelet therapy. Participants were *randomly allocated* to clopidogrel 75 mg daily and placebo or to aspirin 80 mg and esomeprazole (a potent proton-pump inhibitor) 20 mg twice daily for 12 months. The primary *outcome* was recurrent ulcer bleeding, and secondary outcomes included lower gastrointestinal bleeding and adverse effects.

The Users' Guides

Table 6-1 presents our usual 3-step approach to using an article from the medical literature to guide your practice. You will find these criteria useful for a variety of therapy-related questions, including treating symptomatic illnesses (eg, asthma or arthritis), *preventing* distant complications of illness (eg, cardiovascular death after myocardial infarction), and *screening* for silent but treatable disease (eg, colon cancer screening).

If the answer to one key question (Were patients randomized?) is no, some of the other questions (Was randomization *concealed*? Were patients analyzed in the groups to which they were randomized?) will lose their relevance. As you will see, nonrandomized *observational studies* yield far weaker inferences than *randomized controlled trials* (*RCTs*). Nevertheless, clinicians must use the best evidence available in managing their patients, even if the quality of that evidence is limited (see Chapter 2, The Philosophy of Evidence-Based Medicine). The criteria in Chapter 12 (Harm [Observational Studies]) will help

TABLE 6-1

Users' Guides for an Article About Therapy

Are the results valid?
- Did intervention and control groups start with the same prognosis?
  - Were patients randomized?
  - Was randomization concealed?
  - Were patients in the study groups similar with respect to known prognostic factors?
- Was prognostic balance maintained as the study progressed?
  - To what extent was the study blinded?
- Were the groups prognostically balanced at the study's completion?
  - Was follow-up complete?
  - Were patients analyzed in the groups to which they were randomized?
  - Was the trial stopped early?

What are the results?
- How large was the treatment effect?
- How precise was the estimate of the treatment effect?

How can I apply the results to patient care?
- Were the study patients similar to my patient?
- Were all patient-important outcomes considered?
- Are the likely treatment benefits worth the potential harm and costs?

you assess an observational study addressing a potential treatment that has not yet been evaluated in an RCT.

ARE THE RESULTS VALID?

Did Intervention and Control Groups Start With the Same Prognosis?

Were Patients Randomized?

Consider the question of whether hospital care prolongs life. A study finds that more sick people die in the hospital than in the community. We would easily reject the naive conclusion that hospital care kills because we understand that hospitalized patients are sicker than patients in the community.

Although the logic of prognostic balance is clear in comparing hospitalized patients with those in the community, it may be less obvious in other contexts. Until recently, clinicians and epidemiologists (and almost everyone else) believed that hormone replacement therapy (HRT) could decrease the *risk* of coronary events (death and myocardial infarction) in postmenopausal women. The belief arose from the results of many studies that found women taking HRT to have a decreased risk of coronary events.[5] Results of the first large randomized trial of women with established coronary artery disease (CAD) provided a surprise: HRT failed to reduce the risk of coronary events.[6] Even more recently, the Women's Health Initiative demonstrated that HRT also failed in the primary prevention of CAD.[7]

Other surprises generated by randomized trials include the demonstration that antioxidant vitamins fail to reduce gastrointestinal cancer[8]—and one such agent, vitamin E, may actually increase all-cause mortality[9]—and that a variety of initially promising drugs increase mortality in patients with heart failure.[10-15] Such surprises occur periodically when investigators conduct randomized trials to test the observations from studies in which patients and physicians determine which treatment a patient receives (see Chapter 9.2, Surprising Results of Randomized Trials).

The reason that studies in which patient or physician preference determines whether a patient receives treatment or control (observational studies) often yield misleading results is that morbidity and mortality result from many causes, of which treatment is only one. Treatment studies attempt to determine the impact of an intervention on such events as stroke, myocardial infarction, and death—occurrences that we call the trial's *target outcomes*. A patient's age, the underlying severity of illness, the presence of *comorbidity*, and a host of other factors typically determine the frequency with which a trial's target outcome occurs (*prognostic factors* or *determinants of outcome*). If prognostic factors—either those we know about or those we do not know about—prove unbalanced between a trial's treatment and *control groups*, the study's outcome will be biased, either underestimating or overestimating the treatment's effect. Because known prognostic factors often influence clinicians' recommendations and patients' decisions about taking treatment, observational studies often yield biased results.

Observational studies can theoretically match patients, either in the selection of patients for study or in the subsequent statistical analysis, for known prognostic factors (see Chapter 12, Harm [Observational Studies], and Chapter 5, Why Study Results Mislead: Bias and Random Error). The power of randomization is that treatment and control groups are more likely to be balanced with respect to both known and unknown determinants of outcome.

What was the cause of *bias* in the HRT observational studies? Evidence suggests that women who took HRT enjoyed a higher socioeconomic status.[16] Their apparent benefit from HRT was probably due to factors such as a healthier lifestyle and a greater sense of control over life. Whatever the explanation, we are now confident that it was their previous *prognosis*, rather than the HRT, that led to lower rates of CAD.

Although randomization is a powerful technique, it does not always succeed in creating groups with similar prognosis. Investigators may make mistakes that compromise randomization, or randomization may fail because of simple bad luck. The next 2 sections address these issues.

Was Randomization Concealed?

Some years ago, a group of Australian investigators undertook a randomized trial of open vs laparoscopic appendectomy.[17] The trial ran smoothly during the day. At night, however, the attending surgeon's presence was required for the laparoscopic procedure but not the open one, and limited operating room availability made the longer laparoscopic procedure an annoyance. Reluctant to call in a consultant, the residents sometimes adopted what they saw as a practical solution. When an eligible patient appeared, the residents held the semiopaque envelopes containing the study assignment up to the light. They opened the first envelope that dictated an open procedure. The first eligible patient in the morning would then be allocated to the laparoscopic appendectomy group according to the passed-over envelope (D. Wall, written communication, June 2000). If patients who presented at night were sicker than those who presented during the day, the residents' behavior would bias the results against the open procedure.

When those enrolling patients are unaware and cannot control the arm to which the patient is allocated, we refer to randomization as concealed. In unconcealed trials, those responsible for recruitment may systematically enroll sicker—or less sick—patients to either treatment or control groups. This behavior will defeat the purpose of randomization and the study will yield a biased result.[18-20] Careful investigators will ensure that randomization is concealed through strategies such as remote randomization, in which the individual recruiting the patient makes a call to a methods center to discover the arm of the study to which the patient is assigned.

Were Patients in the Treatment and Control Groups Similar With Respect to Known Prognostic Factors?

The purpose of randomization is to create groups whose prognosis, with respect to the target outcomes, is similar. Sometimes, through bad luck, randomization will fail to achieve this goal. The smaller the sample size, the more likely the trial will have prognostic imbalance.

> Picture a trial testing a new treatment for heart failure enrolling patients in New York Heart Association functional class III and class IV. Patients in class IV have a much worse prognosis than those in class III. The trial is small, with only 8 patients. One would not be surprised if all 4 class III patients were allocated to the treatment group and all 4 class IV patients were allocated to the control group. Such a result of the allocation process would seriously bias the study in favor of the treatment. Were the trial to enroll 800 patients, one would be startled if randomization placed all 400 class III patients in the treatment arm. The larger the sample size, the more likely randomization will achieve its goal of prognostic balance.

You can check how effectively randomization has balanced prognostic factors by looking for a display of patient characteristics of the treatment and control groups at the study's commencement—the baseline or entry prognostic features. Although we will never know whether similarity exists for the unknown prognostic factors, we are reassured when the known prognostic factors are well balanced.

All is not lost if the treatment groups are not similar at baseline. Statistical techniques permit adjustment of the study result for baseline differences. *Adjusted analyses* may not be preferable to unadjusted analyses, but when both analyses generate the same conclusion, readers gain confidence in the *validity* of the study result.

Was Prognostic Balance Maintained as the Study Progressed?
To What Extent Was the Study Blinded?

If randomization succeeds, treatment and control groups in a study begin with a similar prognosis. Randomization, however, provides no guarantees that the 2 groups will remain prognostically balanced. *Blinding* is, if possible, the optimal strategy for maintaining prognostic balance.

Table 6-2 describes 5 groups involved in clinical trials that, ideally, will remain unaware of whether patients are receiving the *experimental therapy* or control therapy. You are probably aware that patients who take a treatment that they believe is effective may feel and perform better than those who do not, even if the treatment has no biologic activity. Although the magnitude and consistency of this

TABLE 6-2

Five Groups That Should, if Possible, Be Blind to Treatment Assignment

Patients	To avoid placebo effects
Clinicians	To prevent differential administration of therapies that affect the outcome of interest (cointervention)
Data collectors	To prevent bias in data collection
Adjudicators of outcome	To prevent bias in decisions about whether or not a patient has had an outcome of interest
Data analysts	To avoid bias in decisions regarding data analysis

placebo effect remain uncertain,[21-24] investigators interested in determining the biologic impact of a pharmacologic or nonpharmacologic treatment will ensure patients are blind to treatment allocation. Similarly, rigorous research designs will ensure blinding of those collecting, evaluating, and analyzing data (Table 6-2). Demonstrations of bias introduced by unblinding—such as the results of a trial in multiple sclerosis in which a treatment benefit judged by unblinded outcome assessors disappeared when adjudicators of outcome were blinded[25]—highlight the importance of blinding. The more that judgment is involved in determining whether a patient has had a target outcome (blinding is less crucial in studies in which the outcome is all-cause mortality, for instance), the more important blinding becomes.

Finally, differences in patient care other than the intervention under study—*cointervention*—can, if they affect study outcomes, bias the results. Effective blinding eliminates the possibility of either conscious or unconscious differential administration of effective interventions to treatment and control groups. When effective blinding is not possible, documentation of potential cointervention becomes important.

Were the Groups Prognostically Balanced at the Study's Completion?

Unfortunately, investigators can ensure concealed random allocation and effective blinding and still fail to achieve an unbiased result.

Was Follow-up Complete?

Ideally, at the conclusion of a trial, you will know the status of each patient with respect to the target outcome. The greater the number of patients whose outcome is unknown—patients lost to follow-up—the more a study's validity is potentially compromised. The reason is that patients who are lost often have different prognoses from those who are retained—they may disappear because they have adverse outcomes or because they are doing well and so did not return for assessment.[26]

When does loss to follow-up seriously threaten validity? Rules of thumb (you may run across thresholds such as 20%) are misleading. Consider 2 hypothetical randomized trials, each of which enters 1000 patients into both treatment and control groups, of whom 30 (3%) are lost to follow-up (Table 6-3). In trial A, treated patients die at half the rate of the control group (200 vs 400), a *relative risk reduction (RRR)* of 50%. To what extent does the loss to follow-up potentially threaten our inference that treatment reduces the death rate by half? If we assume the worst (ie, that all treated patients lost to follow-up died), the number of deaths in the experimental group would be 230 (23%). If there were no deaths among the control patients who were lost to follow-up, our best estimate of the effect of treatment in reducing the risk of death drops from 200/400, or 50%, to (400 − 230)/400 or 170/400, or 43%. Thus, even assuming the worst makes little difference to the best estimate of the magnitude of the *treatment effect*. Our inference is therefore secure.

TABLE 6-3

When Does Loss to Follow-up Seriously Threaten Validity?

	Trial A		Trial B	
	Treatment	Control	Treatment	Control
Number of patients randomized	1000	1000	1000	1000
Number (%) lost to follow-up	30 (3)	30 (3)	30 (3)	30 (3)
Number (%) of deaths	200 (20)	400 (40)	30 (3)	60 (6)
RRR not counting patients lost to follow-up	0.2/0.4 = 0.50		0.03/0.06 = 0.50	
RRR—worst-case scenario[a]	0.17/0.4 = 0.43		0.00/0.06 = 0	

Abbreviation: RRR, relative risk reduction.

[a]The worst-case scenario assumes that all patients allocated to the treatment group and lost to follow-up died and all patients allocated to the control group and lost to follow-up survived.

Contrast this with trial B. Here, the reduction in the *relative risk (RR)* of death is also 50%. In this case, however, the total number of deaths is much lower; of the treated patients, 30 die, and the number of deaths in control patients is 60. In trial B, if we make the same worst-case assumption about the fate of the patients lost to follow-up, the results would change markedly. If we assume that all patients initially allocated to treatment— but subsequently lost to follow-up—die, the number of deaths among treated patients rises from 30 to 60, which is exactly equal to the number of control group deaths. Let us assume that this assumption is accurate. Because we would have 60 deaths in both treatment and control groups, the effect of treatment drops to 0. Because of this dramatic change in the treatment effect (50% RRR if we ignore those lost to follow-up; 0% RRR if we assume all patients in the treatment group who were lost to follow-up died), the 3% loss to follow-up in trial B threatens our inference about the magnitude of the RRR.

Of course, this worst-case scenario is unlikely. When a worst-case scenario, were it true, substantially alters the results, you must judge the plausibility of a markedly different outcome *event rate* in the treatment and control group patients lost to follow-up.

In conclusion, loss to follow-up potentially threatens a study's validity. If assuming a worst-case scenario does not change the inferences arising from study results, then loss to follow-up is not a problem. If such an assumption would significantly alter the results, the extent to which validity is compromised depends on how likely it is that treatment patients lost to follow-up did badly while control patients lost to follow-up did well. That decision is a matter of judgment.

Was the Trial Stopped Early?

Although it is becoming increasingly popular, stopping trials early when one sees an apparent large benefit is risky.[27] Trials terminated early will compromise randomization if they stop at a "random high" when prognostic factors temporarily favor the intervention group. Particularly when sample size and the number of events are small, trials stopped early run the risk of greatly overestimating the treatment effect (see Chapter 9.3, Randomized Trials Stopped Early for Benefit).

Were Patients Analyzed in the Groups to Which They Were Randomized?

Investigators can also undermine randomization if they omit from the analysis patients who do not receive their assigned treatment or, worse yet, count events that occur in *nonadherent* patients who were assigned to treatment against the control group. Such analyses will bias the results if the reasons for nonadherence are related to prognosis. In a number of randomized trials, patients who did not adhere to their assigned drug regimens have fared worse than those who took their medication as instructed, even after taking into account all known prognostic factors and even when their medications were placebos.[28-33] When adherent patients are destined to have a better outcome, omitting those who do not receive assigned treatment undermines the unbiased comparison provided by randomization. Investigators prevent this bias when they follow the *intention-to-treat* principle and analyze all patients in the group to which they were randomized (see Chapter 9.4, The Principle of Intention to Treat).

USING THE GUIDE

Returning to our opening clinical scenario, did the experimental and control groups begin the study with a similar prognosis? The study was randomized and allocation was concealed; 320 patients participated and 99% were followed up. The investigators followed the intention-to-treat principle, including all patients in the arm to which they were randomized, and stopped when they reached the planned sample size. There were more patients who smoked (13% vs 8.2%) and regularly consumed alcohol (8.1% vs 5%) in the clopidogrel group compared with the aspirin-esomeprazole group. This could bias the results in favor of the aspirin-esomeprazole, and the investigators do not provide an adjusted analysis for the baseline differences. Clinicians, patients, data collectors, outcomes assessors, and data analysts were all blind to allocation.

The final assessment of validity is never a yes-or-no decision. Rather, think of validity as a continuum ranging from strong studies that are very likely to yield an accurate estimate of the treatment effect to weak studies that are very likely to yield a biased estimate of effect. Inevitably, the judgment as to where a study lies in this continuum involves some subjectivity. In this case, despite uncertainty about baseline differences between the groups, we conclude that the methods were strong.

WHAT ARE THE RESULTS?

How Large Was the Treatment Effect?

Most frequently, RCTs carefully monitor how often patients experience some adverse event or outcome. Examples of these dichotomous outcomes (yes-or-no outcomes, ones that either happen or do not happen) include cancer recurrence, myocardial infarction, and death. Patients either have an event or they do not, and the article reports the proportion of patients who develop such events. Consider, for example, a study in which 20% of a control group died, but only 15% of those receiving a new treatment died (Table 6-4). How might one express these results?

One possibility would be the absolute difference (known as the *absolute risk reduction [ARR]*, or *risk difference*), between the proportion who died in the control group (*baseline risk* or *control group risk [CGR]*) and the proportion who died in the experimental group (*experimental group risk [EGR]*), or CGR − EGR = 0.20 − 0.15 = 0.05. Another way to express the impact of treatment is as an RR: the risk of events among patients receiving the new treatment relative to that risk among patients in the control group, or EGR/CGR = 0.15/0.20 = 0.75.

The most commonly reported measure of dichotomous treatment effects is the complement of the RR, the RRR. It is expressed as a percentage: 1 − (EGR/CGR) × 100% = (1 − 0.75) × 100% = 25%. An RRR of 25% means that the new treatment reduced the risk of death by 25% relative to that occurring among control patients; the greater the RRR, the more effective the therapy. Investigators may compute the RR over a period of time, as in a *survival analysis*, and call it a *hazard ratio* (see Chapter 7, Does Treatment Lower Risk? Understanding the Results). When people do not specify whether they are talking about RRR or ARR—for instance, "Drug X was 30% effective in reducing the risk of death," or "The efficacy of the vaccine was 92%"—they are almost invariably talking about RRR (see Chapter 7, Does Treatment Lower Risk? Understanding the Results, for more detail about how the RRR results in a subjective impression of a larger treatment effect than do other ways of expressing treatment effects).

TABLE 6-4

Results From a Hypothetical Randomized Trial

	Outcome		
Exposure	Death	Survival	Total
Treatment (experimental)	15	85	100
Control	20	80	100

Control group risk (CGR): 20/100 = 20%.
Experimental group risk (EGR): 15/100 = 15%.
Absolute risk reduction or risk difference: CGR − EGR, 20% − 15% = 5%.
Relative risk: EGR/CGR = (15/100)/(20/100) × 100% = 75%.
Relative risk reduction: [1 − (EGR/CGR)] × 100% = 1 − 75% = 25%.

How Precise Was the Estimate of the Treatment Effect?

We can never be sure of the true risk reduction; the best estimate of the true treatment effect is what we observe in a well-designed randomized trial. This estimate is called a *point estimate* to remind us that, although the true value lies somewhere in its neighborhood, it is unlikely to be precisely correct. Investigators often tell us the neighborhood within which the true effect likely lies by calculating CIs, a range of values within which one can be confident the true effect lies.[34]

We usually use the 95% CI (see Chapter 8, Confidence Intervals). You can consider the 95% CI as defining the range that—assuming the study was well conducted and has minimal bias—includes the true RRR 95% of the time. The true RRR will generally lie beyond these extremes only 5% of the time, a property of the CI that relates closely to the conventional level of *statistical significance* of $P < .05$ (see Chapter 10.1, Hypothesis Testing). We illustrate the use of CIs in the following examples.

Example 1

If a trial randomized 100 patients each to experimental and control groups, and there were 20 deaths in the control group and 15 deaths in the experimental group, the authors would calculate a point estimate for the RRR of 25% (CGR = 20/100 or 0.20, EGR = 15/100 or 0.15, and $1 - EGR/CGR = (1 - 0.75) \times 100 = 25\%$). You might guess, however, that the true RRR might be much smaller or much greater than 25%, based on a difference of only 5 deaths. In fact, you might surmise that the treatment might provide no benefit (an RRR of 0%) or might even do harm

FIGURE 6-1

Confidence Intervals in Trials of Various Sample Size

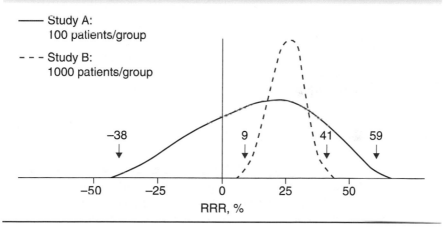

Abbreviations: CI, confidence interval; RRR, relative risk reduction.

Two studies with the same point estimate, a 25% RRR, but different sample sizes and correspondingly different CIs. The x-axis represents the different possible RRR, and the y-axis represents the likelihood of the true RRR having that particular value. The solid line represents the CI around the first example, in which there were 100 patients per group, and the number of events in active and control was 15 and 20, respectively. The broken line represents the CI around the second example in which there were 1000 patients per group, and the number of events in active and control was 150 and 200, respectively.

(a negative RRR). And you would be right; in fact, these results are consistent with both an RRR of −38% (that is, patients given the new treatment might be 38% more likely to die than control patients) and an RRR of nearly 59% (that is, patients subsequently receiving the new treatment might have a risk of dying almost 60% less than those who are not treated). In other words, the 95% CI on this RRR is −38% to 59%, and the trial really has not helped us decide whether or not to offer the new treatment.

Example 2

What if the trial enrolled 1000 patients per group rather than 100 patients per group, and the same event rates were observed as before, so that there were 200 deaths in the control group (CGR = 200/1000 = 0.20) and 150 deaths in the experimental group (EGR = 150/1000 = 0.15)? Again, the point estimate of the RRR is 25% (1 − EGR/CGR = 1 − (0.15/0.20) × 100 = 25%).

In this larger trial, you might think that our confidence that the true reduction in risk is close to 25% is much greater, and, again, you would be right. The 95% CI on the RRR for this set of results is all on the positive side of zero and runs from 9% to 41%.

What these examples show is that the larger the sample size of a trial, the larger the number of outcome events and the greater our confidence that the true RRR (or any other measure of effect) is close to what we have observed. In the second example, the lowest plausible value for the RRR was 9% and the highest value was 41%. The point estimate—in this case, 25%—is the one value most likely to represent the true RRR. As one considers values farther and farther from the point estimate, they become less and less consistent with the observed RRR. By the time one crosses the upper or lower boundaries of the 95% CI, the values are very unlikely to represent the true RRR, given the point estimate (that is, the observed RRR). All this, of course, assumes the study has satisfied the validity criteria we discussed earlier.

Figure 6-1 represents the CIs around the point estimate of an RRR of 25% in these 2 examples, with a risk reduction of 0 representing no treatment effect. In both scenarios, the point estimate of the RRR is 25%, but the CI is far narrower in the second scenario.

Not all randomized trials have dichotomous outcomes, nor should they. In a study of respiratory muscle training for patients with chronic airflow limitation, one primary outcome measured how far patients could walk in 6 minutes in an enclosed corridor.[35] This 6-minute walk improved from an average of 406 to 416 m (up 10 m) in the experimental group receiving respiratory muscle training and from 409 to 429 m (up 20 m) in the control group. The point estimate for improvement in the 6-minute walk due to respiratory muscle training therefore was negative, at −10 m (or a 10-m difference in favor of the control group).

Here, too, you should look for the 95% CIs around this difference in changes in exercise capacity and consider their implications. The investigators tell us that the lower boundary of the 95% CI was −26 (that is, the results are consistent with a difference of 26 m in favor of the control treatment) and the upper boundary was +5 m. Even in the best of circumstances, patients are unlikely to perceive adding 5 m to the 400 recorded at the start of the trial as important, and this result effectively excludes an important benefit of respiratory muscle training as applied in this study.

It will not surprise you that the larger the sample size, the narrower the CI. If you want to learn more about CIs, including finding out when the sample size is sufficiently large, see Chapter 8, Confidence Intervals.

Having determined the magnitude and precision of the treatment effect, clinicians can turn to the final question of how to apply the article's results to their patients.

USING THE GUIDE

Using the raw numbers provided in the article, 1 of 159 people (0.6%) in the aspirin-esomeprazole group and 13 of the 161 people (8%) in the clopidogrel group experienced a recurrence of ulcer. The RRR is 92%, and the 95% CI extends from 41% to 99%. The very large effect and the small number of events somewhat reduce your confidence in this result; 4.4% of the aspirin-esomeprazole group and 9.4% of the clopidogrel group had an adverse effect (defined as dyspepsia or an allergy). The investigators also reported that 11 patients in the aspirin-esomeprazole group and 9 patients in the clopidogrel group experienced recurrent ischemic events

How Can I Apply the Results to Patient Care?

Were the Study Patients Similar to the Patient in My Practice?
Often, the patient before you has different attributes or characteristics from those enrolled in the trial. He or she may be older or younger, sicker or less sick, or may have comorbid disease that would have excluded him or her from participation in the research study. If the patient qualified for enrollment in the study, you can apply the results with considerable confidence.

What if that individual does not meet a study's eligibility criteria? The study result probably applies even if, for example, he or she was 2 years too old for the study, had more severe disease, had previously been treated with a competing therapy, or had a comorbid condition. A better approach than rigidly applying the study's *inclusion and exclusion criteria* is to ask whether there is some compelling reason why the results do not apply to the patient. You usually will not find a compelling reason, and most often you can generalize the results to your patient with confidence (see Chapter 11.1, Applying Results to Individual Patients).

A related issue has to do with the extent to which we can generalize findings from a study using a particular drug to another closely (or not so closely) related agent. The issue of drug class effects and how conservative one should be in assuming class effects remains controversial (see Chapter 22.5, Drug Class Effects). Generalizing findings of surgical treatment may be even riskier. Randomized trials of carotid endarterectomy, for instance, demonstrate much lower perioperative rates of stroke and death than one might expect in one's own community.[36]

A final issue arises when a patient fits the features of a subgroup of patients in the trial report. We encourage you to be skeptical of *subgroup analyses*[37] (see Chapter 20.4, When to Believe a Subgroup Analysis). The treatment is likely to benefit the subgroup more or less than the other patients only if the difference in the effects of treatment in the subgroups is large and very unlikely to occur by chance. Even when these conditions apply, the results may be misleading if investigators did not specify their hypotheses before the study began, if they had a very large number of hypotheses, or if other studies fail to replicate the finding.

Were All Patient-Important Outcomes Considered?

Treatments are indicated when they provide important benefits. Demonstrating that a bronchodilator produces small increments in forced expired volume in patients with chronic airflow limitation, that a vasodilator improves cardiac output in heart failure patients, or that a lipid-lowering agent improves lipid profiles does not provide a sufficient reason for administering these drugs (see Chapter 11.4, Surrogate Outcomes). Here, investigators have chosen *substitute* or *surrogate outcomes* rather than those that patients would consider important. What clinicians and patients require is evidence that the treatments improve outcomes that are important to patients (*patient-important outcomes*), such as reducing shortness of breath during the activities required for daily living, avoiding hospitalization for heart failure, or decreasing the risk of myocardial infarction.[38]

> Trials of the impact of antiarrhythmic drugs after myocardial infarction illustrate the danger of using *substitute outcomes* or *endpoints*. Because such drugs had demonstrated a reduction in abnormal ventricular depolarizations (the substitute endpoints), it made sense that they should reduce the occurrence of life-threatening arrhythmias. A group of investigators performed randomized trials on 3 agents (encainide, flecainide, and moricizine) that were previously shown to be effective in suppressing the substitute endpoint of abnormal ventricular depolarizations. The investigators had to stop the trials when they discovered that mortality was substantially higher in patients receiving antiarrhythmic treatment than in those receiving placebo.[39,40] Clinicians relying on the substitute endpoint of arrhythmia suppression would have continued to administer the 3 drugs, to the considerable detriment of their patients.

Even when investigators report favorable effects of treatment on one patient-important outcome, you must consider whether there may be deleterious effects on other outcomes. For instance, cancer chemotherapy may lengthen life but decrease its quality (see Chapter 10.5, Measuring Patients' Experience). Randomized trials often fail to adequately document the toxicity or adverse effects of the experimental intervention.[41]

Composite endpoints represent a final dangerous trend in presenting outcomes. Like surrogate outcomes, composite endpoints are attractive for reducing sample size and decreasing length of follow-up. Unfortunately, they can mislead. We may find that a trial that reduced a composite outcome of death, renal failure requiring dialysis, and doubling of serum creatinine level actually demonstrated a trend toward increased mortality with the experimental therapy and showed convincing effects only on doubling of serum creatinine level[42] (see Chapter 10.4, Composite Endpoints).

Another long-neglected outcome is the resource implications of alternative management strategies. Health care systems face increasing resource constraints that mandate careful attention to *economic analysis* (see Chapter 22.1, Economic Analysis).

Are the Likely Treatment Benefits Worth the Potential Harm and Costs?

If you can apply the study's results to a patient, and its outcomes are important, the next question concerns whether the probable treatment benefits are worth the effort that you and the patient must put into the enterprise. A 25% reduction in the RR of death may sound quite impressive, but its impact on your patient and practice may nevertheless be minimal. This notion is illustrated by using a concept called *number needed to treat (NNT)*, the number of patients who must receive an intervention of therapy during a specific period to prevent 1 adverse outcome or produce 1 positive outcome.[43]

The impact of a treatment is related not only to its RRR but also to the risk of the adverse outcome it is designed to prevent. One large trial in myocardial infarction suggests that tissue plasminogen activator (tPA) administration reduces the RR of death by approximately 12% in comparison to streptokinase.[44] Table 6-5 considers 2 patients presenting with acute myocardial infarction associated with elevation of ST segments on their electrocardiograms.

In the first case, a 40-year-old man presents with electrocardiographic findings suggesting an inferior myocardial infarction. You find no signs

TABLE 6-5

Considerations in the Decision to Treat 2 Patients With Myocardial Infarction With Tissue Plasminogen Activator or Streptokinase

	Risk of Death 1 Year After MI With Streptokinase (CER)	Risk With tPA (EGR) (ARR = CGR − EGR)	Number Needed to Treat (100/ARR When ARR Is Expressed as a Percentage)
40-Year-old man with small MI	2%	1.76% (0.24% or 0.0024)	417
70-Year-old man with large MI and heart failure	40%	35.2% (4.8% or 0.048)	21

Abbreviations: ARR, absolute risk reduction; CGR, control group risk; EGR, experimental group risk; tPA, tissue plasminogen activator; MI, myocardial infarction.

of heart failure, and the patient is in normal sinus rhythm, with a rate of 90/min. This individual's risk of death in the first year after infarction may be as low as 2%. In comparison to streptokinase, tPA would reduce this risk by 12% to 1.76%, an ARR of 0.24% (0.0024). The inverse of this ARR (that is, 100 divided by the ARR expressed as a percentage) is equal to the number of such patients we would have to treat to prevent 1 event (in this case, to prevent 1 death after a mild heart attack in a low-risk patient), the NNT. In this case, we would have to treat approximately 417 such patients to save a single life (100/0.24 = 417). Given the small increased risk of intracerebral hemorrhage associated with tPA, and its additional cost, many clinicians might prefer streptokinase in this patient.

In the second case, a 70-year-old man presents with electrocardiographic signs of anterior myocardial infarction with pulmonary edema. His risk of dying in the subsequent year is approximately 40%. A 12% RRR of death in such a high-risk patient generates an ARR of 4.8% (0.048), and we would have to treat only 21 such individuals to avert a premature death (100/4.8 = 20.8). Many clinicians would consider tPA the preferable agent for this man.

A key element of the decision to start therapy, therefore, is to consider the patient's risk of the adverse event if left untreated.

For any given RRR, the higher the probability that a patient will experience an adverse outcome if we do not treat, the more likely the patient will benefit from treatment and the fewer such patients we need to treat to prevent 1 adverse outcome (see Chapter 7, Does Treatment Lower Risk? Understanding the Results). Knowing the NNT helps clinicians in the process of weighing the benefits and downsides associated with the management options (see Chapter 11.1, Applying Results to Individual Patients). Chapter 11.2 (Example Numbers Needed to Treat) presents NNTs associated with clearly defined risk groups in a number of common therapeutic situations.

Tradeoff of benefit and risk also requires an accurate assessment of treatment adverse effects. Randomized trials, with relatively small sample sizes, are unsuitable for detecting rare but catastrophic adverse effects of therapy. Clinicians must often look to other sources of information—often characterized by weaker methodology— to obtain an estimate of the adverse effects of therapy (see Chapter 12, Harm [Observational Studies]).

The preferences or values that determine the correct choice when weighing benefit and risk are those of the individual patient. Great uncertainty about how best to communicate information to patients and how to incorporate their values into clinical decision making remains. Vigorous investigation of this frontier of evidence-based medicine is, however, under way (see Chapter 22.2, Decision Making and the Patient).

Clinicians may find it tempting to turn to the article's authors for guidance about tradeoffs between benefits and risks. Because of the possibility of conflict of interest, this can be dangerous. If you are nervous about this danger, check out our strategies to avoid being misled (see Chapter 11.3, Dealing With Misleading Presentations of Clinical Trial Results).

CLINICAL RESOLUTION

The study that we identified showed a decrease in the recurrence of ulcer bleeding in high-risk patients receiving aspirin-esomeprazole in comparison with those taking clopidogrel. The authors also found that more people in the clopidogrel group experienced an adverse effect from the therapy and that there was no significant difference in the risk of ischemic events, although the small number of outcomes leaves any inferences from this result extremely weak.

Our patient is at a high risk of a recurrent ulcer, given his recent gastrointestinal bleed secondary to an aspirin-induced ulcer. His case is similar to those of patients included in this study. You translate the reduction in risk of bleeding into an NNT of approximately 13 (clopidogrel risk of 8.1% – aspirin/esomeprazole of 0.6% = 7.5%; NNT = 100/7.5). Given the very large effect, the NNT using the more conservative boundary of the CI of an RRR of approximately 40%—and thus an NNT of approximately 30—may be more realistic. In combination with the reduction in less-important adverse effects, this seems to be a clear patient-important benefit.

The patient found his bleeding episode terrifying, and he also believes that lowering his risk of bleeding by even as little as 3% during a year would be worthwhile. He gulps, however, when you tell him that esomeprazole costs $2.20 per pill, and if he takes the drug as administered in the trial, it will cost him more than $1600 in the next year. You then explain that the investigators' choice of medication leaves some doubt about the best drug to use along with aspirin. Esomeprazole is still under patent, explaining the high cost. The investigators could have chosen omeprazole, a proton-pump inhibitor with marginal differences in effectiveness relative to esomeprazole, which the patient can purchase for approximately half the price. Ultimately, the patient chooses the aspirin/omeprazole combination.

References

1. Hankey G, Sudlow C, Dunbabin D. Thienopyridine derivatives (ticlopidine, clopidogrel) versus aspirin for preventing stroke and other serious vascular events in high vascular risk patients. *Cochrane Database Syst Rev*. 2000;3(1):CD001246.

2. CAPRIE Steering Committee. A randomised, blinded, trial of clopidogrel versus aspirin in patients at risk of ischaemic events (CAPRIE). *Lancet*. 1996;348(9038):1329-1339.

3. Chan K, Peterson W. Aspirin plus esomeprazole reduced recurrent ulcer bleeding more than clopidogrel in high-risk patients. *ACP J Club*. 2005;143(1):9.

4. Chan K, Ching J, Hung L, et al. Clopidogrel versus aspirin and esomeprazole to prevent recurrent ulcer bleeding. *N Engl J Med*. 2005;352(3):238-244.

5. Stampfer M, Colditz G. Estrogen replacement therapy and coronary heart disease: a quantitative assessment of the epidemiologic evidence. *Prev Med.* 1991;20(1):47-63.

6. Hulley S, Grady D, Bush T, et al. Randomized trial of estrogen plus progestin for secondary prevention of coronary heart disease in postmenopausal women. *JAMA.* 1998;280(7):605-613.

7. Rossouw J, Anderson G, Prentice R, et al. Risks and benefits of estrogen and progestin in healthy postmenopausal women: principal results from the Women's Health Initiative randomized controlled trial. *JAMA.* 2002;288(3):321-323.

8. Vasotec tablets: enalapril maleate. In: *Physician's Desk Reference.* 52nd ed. Montvale, NJ: Medical Economics; 1998:1771-1774.

9. Pitt B, Zannad F, Remme W, et al. The effect of spironolactone on morbidity and mortality in patients with severe heart failure. *N Engl J Med.* 1999;341(10):709-717.

10. Xamoterol in Severe Heart Failure Group. Xamoterol in severe heart failure. *Lancet.* 1990;336(8706):1-6.

11. Packer M, Carver J, Rodeheffer R, et al. Effects of oral milrinone on mortality in severe chronic heart failure for the PROMISE Study Research Group. *N Engl J Med.* 1991;325(21):1468-1475.

12. Packer M, Rouleau J, Svedberg K, Pitt B, Fisher L. Effect of flosequinan on survival in chronic heart failure: preliminary results of the PROFILE study: the Profile Investigators [abstract]. *Circulation.* 1993;88(suppl 1):I-301.

13. Hampton J, van Veldhuisen D, Kleber F, et al. Randomised study of effect of ibopamine on survival in patients with advanced severe heart failure for the Second Prospective Randomized Study of Ibopamine on Mortality and Efficacy (PRIME II) Investigators. *Lancet.* 1997;349(9057):971-977.

14. Califf R, Adams K, McKenna W, et al. A randomized controlled trial of epoprostenol therapy for severe congestive heart failure: the Flolan International Randomized Survival Trial (FIRST). *Am Heart J.* 1997;134(1):44-54.

15. Haynes R, Mukherjee J, Sackett D, et al. Functional status changes following medical or surgical treatment for cerebral ischemia: results in the EC/IC Bypass Study. *JAMA.* 1987;257(15):2043-2046.

16. Humphrey L, Chan B, Sox H. Postmenopausal hormone replacement therapy and the primary prevention of cardiovascular disease. *Ann Intern Med.* 2002;137(4): 273-284.

17. Hansen J, Smithers B, Sachache D, Wall D, Miller B, Menzies B. Laparoscopic versus open appendectomy: prospective randomized trial. *World J Surg.* 1996; 20(1):17-20.

18. Schulz K, Chalmers I, Hayes R, Altman D. Empirical evidence of bias: dimensions of methodological quality associated with estimates of treatment effects in controlled trials. *JAMA.* 1995;273(5):408-412.

19. Moher D, Jones A, Cook D, et al. Does quality of reports of randomised trials affect estimates of intervention efficacy reported in meta-analyses? *Lancet.* 1998;352(9128):609-613.

20. Balk EM, Bonis PA, Moskowitz H, et al. Correlation of quality measures with estimates of treatment effect in meta-analyses of randomized controlled trials. *JAMA.* 2002;287(22):2973-2982.

21. Kaptchuk T. Powerful placebo: the dark side of the randomised controlled trial. *Lancet.* 1998;351(9117):1722-1725.

22. Hrobjartsson A, Gotzsche P. Is the placebo powerless? an analysis of clinical trials comparing placebo with no treatment. *N Engl J Med.* 2001;344(21):1594-1602.

23. McRae C, Cherin E, Yamazaki T, et al. Effects of perceived treatment on quality of life and medical outcomes in a double-blind placebo surgery trial. *Arch Gen Psychiatry.* 2004;61(4):412-420.

24. Rana J, Mannam A, Donnell-Fink L, Gervino E, Sellke F, Laham R. Longevity of the placebo effect in the therapeutic angiogenesis and laser myocardial revascularization trials in patients with coronary heart disease. *Am J Cardiol.* 2005;95(12):1456-1459.

25. Noseworthy JH, Ebers GC, Vandervoort MK, Farquhar RE, Yetisir E, Roberts R. The impact of blinding on the results of a randomized, placebo-controlled multiple sclerosis clinical trial. *Neurology.* 1994;44(1):16-20.

26. Ioannidis JP, Bassett R, Hughes MD, Volberding PA, Sacks HS, Lau J. Predictors and impact of patients lost to follow-up in a long-term randomized trial of immediate versus deferred antiretroviral treatment. *J Acquir Immune Defic Syndr Hum Retrovirol.* 1997;16(1):22-30.

27. Montori VM, Devereaux PJ, Adhikari NK, et al. Randomized trials stopped early for benefit: a systematic review. *JAMA.* 2005;294(17):2203-2209.

28. Coronary Drug Project Research Group. Influence of adherence to treatment and response of cholesterol on mortality in the Coronary Drug Project. *N Engl J Med.* 1980;303(18):1038-1041.

29. Asher W, Harper H. Effect of human chorionic gonadotropin on weight loss, hunger, and feeling of well-being. *Am J Clin Nutr.* 1973;26(2):211-218.

30. Hogarty G, Goldberg S. Drug and soclotherapy in the aftercare of schizophrenic patients: one-year relapse rates. *Arch Gen Psychiatry.* 1973;28(1):54-64.

31. Fuller R, Roth H, Long S. Compliance with disulfiram treatment of alcoholism. *J Chronic Dis.* 1983;36(2):161-170.

32. Pizzo P, Robichaud K, Edwards B, Schumaker C, Kramer B, Johnson A. Oral antibiotic prophylaxis in patients with cancer: a double-blind randomized placebo-controlled trial. *J Pediatr.* 1983;102(1):125-133.

33. Horwitz R, Viscoli C, Berkman L, et al. Treatment adherence and risk of death after myocardial infarction. *Lancet.* 1990;336(8714):542-545.

34. Altman D, Gore S, Gardner M, Pocock S. Statistical guidelines for contributors to medical journals. In: Gardner M, Altman D, eds. *Statistics With Confidence Intervals and Statistical Guidelines.* London, England: British Medical Journal; 1989:83-100.

35. Guyatt G, Keller J, Singer J, Halcrow S, Newhouse M. Controlled trial of respiratory muscle training in chronic airflow limitation. *Thorax.* 1992;47(8):598-602.

36. Asymptomatic Carotid Atherosclerosis Study Group. Endarterectomy for asymptomatic carotid artery stenosis. *JAMA.* 1995;273(18):1421-1428.

37. Oxman A, Guyatt G. A consumer's guide to subgroup analysis. *Ann Intern Med.* 1992;116(1):78-84.

38. Guyatt G, Montori V, Devereaux P, Schunemann H, Bhandari M. Patients at the center: in our practice, and in our use of language. *ACP J Club.* 2004;140(1):A11-A12.

39. Echt D, Liebson P, Mitchell L, et al. Mortality and morbidity in patients receiving encainide, flecainide, or placebo: the Cardiac Arrhythmia Suppression Trial. *N Engl J Med.* 1991;324(12):781-788.

40. Cardiac Arrhythmia Suppression Trial II Investigators. Effect of antiarrhythmic agent moricizine on survival after myocardial infarction. *N Engl J Med.* 1992;327(4):227-233.

41. Ioannidis J, Lau J. Completeness of safety reporting in randomized trials: an evaluation of 7 medical areas. *JAMA.* 2001;285(4):437-443.

42. Carette S, Marcoux S, Treuchon R, et al. A controlled trial of corticosteroid injections into facet joints for chronic low back pain. *N Engl J Med.* 1991; 325(14):1002-1007.

43. Laupacis A, Sackett D, Roberts R. An assessment of clinically useful measures of the consequences of treatment. *N Engl J Med.* 1988;318(26):1728-1733.

44. Malenka DJ, Baron JA, Johansen S, Wahrenberger JW, Ross JM. The framing effect of relative and absolute risk. *J Gen Intern Med.* 1993;8(10):543-548.

7

DOES TREATMENT LOWER RISK? UNDERSTANDING THE RESULTS

Roman Jaeschke, Gordon Guyatt,
Alexandra Barratt, Stephen Walter,
and Deborah J. Cook

IN THIS CHAPTER:

When clinicians consider the results of clinical trials, they are interested in the association between a treatment and an *outcome*. This chapter will help you to understand and interpret study results related to outcomes that are either present or absent (*dichotomous*) for each patient, such as death, stroke, or myocardial infarction. A guide for teaching the *concepts* in this chapter is also available[1] (see http://www.cmaj.ca/cgi/data/171/4/353/DC1/1).

THE 2 × 2 TABLE

Table 7-1 depicts a 2 × 2 table that captures the information for a dichotomous outcome of a clinical trial.

> For instance, in the course of a *randomized trial* comparing *mortality rates* in patients with bleeding esophageal varices that were controlled either by endo-scopic ligation or by endoscopic sclerotherapy,[2] 18 of 64 participants assigned to ligation died, as did 29 of 65 patients assigned to sclerotherapy (Table 7-2).

THE RISK

The simplest measure of occurrence to understand is the *risk* (or *absolute risk*). We often refer to the risk of the adverse outcome in the *control group* as the *baseline risk* or the *control group risk*.

TABLE 7-1

The 2 × 2 Table

Exposure	Outcome	
	Yes	No
Yes	a	b
No	c	d

Relative risk $= \dfrac{a/(a+b)}{c/(c+d)}$

Relative risk reduction $= \dfrac{c/(c+d)-a/(a+b)}{c/(c+d)}$

Risk difference[a] $= \dfrac{c}{c+d} - \dfrac{a}{a+b}$

Number needed to treat = 100/(risk difference expressed as %)

Odds ratio $= \dfrac{a/b}{c/d} = \dfrac{ad}{cb}$

[a]Also known as the absolute risk reduction.

TABLE 7-2

Results From a Randomized Trial of Endoscopic Sclerotherapy as Compared With Endoscopic Ligation for Bleeding Esophageal Varices[a]

| | Outcome | | |
Exposure	Death	Survival	Total
Ligation	18	46	64
Sclerotherapy	29	36	65

Relative risk = (18/64) / (29/65) = 0.63

Relative risk reduction = 1 – 0.63 = 0.37

Risk difference = 0.446 – 0.281 = 0.165

Number needed to treat = 100/16.5 = 6

Odds ratio = (18/46) / (29/36) = 0.39 / 0.80 = 0.49

[a]Data from Stiegmann et al.[2]

The risk of dying in the ligation group is 28% (18/64, or $[a/(a + b)]$), and the risk of dying in the sclerotherapy group is 45% (29/65, or $[c/(c + d)]$).

THE RISK DIFFERENCE (ABSOLUTE RISK REDUCTION)

One way of comparing 2 risks is by calculating the absolute difference between them. We refer to this difference as the *absolute risk reduction (ARR)* or the *risk difference (RD)*. Algebraically, the formula for calculating the RD is $[c/(c + d)] – [a/(a + b)]$ (see Table 7-1). This measure of effect uses absolute rather than relative terms in looking at the proportion of patients who are spared the adverse outcome.

In our example, the RD is 0.446 – 0.281, or 0.165 (ie, an RD of 16.5%).

THE RELATIVE RISK

Another way to compare the risks in the 2 groups is to take their ratio; this is called the *relative risk* or *risk ratio (RR)*. The RR tells us the proportion of the original risk (in this case, the risk of death with sclerotherapy) that is still present when patients receive the *experimental treatment* (in this case, ligation). From our 2 × 2 table, the formula for this calculation is $[a/(a + b)]/[c/(c + d)]$ (see Table 7-1).

In our example, the RR of dying after receiving initial ligation vs sclerotherapy is 18/64 (the risk in the ligation group) divided by 29/65 (the risk in the sclerotherapy group), or 0.63. In everyday English, we would say the risk of death with ligation is about two-thirds that with sclerotherapy.

THE RELATIVE RISK REDUCTION

An alternative relative measure of treatment effectiveness is the *relative risk reduction* (*RRR*), an estimate of the proportion of baseline risk that is removed by the therapy. It may be calculated as 1 − RR. One can also calculate the RRR by dividing the RD (amount of risk removed) by the absolute risk in the control group (see Table 7-1).

> In our bleeding varices example, where RR was 0.63, the RRR is thus 1 − 0.63 (or 16.5% divided by 44.6%, the risk in the sclerotherapy group)—either way, it comes to 0.37. In other words, ligation decreases the risk of death by about a third compared with sclerotherapy.

THE ODDS RATIO

Instead of looking at the risk of an event, we could estimate the odds of having vs not having an event. When considering the effects of therapy, you usually will not go far wrong if you interpret the *odds ratio* (*OR*) as equivalent to the RR. The exception is when event rates are very high—more than 40% of control patients experience myocardial infarction or death, for instance. If you are interested in learning more about the OR, you can refer to Chapter 10.2, Understanding the Results: More About Odds Ratios.

RELATIVE RISK VS RISK DIFFERENCE: WHY THE FUSS?

Failing to distinguish between the OR and the RR when interpreting randomized trial results will seldom mislead you; you must, however, distinguish between the RR and the RD. The reason is that the RR is generally far larger than the RD, and presentations of results in the form of RR (or RRR) can convey a misleading message. Reducing a patient's risk by 50% sounds impressive. That may, however, represent a reduction in risk from 2% to 1%. The corresponding 1% RD sounds considerably less impressive.

As depicted in Figure 7-1, consider a treatment that is administered to 3 different subpopulations of patients and which, in each case, decreases the risk by 1/3 (RRR, 0.33; RR, 0.67). When administered to a subpopulation with a 30% risk of dying, treatment reduces the risk to 20%. When administered to a population with a 10% risk of dying, treatment reduces the risk to 6.7%. In the third population, treatment reduces the risk of dying from 1% to 0.67%.

Although treatment reduces the risk of dying by a third in each population, this piece of information is not adequate to fully capture the impact of treatment. What if

FIGURE 7-1

Constant Relative Risk With Varying Risk Differences

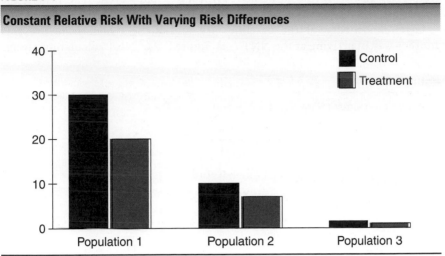

the treatment under consideration is a toxic cancer chemotherapy in which 10% of those treated experience severe adverse effects? Under these circumstances, we would probably not recommend the treatment to most patients in the lowest risk group in Figure 7-1, whose RD is only 0.3%. We would certainly explain the benefits and risks of treatment to the intermediate population, those with an absolute reduction in risk of death of about 3%. In the highest risk population with an absolute benefit of 10%, we could confidently recommend the treatment to most patients.

We suggest that you consider the RRR in the light of your patient's baseline risk. For instance, you might expect an RRR of approximately 30% in vascular events in patients with possible cardiovascular disease with administration of statins. You would view this RRR differently in a 40-year-old female normotensive nondiabetic nonsmoker with a mildly elevated LDL (low-density lipoprotein) (5-year risk of a cardiovascular event of approximately 2%, ARR of about 0.7%) and a 70-year-old hypertensive diabetic smoker (5-year risk of 30%, ARR of 10%). All this assumes a constant RRR across risk groups; fortunately, a more or less constant RRR is usually the case, and we suggest you make that assumption unless there is evidence that suggests it is incorrect.[3-5]

THE NUMBER NEEDED TO TREAT

One can also express the impact of treatment by the number of patients one would need to treat to prevent an adverse event, the *number needed to treat (NNT)*.[6] Table 7-2 shows that the risk of dying in the ligation group is 28.1%; and in the sclerotherapy group, it is 44.6%, an RD of 16.5%. If treating 100 patients results in avoiding 16.5

events, how many patients do we need to treat to avoid 1 event? The answer, 100 divided by 16.5, or approximately 6, is the NNT.

Given knowledge of the baseline risk and RRR, a *nomogram* presents another way of arriving at the NNT (see Figure 7-2).[7] NNT calculation always

FIGURE 7-2

Nomogram for Calculating the Number Needed to Treat

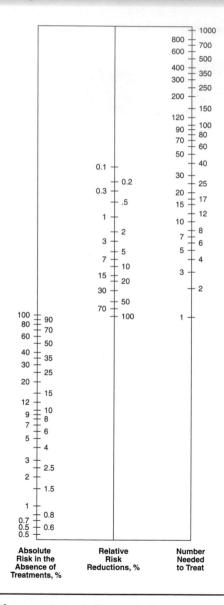

Absolute Risk in the Absence of Treatments, %	Relative Risk Reductions, %	Number Needed to Treat

implies a given time of *follow-up* (ie, do we need to treat 50 patients for 1 year or 5 years to prevent an event?). When trials with long follow-ups are analyzed by survival methods (see following), there are a variety of ways of calculating the NNT. The impact of these different methods will, however, almost never be important.[8]

Assuming a constant RRR, the NNT is inversely related to the proportion of patients in the control group who have an adverse event. If the risk of an adverse event doubles (for example, if we deal with patients at a higher risk of death than those included in the clinical trial), we need to treat only half as many patients to prevent an adverse event; if the risk decreases by a factor of 4 (patients are younger, have less *comorbidity* than those in the study), we will have to treat 4 times as many people.

The NNT is also inversely related to the RRR. With the same baseline risk, a more effective treatment with twice the RRR will reduce the NNT by half. If the RRR with 1 treatment is only a quarter of that achieved by an alternative strategy, the NNT will be 4 times greater.

Table 7-3 presents hypothetical data that illustrate these relationships.

THE NUMBER NEEDED TO HARM

Clinicians can calculate the *number needed to harm* (*NNH*) in a similar way. If you expect 5 of 100 patients to become fatigued when taking a β-blocker for a year, you will have to treat 20 patients to cause 1 to become tired; and the NNH is 20.

TABLE 7-3

Relationship Among the Baseline Risk, the Relative Risk Reduction, and the Number Needed to Treat[a]

Control Group Risk	Experimental Group Risk	Relative Risk, %	Relative Risk Reduction, %	Risk Difference	Number Needed to Treat
0.02	0.01	50	50	0.01	100
0.4	0.2	50	50	0.2	5
0.04	0.02	50	50	0.02	50
0.04	0.03	75	25	0.01	100
0.4	0.3	75	25	0.1	10
0.01	0.005	50	50	0.005	200

[a]Relative risk = experimental group risk/control group risk; relative risk reduction = 1 – relative risk; risk difference = control group risk – experimental group risk; number needed to treat = 1/risk difference (in decimal).

CONFIDENCE INTERVALS

We have presented all of the measures of association of the treatment with ligation vs sclerotherapy as if they represented the true effect. The results of any experiment, however, represent only an estimate of the truth. The true effect of treatment may be somewhat greater—or less—than what we observed. The *confidence interval* tells us, within the bounds of plausibility, how much greater or smaller the true effect is likely to be (see Chapter 8, Confidence Intervals).

SURVIVAL DATA

Analysis of a 2 × 2 table implies an examination of the data at a specific point in time. This analysis is satisfactory if we are looking for events that occur within relatively short periods and if all patients have the same duration of follow-up. In longer-term studies, however, we are interested not only in the total number of events but also in their timing. For instance, we may focus on whether therapy for patients with a uniformly fatal condition (unresectable lung cancer, for example) delays death.

When the timing of events is important, investigators could present the results in the form of several 2 × 2 tables constructed at different points of time after the study began. For example, Table 7-2 represents the situation after the study was finished. Similar tables could be constructed describing the fate of all patients available for analysis after their enrollment in the trial for 1 week, 1 month, 3 months, or whatever time we choose to examine. The analysis of accumulated data that takes into account the timing of events is called *survival analysis*. Do not infer from the name, however, that the analysis is restricted to deaths; in fact, any dichotomous outcome occurring over time will qualify.

The *survival curve* of a group of patients describes their status at different times after a defined starting point.[9] In Figure 7-3, we show the survival curve from the bleeding varices trial. Because the investigators followed some patients for a longer time, the survival curve extends beyond the mean follow-up of about 10 months. At some point, prediction becomes very imprecise because there are few patients remaining to estimate the *probability* of survival. Confidence intervals around the survival curves capture the precision of the estimate.

Even if the true RR, or RRR, is constant throughout the duration of follow-up, the play of chance will ensure that the *point estimates* differ. Ideally then, we would estimate the overall RR by applying an average, weighted for the number of patients available, for the entire survival experience. Statistical methods allow just such an estimate. The weighted RR over the entire study is known as the *hazard ratio*.

FIGURE 7-3

Survival Curves for Ligation and Sclerotherapy

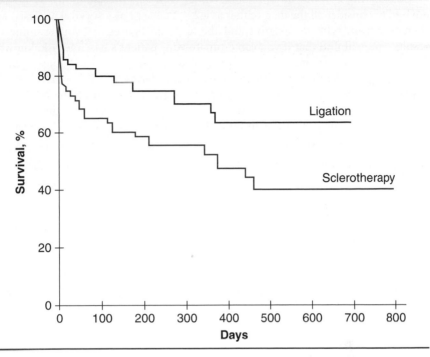

WHICH MEASURE OF ASSOCIATION IS BEST?

As evidence-based practitioners, we must decide which measure of association deserves our focus. Does it matter? The answer is yes. The same results, when presented in different ways, may lead to different treatment decisions.[10-14] For example, Forrow et al[10] demonstrated that clinicians were less inclined to treat patients after presentation of trial results as the absolute change in the outcome compared with the relative change in the outcome. In a similar study, Naylor et al[11] found that clinicians rated the effectiveness of an intervention lower when events were presented in absolute terms rather than using RRR. Moreover, clinicians offered lower effectiveness ratings when they viewed results expressed in terms of NNT than when they saw the same data as RRRs or ARRs. The pharmaceutic industry's awareness of this phenomenon may be responsible for their propensity to present physicians with treatment-associated RRRs.

Patients are as susceptible as clinicians to how results are communicated.[7,15-17] In one study, when researchers presented patients with a hypothetical scenario of life-threatening illness, the patients were more likely to choose a treatment described in terms of RRR than in terms of the corresponding ARR.[15]

Considering how our interpretations differ with data presentations, we are best advised to consider all the data (either as a 2 × 2 table or as a survival analysis) and then reflect on both the relative and the absolute figures. As you examine the results, you will find that if you can estimate your patient's baseline risk, knowing how well the treatment works—expressed as an RR or RRR—allows you to estimate the patient's risk with treatment. Considering the RD—the difference between the risk with and without treatment—and its reciprocal, the NNT, in an individual patient, will be most useful in guiding the treatment decision (see Chapter 11.1, Applying Results to Individual Patients, and Chapter 11.2, Example Numbers Needed to Treat).

References

1. Barratt A, Wyer PC, Hatala R, et al. Tips for learners of evidence-based medicine, 1: relative risk reduction, absolute risk reduction and number needed to treat. *CMAJ.* 2004;171(4:online-1 to online-8):353-358.

2. Stiegmann GV, Goff JS, Michaletz-Onody PA, et al. Endoscopic sclerotherapy as compared with endoscopic ligation for bleeding esophageal varices. *N Engl J Med.* 1992;326(23):1527-1532.

3. Deeks JJ. Issues in the selection of a summary statistic for meta-analysis of clinical trials with binary outcomes. *Stat Med.* 2002;21(11):1575-1600.

4. Schmid CH, Lau J, McIntosh MW, Cappelleri JC. An empirical study of the effect of the control rate as a predictor of treatment efficacy in meta-analysis of clinical trials. *Stat Med.* 1998;17(17):1923-1942.

5. Furukawa TA, Guyatt GH, Griffith LE. Can we individualize the "number needed to treat"? an empirical study of summary effect measures in meta-analyses. *Int J Epidemiol.* 2002;31(1):72-76.

6. Laupacis A, Sackett DL, Roberts RS. An assessment of clinically useful measures of the consequences of treatment. *N Engl J Med.* 1988;318(26):1728-1733.

7. Chatellier G, Zapletal E, Lemaitre D, Menard J, Degoulet P. The number needed to treat: a clinically useful nomogram in its proper context. *BMJ.* 1996;312 (7028):426-429.

8. Barratt AW, Guyatt G, Simpsons J. NNT for studies with long-term follow-up. *CMAJ.* 2005;172(5):613-615.

9. Coldman AJ, Elwood JM. Examining survival data. *CMAJ.* 1979;121(8):1065-1068, 1071.

10. Forrow L, Taylor WC, Arnold RM. Absolutely relative: how research results are summarized can affect treatment decisions. *Am J Med.* 1992;92(2):121-124.

11. Naylor CD, Chen E, Strauss B. Measured enthusiasm: does the method of reporting trial results alter perceptions of therapeutic effectiveness? *Ann Intern Med.* 1992;117(11):916-921.

12. Hux JE, Levinton CM, Naylor CD. Prescribing propensity: influence of life-expectancy gains and drug costs. *J Gen Intern Med.* 1994;9(4):195-201.

13. Redelmeier DA, Tversky A. Discrepancy between medical decisions for individual patients and for groups. *N Engl J Med.* 1990;322(16):1162-1164.

14. Bobbio M, Demichelis B, Giustetto G. Completeness of reporting trial results: effect on physicians' willingness to prescribe. *Lancet.* 1994;343(8907):1209-1211.

15. Malenka DJ, Baron JA, Johansen S, Wahrenberger JW, Ross JM. The framing effect of relative and absolute risk. *J Gen Intern Med.* 1993;8(10):543-548.

16. McNeil BJ, Pauker SG, Sox HC Jr, Tversky A. On the elicitation of preferences for alternative therapies. *N Engl J Med.* 1982;306(21):1259-1262.

17. Hux JE, Naylor CD. Communicating the benefits of chronic preventive therapy: does the format of efficacy data determine patients' acceptance of treatment? *Med Decis Making.* 1995;15(2):152-157.

8

CONFIDENCE INTERVALS

Gordon Guyatt, Stephen Walter, Deborah J. Cook,
Peter Wyer, and Roman Jaeschke

IN THIS CHAPTER:

Hypothesis testing involves estimating the probability that observed results would have occurred by chance if a *null hypothesis*, which most commonly states that there is no difference between a treatment condition and a control condition, were true (see Chapter 10.1, Hypothesis Testing). Health researchers and medical educators have increasingly recognized the limitations of hypothesis testing; consequently, an alternative approach, estimation, is becoming more popular. Several authors[1-5]—including ourselves, in an article on which this chapter is based[6]—have outlined the *concepts* that we will introduce here; and you can use their discussions to supplement our presentation.

HOW SHOULD WE TREAT PATIENTS WITH HEART FAILURE? A PROBLEM IN INTERPRETING STUDY RESULTS

In a *blinded randomized controlled trial* of 804 men with heart failure, investigators compared treatment with enalapril to that with a combination of hydralazine and nitrates.[7] In the *follow-up* period, which ranged from 6 months to 5.7 years, 132 of 403 patients (33%) assigned to receive enalapril died, as did 153 of 401 patients (38%) assigned to receive hydralazine and nitrates. The *P* value associated with the difference in mortality is .11.

Looking at this study as an exercise in hypothesis testing (see Chapter 10.1, Hypothesis Testing) and adopting the usual 5% risk of obtaining a false-positive result, we would conclude that chance remains a plausible explanation of the apparent differences between groups. We would classify this as a *negative study*; ie, we would conclude that no important difference existed between the treatment and *control groups*.

The investigators also conducted an analysis that compared not only the proportion of patients surviving at the end of the study but also the time pattern of the deaths occurring in both groups. This *survival analysis*, which generally is more sensitive than the test of the difference in proportions (see Chapter 7, Does Treatment Lower Risk? Understanding the Results), showed a nonsignificant *P* value of .08, a result that leads to the same conclusion as the simpler analysis that focused on relative proportions at the end of the study. The authors also tell us that the *P* value associated with differences in mortality at 2 years (a point predetermined to be a major *endpoint* of the trial) was significant at .016.

At this point, one might excuse clinicians who feel a little confused. Ask yourself, is this a *positive trial* dictating use of an angiotensin-converting enzyme (ACE) inhibitor instead of the combination of hydralazine and nitrates, or is it a negative study, showing no difference between the 2 regimens and leaving the choice of drugs open?

SOLVING THE PROBLEM: WHAT ARE CONFIDENCE INTERVALS?

How can clinicians deal with the limitations of hypothesis testing and resolve the confusion? The solution involves posing 2 questions (1) What is the single value most likely to represent the true difference between experimental and control?; and (2) Given the observed difference between experimental and control, what is the plausible range of differences between them within which the true difference might actually lie? *Confidence intervals* provide an answer to this second question. Before applying confidence intervals to resolve the issue of enalapril vs hydralazine and nitrates in patients with heart failure, we will illustrate the use of confidence intervals with a thought experiment.

Imagine a series of 5 trials (of equal duration but different sample sizes) wherein investigators have experimented with treating patients with a particular condition (elevated low-density-lipoprotein cholesterol) to determine whether a drug (a novel cholesterol-lowering agent) would work better than a *placebo* to *prevent* strokes (Table 8-1). The smallest trial enrolled only 8 patients, and the largest enrolled 2000 patients.

Now imagine that all the trials showed a *relative risk reduction (RRR)* for the treatment group of 50% (meaning that patients in the drug treatment group were 50% as likely as those in the placebo group to have a stroke). In each trial, how confident can we be that the true value of the RRR is *patient-important?*[8] If you were looking at the studies individually, which ones would lead your patients to use the treatment?

Most clinicians know intuitively that we can be more confident in the results of a larger vs a smaller trial. Why is this? In the absence of *bias* or *systematic*

TABLE 8-1

Relative Risk Reduction Observed in 5 Successively Larger Hypothetical Trials

Control Group Risk	Experimental Group Risk	Relative Risk, %	Relative Risk Reduction, %[a]
2/4	1/4	50	50
10/20	5/20	50	50
20/40	10/40	50	50
50/100	25/100	50	50
500/1000	250/1000	50	50

[a]Expressing event rates as a fraction, if the control group risk were 3/4 and the experimental group risk were 1/4 or 2/4, the relative risk reduction would be [(3/4) – (1/4)]/(3/4) = 2/3 or [(3/4) – (2/4)]/(3/4) = 1/3, respectively. Expressing event rates as percentage, if the control group risk were 75% and the experimental group risk were 25% or 50%, the relative risk reduction would be (75% – 25%)/75% = 67% or (75% – 50%)/75% = 33%, respectively.

Reprinted from Montori et al,[6] by permission of the publisher. Copyright © 2005, Canadian Medical Association.

error, one can interpret the trial as providing an estimate of the true magnitude of effect that would occur if all possible eligible patients had participated. When only a few patients participate, chance may lead to a best estimate of the *treatment effect*—the *point estimate*—that is far removed from the true value. Confidence intervals are a numeric measure of the range within which such variation is likely to occur. The 95% confidence intervals that we often see in biomedical publications represent the range in which we can be 95% certain of finding the underlying true treatment effect.

To gain a better appreciation of confidence intervals, go back to Table 8-1 (do not look at Table 8-2 yet!) and take a guess at what you think the confidence intervals might be for the 5 trials presented. In a moment, you will see how your estimates compare with the actual calculated 95% confidence intervals, but for now, try figuring out an interval that you think would be intuitive.

Now consider the first trial, in which 2 of 4 patients receiving the control intervention and 1 of 4 patients receiving the experimental treatment intervention have a stroke. The risk in the experimental group was thus half of that in the control group, giving a *relative risk (RR)* of 50% and an RRR of 50%.

Would you be ready to recommend this treatment to a patient in view of the substantial RRR? Before you answer this, consider whether it is plausible that, with so few patients in the study, we could have just been lucky in our sample and the true treatment effect could really be a 50% increase in RR. In other words, is it plausible that the true *event rate* in the group that received treatment was 3 of 4 instead of 1 of 4? If you accept that this large, harmful effect may represent the underlying truth, would an RRR of 90% (ie, a large benefit of treatment) also be consistent with the experimental data in these few patients? To the extent that these suggestions are plausible, we can intuitively create a range of plausible truth of −50% to 90% surrounding the RRR of 50% that we actually observed in the study.

Now do this for each of the other 4 trials. In the trial with 20 patients in the experimental group and 20 in the control group, 10 of 20 patients in the control group had a stroke, as did 5 of 20 patients in the experimental group. The RR and RRR are again 50%. Do you still consider plausible that the true event rate in the experimental group is really 15 of 20 rather than 5 of 20? If not, what about 12 of 20? The latter would yield an increase in the RR of 20%. A true RRR of 90% may still remain plausible, given the observed results and numbers of patients involved. In short, given this larger number of patients and lower chance of a bad sample, your range of plausible truth around the observed RRR of 50% might be narrower, perhaps from −20% (an RR increase of 20%) to a 90% RRR.

For the larger and larger trials, you could provide similar intuitively derived confidence intervals. We have done this in Table 8-2, and also provided the 95% confidence intervals (calculated using a statistical program). You can see that, in some instances, we intuitively overestimated or underestimated the calculated intervals.

TABLE 8-2

Confidence Intervals Around the Relative Risk Reduction for the Hypothetical Results of 5 Successively Larger Trials

Control Group Risk	Experimental Group Risk	Relative Risk, %	Relative Risk Reduction (RRR), %	Intuitive Confidence Interval, %	Calculated 95% Confidence Interval Around the RRR, %
2/4	1/4	50	50	−50 to 90	−174 to 92
10/20	5/20	50	50	−20 to 90	−14 to 79.5
20/40	10/40	50	50	0 to 90	9.5 to 73.4
50/100	25/100	50	50	20 to 80	26.8 to 66.4
500/1000	250/1000	50	50	40 to 60	43.5 to 55.9

Reprinted from Montori et al,[6] by permission of the publisher. Copyright © 2005, Canadian Medical Association.

Confidence intervals inform clinicians about the range within which, given the trial data, the true treatment effect might plausibly lie. More precision (narrower confidence intervals) results from larger sample sizes and consequently larger number of events. Statisticians (and clinician-friendly statistical software) can calculate 95% confidence intervals around any estimate of treatment effect.

USING CONFIDENCE INTERVALS TO INTERPRET THE RESULTS OF CLINICAL TRIALS

How do confidence intervals help us understand the results of the trial of vasodilators in patients with heart failure? Throughout the entire study, the mortality in the ACE inhibitor arm was 33% and in the hydralazine plus nitrate group it was 38%, an *absolute difference* of 5% and an RR of 0.86. The 5% absolute difference and the 14% RRR represent our best single estimate of the mortality benefit from using an ACE inhibitor. The 95% confidence interval around the RRR works out to −3.5% to 29% (that is, 3.5% RRR with hydralazine and nitrates, to a 29% RRR with the ACE inhibitor).

How can we now interpret the study results? We can conclude that patients offered ACE inhibitors will most likely (but not certainly) die later than patients offered hydralazine and nitrates—but the magnitude of the difference may be either trivial or quite large, and there remains the possibility of a marginally lower mortality with the hydralazine-nitrate regimen.

Using the confidence interval avoids the yes/no dichotomy of hypothesis testing. It also obviates the need to argue whether the study should be considered positive or negative. One can conclude that, all else being equal, an ACE inhibitor is the appropriate choice for patients with heart failure, but the strength of this inference is weak. Toxicity, expense, and *evidence* from other studies would all bear on the final treatment decision (see Chapter 21, How to Use a Patient Management Recommendation). Because a number of large randomized trials have now shown a mortality benefit from ACE inhibitors in patients with heart failure,[9] one can confidently recommend this class of agents as the treatment of choice. Another study has suggested that for black patients, the hydralazine-nitrate combination offers additional mortality reduction beyond ACE inhibitors.[10]

INTERPRETING APPARENTLY "NEGATIVE" TRIALS

Another example of the use of confidence intervals in interpreting study results comes from a randomized trial of low vs high positive end expiratory pressure (PEEP) in patients with adult respiratory distress syndrome.[11] Of 273 patients in the low-PEEP group, 24.9% died; of 276 in the high-PEEP group, 27.5% died. The point estimate from these results is a 2.6% *absolute risk increase* in deaths in the high-PEEP group.

This trial of more than 500 patients might appear to exclude any possible benefit from high PEEP. The 95% confidence interval on the absolute difference of 2.6% in favor of low PEEP, however, is from 10.0% in favor of low PEEP to 4.7% in favor of high PEEP. Were it true that 4.7% of the patients who would have died if given low PEEP would survive if treated with high PEEP, all patients would want to receive the high-PEEP strategy. This would mean one would need to treat only 21 patients to prevent a premature death. One can thus conclude that the trial has not excluded a patient-important benefit and, in that sense, was not large enough.

This example emphasizes that many patients must participate if trials are to generate precise estimates of treatment effects. In addition, it illustrates why we recommend that, whenever possible, clinicians turn to systematic reviews that pool data from the most valid studies.

When you see an apparently *negative trial* (one with a *P* value greater than .05 that, using conventional criteria, fails to exclude the null hypothesis that treatment and control interventions do not differ), you can focus on the upper end of the confidence interval (that is, the end that suggests the largest benefit from treatment). If the upper boundary of the confidence interval excludes any important benefit of treatment, you can conclude that the trial is definitively negative. If, on the other hand, the confidence interval includes an important benefit, the possibility should not be ruled out that the treatment still might be worthwhile.

This logic of the negative trial is crucial in the interpretation of studies designed to help determine whether we should substitute a treatment that is less expensive, easier to administer, or less toxic for an existing treatment. In such *noninferiority studies*, we will be ready to make the substitution only if we are sure that the standard treatment does not have important additional benefits beyond the less expensive or more convenient substitute.[12-15] We will be confident that we have excluded the possibility of important additional benefits of the standard treatment if the boundary of the confidence interval representing the largest plausible treatment effect is below our threshold.

Interpreting Apparently "Positive" Trials

How can confidence intervals be informative in a positive trial (one that, yielding a *P* value less than .05, makes chance an unlikely explanation for observed differences between treatments)? In a blinded trial in patients with vascular disease, 19 185 patients were randomized to clopidogrel or aspirin. Patients receiving clopidogrel experienced a 5.32% annual risk of ischemic stroke, myocardial infarction, or vascular death vs 5.83% with aspirin, an RRR of 8.7% in favor of clopidogrel (95% confidence interval, 0.3%-16.5%; *P* = .043). In absolute terms, the difference between treatments is 0.5%, with a 95% confidence interval of 0.02%—that is, 2 in 10 000—to 0.9%, or just less than 1 in 100. For the average patient, one could argue whether the point estimate of 0.5% absolute difference—a *number needed to treat* (*NNT*) of 200—represents an important difference. Few patients are likely to find the lower boundary of the confidence interval, representing an NNT of 5000, an important difference. This trial does not establish clopidogrel's superiority over aspirin. The sample size— almost 20 000 patients—was insufficient to provide a definitive answer.

Was the Trial Large Enough?

As implied in our discussion to this point, confidence intervals provide a way of answering the question: was the trial large enough? We illustrate the approach in Figure 8-1. In this figure, we present the results of 4 randomized trials. Although most forest plots (visual plots of trial results) focus on RR or odds ratios, Figure 8-1 presents the results in absolute terms. Thus, the solid vertical line in the center of the figure represents a *risk difference* (*RD*) (or *absolute risk reduction*) of zero, when the experimental and control groups have the same mortality. Values to the left of the vertical line represent results in which the treated group had a lower mortality than the control group. Values to the right of the vertical line represent results in which the treated group fared worse and had a higher mortality rate than the control group.

Assume that the treatment carries sufficient toxicity or risk such that, in each case, patients would choose treatment only if the RD were 1% or greater. That is, if the reduction in death rates were greater than 1%, patients would consider it worth enduring the toxicity and risk of treatment, but if the reduction in event rates were less than 1%, they would not. The broken line in Figure 8-1 represents the threshold reduction in death rates of 1%.

FIGURE 8-1

When Is Trial Sample Size Sufficiently Large? Four Hypothetical Trial Results

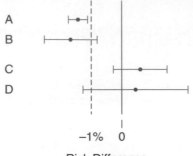

−1%   0

Risk Difference

For the medical condition under investigation, a risk difference of −1% (broken line) is the smallest benefit that patients would consider important enough to warrant undergoing treatment.

Reprinted from Montori et al,[6] by permission of the publisher. Copyright © 2005, Canadian Medical Association.

Now consider trial A: would you recommend this therapy to your patients if the point estimate represented the truth? What if the upper boundary of the confidence interval represented the truth? What about the lower boundary?

For all 3, the answer is yes, given that 1% is the smallest patient-important difference, and all suggest a benefit of greater than 1%. Thus, the trial is definitive and provides a strong inference about the treatment decision.

In the case of trial B, would your patients choose to take the treatment if either the point estimate or the upper boundary of the confidence interval represented the true effect? The answer is yes, the patients would, for the reduction in death rate would be greater than the 1% threshold. What about the lower boundary? The answer here is no, for the effect is less than the smallest difference that patients would consider large enough to take the treatment. Although trial B shows a positive result (ie, the confidence interval excludes an effect of zero), the sample size was inadequate and yielded a result that remains compatible with risk reductions below the minimal patient-important difference.

For negative studies, those that fail to exclude a true treatment effect of zero, you should focus on the other end of the confidence interval, that which represents the largest plausible treatment effect consistent with the trial data. You should consider whether that upper boundary of the confidence interval falls below the smallest difference that patients might consider important. If so, the sample size is adequate and the trial is negative and definitive (Figure 8-1, trial C). If the boundary representing the largest plausible effect exceeds the smallest patient-important difference, then the trial is not definitive and more trials with larger sample sizes are needed (Figure 8-1, trial D).[6]

We can state our message as follows: In a positive trial establishing that the effect of treatment is greater than zero, look to the lower boundary of the confidence interval to determine whether sample size has been adequate. If this lower boundary—the smallest plausible treatment effect compatible with the data—is greater than the smallest difference that you consider important, the sample size is adequate and the trial is definitive. If the lower boundary is less than this smallest important difference, the trial is nondefinitive and further trials are required.

In a negative trial, look to the upper boundary of the confidence interval to determine whether sample size has been adequate. If this upper boundary, the largest treatment effect plausibly compatible with the data, is less than the smallest difference that you consider important, the sample size is adequate and the trial is definitively negative. If the upper boundary exceeds the smallest important difference, there may still be an important positive treatment effect, the trial is nondefinitive, and further trials are required.

Acknowledgment

Portions of this material were previously published from Montori et al.[6]

References

1. Simon R. Confidence intervals for reporting results of clinical trials. *Ann Intern Med.* 1986;105(3):429-435.

2. Gardner M. *Statistics With Confidence: Confidence Intervals and Statistical Guidelines*. London, England: BMJ Publishing Group; 1989.

3. Bulpitt CJ. Confidence intervals. *Lancet.* 1987;1(8531):494-497.

4. Pocock SJ, Hughes MD. Estimation issues in clinical trials and overviews. *Stat Med.* 1990;9(6):657 671.

5. Braitman LE. Confidence intervals assess both clinical significance and statistical significance. *Ann Intern Med.* 1991;114(6):515-517.

6. Montori VM, Kleinbart J, Newman TB, et al. Tips for learners of evidence-based medicine, 2: measures of precision (confidence intervals). *CMAJ.* 2004;171 (6):611-615.

7. Cohn JN, Johnson G, Ziesche S, et al. A comparison of enalapril with hydralazine-isosorbide dinitrate in the treatment of chronic congestive heart failure. *N Engl J Med.* 1991;325(5):303-310.

8. Guyatt G, Montori V, Devereaux PJ, Schunemann H, Bhandari M. Patients at the center: in our practice, and in our use of language. *ACP J Club.* 2004;140(1):A11-A12.

9. Garg R, Yusuf S. Overview of randomized trials of angiotensin converting enzyme inhibitors on mortality and morbidity in patients with heart failure: Collaborative Group on ACE Inhibitor Trials. *JAMA.* 1995;273(18):1450-1456.

10. Taylor AL, Ziesche S, Yancy C, et al. Combination of isosorbide dinitrate and hydralazine in blacks with heart failure. *N Engl J Med.* 2004;351(20):2049-2057.

11. Brower RG, Lanken PN, MacIntyre N, et al. Higher versus lower positive end-expiratory pressures in patients with the acute respiratory distress syndrome. *N Engl J Med.* 2004;351(4):327-336.

12. D'Agostino RB Sr, Massaro JM, Sullivan LM. Non-inferiority trials: design concepts and issues—the encounters of academic consultants in statistics. *Stat Med.* 2003;22(2):169-186.

13. Gotzsche PC. Lessons from and cautions about noninferiority and equivalence randomized trials. *JAMA.* 2006;295(10):1172-1174.

14. Piaggio G, Elbourne DR, Altman DG, Pocock SJ, Evans SJ. Reporting of noninferiority and equivalence randomized trials: an extension of the CONSORT statement. *JAMA.* 2006;295(10):1152-1160.

15. Le Henanff A, Giraudeau B, Baron G, Ravaud P. Quality of reporting of noninferiority and equivalence randomized trials. *JAMA.* 2006;295(10):1147-1151.

ADVANCED TOPICS IN THE
VALIDITY OF THERAPY TRIALS

AN ILLUSTRATION OF BIAS AND RANDOM ERROR

Gordon Guyatt and Toshi Furukawa

As is true of any area of intellectual endeavor, students of *evidence-based medicine* face challenges both in understanding *concepts* and in becoming familiar with technical language. When asked to say what makes a study valid, students often respond, "large sample size." Small sample size does not produce *bias* (and, thus, compromised *validity*), but it can increase the likelihood of a misleading result through *random error*. You may find the following exercise helpful in clarifying notions of bias—*systematic error* or deviation from the truth—vs random error.

Consider a set of studies with identical design and sample size. Each study recruits from the same patient pool. Will these studies, with exactly the same type of patients and exactly the same study design, yield identical results? No, they will not. Just as an experiment of 10 coin flips will not always yield 5 heads and 5 tails, the play of chance will ensure that, despite their identical design, each study will have a different result.

Consider 4 sets of such studies. Within each set, the design and sample size of each individual trial are identical. Two of the 4 sets of studies have a small sample size and 2 have a large sample size.

Two sets of studies include only *randomized controlled trials* (*RCTs*) in which patients, caregivers, and those assessing outcome are all *blinded*. Design features, such as blinding and *complete follow-up*, reduce bias. The remaining sets of studies use an observational design (eg, patients are in treatment or *control groups* according to their choice or their clinician's choice), which is far more vulnerable to bias. In this exercise, we are in the unique position of knowing the true *treatment effect*. In Figure 9.1-1, each of the bull's-eyes in the center of the 4 components of the figure represents the truth. Each smaller dot represents not a single patient but the results of 1 repetition of the study. The farther a smaller dot lies from the central bull's-eye, the larger the difference between the study result and the underlying true treatment effect.

Each set of studies represents the results of RCTs or *observational studies* and of studies of large or small sample size. Before reading further, examine

FIGURE 9.1-1

Four Sets of Identically Conducted Studies Demonstrating Various Degrees of Bias and Random Error

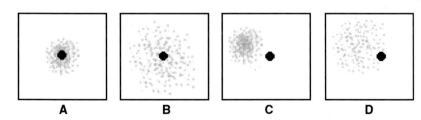

| A | B | C | D |

A and B represent randomized trials. C and D represent observational studies. In each part, the studies are of identical sample size and identical design.

Figure 9.1-1 and draw your own conclusions about the study designs and number of patients in each of the 4 (A through D) components.

Figure 9.1-1A represents the results of a series of randomized trials with large sample size. The results are valid and are thus uniformly distributed around the true effect, represented by the central bull's-eye, resulting from the strong study design. The results also do not fall exactly on target because of chance or random error. Nevertheless, the large sample size, which minimizes random error, ensures that the result of any individual study is relatively close to the truth.

Contrast this set of results with those depicted in Figure 9.1-1B. Again, the strong study design results in the individual study results being distributed uniformly around the truth. Because the sample size is small and random error is large, however, the results of individual studies may be far from the truth.

Thinking back to the coin flip experiments from Chapter 5 (Why Study Results Mislead: Bias and Random Error) clarifies the difference between the studies in Figure 9.1-1A and 9.1-1B. In a series of experiments in which each study involves 10 flips of a true coin, individual results may fall far from the truth. Findings of 7 to 3, 70%—or even 8 to 2, 80%—heads (or tails) will not be unusual. This situation is analogous to Figure 9.1-1B. If our experiments each involve 1000 coin flips, analogous to Figure 9.1-1A, we will seldom see distributions more extreme than, say, 540 to 460, or a 54% probability of heads or tails. With the smaller sample size, individual results are far from the truth; with the larger sample size, they are all close to the truth.

Figure 9.1-1A and 9.1-1B illustrates the rationale for pooling results of different studies, a process called *meta-analysis*. We can assume that the available evidence about therapeutic effectiveness comes from a series of small RCTs. There is a problem, however: chance will ensure that the study results vary widely, and we will not know which one to believe. However, because of a strong study design, the distribution of the results is centered on the truth. As a result of this favorable situation, we can, by pooling the results of the studies, decrease random error and increase the strength of our inferences from the uncertainty of Figure 9.1-1B to the confidence of Figure 9.1-1A.

In Figure 9.1-1C, the center of the set of dots is far from the truth because studies with observational designs, even large ones, are vulnerable to bias. Because the studies share an identical design, each one will be subject to the same magnitude and direction of bias. The results are precise, with minimal random error; however, they are wrong.

One example of this phenomenon is the apparent benefit of vitamin E on reducing mortality from coronary artery disease, suggested by the results of a number of large observational studies. By contrast, a subsequent, very large, well-conducted RCT and a meta-analysis of all available randomized trials failed to demonstrate any beneficial effect of vitamin E on coronary deaths or all-cause mortality. There are many additional examples of this phenomenon (see Chapter 9.2, Surprising Results of Randomized Trials).

The situation depicted in Figure 9.1-1C is a particularly dangerous one because the large size of the studies instills confidence in clinicians that their results are accurate. For example, some clinicians, fed by the consistent results of very large observational studies, still believe the discredited dogma of the beneficial effect of hormone replacement therapy on coronary artery disease mortality.

Like Figure 9.1-1C, Figure 9.1-1D depicts a series of observational studies leading to biased results that are far from the truth. However, because the sample sizes are all small, the results vary widely from study to study. One might be tempted to conduct a meta-analysis of these data. This is dangerous because we risk converting imprecise estimates with large random error to precise estimates with small random error; both, however, are biased and will therefore yield misleading estimates of the true effect.

ADVANCED TOPICS IN THE
VALIDITY OF THERAPY TRIALS

SURPRISING RESULTS OF RANDOMIZED TRIALS

Christina Lacchetti, John Ioannidis,
and Gordon Guyatt

IN THIS CHAPTER:

MOST MAJOR BASIC SCIENCE AND PRECLINICAL PROMISES FOR EFFECTIVE INTERVENTIONS DISAPPOINT IN CLINICAL TRIALS

Ideally, *evidence* for the effectiveness of diagnostic, preventive, or therapeutic interventions will come from rigorous *randomized controlled trials (RCTs)* measuring effects on *patient-important outcomes* such as stroke, myocardial infarction, and death. Historically, however, clinicians have often relied on weaker evidence. Whenever an intervention is tested to see whether it is effective or not for patient-important outcomes, typically some other evidence of variable quantity and quality already exists. This evidence includes combinations of basic science findings, preclinical results, *observational studies*, and earlier *phase I or II clinical trials*.

Sometimes, clinicians adopt interventions even though randomized trials have never been performed to test their effect on patient-important outcomes. This is very common for acute surgical interventions, common for elective surgical interventions and mental health interventions, and somewhat less common for medical interventions.[1] Nevertheless, even for medical interventions, randomized evidence is usually absent when it comes to interventions that need to be applied for specialized decisions after some major first decision has been made.[2] For these interventions, their adoption and continued use in clinical practice has been based on various combinations of basic science, preclinical, and observational evidence.

Moreover, there is a strong undercurrent in many scientific circles supporting the use of *surrogate endpoints* for adopting interventions for common diseases. Trials using surrogate endpoints require smaller sample sizes and shorter *follow-up* periods than trials of patient-important *endpoints*. Thus, drugs and other interventions can be rapidly tested and approved for clinical use.[3]

Given this patchy and uneven availability of evidence, surprises often occur when interventions that seem promising or have even been established according to relatively strong evidence prove disappointing in randomized trials. Typically, fewer and fewer promising interventions retain their postulated claims to effectiveness as we move from basic science experimentation to RCTs with objective outcomes. An empirical evaluation[4] examined 101 major findings published in the top basic science journals between 1979 and 1983 in which the investigators made a clear promise that their work will be translated to a major therapeutic or preventive intervention. Of those, only 27 eventually materialized to have a randomized trial, and only 19 had positive results in at least 1 randomized trial with any kind of endpoint by 2002. At that time, only 5 interventions were approved for clinical use, and only 1 of them has had a major effect in therapeutics, the other 4 having uncommon or questionable clinical indications. The credibility of basic science and preclinical claims or observational discoveries, fascinating as they may be, is often low.[5]

TYPES OF WEAK EVIDENCE

Evidence may be weak in 3 ways. First, the methodology may be pristine—as is the case in rigorous RCTs—but the participants may be very different from those of interest. For instance, demonstrating that a type of therapy hastens the resolution of experimentally induced renal failure in rats is provocative, but it provides weak evidence for administration of that therapy to human beings.

Second, the outcomes may be interesting but not important to patients. For example, demonstrating the effect of an intervention on cardiac output or pulmonary capillary wedge pressure may herald the introduction of a beneficial drug for patients with heart failure, but trials examining the frequency of hospitalization and mortality are essential before clinicians can confidently offer the medication to patients.

Third, examining the apparent effect of a drug, device, procedure, or program on patient-important outcomes such as stroke, myocardial infarction, or death may choose the right population and outcome but a weak study design (eg, observational studies) that leads to a biased estimate of the *treatment effect.*

Evidence may have combinations of these limitations. For example, investigators have may used observational study designs to test the effects of interventions using surrogate outcomes on other species.

Our message is not to dismiss weaker forms of evidence. Studies of weaker design may occasionally provide such compelling results that they strongly support clinical use of an intervention. They may even dissuade patients, clinicians, and researchers from performing large clinical trials with patient-important outcomes because of perceived ethical constraints. Evidence-based decision making demands reliance on the best available evidence, even if that evidence is weak. Moreover, sometimes RCTs with patient-important outcomes may still be heavily biased, whereas "weaker" forms of evidence on the same question may be more rigorous and their results closer to the truth.

Allowing for these caveats, we suggest that when clinicians rely on weak evidence, they acknowledge the risk of administering useless or even harmful interventions.[6] Our concern is empirically strengthened by examples of conclusions clinicians have drawn based on nonhuman, surrogate endpoint, or observational studies subsequently refuted by RCTs. In the majority of cases, the weaker evidence suggested that a therapy should be used but this proved misleading. In a few cases, the opposite was seen: an intervention deemed useless or harmful according to weak evidence was eventually found to be effective with higher quality evidence.

In the following sections, we present examples of instances in which RCT results on patient-important endpoints contradicted those of previous studies. We have categorized the examples according to the type of weak previous evidence. All these examples suggest the same message: clinician, beware!

WHEN RANDOMIZED CONTROLLED TRIAL RESULTS HAVE CONTRADICTED NONHUMAN STUDIES

Table 9.2-1 provides examples in which animal or tissue studies gave misleading inferences. In the typical scenario, an attractive promise in nonhuman research is not validated when tested in humans. It is uncommon to see negative results in nonhuman experiments being followed by proof of effectiveness on human studies, probably because interventions that do not show promise at the basic science and animal experimentation level are unlikely to move toward human experimentation.

TABLE 9.2-1

Refuted Evidence From Nonhuman Studies[a]

Question	Evidence From Nonhuman Studies	RCT Evidence in Humans
What effect does atrial natriuretic peptide (anaritide) have on renal function?	An experiment evaluated α-human atrial natriuretic peptide in experimental ischemic renal failure, induced by renal artery occlusion in renally intact rats. After ischemia, a 4-h intrarenal infusion restored 14C-inulin clearances ($P <$ .001). There was progressive decrease in medullary hyperemia and prevention of intratubular cell shedding and granulocyte margination; at 24-48 h, tissue histology was essentially normal.[7]	A multicenter RCT studied administration of anaritide in 504 critically ill patients with acute tubular necrosis. Among 120 patients with oliguria, dialysis-free survival was 8% in the placebo group and 27% in the anaritide group ($P =$ .008). However, among the 378 patients without oliguria, dialysis-free survival was 59% in the placebo group and 48% in the anaritide group ($P =$ .03).[8]
Does acetylcysteine prevent doxorubicin-induced acute myocardial morphologic damage?	An experiment investigated the effect of acetylcysteine administration on the toxicity of doxorubicin in mice. Results suggested that pretreatment with acetylcysteine 1 h before doxorubicin significantly decreased lethality, long-term mortality, and loss in total body weight and heart weight. Acetylcysteine pretreatment also ablated electron microscopic evidence of doxorubicin cardiomyopathy.[9]	Twenty patients with normal cardiovascular function were randomized to 2 groups. Group I received placebo and group II received acetylcysteine (Nac), both 1 h before doxorubicin. Endomyocardial biopsies were performed and were viewed by electron microscopy and stereoscopic techniques. The change of the tubular area and mitochondrial swelling were similar in the 2 groups and were proportionate throughout the cell. This study demonstrated that the acute doxorubicin-induced damage was diffuse and not prevented by Nac.[10]

(Continued)

TABLE 9.2-1

Refuted Evidence From Nonhuman Studies[a] (*Continued*)

Question	Evidence From Nonhuman Studies	RCT Evidence in Humans
Does treatment with naloxone (opiate antagonist) improve neurologic outcomes in patients with spinal cord injury?	The opiate antagonist naloxone has been used to treat cats subjected to cervical spinal trauma. In contrast to saline-treated controls, naloxone treatment significantly improved the hypotension observed after cervical spinal injury. More critically, naloxone therapy significantly improved neurologic recovery.[11]	A multicenter, randomized, blinded trial evaluated the efficacy and safety of naloxone (and other drugs) in patients with acute spinal cord injury. Naloxone was given to 154 patients and placebo to 171 patients. Motor and sensory functions were assessed by systematic neurologic examination. Results show that patients treated with naloxone did not differ in their neurologic outcomes from those given placebo. Mortality and major morbidity were also similar between groups. Investigators concluded that treatment with naloxone in the dose used in this study does not improve neurologic recovery after acute spinal cord injury.[12]
What is the efficacy of recombinant human relaxin (rhRlx) as a cervical ripening agent?	Relaxin, a peptide hormone synthesized in the corpora lutea of ovaries during pregnancy, is released into the bloodstream before parturition. Synthetic relaxin exhibited relaxin-like bioactivity assessed by the standard uterine contraction bioassay. Results suggested "synthetic human relaxin... may lead to the development of clinical treatments to alleviate some of the problems encountered at childbirth."[13]	A multicenter, blinded, placebo-controlled trial evaluated the efficacy and safety of rhRlx as a cervical ripening agent in women with an unfavorable cervix before induction of labor. Ninety-six women at 37 to 42 wk of gestation were treated with 0, 1, 2, or 4 mg of rhRlx. Results showed no significant differences in the change in modified Bishop score between the 4 treatment groups, and the lengths of the first and second stages of labor were similar in all 4 groups. Investigators conclude that rhRlx 1 to 4 mg has no effect as a cervical ripening agent before induction of labor at term.[14]

(*Continued*)

TABLE 9.2-1

Refuted Evidence From Nonhuman Studies[a] *(Continued)*

Question	Evidence From Nonhuman Studies	RCT Evidence in Humans
What is the therapeutic effect of vitamin D3 metabolite in patients with leukemia?	HL-60 cells from patients with promyelocytic leukemia respond to near physiologic levels of vitamin D3 by rapidly acquiring a number of monocyte-like features. These phenotypic changes are preceded by a marked decrement in the expression of the *c-myc* oncogene (a gene related to the process of development of cancer). In addition, removal of vitamin D3, after the onset of maturational change, resulted in the reappearance of elevated *myc* mRNA levels. The authors conclude that "this is the first demonstration of a sequential relationship between the application of an exogenous inducing agent, a reduction in *myc* mRNA levels and the development of characteristics associated with normal cell maturation."[15]	An RCT evaluated 63 patients with myelodysplastic syndromes (MDS) and 15 with acute myelogenous leukemia (AML). Patients were randomized between low-dose cytosine arabinoside (ara-C) (arm A) and low-dose ara-C in combination with 13-*cis*-retinoic acid (13-CRA) and vitamin D3 (arm B). Results suggested the addition of 13-CRA and vitamin D3 had no positive influence on survival of the patients, remission rates, or duration of remissions.[16]
What is the efficacy of treatment with cytosine arabinoside (CA) in patients with herpes zoster?	Several investigations of the in vitro antiviral action of CA showed that CA had antiviral activity in cell cultures against DNA viruses, including herpes. Results also suggested that the presence of CA in the medium feeding actively growing cells inhibited some cellular function necessary for replication.[43]	A randomized, blinded, controlled study investigating the treatment of disseminated herpes zoster with CA found that the duration of the dissemination was greater in the treated than placebo group ($P = .03$). The authors concluded that CA at a dose of 100 mg/m^2/24 h has no beneficial effects on the disease.[44]

Abbreviations: 1-α-D3, 1 α-hydroxy-vitamin D3; ara-C, cytarabine; CA, cytosine arabinoside; 13-CRA, 13-*cis*-retinoic acid; mRNA, messenger ribonucleic acid; Nac, acetylcysteine; RCT, randomized controlled trial; rhRlx, recombinant human relaxin.

[a]Data are expressed here as reported in the original literature.

When Randomized Controlled Trials Have Contradicted Human Studies of Surrogate Endpoints

Table 9.2-2 shows examples in which RCTs of patient-important outcomes refuted results of studies using physiologic or surrogate endpoints. Surrogate endpoint studies were either observational or randomized. Whereas in most cases the surrogate studies were overly optimistic, in some, surrogates did not suggest any benefit (or even suggested *harm*), but patient-important outcomes demonstrated benefit.

Surrogates can give misleading inferences both for the efficacy and the harms of an intervention. Surrogates that capture adequately both the eventual clinical benefits and the clinical harms of an intervention are difficult to develop, let alone validate.[3,6,17] In some of the examples below, both study design and reliance on a surrogate were problematic (the RCT failed to demonstrate the apparent effect on the surrogate demonstrated in a study of weaker design).

TABLE 9.2-2

Refuted Evidence From Studies of Physiologic or Surrogate Endpoints

Question	Evidence From Surrogate Endpoints	RCT Evidence of Patient-Important Endpoints
In patients with chronic heart failure, what impact does β-adrenergic blockade have on mortality?	In a before-after study, intravenous propranolol demonstrated declines in ejection fraction (range, 0.05-0.22) and increases in end-diastolic volume (range, 30-135 mL) in 4 patients with advanced coronary disease and previous myocardial infarction. Abnormalities of wall motion after propranolol developed in 2 patients. Investigators suggested that "results are consistent with the thesis that β-adrenergic blocking drugs may inhibit compensatory sympathetic mechanisms."[18]	A meta-analysis of 18 RCTs of β-blockers in patients with heart failure found a 32% reduction in the RR of death (95% CI, 12%-47%; $P = .003$) and a 41% reduction in the RR of hospitalization for heart failure (95% CI, 26%-52%; $P < .001$) with β-blockers. Significant improvements were also seen in New York Heart Association status.[19]

(Continued)

TABLE 9.2-2

Refuted Evidence From Studies of Physiologic or Surrogate Endpoints (*Continued*)

Question	Evidence From Surrogate Endpoints	RCT Evidence of Patient-Important Endpoints
What effect does clofibrate have on mortality in men without clinically evident ischemic heart disease?	A before-after study of the effects of clofibrate on total and β-cholesterol found, after a 4-wk treatment regimen with 750-1500 mg of clofibrate, a significant reduction in total cholesterol level in 86% of patients (30/35) and a significant decrease in β-cholesterol in 91% of patients (21/23). Furthermore, in every case, the tolerance to clofibrate was excellent and no adverse effects could be observed.[20]	An RCT of men without clinical ischemic heart disease randomized participants in the upper third of the cholesterol distribution to clofibrate therapy or placebo. After a mean observation of 9.6 y, there were 20% fewer incidents of ischemic heart disease ($P <$ .05), but 25% more deaths ($P <$ .01) in the clofibrate group compared with those in the high-cholesterol control group ($P <$ .05).[21]
What impact do the antiarrhythmic drugs encainide and flecainide have on mortality from ventricular arrhythmias in patients after myocardial infarction?	A before-after study of patients with symptomatic, recurrent, previously drug-refractory ventricular tachycardia found that encainide completely eliminated recurrence of ventricular tachycardia in 54% of patients after 6 mo of therapy and in 29% of patients after 18-30 mo of therapy. Investigators concluded that "encainide is a safe, well-tolerated antiarrhythmic agent."[22]	An RCT evaluating the effect of encainide and flecainide in survivors of acute myocardial infarction with ventricular ectopy found an RR of 2.64 (95% CI, 1.60-4.36) for cardiac deaths and cardiac arrests among patients receiving active drug vs those receiving placebo.[23]
In patients with chronic heart failure, does treatment with milrinone alter mortality?	A before-after study in 12 patients with congestive heart failure found that milrinone treatment produced an improvement in left ventricular function during exercise, with significant changes in cardiac index, stroke volume index, and pulmonary capillary wedge pressure ($P <$ .001). Systemic oxygen consumption increased ($P <$ .05), as did maximum exercise capacity ($P <$ .001). Beneficial effects on exercise hemodynamics and tolerance were sustained throughout the 4-wk treatment period. No drug-related adverse effects occurred.[24]	In an RCT of 1088 patients with severe chronic heart failure and advanced left ventricular dysfunction, milrinone (compared with placebo) was associated with a 28% relative increase in overall mortality (95% CI, 1%-61%; $P =$ .04) and 34% increase in cardiovascular mortality (95% CI, 6%-69%; $P =$ .02). The effect of milrinone was adverse in all predefined subgroups, defined by left ventricular fraction, cause of heart failure, functional class, serum sodium and creatinine levels, age, sex, angina, cardiothoracic ratio, and ventricular tachycardia.[25]

(Continued)

TABLE 9.2-2

Refuted Evidence From Studies of Physiologic or Surrogate Endpoints (*Continued*)

Question	Evidence From Surrogate Endpoints	RCT Evidence of Patient-Important Endpoints
In patients with chronic heart failure, does treatment with ibopamine alter mortality?	The effects of ibopamine were studied in 8 patients with idiopathic dilatative cardiomyopathy. After 2 h, ibopamine increased cardiac output (+16%; $P < .05$), stroke volume (+12%; $P < .05$), and ejection fraction (+10%; $P < .01$). Patients were then randomly treated with placebo or ibopamine according to a blinded crossover design for 2 periods of 15 d each. Cardiac output and stroke volume were higher after ibopamine than after placebo ($P < .05$). Treatment was well tolerated.[26]	Investigators conducted an RCT to assess the effect of ibopamine vs placebo on survival in patients with advanced heart failure and evidence of severe left ventricular disease, who were already receiving optimum treatment for heart failure. After 1906 patients had been recruited, the trial was stopped early because of an excess of deaths among patients in the ibopamine group (RR, 1.26; 95% CI, 1.04-1.53; $P = .02$).[27]
In patients with heart failure, what is the effect of treatment with vesnarinone on morbidity and mortality?	A before-after study of 11 patients with moderate congestive heart failure receiving OPC-8212 found, after 8 h, that cardiac and stroke work indexes increased by 11% ($P < .01$) and 20% ($P < .005$), respectively, with concomitant decreases in diastolic pulmonary-artery (25%; $P < .005$) and right atrial pressures (33%; $P < .01$). Inotropic effects were confirmed by a shifting function curve. Researchers claimed that "OPC-8212 clearly improves rest hemodynamics... and may be particularly useful for the treatment of mild to moderate cardiac failure."[28]	An RCT evaluated the effects of daily doses of 60 mg or 30 mg of vesnarinone, as compared with placebo, on mortality and morbidity. Results demonstrated 18.9%, 21.0%, and 22.9% death rates in the placebo, 30-mg, and 60-mg vesnarinone groups, respectively. The hazard ratio for sudden death was 1.35 (95% CI, 1.08-1.69) in the 60-mg group and 1.15 (95% CI, 0.91-1.17) in the 30-mg group compared with the placebo group. The increase in mortality with vesnarinone was attributed to an increase in sudden death, presumably from arrhythmia.[29]
In patients with heart failure, what is the effect of xamoterol on mortality?	A single-blind trial assessed the efficacy of xamoterol in 14 patients with mild to moderate heart failure during 18 mo. At both 1 mo and 18 mo, xamoterol, compared with placebo, produced a significant increase in endurance ($P < .005$) and the amount of work achieved ($P < .05$), plus a decrease in maximum exercise heart rate ($P < .005$).[30]	Investigators randomized 516 patients with heart failure to xamoterol vs placebo for 13 wk; 9.2% of patients in the xamoterol group vs 3.7% in the placebo group died within 100 days of randomization ($P = .02$, hazard ratio 2.54 [95% CI, 1.04-6.18]).[31]

(Continued)

TABLE 9.2-2

Refuted Evidence From Studies of Physiologic or Surrogate Endpoints (*Continued*)

Question	Evidence From Surrogate Endpoints	RCT Evidence of Patient-Important Endpoints
In cardiac arrest patients, what is the effect of active compression-decompression (ACD) cardiopulmonary resuscitation (CPR) vs standard CPR on mortality?	Patients in cardiac arrest were randomized to receive 2 min of either standard CPR or ACD CPR followed by 2 min of the alternate technique. The mean end-tidal carbon dioxide was 4.3 ± 3.8 mm Hg vs 9.0 ± 0.9 mm Hg, respectively ($P < .001$). Systolic arterial pressure was 52.5 ± 14.0 mm Hg vs 88.9 ± 24.7 mm Hg, respectively ($P < .003$). The velocity time integral increased from 7.3 ± 2.6 cm to 17.5 ± 5.6 cm ($P < .001$), and diastolic filling times increased from 0.23 ± 0.09 s to 0.37 ± 0.12 s, respectively ($P < .004$).[32]	An RCT allocated 1784 adults in cardiac arrest to receive either standard CPR or ACD CPR throughout resuscitation and found, in patients who arrested in the hospital, no significant difference between the standard and ACD CPR groups in survival for 1 h (35.1% vs 34.6%; $P = .89$) or until hospital discharge (11.4% vs 10.4%; $P = .64$). For patients who collapsed outside of the hospital, there were no significant differences in survival between the standard and ACD CPR groups for 1 h (16.5% vs 18.2%; $P = .48$) or until hospital discharge (3.7% vs 4.6%; $P = .49$).[33]
In patients with myocarditis, what is the effect of immunosuppressive therapy on mortality?	Authors of a before-after study of 16 patients with myocarditis receiving azathioprine and prednisolone in addition to standard measures found a significant decrease in cardiothoracic ratio ($62.3\pm4.7\%$ to $50.6\pm1.5\%$; $P < .001$), mean pulmonary-artery pressure (34.3 ± 13.05 to 20.0 ± 2.75 mm; $P < .01$) and mean pulmonary wedge pressure (26.0 ± 9.1 to 13.2 ± 4.6 mm; $P < .001$) after 6 mo of therapy. Left ventricular ejection fraction improved from $24.3\pm8.4\%$ to $49.8\pm18.2\%$ ($P < .001$).[34]	An RCT assigned 111 patients with myocarditis to receive conventional therapy either alone or combined with a 24-wk regimen of immunosuppressive therapy (prednisolone plus cyclosporine or azathioprine). A change in the left ventricular ejection fraction at 28 wk did not differ significantly between the compared groups. There was no significant difference in survival between the 2 groups (RR, 0.98; 95% CI, 0.52-1.87; $P = .96$).[35]

(Continued)

TABLE 9.2-2

Refuted Evidence From Studies of Physiologic or Surrogate Endpoints (*Continued*)

Question	Evidence From Surrogate Endpoints	RCT Evidence of Patient-Important Endpoints
In ventilated preterm neonates, is morphine safe and effective?	26 Preterm infants with hyaline membrane disease requiring ventilatory assistance were randomized to morphine or placebo. Results showed that morphine-treated infants spent a significantly greater percentage of total ventilated time breathing in synchrony with their ventilators (median [IQ] = 72% [58%-87%] vs 31% [17%-51%]; $P = .001$). Heart rate and respiratory rate were reduced in morphine-treated infants. Duration of oxygen therapy was reduced (median [IQ] = 4.5 d [3-7 d] vs 8 d [4.75-12.5 d]; $P = .046$).[36]	Ventilated preterm neonates were randomly assigned masked placebo (n = 449) or morphine (n = 449). Open-label morphine could be given on clinical judgment. The placebo and morphine groups had similar rates of neonatal death (11% vs 13%), severe intraventricular hemorrhage (11% vs 13%), and periventricular leukomalacia (9% vs 7%).[37]
In patients with advanced colorectal cancer, what is the effect of fluorouracil (5-FU) plus leucovorin (LV) on survival?	A total of 343 patients with previously untreated metastatic measurable colorectal carcinoma were studied to evaluate the effect on toxicity, response and survival of LV-modulated 5-FU. A maximally tolerated intravenous bolus loading-course regimen of 5-FU alone was compared with a high-dose LV regimen and with a similar low-dose LV regimen. Significant improvements in response rates were observed, with a response rate of 30.3% on the high-dose LV regimen ($P < .01$ vs control), 12.1% on the 5-FU control, and 18.8% on the low-dose LV regimen. Authors concluded that "leucovorin was shown to significantly enhance the therapeutic effect of 5-FU in metastatic colorectal carcinoma."[38]	A meta-analysis was performed on 9 RCTs that compared 5-FU with 5-FU plus intravenous LV for the treatment of advanced colorectal cancer. The endpoints of interest were tumor response and overall survival. Results showed that therapy with 5-FU plus LV had a highly significant benefit over single-agent 5-FU in terms of tumor response rate (23% vs 11%; response OR, 0.45; $P < .001$). This increase in response did not result in a discernable improvement of overall survival (survival OR, 0.97; $P = .57$). Authors concluded that "... In planning future trials, tumor response should not be considered a valid surrogate endpoint for survival in patients with advanced colorectal cancer."[39]

(Continued)

TABLE 9.2-2

Refuted Evidence From Studies of Physiologic or Surrogate Endpoints (*Continued*)

Question	Evidence From Surrogate Endpoints	RCT Evidence of Patient-Important Endpoints
In patients with breast cancer, what is the effect of neoadjuvant therapy on mortality?	An RCT in 196 premenopausal and postmenopausal patients with operable breast cancer compared neoadjuvant and adjuvant regimens of chemotherapy with radiotherapy with or without surgery. Results showed that tumor response, evaluated after 2 cycles of neoadjuvant chemotherapy, was significantly associated with dose ($P = .003$).[40]	Clinical endpoints of patients with breast cancer treated preoperatively with systemic therapy (neoadjuvant therapy) and of those treated postoperatively with the same regimen (adjuvant therapy) were compared in a meta-analysis of RCTs. Nine randomized studies compared neoadjuvant therapy with adjuvant. No statistically or clinically significant difference was found between neoadjuvant therapy and adjuvant therapy arms associated with death (RR = 1.00; 95% CI, 0.90-1.12), disease progression (RR, 0.99; 95% CI, 0.91-1.07), or distant disease recurrence (RR, 0.94; 95% CI, 0.83-1.06). However, neoadjuvant therapy was statistically significantly associated with an increased risk of locoregional disease recurrences (RR, 1.22; 95% CI, 1.04-1.43) compared with adjuvant therapy, especially in trials in which more patients in the neoadjuvant than the adjuvant arm received radiation therapy without surgery (RR, 1.53; 95% CI, 1.11-2.10).[41]
In patients with chronic granulomatous disease, what is the effect of interferon-γ treatment on infection?	A blinded study randomized 128 patients with chronic granulomatous disease to receive interferon-γ or placebo subcutaneously 3 times a week for up to a year. As a secondary measure, phagocyte function was monitored. Results showed no significant changes in the measures of superoxide production by phagocytes.[42]	The same randomized, double-blind, placebo-controlled study in 128 patients with chronic granulomatous disease considered time to the first serious infection, defined as an event requiring hospitalization and parenteral antibiotics as a primary outcome. Results showed a clear benefit from interferon-γ as compared with placebo in time to the first serious infection ($P = .001$). Of the 63 patients assigned to interferon-γ, 14 had serious infections compared with 30 of the 65 patients assigned to placebo ($P = .002$). There was also a reduction in the total number of serious infections—20 with interferon-γ compared with 56 with placebo ($P < .001$).[42]

(*Continued*)

TABLE 9.2-2

Refuted Evidence From Studies of Physiologic or Surrogate Endpoints (*Continued*)

Question	Evidence From Surrogate Endpoints	RCT Evidence of Patient-Important Endpoints
In adult victims of cardiac arrest, what is the effect of treatment with high-dose epinephrine on mortality?	The effect of standard and high doses of epinephrine on coronary perfusion pressure was studied in 32 patients. Patients remaining in cardiac arrest after multiple 1-mg doses of epinephrine received a high dose of 0.2 mg/kg. The increase in the coronary perfusion pressures after a standard dose was not statistically significant. The increase after a high dose was both statistically different from before administration and larger than after a standard dose. High-dose epinephrine was more likely to raise the coronary perfusion pressure above the previously demonstrated critical value of 15 mm Hg. Authors concluded that because coronary perfusion pressure is a good predictor of outcome in cardiac arrest, the increase after high-dose epinephrine may improve rates of return of spontaneous circulation.[45]	An RCT randomly assigned 650 cardiac arrest patients to receive up to 5 doses of high-dose (7 mg) or standard-dose (1 mg) epinephrine at 5-min intervals according to standard protocols for advanced cardiac life support. Results showed no significant difference between the high-dose group and the standard-dose group in the proportions of patients who survived for 1 h (18% vs 23%, respectively) or who survived until hospital discharge (3% vs 5%). Among the survivors, there was no significant difference in the proportions that remained in the best category of cerebral performance (90% vs 94%) and no significant difference in the median Mini-Mental State score (36 vs 37). The exploration of subgroups, including those with out-of-hospital arrest and those with in-hospital arrest, failed to identify any patients who appeared to benefit from high-dose epinephrine and suggested that some patients may have worse outcomes after high-dose epinephrine.[46]

(Continued)

TABLE 9.2-2

Refuted Evidence From Studies of Physiologic or Surrogate Endpoints (*Continued*)

Question	Evidence From Surrogate Endpoints	RCT Evidence of Patient-Important Endpoints
In patients with acute lung injury or acute respiratory distress syndrome, what is the effect of inhaled nitric oxide (NO) on mortality?	9 Of 10 consecutive patients with severe adult respiratory distress syndrome were made to inhale NO in 2 concentrations for 40 min each to investigate whether inhaling NO gas would cause selective vasodilation of ventilated lung regions, thereby reducing pulmonary hypertension and improving gas exchange. Results showed that inhalation of NO in a concentration of 18 ppm reduced the mean pulmonary-artery pressure ($P = .008$) and decreased intrapulmonary shunting ($P = .03$). The ratio of the partial pressure of arterial oxygen to the fraction of inspired oxygen (PaO_2/FiO_2) increased during NO administration ($P = .03$). Authors concluded inhalation of NO by patients with severe adult respiratory distress syndrome reduces the pulmonary-artery pressure and increases arterial oxygenation by improving the matching of ventilation with perfusion, without producing systemic vasodilation.[47]	To evaluate the clinical efficacy of low-dose inhaled NO in patients with acute lung injury, a multicenter, randomized, placebo-controlled study was conducted in the intensive care units of 46 hospitals in the United States. Patients (n = 385) were randomly assigned to placebo (nitrogen gas) or inhaled NO at 5 ppm until 28 d, discontinuation of assisted breathing, or death. An intention-to-treat analysis revealed that inhaled NO at 5 ppm did not increase the number of days patients were alive and not receiving assisted breathing ($P = .97$). Mortality was similar between groups (20% placebo vs 23% NO; $P = .54$). Days patients were alive after a successful 2-h unassisted ventilation trial were a mean (SD) of 11.9 (9.9) for placebo and 11.4 (9.8) for NO patients ($P = .54$).[48]

(Continued)

TABLE 9.2-2

Refuted Evidence From Studies of Physiologic or Surrogate Endpoints (*Continued*)

Question	Evidence From Surrogate Endpoints	RCT Evidence of Patient-Important Endpoints
What are the efficacy and safety of moxonidine in patients with heart failure?	An RCT designed to evaluate the effects of central sympathetic inhibition on clinical and neurohumoral status in patients with congestive heart failure evaluated 25 patients with symptomatic heart failure, stabilized while receiving standard therapy. Patients were titrated in a blinded fashion to 11 wk of oral therapy with placebo (n = 9) or sustained-release (SR) moxonidine (n = 16). Plasma norepinephrine (PNE) was substantially reduced after 6 wk at the maximum dose by 50% vs placebo ($P < .001$). A reduction in 24-h mean heart rate ($P < .01$) was correlated to the reduction in PNE ($r = 0.70$; $P < .05$). Abrupt cessation of chronic therapy resulted in substantial increases in PNE, blood pressure, and heart rate.[49]	An RCT of SR moxonidine or matching placebo found an early increase in death rate and adverse events in the moxonidine SR group. This led to the premature termination of the trial because of safety concerns after 1934 patients were entered. Final analysis revealed 54 deaths (5.5%) in the moxonidine SR group and 32 deaths (3.4%) in the placebo group during the active treatment phase. Survival curves revealed a significantly worse outcome ($P = .012$) in the moxonidine SR group. Hospitalization for heart failure, acute myocardial infarction, and adverse events was also more frequent in the moxonidine SR group.[50]

(*Continued*)

TABLE 9.2-2

Refuted Evidence From Studies of Physiologic or Surrogate Endpoints (*Continued*)

Question	Evidence From Surrogate Endpoints	RCT Evidence of Patient-Important Endpoints
In patients with hypoxemic acute respiratory failure (ARF), what is the effect of prone positioning on mortality?	A clinical follow-up study in an intensive care setting examined 13 patients with severe acute lung insufficiency caused by trauma, septicemia, aspiration, and burn injury. Patients were treated in the prone position, without changing of other ventilatory settings other than FiO$_2$ when saturation increased. Results showed that 12 of the 13 patients responded to treatment in the prone position. No patient needed extracorporeal membrane oxygenation. In the prone position, the oxygenation index increased ($P < .001$) and the alveolar-arterial oxygen gradient, P(A-a)O$_2$, decreased dramatically ($P < .001$). The authors concluded that the prone position significantly improves impaired gas exchange caused by severe acute lung insufficiency and suggested that this treatment be used before more complex modalities.[51]	A multicenter RCT of 791 ARF patients investigated whether prone positioning improves mortality in ARF patients. Patients were randomly assigned to prone position placement (n = 413), applied as early as possible for at least 8 h/d on standard beds, or to supine position placement (n = 378). The 28-d mortality rate was 31.5% in the supine group and 32.4% in the prone group (RR, 0.97; 95% CI, 0.79-1.19; $P = .77$). Ninety-day mortality for the supine group was 42.2% vs 43.3% for the prone group (RR, 0.98; 95% CI, 0.84-1.13; $P = .74$). Authors concluded that this trial demonstrated no beneficial outcomes and some safety concerns associated with prone positioning.[52]

(Continued)

TABLE 9.2-2

Refuted Evidence From Studies of Physiologic or Surrogate Endpoints (*Continued*)

Question	Evidence From Surrogate Endpoints	RCT Evidence of Patient-Important Endpoints
In patients with severe emphysema, what is the effect of lung volume reduction surgery (LVRS) on mortality?	Eighty-nine consecutive patients with severe emphysema who underwent bilateral LVRS were prospectively followed up for up to 3 y. Patients underwent preoperative pulmonary function testing, 6-min walk, and chest computed tomography (CT) and answered a baseline dyspnea questionnaire. CT scans in 65 patients were analyzed for emphysema extent and distribution using the percentage of emphysema in the lung, percentage of normal lower lung, and the CT emphysema ratio. Results showed that, compared with baseline, FEV_1 was significantly increased up to 36 mo after surgery ($P \leq .008$). The 6-min walk distance increased from 871 feet (baseline) to 1326 feet (12 mo), 1342 feet (18 mo), 1371 feet (24 mo), and 1390 feet (36 mo) after surgery. Despite a decline in FEV_1 over time, 6-min walk distance was preserved. Dyspnea improved at 3, 6, 12, 18, 24, and 36 mo after surgery. Authors concluded that LVRS improves pulmonary function, decreases dyspnea, and enhances exercise capacity in many patients with severe emphysema.[53]	A multicenter RCT randomly assigned 1033 patients to undergo LVRS or receive medical treatment. Results showed that for 69 patients who had an FEV_1 that was no more than 20% of their predicted value and either a homogeneous distribution of emphysema on CT or a carbon monoxide–diffusing capacity that was no more than 20% of their predicted value, the 30-d mortality rate after surgery was 16% (95% CI, 8.2%-26.7%) compared with a rate of 0% among 70 medically treated patients ($P < .001$). Among these high-risk patients, the overall mortality rate was higher in surgical patients than medical patients (0.43 deaths per person-year vs 0.11 deaths per person-year; RR, 3.9; 95% CI, 1.9-9.0). Authors cautioned that the use of LVRS in patients with emphysema who have a low FEV_1 and either homogeneous emphysema or a very low carbon monoxide–diffusing capacity comes with a high risk for death after surgery and that such patients are unlikely to benefit from the surgery.[54]

(*Continued*)

TABLE 9.2-2

Refuted Evidence From Studies of Physiologic or Surrogate Endpoints (Continued)

Question	Evidence From Surrogate Endpoints	RCT Evidence of Patient-Important Endpoints
What is the efficacy of indomethacin therapy in low-birth-weight infants?	Thirty-seven infants with symptomatic patent ductus arteriosus (PDA) were in the historical comparison group, and 39 infants were given low-dose indomethacin continuously from 6 to 12 postnatal hours until the recognition of closing PDA. Low-dose continuous indomethacin significantly decreased the incidence of symptomatic PDA at 5 d of age (P < .01) compared with the historical comparison group. There was no episode of decreasing urinary output and necrotizing enterocolitis in the indomethacin group. Authors concluded that the low-dose continuous indomethacin therapy results in a decrease in the incidence of symptomatic PDA, without significant adverse reactions.[55]	An RCT randomly assigned 1202 infants with birth weights of 500-999 g to receive either indomethacin or placebo once daily for 3 d. Results showed that, of the 574 infants with data on the primary outcome who were assigned to indomethacin, 271 (47%) died or survived with impairments compared with 261 of the 569 infants (46%) assigned to placebo (OR, 1.1; 95% CI, 0.8-1.4; P = .61). Indomethacin reduced the incidence of PDA (24% vs 50% in the placebo group; OR, 0.3; P < .001) and of severe periventricular and intraventricular hemorrhage (9% vs 13% in the placebo group; OR, 0.6; P = .02). Authors concluded that in extremely-low-birth-weight infants, prophylaxis with indomethacin does not improve the rate of survival without neurosensory impairment at 18 mo, despite a reduction in the frequency of PDA and severe periventricular and intraventricular hemorrhage.[56]

Abbreviations: ACD, active compression-decompression; ARF, acute respiratory failure; CA, cytosine arabinoside; CI, confidence interval; CPR, cardiopulmonary resuscitation; CT, computed tomography; 5-FU, fluorouracil; FEV_1, forced expiratory volume in 1 second; IQR, interquartile range; LV, leucovorin; LVRS, lung volume reduction surgery; NO, nitric oxide; OR, odds ratio; PDA, patent ductus arteriosus; PNE, plasma norepinephrine; RCT, randomized controlled trial; RR, relative risk; SD, standard deviation; SR, sustained release.

WHEN RANDOMIZED CONTROLLED TRIAL RESULTS HAVE CONTRADICTED OBSERVATIONAL STUDIES OF PATIENT-IMPORTANT ENDPOINTS

Table 9.2-3 demonstrates that the results of observational studies are often an inadequate guide for therapeutic decisions, even if they pertain to patient-important outcomes. Some investigators have suggested that usually randomized and observational evidence agree with similar evidence.[57-59] An empirical evaluation, however, examined 45 topics for which both RCTs and observational studies were available on the same clinical question and used the same outcome. Observational studies showed, on average, larger benefits, and in 7 of these questions, the 2 designs gave results that were different beyond chance.[60] Overall, observational studies may be subject to more noise in their estimates compared with randomized trials after accounting for differences in sample size.[61] Some observational studies may use very large sample sizes (much larger than what randomized trials can achieve), and therefore they produce spuriously tight *confidence intervals*, whereas the true uncertainty associated with their findings is much larger.

Most of the evidence that we have on the comparison of randomized and observational studies comes from comparisons pertaining to the efficacy of interventions. There are more limited data on harms (adverse effects of interventions). Traditionally, harms (especially serious but uncommon ones) have been studied with observational study designs, but there is an increasing recognition that randomized evidence on harms may offer useful information and its quality and quantity should be improved.[62] An empirical evaluation[63] of 15 topics for which large-scale evidence was available from both randomized and observational studies on the same harm suggested that the estimated relative risk may be higher either in randomized or in observational studies. However, the absolute risk is often smaller in observational studies compared with what is seen in randomized trials, which suggests that if an adverse effect is suggested in observational studies, it may be even more common in reality. This may be because many observational studies collect data passively and may therefore record only a portion of the adverse events. Lack of documentation of harm in observational studies may not necessarily exclude the presence of harm.

TABLE 9.2-3

Refuted Evidence From Observational Studies[a]

Question	Evidence From Same Endpoints	RCT Evidence
In patients with cerebral malaria, what is the effect of dexamethasone on morbidity and mortality?	A case report of a 40-y-old man with cerebral malaria in a coma for 24 h suggested dexamethasone had a dramatic life-saving effect and thus "dexamethasone should be given routinely, together with antimalarial therapy, to patients with cerebral malaria."[64]	A blinded placebo-controlled trial of 100 comatose patients demonstrated no significant difference in total deaths between the dexamethasone and placebo groups, but dexamethasone prolonged coma among survivors ($P = .02$). Complications, including pneumonia and gastrointestinal bleeding, occurred in 52% of patients given dexamethasone vs 22% given placebo ($P = .004$).[65]

(Continued)

TABLE 9.2-3

Refuted Evidence From Observational Studies[a] *(Continued)*

Question	Evidence From Same Endpoints	RCT Evidence
Does extracranial to intracranial (EC/IC) bypass surgery alter the risk of ischemic stroke?	A before-after study examined 110 patients with cerebrovascular disease undergoing EC/IC arterial bypass. Stroke rate was 4.3% in 70 patients with transient ischemic attacks (TIAs) compared with literature-cited rates of 13%-62% in TIA patients who have not undergone surgery. Stroke rate was 5% across all 110 patients followed for more than 3 y. Researchers claimed a "dramatic improvement in the symptomatology of virtually all patients" undergoing this bypass procedure.[66]	An RCT of 1377 patients, studying whether bypass surgery benefits patients with symptomatic atherosclerotic disease of the internal carotid artery, found a 14% increase in the RR of fatal and nonfatal stroke throughout the entire trial for the group receiving surgery over those treated with best medical care (95% CI, 3%-34%).[67]
In patients in need of a pacemaker to correct symptomatic bradycardia, what effect does physiologic (AAI) and ventricular (VVI) pacing have on risks of cardiovascular morbidity and death?	A cohort study of the effect of AAI vs VVI pacing with respect to cardiovascular morbidity and mortality found, after an average follow-up of 4 y in 168 patients, significantly higher incidence of permanent physiologic fibrillation in patients treated with VVI pacing (47%) compared with AAI pacing (6.7%) (RR, 7.0; $P < .001$). Congestive heart failure occurred significantly more often in the VVI group than in the AAI group (37% vs 15%; RR, 2.5; $P < .005$). Analysis of survival data showed a higher overall mortality rate in the VVI group (23%) than in the AAI group (8%) (RR, 2.9; $P < .05$).[68]	Investigators randomized 2568 patients to an AAI or VVI pacemaker and found that the type of pacemaker had virtually no effect on the annual rate of death (6.3% in the AAI group vs 6.6% in the VVI group; RRR, 4%; 95% CI, −29% to 29%). There was no significant difference in the incidence of hospitalization for congestive heart failure between the 2 groups (3.1% vs 3.5%; RRR, 12%; 95% CI, −35% to 42%). The annual stroke rate was 1.0 vs 1.1%, respectively. There were significantly more perioperative complications with AAI pacing than with VVI pacing (9.0% vs 3.8%, respectively; $P < .001$).[69]

(Continued)

TABLE 9.2-3

Refuted Evidence From Observational Studies[a] (Continued)

Question	Evidence From Same Endpoints	RCT Evidence
What effect does plasma exchange have in patents with dermatomyositis and polymyositis?	Authors of a before-after study of 38 patients who had undergone plasma exchanges between 1980 and 1986 found that, according to changes in muscle force, 24 patients (63%) improved (10 appreciably and 14 moderately) and 14 remained unchanged. Plasma exchange was well tolerated in 23 patients.[70]	An RCT of 39 patients with definite polymyositis or dermatomyositis assigned to receive plasma exchange, leukapheresis, or sham apheresis found no significant differences among the 3 treatment groups in final muscle strength or functional capacity; investigators concluded that leukapheresis and plasma exchange are no more effective than sham apheresis.[71]
What is the effect of sodium fluoride on vertebral fractures?	In a before-after study using quantitative computed tomography to measure trabecular vertebral body density (TVBD) in the lumbar spine of 18 female patients with osteoporosis, TVBD was significantly greater in the experimental group than mean TVBD for an age-matched group of untreated female patients with osteoporosis ($P < .001$). Only 1 of the 18 fluoride-treated patients had spinal fractures during therapy. Incidence (4 fractures per 87.2 patient-years of observation) was significantly lower than the published incidence of 76 fractures per 91 patient-years for untreated patients ($P < .001$).[72]	An RCT studied patients receiving either sodium fluoride or placebo, in addition to daily supplements of calcium. Compared with the placebo group, the treatment group had increases in median bone mineral density of 35% ($P < .001$) in the lumbar spine, 12% ($P < .001$) in the femoral neck, and 10% ($P < .001$) in the femoral trochanter. However, the number of new vertebral fractures was similar in the 2 groups (163 and 136, respectively; $P = .32$), whereas the fluoride-treated patients had nonvertebral fractures 3.2 times more often than patients given placebo (95% CI, 1.8-5.6; $P < .01$).[73]

(Continued)

TABLE 9.2-3

Refuted Evidence From Observational Studies[a] (*Continued*)

Question	Evidence From Same Endpoints	RCT Evidence
Does estrogen replacement therapy (ERT) alter the risk for coronary heart disease (CHD) events in postmenopausal women with established coronary disease?	A meta-analysis of 16 cohort studies with internal controls and 3 cross-sectional angiography studies (including studies of women with established CHD) demonstrated an RR of 0.50 (95% CI, 0.44-0.57) for CHD among estrogen users. Investigators concluded that "... the preponderance of the evidence strongly suggests women taking postmenopausal estrogen therapy are at a decreased risk for CHD."[74]	A randomized, blinded, placebo-controlled trial of 4.1-y duration (Response to Heart and Estrogen-Progestin Replacement Study) randomly assigned patients to receive conjugated estrogens and medroxyprogesterone acetate or placebo. Results showed a hazard ratio (HR) for CHD of 0.99 (95% CI, 0.81-1.22).[75] Another larger trial in women without underlying coronary artery disease suggested a significantly increased risk of coronary events.[76]
Does ERT alter the risk for stroke in postmenopausal women?	A national sample of 1910 (of 2371 eligible) white postmenopausal women who were 55 to 74 y old and who did not report a history of stroke at that time were examined. Results showed that there were 250 incident cases of stroke identified, including 64 deaths with stroke listed as the underlying cause. The age-adjusted incidence rate of stroke among postmenopausal hormone ever-users was 82 per 10000 woman-years of follow-up compared with 124 per 10000 among never-users. Postmenopausal hormone use remained a protective factor against stroke incidence (RR, 0.69; 95% CI, 0.47-1.00) and stroke mortality (RR, 0.37; 95% CI, 0.14-0.92) after adjustment for the baseline risk factors.[77]	A multicenter, blinded, placebo-controlled RCT involving 16 608 women aged 50 through 79 y assigned patients to receive conjugated equine estrogen plus medroxyprogesterone acetate (n = 8506) or placebo (n = 8102). Results showed that 1.8% of patients in the estrogen plus progestin and 1.3% in the placebo groups had strokes. For combined ischemic and hemorrhagic strokes, the intention-to-treat HR for estrogen plus progestin vs placebo was 1.31 (95% CI, 1.02-1.68). The HR for ischemic stroke was 1.44 (95% CI, 1.09-1.90), and for hemorrhagic stroke, it was 0.82 (95% CI, 0.43-1.56).[78]

(Continued)

TABLE 9.2-3

Refuted Evidence From Observational Studies[a] (*Continued*)

Question	Evidence From Same Endpoints	RCT Evidence
Does ERT alter the risk for dementia in postmenopausal women?	A prospective, longitudinal study of 472 postmenopausal or perimenopausal women, followed for up to 16 y, found that approximately 45% of the women in the cohort had used ERT and diagnosed 34 incident cases of Alzheimer disease (AD) (National Institute of Neurological and Communicative Disorders and Stroke and the Alzheimer's Disease and Related Disorders Association criteria) during follow-up, including 9 estrogen users. After adjusting for education, the RR for AD in ERT users compared with nonusers was 0.46 (95% CI, 0.21-1.00), suggesting a reduced risk of AD for women who had reported the use of estrogen.[77]	4532 Eligible postmenopausal women aged 65 y or older and free of probable dementia at baseline were enrolled in a randomized, blinded, placebo-controlled clinical trial. Participants received either conjugated equine estrogen with medroxyprogesterone acetate (n = 2145) or matching placebo (n = 2236). More women in the estrogen plus progestin group had a substantial and clinically important decline (≥ 2 SDs) in Modified Mini-Mental State Examination total score (6.7%) compared with the placebo group (1.8%) ($P = .008$) [78]
In patients with diabetes who have isolated systolic hypertension (ISH), what is the effect of diuretic-based antihypertensive treatment on mortality?	In a cohort analytic study of 759 participants aged 35 to 69 y with normal serum creatinine levels, cardiovascular mortality in individuals with diabetes, after adjusting for differences in risk factors, was 3.8 times higher in patients treated with diuretics alone than in patients with untreated hypertension ($P < .001$). Investigators concluded that "there is an urgent need to reconsider its continued usage in this population."[79]	Authors of an RCT of diuretic treatment vs placebo in 4736 patients aged ≥ 60 y with ISH found an RRR in 5-y major cardiovascular death rate of 34% for active treatment compared with placebo for patients with diabetes (95% CI, 6%-54%) and for those without diabetes (95% CI, 21%-45%). Absolute risk reduction with active treatment compared with placebo was twice as great for patients with vs without diabetes (101/1000 vs 51/1000, respectively, at 5 y).[80]

(*Continued*)

TABLE 9.2-3

Refuted Evidence From Observational Studies[a] (*Continued*)

Question	Evidence From Same Endpoints	RCT Evidence
Does a diet low in fat and high in fiber alter the risk of colorectal adenomas?	Authors of a cohort study prospectively examining the risk of colorectal adenoma of 7284 male health professionals according to quintiles of nutrient intake found that dietary fiber was inversely associated with the risk of adenoma ($P < .001$); RR for men in the highest vs the lowest quintile was 0.36 (95% CI, 0.22-0.60). Furthermore, for subjects receiving a high-saturated-fat, low-fiber diet, the RR was 3.7 (95% CI, 1.5-8.8) compared with those receiving a low-saturated-fat, high-fiber diet.[81]	Investigators randomly allocated 2079 subjects who had 1 or more histologically confirmed colorectal adenomas removed within 6 mo to one of 2 groups: an intervention group (given intensive counseling and assigned to follow a low-fat, high-fiber diet) and a control group (given a standard brochure on healthy eating and assigned to follow their usual diet). Results showed that 39.7% of participants in the intervention group and 39.5% in the control group had at least 1 recurrent adenoma (RR, 1.00; 95% CI, 0.90-1.12). Moreover, among subjects with recurrent adenomas, the mean number of such lesions was 1.85 ± 0.08 and 1.84 ± 0.07 in the intervention and control groups, respectively ($P = .93$).[82]
Does supplementation with beta carotene alter the risk of major coronary events?	An analysis of a cohort from the Lipid Research Clinics Coronary Primary Prevention Trial and Follow-up Study found that, after adjustment for known CHD risk factors, including smoking, serum carotenoid levels were inversely related to CHD events. Men in the highest quartile of serum carotenoid levels had an adjusted RR of 0.64 (95% CI, 0.44-0.92) compared with the lowest quartile for CHD. For men who never smoked, this RR was 0.28 (95% CI, 0.11-0.73).[83] Authors of approximately 8 other observational studies found similar results.	An RCT, the Physicians' Health Study, involving 22 071 male physicians, showed no statistically significant benefit or harm from beta carotene with respect to the number of myocardial infarctions (RR, 0.96; 95% CI, 0.84-1.09), strokes (RR 0.96; 95% CI, 0.83-1.11), deaths from cardiovascular causes (RR, 1.09; 95% CI, 0.93-1.27), all important cardiovascular events (RR, 1.00; 95% CI, 0.91-1.09), or deaths from all causes (RR, 1.02; 95% CI, 0.93-1.11). Moreover, there was no significant trend toward greater benefit or harm with an increasing duration of treatment, even 5 or more years after randomization.[84]

(*Continued*)

TABLE 9.2-3

Refuted Evidence From Observational Studies[a] (Continued)

Question	Evidence From Same Endpoints	RCT Evidence
Does dietary supplementation with vitamin E alter the risk of major coronary events?	A cohort of 5133 Finnish men and women showed an inverse association between dietary vitamin E intake and coronary mortality in both men and women with RRs of 0.68 (P for trend = .01) and 0.35 (P for trend < .01), respectively, between the highest and lowest tertiles of intake.[85] Approximately 12 other observational or experimental studies have shown similar results.	Authors of an RCT of 2545 women and 6996 men at high risk for cardiovascular events found an RR of 1.05 (95% CI, 0.95-1.16) for myocardial infarction, stroke, and death among patients assigned to vitamin E vs placebo. There were no significant differences in the numbers of deaths from cardiovascular causes (RR, 1.05; 95% CI, 0.90-1.22), myocardial infarction (RR, 1.02; 95% CI, 0.90-1.15), or stroke (RR, 1.17; 95% CI, 0.95-1.42).[86]
In critically ill patients, what is the effect of treatment with growth hormone on mortality?	A before-after study of 53 patients who had failed standard ventilator weaning protocols and who were subsequently treated with human growth hormone (HGH) found that 81% of the previously unweanable patients were eventually weaned from mechanical ventilation, with overall survival of 76%. Predicted mortality of the study group was significantly greater than the actual mortality rate (P < .05). Researchers concluded that "this study presents clinical evidence supporting the safety and efficacy of HGH in promoting respiratory independence in a selected group of surgical ICU patients."[87]	Two multicenter RCTs were carried out in patients in intensive care units (ICUs). The patients received either HGH or placebo until discharge from intensive care or for a maximum of 21 d. The in-hospital mortality rate was higher in the HGH arms (P < .001 for both studies). The RR of death was 1.9 (95% CI, 1.3-2.9) in the Finnish study and 2.4 (95% CI, 1.6-3.5) in the multinational study. Among survivors, the length of stay in ICU and in the hospital and the duration of mechanical ventilation were prolonged in the HGH group.[88]

(Continued)

TABLE 9.2-3

Refuted Evidence From Observational Studies[a] (Continued)

Question	Evidence From Same Endpoints	RCT Evidence
In patients with deep venous thrombosis (DVT), what is the effect of vena cava filters (vs no filter) on pulmonary embolism and recurrent DVT?	A before-after study followed the insertion of 61 vena cava filters (47 permanent and 14 temporary) in patients with DVT and recorded no deaths or clinically evident pulmonary embolism in any patient in whom a vena cava filter was inserted. Researchers concluded that "vena cava filters represent an effective prevention of pulmonary embolism together with medical and surgical treatment."[89]	Investigators randomized 400 patients with proximal DVT who were at risk for pulmonary embolism to receive a vena caval filter or no filter. Results showed an odds ratio (OR) of 0.22 (95% CI, 0.05-0.90) for pulmonary embolism at 12 d. However, this benefit was counterbalanced by an excess of recurrent DVT (OR, 1.87; 95% CI, 1.10-3.20) at 2 y, without any significant differences in mortality.[90]
Is low-dose aspirin as effective as high-dose aspirin for reducing stroke, myocardial infarction, and death?	An observational investigation resulting from a secondary analysis of data from an RCT of low-dose and high-dose aspirin for patients undergoing carotid endarterectomy found an association between perioperative stoke and death and the amount of aspirin taken before surgery. The risk of perioperative stroke and death was 1.8% for patients taking 650-1300 mg daily compared with 6.9% for patients taking 0-325 mg daily.[91]	An RCT allocated 4 different doses of aspirin to 2849 patients scheduled for carotid endarterectomy. Results demonstrated the combined RR of stoke, myocardial infarction, and death at 3 mo was 1.34 (95% CI, 1.03-1.75; $P = $ .03) with high-dose aspirin. Efficacy analysis (excluding patients receiving aspirin before randomization) showed even more prominent superiority of low-dose aspirin.[91]
Do educational and community interventions modify the risk of adolescent pregnancy?	A meta-analysis of observational studies demonstrated a statistically significant delay in initiation of sexual intercourse (OR, 0.64; 95% CI, 0.44-0.93) and a reduction in pregnancy (OR, 0.74; 95% CI, 0.56-0.98) with educational and community interventions.[92]	A meta-analysis of randomized trials provided no support for the effect of educational or community interventions on initiation of sexual intercourse (OR, 1.09; 95% CI, 0.90-1.32) or pregnancy (OR, 1.08; 95% CI, 0.91-1.27).[92]

(Continued)

TABLE 9.2-3

Refuted Evidence From Observational Studies[a] (*Continued*)

Question	Evidence From Same Endpoints	RCT Evidence
What is the efficacy of arthroscopic surgery of the knee in relieving pain and improving function?	A retrospective review of medical records and operative videotapes, along with follow-up evaluation, was undertaken for 43 knees in 40 patients with degenerative joint disease. Average follow-up was 24 months; 72.1% of patients had good results at follow-up, 16.3% had fair results, and 11.6% had treatment failures. Preoperative clinical status, severity of degenerative changes, and number of pathologic entities encountered at surgery correlated with the results of treatment. The authors concluded that arthroscopic debridement is an effective means of treatment for mild to moderate degenerative joint disease after failure of conservative measures.[93]	A randomized, blinded, placebo-controlled trial of 180 patients with osteoarthritis of the knee randomly assigned patients to receive arthroscopic debridement, arthroscopic lavage, or placebo surgery. Patients in the placebo group received skin incisions and underwent a simulated debridement without insertion of the arthroscope. Results showed that at no point did either of the intervention groups report less pain or better function than the placebo group. The 95% CIs for the differences between the placebo group and intervention groups exclude any patient-important differences.[94]
Is long-term survival improved in patients undergoing coronary artery revascularization (CR) before elective major vascular surgery?	A cohort of patients scheduled for vascular surgery underwent preoperative thallium scanning (PTS). Seventy-four of 136 patients with moderate to severe reversible ischemia underwent CR. Results by multivariate analysis showed preoperative CR was associated with improved survival (OR, 0.52; $P = .02$). Authors concluded that long-term survival after major vascular surgery is significantly improved if patients with moderate-severe ischemia, who are receiving PTS, undergo selective CR.[95]	An RCT assigned 510 patients at increased risk for perioperative cardiac complications and clinically significant coronary artery disease to undergo either CR before surgery or no revascularization before surgery. At 2.7 y after randomization, mortality in the revascularization group was 22%, and in the no-revascularization group, it was 23% (RR, 0.98; 95% CI, 0.70-1.37; $P = .92$). Authors concluded that "coronary artery revascularization before elective vascular surgery does not significantly alter the long-term outcome and, on the basis of these data, a strategy of coronary artery revascularization before elective vascular surgery among patients with stable cardiac symptoms cannot be recommended."[96]

(Continued)

TABLE 9.2-3

Refuted Evidence From Observational Studies[a] *(Continued)*

Question	Evidence From Same Endpoints	RCT Evidence
Is coronary artery bypass grafting (CABG) equivalent to percutaneous transluminal coronary angioplasty (PTCA) for reducing death?	Mortality rates for Medicare patients who underwent coronary artery bypass surgery were compared with those who had angioplasty or angioplasty and bypass surgery. From a national data set, 30-d and 1-y mortality rates were 3.8% and 8.2% for 25423 angioplasty patients and 6.4% and 11.8% for 71243 bypass surgery patients ($P < .001$ for both periods). The risk-adjusted RR of mortality for bypass surgery vs angioplasty was 1.72 ($P = .001$).[97]	A multinational, multicenter RCT randomized 1054 patients to CABG (n = 513) or PTCA (n = 541). Results showed that, after 1 y of follow-up, 14 (2.7%) of those randomized to CABG and 21 (3.9%) of those randomized to PTCA had died. The PTCA group's RR of death was 1.42 (95% CI, 0.73-2.76).[98]
What effect do statins have on cancer incidence and mortality?	Using administrative health databases, a nested case-control study was performed on a cohort of 6721 beneficiaries of the health care plan of Quebec who were free of cancer for at least 1 y at cohort entry, 65 y and older, and treated with lipid-modifying agents. From the cohort, 542 cases of first malignant neoplasm were identified, and 5420 controls were randomly selected. Users of HMG-CoA reductase inhibitors were compared with users of bile acid–binding resins as to their risk of cancer. Specific cancer sites were also considered. Results: Users of HMG-CoA reductase inhibitors were found to be 28% less likely than users of bile acid–binding resins to be diagnosed as having any cancer (RR, 0.72; 95% CI, 0.57-0.92). All specific cancer sites under study were found to be not or inversely associated with the use of HMG-CoA reductase inhibitors.[99]	A meta-analysis of 26 RCTs investigated the effect of statin therapy on cancer incidence and cancer death. Analyses including 6662 incident cancers and 2407 cancer deaths showed that statins did not reduce the incidence of cancer (OR, 1.02; 95% CI, 0.97-1.07) or cancer deaths (OR, 1.01; 95% CI, 0.93-1.09). No reductions were noted for any individual cancer type. Authors concluded that statins have a neutral effect on cancer and cancer death risk in randomized controlled trials. They found that no type of cancer was affected by statin use and no subtype of statin affected the risk of cancer.[100]

(Continued)

TABLE 9.2-3

Refuted Evidence From Observational Studies[a] (Continued)

Question	Evidence From Same Endpoints	RCT Evidence
What effect does gastric freezing have on duodenal ulcers?	Clinical observations in 24 patients with duodenal ulcers demonstrated that short periods of gastric freezing, with inflowing coolant temperatures of −17°C to −20°C, were well tolerated. Patients had subjective relief of symptoms, disappearance of duodenal ulcer craters, and significant decreases in gastric secretory responses.[101]	A blinded, randomized trial of gastric freezing in the treatment of duodenal ulcer allocated patients to either a true freeze with coolant at −10°C or a sham procedure with coolant at 37°C. The results showed no significant difference in the relief of pain, secretory suppression, the number and severity of recurrences, development of perforation, hospitalization, obstruction, hemorrhage, surgery, repeated hypothermia, or radiograph therapy to the stomach in the 2 groups.[102]
Do occlusive hydrocolloid wound dressings heal venous leg ulcers quicker than simple nonadherent (NA) dressings?	Eighteen patients with a total of 24 dermal ulcers of varying causes and unresponsive to other conservative treatments were treated with a new hydrocolloid dressing. The case report showed that all lesions healed in less time than with other modalities. Authors concluded that the hydrocolloid dressing is more effective than others presently available for the treatment of noninfected dermal ulcers.[103]	An RCT of 56 patients with chronic venous ulcers, present for a mean of 2.4 y, randomized the patients to either a new occlusive hydrocolloid dressing or a porous NA dressing. In all patients, dressings were applied beneath a standard graduated compression bandage. There was no difference between the 2 groups, with complete healing in 21 of 28 (75%) occlusive dressing patients and 22 of 28 (78%) with NA dressings by 12 wk. Careful graduated compression bandaging achieves healing even in the majority of so-called resistant chronic venous ulcers; there was no additional benefit from applying occlusive dressings, which tend to be expensive.[104]

Abbreviations: AAI, atrium-atrium-inhibit; AD, Alzheimer disease; CABG, coronary artery bypass grafting; CHD, coronary heart disease; CI, confidence interval; CR, coronary artery revascularization; DVT, deep venous thrombosis; EC/IC, extracranial to intracranial; ERT, estrogen replacement therapy; HGH, human growth hormone; HMG-CoA, 3-hydroxy-3-methylglutaryl coenzyme A; HR, hazard ratio; ICU, intensive care unit; ISH, isolated systolic hypertension; NA, nonadherent; OR, odds ratio; PTCA, percutaneous transluminal coronary angioplasty; PTS, preoperative thallium scanning; RCT, randomized controlled trial; RR, relative risk; RRR, relative risk reduction; TIA, transient ischemic attack; TVBD, trabecular vertebral body density; VVI, ventricular pacing.

[a]Data are expressed as reported in the original literature.

Randomized Controlled Trials May Also Contradict Other Previous Randomized Controlled Trials

Although well-designed RCTs with patient-important outcomes (and their *meta-analyses*) represent the *reference standard* for therapeutic decisions, even this reference standard is not always perfect. There are an accumulating number of examples in which such trials have been refuted by subsequent trials that were larger and even better designed, more carefully protected from *bias*, or more *generalizable*.[5] Even large, confirmatory, randomized trials with little or no obvious bias and statistically significant results ($P < .05$) may ultimately prove misleading. For small, underpowered randomized trials with considerable bias, a statistically significant result is likely to be misleading more often that it is accurate.[5,105] The interplay of small sample sizes, small or negligible true effects, bias, and significance-chasing can generate a spurious literature even for trials with patient-important outcomes. A number of small trials in early human immunodeficiency virus research before the advent of truly effective treatments showed major differences in survival that seemed unexplained, implausible, and probably false[106] based on subsequent evidence.

Although small and poorly designed and reported trials are most likely to be refuted, even the most prominent, highly cited randomized trials are sometimes refuted.[107] Among the 39 randomized trials published between 1990 and 2003 that received more than 1000 citations each, 9 had been entirely contradicted or found to have had potentially exaggerated results by 2004, according to subsequent better and larger evidence bases. A typical example of an initially widely cited RCT, the results of which ultimately proved misleading, is an RCT of monoclonal antibody to endotoxin for the treatment of gram-negative sepsis. A trial of 200 patients found that mortality could be halved with this intervention.[108] However, a 10-fold larger trial[109] found that this antibody actually tended to increase mortality in these patients.

Also, in the previous chapter, we discussed the example of observational studies claiming that vitamin E decreases cardiovascular mortality and subsequent randomized evidence suggesting this was a false claim. In fact, not only observational studies but also a relatively large randomized trial of 2002 patients[110] randomized to vitamin E vs placebo found a significant 47% relative risk reduction in cardiovascular death and nonfatal myocardial infarction with vitamin E supplementation. This was refuted by the much larger Heart Outcomes Prevention Evaluation trial.[86] A subsequent meta-analysis and *meta-regression*[111] actually suggests that vitamin E not only does not reduce mortality but also may increase mortality when given in high doses.

Evolution of Evidence

Clinicians should view evidence on any therapeutic question as a continuum that evolves across time and research designs. The composite evidence may change little or a lot over time as more results become available. Surprises, as those described above, comprise the end of the spectrum in these continuous fluctuations. Ideally, one would like to be able to know that once a certain amount of evidence of a certain quality has been reached, then results are not going to change in any important manner even if more studies are conducted. Unfortunately, this point is not reached in practice for many important medical questions.[112,113]

Conclusion

Physiologic and pathophysiologic rationale—or an observational study—often accurately predicts the results of RCTs. However, this is not always the case. The problem is, one never knows in advance if the particular instance is one in which the preliminary data reflect the truth or whether they are misleading. Some hints may help occasionally, but confident clinical action must generally await the results of RCTs. Even then, evidence may not be final. Clinicians should see evidence as an evolving continuum in which even the best classics of old may not stand the test of time.

References

1. Gray JAM. *Evidence-Based Healthcare*. London, England: Churchill Livingstone; 1997.

2. Djulbegovic B, Loughran TP Jr, Hornung CA, et al. The quality of medical evidence in hematology-oncology. *Am J Med*. 1999;106(2):198-205.

3. Fleming TR. Surrogate endpoints and FDA's accelerated approval process. *Health Aff (Millwood)*. 2005;24(1):67-78.

4. Contopoulos-Ioannidis DG, Ntzani E, Ioannidis JP. Translation of highly promising basic science research into clinical applications. *Am J Med*. 2003;114(6):477-484.

5. Ioannidis JP. Why most published research findings are false. *PLoS Med*. 2005;2(8):e124.

6. Fleming TR, DeMets DL. Surrogate end points in clinical trials: are we being misled? *Ann Intern Med*. 1996;125(7):605-613.

7. Shaw SG, Weidmann P, Hodler J, Zimmermann A, Paternostro A. Atrial natriuretic peptide protects against acute ischemic renal failure in the rat. *J Clin Invest*. 1987;80(5):1232-1237.

8. Allgren RL, Marbury TC, Rahman SN, et al. Anaritide in acute tubular necrosis: Auriculin Anaritide Acute Renal Failure Study Group. *N Engl J Med*. 1997; 336(12):828-834.

9. Doroshow JH, Locker GY, Ifrim I, Myers CE. Prevention of doxorubicin cardiac toxicity in the mouse by N-acetylcysteine. *J Clin Invest*. 1981;68(4):1053-1064.

10. Unverferth DV, Jagadeesh JM, Unverferth BJ, Magorien RD, Leier CV, Balcerzak SP. Attempt to prevent doxorubicin-induced acute human myocardial morphologic damage with acetylcysteine. *J Natl Cancer Inst.* 1983;71(5):917-920.

11. Faden AI, Jacobs TP, Holaday JW. Opiate antagonist improves neurologic recovery after spinal injury. *Science.* 1981;211(4481):493-494.

12. Bracken MB, Shepard MJ, Collins WF, et al. A randomized, controlled trial of methylprednisolone or naloxone in the treatment of acute spinal-cord injury: results of the Second National Acute Spinal Cord Injury Study. *N Engl J Med.* 1990;322(20):1405-1411.

13. Hudson P, Haley J, John M, et al. Structure of a genomic clone encoding biologically active human relaxin. *Nature.* 1983;301(5901):628-631.

14. Brennand JE, Calder AA, Leitch CR, Greer IA, Chou MM, MacKenzie IZ. Recombinant human relaxin as a cervical ripening agent. *Br J Obstet Gynaecol.* 1997; 104(7):775-780.

15. Reitsma PH, Rothberg PG, Astrin SM, et al. Regulation of myc gene expression in HL-60 leukaemia cells by a vitamin D metabolite. *Nature.* 1983;306(5942):492-494.

16. Hellstrom E, Robert KH, Samuelsson J, et al. Treatment of myelodysplastic syndromes with retinoic acid and 1 alpha-hydroxy-vitamin D3 in combination with low-dose ara-C is not superior to ara-C alone: results from a randomized study: the Scandinavian Myelodysplasia Group (SMG). *Eur J Haematol.* 1990; 45(5):255-261.

17. Albert JM, Ioannidis JP, Reichelderfer P, et al. Statistical issues for HIV surrogate endpoints: point/counterpoint: an NIAID workshop. *Stat Med.* 1998;17(21):2435-2462.

18. Coltart J, Alderman EL, Robison SC, Harrison DC. Effect of propranolol on left ventricular function, segmental wall motion, and diastolic pressure-volume relation in man. *Br Heart J.* 1975;37(4):357-364.

19. Lechat P, Packer M, Chalon S, Cucherat M, Arab T, Boissel JP. Clinical effects of beta-adrenergic blockade in chronic heart failure: a meta-analysis of double-blind, placebo-controlled, randomized trials. *Circulation.* 1998;98(12):1184-1191.

20. Delcourt R, Vastesaeger M. Action of Atromid on total and beta-cholesterol. *J Atheroscler Res.* 1963 Sep-Dec;3:533-537.

21. A co-operative trial in the primary prevention of ischaemic heart disease using clofibrate. Report from the Committee of Principal Investigators. *Br Heart J.* 1978;40(10):1069-1118.

22. Mason JW, Peters FA. Antiarrhythmic efficacy of encainide in patients with refractory recurrent ventricular tachycardia. *Circulation.* 1981;63(3):670-675.

23. Echt DS, Liebson PR, Mitchell LB, et al. Mortality and morbidity in patients receiving encainide, flecainide, or placebo: the Cardiac Arrhythmia Suppression Trial. *N Engl J Med.* 1991;324(12):781-788.

24. Timmis AD, Smyth P, Jewitt DE. Milrinone in heart failure: effects on exercise haemodynamics during short term treatment. *Br Heart J.* 1985;54(1):42-47.

25. Packer M, Carver JR, Rodeheffer RJ, et al. Effect of oral milrinone on mortality in severe chronic heart failure: the PROMISE Study Research Group. *N Engl J Med.* 1991;325(21):1468-1475.

26. Gronda E, Brusoni B, Inglese E, Mangiavacchi M, Gasparini M, Ghirardi P. Effects of ibopamine on heart performance: a radionuclide ventriculography study in patients with idiopathic dilatative cardiomyopathy. *Arzneimittelforschung.* 1986; 36(2A):371-375.

27. Hampton JR, van Veldhuisen DJ, Kleber FX, et al. Randomised study of effect of ibopamine on survival in patients with advanced severe heart failure: second Prospective Randomised Study of Ibopamine on Mortality and Efficacy (PRIME II) Investigators. *Lancet.* 1997;349(9057):971-977.

28. Asanoi H, Sasayama S, Iuchi K, Kameyama T. Acute hemodynamic effects of a new inotropic agent (OPC-8212) in patients with congestive heart failure. *J Am Coll Cardiol.* 1987;9(4):865-871.

29. Cohn JN, Goldstein SO, Greenberg BH, et al. A dose-dependent increase in mortality with vesnarinone among patients with severe heart failure: Vesnarinone Trial Investigators. *N Engl J Med.* 1998;339(25):1810-1816.

30. Sorensen EV, Faergeman O, Day MA, Snow HM. Long-term efficacy of xamoterol (a beta 1-adrenoceptor partial agonist) in patients with mild to moderate heart failure. *Br J Clin Pharmacol.* 1989;28(suppl 1):86S-88S.

31. Xamoterol in Severe Heart Failure Study Group. Xamoterol in severe heart failure. *Lancet.* 1990;336(8706):1-6.

32. Cohen TJ, Tucker KJ, Lurie KG, et al. Active compression-decompression: a new method of cardiopulmonary resuscitation: Cardiopulmonary Resuscitation Working Group. *JAMA.* 1992;267(21):2916-2923.

33. Stiell IG, Hebert PC, Wells GA, et al. The Ontario trial of active compression-decompression cardiopulmonary resuscitation for in-hospital and prehospital cardiac arrest. *JAMA.* 1996;275(18):1417-1423.

34. Talwar KK, Goswami KC, Chopra P, Dev V, Shrivastava S, Malhotra A. Immunosuppressive therapy in inflammatory myocarditis: long-term follow-up. *Int J Cardiol.* 1992;34(2):157-166.

35. Mason JW, O'Connell JB, Herskowitz A, et al. A clinical trial of immunosuppressive therapy for myocarditis: the Myocarditis Treatment Trial Investigators. *N Engl J Med.* 1995;333(5):269-275.

36. Dyke MP, Kohan R, Evans S. Morphine increases synchronous ventilation in preterm infants. *J Paediatr Child Health.* 1995;31(3):176-179.

37. Anand KJ, Hall RW, Desai N, et al. Effects of morphine analgesia in ventilated preterm neonates: primary outcomes from the NEOPAIN randomised trial. *Lancet.* 2004;363(9422):1673-1682.

38. Petrelli N, Douglass HO Jr, Herrera L, et al. The modulation of fluorouracil with leucovorin in metastatic colorectal carcinoma: a prospective randomized phase III trial: Gastrointestinal Tumor Study Group. *J Clin Oncol.* 1989;7(10):1419-1426.

39. Advanced Colorectal Cancer Meta-Analysis Project. Modulation of fluorouracil by leucovorin in patients with advanced colorectal cancer: evidence in terms of response rate. *J Clin Oncol.* 1992;10(6):896-903.

40. Scholl SM, Asselain B, Palangie T, et al. Neoadjuvant chemotherapy in operable breast cancer. *Eur J Cancer.* 1991;27(12):1668-1671.

41. Mauri D, Pavlidis N, Ioannidis JP. Neoadjuvant versus adjuvant systemic treatment in breast cancer: a meta-analysis. *J Natl Cancer Inst.* 2005;97(3):188-194.

42. International Chronic Granulomatous Disease Cooperative Study Group. A controlled trial of interferon gamma to prevent infection in chronic granulomatous disease. *N Engl J Med.* 1991;324(8):509-516.

43. Buthala DA. Cell culture studies on antiviral agents, I: action of cytosine arabinoside and some comparisons with 5-iodo-2-deoxyuridine. *Proc Soc Exp Biol Med.* 1964 Jan;115:69-77.

44. Stevens DA, Jordan GW, Waddell TF, Merigan TC. Adverse effect of cytosine arabinoside on disseminated zoster in a controlled trial. *N Engl J Med.* 1973;289(17):873-878.

45. Paradis NA, Martin GB, Rosenberg J, et al. The effect of standard- and high-dose epinephrine on coronary perfusion pressure during prolonged cardiopulmonary resuscitation. *JAMA.* 1991;265(9):1139-1144.

46. Stiell IG, Hebert PC, Weitzman BN, et al. High-dose epinephrine in adult cardiac arrest. *N Engl J Med.* 1992;327(15):1045-1050.

47. Rossaint R, Falke KJ, Lopez F, Slama K, Pison U, Zapol WM. Inhaled nitric oxide for the adult respiratory distress syndrome. *N Engl J Med.* 1993;328(6):399-405.

48. Taylor RW, Zimmerman JL, Dellinger RP, et al. Low-dose inhaled nitric oxide in patients with acute lung injury: a randomized controlled trial. *JAMA.* 2004;291(13):1603-1609.

49. Dickstein K, Manhenke C, Aarsland T, McNay J, Wiltse C, Wright T. The effects of chronic, sustained-release moxonidine therapy on clinical and neurohumoral status in patients with heart failure. *Int J Cardiol.* 2000;75(2-3):167-176; discussion 176-177.

50. Cohn JN, Pfeffer MA, Rouleau J, et al. Adverse mortality effect of central sympathetic inhibition with sustained-release moxonidine in patients with heart failure (MOXCON). *Eur J Heart Fail.* 2003;5(5):659-667.

51. Mure M, Martling CR, Lindahl SG. Dramatic effect on oxygenation in patients with severe acute lung insufficiency treated in the prone position. *Crit Care Med.* 1997;25(9):1539-1544.

52. Guerin C, Gaillard S, Lemasson S, et al. Effects of systematic prone positioning in hypoxemic acute respiratory failure: a randomized controlled trial. *JAMA.* 2004;292(19):2379-2387.

53. Flaherty KR, Kazerooni EA, Curtis JL, et al. Short-term and long-term outcomes after bilateral lung volume reduction surgery: prediction by quantitative CT. *Chest.* 2001;119(5):1337-1346.

54. National Emphysema Treatment Trial Research Group. Patients at high risk of death after lung-volume-reduction surgery. *N Engl J Med.* 2001;345(15):1075-1083.

55. Nakamura T, Tamura M, Kadowaki S, Sasano T. Low-dose continuous indomethacin in early days of age reduces the incidence of symptomatic patent ductus arteriosus without adverse effects. *Am J Perinatol.* 2000;17(5):271-275.

56. Schmidt B, Davis P, Moddemann D, et al. Long-term effects of indomethacin prophylaxis in extremely-low-birth-weight infants. *N Engl J Med.* 2001;344(26):1966-1972.

57. Benson K, Hartz AJ. A comparison of observational studies and randomized, controlled trials. *N Engl J Med.* 2000;342(25):1878-1886.

58. Concato J, Shah N, Horwitz RI. Randomized, controlled trials, observational studies, and the hierarchy of research designs. *N Engl J Med.* 2000;342(25):1887-1892.

59. Ioannidis JP, Haidich AB, Lau J. Any casualties in the clash of randomised and observational evidence? *BMJ.* 2001;322(7291):879-880.

60. Ioannidis JP, Haidich AB, Pappa M, et al. Comparison of evidence of treatment effects in randomized and nonrandomized studies. *JAMA.* 2001;286(7):821-830.

61. Deeks JJ, Dinnes J, D'Amico R, et al. Evaluating non-randomised intervention studies. *Health Technol Assess.* 2003;7(27):iii-x, 1-173.

62. Ioannidis JP, Evans SJ, Gotzsche PC, et al. Better reporting of harms in randomized trials: an extension of the CONSORT statement. *Ann Intern Med.* 2004;141(10):781-788.

63. Papanikolaou PN, Christidi GD, Ioannidis JP. Comparison of evidence on harms of medical interventions in randomized and nonrandomized studies. *CMAJ.* 2006;174(5):635-641.

64. Woodruff AW, Dickinson CJ. Use of dexamethasone in cerebral malaria. *BMJ.* 1968;3(609):31-32.

65. Warrell DA, Looareesuwan S, Warrell MJ, et al. Dexamethasone proves deleterious in cerebral malaria: a double-blind trial in 100 comatose patients. *N Engl J Med.* 1982;306(6):313-319.

66. Popp AJ, Chater N. Extracranial to intracranial vascular anastomosis for occlusive cerebrovascular disease: experience in 110 patients. *Surgery.* 1977;82(5):648-654.

67. EC/IC Bypass Study Group. Failure of extracranial-intracranial arterial bypass to reduce the risk of ischemic stroke: results of an international randomized trial. *N Engl J Med.* 1985;313(19):1191-1200.

68. Rosenqvist M, Brandt J, Schuller H. Long-term pacing in sinus node disease: effects of stimulation mode on cardiovascular morbidity and mortality. *Am Heart J.* 1988;116(1 pt 1):16-22.

69. Connolly SJ, Kerr CR, Gent M, et al. Effects of physiologic pacing versus ventricular pacing on the risk of stroke and death due to cardiovascular causes: Canadian Trial of Physiologic Pacing Investigators. *N Engl J Med.* 2000;342(19):1385-1391.

70. Herson S, Lok C, Roujeau JC, et al. [Plasma exchange in dermatomyositis and polymyositis: retrospective study of 38 cases of plasma exchange]. *Ann Med Interne (Paris).* 1989;140(6):453-455.

71. Miller FW, Leitman SF, Cronin ME, et al. Controlled trial of plasma exchange and leukapheresis in polymyositis and dermatomyositis. *N Engl J Med.* 1992; 326(21):1380-1384.

72. Farley SM, Libanati CR, Odvina CV, et al. Efficacy of long-term fluoride and calcium therapy in correcting the deficit of spinal bone density in osteoporosis. *J Clin Epidemiol.* 1989;42(11):1067-1074.

73. Riggs BL, Hodgson SF, O'Fallon WM, et al. Effect of fluoride treatment on the fracture rate in postmenopausal women with osteoporosis. *N Engl J Med.* 1990;322(12):802-809.

74. Stampfer MJ, Colditz GA. Estrogen replacement therapy and coronary heart disease: a quantitative assessment of the epidemiologic evidence. *Prev Med.* 1991;20(1):47-63.

75. Grady D, Herrington D, Bittner V, et al. Cardiovascular disease outcomes during 6.8 years of hormone therapy: Heart and Estrogen/progestin Replacement Study follow-up (HERS II). *JAMA.* 2002;288(1):49-57.

76. Rossouw JE, Anderson GL, Prentice RL, et al. Risks and benefits of estrogen plus progestin in healthy postmenopausal women: principal results from the Women's Health Initiative randomized controlled trial. *JAMA.* 2002;288(3):321-333.

77. Finucane FF, Madans JH, Bush TL, Wolf PH, Kleinman JC. Decreased risk of stroke among postmenopausal hormone users: results from a national cohort. *Arch Intern Med.* 1993;153(1):73-79.

78. Wassertheil-Smoller S, Hendrix SL, Limacher M, et al. Effect of estrogen plus progestin on stroke in postmenopausal women: the Women's Health Initiative: a randomized trial. *JAMA.* 2003;289(20):2673-2684.

79. Warram JH, Laffel LM, Valsania P, Christlieb AR, Krolewski AS. Excess mortality associated with diuretic therapy in diabetes mellitus. *Arch Intern Med.* 1991; 151(7):1350-1356.

80. Curb JD, Pressel SL, Cutler JA, et al. Effect of diuretic-based antihypertensive treatment on cardiovascular disease risk in older diabetic patients with isolated systolic hypertension: Systolic Hypertension in the Elderly Program Cooperative Research Group. *JAMA.* 1996;276(23):1886-1892.

81. Giovannucci E, Stampfer MJ, Colditz G, Rimm EB, Willett WC. Relationship of diet to risk of colorectal adenoma in men. *J Natl Cancer Inst.* 1992;84(2):91-98.

82. Schatzkin A, Lanza E, Corle D, et al. Lack of effect of a low-fat, high-fiber diet on the recurrence of colorectal adenomas: Polyp Prevention Trial Study Group. *N Engl J Med.* 2000;342(16):1149-1155.

83. Morris DL, Kritchevsky SB, Davis CE. Serum carotenoids and coronary heart disease: the Lipid Research Clinics Coronary Primary Prevention Trial and Follow-up Study. *JAMA.* 1994;272(18):1439-1441.

84. Hennekens CH, Buring JE, Manson JE, et al. Lack of effect of long-term supplementation with beta carotene on the incidence of malignant neoplasms and cardiovascular disease. *N Engl J Med.* 1996;334(18):1145-1149.

85. Knekt P, Reunanen A, Jarvinen R, Seppanen R, Heliovaara M, Aromaa A. Antioxidant vitamin intake and coronary mortality in a longitudinal population study. *Am J Epidemiol.* 1994;139(12):1180-1189.

86. Yusuf S, Dagenais G, Pogue J, Bosch J, Sleight P. Vitamin E supplementation and cardiovascular events in high-risk patients: the Heart Outcomes Prevention Evaluation Study Investigators. *N Engl J Med.* 2000;342(3):154-160.

87. Knox JB, Wilmore DW, Demling RH, Sarraf P, Santos AA. Use of growth hormone for postoperative respiratory failure. *Am J Surg.* 1996;171(6):576-580.

88. Takala J, Ruokonen E, Webster NR, et al. Increased mortality associated with growth hormone treatment in critically ill adults. *N Engl J Med.* 1999;341 (11):785-792.

89. Cotroneo AR, Di Stasi C, Cina A, Di Gregorio F. Venous interruption as prophylaxis of pulmonary embolism: vena cava filters. *Rays.* 1996;21(3):461-480.

90. Decousus H, Leizorovicz A, Parent F, et al. A clinical trial of vena caval filters in the prevention of pulmonary embolism in patients with proximal deep-vein thrombosis; Prevention du Risque d'Embolie Pulmonaire par Interruption Cave Study Group. *N Engl J Med.* 1998;338(7):409-415.

91. Taylor DW, Barnett HJ, Haynes RB, et al. Low-dose and high-dose acetylsalicylic acid for patients undergoing carotid endarterectomy: a randomised controlled trial: ASA and Carotid Endarterectomy (ACE) Trial Collaborators. *Lancet.* 1999;353(9171):2179-2184.

92. Guyatt GH, DiCenso A, Farewell V, Willan A, Griffith L. Randomized trials versus observational studies in adolescent pregnancy prevention. *J Clin Epidemiol.* 2000;53(2):167-174.

93. Gross DE, Brenner SL, Esformes I, Gross ML. Arthroscopic treatment of degenerative joint disease of the knee. *Orthopedics.* 1991;14(12):1317-1321.

94. Moseley JB, O'Malley K, Petersen NJ, et al. A controlled trial of arthroscopic surgery for osteoarthritis of the knee. *N Engl J Med.* 2002;347(2):81-88.

95. Landesberg G, Mosseri M, Wolf YG, et al. Preoperative thallium scanning, selective coronary revascularization, and long-term survival after major vascular surgery. *Circulation.* 2003;108(2):177-183.

96. McFalls EO, Ward HB, Moritz TE, et al. Coronary-artery revascularization before elective major vascular surgery. *N Engl J Med.* 2004;351(27):2795-2804.

97. Hartz AJ, Kuhn EM, Pryor DB, et al. Mortality after coronary angioplasty and coronary artery bypass surgery (the national Medicare experience). *Am J Cardiol.* 1992;70(2):179-185.

98. CABRI Trial Participants. First-year results of CABRI (Coronary Angioplasty versus Bypass Revascularisation Investigation). *Lancet.* 1995;346(8984):1179-1184.

99. Blais L, Desgagne A, LeLorier J. 3-Hydroxy-3-methylglutaryl coenzyme A reductase inhibitors and the risk of cancer: a nested case-control study. *Arch Intern Med.* 2000;160(15):2363-2368.

100. Dale KM, Coleman CI, Henyan NN, Kluger J, White CM. Statins and cancer risk: a meta-analysis. *JAMA.* 2006;295(1):74-80.

101. Wangensteen OH, Peter ET, Nicoloff DM, Walder AI, Sosin H, Bernstein EF. Achieving "physiological gastrectomy" by gastric freezing: a preliminary report of an experimental and clinical study. *JAMA.* 1962 May 12;180:439-444.

102. Ruffin JM, Grizzle JE, Hightower NC, McHardy G, Shull H, Kirsner JB. A co-operative double-blind evaluation of gastric "freezing" in the treatment of duodenal ulcer. *N Engl J Med.* 1969;281(1):16-19.

103. Mulder GD, Albert SF, Grimwood RE. Clinical evaluation of a new occlusive hydrocolloid dressing. *Cutis.* 1985;35(4):396-397, 400.

104. Backhouse CM, Blair SD, Savage AP, Walton J, McCollum CN. Controlled trial of occlusive dressings in healing chronic venous ulcers. *Br J Surg.* 1987;74(7):626-627.

105. Ioannidis JP, Cappelleri JC, Sacks HS, Lau J. The relationship between study design, results, and reporting of randomized clinical trials of HIV infection. *Control Clin Trials.* 1997;18(5):431-444.

106. Ioannidis JP, Lau J. The impact of high-risk patients on the results of clinical trials. *J Clin Epidemiol.* 1997;50(10):1089-1098.

107. Ioannidis JP. Contradicted and initially stronger effects in highly cited clinical research. *JAMA.* 2005;294(2):218-228.

108. Ziegler EJ, Fisher CJ Jr, Sprung CL, et al. Treatment of gram-negative bacteremia and septic shock with HA-1A human monoclonal antibody against endotoxin: a randomized, double-blind, placebo-controlled trial: the HA-1A Sepsis Study Group. *N Engl J Med.* 1991;324(7):429-436.

109. McCloskey RV, Straube RC, Sanders C, Smith SM, Smith CR. Treatment of septic shock with human monoclonal antibody HA-1A: a randomized, double-blind, placebo-controlled trial: CHESS Trial Study Group. *Ann Intern Med.* 1994;121(1):1-5.

110. Stephens NG, Parsons A, Schofield PM, Kelly F, Cheeseman K, Mitchinson MJ. Randomised controlled trial of vitamin E in patients with coronary disease: Cambridge Heart Antioxidant Study (CHAOS). *Lancet.* 1996;347(9004):781-786.

111. Miller ER 3rd, Pastor-Barriuso R, Dalal D, Riemersma RA, Appel LJ, Guallar E. Meta-analysis: high-dosage vitamin E supplementation may increase all-cause mortality. *Ann Intern Med.* 2005;142(1):37-46.

112. Ioannidis J, Lau J. Evolution of treatment effects over time: empirical insight from recursive cumulative metaanalyses. *Proc Natl Acad Sci U S A*. 2001; 98(3):831-836.

113. Trikalinos TA, Churchill R, Ferri M, et al. Effect sizes in cumulative meta-analyses of mental health randomized trials evolved over time. *J Clin Epidemiol*. 2004;57(11):1124-1130.

ADVANCED TOPICS IN THE VALIDITY
OF THERAPY TRIALS

RANDOMIZED TRIALS STOPPED EARLY FOR BENEFIT

Victor Montori, P. J. Devereaux,
Holger Schünemann, Maureen O. Meade,
Deborah J. Cook, and Gordon Guyatt

IN THIS CHAPTER:

RANDOMIZED CONTROLLED TRIALS STOPPED EARLY FOR BENEFIT PLAY A PROMINENT ROLE IN THE MEDICAL LITERATURE

Investigators may stop *randomized controlled trials (RCTs)* earlier than planned because of perceived *harm* of the *experimental intervention*, because they lose hope in achieving a positive result, or because the sponsor wishes to save money.[1] The most common reason for early stopping, however, is that investigators note *treatment effects* that appear to be unlikely by chance (and that are often large) and that persuade them that the experimental intervention is beneficial. Trials *stopped early* for apparent benefit—which we will refer to as *truncated RCTs*— often receive considerable attention. They enjoy extraordinary success in appearing in the most prominent journals and in the popular press,[2] markedly increasing their likelihood of widespread dissemination and subsequent citation. They may, with remarkable rapidity, form the basis of *practice guidelines* and criteria for quality of medical care. Such has been the fate of stopped-early RCTs documenting the effect of tight glucose control with insulin in patients in the intensive care unit[3] and β-blockers in patients undergoing vascular surgery.[4] Moreover, the frequency of their appearance in the medical literature is growing rapidly; more than 1% of the RCTs published in 15 leading medical journals from 2000 to 2004 were stopped early for benefit, a 100% increase in 1 decade.[2] Because authors may not always report that their trial was stopped early, however, the true frequency may be much greater.[5]

TRUNCATED RANDOMIZED CONTROLLED TRIALS ARE AT RISK OF OVERESTIMATING TREATMENT EFFECTS

Taking the point estimate of the treatment effect at face value will mislead if the decision to stop the trial resulted from catching the apparent benefit of treatment at a random high. Consider a hypothetical set of RCTs testing a treatment with a true, but modest, underlying benefit. Even early in their conduct, results will cluster around the true effect (Figure 9.3-1). Even so, half these trials will, by chance, overestimate the true effect and half will underestimate the true effect (Figure 9.3-1). In some, the overestimates and underestimates will be large. The smaller the number of events, the greater the risk that the play of chance will result in apparent effects far from the truth (Figure 9.3-1).

Let us assume that investigators repeatedly check the results as patients complete the study, in search of a large treatment effect that, to them, presents an ethical mandate to stop early and offer treatment to all subsequent patients. Chance will ensure that an appreciable number of such trials will stop early, creating a false impression of a very large treatment effect (Figure 9.3-1). When this occurs, data from future trials that refrain from early stopping will yield a smaller estimate of

FIGURE 9.3-1

Theoretical Distribution of Randomized Controlled Trial Results as Data Accumulate

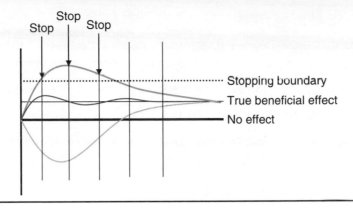

the treatment effect, the so-called regression to the truth effect.[6] If investigators wait long enough for a large number of events to accumulate, the risk of overestimation is far lower (Figure 9.3-1).

Although statistical simulation can readily demonstrate how truncated RCTs will overestimate treatment effects,[7] trials in which investigators have looked at the data as it accumulated, but refrained from early stopping, also provide compelling evidence. Investigators conducted a trial comparing 5 vs 4 courses of chemotherapy for acute myeloid leukemia. They observed an extremely large treatment effect early on in their RCT (Figure 9.3-2).[8] Their results crossed their prespecified stopping boundary. Nevertheless, because they correctly concluded that the effect was too good to be true, they continued recruiting and following patients. Ultimately, the apparent beneficial effect disappeared, and the final result showed a weak trend toward harm. Had the investigators adhered to their initial plan to stop early if they saw a sufficiently large effect and published this erroneous result, subsequent leukemia patients would have undergone additional toxic chemotherapy without benefit.

In a multicenter trial of tifacogin, a tissue-factor pathway inhibitor for treatment of critically ill patients with severe sepsis, an interim analysis conducted after 722 patients were enrolled showed a 10% *absolute risk difference* in 28-day mortality in favor of treated patients. This effect would have occurred by chance fewer than 6 times in 1000 (Figure 9.3-3A).[9] The investigators continued to recruit, the treatment effect vanished, and the trial ultimately showed a weak trend toward harm with treatment (Figure 9.3-3B). Had the trial stopped early, the manufacturers would have ensured that a toxic and expensive therapy was widely disseminated (as occurred for another agent with immune-modulating properties as a result of a stopped-early RCT in severely septic patients[10]).

FIGURE 9.3-2

A Near Miss in a Trial of Chemotherapy for Leukemia

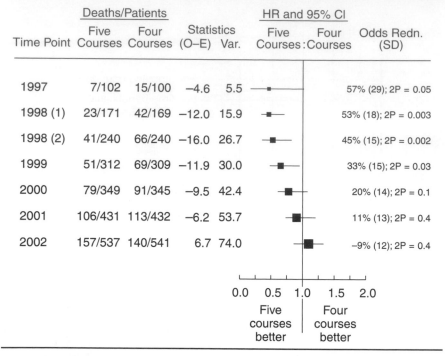

| | Deaths/Patients | | | | HR and 95% CI | | |
Time Point	Five Courses	Four Courses	Statistics (O–E)	Var.	Five Courses :	Four Courses	Odds Redn. (SD)
1997	7/102	15/100	−4.6	5.5			57% (29); 2P = 0.05
1998 (1)	23/171	42/169	−12.0	15.9			53% (18); 2P = 0.003
1998 (2)	41/240	66/240	−16.0	26.7			45% (15); 2P = 0.002
1999	51/312	69/309	−11.9	30.0			33% (15); 2P = 0.03
2000	79/349	91/345	−9.5	42.4			20% (14); 2P = 0.1
2001	106/431	113/432	−6.2	53.7			11% (13); 2P = 0.4
2002	157/537	140/541	6.7	74.0			−9% (12); 2P = 0.4

0.0   0.5   1.0   1.5   2.0

Five courses better | Four courses better

Abbreviations: CI, confidence interval; HR, hazard ratio; P, patients; SD, standard deviation.

Reproduced from Wheatley and Clayton.[8] Copyright © 2003, with permission from Elsevier.

TRUNCATED RANDOMIZED CONTROLLED TRIALS FREQUENTLY SHOW TREATMENT EFFECTS THAT ARE TOO GOOD TO BE TRUE

A systematic review of 143 truncated RCTs found that the majority evaluated cardiovascular or cancer interventions (Table 9.3-1).[2] On average, these RCTs stopped after recruiting approximately 64% of the planned sample and after a median of 13 months of *follow-up* and 1 interim analysis, documenting a median of 68 patients experiencing the *endpoints* driving termination. The RCTs had limited reporting of critical features specific to the decision to stop the trial: only 67 (47%) of the 143 trials reported their planned sample size, the interim analysis after which they decided to stop the RCT, and the stopping rule used to inform this decision (Table 9.3-2).

The median *relative risk* (RR) in these 143 RCTs was 0.53. That is, almost half of the stopped-early trials showed *relative risk reductions* (RRRs) of 50%, and more than a quarter showed RRRs of greater than 70%. Considering what we know about human biology, and our experience with treatment of human disease rarely achieving effects of this size, the magnitude of these average effects observed in truncated RCTs is not credible.

FIGURE 9.3-3 A, B

A Near Miss in a Trial of Tissue Factor Pathway Inhibitor in Critically Ill Patients With Severe Sepsis

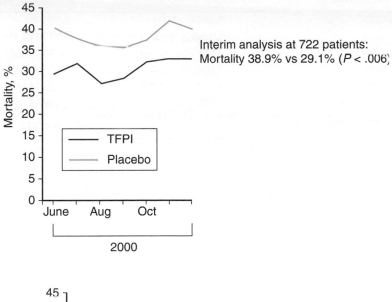

A

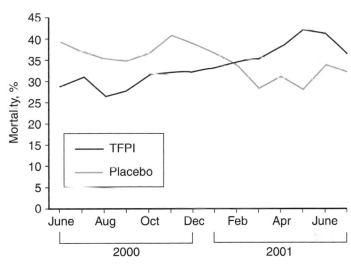

B

A, Results at an interim analysis. B, Final results. Reproduced from Abraham et al,[9] with permission from *JAMA*. Abbreviation: TFPI, tissue factor pathway inhibitor.

TABLE 9.3-1

Characteristics of Randomized Controlled Trials Stopped Early for Benefit

Year of Publication	Truncated RCTs/RCTs Indexed in MEDLINE (%)	Truncated RCTs/RCTs in Top Impact Journals
1975-1979	1/6574 (0.01)	0/620 (0)
1980-1984	1/12653 (0.008)	1/1175 (0.1)
1985-1989	10/21807 (0.05)	9/1938 (0.5)
1990-1994	19/38712 (0.05)	15/3106 (0.5)
1995-1999	41/52060 (0.08)	35/3594 (1.0)
2000-2004	71/58537 (0.12)	47/3859 (1.2)

Characteristic	n = 143
Area of Study	
Cardiology	36
Cancer (hematology/oncology)	30
HIV/AIDS	17
Critical care	10
Other areas	50
Type of Comparisons	
Active medication vs placebo	76
Active medication vs active medication	31
Nonpharmacologic therapeutic interventions (eg, invasive procedures, rehabilitation)	23
Drug vs nonpharmacologic therapeutic intervention	12
Nontherapeutic interventions (eg, education)	1
Type of Endpoint Driving the Decision to Stop the Trial	
Dichotomous single endpoints	95
Dichotomous composite endpoints	32
Continuous	16
Quality of Reporting of Safeguards Against Bias	
Adequate randomization method	84
Adequate allocation concealment	76
Blinding of	
Participants	77
Health care providers	61
Data collectors	39
Data analysts	7
Judicial assessors of outcomes	58
Reported planned sample size	115
Section Reporting RCT Stopped Early	
Title	2
Abstract	95
Introduction	25

(Continued)

TABLE 9.3-1

Characteristics of Randomized Controlled Trials Stopped Early for Benefit (*Continued*)

Characteristic	n = 143
Section Reporting RCT Stopped Early (*Continued*)	
Methods	
Not statistical section	16
Statistical section	38
Results	
First paragraph	57
Elsewhere in the results section	38
Discussion section	57
Funding	
For-profit agency (eg, pharmaceutical industry)	64
Only source reported	36
Along with not-for-profit/government agency only	28
Not-for-profit organization/government agency only	53
Not reported	26
Reports of Competing Interest	
No report of competing interests	100
Reported employment with funding agency	24
Reported potential conflict other than employment	16
Reported no competing interests	3

Abbreviations: HIV, human immunodeficiency virus; RCT, randomized controlled trial.

Reproduced from Montori et al,[2] with permission from *JAMA*.

TABLE 9.3-2

Stopping Characteristics of Randomized Controlled Trials Stopped Early for Benefit

Characteristics	n = 143
Type of Stop	
Stopped recruitment	104
Continue follow-up	51
Stopped follow-up	53
Stopped follow-up after completing recruitment	30
Could not be determined	9
Interim Analyses—Definition of Interval	
After enrolling a set number of participants	51
After a calendar period after date of trial start	32
After a set number of endpoints accrue	6
After a set follow-up (eg, patient-years of observation)	8
Ad hoc	6
Did not report	40

(*Continued*)

TABLE 9.3-2

Stopping Characteristics of Randomized Controlled Trials Stopped Early for Benefit (*Continued*)

Characteristics	n = 143
Monitoring Methods/Stopping Boundaries	
No method or α spending function used	28
Method specified	
O'Brien-Fleming boundary	38
With Lan-DeMets α spending function	15
Haybittle-Peto boundary	16
Pocock boundary	10
Triangular boundaries	3
Prespecified P value (α spending function not reported)	15
Other boundaries/α spending functions	13
Monitoring methods not specified	20
Role of Monitoring Method/Stopping Boundary in Trial Termination	
Results exceeded stopping boundary	90
Unrelated to stopping boundary/no stopping boundaries/rules in place	46
Trial continued despite results exceeding stopping boundary	3
Unclear reasons	7
Adjustments for Early Stop/Interim Analyses	
None reported	129
Adjustment reported	14
On point estimate, confidence interval, and P value	5
On confidence interval or P value only	9
Adjusted estimates reported in the abstract	11
Who Made Decision to Stop	
Executive committee	109
Following recommendation from data safety and monitoring board	84
Data safety and monitoring board	8
Not-for-profit sponsor	2
Not reported	24

Reproduced from Montori et al,[2] with permission from *JAMA*.

TRUNCATED RANDOMIZED CONTROLLED TRIALS MAY PREVENT A COMPREHENSIVE ASSESSMENT OF TREATMENT IMPACT

In 22% of the 143 trials reviewed, the decision to stop was based on a *composite endpoint*. Use of a composite endpoint compounds the risk of misleading results: the least *patient-important outcome* that makes up the composite endpoint (eg, angina in a composite of death, myocardial infarction, and angina) (see Chapter 10.4, Composite Endpoints) may drive the decision to stop early. Consequently, few events that are most important to patients may accrue.

Even when investigators do not use composite endpoints, few events will accrue in the endpoints not driving the decision to stop early for benefit. These endpoints may include patient-important beneficial events (eg, overall survival rather than progression-free survival[11]) or adverse events. Lack of adequate safety data as a result of stopping the trial early may in turn affect the perceived and actual risk-benefit ratios (ie, overestimating the benefit, underestimating the risk) of implementing the intervention in clinical practice.[12]

ETHICAL RESPONSIBILITIES TO PATIENTS RELYING ON TRIAL RESULTS

Readers may, at this point, experience a dilemma. Even if investigators are aware of the dangers of stopping early—overestimating treatment effects and failing to provide precise estimates of effect on all patient-important benefits and risks[13]—how can they continue to ethically enroll patients who have a 50% chance of receiving *placebo* when results show an apparent large benefit of treatment? The answer to the question lies in clinical responsibilities toward the many patients who are at risk of basing their subsequent treatment decisions on false information.[10] The prospect of, for instance, leukemic patients undergoing toxic chemotherapy without benefit is not ethically attractive. Patients deserve robust, accurate estimates of the effects of treatments they are considering.

USERS' GUIDES

Was There a Preplanned Stopping Rule?

If investigators check their data periodically and stop as soon as they observe an apparent large treatment effect, the risk of overestimation of the treatment effect is enormous (Figure 9.3-1). A previous plan to look at the data only periodically (eg, at 250, 500, and 750 completed patients of a trial planning to enroll 1000 patients) and stop only if the results meet certain criteria (eg, $P < .001$) reduces considerably the chances of stopping early.

There are, however, 3 serious limitations of formal *stopping rules*. First, investigators sometimes choose unsatisfactory criteria for termination. In one trial, after finding an apparent trend in favor of treatment after 28 patients, investigators decided to review the data after every subsequent 5 patients and to stop as soon as their P value reached .001 (which it did after another 25 patients, for a total of 53 enrolled, of whom 28 had died).[14]

Second, trials that stop early without formal stopping rules fail to inform you that their trial was indeed stopped early. This is one reason to be skeptical of small trials with very large effects—they may represent instances of stopping in response to a large treatment effect discovered because of repeated looks at the data (see Chapter 11.3, Dealing With Misleading Presentations of Clinical Trial Results).

Sydes et al[15] reported that the problem of unreported early stopping may be appreciable. In an examination of statistical methods in 662 trials, they found that 156 reported either a stopping rule or a data monitoring committee (DMC). Of these 156 trials, 41 reported a DMC without a formal stopping rule (a somewhat anomalous situation).[15] These data suggest that reviews of stopped-early trials based on explicit reports of the decision to stop will underestimate the magnitude of the problem.

Third, trials that hit preplanned stopping boundaries early, after few events, are still likely to represent large overestimates of the treatment effect.

Did the Rule Involve Few Interim Looks and a Stringent *P* Value?

Trials with stopping rules that involve multiple looks at short intervals—such as the every-5-patients criterion described above—provide little protection against the play of chance and the risk of a biased estimate of treatment effect. Somewhat more rigorous criteria with excessively lenient *P* value (for instance, .02) are also problematic.[16,17] More rigorous criteria that demand a *P* value of .001 or less provide increasing protection.

Stringent *P* value, however, still leave a major danger: although they will decrease the likelihood of stopping early, the instances in which the boundary is crossed may still represent a chance finding and a substantially inflated treatment effect.

Take, for example, an RCT evaluating the efficacy of bisoprolol in patients with a positive dobutamine echocardiography result undergoing elective vascular surgery.[4] When the trial was stopped, investigators had enrolled 112 patients (the authors had planned to recruit 266 patients, expecting an RR of 0.50), and the results had exceeded the $P < .001$ O'Brien-Fleming boundary for benefit. The RR for the primary endpoint (cardiac death or nonfatal myocardial infarction) was 0.09 (nominal 95% confidence interval [CI], 0.02-0.37) or a 91% RRR.

This very large treatment effect is far too good to be true. It is inconsistent with the researchers' expectations, with the magnitude of effect (ie, RRs, 0.65-0.85) of β-blockers in tens of thousands of patients with acute myocardial infarction or chronic management of congestive heart failure, and with results in day-to-day clinical practice.[18] Further, the very large treatment effect in the stopped-early trial[4] contrasts with the results of 2 recently reported RCTs.[19,20] Both much larger than the stopped-early trial that suggests a large benefit from β-blockers (491 patients[19] and 921 patients[20]), neither suggest an important benefit from the peri-operative administration of β-blockers.

Thus, you must maintain your skepticism even in the face of apparently conservative stopping rules. The risk of a *false-positive trial* decreases if the trialist or the DMC chooses to enroll further and have another look after the stopping criteria are met. Even so, the remaining risk of an inflated treatment effect suggests the need for yet an additional criterion.

Were There a Large Number of Events?

As events accumulate, the likelihood of chance producing a substantially inflated effect decreases (Figure 9.3-1). The smaller trials among the 143 truncated RCTs in the systematic review showed, on average, a far greater magnitude of effect than the larger trials. Trials that included fewer than the median number of events (66) were far more likely (odds ratio, 28; 95% CI, 11%-73%) to show a large treatment effect (greater than the median RRR of 47%) than trials with more events. Thus, if investigators and DMCs refrain from peeking at their data until a large number of patients have experienced events, and also choose a stringent P value, their risk of spurious results decreases appreciably.

How many events is enough? In a look at 143 trials stopped early for benefit, no RCT with greater than 200 events showed an RRR of more than 50%. The more conservative among us would suggest that more than 300 events are required before the risk of an inflated treatment effect becomes minimal, and the most conservative, that we must vary the threshold depending on the *event rate*. Although future research may well provide further insight into the optimal threshold, we can confidently suggest that you should not believe RRRs of more than 50% generated in truncated trials with fewer than 100 events. The larger the number of events and the more plausible the RRRs (on the order of 20%-35%), the less skeptical you need to be about the result.

CONCLUSION—GUIDANCE FOR THE CLINICIAN

How should a clinician respond to a trial stopped early? If all the *validity* criteria we have presented are met, the trial may well represent an accurate estimate of the true patient benefit, and the clinician can proceed with confidence. If not, the clinician faces a situation not dissimilar to acting on the basis of trials with limited validity or inadequate sample size: the results are likely to represent an overestimate of the effect, and the degree of the overestimate may be large. In such situations, patients' underlying *values and preferences* (how they feel about receiving treatment with uncertain benefit, and some inconvenience, risk, and possibly cost) become particularly salient in decision making.

References

1. Psaty BM, Rennie D. Stopping medical research to save money: a broken pact with researchers and patients. *JAMA*. 2003;289(16):2128-2131.

2. Montori VM, Devereaux PJ, Adhikari NK, et al. Randomized trials stopped early for benefit: a systematic review. *JAMA*. 2005;294(17):2203-2209.

3. van den Berghe G, Wouters P, Weekers F, et al. Intensive insulin therapy in the critically ill patients. *N Engl J Med.* 2001;345(19):1359-1367.

4. Poldermans D, Boersma E, Bax JJ, et al. The effect of bisoprolol on perioperative mortality and myocardial infarction in high-risk patients undergoing vascular surgery: Dutch Echocardiographic Cardiac Risk Evaluation Applying Stress Echocardiography Study Group. *N Engl J Med.* 1999;341(24):1789-1794.

5. Kiri A, Tonascia S, Meinert CL. Treatment effects monitoring committees and early stopping in large clinical trials. *Clin Trials.* 2004;1(1):40-47.

6. Pocock SJ, Hughes MD. Practical problems in interim analyses, with particular regard to estimation. *Control Clin Trials.* 1989;10(suppl 4):209S-221S.

7. Pocock S, White I. Trials stopped early: too good to be true? *Lancet.* 1999;353(9157):943-944.

8. Wheatley K, Clayton D. Be skeptical about unexpected large apparent treatment effects: the case of an MRC AML12 randomization. *Control Clin Trials.* 2003;24(1):66-70.

9. Abraham E, Reinhart K, Opal S, et al. Efficacy and safety of tifacogin (recombinant tissue factor pathway inhibitor) in severe sepsis: a randomized controlled trial. *JAMA.* 2003;290(2):238-247.

10. Bernard GR, Vincent JL, Laterre PF, et al. Efficacy and safety of recombinant human activated protein C for severe sepsis. *N Engl J Med.* 2001;344(10):699-709.

11. Cannistra SA. The ethics of early stopping rules: who is protecting whom? *J Clin Oncol.* 2004;22(9):1542-1545.

12. Juurlink DN, Mamdani MM, Lee DS, et al. Rates of hyperkalemia after publication of the Randomized Aldactone Evaluation Study. *N Engl J Med.* 2004;351(6):543-551.

13. Guyatt G, Montori V, Devereaux PJ, Schunemann H, Bhandari M. Patients at the center: in our practice, and in our use of language. *ACP J Club.* 2004;140(1):A11-12.

14. Amato MB, Barbas CS, Medeiros DM, et al. Effect of a protective-ventilation strategy on mortality in the acute respiratory distress syndrome. *N Engl J Med.* 1998;338(6):347-354.

15. Sydes MR, Altman DG, Babiker AB, Parmar MK, Spiegelhalter DJ. Reported use of data monitoring committees in the main published reports of randomized controlled trials: a cross-sectional study. *Clin Trials.* 2004;1(1):48-59.

16. Pocock SJ. When (not) to stop a clinical trial for benefit. *JAMA.* 2005;294(17):2228-2230.

17. A proposed charter for clinical trial data monitoring committees: helping them to do their job well. *Lancet.* 2005;365(9460):711-722.

18. Devereaux PJ, Yusuf S, Yang H, Choi PT, Guyatt GH. Are the recommendations to use perioperative beta-blocker therapy in patients undergoing noncardiac surgery based on reliable evidence? *CMAJ.* 2004;171(3):245-247.

19. Yang H, Raymer K, Butler R, Parlow J, Roberts R. The effects of perioperative beta-blockade: results of the Metoprolol after Vascular Surgery (MaVS) study, a randomized controlled trial. *Am Heart J*. 2006;152(5)983-90.

20. Juul AB, Wetterslev J, Gluud C, et al; DIPOM Trial Group. Effect of perioperative beta-blockade in patients with diabetes undergoing major non-cardiac sugery: randomized, placebo controlled, blinded multicentre trial. *BMJ*. 2006;332 (7556):1482.

THE PRINCIPLE
OF INTENTION
TO TREAT

Gordon Guyatt, Victor Montori, P. J. Devereaux,
and Pierre Durieux

IN THIS CHAPTER:

HOW SHOULD RANDOMIZED TRIALS DEAL WITH TREATMENT-ARM PATIENTS WHO DO NOT RECEIVE TREATMENT?

If patients do not take their medication, they are not going to get any benefit. Furthermore, we do not need randomized trials—or studies of any kind—to demonstrate this lack of benefit. One might therefore reason that, in a randomized trial, investigators should compare patients in the experimental group who received treatment with patients in the control group who did not. As it turns out, however, doing so is a mistake. We need to know about all the patients in a trial, including those in the experimental group who do not adhere to or complete therapy.

One argument for incorporating all patients in the final analysis, including those who did not adhere to treatment, has to do with the effect of the treatment on members of the community. If one is interested in knowing the effect of a drug on a given population, one must include all members of that population. When patients do not adhere to a regimen, particularly if adverse effects have caused nonadherence, reservations will arise about the effect on a community of a medication.

As clinicians, however, we are more interested in the effect of our interventions on individual patients than on populations. Consider the viewpoint of a patient who is determined to adhere to a treatment regimen and is destined to succeed. Let us assume that 50% of treated patients in a trial did not comply with the treatment regimen. Does the motivated patient wish to know the average effect of the treatment in a group of people of whom 50% did not comply? No; he or she wants the best estimate of the effect the medication will have when taken, which would come from a population of other patients who succeeded in adhering to the treatment regimen.

A HYPOTHETICAL SURGICAL RANDOMIZED CONTROLLED TRIAL

Imagine a randomized trial studying patients with cerebrovascular disease. The trial compares administration of aspirin alone with that of aspirin along with an experimental surgical procedure. Assume that, although the investigators conducting the trial do not know it, the underlying true effect of the surgical procedure is zero; patients in the surgical arm of the study do neither better nor worse than those in the aspirin-only arm.

Of 100 patients randomized to surgery, 10 experience the primary outcome of the trial, a stroke, during the 1-month preoperative period, and their surgery is cancelled. Of the 90 patients who go to surgery, 10 have a stroke in the subsequent year (Figure 9.4-1). What will happen to the patients in the control group? Because randomization will, on average, create groups with the same fate or destiny and because we have already established that the surgical procedure has no effect on outcome, we predict that 10 control group patients will have a stroke in the month after randomization and another 10 will have a stroke in the subsequent year.

FIGURE 9.4-1

Results of a Hypothetical Trial of Surgical Therapy in Patients With Cerebrovascular Disease

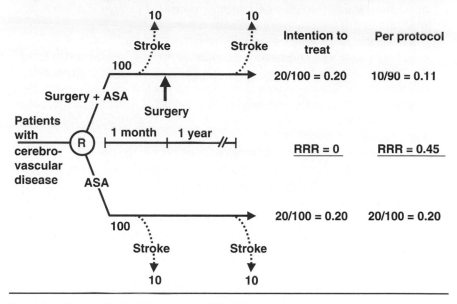

Abbreviations: ASA, acetylsalicylic acid; R, randomization; RRR, relative risk reduction.

Reprinted from Montori and Guyatt,[1] by permission of the publisher. Copyright © 2001, Canadian Medical Association.

The principle that dictates that we count events in all randomized patients, regardless of whether they received the intended intervention, is the *intention-to-treat principle*. When we apply the intention-to-treat principle in our study of cerebrovascular surgery for stroke, we find 20 events in each group and, therefore, no evidence of a positive treatment effect. If we use the logic that we should not count events in patients in the surgical group who did not receive surgery, however, the event rate in the experimental groups would be 10/90 (or 11%), in comparison to the 20% event rate in the control group—a reduction in relative risk of 45% instead of the true *relative risk reduction* (*RRR*) of 0. These data show how analyses restricted to patients who adhered to assigned treatment (sometimes referred to *per-protocol*, efficacy, or explanatory analyses) can provide a misleading estimate of surgical therapy's effect.

A SECOND HYPOTHETICAL SURGICAL RANDOMIZED TRIAL

Consider a second surgical example made more complex by the fact that not only do some patients allocated to surgery not undergo surgery but also some of the patients allocated to the medical arm receive surgery not dictated by the protocol. Once again, we specify that the true underlying effect of the surgical procedure is zero, and the overall event rate of adverse outcomes—that is, strokes—is 20%.

In this example, of 100 patients randomized to surgery, 20 did not get surgery, and of 100 patients randomized to medical treatment alone, 20 underwent surgery (groups e and g in Figure 9.4-2, respectively). This situation can occur, for example, when investigators can identify patients at different risk levels for stroke and tend to favor surgery for patients at low risk.

Because they are a prognostically lower-risk group, the event rate will be lower for patients who underwent surgery in the medical treatment arm (say, 10%). The remaining higher-risk medical patients have a higher stroke rate. At the same time, the event rate will be higher for the high-risk patients in the surgery arm who do not receive surgery (say, 30%) and lower for the patients who do undergo surgery, again considered prognostically a lower-risk group (Figure 9.4-2).

Of 100 patients randomized to surgery, 20 experience the primary outcome (among whom 6 did not receive surgery [group a] and 14 did [group b]). Of 100 patients randomized to medical treatment, 20 experience the primary outcome (among whom 2 received surgery [group c] and 2 received the medical treatment [group d] [Figure 9.4-2]). Applying the intention-to-treat principle, we find no evidence of a positive treatment effect (RRR = 0, the

FIGURE 9.4-2

Results of a Second Hypothetical Trial of Surgical Therapy in Patients With Cerebrovascular Disease

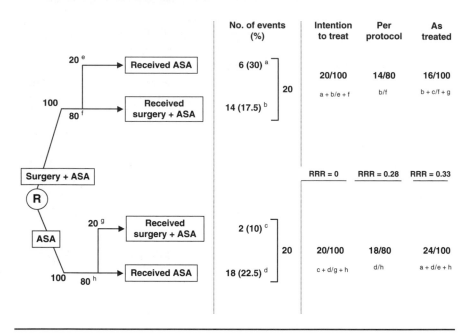

Abbreviations: ASA, acetylsalicylic acid; R, randomization; RRR, relative risk reduction.

Notes a-h refer to groups as discussed in text.

accurate result) (Figure 9.4-2). If we count only patients who adhered to the assigned arm (per-protocol analysis), the results are in favor of surgery (RRR = 0.28). The results are even more in favor of surgery if we compare all patients who received surgery (80 in the surgical arm, group f; and 20 in the medical arm, group g) with all patients who received the medical treatment (80 in the medical arm, group h; 20 in the surgical arm, group e) (RRR = 0.33) (Figure 9.4-2). This "as-treated" analysis is the most misleading.

A Hypothetical Randomized Trial of Drug Therapy

Now consider a trial of a new drug in which 20 of 100 patients are *nonadherent* (Figure 9.4-3). Under what circumstances would a comparison of the 80 patients who took their active medication with the control group yield an unbiased comparison? This would be true only if the underlying prognosis in the 80 adherent patients were identical to that of the 20

FIGURE 9.4-3

Results of a Hypothetical Trial of Drug Therapy in Patients With Cerebrovascular Disease

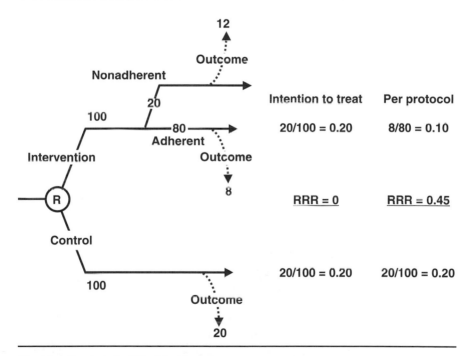

Abbreviations: R, randomization; RRR, relative risk reduction.

Reproduced with permission of Victor Montori.

nonadherent patients. If the 20 nonadherent patients were destined to do better than the other members of their group, the per-protocol analysis would provide a misleading underestimate of the true treatment effect. If, as is more often the case, the nonadherent group were more likely to have an adverse outcome, their omission would lead to a spurious overestimate of treatment benefit.

To make our demonstration more vivid, we can illustrate with additional hypothetical data. Let us assume that the treatment is once again ineffective and that the true underlying event rate in both treatment and control patients is 20%. Again, the 20 nonadherent patients are sicker, but their event rate (60%) is now much higher. Under these circumstances, the nonadherent patients will experience 12 of the 20 events destined to occur in the treated patients. If one compares only the adherent patients (with an event rate of 8/80, or 10%) with the control group (event rate 20/100, or 20%), one will mistakenly conclude that treatment cuts the event rate in half (Figure 9.4-3).

Our hypothetical examples have included 2 surgical trials and a trial of a medication.[1] The intention-to-treat principle applies regardless of the intervention (surgery, medication, or a behavioral therapy) and regardless of the outcome (mortality, morbidity, or a behavioral outcome such as smoking cessation). Removing patients after randomization always risks introducing bias by creating noncomparable groups.

A REAL-WORLD EXAMPLE

Perhaps the most dramatic example of how misleading a per-protocol analysis can be occurred many years ago in a trial testing the effect of clofibrate, a lipid-lowering agent, in reducing mortality in men between ages 30 and 64 years who had experienced a myocardial infarction.[2] After 5 years of follow-up, slightly fewer (20.0% of 1103) patients randomized to clofibrate had died than those randomized to placebo (20.9% of 2789; P value on the difference, .55). However, the mortality rate in 357 patients treated with clofibrate who took less than 80% of their prescribed treatment was 24.6%, whereas among those who had taken more than 80% of the medication, it was 15.0% (P value on the difference < .001). The study found parallel results among placebo-treated patients: the mortality rate in low-adherent patients was 28.2%, and in high-adherent patients it was 15.1% (P < .001). Patients with high adherence both in the experimental group and in the control group clearly represent a prognostically better group. Any inferences about treatment effects based on a selective focus on adherent patients would be extremely misleading.

Adhering to the Intention-to-Treat Principle Does Not Mean That All Patients Randomized Must Be Included in the Analysis

The goal of the intention-to-treat principle is to prevent bias introduced by prognostic differences between patients in the treatment and control groups included in the analysis. There are circumstances in which one can achieve efficiencies by excluding randomized patients and still avoid prognostic imbalance.[3] This requires meeting 2 conditions: (1) allocation to treatment or control could not possibly influence whether a particular randomized patient met criteria for postrandomization exclusion; and (2) the decision about postrandomization exclusion is made without possible bias (usually achieved by a review that is blinded to allocation).

> For instance, in a recently completed randomized trial of different ways of nailing tibial fractures, because the nailing approach is unlikely to be an important determinant of outcome among patients with previous osteomyelitis in the affected limb, the investigators planned to exclude such individuals. However, when study personnel fail to identify this exclusion criterion, they will occasionally enroll such a patient in error. For these patients, study investigators planned for postrandomization exclusion. A team of reviewers blinded to allocation routinely reviewed information available at randomization and, if there was evidence of osteomyelitis in the affected limb, made the decision to exclude patients from the analysis.

Intention to Treat and Toxicity

Investigators sometimes adhere to the intention-to-treat principle in terms of assessing endpoints that reflect potential treatment benefit but not for toxicity outcomes. Considering only those exposed to an intervention is appropriate if the adverse outcomes occur exclusively in this population (wound dehiscence can only occur in those who have undergone a surgical procedure).

In other instances, unbiased assessment of intervention toxicity requires as strict an adherence to the intention-to-treat principle as does assessment of benefit. The reason is that noncompliers in the experimental and control groups may have a different risk of adverse effects or toxicity than compliers in the same way that they may have a differential risk of the adverse outcomes that treatment is designed to prevent.

Limitations of the Intention-to-Treat Principle

Even after understanding the logic of the intention-to-treat principle, clinicians may find it unpalatable to count target adverse events in large numbers of patients who did not receive an experimental treatment against the treatment group. After all, the patient we considered at the beginning of this chapter was interested in the effect the medication would have if he or she were to take it. The best estimate of this effect would come from a group of patients who all received the experimental intervention, rather than from a group in which some did and some did not receive that intervention. Regrettably, following the intention-to-treat principle does not produce this best estimate, and the higher the level of nonadherence, the farther an analysis that adheres to the intention-to-treat principle will be from that best estimate. Unfortunately, as we have pointed out, possible solutions (per-protocol analyses, as-treated analysis, findings from observational studies) are extremely vulnerable to bias.

Differential nonadherence can produce potentially misleading results even in an appropriate analysis. Let us say, for instance, that surgery reduces the relative risk of stroke in patients with cerebrovascular disease by 40%, but 50% of the patients assigned to the no-surgery group receive surgery shortly after randomization. The intention-to-treat analysis will show an apparent treatment effect that is only 50% of what investigators would have observed if all medical patients had adhered to their assigned therapy. The apparent RRR with surgery will be even less if the patients allocated to medical treatment who nevertheless receive surgery are those at the highest risk of adverse events.

Unfortunately, the per-protocol analysis cannot solve the problem because we cannot distinguish between treatment effects and bias introduced by baseline differences in prognosis. When substantial noncompliance exists, our choice is between a biased estimate of the treatment effect from a per-protocol analysis and an unbiased estimate of the effect of the treatment as administered (rather than as intended) from the analysis that attributes events in all patients to the arm to which they were allocated. Statistical methods to "correct" for nonadherent methods are available, but they are either limited in their applicability or complex and not widely used.[4] The result from applying the intention-to-treat principle may have limited applicability to adherent patients. The best solution to this dilemma is for investigators to design their trials to ensure the highest possible level of adherence and for clinicians to understand the many pitfalls of studies that fail to follow an intention-to-treat approach to the analysis of their results.

The safest action for the clinician when faced with a trial that demonstrates an apparent effect of treatment, but in which nonadherence was substantial, is to treat the apparent treatment effect as a likely underestimate of the true treatment effect. For instance, in the Heart Protection Study, the overall compliance with simvastatin was approximately 85%, and the overall use of statins in the control group was approximately 17%.[5] Thus, one can consider the apparent 17% RRR in vascular deaths with simvastatin a likely underestimate of the benefit a fully compliant patient might expect from taking the drug vs not taking it.

MISLEADING USE OF "INTENTION TO TREAT"

We have been careful to talk about the "intention-to-treat principle" rather than the commonly used "intention-to-treat analysis." The reason is that there is considerable ambiguity in the term "intention-to-treat analysis," and its use can be very misleading.

For instance, picture a trial in which 20% of treated patients and 20% of control patients stop taking medication, and investigators elect to terminate their follow-up at that point. At the end of the trial, the investigators count events in all patients whose status they are aware of in the groups to which they are allocated. Technically, they could say they had conducted an intention-to-treat analysis in that they counted all events of which they were aware against the group to which the patient was allocated. Of course, the intention-to-treat analysis has in no way avoided the possible bias introduced by omission of outcome events in patients who discontinued treatment. The investigators could have avoided this problem had they chosen to follow all patients, irrespective of adherence to treatment.

Clinicians evaluating a randomized trial need to know whether the researchers followed the intention-to-treat principle. A quick approach is to scan the methods section of the *randomized controlled trial (RCT)*, looking for the phrase "intention-to-treat analysis." Two surveys of RCTs published in major medical journals during 1993-1995[6] and 1997[7] found that half of the RCTs used the term "intention-to-treat analysis." Unfortunately, the term was not always used appropriately. Thus, readers must look carefully at what was actually done, rather than look only for the "intention-to-treat" term.

In particular, a large loss to follow-up may introduce the same bias as a per-protocol analysis. This is particularly so because patients lost to follow-up tend to have poorer outcomes than patients whom investigators successfully follow.[8]

For instance, Silverstein et al[9] reported the results of an RCT of 8843 patients taking nonsteroidal anti-inflammatory agents for rheumatoid arthritis, randomized to receive misoprostol (4404 patients) or placebo (4439 patients) to prevent gastroduodenal complications as judged by outcome assessors blinded to treatment allocation. The authors described their analysis as intention to treat. However, they included patients lost to follow-up in the denominator of event rates used for this analysis. Inclusion of these patients in the denominator without including their outcomes in the numerator assumed that no patient lost to follow-up had gastroduodenal ulcerations. The size of the groups lost (1851 patients in the misoprostol arm and 1617 in the placebo arm) eclipsed the number of patients that experienced the primary endpoint in each group (25 in the misoprostol group and 42 in the placebo group), leaving the reader uncertain about the true magnitude of the treatment effect. Again, the investigators could have avoided the problem by rigorously following all patients.

In another example, Harris et al[10] reported the results of an RCT of secondary prevention of vertebral fractures in 1628 postmenopausal women randomized to receive risedronate (813 patients) or placebo (815 patients) to prevent another vertebral fracture as judged by a radiologist blinded to treatment allocation. The authors described their analysis as intention to treat. After 3 years, 324 of 813 patients in the risedronate arm and 365 of 815 patients in the placebo arm were lost to follow-up. The authors reported outcomes up to the point of last follow-up (using *survival analysis*), including 93 patients with new vertebral fractures in the placebo group and 61 in the risedronate group, for an RRR of 41% in favor of risedronate. Those lost to follow-up from the placebo group were at a higher risk (had more vertebral fractures) at baseline than those lost from the risedronate arm, suggesting that the placebo group remaining in the study had, on average, a better prognosis than the remaining risedronate group, thus biasing the results in favor of placebo. Because the risedronate group experienced fewer vertebral fractures than the placebo group, in this case the large loss to follow-up does not weaken the inference that risedronate results in a large reduction in relative risk.

SUMMARY

For RCTs to provide unbiased assessments of treatment efficacy, investigators should apply the intention-to-treat principle. To improve the applicability of the study results to the individual patient, investigators should improve the design of the trial to ensure protocol adherence with minimal loss to follow-up. Finally, loss to follow-up can result in the same sort of bias as a per-protocol analysis. Thus, in the presence of significant loss to follow-up, statements that investigators conducted an "intention-to-treat analysis" generally provide little reassurance.

References

1. Montori VM, Guyatt GH. Intention-to-treat principle. *CMAJ.* 2001;165(10):1339-1341.

2. The Coronary Drug Project Research Group. Influence of adherence to treatment and response of cholesterol on mortality in the coronary drug project. *N Engl J Med.* 1980;303(18):1038-1041.

3. Fergusson D, Aaron SD, Guyatt G, Hebert P. Post-randomisation exclusions: the intention to treat principle and excluding patients from analysis. *BMJ.* 2002; 325(7365):652-654.

4. Dunn G, Maracy M, Tomenson B. Estimating treatment effects from randomized clinical trials with noncompliance and loss to follow-up: the role of instrumental variable methods. *Stat Methods Med Res.* 2005;14(4):369-395.

5. MRC/BHF Heart Protection Study of cholesterol lowering with simvastatin in 20,536 high-risk individuals: a randomised placebo-controlled trial. *Lancet.* 2002; 360(9326):7-22.

6. Ruiz-Canela M, Martinez-Gonzalez MA, de Irala-Estevez J. Intention to treat analysis is related to methodological quality. *BMJ.* 2000;320(7240):1007-1008.

7. Hollis S, Campbell F. What is meant by intention to treat analysis? survey of published randomised controlled trials. *BMJ.* 1999;319(7211):670-674.

8. Ioannidis JP, Bassett R, Hughes MD, Volberding PA, Sacks HS, Lau J. Predictors and impact of patients lost to follow-up in a long-term randomized trial of immediate versus deferred antiretroviral treatment. *J Acquir Immune Defic Syndr Hum Retrovirol.* 1997;16(1):22-30.

9. Silverstein FE, Graham DY, Senior JR, et al. Misoprostol reduces serious gastrointestinal complications in patients with rheumatoid arthritis receiving nonsteroidal anti-inflammatory drugs: a randomized, double-blind, placebo-controlled trial. *Ann Intern Med.* 1995;123(4):241-249.

10. Harris ST, Watts NB, Genant HK, et al. Effects of risedronate treatment on vertebral and nonvertebral fractures in women with postmenopausal osteoporosis: a randomized controlled trial: Vertebral Efficacy With Risedronate Therapy (VERT) Study Group. *JAMA.* 1999;282(14):1344-1352.

N-OF-1 RANDOMIZED CONTROLLED TRIALS

Gordon Guyatt, Roman Jaeschke,
and Thomas McGinn

IN THIS CHAPTER:

INTRODUCTION

Clinicians should use the results of *randomized controlled trials (RCTs)* of groups of patients to guide their clinical practice. When deciding which management approach will be best for an individual patient, however, clinicians cannot always rely on the results of RCTs. An RCT addressing the particular issue may not be available; for example, some conditions are so rare that randomized trials are not feasible. Furthermore, even when a relevant RCT generates a clear answer, its result may not apply to an individual patient. First, if the patient is very different from trial participants, the trial results may not be applicable to that patient (see Chapter 11.1, Applying Results to Individual Patients). Second, regardless of the overall trial results, some similar patients may benefit from a given therapy, whereas others receive no benefit. Clinicians may have particularly strong reservations about applying RCT results to individuals when results have shown small *treatment effects* of questionable importance.

These considerations lead clinicians to conduct *trials of therapy*, in which the patient begins treatment and the subsequent clinical course determines whether treatment is continued. Many factors may, however, mislead physicians conducting conventional trials of therapy. The patient may have improved anyway, even without any medication. Physicians' and patients' optimism may result in misinterpretation of the therapeutic trial results. Finally, people often feel better when they are taking a new medication even when it does not have any specific activity against their illness (the *placebo effect*); this may also lead to a misleading interpretation of the value of the new treatment.

To avoid these pitfalls, clinicians must conduct trials of therapy with safeguards that minimize these *biases*. Potential safeguards include repeatedly administering and withdrawing the *target treatment*, performing quantitative measurements of the *target outcomes*, and keeping both patients and clinicians *blind* to the treatment being administered. Investigators routinely use such safeguards in RCTs involving large numbers of patients.

To determine the best care for an individual patient, clinicians can conduct RCTs in individual patients (*n-of-1 RCTs*). In contrast to most of this book, which provides a guide to using the medical literature, this chaper provides an approach to applying the principles of *evidence-based medicine* to conduct an n-of-1 RCT in your own practice.

N-OF-1 RANDOMIZED CONTROLLED TRIALS: STUDY DESIGN

Although there are many ways of conducting n-of-1 RCTs, the method we have found to be most widely applicable can be summarized as follows:

1. A clinician and patient agree to test a therapy (the *experimental therapy*) for its ability to improve or control the *symptoms, signs,* or other manifestations (the *treatment targets*) of the patient's ailment.

2. The patient then undergoes pairs of treatment periods organized so that one period of each pair applies the experimental therapy and the other period applies either an alternative treatment or placebo (Figure 9.5-1). The order of these 2 periods within each pair is *randomized* by a coin toss or any other method that ensures that the patient is equally likely to receive the experimental or control therapy during any treatment period.

3. Whenever possible, a pharmacist independently prepares medication to ensure that both the clinician and the patient are blind to when the patient is receiving the treatment and alternative therapies (see the section below entitled "Is There a Pharmacist Who Can Help?").

4. The clinician monitors the treatment targets, often through a patient diary, to document the effect of the treatment currently being applied.

5. Pairs of treatment periods are replicated until the clinician and patient are convinced that the experimental therapy is effective, causes *harm*, or has no effect on the treatment targets. This usually requires a minimum of 3 pairs of treatment periods.

We will now describe an n-of-1 RCT in detail. To facilitate its illustration, each step will address a question that must be answered before proceeding to the next step, as summarized in Table 9.5-1.

FIGURE 9.5-1

Basic Design for n-of-1 Randomized Controlled Trial

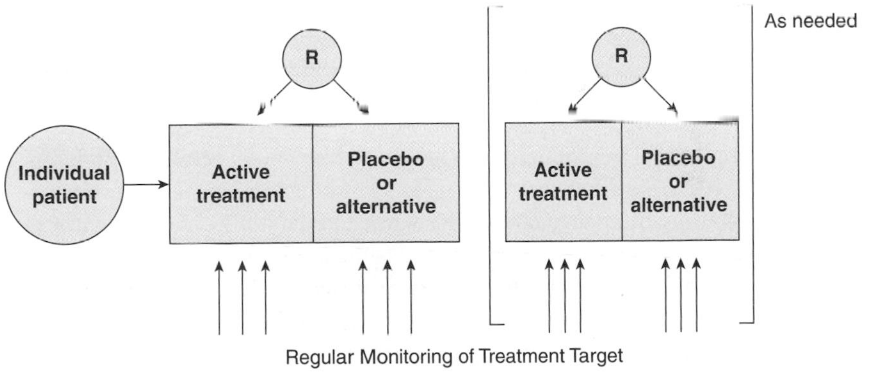

Circled R indicates that the order of placebo and active periods in each pair is determined by random allocation. Bracketed pair with "As needed" indicates that, beyond the first pair of treatment periods, as many additional pairs of treatment periods as necessary are conducted until patient and physician are convinced of the efficacy—or lack of efficacy—of the trial medication.

Reproduced from Carruthers et al.[1] Copyright © 2000, with permission from the McGraw-Hill Companies.

TABLE 9.5-1

Guidelines for n-of-1 Randomized Controlled Trials

Is an n-of-1 RCT indicated for this patient?

Is the effectiveness of the treatment really in doubt?

If effective, will the treatment be continued long term?

Is an n-of-1 RCT feasible in this patient?

Is the patient eager to collaborate in designing and carrying out an n-of-1 RCT?

Does the treatment have rapid onset and termination of action?

Is an optimal duration of treatment feasible?

Are there patient-important targets of treatment amenable to measurement?

Can you identify criteria to end the n-of-1 RCT?

Is there a pharmacist who can help?

Are strategies in place for the interpretation of the data?

Abbreviation: RCT, randomized controlled trial.

Reproduced from Carruthers et al.[1] Copyright © 2000, with permission from the McGraw-Hill Companies.

Is an n-of-1 Randomized Controlled Trial Indicated for This Patient?

Because n-of-1 RCTs are unnecessary for some ailments (such as self-limited illnesses) and unsuited for some treatments (such as acute or rapidly evolving illness, surgical procedures, or the *prevention* of distant adverse outcomes such as death, stroke, or myocardial infarction), at the outset it is important to determine whether an n-of-1 RCT really is indicated for the patient and treatment in question. If an n-of-1 RCT is appropriate, the answer to each of the following questions should be yes.

Is the Effectiveness of the Treatment Really in Doubt?

One or several RCTs may have shown that the treatment in question is highly effective. If, however, 50% or more of patients in such trials have proved unresponsive, an n-of-1 RCT may still be appropriate. Calculations of *numbers needed to treat* suggest that this will almost always be the case, regardless of whether the treatments are designed to prevent major adverse events or to improve health-related quality of life.[2] Numbers needed to treat of 2 or less are extremely uncommon.

For example, in a randomized trial of selective serotonin reuptake inhibitors (SSRIs) to reduce the frequency of hot flashes in women experiencing postmenopausal symptoms, more than 60% of the women in the study experienced a 50% reduction in symptoms.[3] Although these results are impressive, the treatment still leaves a large percentage of women to experience significant symptoms despite effective therapy. In a woman with an equivocal response to SSRIs, an n-of-1 trial may be appropriate to definitively sort out treatment effectiveness.

On the other hand, a patient may have exhibited such a dramatic response to the treatment that both clinician and patient are convinced that it works. N-of-1 RCTs are best reserved for the situations presented in Table 9.5-2.

TABLE 9.5-2

When to Conduct an n-of-1 Randomized Controlled Trial

1. The clinician is uncertain whether a treatment that has not yet been started will work in a particular patient.

2. The patient has started taking a medication, but neither patient nor clinician is confident that a treatment is really providing benefit.

3. Neither the clinician nor the patient is confident of the optimal dose of a medication the patient is receiving or should receive.

4. A patient has symptoms that both the clinician and the patient suspect—but are not certain—are caused by the adverse effects of the medications.

5. The patient has so far insisted on taking a treatment that the clinician believes is useless or harmful, and although logically constructed arguments have not persuaded a patient, a negative result of an n-of-1 RCT might.

Abbreviation: RCT, randomized controlled trial.

Reproduced from Carruthers et al.[1] Copyright © 2000, with permission from the McGraw-Hill Companies.

If Effective, Will the Treatment Be Continued on a Long-Term Basis?

If the underlying condition is self-limited and treatment will be continued only during the short term, an n-of-1 RCT may not be worthwhile. N-of-1 RCTs are most useful when conditions are chronic and maintenance therapy is likely to be prolonged.

Is an n-of-1 Randomized Controlled Trial Feasible in This Patient?

The clinician may wish to determine the efficacy of treatment in an individual patient, but the patient, the ailment, or the treatment may not lend itself to the n-of-1 approach.

Is the Patient Eager to Collaborate in Designing and Carrying Out an n-of-1 Randomized Controlled Trial?

N-of-1 RCTs are indicated only when patients can fully understand the nature of the experiment and are enthusiastic about participating. The n-of-1 RCT is a cooperative venture between clinician and patient.

Does the Treatment Have Rapid Onset and Termination of Action?

N-of-1 RCTs are much easier to carry out when positive treatment effects, if they are indeed present, manifest themselves within a few days. Although it may be possible to conduct n-of-1 RCTs with drugs that have a longer latency for the development of signs of efficacy (such as disease-remitting therapy in patients with rheumatoid arthritis, or use of antidepressants in patients with depression), the requirement for very long treatment periods before the effect can be evaluated may prove prohibitive.

Similarly, treatments whose effects cease abruptly when they are withdrawn are most suitable for n-of-1 RCTs. If the treatment continues to act long after it is stopped, a prolonged *washout period* may be necessary. If this washout period lasts longer than a few days, the feasibility of the trial is compromised. Similarly, treatments that have the potential to cure the underlying condition—or to lead to a permanent change in the treatment target—are not suitable for n-of-1 RCTs.

Is an Optimal Duration of Treatment Feasible?

Although short periods of treatment boost the feasibility of n-of-1 RCTs, the trials may need to be long to be valid. For example, if active therapy takes a few days to reach full effect and a few days to cease acting once it is stopped, avoiding distortion from these delayed peak effects and washout periods requires relatively long treatment periods. Thus, our n-of-1 RCTs of theophylline in patients with asthma use treatment periods of at least 10 days: 3 days to allow the drug to reach steady state or washout and 7 days thereafter to monitor the patient's response to treatment.

In addition, because many n-of-1 RCTs test a treatment's ability to prevent or mitigate attacks or exacerbations (such as migraines or seizures), each treatment period must be long enough to include an attack or exacerbation. A rough rule of thumb, called the *inverse rule of 3s*, tells us the following: If an event occurs, on average, once every x days, we need to observe $3x$ days to be 95% confident of observing at least 1 event. For example, applying this rule in a patient with familial Mediterranean fever with attacks that occur, on average, once every 2 weeks, we choose treatment periods of at least 6 weeks.

Are There Patient-Important Targets of Treatment Amenable to Measurement?

The targets of treatment, or outcome measures, usually go beyond a set of physical signs (eg, the rigidity and tremor of parkinsonism or the jugular venous distention and the S3, S4, and pulmonary crackles of congestive heart failure), a laboratory test (eg, serum erythrocyte sedimentation rate or serum blood sugar, uric acid, and creatinine levels), or a measure of patient performance (eg, recordings of respiratory peak flow or results of a 6-minute walk test). Each of these is only an indirect measure of the patient's quality of life.

In most situations, it is not only possible but also preferable to assess the patient's symptoms and feelings of well-being (or lack of well-being). Clinicians can, in a simple fashion, apply principles of measurement of quality of life to n-of-1 RCTs (see Chapter 10.5, Measuring Patients' Experience). To begin with, ask the patient to identify the most troubling symptoms or problems he or she is experiencing and then decide which of them is likely to respond to the experimental treatment. This responsive subset of symptoms or problems forms the basis of a self-administered patient diary or questionnaire.

For example, a patient with chronic airflow limitation identified the problem as shortness of breath while walking up stairs, bending, or vacuuming.[4] A patient with fibromyalgia identified fatigue, aches and pains, morning stiffness, and sleep disturbance as problems that became the treatment targets for the illness.[5]

You can use a number of formats for the questionnaire to record the patient's symptoms. Figure 9.5-2 shows a data sheet from an n-of-1 RCT examining the effectiveness of ketanserin in Raynaud phenomenon. For some patients, a daily symptom rating may work best; for others, a weekly summary may be better. The best way of presenting response options to patients is as graded descriptions of

FIGURE 9.5-2

N-of-1 Randomized Controlled Trial—Sample Data Sheet

Physician: _____

Patient: _____

Sex: Male   Female   Date of birth _____ _____ _____

Diagnosis: _____

Occupation: _____

Present medications: _____

Trial medication: Ketanserin   Dose: _____

Duration of study periods: 2 Weeks

Outcomes: Symptom ratings

Informed consent obtained (please sign): _____

Answers to symptom questions, pair 1, period 1:

1. How many episodes of Raynaud phenomenon did you have in the last week?
   First week (to be completed on _____ _____) _____
   Second week (to be completed on _____ _____) _____

2. On average, in comparison with your usual episodes, how long were the attacks?
   1. Very long; as long as or longer than they have ever been
   2. Very long; almost as long as they have ever been
   3. Longer than usual
   4. As long as usual
   5. Not as long as usual
   6. Not nearly as long as usual
   7. Very short; as brief as or briefer than they have ever been

   Write in the number that best describes your experience for each week.
   First week (to be completed on   _____ _____) _____
   Second week (to be completed on _____ _____) _____

3. On average, in comparison with your usual episodes, how severe were the attacks?
   1. Very bad; as severe as or more severe than they have ever been
   2. Very bad; almost as severe as they have ever been
   3. More severe than usual
   4. About as severe as usual
   5. Not as severe as usual
   6. Not nearly as severe as usual
   7. Very mild; as mild as or milder than they have ever been

   Write in the number that best describes your experience for each week.
   First week (to be completed on _____ _____) _____
   Second week (to be completed on _____ _____) _____

symptoms ranging from none to severe. One example of such graded descriptions might be "no shortness of breath," "a little shortness of breath," "moderate shortness of breath," and "extreme shortness of breath." Constructing simple symptom questionnaires allows the patient and the clinician to collaborate in quantifying the patient's symptoms, on which the analysis of the n-of-1 RCT relies.

You can use a patient diary or questionnaire to measure nausea, gastrointestinal disturbances, dizziness, or other common adverse effects, along with symptoms of the primary condition. In n-of-1 RCTs designed to determine whether medication adverse effects are responsible for a patient's symptoms (for example, whether a patient's fatigue is caused by an antihypertensive agent), adverse effects become the primary treatment targets.

Can You Identify Criteria to End the n-of-1 Randomized Controlled Trial?

If the clinician and patient decide not to specify the number of pairs of treatment periods in advance, they can stop anytime they are convinced that the experimental treatment ought to be stopped or continued indefinitely. Thus, if they find a dramatic improvement in the treatment target between the 2 periods of the first pair, both clinician and patient may want to stop the trial immediately and unblind the sequence of medications. On the other hand, if patient and clinician perceive no or only a minimal difference between the 2 periods of each pair, both the clinician and the patient may need 3, 4, or even 5 pairs before confidently concluding that the treatment is or is not effective.

If, however, one wishes to conduct a formal statistical analysis of data from the n-of-1 RCT, specifying in advance the number of pairs will strengthen the analysis. Regardless of whether they specify number of treatment periods in advance, we recommend that clinicians resist the temptation and refrain from breaking the code until they are certain they are ready to terminate the study.

Is There a Pharmacist Who Can Help?

In most instances, conducting an n-of-1 RCT that incorporates all the aforementioned safeguards against bias and misinterpretation requires collaboration between the clinician and a pharmacist who can prepare placebos identical to the active medication in appearance, taste, and texture. Occasionally, pharmaceutical firms can supply such placebos. More often, however, you will want your local pharmacist to repackage the active medication. If it comes in tablet form, the pharmacist can crush and repackage it in capsule form—unless the medication is a modified-release preparation whose absorption characteristics will be altered. Thus, a clinician who is interested in the effect of a modified-release preparation may have to forgo blinding if the duration of action of the medication is a crucial issue.

If you need a placebo, the pharmacist can fill identical-appearing placebo capsules with lactose. Although it is time consuming, preparation of placebos is not technically difficult. Our average cost for preparing medication for n-of-1 studies in which placebos have not been available from a pharmaceutical company has been $200 (Canadian dollars). In considering the cost, the large savings that follow from abandoning a useless or harmful treatment that might otherwise be continued indefinitely, along with the reassurance of knowing that long-term treatment really works, emphasize the relatively trivial medication cost of the n-of-1 RCT.

The pharmacist is also charged with preparing the randomization schedule (which requires nothing more than a coin toss for each pair of treatment periods). This allows the clinician, along with the patient, to remain blind to allocation. The pharmacist also may be helpful in planning the design of the trial by providing information regarding the anticipated time to onset of action and the washout period, thus helping with decisions about the duration of study periods.

Are Strategies for the Interpretation of the Trial Data in Place?

Once you carefully gather data on the treatment targets in your n-of-1 trial, how will you interpret them? One approach is to simply plot the data and visually inspect the results. Evaluation of results by visual inspection has a long and distinguished record in the psychology literature concerning single-subject designs.[6,7] Visual inspection is simple and easy. Its major disadvantage is that it is vulnerable to viewer or *observer bias*.

An alternative approach to analysis of data from n-of-1 RCTs is to use a test of *statistical significance*. The simplest test would be based on the likelihood of a patient's preferring active treatment in each pair of treatment periods. This situation is analogous to the likelihood of heads coming up repeatedly on a series of coin tosses. For example, the likelihood of a patient's preferring active treatment to placebo during 3 consecutive pairs if the treatment were ineffective would be $(1/2) \times (1/2) \times (1/2) = 1/8$, or 0.125. The disadvantage of this approach (which is called the *sign test*) is that it lacks *power*; 5 pairs must be conducted before there is any chance of reaching conventional levels of statistical significance.

A second statistical strategy is to use Student t *test*. The *t* test offers increased power because not only the direction but also the strength of the treatment effect in each pair is taken into account.

To avoid misleading results based on random highs or lows, if you plan a statistical test, you should ideally specify the number of treatment periods before the study begins.

To conduct a paired *t* test, derive a single score for each pair by subtracting the mean score of the placebo period from the mean score of the active period. These differences in scores constitute the data for the paired *t*; the number of *degrees of freedom* is simply the number of pairs minus 1. Statistical software programs that will facilitate quick calculation of the P value are available.

Table 9.5-3 presents the results of an n-of-1 RCT. In this trial, we tested the effectiveness of amitriptyline in a dose of 10 mg at bedtime for a patient with fibromyalgia.[7] Each week, the patient separately rated the severity of a number of symptoms, including fatigue, aches and pains, and sleep disturbance, on a 7-point scale in which a higher score represented better function. The treatment periods were 4 weeks long, and 3 pairs were undertaken. Table 9.5-3 presents the mean scores for each of the 24 weeks of the study.

The first step in analyzing the results of the study is to calculate the mean score for each period (presented in the far right-hand column of Table 9.5-3). In each pair, the score favored the active treatment. The sign test tells us that the *probability* of this result occurring by chance if the treatment was ineffective is $(1/2) \times (1/2) \times 1/2 = 1/8$ (or 0.125).

This analysis, however, ignores the magnitude and consistency of the difference between the active and placebo treatments. A paired *t* test in which data from the same patient during different periods are paired takes these factors into account. We did our *t* test by entering the data from the pairs of results into a simple

TABLE 9.5-3

Results of an n-of-1 Randomized Controlled Trial in a Patient With Fibrositis[a]

	Severity Score				
Treatment	Week 1	Week 2	Week 3	Week 4	Mean Score
Pair 1					
Active	4.43	4.86	4.71	4.71	4.68
Placebo	4.43	4.00	4.14	4.29	4.22
Pair 2					
Active	4.57	4.89	5.29	5.29	5.01
Placebo	3.86	4.00	4.29	4.14	4.07
Pair 3					
Active	4.29	5.00	5.43	5.43	5.04
Placebo	3.71	4.14	4.43	4.43	4.18

[a]The active drug was amitriptyline hydrochloride. Higher scores represent better function.

Reproduced from Carruthers et al.[1] Copyright © 2000, with permission from the McGraw-Hill Companies.

statistical program: 4.68 and 4.22; 5.01 and 4.07; 5.04 and 4.18. The program tells us that the t value is 5.07 and there are 2 degrees of freedom; the associated P value is .04. This analysis makes us considerably more confident that the consistent difference in favor of the active drug is unlikely to have occurred by chance.

The use of n-of-1 RCTs to improve patient care does not depend on statistical analysis of the results. Even if statistical analysis is not used in the interpretation of the trial, the strategies of randomization, blinding, replication, and quantifying *outcomes*, when accompanied by careful visual inspection of the data, still allow a much more rigorous assessment of effectiveness of treatment than is possible in conventional clinical practice.

ETHICS OF N-OF-1 RANDOMIZED CONTROLLED TRIALS

Is conducting an n-of-1 RCT a clinical task or a research undertaking? If the former, is it the sort of clinical procedure, analogous to an invasive diagnostic test, that requires written informed consent? We would argue that the n-of-1 RCT can be—and should be—a part of routine clinical practice.

Nevertheless, there are a number of important ethical issues to consider. Patients should be fully aware of the nature of the study in which they are participating, and there should be no element of deception in the use of placebos as part of the study. Clinicians should obtain written informed consent; see Figure 9.5-3 for an example of a consent form. Patients should be aware that they can terminate the trial at any time without

FIGURE 9.5-3

Consent Form for n-of-1 Randomized Trial

We think that it would help you to take part in one of these therapeutic trials of [NAME OF DRUG]. We will conduct a number of pairs of periods. Each period will be [DURATION OF PERIOD]. During one period of each pair, you will be taking the active treatment, and during the other you will be using the placebo. The placebo is a pill that looks exactly like the medication but does not contain the active ingredients. If at any time during the study you are feeling worse, we can consider that treatment period at an end and can go on to the next treatment. Therefore, if you begin to feel worse, just call my office at [INSERT NUMBER], and I will get in touch with you.

If you don't think this new way of conducting a therapeutic trial is a good idea for you, we will try the new drug in the usual way. Your decision will not interfere with your treatment in any way. You can decide to stop the trial at any time and this will not interfere with your treatment. All information we collect during the trial will remain confidential.

PATIENT SIGNATURE _____

WITNESS SIGNATURE _____

PHYSICIAN SIGNATURE _____

DATE _____

jeopardizing their care or their relationship with their physician. Finally, follow-up should be soon enough to prevent any important deleterious consequences of institution or withdrawal of therapy. Discussing the rationale for, and value of, n-of-1 RCTs with an institutional review board representative can help to clarify local policies.

THE IMPACT OF N-OF-1 RANDOMIZED CONTROLLED TRIALS ON CLINICAL PRACTICE

We have reported a series of more than 50 n-of-1 RCTs, each one designed to improve the care being delivered to an individual patient.[8] Patients had a wide variety of conditions, including chronic airflow limitation, asthma, fibrositis, arthritis, syncope, anxiety, insomnia, and angina pectoris. In general, these trials were successful in sorting out whether the treatment was effective. In approximately a third of the trials, the ultimate treatment differed from that which would have been given had the trial not been conducted. In most of the trials in which treatment differed from that which would have been given had the trial not been conducted, medication that would otherwise have been given during the long term was discontinued. Other clinical groups have reported their experience with n-of-1 RCTs, generally confirming the feasibility and usefulness of the approach.[9-11] Table 9.5-4 presents a set of conditions and therapeutic options that are excellent candidates for n-of-1 RCTs.

These reports do not definitively answer the question about whether patients who undergo n-of-1 RCTs are better off than those whose treatment regimen is determined by conventional methods. The most rigorous test of the usefulness of n-of-1 RCTs would be a randomized trial. Three such trials, in which investigators randomized patients to conventional care or to n-of-1 RCTs, have addressed the effect of n-of-1 RCTs.

The same group of investigators conducted 2 of these studies[12,13]; both examined the use of theophylline in patients with chronic airflow limitation. The investigators found that, although using n-of-1 RCTs did not affect quality of life or functional status of patients initially receiving theophylline, fewer patients in the n-of-1 RCT groups ended up receiving the drug in the long term. Thus, n-of-1 RCTs saved patients the expense, inconvenience, and potential toxicity of long-term theophylline therapy of no use to them.

The third trial randomized 27 patients with osteoarthritis who were uncertain as to whether adding nonsteroidal anti-inflammatory drugs to conventional management reduced their pain, and another 24 similar patients to an n-of-1 randomized

TABLE 9.5-4

Examples of n-of-1 Randomized Controlled Trials

Type of Condition	Possible Outcome Measures	Example of Intervention
Chronic headache	Duration, severity, and frequency of headache	Tricyclic antidepressant or β-blockers
Low back pain	Pain or function	Cyclobenzaprine or acupuncture[a]
Recurrent syncope	Syncopal episodes	β-Blockers
Chronic airway obstruction	Dyspnea, peak flow rates	Aerosolized β-agonists, ipratropium, steroids
Fibromyalgia	Aches and pains, fatigue, sleep disruption	Low-dose tricyclic antidepressant
Fatigue	Fatigue	Ginseng tablets[a]
Insomnia	Sleep disruption, satisfaction	Low-dose tricyclic antidepressant
Anxiety	Anxiety, formal anxiety questionnaire such as Beck	Black cohosh[a]
Hot flashes of menopause	Frequency and severity of hot flashes	Clonidine or soy milk[a]

[a]Alternative therapies with limited evidence to support efficacy but frequently used by patients, sometimes with substantial costs.

trial comparing diclofenac and misoprostol (the latter agent to avoid gastrointestinal adverse effects) to placebo.[14] The results showed few differences between groups (similar proportion of patients ended up taking diclofenac, similar quality of life), though all quality-of-life measures showed trends in favor of the n-of-1 arm. Costs were higher in the n-of-1 arm. These results suggest that n-of-1 RCTs are unlikely to be uniformly superior to conventional trials. Understanding when n-of-1 RCTs will benefit patients will require further study.

In summary, the n-of-1 approach clearly has potential for improving the quality of medical care and the judicious use of medication in patients with chronic disease. Using the guidelines offered here, clinicians will find conducting n-of-1 RCTs feasible, highly informative, and stimulating.

References

1. Carruthers SG, Hoffman BB, Melmon KL, Nierenberg DF, eds. *Melmon and Morelli's Clinical Pharmacology: Basic Principles in Therapeutics*, 4th ed. New York, NY: McGraw-Hill; 2000.

2. Guyatt G, Juniper E, Walter S, Griffith L, Goldstein R. Interpreting treatment effects in randomised trials. *BMJ.* 1998;316(7132):690-693.

3. Stearns V, Beebe K, Iyengar M, Dube E. Paroxetine controlled release in the treatment of menopausal hot flashes: a randomized controlled trial. *JAMA.* 2003;289(2):2827-2834.

4. Patel A, Jaeschke R, Guyatt G, Newhouse M, Keller J. Clinical usefulness of n of 1 randomized controlled trials in patients with nonreversible chronic airflow limitation. *Am Rev Respir Dis.* 1991;144(4):962-964.

5. Jaeschke R, Adachi J, Guyatt G, Keller J, Wong B. Clinical usefulness of amitriptyline in fibromyalgia: the results of 23 N-of-1 randomized controlled trials. *J Rheumatol.* 1991;18(3):447-451.

6. Kratchowill T. *Single Subject Research: Strategies for Evaluating Change*. New York, NY: Academic Press; 1978.

7. Kazdin A. *Single-case Research Designs: Methods for Clinical and Applied Settings*. New York, NY: Oxford University Press; 1982.

8. Guyatt G, Keller J, Jaeschke R, Rosenbloom D, Adachi J, Newhouse M. The n-of-1 randomized controlled trial: clinical usefulness: our three-year experience. *Ann Intern Med.* 1990;112(4):293-299.

9. Menard J, Serrurier D, Bautier P, Plouin P, Corvol P. Crossover design to test antihypertensive drugs with self-recorded blood pressure. *Hypertension.* 1988;11(2):153-159.

10. Johannessen T. Controlled trials in single subject, 1: value in clinical medicine. *BMJ.* 1991;303(6795):173-174.

11. Larson E, Ellsworth A, Oas J. Randomized clinical trials in single patients during a 2-year period. *JAMA.* 1993;270(22):2708-2712.

12. Mahon J, Laupacis A, Donner A, Wood T. Randomised study of no of 1 trials versus standard practice. *BMJ.* 1996;312(7038):1069-1074.

13. Mahon J, Laupacis A, Hodder R, et al. Theophylline for irreversible chronic airflow limitation: a randomized study comparing n of 1 trials to standard practice. *Chest.* 1999;115(1):38-48.

14. Pope J, Prashker M, Anderson J. The efficacy and cost effectiveness of N of 1 studies with diclofenac compared to standard treatment with nonsteroidal antiinflammatory drugs in osteoarthritis. *J Rheumatol.* 2004;31(1):140-149.

ADVANCED TOPICS IN THE VALIDITY
OF THERAPY TRIALS

CLINICAL
DECISION
SUPPORT
SYSTEMS

Adrienne Randolph, Anne Holbrook, Amit Garg,
Brian Haynes, Pierre Durieux, Deborah J. Cook,
and Gordon Guyatt

IN THIS CHAPTER:

What Are the Results?

What Is the Effect of the Clinical Decision Support System?

How Precise Is the Estimate of the Effect?

How Can I Apply the Results to Patient Care?

What Elements of the Clinical Decision Support System Are Required?

Is the Clinical Decision Support System Exportable to a New Site?

Are Clinicians in Your Setting Likely to Accept the Clinical Decision Support System?

Do the Benefits of the Clinical Decision Support System Justify the Risks and Costs?

Clinical Resolution

CLINICAL SCENARIO

Can Clinical Decision Support Systems Change Prescribing Behavior?

As director of a hospital-based pediatric outpatient clinic, you oversee the care delivered by 45 pediatric residents and 5 nurse practitioners. Last year, the hospital infection control audit of charts in your clinic revealed that antibiotic use was inappropriate for 47% of children presenting with respiratory symptoms most likely of viral origin. They urged you to decrease the inappropriate use of antibiotics in your clinic and set a target of a 50% reduction throughout the next 12 months. Your response included education of trainees on appropriate evidence-based antibiotic prescribing during 4 lunches throughout the year, insistence that trainees complete a relevant test administered in an online scenario-based format, and reminders to attending physicians to carefully oversee resident prescribing, emphasizing the need to decrease inappropriate antibiotic use. You just received the results of this year's audit, and it shows only a 2% decrease in the overall rate of inappropriate antibiotic prescribing. In thinking about further strategies that you need, you remember that all the residents now have a handheld personal digital assistant (PDA) in preparation for a computer-based order entry system. Could you use this tool to more effectively decrease inappropriate antibiotic prescribing?

FINDING THE EVIDENCE

When you return home that night, you use PubMed (http://www.ncbi.nlm.nih.gov) to search for information regarding use of computers for decision support in antibiotic prescribing. You click on "Clinical Queries" on the left side of the page under "PubMed Services." You are taken to the "Search by Clinical Category" section, where you click on "therapy" and "broad, sensitive search." You type in "decision support antibiotics computer" (without the quotes). One citation impresses you because its title suggests that it represents a directly relevant randomized trial: "Clinical Decision Support and Appropriateness of Antimicrobial Prescribing: A Randomized Trial." The abstract of this article concludes that "...CDSSs [*clinical decision support systems*] implemented in rural primary care settings reduced overall antimicrobial use and improved appropriateness of antimicrobial selection for acute respiratory tract infections."[1]

The green bar on the icon to the left of the citation indicates that the full text of the article is freely available. You left click on the icon, click the red "JAMA" in the upper right-hand corner of the screen, and follow instructions to obtain your free download. In this study,[1] 12 rural communities in 2 US states (2 larger and 4 smaller communities in each state) were *randomly allocated* to a community intervention plus CDSS or to the same community intervention alone. The intervention was complex, with each community receiving 2 waves of education directed at community leaders, parents, media, physician offices, and pharmacies during the first year, followed by patient self-management tips for respiratory infections and key questions to ask clinicians. In addition, all the participating primary-care clinicians in the 6 communities randomized to CDSS received 3 types of CDSS, 2 paper based and 1 PDA based (Table 9.6-1). The rationale for providing more than 1 type of CDSS was to increase the number of choices and, therefore, the willingness of clinicians to participate. Each intervention was aimed at reducing inappropriate prescribing of antimicrobial drugs for acute respiratory tract infections. As an extra precaution, another *control group* of 6 additional eligible but nonselected communities served as a randomly chosen nonstudy reference group using retail pharmacy data.

TABLE 9.6-1

Description of the Community-Based Intervention and the Clinical Decision Support System (CDSS) Intervention

1. Community intervention alone: Multifaceted education and media regarding antimicrobial resistance, self-management of common respiratory infections, and questions for patients to ask their clinicians

2. CDSS intervention: Community intervention (described above) plus 3 CDSS acute respiratory tract management tools (described below) to be used with individual patients to guide diagnosis and therapy, plus feedback on performance and tips on patient management. Clinicians could choose to use any or all of the tools:

   i. PDA-based diagnostic and therapeutic recommendations based on patient-specific information plus a pneumonia severity index score

   ii. Paper-based chart documentation tool leading to appropriate treatment recommendations

   iii. Paper-based graphic flowchart guiding diagnosis and treatment options

WHAT ARE CLINICAL DECISION SUPPORT SYSTEMS?

Clinicians depend on computers. Laboratory data management software, pharmacy information management systems, applications for tracking patient location through admission and discharge, and advanced life support technologies such as mechanical ventilators and dialysis machines are among the many types of computerized systems that have become integral to the modern hospital. These devices and systems capture, transform, display, or analyze data for use in clinical decision making. The term *clinical decision support systems (CDSSs)* is defined by the MEDLINE Medical Subject Headings (MeSH) scope notes as "computer-based information systems used to integrate clinical and patient information and provide support for decision-making in patient care."

In CDSSs that are computer based, detailed individual patient data are entered into a computer program that sorts and matches data to *algorithms*, ultimately generating patient-specific assessments or recommendations for clinicians.[2] Table 9.6-2 describes the general types of CDSSs according to their function.[3]

As an example of one type of CDSS, the Antibiotic Assistant[10] is a CDSS that implements guidelines to assist physicians in ordering antibiotic agents. This system recommends the most cost-effective antibiotic regimen while taking into account the site of infection, the epidemiology of organisms in patients with this infection at the particular hospital, the efficacy of the chosen antibiotic regimen, the patient's renal function and drug allergies, and the cost of therapy.

The primary reason to invest in computer support is to improve *quality of care* and, ultimately, *health outcomes*. If a computer system purports to aid clinical decisions, enhance patient care, and improve outcomes, then it should be subject to the same rules of testing as any other health care intervention. In this chapter, we describe how to use articles that evaluate the influence of a CDSS. We will limit our discussion to CDSSs that are designed to alter clinician behavior and thereby patient outcomes and in which initial evaluation has been completed and implementation has begun.

TABLE 9.6-2

Functions of Computer-Based Clinical Decision Support System

Function	Example
Alerting[4]	Highlighting out-of-range (either too high or too low) laboratory values
Reminding[4]	Reminding the clinician to schedule a mammogram
Critiquing[3,5]	Rejecting an inappropriate electronic order for a new drug
Interpreting[6]	Analyzing an electrocardiogram
Predicting[7]	Calculating risk of mortality from a severity of illness score
Diagnosing[8,9]	Listing a differential diagnosis for a patient with chest pain
Assisting[10]	Tailoring antibiotics for liver transplant and renal failure patients
Suggesting[11]	Generating suggestions for adjusting a mechanical ventilator

ARE THE RESULTS VALID?

In keeping with the approach of other chapters of this book, we will consider 3 primary questions related to the *validity* of research methods, the results, and clinical application of the results (Table 9.6 3). We will periodically refer to the article by Samore et al[1] evaluating the effect of clinical decision support on antibiotic prescribing.

When clinicians examine the effect of a CDSS on patient management or outcome, they should use the usual criteria for assessing an intervention. Thus, you will find that Table 9.6-3, which summarizes our approach to evaluating an article evaluating the influence of a CDSS, includes some of the criteria from our guide to therapy (see Chapter 6, Therapy) and some criteria from our guide to articles concerning harm (see Chapter 12, Harm) because randomization and other strategies used to reduce bias in *randomized controlled trials (RCTs)* may not be feasible in a CDSS evaluation. Our discussion includes only issues of particular importance in the evaluation of a CDSS.

Were Study Participants Randomized?
If Not, Did the Investigators Demonstrate Similarity in All Known Determinants of Prognosis or Adjust for Differences in the Analysis?
The validity of *observational studies* often used to evaluate a CDSS is limited (see Chapter 5, Why Study Results Mislead: Bias and Random Error). One observa-

TABLE 9.6-3

Using Articles Describing Clinical Decision Support Systems (CDSS)

Are the Results Valid?

   Were study participants randomized?

      If not, did the investigators demonstrate similarity in all known determinants of prognosis or adjust for differences in the analysis?

   If the intervention primarily targeted clinicians, was the clinician or clinician group the unit of analysis?

      Were study participants analyzed in the groups to which they were randomized?

      Was the control group unaffected by the CDSS?

   Was follow-up complete?

   Aside from the experimental intervention(s), were the groups treated equally?

   Was outcome assessed uniformly between the experimental and control groups?

What Are the Results?

   How large was the treatment effect?

   How precise was the estimate of the treatment effect?

How Can I Apply the Results to Patient Care?

   Were all clinically important outcomes considered?

   What elements of the CDSS are required?

   Is the CDSS exportable to a new site?

   Is the CDSS likely to be accepted by clinicians in your setting?

   Do the benefits of the CDSS justify the potential risks and costs?

tional design, the *before-after design*, compares outcomes before a technology is implemented with those after the system is implemented. The validity of this approach is threatened by the possibility that changes over time (called *secular trends*) in patient mix or in other aspects of health care delivery are responsible for changes that investigators may be tempted to attribute to the CDSS.

Consider a CDSS assisting physicians with the ordering of antibiotic drugs[10] implemented in the late 1980s that was associated with improvements in the cost-effectiveness of antibiotic ordering throughout the subsequent 5 years. Although this before-after study may appear compelling, changes in the health care system, including the advent of managed care, were occurring simultaneously during the study period. To control for secular trends, study investigators[10] compared antibiotic-prescribing practices to those of other US acute-care hospitals for the duration of the study. Of course, these other hospitals differed in many ways aside from the CDSS, limiting the validity of the comparison. Nevertheless, the addition of a concurrent control group strengthens the study design.

Investigators may also strengthen the before-after design by turning the intervention on and off multiple times, a type of *time series design*. Durieux et al[12] used such a design to evaluate whether a CDSS that provided recommendations for venous thromboembolism prevention for surgical patients improved prophylaxis use. There were three 10-week intervention periods alternating with four 10-week control periods, with a 4-week washout between each period. During each intervention period, *compliance* with practice guidelines improved significantly and then reverted to baseline during each control period.

Although alternating intervention and control periods strengthen a before-after design, random allocation of patients to a concurrent control group remains the strongest study design for evaluating therapeutic or *preventive* interventions. Of more than 100 CDSS studies considered in a recent review, 88% were randomized.[13]

If the Intervention Primarily Targeted Clinicians, Was the Clinician or Clinician Group the Unit of Analysis?

The *unit of analysis* is a special issue for CDSS evaluation. For most RCTs, the *unit of allocation* is the patient. Most CDSS evaluations target clinician behavior. Hence, investigators may randomize individual clinicians or clinician clusters such as health care teams, hospital wards, or outpatient practices.[14] Unfortunately, investigators using such designs often analyze their data as if they had randomized patients.[15,16] This mistake, the *unit of analysis error*, occurs frequently and can generate artificially low *P* values. Suspect a unit of analysis error if an article does not describe the number and characteristics (eg, level of clinical experience, sex, clinical specialties) of clinicians in each arm of a trial.[15,16]

To deepen your understanding of the problem, we will use an extreme example. Consider a study in which an investigator randomizes 2 teams of clinicians to a CDSS and randomizes another 2 teams to standard practice. During the course of the study, each team sees 10 000 patients. If the investigator analyzes the data as if patients were individually randomized, the sample size appears huge. However, it is plausible, perhaps even likely, that the teams' performance differed at baseline and those differences persisted throughout the study, independent of the CDSS. The actual sample size in this study is somewhere between 2 per group (the 4 teams; this would be the case if the teams were inherently different) and 10000 per group (which would be the case if the teams' performance were identical aside from the intervention).

A statistic called the *intraclass correlation* tells us about the strength of the relation between team and outcome (the more the teams are inherently different, the higher the correlation) and thus where in this spectrum the particular situation lies. If the intraclass correlation is high, then the sample size is closer to 2 (in this case) or the number of teams (in general). If it is low, the effective sample size is closer to the number of patients.

Obtaining a sufficient sample size can be difficult when randomizing physicians and health care teams. If only a few health care teams are available, investigators can pair them according to their similarities on numerous factors, and they can randomly allocate the intervention within each matched pair and use optimal techniques available for RCTs that use cluster randomization.[17-20] A *systematic review* of 88 RCTs evaluating the effect of CDSSs found that 43 of 88 used cluster randomization and 35 of 88 used cluster as the unit of analysis or adjusted for clustering in the analysis (*cluster analysis*).[13]

Were Participants Analyzed in the Groups to Which They Were Randomized?

Clinicians should attend to one other issue regarding randomization. Computer competency varies, and it is common for some clinicians to not use a CDSS, even when they are assigned to do so. Consider the following: If some clinicians assigned to CDSS fail or refuse to receive the intervention, should these clinicians be included in the analysis? The answer, counterintuitive to some, is yes (see Chapter 9.4, The Principle of Intention to Treat).

Randomization can accomplish the goal of balancing groups with respect to both known and unknown determinants of outcome only if patients (or clinicians) are analyzed according to the groups to which they are randomized, the *intention-to-treat principle*. Deleting or moving patients after randomization compromises or destroys the balance that randomization is designed to achieve (see Chapter 9.4, The Principle of Intention to Treat).

Was the Control Group Unaffected by the Clinical Decision Support System?

The extent to which physicians in the control group have access to all or part of the CDSS intervention threatens the validity of randomized trials. CDSS evaluations are particularly vulnerable to this problem of *contamination*. When the control group is influenced by the intervention, the effect of the CDSS may be diluted. Contamination may decrease or even eliminate a true intervention effect.

For example, Strickland and Hasson[21] randomly allocated patients to have changes in their level of mechanical ventilator support directed by a computer protocol or according to clinical judgment. Because the same physicians and respiratory therapists using the computer protocol were also managing the care of patients not assigned to the protocol, the apparent effect on weaning duration that the investigators observed might have been even larger had clinicians managing control-group patients been unaware of the computer protocol.

One method of preventing exposure of the control group to the CDSS—contamination—is to assign individual clinicians to use or not use the CDSS, which is often problematic because of cross-coverage of patients. Comparing the performance of wards or hospitals that do or do not use the CDSS is another possibility. Unfortunately, it is not always feasible to enroll a sufficient number of hospitals to avoid the unit of analysis problem that we described earlier: When sample size is small, randomization may fail to ensure prognostically similar groups.

Imaginative study designs can deal with this problem. For instance, in one study, one group of physicians received computerized guidelines for the management of asthma, whereas the other group received guidelines for the management of angina.[22] The 2 groups serve as a control for each other.

Aside From the Experimental Intervention, Were the Groups Treated Equally?

The results of studies evaluating interventions aimed at therapy or prevention are more believable if patients, their caregivers, and study personnel are *blind* to the treatment (see Chapter 6, Therapy). Blinding also diminishes the *placebo effect*, which in the case of CDSS may be the tendency of practitioners and patients to ascribe positive attributes to the use of a computer workstation. Although blinding the clinicians, patients, and study personnel to the presence of the computer-based CDSS may prevent this type of *bias*, blinding is usually not possible.

Lack of blinding can result in bias if interventions other than the treatment are differentially applied to the treatment and control groups, particularly if the use of effective nonstudy treatments is permitted at the physicians' discretion. Investigators can ameliorate concerns regarding lack of blinding if they describe permissible *cointerventions* and their differential use, standardize cointerventions,[23] or both to ensure that their application was similar in the treatment group and in the control group.

There are many elements of a CDSS unrelated to the computer. The CDSS may have a positive influence for unintended reasons, such as use of structured data collection forms and performance evaluations (respectively called the *checklist effect* and the *feedback effect*).[4,24] A related issue is the possible effect of observation on the CDSS group but not on the control group. Human performance may improve when participants are aware that their behavior is being observed (the *Hawthorne effect*)[25] or evaluated (the *sentinel effect*). The same behavior may not be exhibited when the monitoring of outcomes has stopped. Clinicians should consider the possibility of these effects in a study evaluating a CDSS and determine whether investigators have instituted strategies to minimize their effect. One such strategy is the uniform assessment of outcome that we describe in the next section.

Was Outcome Assessed Uniformly in the Experimental and Control Groups?

Unblinded study personnel who measure outcomes may provide different interpretations of marginal findings or differential encouragement during performance tests.[24] In some studies, the computer system may be used as a data collection tool to evaluate the outcome in the CDSS group. Using the information system to log episodes in the treatment group and using a manual system in the non-CDSS group can create a *data completeness bias*.[4] If the computer logs more episodes than the manual system, then it may appear that the CDSS group had more events, which could bias the outcome for or against the CDSS group. To prevent this bias, investigators should log outcomes similarly in both groups.

USING THE GUIDE

Returning to our opening scenario, the investigation of a CDSS to improve antimicrobial prescribing,[1] communities (and their indwelling patients and clinicians) were randomized, a cluster randomized study. Because the trial tests a multifaceted educational intervention aimed at the population as a whole, this seems sensible. The authors describe how communities were selected according to population size and the presence of at least 1 primary-care clinic and inpatient facility. The randomization was stratified by state and population size at a cutoff of 25000. Baseline characteristics of the 3 sets of communities (CDSS plus community intervention, community intervention alone, and control nonstudy communities) were similar.

To address their primary outcome, antibiotic use, the investigators chose an analysis plan (called *hierarchical regression*) that accounted for the design and avoided the unit of allocation problem we described earlier. Charts of randomly selected patients who had an acute respiratory illness and presented to any clinician in each of the 2 intervention communities were selected and reviewed for diagnoses and antibiotic appropriateness. Case-specific use of CDSS tools was not identifiable by the chart reviewers. The actual prescribing of antibiotics, derived from retail pharmacy volume of new prescriptions per month per community, was obtained from an international pharmacy data supplier. Although the movement of clinicians and patients between the study communities is not described, substantial relocation would be unlikely in a 21-month intervention period. All communities were followed for the study's duration.

In terms of cointerventions, it would be difficult in a large, multicenter RCT with hundreds of clinicians to be sure that other factors that might influence antibiotic prescribing were not at play. Pharmaceutic sales representative detailing, for example, might have changed. The presence of 2 control groups—one a less intensive intervention and the second a concurrent, nonstudy group—revealed a secular trend of increasing antibiotic prescribing during the monitoring period. The outcome, antimicrobial prescribing, was ascertained equally for the 2 intervention groups by using retail pharmacy volume and chart review, but only retail pharmacy prescribing could be ascertained for the nonstudy control group.

WHAT ARE THE RESULTS?

What Is the Effect of the Clinical Decision Support System?

The *Users' Guide* (see Chapter 6, Therapy) provides a discussion of *relative risk (RR)* and *relative risk reduction (RRR)*, *risk difference (RD)*, and *absolute risk reduction (ARR)*, which we use to provide a sense of the magnitude of a *treatment effect*. As we have discussed, for patients to benefit, a CDSS must change physician behavior, and that behavior change should positively affect the outcomes of patients. A CDSS could change physician behavior but have no influence on patient health outcomes. If implementation of a CDSS leads to improved patient health outcomes, it is more convincing that the outcome change is due to the CDSS if there is also proof that the CDSS altered the clinician behavior it was targeted to change (eg, if rates of deep venous thrombosis were reduced, this is more likely due to a CDSS if the targeted rates of effective thromboprophylaxis were increased).

How Precise Is the Estimate of the Effect?

Given a study of high validity, the *confidence interval* reflects the range in which the true effect of a CDSS might actually lie (see Chapter 6, Therapy; and Chapter 8, Confidence Intervals).

USING THE GUIDE

Returning to our opening clinical scenario, the investigators in the antimicrobial-prescribing CDSS study[1] report that the overall antimicrobial-prescribing rate decreased from 84.1 to 75.3 per 100 person-years in the CDSS arm vs 84.3 to 85.2 in community intervention alone and remained stable in the other communities ($P = .03$). In addition, antimicrobial prescribing for visits in the antibiotics "never-indicated" category during the postintervention period decreased from 35% to 24% (32% RRR) in CDSS communities and from 40% to 38% (5% RRR) in community intervention–alone communities ($P = .03$). A concomitant significant decrease in use of macrolides in CDSS communities but not in community intervention–alone communities was also reported.

HOW CAN I APPLY THE RESULTS TO PATIENT CARE?

Many of the issues specific to a CDSS arise in its application. Implementing the CDSS within your own environment may be challenging.

What Elements of the Clinical Decision Support System Are Required?

There are 2 major elements composing a CDSS: the logic that has been incorporated and the interface used to present the logic. Generally, RCTs of CDSSs cannot tell us the extent to which the logic of the system contributed to a difference in outcomes or whether the computer application was critical. To test whether the computer is needed requires that one group apply the protocol logic as written on paper and the other group use the same logic implemented in the computer. However, sometimes the logic is so complex that a computer is required for implementation. In addition, the CDSS intervention itself may be administered by research personnel or paid clinical staff receiving scant mention in the published report but without whom the effect of the system is seriously undermined.

Is the Clinical Decision Support System Exportable to a New Site?

For a CDSS to be exported to a new site, it must have the ability to be integrated with existing information systems and software. In addition, users at the new site must be able to maintain the system, and they must accept the system and ensure that it is kept up to date. Double charting occurs when systems require staff (usually nurses) to enter the data once into the computer and once again on a flow sheet. Systems that require double charting increase staff time devoted to documentation, frustrate users, and divert time that could be devoted to patient care. In general, experience suggests that systems that require double entry of data fail in clinical use.

Successful systems are easily integrated into the workflow and are time saving or time neutral for the clinician. Therefore, it is important to assess how the information necessary to run the decision support gets into the system—ideally, through automatic electronic interfaces to existing data-producing systems. Unfortunately, building interfaces to diverse computer systems is often challenging and sometimes impossible.

Many successful CDSS applications are built on top of proprietary custom-built computer systems that provide an electronic medical record system and usually a physician order entry system. Although it may be possible to take the knowledge built into the system and use it in a health care environment in which the patients are similar to those enrolled in the study, the inference engine used to compare the rules against the order entered into the database is usually not easily exported to other locations. If, after critically appraising a study describing the effect of a CDSS, you are convinced that a system for implementing clinical decision support would be useful, you would need sufficient resources to either rebuild the system at your own site or to purchase an off-the-shelf system that you believe could be customized to perform the same functions and that could maintain your customizations with each system upgrade. To accomplish this, you may need a local champion, someone who is willing and able to introduce the system, arrange for it to be customized for local use, troubleshoot its problems, and educate and encourage others to use the system.

Are Clinicians in Your Setting Likely to Accept the Clinical Decision Support System?

Clinicians who differ in important ways from those in the study may not accept the CDSS. The choice of the evaluative group may limit the generalizability of the conclusions if recruitment is based on a zest for new technology. Innovators in a new setting may be surprised when their colleagues do not use a CDSS with the same enthusiasm as the original participants.

The user interface is an important component of the effectiveness of a CDSS. The CDSS interface should be developed according to potential users' capabilities and limitations, the users' tasks, and the environment in which those tasks are performed.[26] One of the main difficulties with alerting systems is getting the information that there is a potential problem (such as an abnormal laboratory value) as rapidly as possible to the individual with the decision-making capability. A group of investigators tried a number of different alerting methods, from a highlighted icon on the computer screen to a flashing yellow light placed on the top of the computer.[27] These investigators later gave the nurses pagers to alert them about abnormal laboratory values.[28] The nurses could then decide how to act on the information and when to alert the physician.

To ensure acceptance, users must believe that they can count on the system to be available whenever they need it. The amount of downtime needed for data backup, troubleshooting, and upgrading should be minimal. The response time must be fast, data integrity maintained, data redundancy minimized, and system downtime minimized. It is also important to provide training required for users to feel comfortable with the system. If users become frustrated with the system, system performance will be suboptimal.

Many computer programs may function well at the site where the program was developed. Unfortunately, the staff at your institution may have objections to the approaches taken elsewhere. For example, an expert system for managing patients with ventilators who have adult respiratory distress syndrome may use continuous positive-airway-pressure trials to wean patients from the ventilator, whereas clinicians at your institution may prefer pressure-support weaning. Syntax, laboratory coding, and phrasing of diagnoses and therapeutic interventions can vary markedly across institutions. Customizing the application to the environment may not be feasible, and additional expense may be required when vocabulary is mapped to synonyms, unless a mechanism to do so has already been incorporated. To ensure user acceptance, users should participate in the decision-making and implementation stages.

Another issue is whether the logic that the system is based on is evidence based. Use of strong evidence from the literature could enhance clinician acceptance by convincing physicians that the rules positively affect patient outcomes. However, evidence-based practices do not ensure acceptance, so you would be advised to develop *local consensus* and endorsement in your setting. Additionally, any evidence-based system must be updated as important new evidence becomes available.

Do the Benefits of the Clinical Decision Support System Justify the Risks and Costs?

The real cost of the CDSS is usually much higher than the initial hardware, software, interface, training, maintenance fees, and upgrade costs. Often the CDSS is designed and maintained by staff whose actions are critical to the success of the intervention. Your institution might not want to pay for the time of such people in addition to the cost of the computer software and hardware. Indeed, it can be difficult to estimate the costs of purchasing or building and implementing an integrated CDSS. On the other hand, investing in employees to create or manage a CDSS is usually a wise institutional investment because current trends toward more efficient information management are likely to continue as health care catches up with the business world.

A computer-based CDSS evaluation involves the interplay between 3 complex elements:

- one or more human intermediaries;
- an integrated computerized system and its interface; and
- the knowledge in the decision support.

This makes evaluation of a computer-based CDSS a complex undertaking. Taking into account the influence of a study environment, a published systematic review of studies assessing CDSSs used in inpatient and outpatient clinical settings by physicians and other health care providers[2] was recently updated.[13] Of the 97 controlled trials assessing practitioner performance, the majority (64%) improved processes of care: 4 (40%) of 10 diagnostic systems, 16 (76%) of 21 reminder systems, 23 (62%) of 37 disease management systems, and 19 (66%) of 29 drug-dosing or prescribing systems. The effects of these systems on patient health, however, remain understudied and inconsistent when studied. In the recent review, 52 of 100 trials assessed patient outcomes, often in a limited capacity without adequate statistical power to detect important differences. Only 7 trials reported improved patient outcomes with the CDSS, and no study reported benefits for major outcomes such as mortality. Surrogate outcomes such as blood pressure and glycosylated hemoglobin did not show important improvements in most studies.

The best reason for evaluating processes of care is if RCTs have previously shown that those processes improve patient outcomes. Interventions that increase the proportion of patients receiving aspirin or a statin after a myocardial infarction,[29] an inhaled steroid in the presence of uncontrolled asthma, or thromboprophylaxis after a hip fracture provide indisputable benefit.

A less attractive reason for evaluating health care processes rather than health outcomes is that failures of process occur more frequently than major adverse health outcomes. For example, an RCT designed to show a 25% RRR in failure to follow a process criterion (from 50% to 32.5%) would need to enroll 246 patients per group. An RCT designed to show that this intervention reduces mortality in relative terms by 25% (from 5% to 3.75%) would need to enroll 4177 patients per group. Furthermore, demonstrating that preventive interventions improve patient health outcomes demands long follow-up periods.

CLINICAL RESOLUTION

As program director, you now face 2 separate but related questions: In an ideal world, should you implement this type of CDSS, and in reality, could you implement this type of CDSS? You are impressed at the RRR in inappropriate prescribing of 32% but wonder whether your 45 pediatric residents with their high rate (47%) of inappropriate prescribing will respond similarly. Not only is the study intervention very complex but also the authors did not present its cost and it is likely expensive. Although reducing the rate of inappropriate antibiotic prescribing is of some importance in itself (reduced adverse effects and cost), a decrease in return visits or antibiotic resistance would be even more compelling.

As is typical of CDSS trial reports, the authors are not able to identify the specific facets of the intervention that had the most effect. Because all your residents have PDAs, you are especially interested in whether the PDA-based CDSS worked better than the paper-based interventions; the study design did not, however, address this issue. Likewise, you observe that the study population was approximately 70% adults, whereas your patients are children, and you wonder whether the community-based clinicians in the study were more or less amenable to change compared with your colleagues. Finally, the details of the algorithms themselves, particularly the evidence base of the logic behind the adjudication of a prescription as inappropriate or not, are missing.

In the end, you decide that the goal of decreasing inappropriate antibiotic prescribing in the clinic is important enough to form a more focused *quality improvement* (QI) initiative. You gather a group of residents interested in carrying out a QI project, along with some of their attending physicians. They are particularly keen to try the PDA intervention in the study, so they agree to begin a formal chart abstraction process on respiratory tract infection prescribing. The clinical pharmacists offer to develop an algorithm that considers the marked differences in costs among antibiotics. You contact the authors of the CDSS study about further details of the antibiotic-prescribing algorithm and ask them whether they are willing to discuss in more detail the algorithms, the PDA component, and the factors that seemed to contribute to the study's success.

References

1. Samore MH, Bateman K, Alder SC, et al. Clinical decision support and appropriateness of antimicrobial prescribing: a randomized trial. *JAMA*. 2005;294(18): 2305-2314.

2. Johnston M, Langton K, Haynes R, Mathieu A. Effects of computer-based clinical decision support systems on clinician performance and patient outcome: a critical appraisal of research. *Ann Intern Med*. 1994;120(2):135-142.

3. Pryor TA. Development of decision support systems. *Int J Clin Monit Comput*. 1990;7(3):137-146.

4. Friedman CP, Wyatt JC. *Evaluation Methods in Medical Informatics*. New York, NY: Springer-Verlag; 1997.

5. Lepage E, Gardner R, Laub R, Golubjatnikov O. Improving blood transfusion practice: role of a computerized hospital information system. *Transfusion*. 1992;32(3):253-259.

6. Weinfurt PT. Electrocardiographic monitoring: an overview. *J Clin Monit*. 1990;6(2):132-138.

7. Knaus WA, Wagner DP, Draper EA, et al. The APACHE III prognostic system: risk prediction of hospital mortality for critically ill hospitalized adults. *Chest*. 1991;100(6):1619-1636.

8. Berner E, Webster G, Shugerman A, et al. Performance of four computer-based diagnostic systems. *N Engl J Med*. 1994;330(25):1792-1796.

9. Kennedy R, Harrison R, Burton A, et al. An artificial neural network system for diagnosis of acute myocardial infarction (AMI) in the accident and emergency department: evaluation and comparison with serum myoglobin measurements. *Comput Methods Prog Biomed*. 1997;52(2):93-103.

10. Evans RS, Pestotnik SL, Classen DC, et al. A computer-assisted management program for antibiotics and other antiinfective agents. *N Engl J Med*. 1998; 38(4):232-238.

11. Morris AH, Wallace CJ, Menlove RL, et al. Randomized clinical trial of pressure-controlled inverse ratio ventilation and extracorporeal CO_2 removal for adult respiratory distress syndrome. *Am J Respir Crit Care Med*. 1994;149(2 pt 1):295-305.

12. Durieux P, Nizard R, Ravaud P, Mounier N, Lepage E. A clinical decision support system for prevention of venous thromboembolism: effect on physician behavior. *JAMA*. 2000;283(21):2816-2821.

13. Garg AX, Adhikari NK, McDonald H, et al. Effects of computer-based clinical decision support systems on practitioner performance and patient outcomes: a systematic review. *JAMA*. 2005;293(10):1223-1238.

14. Cornfield J. Randomization by group: a formal analysis. *Am J Epidemiol*. 1978;108(2):100-102.

15. Whiting-O'Keefe Q, Henke C, Simborg D. Choosing the correct unit of analysis in medical care experiments. *Med Care*. 1984;22(12).1101-1114.

16. Divine GW, Brown JT, Frazier LM. The unit of analysis error in studies about physicians' patient care behaviour. *J Gen Intern Med*. 1992;7(6):623-629.

17. Klar N, Donner A. The merits of matching in community intervention trials: a cautionary tale. *Stat Med*. 1997;16(15):1753-1764.

18. Thompson SG, Pyke SD, Hardy RJ. The design and analysis of paired cluster randomized trials: an application of meta-analysis techniques. *Stat Med*. 1997; 16(18):2063-2079.

19. Campbell MK, Mollison J, Steen N, Grimshaw JM, Eccles M. Analysis of cluster randomized trials in primary care: a practical approach. *Fam Pract.* 2000; 17(2):192-196.

20. Mollison J, Simpson JA, Campbell MK, Grimshaw JM. Comparison of analytic methods for cluster randomized trials: an example from a primary care setting. *J Epidemiol Biostat.* 2000;5(6):339-348.

21. Strickland JH, Hasson JH. A computer-controlled ventilator weaning system. *Chest.* 1993;103(4):1220-1226.

22. Eccles M, McColl E, Steen N, et al. Effect of computerised evidence based guidelines on management of asthma and angina in adults in primary care: cluster randomised controlled trial. *BMJ.* 2002;325(7370):941.

23. Morris A, East T, Wallace C, et al. Standardization of clinical decision making for the conduct of credible clinical research in complicated medical environments. *Proc AMIA Annu Fall Symp.* 1996:418-422.

24. Guyatt GH, Pugsley SO, Sullivan MJ, et al. Effect of encouragement on walking test performance. *Thorax.* 1984;39(11):818-822.

25. Roethligsburger FJ, Dickson WJ. *Management and the Worker.* Cambridge, MA: Harvard University Press; 1939.

26. Adams ID, Chan M, Clifford PC, et al. Computer aided diagnosis of acute abdominal pain: a multicentre study. *BMJ.* 1986;293(6550):800-804.

27. Bradshaw K, Gardner R, Pryor T. Development of a computerized laboratory alerting system. *Comput Biomed Res.* 1989;22(6):575-587.

28. Tate K, Gardner R, Scherting K. Nurses, pagers, and patient-specific criteria: three keys to improved critical value reporting. *Proc Annu Symp Comput Appl Med Care.* 1995:164-168.

29. Mant J, Hicks N. Detecting differences in quality of care: the sensitivity of measures of process and outcome in treating acute myocardial infarction. *BMJ.* 1995;311(7008):793-796.

ADVANCED TOPICS IN THE RESULTS
OF THERAPY TRIALS

HYPOTHESIS TESTING

Gordon Guyatt, Kameshwar Prasad,
Roman Jaeschke, Deborah J. Cook,
and Stephen Walter

IN THIS CHAPTER:

For every treatment, there is a true, underlying effect that any individual experiment can only estimate (see Chapter 5, Why Study Results Mislead: Bias and Random Error). Investigators use statistical methods to advance their understanding of this true effect. One approach to statistical exploration is to begin with what is called a *null hypothesis* and try to disprove that hypothesis. Typically, the null hypothesis suggests there is no difference between treatments being compared.

> For instance, in a comparison of vasodilator treatment in 804 men with heart failure, investigators compared the proportion of enalapril-treated survivors with the proportion of survivors receiving a combination of hydralazine and nitrates.[1] We start with the assumption that the treatments are equally effective, and we adhere to this position unless the results make it untenable. One could state the null hypothesis in the vasodilator trial more formally as follows: The true difference in the proportion of patients surviving between those treated with enalapril and those treated with hydralazine and nitrates is zero.

In this hypothesis-testing framework, the statistical analysis addresses the question of whether the observed data are consistent with the null hypothesis. Even if the treatment truly has no positive or negative effect on the *outcome* (that is, the *effect size* is zero), the results observed will seldom show exact equivalence. For instance, even if there is actually no difference between treatments, seldom will we see exactly the same proportion of deaths in treatment and *control groups*. As the results diverge farther and farther from the finding of "no difference," however, the null hypothesis that there is no true difference between the treatments becomes progressively less credible. If the difference between results of the treatment and control groups becomes large enough, clinicians abandon belief in the null hypothesis. We will further develop the underlying logic by describing the role of chance in clinical research.

THE ROLE OF CHANCE

In Chapter 5, Why Study Results Mislead: Bias and Random Error, we considered a balanced coin with which the true *probability* of obtaining either heads or tails in any individual coin toss is 0.5. We noted that if we tossed such a coin 10 times, we would not be surprised if we did not see exactly 5 heads and 5 tails. Occasionally, we would get results quite divergent from the 5:5 split, such as 8:2, or even 9:1. Furthermore, very infrequently, the 10 coin tosses would result in 10 consecutive heads or tails.

Chance is responsible for this variability in results. Certain recreational games illustrate the way chance operates. On occasion, the roll of 2 unbiased dice (dice with an equal probability of rolling any number between 1 and 6) will yield 2 ones or 2 sixes. On occasion (much to the delight of the recipient), the dealer at a poker game will dispense a hand consisting of 5 cards of a single suit. Even less frequently, the 5 cards will not only belong to a single suit but also have consecutive face values.

Chance is not restricted to the world of coin tosses, dice, and card games. If we take a sample of patients from a community, chance may result in unusual and potentially misleading distributions of chronic disease such as hypertension or diabetes. Chance also may be responsible for substantial imbalance in *event rates* in 2 groups of patients given different treatments that are, in fact, equally effective. Much statistical inquiry is geared toward determining the extent to which unbalanced distributions could be attributed to chance and the extent to which one should invoke other explanations (differential *treatment effects*, for instance). As we demonstrate here, the size of the study to a large extent determines the conclusions of its statistical inquiry.

THE *P* VALUE

One way that an investigator can err is to conclude that there is a difference between a treatment group and a control group when, in fact, no such difference exists. In statistical terminology, making the mistake of concluding that treatment and control differ when, in truth, they do not is called a *type I error* and the probability of making such an error is referred to as α *level.*

Imagine a situation in which we are uncertain whether a coin is biased. One could construct a null hypothesis that the true proportions of heads and tails are equal (that is, the coin is unbiased). With this scenario, the probability of any given toss landing heads is 50%, as is the probability of any given toss landing tails. We could test this hypothesis by an experiment in which we conduct a series of coin tosses. Statistical analysis of the results of the experiment would address the question of whether the results observed were consistent with chance.

Let us conduct a hypothetical experiment in which the suspected coin is tossed 10 times, and on all 10 occasions, the result is heads. How likely is this to have occurred if the coin were indeed unbiased? Most people would conclude that it is highly unlikely that chance could explain this extreme result. We would therefore be ready to reject the hypothesis that the coin is unbiased (the null hypothesis) and conclude that the coin is biased.

Statistical methods allow us to be more precise by ascertaining just how unlikely the result is to have occurred simply as a result of chance if the null hypothesis is true. The *law of multiplicative probabilities* for independent events (in which one event in no way influences the other) tells us that the probability of 10 consecutive heads can be found by multiplying the probability of a single head (1/2) 10 times over; that is, $(1/2) \times (1/2) \times (1/2)$, and so on, which, it turns out, yields a value of slightly less than 1 in a 1000.

In a journal article, one would likely see this probability expressed as a P value, $P < .001$. What is the precise meaning of this *P* value? If the coin were unbiased (that is, if the null hypothesis were true) and one were to repeat the experiment of the 10 coin tosses many times, 10 consecutive heads would be expected to occur by chance in less than 1 in 1000 of these repetitions.

The framework of hypothesis testing involves a yes-no decision. Are we willing to reject the null hypothesis? This choice involves a decision about how much risk or chance of making a type I error we are willing to accept. The reasoning implies a threshold value that demarcates a boundary. On one side of this boundary, we are unwilling to reject the null hypothesis; on the other side, we are ready to conclude that chance is no longer a plausible explanation for the results.

To return to the example of 10 consecutive heads, most people would be ready to reject the null hypothesis when the results observed would be expected to occur by chance alone less than 1 in a 1000 times. What if we repeat the thought experiment? This time we obtain 9 tails and 1 head. Once again, it is unlikely that the result is because of the play of chance alone. This time, as shown in Figure 10.1-1 (which you will recognize from Chapter 5; the theoretical distribution of the distribution of results on an infinite number of repetitions of the 10-coin flip experiment when the coin is unbiased), the P value is .02, or 2 in 100. That is, if the coin were unbiased and the null hypothesis were true, we would expect results as extreme as—or more extreme than—those observed (that is, 10 heads or 10 tails, 9 heads and 1 tail, or 9 tails and 1 head) to occur by chance alone 2 times per 100 repetitions of the experiment.

Where we set this threshold or boundary is arbitrary and is a matter of judgment. Statistical convention suggests a threshold that demarcates the plausible from the implausible at 5 times per 100, which is represented by a P value of .05. We call results that fall beyond this boundary (that is, $P < .05$) *statistically significant*. The meaning of statistically significant, therefore, is "sufficiently unlikely to be due to chance alone that we are ready to reject the null hypothesis."

Let us repeat our experiment twice more, both times with a new coin. On the first repetition, we obtain 8 heads and 2 tails. Calculation of the P value associated with an 8/2 split tells us that, if the coin were unbiased, results as extreme as or more extreme than 8/2 (or 2/8) would occur solely as a result of the play of chance 11 times per 100 ($P = .11$) (Figure 10.1-1). We have crossed to the other side of the conventional boundary between what is plausible and what is implausible. If we accept the convention, the results are not statistically significant and we will not reject the null hypothesis.

On our final repetition of the experiment, we obtain 7 tails and 3 heads. Experience tells us that such a result, although not the most common, would not be unusual even if the coin were unbiased. The P value confirms our intuition: Results as extreme as, or more extreme than, this 7/3 split would occur under the null hypothesis 34 times per 100 ($P = .34$) (Figure 10.1-1). Again, we will not reject the null hypothesis.

When investigators compare 2 treatments, the question they ask is, how likely is it that the observed difference is due to chance alone? If we accept the conventional boundary or threshold ($P < .05$), we will reject the null hypothesis and conclude that the treatment has some effect when the answer to this question is that

FIGURE 10.1-1

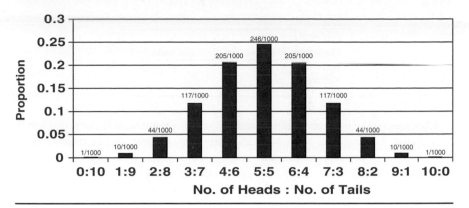

Theoretical Distribution of Results of an Infinite Number of Repetitions of 10 Flips of an Unbiased Coin

repetitions of the experiment would yield differences as extreme as or more extreme than those we have observed less than 5% of the time. Generally, the 5% refers to both tails of the distribution of possible results (analogous to 0 or 1 head *or* 0 or 1 tail), though investigators sometimes conduct *1-sided significance tests*.

Let us return to the example of the randomized trial in which investigators compared enalapril to the combination of hydralazine and nitrates in 804 men with heart failure. The results of this study illustrate hypothesis testing using a dichotomous (yes/no) outcome; in this case, mortality.[1] During the *follow-up* period, which ranged from 6 months to 5.7 years, 132 of 403 patients (33%) assigned to enalapril died, as did 153 of 401 (38%) of those assigned to hydralazine and nitrates. Application of a statistical test that compares proportions (the χ^2 *test*) reveals that if there were actually no difference in mortality between the 2 groups, differences as large as or larger than those actually observed would be expected 11 times per 100 ($P = .11$). Using the hypothesis-testing framework and the conventional threshold of $P < .05$, we would conclude that we cannot reject the null hypothesis and that the difference observed is compatible with chance.

Readers interested in how to teach the *concepts* we have reviewed in this chapter to clinical learners may be interested in an interactive script we have developed for this purpose.[2]

TYPE I AND TYPE II ERRORS

Consider a woman who suspects she is pregnant and is undertaking a pregnancy test. The test has possible errors associated with its result. Figure 10.1-2 represents the 4

FIGURE 10.1-2

Four Possible Results of a Pregnancy Test

	Pregnancy present	
	Yes	No
Test positive	**a** *True positive*	**b** *False positive*
Test negative	**c** *False negative*	**d** *True negative*

possible results: the woman is either pregnant or not pregnant, and the test result is either positive or negative. If the woman is pregnant, the test may be positive (*true positive*, cell a) or negative (*false negative*, cell c). If the woman is not pregnant, the test may be positive (*false positive*, cell b) or negative (*true negative*, cell d).

We can apply the same logic to the result of an experiment testing the effect of a treatment. The treatment either has an effect or it does not; the experiment is either positive ($P \leq .05$) or negative ($P > .05$) (Figure 10.1-3). Here, a true positive occurs when there is a real treatment effect and the study results yield a $P \leq .05$ (cell a), and a true negative occurs when treatment has no effect and the study P value is greater than .05. We refer to a false positive (no true treatment effect, $P \leq .05$, cell b) as a type I or α error. When we set our threshold P at .05, the likelihood of a type I error when the null hypothesis is true is 5%. We refer to a false negative (treatment truly effective, $P > .05$, cell c) as a type II or β error. We expand on this logic in the following discussion.

THE RISK OF A FALSE-NEGATIVE RESULT

A clinician might comment on the results of the comparison of treatment with enalapril with that of a combination of hydralazine and nitrates as follows: "Although I accept the 5% threshold and therefore agree that we

FIGURE 10.1-3

Four Possible Results of a Randomized Trial of an Experimental Intervention

	Treatment effect present	
	Yes	No
Study result positive	**a** *True positive*	**b** *False positive type I error*
Study result negative	**c** *False negative type II error*	**d** *True negative*

cannot reject the null hypothesis, I am nevertheless still suspicious that enalapril results in a lower mortality than does the combination of hydralazine and nitrates. The experiment still leaves me in a state of uncertainty." In making these statements, the clinician is recognizing the possibility of a second type of error in hypothesis testing.

The second type of error that an investigator can make is falsely concluding that an effective treatment is useless. A *type II error* occurs when one erroneously dismisses an actual treatment effect—and a potentially useful treatment.

In the comparison of enalapril with hydralazine and nitrates, the possibility of erroneously concluding that there is no difference between the 2 treatments is great. The investigators found that 5% fewer patients receiving enalapril died than those receiving the alternative vasodilator regimen. If the true difference in mortality really were 5%, we would readily conclude that patients will receive an important benefit if we prescribe enalapril. Despite this, we were unable to reject the null hypothesis. Why is it that the investigators observed an important difference between the mortality rates and yet were unable to conclude that enalapril is superior to hydralazine and nitrates?

Whenever one observes a large difference between treatment and control groups and yet cannot reject the null hypothesis, one should consider the possibility that the problem is failure to enroll enough patients. The likelihood of missing an important difference (and, therefore, of making a type II error) decreases as the sample size and thus the number of events gets larger. When a study is at high risk of making a type II error, we say it has inadequate *power*. The larger the sample size, the lower the risk of type II error and the greater the power.

Although the 804 patients recruited by the investigators conducting the vasodilator trial may sound like a substantial number, for dichotomous outcomes such as mortality, even larger sample sizes are often required to detect small treatment effects. For example, researchers conducting the trials that established the optimal treatment of acute myocardial infarction with thrombolytic agents both anticipated and found *absolute differences* between treatment and control mortalities of less than 5%. Because of these small absolute differences between treatment and control, they required—and recruited—thousands of patients to ensure adequate power.

Whenever a trial has failed to reject the null hypothesis (ie, when $P > .05$), the investigators may have missed a true treatment effect, and you should then consider whether the power of the trial was adequate. In these negative studies, the stronger the nonsignificant trend in favor of the experimental treatment, the more likely it is that the investigators missed a true treatment effect.[3] Another chapter in this book describes how to decide whether a study is large enough (see Chapter 8, Confidence Intervals).

NONINFERIORITY TRIALS

Some studies are not designed to determine whether a new treatment is better than the current one, but rather, whether a treatment that is less expensive, easier to administer, or less toxic yields more or less the same treatment effect as standard therapy. Such studies are often referred to as *equivalence trials* or, more commonly, *noninferiority trials*.[4]

In noninferiority studies, considering whether investigators have recruited an adequate sample size to make sure they will not miss small but important treatment effects is even more important. If the sample size of a noninferiority study is inadequate, the investigator runs the risk of a β error: concluding that the treatments are equivalent when, in fact, patients given standard therapy derive important benefits in comparison to the easier, less expensive, or less toxic alternative.

CONTINUOUS MEASURES OF OUTCOME

To this point, all of our examples have used outcomes such as yes/no, heads or tails, or dying or not dying, all of which we can express as a proportion. Often, investigators compare the effects of 2 or more treatments using a variable such as spirometric measurements, cardiac output, creatinine clearance, or score on a quality-of-life questionnaire. We call such variables, in which results can take a large number of values with small differences between those values, *continuous variables*. When one compares differences between groups using continuous outcomes, one typically asks the question whether one can exclude chance as the explanation of a difference in means.

The study of enalapril vs hydralazine and nitrates in patients with heart failure described above[1] provides an example of the use of a continuous variable as an outcome in a hypothesis test. The investigators compared the effect of the 2 regimens on exercise capacity. In contrast to the effect on mortality, which favored enalapril, exercise capacity improved with hydralazine and nitrates but not with enalapril. Using a test (the *t* test) appropriate for continuous variables, the investigators compared the changes in exercise capacity from baseline to 6 months in the patients receiving hydralazine and nitrates to those changes in the enalapril group during the same period. Exercise capacity in the hydralazine group improved more, and the differences between the 2 groups are unlikely to have occurred by chance ($P = .02$).

MULTIPLE TESTS

Picture a medical school in which 2 instructors with differing approaches teach an introductory course on medical statistics. The instructors wish to see whether the 2 approaches lead to different results on a final common examination. To do so, they assign the 200 medical students in the first-year class to one instructor or the other by a process of *random allocation*, through which each student has an equal chance (50%) of being allocated to either of the 2 instructors.

The instructors decide to take advantage of this process to illustrate some important principles of medical statistics. They therefore ask the question, are there characteristics of the 2 groups of students that differ beyond a level that could be explained by the play of chance? The characteristics they choose include sex distribution, eye color, height, grade point average in the last year of college before entering medical school, socioeconomic status, and favorite type of music.

The instructors formulate null hypotheses for each of their tests. For instance, the null hypothesis associated with sex distribution is as follows: The students are drawn from the same group of people and, therefore, the true proportion of females in the 2 groups is identical. You will note that the students were drawn from the same underlying population and were assigned to the 2 groups by random allocation. The null hypothesis in each case is true; therefore, anytime in this experiment in which the hypothesis is rejected will represent a false-positive result (a type I error).

The instructors survey their students to determine their status on each of the 6 variables of interest. For 5 of these variables, they find that the distributions are similar in the 2 groups; and all of the P values associated with formal tests of the differences between groups are greater than .10. The instructors find that for eye color, however, 25 of 100 students in one group have blue eyes, whereas 38 of 100 in the other group have blue eyes. A formal statistical analysis reveals that if the null hypothesis were true (which it is), then differences in the proportion of people with blue eyes in the 2 groups as large as or larger than the difference observed would occur slightly less than 5 times per 100 repetitions of the experiment. Using the conventional boundary, the instructors would reject the null hypothesis, even though it is in fact true. The example shows, among other things, the potential for error in testing for differences between groups that have been allocated through well-conducted *randomization*.

The assumptions underlying hypothesis testing break down if we are simultaneously considering more than 1 hypothesis. For instance, consider how likely it is that in testing 6 independent hypotheses, one would find at least 1 that crossed the threshold of .05 by chance alone. By independent, we mean that the result of a test of one hypothesis does not depend in any way on the results of tests of any of the other hypotheses. Because our likelihood of crossing the significance threshold for any one characteristic is .05, the likelihood of not crossing the threshold for that same characteristic is 1.0 − .05, or .95. When 2 hypotheses are tested, the probability that neither one would cross the threshold would be .95 multiplied by .95 (or the square of .95); when 6 hypotheses are tested, the probability that not a single one would cross the 5% threshold is .95 to the sixth power, or 74%. When 6 independent hypotheses are tested, the probability that at least 1 result is statistically significant is therefore 26% (100% − 74%), or approximately 1 in 4, rather than 1 in 20. If we wished to maintain our overall standard of .05, we would have to divide the threshold P value by 6, so that each of the 6 tests would use a boundary value of approximately .0085.[5]

The message here is 2-fold. First, rare findings do occasionally happen by chance. Even with a single test, a finding with a P value of .01 will happen 1% of the time. Second, one should be aware of multiple hypotheses testing that may yield misleading results. Examples of this phenomenon abound in the clinical literature. For example, in a survey of 45 trials from 3 leading medical journals, Pocock et al[7] found that the median number of *endpoints* mentioned was 6, and most were tested for statistical significance.

We find an example of the dangers of using multiple endpoints in a randomized trial of the effect of rehabilitation on quality of life after myocardial infarction in which investigators randomized patients to receive standard care, an exercise program, or a counseling program. They obtained patient reports of work, leisure, quality of work and leisure, sexual activity, compliance with advice, cardiac symptoms, psychiatric symptoms, general health, and satisfaction with outcome.[6] For almost all of these variables, there was no difference between the 3 groups. However, at follow-up after 18 months, patients were more satisfied with the exercise regimen than with the other 2 regimens, families in the counseling group were less protective than in the other groups, and patients participating in the counseling group worked more hours and had sexual intercourse more frequently.

Does this mean that both exercise and rehabilitation programs should be implemented because of the small number of outcomes that changed in their favor or that they should be rejected because most of the outcomes showed no difference? The authors themselves concluded that their results did not support the effectiveness of rehabilitation in improving quality of life. However, a program's advocate might argue that if even some of the ratings favored treatment, the intervention is worthwhile. The use of multiple instruments opens the door to such potential controversy.

A number of statistical strategies exist for dealing with the issue of multiple hypotheses testing on the same data set. We have illustrated one of these in a previous example: dividing the P value by the number of tests. One can also specify, before the study is undertaken, a single primary outcome on which the major conclusions of the study will hinge. A third approach is to derive a single global test statistic (a pooled effect size, for instance) that effectively combines the multiple outcomes into a single measure.

Finally, one might argue that in some situations, one can carry out several hypothesis tests without making a multiple comparisons adjustment. When the hypotheses being tested represent distinct scientific questions, each of interest in its own right, it may be that interpretation of each hypothesis should not be influenced by the number of other hypotheses being tested.[1]

A full discussion of strategies for dealing with multiple outcomes is beyond the scope of this book, but the interested reader can find a cogent discussion elsewhere.[7]

Limitations of Hypothesis Testing

At this point, you may be entertaining a number of questions that leave you uneasy. Why use a single cut point for rejecting the null hypothesis when the choice of a cut point is so arbitrary? Why dichotomize the question of whether a treatment is effective into a yes/no issue when it may be viewed more appropriately as a continuum (from, for instance, "very unlikely to be effective" to "almost certainly effective")? We direct these clinicians to another part of this book (see Chapter 8, Confidence Intervals) for an explanation of why we consider an alternative to hypothesis testing a superior approach.

References

1. Cohn J, Johnson G, Ziesche S, et al. A comparison of enalapril with hydralazine-isosorbide dinitrate in the treatment of chronic congestive heart failure. *N Engl J Med.* 1991;325(5):303-310.

2. Montori VM, Kleinbart J, Newman TB, et al. Tips for learners of evidence-based medicine, 2: measures of precision (confidence intervals). *CMAJ.* 2004;171: online-1 to online-12. http://www.cmaj.ca/cgi/data/171/6/611/DC1/1. Accessed February 24, 2008.

3. Detsky A, Sackett D. When was a "negative" trial big enough? how many patients you needed depends on what you found. *Arch Intern Med.* 1985;145(4):709-715.

4. Kirshner B. Methodological standards for assessing therapeutic equivalence. *J Clin Epidemiol.* 1991;44(8):839-849.

5. Cook R, Dunnett C. Multiple comparisons. In: Armitage P, Colton T, eds. *Encyclopedia of Biostatistics.* New York, NY: Wiley; 1999:2736-2746.

6. Mayou R, MacMahon D, Sleight P, Florencio M. Early rehabilitation after myocardial infarction. *Lancet.* 1981;2(8260-8261):1399-1401.

7. Pocock S, Geller N, Tsiatis A. The analysis of multiple endpoints in clinical trials. *Biometrics.* 1987;43(3):487-498.

ADVANCED TOPICS IN THE RESULTS
OF THERAPY TRIALS

UNDERSTANDING THE RESULTS: MORE ABOUT ODDS RATIOS

Roman Jaeschke, Stephen Walter,
Mahmoud El Barbary, and Gordon Guyatt

IN THIS CHAPTER:

Odds in Ordinary Life

The 2 × 2 Table

Odds vs Risks

The Merits of the Odds Ratio

Substitution of Relative Risk for Odds Ratio

Case-Control Studies

ODDS IN ORDINARY LIFE

You might be most familiar with *odds* in the context of sporting events, when bookmakers or newspaper commentators quote the odds for and against a horse, a boxer, or a tennis player winning a particular event.

In the context of games, suppose you have a die that has 6 faces. What is the likelihood of getting the face that has 4 dots vs getting some other face on a single throw? What are the odds of that particular event occurring vs not occurring? Is it 1:5 or 1:6? The correct answer to this question is 1:5, representing the ratio of *probability* that the event (having the face of 4 dots) will happen relative to the probability that it will not happen (ie, having one of the other possible 5 faces). The corresponding probability of rolling a 4 is 1/6, and of rolling some face other than the 4 is 5/6.

THE 2 × 2 TABLE

As clinicians, we are interested less in rolling dice than in treating patients. So, in terms of odds, we are interested in the odds of experiencing an adverse *outcome* vs avoiding that outcome. Further, we are interested in those odds in patients exposed to treatment vs those not exposed. When we compare odds from treated and untreated groups, we will end up with the ratio of 2 odds, not surprisingly called *odds ratio* (OR). In Chapter 7, Does Treatment Lower Risk? Understanding the Results, in which we discussed ways of presenting the magnitude of a *treatment effect*, we introduced the concept of the OR. To help understand it, we present once again the 2 × 2 table (Table 10.2-1) and the results from ligation vs sclerotherapy of bleeding esophageal varices (Table 10.2-2).[1] In this and other examples in this chapter, we look at situations in which a treatment may reduce the probability of an adverse event, and thus an OR less than 1.0 represents a benefit of treatment (OR > 1 is associated with increased odds of that event happening, whereas OR of 1 describes no effect).

ODDS VS RISKS

In Chapter 7, Does Treatment Lower Risk? Understanding the Results, we expressed the results in terms of *risks* and then in terms of *risk reduction*, either relative or absolute. The OR represents an alternative: instead of looking at the risk of an event, we could estimate the odds of having vs not having an event.

When used in medicine, the odds represent the number of patients in a given group with an event divided by number of patients in the same group without it.

TABLE 10.2-1

The 2 × 2 Table

	Outcome	
Exposure[a]	Yes	No
Yes	a	b
No	c	d

Odds ratio $= \dfrac{a/b}{c/d} = \dfrac{ad}{cb}$

Relative risk $= \dfrac{a/(a+b)}{c/(c+d)}$

Relative risk reduction $= 1 - \text{RR} = \dfrac{c/(c+d) - a/(a+b)}{c/(c+d)}$

Risk difference (RD) $= \dfrac{c}{c+d} - \dfrac{a}{a+b}$

Number needed to treat $= 100/(\text{RD} \times 100\%)$

[a]The exposure may be a putatively beneficial therapy or a possibly harmful agent.

The ratio of odds in one group to the odds in the other group is the OR. You will find that sometimes authors calculate the OR and then report the results as *relative risks* (*RRs*). In most instances in medical investigation, when odds and risks are approximately equal, this is not a problem. On the relatively infrequent occasions when odds and risks are widely divergent, this practice will be misleading.

You may sometimes be in the position in which you would like to convert odds to risk. To do so, you divide the odds by (1 plus those odds). For instance, if the odds of a poor surgical outcome is 0.5 (or 1:2), the risk is [0.5/(0.5 + 1)], or 0.33. To

TABLE 10.2-2

Results From a Randomized Trial of Endoscopic Sclerotherapy Compared With Endoscopic Ligation for Bleeding Esophageal Varices[a]

	Outcome		
Exposure	Death	Survival	Total
Ligation	18	46	64
Sclerotherapy	29	36	65

Odds ratio = (18/46)/(29/36) = 0.39/0.81 = 0.49
Relative risk = (18/64)/(29/65) = 0.63
Relative risk reduction = 1 − 0.63 = 0.37
Risk difference = 0.455 − 0.28 = 0.165
Number needed to treat = 100%/16.5% = 6

[a]Data from Stiegmann et al.[1]

TABLE 10.2-3

Risks and Odds[a]

Risk	Odds
0.05	$0.05/0.95 = 0.053$
0.1	$0.1/0.9 = 0.11$
0.2	$0.2/0.8 = 0.25$
0.25	$0.25/0.75 = 0.33$
0.33	$0.33/0.66 = 0.5$
0.4	$0.4/0.6 = 0.67$
0.5	$0.5/0.5 = 1.0$
0.6	$0.6/0.4 = 1.5$
0.8	$0.8/0.2 = 4.0$

[a]Risks are equal to [odds/(1 + odds)]. Odds are equal to [risks/(1 − risk)].

convert from risks to odds, divide risk by (1 − risk). Table 10.2-3 presents the relationship between risk and odds. Note that the greater the magnitude of the risk, the greater the numeric difference between the risk and odds.

THE MERITS OF THE ODDS RATIO

One can create a measure of association or effect by creating a ratio of odds. The OR, then, is the ratio of the odds of having the event in one (exposed or experimental) group relative to the odds of having the event in another group (unexposed or *control group*). In our example, the odds of dying in the ligation group are 18 (death) vs 46 (survival), or 18 to 46, or 18/46 (*a/b*), and the odds of dying in the sclerotherapy group are 29 to 36 (*c/d*). The formula for the ratio of these odds is (*a/c*)/(*b/d*) (Table 10.2-1); in our example, this yields (18/46)/(29/36), or 0.49. If one were formulating a terminology parallel to risk (in which we call a ratio of risks an RR), one would call a ratio of odds a *relative odds*. Epidemiologists have chosen RR as the preferred term for a ratio of risks and OR for a ratio of odds.

Historically, the OR, which has a number of points (Table 10.2-4) in its favor, has been the predominant measure of association[2] because the OR has a statistical advantage in that it is essentially independent of the arbitrary choice between a comparison of the risks of an event (such as death) or the corresponding "nonevent" (such as survival), which is not necessarily true of the RR.[3-5]

TABLE 10.2-4

Merits of the Odds Ratio (OR)

1. Apparent prevalence in *case-control studies* depends on the ratio of sampling cases to controls, which is determined by the investigator. Effect measure that is unaltered by *prevalence (a + b)* required—OR only appropriate measure

2. May be desirable if we are performing a *meta-analysis* in trials with greatly different *event rates*

3. If we reverse the outcomes in the analysis and look at good outcome (survival) rather than bad outcome (mortality), the latter relationship will have a reciprocal OR (not true of relative risk [RR])

4. OR appropriate whatever the baseline event rate (RR becomes problematic if high event rates; for example, if risk > 0.5, we cannot have RR > 2)

5. OR is the measure of association or effect that we use in *logistic regression* (see Chapter 13, Correlation and Regression)

SUBSTITUTION OF RELATIVE RISK FOR ODDS RATIO

As clinicians, we would like to be able to substitute the RR, which we intuitively understand, for the OR, which we do not understand. Looking back at our 2×2 table (see Table 10.2-1), we see that the validity of this substitution requires that the RR, $[a/(a + b)]/[c/(c + d)]$, be more or less equal to the OR, $(a/b)/(c/d)$. For this to be the case, a must be much less than b, and c much less than d (look at denominators in the formula); in other words, the outcome must occur infrequently in both the experimental and the control groups.

For low event rates, common in most randomized trials, the OR and RR are numerically very close. The RR and OR will also be closer together when the magnitude of the treatment effect is small (that is, OR and RR are close to 1.0) than when the treatment effect is large. With both low event rates (in which OR is numerically close to RR) and with higher event rates (in which they may be farther apart), the OR will always make a treatment appear more effective than RR (ie, for the same results, the OR will be farther from 1.0 than the RR). With low event rates, this tendency is minimal; with higher event rates, it is more pronounced (Table 10.2-5).

When event rates are high and effect sizes are large, there are ways of converting the OR to RR.[6,7] Fortunately, clinicians will rarely need to consult such tables. To see why, consider a meta-analysis of ligation vs sclerotherapy for esophageal varices[8] that demonstrated a rebleeding rate of 0.47 with sclerotherapy, as high an event rate as one is likely to find in most trials. The OR associated with treatment with ligation was 0.52, a large effect. Despite the high event rate and large effect, the RR (0.67) is not practically very different from the OR. The 2 are close enough— and this is the crucial point—so that choosing one relative measure or the other is unlikely to have an important influence on treatment decisions.

TABLE 10.2-5

Comparison of Relative Risks and Odds Ratios

Risk Control, %	Risk Exposure, %	Odds Control	Odds Exposure	Relative Risk	Odds Ratio
Undesirable Event					
4	3	0.042	0.031	0.75	0.74
40	30	0.67	0.43	0.75	0.64
Desirable Event					
10	15	0.11	0.18	1.5	1.59
30	45	0.43	0.82	1.5	1.91

The calculation of *number needed to treat* (NNT) and *number needed to harm* (NNH) provides another problem when investigators report ORs instead of RRs. As we stated before, the best way of dealing with this situation when event rates are low is to assume that the RR will be very close to the OR. The higher the risk, the less secure the assumption. Tables 10.2-6 and 10.2-7 provide a guide for making an accurate estimate of the NNT and NNH when you estimate the patient's baseline risk and the investigator has provided only an OR.

TABLE 10.2-6

Deriving the NNT From the Odds Ratio (OR)

Control Group Risk	Therapeutic Intervention (OR)								
	0.5	0.55	0.6	0.65	0.7	0.75	0.8	0.85	0.9
0.05	41	46	52	59	69	83	104	139	209
0.1	21	24	27	31	36	43	54	73	110
0.2	11	13	14	17	20	24	30	40	61
0.3	8	9	10	12	14	18	22	30	46
0.4	7	8	9	10	12	15	19	26	40
0.5	6	7	8	9	11	14	18	25	38
0.7	6	7	9	10	13	16	20	28	44
0.9	12	15	18	22	27	34	46	64	101

The formula for determining the NNT: $\dfrac{1 - CGR(1 - OR)}{CGR(1 - CGR)(1 - OR)}$

Abbreviations: CGR, control group risk; NNT, number needed to treat; OR, odds ratio.
Adapted from Hux et al.[9]

TABLE 10.2-7

Deriving the NNH From the Odds Ratio

Control Group Risk	Therapeutic Intervention (OR)								
	1.1	1.2	1.3	1.4	1.5	2	2.5	3	3.5
0.05	212	106	71	54	43	22	15	12	9
0.1	112	57	38	29	23	12	9	7	6
0.2	64	33	22	17	14	8	5	4	4
0.3	49	25	17	13	11	6	5	4	3
0.4	43	23	16	12	10	6	4	4	3
0.5	42	22	15	12	10	6	5	4	4
0.7	51	27	19	15	13	8	7	6	5
0.9	121	66	47	38	32	21	17	16	14

The formula for determining the NNH: $\dfrac{CGR(OR-1)+1}{CGR(OR-1)(1-CGR)}$

Abbreviations: CGR, control group risk; NNH, number needed to harm; OR, odds ratio.

Adapted from Hux et al.[9]

CASE-CONTROL STUDIES

Up to now, our examples have come from prospective *randomized controlled trials.* In these trials, we start with a group of patients who are *randomly allocated* to an intervention and a group of patients who are allocated to a control intervention. The investigators follow the patients over time and record the frequency of events. The process is similar in observational studies termed "prospective cohort studies," although in this study, the investigators do not control the *exposure* or treatment. For randomized trials and prospective cohort studies, we can calculate risks, odds, *risk difference*, RRs, ORs, and even odds reductions.

In case-control studies, investigators choose or sample participants not according to whether they have been exposed to the treatment or *risk factor*, but according to whether they have experienced a *target outcome*. Participants start the study with or without the event, rather than with or without the exposure or intervention. Investigators compare patients with the adverse outcome, be it stroke, myocardial infarction, or cancer, with controls who have not had the outcome. The usual question asked is whether there are any factors that seem to be more commonly present in one of these groups than in the other group.

In one case-control study, investigators examined the question of whether sunbeds or sunlamps increase the risk of skin melanoma.[10] The control patients and the cases had similar distributions of age, sex, and residence. Table 10.2-8 presents some of the findings from this study.

TABLE 10.2-8

Results From a Case-Control Study Examining the Association of Cutaneous Melanoma and the Use of Sunbeds and Sunlamps[a]

Exposure	Cases	Controls
Yes	67	41
No	210	242

[a]Data from Walter et al,[10] men only.

If the information in Table 10.2-8 had come from a prospective cohort study or a randomized controlled trial, we could have begun by calculating the risk of an event in the exposed and control groups. This would not make sense in the case-control study because the number of patients who did or did not have melanoma was chosen by the investigators. The OR provides the only sensible measure of association in a case-control study. One can ask whether the odds of having been exposed to sunbeds or sunlamps among people with melanoma were the same as the odds of exposure among the control patients. In the study, the odds of exposure (in men) were 67 of 210 in the melanoma patients and 41 of 242 in the control patients. The OR is therefore (67/210)/(41/242), or 1.88 (95% *confidence interval*, 1.20-2.98), suggesting an association between using sunbeds or sunlamps and developing melanoma. The fact that the confidence interval does not overlap or include 1.0 suggests that the association is unlikely to have resulted from chance.

Even if the association were not chance related, it does not necessarily mean that the sunbeds or sunlamps were the cause of melanoma. Potential explanations could include greater recollection of using these devices among people with melanoma (*recall bias*), longer sun exposure among these people, and different skin color; of these explanations, the investigators addressed many. To be confident that exposure to sunbeds or sunlamps was the cause of melanoma would require additional confirmatory studies.

References

1. Stiegmann GV, Goff JS, Michaletz-Onody PA, et al. Endoscopic sclerotherapy as compared with endoscopic ligation for bleeding esophageal varices. *N Engl J Med*. 1992;326(23):1527-1532.

2. Laird NM, Mosteller F. Some statistical methods for combining experimental results. *Int J Technol Assess Health Care*. 1990;6(1):5-30.

3. Walter SD. Choice of effect measure for epidemiological data. *J Clin Epidemiol*. 2000;53(9):931-939.

4. Deeks JJ. Issues in the selection of a summary statistic for meta-analysis of clinical trials with binary outcomes. *Stat Med*. 2002;21(11):1575-1600.

5. Bland JM, Altman DG. Statistics notes: the odds ratio. *BMJ*. 2000;320 (7247):1468.

6. Davies HT, Crombie IK, Tavakoli M. When can odds ratios mislead? *BMJ*. 1998;316(7136):989-991.

7. Zhang J, Yu KF. What's the relative risk? a method of correcting the odds ratio in cohort studies of common outcomes. *JAMA*. 1998;280(19):1690-1691.

8. Laine L, Cook D. Endoscopic ligation compared with sclerotherapy for treatment of esophageal variceal bleeding: a meta-analysis. *Ann Intern Med*. 1995;123(4): 280-287.

9. Hux JE, Levinton CM, Naylor CD. Prescribing posterity: influence of life-expectancy gains and drug costs. *J Gen Intern Med*. 1994;9(4):195-201.

10. Walter SD, Marrett LD, Shannon HS, From L, Hertzman C. The association of cutaneous malignant melanoma with the use of sunbeds and sunlamps. *Am J Epidemiol*. 1990;131(2):232-243.

WHAT DETERMINES THE WIDTH OF THE CONFIDENCE INTERVAL?

Jan Brożek

IN THIS CHAPTER:

Sample Size Does Not Determine the Width of the Confidence Interval

Small Sample Sizes Can Give More Precise Results Than Large Sample Sizes

Precision Increases as the Number of Events Increases

Beware of Randomized Controlled Trials With Too Few Events

SAMPLE SIZE DOES NOT DETERMINE THE WIDTH OF THE CONFIDENCE INTERVAL

Clinicians sometimes equate the size of a *randomized trial* or the number of participants in a *trial of therapy* with its precision, and thus the width of the *confidence interval (CI)*. This chapter deals with issues of precision and the resulting confidence in estimates of treatment effects in studies in which the *outcomes* are *dichotomous* (yes/no) events such as death, stroke, or myocardial infarction. As it turns out, the number of patients is a secondary determinant of our confidence in estimates of reduction in adverse outcomes associated with an *experimental intervention.*

SMALL SAMPLE SIZES CAN GIVE MORE PRECISE RESULTS THAN LARGE SAMPLE SIZES

Consider 2 studies. Both show a *relative risk reduction (RRR)* of 33%—a reduction in adverse events of 1/3—with intervention A vs control. Study 1 has enrolled 100 patients in each of the experimental and *control groups*, and study 2 has enrolled 1000 patients in each group. Which of the 2 studies will generate a more precise estimate of treatment effect, represented by a narrower CI? The apparently obvious answer is study 2, with its sample size an order of magnitude larger than that of study 1.

Suppose, however, that study 2—the study with the larger sample size—generated its RRR of 33% on the basis of 2 of 1000 people receiving intervention A vs 3 of 1000 in the control group having an adverse outcome. Study 1 demonstrated its RRR of 33% on the basis of 20 of 100 people receiving intervention A having an adverse outcome vs 30 of 100 people in the control group.

Which RRR of 33% do you trust more? Which one is more precise? Which has the narrower associated CI? As shown in Table 10.3-1, study 1 is the more reliable

TABLE 10.3-1

Study	No. of Events in Control Group	Total No. in Control Group	No. of Events in Experimental Group	Total No. in Experimental Group	RRR	95% CI Around RRR
Sample Size, Event Rate, and the Width of the Confidence Interval						
1	30	100	20	100	33%	−8 to 59
2	3	1000	2	1000	33%	−233 to 87

Abbreviations: CI, confidence interval; RRR, relative risk reduction.

because it is not the number of participants, but rather the number of outcome events that matters most.

PRECISION INCREASES AS THE NUMBER OF EVENTS INCREASES

In the following figures, we explore the relationship between sample size, number of events, and the precision of the study results by calculating CIs around the RRR from a set of hypothetical studies. The starting point is 100 patients per group, with 12 patients having an event in the control group and 8 patients in the group receiving treatment A. The RRR is 33%, with a corresponding 95% CI of –52% to 71%. This CI tells us that it is extremely likely that, compared with control, treatment A reduces the risk of an event by no more than 71% and that it increases the risk of an event by no more than 52% (not very useful information). We then explore the effects of increasing the sample size while leaving the *event rates* constant (Figure 10.3-1) and the effects of increasing the event rate while keeping the sample size constant (Figure 10.3-2). Investigators may achieve the former by enrolling more patients and the latter by extending the study duration or enrolling patients at higher risk of the outcome.

Figure 10.3-1 shows that as one increases the sample size while holding the event rate in both groups constant, the width of the CI decreases, eventually becoming narrow enough to be *statistically significant*, and then even narrower, providing a very precise estimate of the true RRR (assuming optimal *validity*).

Figure 10.3-2 shows an example of what would happen if we hold the sample size constant at 100 patients per group and increased the event rate.

FIGURE 10.3-1

Sample Size and the Width of the Confidence Interval (Assuming Constant Event Rate)

Control Events/total no.		Experimental Events/total no.		Sample size multiplied by	RRR (95% CI)	Favors control ⟷ Favors treatment
12	100	8	100	1	33% (–52% to 71%)	
24	200	16	200	2	33% (–20% to 63%)	
36	300	24	300	3	33% (–8% to 59%)	
48	400	32	400	4	33% (–2% to 56%)	
60	500	40	500	5	33% (2% to 54%)	
120	1000	80	1000	10	33% (13% to 49%)	
240	2000	160	2000	20	33% (19% to 45%)	

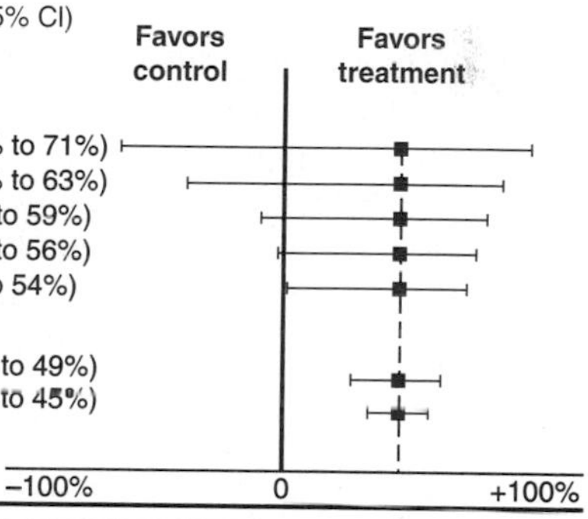

–100%　　0　　+100%

Abbreviations: CI, confidence interval; RRR, relative risk reduction.

FIGURE 10.3-2

Event Rate and the Width of the Confidence Interval (With a Constant Sample Size)

Control		Experimental		Event rate multiplied by	RRR (95% CI)	Favors control	Favors treatment
Events/total no.		Events/total no.					
12	100	8	100	1	33% (−52% to 71%)		
24	100	16	100	2	33% (−16% to 62%)		
36	100	24	100	3	33% (−2% to 57%)		
48	100	32	100	4	33% (6% to 53%)		

−100%   0   +100%

Abbreviations: CI, confidence interval; RRR, relative risk reduction.

Closer inspection of these figures allows 2 more observations. First, the width of the CI does not narrow linearly with the increase in sample size or event rate. In fact, it narrows proportionally to their square root. So, for instance, increasing the sample size from 100 to 200 has more effect than increasing it from 200 to 300, and from 200 to 300 more than increasing from 300 to 400, etc. Second, doubling the number of events by increasing the event rate while holding sample size constant decreases the width of the CI more than doubling the number of events by increasing the number of participants. Another way to state this phenomenon is this: for a constant number of events, the CI is narrower when the denominator (the number of patients) is small than when it is large.

For example, one recent report from the Women's Health Study,[1] a randomized *placebo*-controlled trial in primary prevention of cardiovascular disease, which enrolled almost 20000 women per group, showed a barely significant benefit in stroke reduction with low-dose aspirin compared with placebo after 10 years of observation (RRR, 17%; 95% CI, 1%-31%). Despite the substantial sample size, the estimate of the effect was imprecise—a wide CI allowing for an RRR of as much as 31% or as little as 1%. This lack of precision was due to the low stroke event rate of 266 of 19942 (1.3%) in the placebo group vs the even (though slightly) lower event rate of 221 of 19934 (1.1%) in the aspirin group.

In contrast, a much smaller trial of mechanical ventilation that compared low vs high tidal volume in patients with the acute respiratory distress syndrome[2] and which enrolled approximately 430 patients per group (40 times fewer than in Women's Health Study) showed an RRR of death of 22% (95% CI, 7%-35%) during 180 days. The width of the CI is almost the same as in the previous example because, despite a much smaller sample size, the risk of death in this population was high: 40% in the high-tidal-volume ventilated patients vs 31% in the lower-tidal-volume group.

Beware of Randomized Controlled Trials With Too Few Events

The fundamental implication of this discussion is that estimates of treatment effects derived from randomized trials become more exact not as their sample size increases, but rather as the number of events increases. Over and over again in this book, we caution you against trials with too few events and suggest you demand large numbers of events before you make strong inferences about treatment effects in the management of your patients (see Chapter 9.3, Randomized Trials Stopped Early for Benefit, and Chapter 11.3, Dealing with Misleading Presentations of Clinical Trial Results).

References

1. Ridker PM, Cook NR, Lee IM, et al. A randomized trial of low-dose aspirin in the primary prevention of cardiovascular disease in women. *N Engl J Med*. 2005; 352(13):1293-1304.

2. Acute Respiratory Distress Syndrome Network. Ventilation with lower tidal volumes as compared with traditional tidal volumes for acute lung injury and the acute respiratory distress syndrome. *N Engl J Med*. 2000;342(18):1301-1308.

COMPOSITE ENDPOINTS

Gordon Guyatt, Victor Montori,
Ignacio Ferreira-González, Jason W. Busse,
Holger Schünemann, Roman Jaeschke,
and Gaietà Permanyer-Miralda

IN THIS CHAPTER:

An Elderly Patient With Angina Considering Angiography and Possible Revascularization

You are an internist seeing a 76-year-old man who, despite taking carefully titrated β-blockers, nitrates, aspirin, an angiotensin-converting enzyme inhibitor, and a statin, has angina that significantly restricts his activities. Throughout the last year, his symptoms have worsened and now significantly limit his quality of life. You suggest to him the possibility of referral to a cardiologist for cardiac catheterization and possible revascularization. The patient expresses reluctance to undergo invasive management and wonders how much benefit he might expect from an invasive approach.

FINDING THE EVIDENCE

You wonder what recent *evidence* might bear on the patient's dilemma. You ask the patient to join you in front of your computer and go straight to your favorite source of information, ACP Journal Club, which you can review from your library's Ovid Evidence-Based Medicine Reviews system. To guide your search, you quickly jot down your question in *PICO* (patient, intervention, comparison, outcome) format (see Chapter 3, What Is the Question?). Your clinical question in PICO format is, In elderly patients with coronary artery disease, will invasive treatment with revascularization improve quality of life? You enter the search term "coronary artery disease" and restrict to "therapy" (146 citations) and combine this with "elderly" (272 citations). The search yields 20 citations, the first of which is a *randomized controlled trial* (*RCT*) of invasive vs noninvasive management of coronary artery disease in the elderly, with the acronym TIME that looks applicable.[1] You tell the patient you will review this study carefully and discuss the results with him in a week.

In the TIME study, you find that 301 patients 75 years or older who had Canadian Cardiac Society Class 2 or worse angina despite receiving at least 2 antianginal medications were randomized to optimized medical therapy or cardiac catheterization and, if appropriate, revascularization. The authors report their primary *endpoints* as quality of life, which showed equivalence at 12 months, and a *composite endpoint* (*CEP*) of death, nonfatal myocardial infarction (MI), and hospitalization for acute coronary syndrome (ACS). The frequency of this CEP was much lower in the revascularization (25.5%) than in the medical management arm (64.2%) (*hazard ratio* 0.31; 95% *confidence interval* [*CI*], 0.21-0.45; $P < .001$).

How should you interpret these results to best inform your patient's decision? Should you assume that the effect of treatment on the CEP accurately captures the effect on its components (death, nonfatal MI, and hospitalization for ACS)? Or, rather, should you abjure assumptions about the effect of treatment on component endpoints based on the effect of treatment on the CEP?

In this chapter, we offer clinicians a strategy to interpret the results of clinical trials when investigators measure the effect of treatment on an aggregate of endpoints of varying importance, as was the case with the TIME trial.

COMPOSITE ENDPOINTS

In the last 2 decades, as medical care has improved, the frequency with which patients with common conditions such as MI have subsequent adverse events, including death, recurrent MI, or stroke, has decreased. Although welcome for patients, low event rates provide challenges for clinical investigators who consequently require very large sample sizes and longer *follow-up* to test the incremental benefits of new therapies.

Clinical trialists have increasingly responded to these challenges by using CEPs that capture the number of patients experiencing any one of several adverse events—death, MI, or hospitalization, for example—as a primary study endpoint.[2] Investigators interested in decreasing the necessary sample size and duration of follow-up may assemble a CEP with a group of events that are important to patients and on which one anticipates treatment will have a similar effect. This justification—a paucity of events in any single category and a presumption that treatment will act in more or less the same way across categories of adverse events—provides the most compelling rationale for CEPs in contemporary clinical trials.[2]

INTERPRETATIONS OF COMPOSITE ENDPOINTS— WHAT ARE THE CLINICIAN'S OPTIONS?

Potentially, clinicians can base clinical decisions on the effect of treatment on a CEP. One might be safe in taking this approach if the reduction in *risk* were the same (in absolute and relative terms) on all components of the CEP. In the TIME trial, this would mean that the invasive strategy reduces the risk of each—death, nonfatal MI, and hospitalization for ACS—to the same extent. Table 10.4-1, which summarizes the results of the TIME trial, shows that in the invasive arm, 5 more patients died, and there were 6 fewer MIs and 78 fewer hospitalizations. This variation makes the assumption of similar reductions in *absolute risk* untenable. This result—appreciable variability in absolute reductions in component endpoints—is the rule in most trials including CEPs.

Alternatively, clinicians might legitimately maintain their focus on the CEP by considering the effect of treatment on the combination of death, MI, and hospitaliza-

TABLE 10.4-1

Results From the TIME Trial[a]

Endpoints	Invasive (n = 153)	Medical (n = 148)	Absolute Risk Difference (95% CI)	Hazard Ratio (95% CI)
Patients with a composite endpoint[a]	39 (25.5%)	95 (64.2%)	38.7 (27.9 to 48.5)	0.31 (0.21 to 0.45)
Deaths	17 (11.1%)	12 (8.1%)	−3.0 (−9.9 to 3.8)	1.51 (0.72 to 3.16)
Nonfatal myocardial infarctions[b]	14	20		0.75 (0.36 to 1.55)
Number of hospitalizations for ACS[b]	28	106		0.19 (0.12 to 0.30)

Abbreviations: ACS, acute coronary syndrome; CI, confidence interval.

[a]The composite endpoint included mortality, nonfatal myocardial infarction, and hospitalization for ACS.
[b]Authors report the number of events, rather than patients, so we cannot provide percentages of patients who had the event.

BMJ. 2005;330(7491):594-596. Reproduced with permission of the BMJ Publishing Group.

tion for ACS as just that, a combination, and eschew any inferences about the effect of treatment on each of the component endpoints. Adopting this interpretation, the clinician would answer the patient's question about the benefits of the invasive strategy by stating that "it will decrease your risk of serious cardiac events by, in relative terms, about 70%."

For the clinicians and patients who want specific information about the magnitude of the *relative risk reduction (RRR)* and *absolute risk reduction (ARR)* on endpoints of differing importance, this interpretation is of limited utility. For instance, the patient in the scenario might ask, "Doctor, what serious cardiac events are you talking about?" and subsequently, "Given that I am much more interested in avoiding death than MI and serious MI than a brief hospitalization without cardiac damage, can you please tell me the specific effect of surgery on death, on MI, and on hospitalization?"

Adhering to the interpretation that the data allow no statements about treatment effect on components of the CEP, the clinician can provide no guarantee that the 70% reduction in hazard applies to the most serious component, death, and can say nothing about the absolute reduction in likelihood of dying that the patient can anticipate. This limitation argues for abandoning the effect of treatment on the CEP as the basis for clinical decision making and focusing instead on its effects on each component endpoint.

Both investigators and pharmaceutical companies would often prefer that clinicians focus on CEPs. After all, a statement that treatment reduces the risk of a CEP of death, MI, and hospitalization is compelling because it gives us a sense of an important impact on all 3 endpoints. On the other hand, stating that we can be confident that treatment reduces the risk of hospitalizations but are uncertain about its effects on death and MI carries appreciably less force.

Table 10.4-2 presents a set of 3 questions to guide clinicians pondering whether to base a clinical decision on the effect of treatment on a CEP or on the component endpoints. The following is a description of how to apply these criteria.

TABLE 10.4-2

Users' Guides to Interpreting Composite Endpoints

1. Are the component endpoints of the composite endpoint of similar importance to patients?

2. Did the more and less important endpoints occur with similar frequencies?

3. Can one be confident that the component endpoints share similar relative risk reductions?

   • Is the underlying biology of the component endpoints similar enough such that one would expect similar relative risk reductions?

   • Are the point estimates of the relative risk reductions similar, and are the confidence intervals sufficiently narrow?

To the extent that one can answer yes to these questions, one can feel confident about using the effect of treatment on the combined endpoint as the basis for decision making.

To the extent that one answers no to these questions, one should look separately at the effect of treatment on the component endpoints as the basis for decision making.

BMJ. 2005;330(7491):594-596. Reproduced with permission of the BMJ Publishing Group.

ARE THE COMPONENT ENDPOINTS OF THE COMPOSITE ENDPOINT OF SIMILAR IMPORTANCE TO PATIENTS?

Consider a situation in which all components of a CEP are of equal importance to the patient. Were this true, making the assumption that the effect of the intervention on each component endpoint is similar in both relative and absolute terms will not be misleading. If patients consider death, stroke, and MI to be of equal importance, it does not much matter how a 5% ARR in the CEP is distributed across a CEP including these 3 components. Assuming similar effects across components will not adversely affect decision making, even if treatment effects differ substantially.

Patients almost invariably, however, assign varying importance to different health *outcomes*. As a result, ignoring possible difference of treatment effect on component endpoints on the grounds that they share identical patient-importance will seldom be justified. The magnitude of the gradient in importance between endpoints therefore becomes the issue.

Consider an RCT of corticosteroids in patients with an acute exacerbation of chronic obstructive lung disease. The investigators chose a CEP of death from any cause, need for intubation and mechanical ventilation, and administration of open-label corticosteroids.[3] Patients are likely to consider the need for short-term steroids of trivial importance in comparison to the requirement for mechanical ventilation, and particularly in relation to death. The large gradient in importance increases our skepticism about the combined endpoint.

On the other hand, consider a trial of 4 doses of perioperative aspirin in patients undergoing carotid endarterectomy in which one of the CEPs comprised death and stroke.[4] Many patients would consider a severe stroke with permanent residual deficits as having a low value approaching that of death. The relatively small gradient in importance between the components increases the usefulness of the CEP in clinical decision making.

DID THE COMPONENT ENDPOINTS OCCUR WITH SIMILAR FREQUENCIES?

Consider the following statement: In patients with in-stent stenosis of coronary artery bypass grafts, γ-radiation reduced the CEP of death from cardiac causes, Q-wave MI, and revascularization of the target vessel. This result seems impressive because it suggests that γ-radiation reduces the incidence of death and MI, as well as the need for revascularization. The trial from which we draw this result randomized 120 patients with in-stent stenosis of a saphenous vein graft to γ-radiation (iridium 192) or *placebo*.[5] Of those in the iridium 192 arm, 32% experienced the primary CEP of death from cardiac causes, Q-wave MIs, or revascularization of the target vessel at 12 months, as did 63% in the placebo arm (RRR 50%; 95% CI, 25%-68%).

Although this result appears compelling, only 2 patients in the placebo arm (3.3%) and 1 patient in the iridium 192 arm (1.7%) sustained an MI (*risk difference [RD]*, 1.7%; 95% CI, −5.9% to 9.9%). The story is similar for cardiac death, which occurred in 4 patients (7%) in each arm (RD, 0%; 95% CI, −10.3% to 10.3%). Revascularizations constituted the majority of the events: 32 of 38 patients who experienced events in the placebo arm experienced only revascularization; the same was true of 14 of 19 who experienced events in the radiated group. Because of the very large discrepancy in the frequency of the more important and less important endpoints in this trial, the most reasonable conclusion is that the intervention reduced the *relative risk* (RR) of revascularization of the target vessel by 54% (95% CI, 29%-71%), an RD of 33% (95% CI, 16%-49%). The trial provides, however, essentially no information about the effect of the intervention on MI or death.

Contrast this result with that of the Heart Outcomes Prevention Evaluation (HOPE) trial,[6] which randomized 9297 patients at high risk of cardiac events to ramipril or placebo. Ramipril reduced cardiovascular deaths from 8.1% to 6.1% (RRR, 26%; 95% CI, 13%-36%), MI from 12.3% to 9.9% (RRR, 20%; 95% CI, 10%-30%), and stroke from 4.9 to 3.4% (RRR, 32%; 95% CI, 16%-44%). Here, the gradient in rates of death, MI, and stroke in the control group (8.1%, 12.3%, and 4.9%) is relatively small. The difference in events between treatment and control (2.0% for deaths, 2.4% for MI, and 1.5% for stroke) is even more similar. This similar frequency of occurrence of the more and less important endpoints provides support for relying on the CEP in clinical decision making.

If the more patient-important components occur with far less frequency than the less patient-important components of a CEP, the CEP becomes uninformative, if not frankly misleading. Clinicians must look carefully at the results of each component to interpret the results for their patients.

Can One Be Confident That the Component Endpoints Share Similar Relative Risk Reductions?

Is the Underlying Biology of the Component Endpoints Similar Enough That One Would Expect Similar Relative Risk Reductions?

Comfort with using a CEP as the basis of clinical decision making rests in part on confidence that similar RRRs apply to the more and the less important components. Investigators should therefore construct CEPs in which the biology would lead us to expect similar effects across components.

The Irbesartan Diabetic Nephropathy Trial[7] randomized 1715 hypertensive patients with nephropathy and type 2 diabetes to irbesartan, amlodipine, or placebo. The primary endpoint was the composite of a doubling of the baseline serum creatinine concentration, the onset of end-stage renal disease (serum creatinine level > 6.0 mg/dL, initiation of dialysis, or transplantation), or death from any cause. It is extremely plausible that, for 2 of these 3 components, doubling of creatinine level and crossing the creatinine-level threshold of 6.0 mg/dL, any treatment effects would be similar—indeed, one would be surprised if results showed otherwise. On the other hand, there are many contributors to all-cause mortality aside from renal failure (including, for instance, cardiac disease), and it might well be that treatments have different effects on these contributors. Thus, the biological rationale that the treatments would have similar effects on all 3 components is weak. The relatively weak biological rationale increases our reluctance to base treatment decisions on the composite, as opposed to its components. Indeed, in this instance, irbesartan lowered the incidence of both, doubling of creatinine level and end-stage renal disease, but without apparent effect on all-cause mortality (Figure 10.4-1).

In contrast, the authors of the Clopidogrel Versus Aspirin in Patients at Risk of Ischaemic Events (CAPRIE) study, an RCT of aspirin vs clopidogrel in patients with a variety of manifestations of atherosclerosis, argued explicitly for the biological sense of their CEP.[8] Citing results of previous trials of antiplatelet agents vs placebo, they note the similar biological determinants of ischemic stroke, MI, and vascular death: "A *meta-analysis* of 142 trials…shows clearly that antiplatelet drugs reduce the incidence of a CEP of ischemic stroke, MI, and vascular death, the odds reduction being 27%, which is consistent over a wide range of clinical manifestations."[8] Their argument strengthens the case for assuming, until evidence suggests otherwise, that RRRs are consistent across components of the authors' CEP.

FIGURE 10.4-1

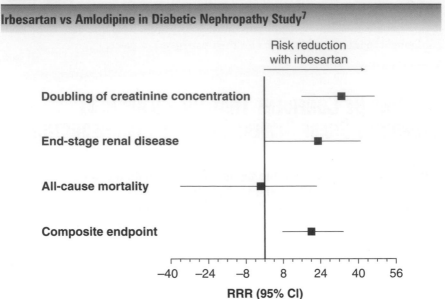

Irbesartan vs Amlodipine in Diabetic Nephropathy Study[7]

Abbreviations: CI, confidence interval; RRR, relative risk reduction.

BMJ. 2005;330(7491):594-596. Reproduced with permission of the BMJ Publishing Group.

Are the Point Estimates of the Relative Risk Reductions Similar and Confidence Intervals Sufficiently Narrow?

No matter how compelling the authors' biological rationale, only the demonstration of similar RRRs can strongly increase our comfort with a CEP.

The LIFE trial[9] investigators randomized 9193 patients older than 55 years, with hypertension and left ventricular hypertrophy, to receive either a losartan-based or an atenolol-based antihypertensive treatment and followed them for a median of 4.8 years. They used exactly the same rationale as the CAPRIE investigators to choose a primary CEP of cardiovascular mortality, MI, and stroke. Figure 10.4-2 depicts the results showing that patients allocated to losartan had 2.38 CEP events per 100 patient-years and those allocated to atenolol had 2.79 CEP events per 100 patient-years, an RRR for the CEP of 13% (95% CI, 2%-23%). The point estimates (RRR) for the components, however, show important differences: −7% for MI, 25% for stroke, and 11% for cardiovascular death. This variability suggests that clinicians should focus on individual endpoints. The LIFE trial suggests that a losartan-based regimen, compared with one based on atenolol, may reduce the risk for strokes but has uncertain effects on cardiovascular mortality and MI in patients with hypertension and left ventricular hypertrophy.

The UK Prospective Diabetes Study (UKPDS) trial of intensive glycemic control vs conventional control in patients with type 2 diabetes provides another example. This study reported that the primary endpoint of the trial was time to first "diabetes-related endpoint" (sudden death, death from hyperglycemia or

FIGURE 10.4-2

Randomized Trial of Losartan vs Atenolol[9]

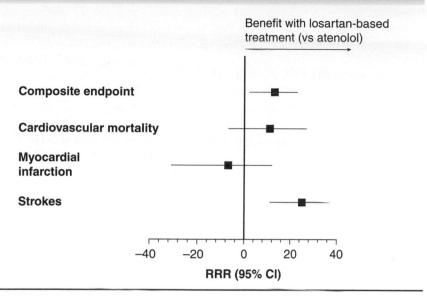

Abbreviations: CI, confidence interval; RRR, relative risk reduction.

hypoglycemia, fatal or nonfatal MI, angina, heart failure, stroke, renal failure, amputation [of at least 1 digit], vitreous hemorrhage, retinal photocoagulation, blindness in 1 eye, or cataract extraction), "diabetes-related death" (death from MI, stroke, peripheral vascular disease, renal disease, hyperglycemia or hypoglycemia, and sudden death), or all-cause mortality.[10] Although the investigators reported a significant 12% reduction in the RR in the CEP (95% CI, 1%-21%), the results do not exclude a harmful effect on diabetes-related deaths (RRR, 0.90; 95% CI, 0.73-1.11) and all-cause mortality (RR, 0.94; 95% CI, 0.80-1.10).[10] Moreover, they identify that most of the apparent effect was a reduction (2.7% of the 3.2%, or 80% of the absolute reduction in risk of microvascular complications) in retinal photocoagulation.[10,11] Reviewers typically summarize the results as showing a reduction in any of 21 diabetes-related endpoints with intensive glycemic control, and only 1 in 35 reviews of the UKPDS results highlighted the dominance of the overall effect of the reduction in the risk of photocoagulation.[12]

These results contrast with those of the HOPE trial of ramipril vs placebo in patients at high risk of vascular events we described earlier.[6] Here, the RRRs in the same 3 endpoints were 26% (95% CI, 13%-36%) for cardiovascular death, 20% (95% CI, 10%-30%) for MI, and 32% (95% CI, 16%-44%) for stroke. Although one might challenge these CIs on the basis that reporting 3 separate endpoints mandates adjustment for multiple statistical tests, the observation that the lower boundary—the boundary closest to no effect—of all 3 CIs is well above 0% is reassuring. For each of the 3 components of the CEP, then, the clinician can be confident that treatment effect is favorable.

Finally, consider the results of the Clopidogrel in Unstable Angina to Prevent Recurrent Events (CURE) trial, in which investigators randomized 12 562 patients with ACS to clopidogrel or placebo and examined the effect on the same CEP: cardiovascular death, MI, or stroke.[13] Here, although one could interpret the point estimates of the RRR as consistent (23%, 7%, and 14% for MI, cardiovascular death, and stroke, respectively), the range of the CIs should give us pause. Although the point estimate and 95% CI on the RRR leave us reasonably confident of an important treatment effect on MI (23%; 95% CI, 11%-33%), the same is not true of either cardiovascular death (7%; 95% CI, −8% to 21%) or stroke (14%; 95% CI, −18% to 37%). As a result, the statement that clopidogrel reduced a CEP of cardiovascular death, stroke, and MI by 20% (the RRR associated with the CEP) is potentially misleading, and using the CEP as a basis for clinical decision making is problematic.

Many of the examples we have presented highlight the typical situation. Here, the RRR associated with components that represent the most *patient-important outcomes* may or may not be similar to that for the less important components, but the low event rate of the former precludes confident inferences about the true treatment effect. Sometimes, however, when data accumulate from many trials, it becomes clear that skepticism about treatment effect on the most important outcomes, even in the presence of convincing evidence of effect on outcomes of lesser seriousness, was well warranted.

Consider that, for example, trials comparing drug-eluting stents vs bare-metal stents show conclusively that the former type of stent reduces the CEP "MACE" ("major adverse cardiac events") compared with the latter type of stent. However, meta-analyses of several RCTs show that drug-eluting stents show no benefit in survival or Q-wave MI (in fact there is an unfavorable trend for Q-wave MI), whereas there is a large benefit in reducing the need for revascularization.[14,15] Similarly, percutaneous coronary intervention in patients with stable coronary artery disease decreases the risk of recurrent angina[16] but has no effect on death or MI risk.[17]

TIME TRIAL—RESOLUTION

Let us return to the scenario with which our discussion began, that of the patient reluctant to undergo invasive interventions to control his angina. Is it reasonable to use the CEP from the TIME trial—death, MI, and hospitalization for ACS—to guide the decision, or should we focus on individual results of the 3 components?

To address this issue, we can ask the 3 questions in our Users' Guides (Table 10.4-2). Most patients will find death and large MI with subsequent disability far more important than a short hospital admission for ACS with rapid return to previous function. Hospitalization occurred far more frequently than the 2 more important events (Table 10.4-2). Biological rationale fails to support a presumption that the invasive strategy will have similar effects on all 3 endpoints, particularly during the short term. Indeed, the investigators explicitly state that they might anticipate an increase in short-term deaths with surgery while achieving benefits in terms of decreased angina and associated hospital admissions. Although CIs are wide, the data provide support for this hypothesis, with a trend toward increased deaths but with a large reduction in admissions, with the invasive strategy. In the TIME trial, the CEP fails all 3 criteria and thus provides little useful information for clinical decision making. Your patient's decision will be best informed by discussion of the treatment's effect on each component endpoint.

CONCLUSION

The widespread use of CEPs reflects their utility as a solution to the problem of declining event rates and the resultant need for very large RCTs with long duration of follow-up to reliably detect small treatment effects. Unfortunately, use of CEPs as major endpoints makes the interpretation of the results of RCTs challenging.

At one extreme, one may find trials in which (1) the component endpoints are of similar but not identical importance, (2) the endpoints that are more important occur with a frequency similar to those that are less important, and (3) strong biological rationale supports results that, across component endpoints, show similar RRRs with CIs excluding minimal effects. Under such circumstances, clinicians can, with confidence, use the CEP as the primary basis for decision making.

At the other extreme, (1) the component endpoints have very different patient importance, (2) the more important endpoints occur far less often than the less important endpoints, and (3) biological rationale is weak, RRRs differ widely, and CIs for the more important endpoints include the possibility of harm. Under these circumstances, the point estimates and CIs for individual component endpoints should provide the basis for clinical decisions. Although situations between these extremes may leave reasonable people disagreeing about the most appropriate interpretation of the results, these Users' Guides will help clinicians navigate the treacherous waters of CEPs.

References

1. Pfisterer M, Buser P, Osswald S, et al. Outcome of elderly patients with chronic symptomatic coronary artery disease with an invasive vs optimized medical treatment strategy: one-year results of the randomized TIME trial. *JAMA.* 2003;289(9):1117-1123.

2. Freemantle N, Calvert M, Wood J, Eastaugh J, Griffin C. Composite outcomes in randomized trials: greater precision but with greater uncertainty? *JAMA.* 2003; 289(19):2554-2559.

3. Niewoehner D, Erbland M, Deupree R, et al. Effect of systemic glucocorticoids on exacerbations of chronic obstructive pulmonary disease. *N Engl J Med.* 1999; 340(25):1941-1947.

4. Taylor DW, Barnett HJ, Haynes RB, et al. Low-dose and high-dose acetylsalicylic acid for patients undergoing carotid endarterectomy: a randomised controlled trial: ASA and Carotid Endarterectomy (ACE) Trial Collaborators. *Lancet.* 1999;353(9171):2179-2184.

5. Waksman R, Ajani AE, White RL, et al. Intravascular gamma radiation for in-stent restenosis in saphenous-vein bypass grafts. *N Engl J Med.* 2002;346(16):1194-1199.

6. Yusuf S, Sleight P, Pogue J, Bosch J, Davies R, Dagenais G. Effects of an angiotensin-converting-enzyme inhibitor, ramipril, on cardiovascular events in high-risk patients: the Heart Outcomes Prevention Evaluation Study Investigators. *N Engl J Med.* 2000;342(3):145-153.

7. Lewis EJ, Hunsicker LG, Clarke WR, et al. Renoprotective effect of the angiotensin-receptor antagonist irbesartan in patients with nephropathy due to type 2 diabetes. *N Engl J Med.* 2001;345(12):851-860.

8. CAPRIE Steering Committee. A randomised, blinded, trial of clopidogrel versus aspirin in patients at risk of ischaemic events (CAPRIE). *Lancet.* 1996;348 (9038):1329-1339.

9. Dahlof B, Devereux RB, Kjeldsen SE, et al. Cardiovascular morbidity and mortality in the Losartan Intervention For Endpoint reduction in hypertension study (LIFE): a randomised trial against atenolol. *Lancet.* 2002;359(9311):995-1003.

10. UK Prospective Diabetes Study (UKPDS) Group. Intensive blood-glucose control with sulphonylureas or insulin compared with conventional treatment and risk of complications in patients with type 2 diabetes (UKPDS 33). *Lancet.* 1998;352 (9131):837-853.

11. McCormack J, Greenhalgh T. Seeing what you want to see in randomised controlled trials: versions and perversions of UKPDS data: United Kingdom Prospective Diabetes Study. *BMJ.* 2000;320(7251):1720-1723.

12. Shaughnessy AF, Slawson DC. What happened to the valid POEMs? a survey of review articles on the treatment of type 2 diabetes. *BMJ.* 2003;327(7409):266.

13. Yusuf S, Zhao F, Mehta SR, Chrolavicius S, Tognoni G, Fox KK. Effects of clopidogrel in addition to aspirin in patients with acute coronary syndromes without ST-segment elevation. *N Engl J Med.* 2001;345(7):494-502.

14. Katritsis DG, Karvouni E, Ioannidis JP. Meta-analysis comparing drug-eluting stents with bare metal stents. *Am J Cardiol.* 2005;95(5):640-643.

15. Babapulle MN, Joseph L, Belisle P, Brophy JM, Eisenberg MJ. A hierarchical Bayesian meta-analysis of randomised clinical trials of drug-eluting stents. *Lancet.* 2004;364(9434):583-591.

16. Bucher HC, Hengstler P, Schindler C, Guyatt GH. Percutaneous transluminal coronary angioplasty versus medical treatment for non-acute coronary heart disease: meta-analysis of randomised controlled trials. *BMJ.* 2000;321(7253):73-77.

17. Katritsis DG, Ioannidis JP. Percutaneous coronary intervention versus conservative therapy in nonacute coronary artery disease: a meta-analysis. *Circulation.* 2005;111(22):2906-2912.

ADVANCED TOPICS IN THE RESULTS
OF THERAPY TRIALS

MEASURING PATIENTS' EXPERIENCE

Toshi A. Furukawa, Roman Jaeschke,
Deborah J. Cook, and Gordon Guyatt

IN THIS CHAPTER:

Clinical Resolution

Conclusion

CLINICAL SCENARIO

Which Drug Is Best for a Patient With Chronic Schizophrenia?

You are a psychiatrist following a 49-year-old man who has had schizophrenia for more than 20 years. He had an acute psychotic episode in his mid-20s and was admitted to a psychiatric hospital for 3 weeks. He made good recovery and has managed to continue work in a small factory. He has been taking chlorpromazine 200 mg/d for many years, still hears occasional hallucinations, and has no close friends except for his sister's family, who live a block away. Half a year ago, work stress increased, the patient began to take medication only irregularly, and he experienced a mild exacerbation, becoming fearful, developing insomnia, and hearing more voices. You increased his chlorpromazine dosage to 300 mg/d, and the patient became less agitated but is still moderately symptomatic. Taking 300 mg/d of chlorpromazine, the patient has hand tremors that trouble him, and his movements are stiff. He does not mind the stiffness, but his family worries because "he looks odd, aloof, and ill." He and his family now wonder whether he should try a new antipsychotic drug that had been publicized at schizophrenia support group meetings they have attended.

You are impressed with the recent report of a government-funded large pragmatic trial comparing 4 newer antipsychotic drugs and 1 old-generation drug (chlorpromazine belongs to this latter class) among 1500 patients with chronic schizophrenia.[1] The authors concluded that, although the majority of the patients in each group discontinued their medication, olanzapine proved the most effective in terms of the rates of overall discontinuation and *symptom* reduction. Patients did not, however, tolerate olanzapine as well, and the drug can produce weight gain and elevations in blood glucose and lipid levels.

After hearing about the treatment options, the patient comments, "Doctor, tell me how much better I will actually feel while taking these medications and also what side effects I might get. I care more about these than being able to stay on one medication longer than the others." Skimming the article in question, you feel you are incompetent to answer this patient's questions. You promise him and his family that you will get back with more information in understandable terms in a week and advise him to continue taking chlorpromazine until then.

TYPES OF INSTRUMENTS AND TESTS IN MEDICINE

Why do we offer treatment to patients? There are 3 reasons. We believe that our interventions increase longevity, decrease symptoms, or prevent future morbidity.

Decreasing symptoms or feeling better includes avoiding discomfort (pain, nausea, breathlessness, and so forth), distress (emotional suffering), and disability (loss of function).[2]

At least in part because of the difficulty in measurement, for many years, clinicians were willing to substitute physiologic or laboratory tests for the direct measurement of these *endpoints*, or tended even to ignore them altogether. During the past 20 years, however, the growing prevalence of chronic diseases has led clinicians to recognize the importance of direct measurement of how people are feeling and the extent to which they are functioning in daily activities. Investigators have developed sophisticated methods to measure people's experience. Because, as clinicians, we are most interested in aspects of life that are directly related to health rather than issues such as financial solvency or the quality of the environment, we frequently refer to measurements of how people are feeling as *health-related quality of life (HRQL)*. In this chapter, we use the generic term HRQL to refer to all self-reported or observer-rated assessments of patients' discomfort, distress, and disability.

Before launching into the details, it is useful to review what we loosely call "measures," "assessments," "instruments," "indexes," "scales," or "tests" in medicine. When we practice medicine, we are constantly assessing and measuring patients' status. One can categorize these clinical assessments or tests depending on their purpose and their format (Table 10.5-1). A test may aim to screen for disease, to diagnose disease, to measure disease severity, or to evaluate change in severity. In terms of format, clinicians can rely on self-report, rate patient status themselves, or carry out physiologic measurements.

This chapter focuses on the instruments shown in italics in Table 10.5-1: those that either measure severity (in this instance, degree of patients' discomfort, distress, and disability) or assess change in severity, according to patients' self-report or clinicians' assessments. (For a critical appraisal of screening tests, see Chapter 22.3, Moving From Evidence to Action: Recommendations About Screening; and for a critical appraisal of diagnostic tests, see Chapter 17, Advanced Topics in Diagnosis and related sections 17.1 to 17.4.) Investigators typically measure HRQL by using self-report questionnaires asking patients how they are feeling or what they are experiencing. Such questionnaires may use *dichotomous* response options such as yes/no, or 5-point (or any other number) *Likert scales* (feeling great, good, OK, bad, or terrible), or *visual analog scales*. Investigators aggregate responses to these questions into domains or dimensions that yield a single score for aspects of HRQL (for example, 5 individual questions may yield a single measure of physical function, and 7 different questions may yield a measure of emotional function).

Physicians often have limited familiarity with methods of measuring patients' experience. At the same time, they read articles that recommend administering or withholding treatment on the basis of its effect on patients' well-being. This chapter is designed for clinicians asking the question, Will this treatment make the patient feel better? As in other chapters of this book, we will use the framework of assessing the *validity* of the methods, interpreting the results, and applying the results to patients (Table 10.5-2). In this case, however, we have added a preliminary question regarding whether you should or should not be concerned with measure-

TABLE 10.5-1

Examples of Instruments and Tests in Medicine, Categorized by Their Format and Purpose[a]

Purpose	Format		
	Self-report	Clinician Rated	Physiologic
Screening test	Beck Depression Inventory[3]	Mini-Mental State Examination[4]	Urine glucose
		Six-Item Screener[5]	Blood pressure
			Mammography
			Fecal occult blood test
Diagnostic test		History taking	OGTT
		Physical examination	Blood pressure
			Biopsy
Severity Measure (Discriminative Instrument)			
	Chronic Respiratory Questionnaire[6]	*NYHA functional classification*	HbA1c
	Asthma Quality of Life Questionnaire[7]	*ECOG performance status*	Blood pressure
	Short Form-36[8]	*Hamilton Rating Scale for Depression[10]*	
	Sickness Impact Profile[9]	*Positive and Negative Syndrome Scale[11]*	
	Beck Depression Inventory[3]	*Clinical Global Impression-Severity[12]*	
Change Measure (Evaluative Instrument)			
Serial assessments with severity measure	*Chronic Respiratory Questionnaire*	(NYHA is apparently unsuitable here)	HbA1c
	Asthma Quality of Life Questionnaire	*Hamilton Rating Scale for Depression[10]*	Blood pressure
	Short Form-36 (Sickness Impact Profile is not good)	*Positive and Negative Syndrome Scale[11]*	
Transition measure[b]	*Patient-specific measure of change*	*Transition Dyspnea Index[13]*	
		Clinical Global Impression-Improvement[12]	

Abbreviations: ECOG, Eastern Cooperative Oncology Group; HbA1c, glycosylated hemoglobin; NYHA, New York Heart Association; OGTT, oral glucose tolerance test.

[a]Italicized text corresponds to instruments that are examples of measures of patients' experience that are subjects of this chapter.
[b]Transition measures ask the patients how much better or worse they are feeling or functioning, or ask the clinicians to assess how much better or worse the patients are feeling or functioning.

TABLE 10.5-2

Guidelines for Using Articles About Health-Related Quality of Life (HRQL)

Is measurement of HRQL important?

Are the results valid?

Primary guides

- Have the investigators measured aspects of patients' lives that patients consider important?
- Is the instrument reliable (when measuring severity) or responsive (when measuring change)?
- Does the instrument relate to other measurements in the way it should?

Secondary guides

- Have the investigators omitted important aspects of patients' HRQL?

What are the results?

- How can we interpret the scores?

How can I apply the results to patient care?

- Has the information from the study addressed aspects of life that your patient considers important?

---

ment of how patients feel. We hope that this chapter will help you improve your clinical care by emphasizing certain aspects of patients' experience, including functional, emotional, and social limitations that may sometimes be less salient than you and your patients would consider ideal.

IS MEASUREMENT OF HEALTH-RELATED QUALITY OF LIFE IMPORTANT?

Most patients will agree that, under most circumstances, prolonging their lives is a sufficient reason to accept a course of treatment. Under these circumstances, measurement of HRQL may be of little relevance.

> For instance, some years ago, investigators showed that 24-hour oxygen administration in patients with severe chronic airflow limitation reduced mortality.[14] The omission of HRQL data from the original article ultimately was not an important one. Because the intervention prolongs life, our enthusiasm for continuous oxygen administration is not diminished by a subsequent report suggesting that more intensive oxygen therapy had little or no impact on HRQL.[15]

Measurement of HRQL becomes important in 3 circumstances. First, although many of our life-prolonging treatments have a negligible impact on HRQL, when they do lead to a deterioration in HRQL, patients may be concerned that small gains in life expectancy come at too high a cost. For instance, patients may not accept toxic cancer chemotherapy that will provide marginal gains in longevity. In the extreme, an intervention such as mechanical ventilation may prolong the life of a patient in a vegetative state, but the patient's family may wonder whether their loved one would really want it. Unfortunately, underdevelopment of appropriate measures may have hindered clinicians from paying due attention to patients' symptoms, such as fatigue and dyspnea in cancer patients.[16,17]

When the goal of treatment is to improve how people are feeling (rather than to prolong their lives) and physiologic correlates of patients' experience are lacking, HRQL measurement is imperative. For example, we would pay little attention to studies of antidepressant medications that failed to measure patients' mood or to trials of migraine medication that failed to measure pain.

The more difficult decisions occur when the relationship between physiologic or laboratory measures and HRQL *outcomes* is uncertain. Practitioners tended to rely on substitute endpoints not because they were uninterested in making patients feel better, but because they assumed a strong link between physiologic measurements and patients' well-being. As we argue in another chapter of this book (see Chapter 11.4, Surrogate Outcomes), *substitute endpoints* or *surrogate outcomes* such as bone density for fractures, cholesterol level for coronary artery disease deaths, and laboratory exercise capacity for ability to undertake day-to-day activities have often proved misleading. Changes in conventional measures of clinical status often show only weak to moderate correlations with changes in HRQL[18] and fail to detect patient-important changes in HRQL.[18] *Randomized trials* that measure both physiologic endpoints and HRQL may show effects on one but not on the other. For example, trials in patients with chronic lung disease have shown treatment effects on peak flow rate without improvement in HRQL.[19] We therefore advocate great caution when relying on surrogate outcomes.

USING THE GUIDE

Referring to our opening scenario, in this landmark study of antipsychotics, 1493 adults with chronic schizophrenia at 57 US clinical sites were randomly assigned to one of the following agents: olanzapine, quetiapine, risperidone, ziprasidone (all newer or second-generation or atypical antipsychotics), or perphenazine (a first-generation antipsychotic). Patients had a mean age of 41 years and had had the disease for a mean of 24 years.

Patients with tardive dyskinesia at baseline were allocated to newer antipsychotics only. Despite this, the rates of discontinuation because of intolerable extrapyramidal adverse effects were greater among those receiving perphenazine than among those receiving newer antipsychotics ($P = .002$). You therefore decide to focus your inquiry on comparisons of newer antipsychotics, and especially on olanzapine and risperidone, because the other 2 newer antipsychotics (quetiapine and ziprasidone) proved no better than the other 2 in any respect.

Half of the patients assigned to olanzapine kept receiving that medication for 3 months, whereas half of those assigned to risperidone had discontinued the medication after only 1 month. By 18 months, 64% of those assigned to olanzapine and 74% of those assigned to risperidone discontinued the study medication ($P = .002$).

Olanzapine led to a 5- to 7-point improvement in the Positive and Negative Sydrome Scale (PANSS), a standard measure to assess schizophrenia symptoms, with a possible score range of 30 to 210,[11] through 1 to 3 months, whereas risperidone resulted in improvements of about 3 or 4 points ($P = .002$). You wonder whether this represents an important difference in the degree of improvement in the patient's psychiatric symptoms and, if so, whether adverse effects might outweigh the difference. The article itself provides no clue to the first question, and you set out to find the answers.

FINDING THE EVIDENCE

Definitively establishing a measurement instrument's usefulness requires several studies. As a result, critically appraising an HRQL measure requires a review of several articles. A good first step is to identify the original report of the instrument, where you will usually find a detailed description of the instrument and initial data about its measurement properties. You enter "PANSS" in PubMed, hit 858 articles, jump to the last page of the retrieved studies, and identify the first reports of the PANSS.[11,20] For some well-established instruments, you may sometimes wish to purchase a published manual, if the instrument is very important for many of your patients. The manual for PANSS is available from Multi-Health Systems, Inc. (https://www.mhs.com/ecom/(ck2jpcn4lciyioafxle32a55)/product.aspx?RptGrpID=PAN).

Sometimes, initial studies may provide sufficient data for your critical appraisal. When they do not (as in the case of PANSS, whose responsiveness—which we explain shortly—was not evident in the first reports), we need to look for additional studies. To identify an article that deals with responsiveness or sensitivity to change, you enter "response OR sensitivity" as free text words and "PANSS" in the title field, and the search yields 8 citations. The title of one article ("What Does the PANSS Mean?")[21] promises it will provide the data you need.

ARE THE RESULTS VALID?

Have the Investigators Measured Aspects of Patients' Lives That Patients Consider Important?

We have described how investigators often substitute endpoints that make intuitive sense to them for those that patients value. Clinicians can recognize these situations by asking themselves the following question: if the endpoints measured by the investigators were the only thing that changed, would patients be willing to take the treatment? In addition to changes in clinical or physiologic variables, patients would require that they feel better or live longer. For instance, if a treatment for osteoporosis increased bone density without preventing back pain, loss of height, or fractures, patients would not be interested in risking the adverse effects—or incurring the costs and inconvenience—of treatment.

How can clinicians be sure that investigators have measured aspects of life that patients value? Investigators may show that the outcomes they have measured are important to patients by asking them directly.

> For example, in a study examining HRQL in patients with chronic airflow limitation who were recruited from a secondary-care respiratory care clinic, the investigators used a literature review and interviews with clinicians and patients to identify 123 items reflecting possible ways that patients' illness might affect their quality of life.[6] They then asked 100 patients to identify the items that were problems for them and to indicate how important those items were. They found that the most important problem areas for patients were their dyspnea during day-to-day activities and their chronic fatigue. An additional area of difficulty was emotional function, including having feelings of frustration and impatience.

If the authors do not present direct evidence that their outcome measures are important to patients, they may cite previous work. For example, researchers conducting a randomized trial of respiratory rehabilitation in patients with chronic lung disease used an HRQL measure based on the responses of patients in the study described just above, and they referred to that study.[22] Ideally, the report will include enough information about the questionnaire to obviate the need to review previous reports.

Another alternative is to describe the content of the outcome measures in detail. An adequate description of the content of a questionnaire allows clinicians to use their own experience to decide whether what is being measured is important to patients.

> For instance, the authors of an article describing a randomized trial of surgery vs watchful waiting for benign prostatic hyperplasia assessed the degree to which urinary difficulties bothered the patients or interfered with their activities of daily living, sexual function, social activities, and general well-being.[23] Few would doubt the importance of these items and—because patients in primary care often are untroubled by minor symptoms of benign prostatic hyperplasia—the importance of including them in the results of the trial.

USING THE GUIDE

The PANSS, used in the study of antipsychotics for chronic schizophrenia, covers a wide range of psychopathologic symptoms that patients with schizophrenia may experience, including the so-called positive symptoms (7 items for delusions, hallucinations, etc), the so-called negative symptoms (7 items for blunted affect, withdrawal, etc), and the general psychopathology (16 items for anxiety, depression, etc).[11] These items can capture the overall picture of the patient's symptoms well but may miss more general aspects of HRQL such as a sense of well-being or satisfaction with life.

Is the Instrument Reliable (When Measuring Severity) or Responsive (When Measuring Change)?

There are 2 distinct ways in which investigators use HRQL instruments. They may wish to help clinicians distinguish between people who have a better or worse level of HRQL or to measure whether people are feeling better or worse over time[24] (see Table 10.5-1).

For instance, suppose a trial of a new drug for patients with heart failure shows that it works best in patients with the New York Heart Association (NYHA) functional classification class III and IV symptoms. We could use the NYHA classification for 2 purposes. First, for treatment decisions, we might use it as a tool by which to discriminate between patients who do and do not warrant therapy. Indeed, a single trial has suggested that spironolactone reduces mortality in NYHA class III and IV patients. One might choose to restrict therapy to this group, in which the intervention has been tested directly.[25] We might also want to determine whether the drug was effective in improving an individual patient's functional status and, in so doing, monitor changes in the patient's NYHA functional class. However, in this instance, the NYHA classification, which has only 4 levels, would likely not perform very well in assessing the important changes in the patients.

When Measuring Severity

If, when we are trying to discriminate among people at a single point in time, everyone gets the same score, we will not be able to tell who is better and who is worse than others—in this case, who should receive therapy and who should not. The key differences we are trying to detect—the signal—come from cross-sectional differences in scores among patients. The bigger these differences are, the better off we will be.

At the same time, if stable patients' scores on repeated measurements fluctuate wildly—we call this fluctuation the noise—we will not be able to say much about their relative well-being.[26] The greater the noise, which comes from variability within patients, the more difficulty we will have detecting the signal.

The technical term usually used to describe the ratio of variability between patients—the signal—to the total variability—the signal plus the noise—is *reliability*. If patients' scores change little over time (when in fact the patients' statuses are not changing) but are very different from patient to patient, reliability will be high. If the changes in score within patients are high in relation to differences among patients, reliability will be low.

The mathematical expression of reliability is the variance (or variability) among patients divided by the variance among patients and the variance within patients. One index of reliability measures homogeneity or internal consistency of items, constituting a scale expressed by *Cronbach α coefficient*. Cronbach α ranges between 0 and 1, and values of at least .7 are desirable. A more useful measure, expressed as test-retest reliability, refers to reproducibility of measurements when the same instrument is applied to stable patients. Preferred mathematical expressions of this type of reliability are κ, when the scale is dichotomous, and intraclass correlation coefficient (ICC), when the scale is continuous. For an explanation of κ, please refer to Chapter 17.3, Measuring Agreement Beyond Chance. Both measures vary between -1 and 1. As a very rough rule of thumb, values of κ or ICC should exceed .7.

When Measuring Change

Returning to our chronic heart failure example, we might now want to determine whether a drug such as spironolactone was effective in improving an individual patient's functional status and, in so doing, monitor changes in patient's NYHA functional class. When we use instruments to evaluate change over time, they must be able to detect any important changes in the way patients are feeling, even if those changes are small. Thus, the signal comes from the difference in score in patients whose status has improved or deteriorated, and the noise comes from the variability in score in patients whose status has not changed. The term we use for the ability to detect change (*signal-to-noise ratio* over time) is "responsiveness." It is sometimes also referred to as sensitivity to change.

An unresponsive instrument can result in false-negative results, in which the intervention improves how patients feel, yet the instrument fails to detect the improvement. This problem may be particularly salient for questionnaires that have the advantage of covering all relevant areas of HRQL but the disadvantage of covering each area superficially. With only 4 categories, a crude instrument such as the NYHA functional classification may work well for stratifying patients, but it may not be able to detect small but important improvements resulting from treatment.

There is no generally agreed-on mathematical expression for responsiveness. Some studies judge a scale to be responsive when it can find a statistically significant change after an intervention of known efficacy. For example, the Chronic Respiratory Disease Questionnaire (CRQ) was found to be responsive when all of their subscale scores improved substantially after initiation or modification of treatment, despite only small improvements in spirometric values.[6] Despite this high responsiveness, one of the CRQ subscales was subsequently found to have a modest reliability (internal consistency reliability = 0.53; test-retest reliability = 0.73).[27]

In studies that show no difference in change in HRQL when patients receive a treatment vs a control intervention, clinicians should look for evidence that the instruments have been able to detect small- or medium-sized effects in previous investigations. In the absence of this evidence, instrument unresponsiveness becomes a plausible reason for the failure to detect differences in HRQL.

For example, researchers who conducted a randomized trial of a diabetes education program reported no changes in 2 measures of well-being, attributing the result to, among other factors, lack of integration of the program with standard therapy.[28] However, those involved in the educational program, in comparison to a *control group* that did not experience it, showed an improvement in knowledge and self-care, along with a decrease in feelings of dependence on physicians. Given these changes, another explanation for the negative result—no difference between treatments in well-being—is inadequate responsiveness of the 2 well-being measures the investigators used.

USING THE GUIDE

In the trial of antipsychotics for chronic schizophrenia, the report does not examine the responsiveness of the PANSS. A comparison of the PANSS with an independent global assessment of change, however, persuasively demonstrated its responsiveness.[21]

Does the Instrument Relate to Other Measurements in the Way It Should?

Validity has to do with whether the instrument is measuring what it is intended to measure. The absence of a *reference standard* for HRQL creates a challenge for anyone hoping to measure patients' experience. We can be more confident that an instrument is doing its job if the items appear to measure what is intended (the instrument's *face validity*), although face validity alone is of limited help. Empirical evidence that it measures the domains of interest allows stronger inferences.

To provide such evidence, investigators have borrowed validation strategies from psychologists, who for many years have struggled with determining whether questionnaires assessing intelligence and attitudes really measure what is intended.

Establishing validity involves examining the logical relationships that should exist between assessment measures. For example, we would expect that patients with a lower treadmill exercise capacity generally will have more dyspnea in daily life than those with a higher exercise capacity, and we would expect to see substantial correlations between a new measure of emotional function and existing emotional function questionnaires.

When we are interested in evaluating change over time, we examine correlations of change scores. For example, patients who deteriorate in their treadmill exercise capacity should, in general, show increases in dyspnea, whereas those whose exercise capacity improves should experience less dyspnea; a new emotional function measure should show improvement in patients who improve on existing measures of emotional function. The technical term for this process is testing an instrument's "construct validity."

Clinicians should look for evidence of the validity of HRQL measures used in clinical studies. Reports of randomized trials using HRQL measures seldom review evidence of the validity of the instruments they use, but clinicians can gain some reassurance from statements (backed by citations) that the questionnaires have been validated previously. In the absence of evident face validity or empirical evidence of *construct validity*, clinicians are entitled to skepticism about the study's measurement of HRQL.

A final concern about validity arises if the measurement instrument is used in a culturally and linguistically different environment than the one in which it was developed—typically, use of a non-English version of an English-language questionnaire. Ideally, these non–English-language versions have undergone a translation process that ensures that the new version of the questionnaire reflects the idiom and the attitudes of the local population, a process called linguistic and cultural validation.[29] At the very least, the translation of the instrument should follow a procedure known as back-translation, whereby one group of researchers translates the original into a new language, another group blindly back-translates it into English, and a third group ascertains the equivalence of the original and the back-translated versions and resolves any discrepancies. If investigators provide no reassurance of appropriate linguistic validation, the clinician has another reason for caution regarding the results.

USING THE GUIDE

In the antipsychotics study, the investigators provide no citation to support the validity of the PANSS. As noted above, a quick search of PubMed (entering "PANSS" with no restriction) identified 854 articles, showing that it is a widely used measure in psychiatry. The first 2 reports describe extensive validation of the instrument.[11,20]

Are There Important Aspects of Health-Related Quality of Life That Have Been Omitted?

Although investigators may have addressed HRQL issues, they may not have done so comprehensively. When measuring patients' discomfort, distress, and disability, one can think of a hierarchy that begins with symptoms, moves on to the functional consequences of the symptoms, and ends with more complex elements such as emotional function. Exhaustive measurement may be more or less important in a particular context.

If, as a clinician, you believe your patients' sole interest is in whether a treatment relieves the primary symptoms and most important functional limitations, you will be satisfied with a limited range of assessments. Randomized trials in patients with migraine[30] and postherpetic neuralgia[31] restricted themselves primarily to the measurement of pain; studies of patients with rheumatoid arthritis[32] and back pain[33] measured pain and physical function, but not emotional or social function. Depending on the magnitude of effect on pain, the adverse effects of the medication, and the circumstances of the patient (degree of pain, concern about toxicity, degree of impairment of function, or emotional distress), lack of comprehensiveness of outcome measurement may or may not be important.

Thus, as a clinician, you can judge whether or not these omissions are important to you or, more to the point, to your patients. You should consider that although the omissions are unimportant to some patients, they may be critical to others (see Chapter 22.2, Decision Making and the Patient). We therefore encourage you to bear in mind the broader effect of disease on patients' lives.

Disease-specific HRQL measures that explore the full range of patients' problems and experience remind us of domains we might otherwise forget. We can trust these measures to be comprehensive if the developers have conducted a detailed survey of patients with the illness or condition.

For example, the American College of Rheumatology developed the 7-item core set of disease activity measures for rheumatoid arthritis, 3 of which represent patients' own reports of pain, global disease activity, and physical function.[34] Despite the extensive and intensive development process of the 7 core items, the data set, when presented to patients, failed to include one important aspect of disease activity: fatigue.[35]

If you are interested in going beyond the specific illness and comparing the effect of treatments on HRQL across diseases or conditions, you will look for a more comprehensive assessment. These comparisons require *generic HRQL* measures, covering all relevant areas of HRQL, that are designed for administration to people with any kind of underlying health problems (or no problem at all).

One type of generic measure, a *health profile*, yields scores for all domains of HRQL (including, for example, mobility, self-care, and physical, emotional, and social function). The most popular health profiles are short forms of the instruments used in the Medical Outcomes Study.[36,37] Inevitably, such instruments cover each area superficially. This may limit their responsiveness. Indeed, generic instruments are less powerful in detecting treatment effects than specific instruments.[38] Ironically, generic instruments also may not be sufficiently comprehensive; in certain cases, they may completely omit patients' primary symptoms.

Even when investigators use both disease-specific and generic measures of HRQL, these may still fail to adequately address adverse effects or toxicity of therapy.

For example, in a study of methotrexate for patients with inflammatory bowel disease,[39] patients completed the Inflammatory Bowel Disease Questionnaire (IBDQ), which addresses patients' bowel function, emotional function, systemic symptoms, and social function. Coincidentally, it measures some adverse effects of methotrexate, including nausea and lethargy, because they also afflict patients with inflammatory bowel disease who are not taking methotrexate, but it fails to measure others such as rash or mouth ulcers. The investigators could have administered a generic instrument to tap into non–inflammatory-bowel-disease-related aspects of HRQL, but once again, such instruments would also fail to directly address issues such as rash or mouth ulcers. The investigators chose a checklist approach to adverse effects and documented the frequency of occurrence of adverse events that were both severe enough and not severe enough to warrant discontinuation of treatment, but such an approach provides limited information about the influence of adverse effects on patients' lives.

USING THE GUIDE

In the Clinical Antipsychotic Trials of Intervention Effectiveness (CATIE) trial the investigators not only administered the PANSS but also monitored adverse events through systematic query, administered 3 rating scales of extrapyramidal signs, and measured changes in weight, electrocardiogram, and laboratory analyses.[1] The assessment appears adequately comprehensive.

WHAT ARE THE RESULTS?

How Can We Interpret the Scores?

Understanding the results of a trial involving HRQL involves special challenges. Patients who had acute back pain and were prescribed bed rest had mean scores on the Owestry Back-Disability Index, a measure that focuses on disease-specific functional status, that were 3.9 points worse than those of control patients.[33] Patients with severe rheumatoid arthritis allocated to treatment with cyclosporine had a mean disability score that was 0.28 units better than that of control patients.[40] Are these differences trivial, are they small but important, are they of moderate magnitude, or do they reflect large and extremely important differences in efficacy among treatments?

These examples show that the interpretability of most HRQL measures is not self-evident. When trying to interpret HRQL results, we must consider that, depending on the patient, a different value will be placed on the same change in function or capacity. The result is a series of tradeoffs that are often assessed informally in the interaction between physicians and patients. For example, one patient may be desperate for small improvements in a particular domain of HRQL and will be willing to take drugs with severe adverse effects to achieve that improvement. Another patient, by contrast, may be indifferent to small improvements and unwilling to tolerate even mild toxicity. Eliciting these preferences is an integral part of practicing *evidence-based medicine* effectively and sensitively (see Chapter 1, How to Use the Medical Literature—and This Book—to Improve Your Patient Care; see also Chapter 2, The Philosophy of Evidence-Based Medicine, and Chapter 22.2, Decision Making and the Patient).

When reading the literature and advising patients before beginning the treatment, however, clinicians must still arrive at some estimates of how well, on average, a given therapy performs with regard to effecting improvements in HRQL. One can classify ways to establish the interpretability of HRQL measures as anchor based or distribution based. These strategies lead to estimates of change in HRQL measures that, either for individual patients or for a group of patients, constitute trivial, small, medium, and large differences. No approach is without its limitations, but they all contribute important information.

Anchor-Based Approaches to Establishing Interpretability

Anchor-based methods require an independent standard, or *anchor*, that is itself interpretable and at least moderately correlated with the instrument being explored. The anchor is usually so designed as to establish a *minimum important difference (MID)* in change. The MID is the smallest difference in score in the domain of interest that patients perceive as beneficial and that would mandate, in the absence of troublesome adverse effects and excessive cost, a change in the patient's health care management.[41] The typical single anchor used in this approach is a global assessment of change corresponding to "no change," "small but important change," "moderate change," and "large change."

For instance, investigators asked patients with chronic respiratory disease or heart failure about the extent to which their dyspnea, fatigue, and emotional function had changed over time. To establish the MID, they focused on patients whose global rating suggested they had experienced a small but important change. They discovered, for all 3 domains, that the MID was approximately 0.5 on a scale of 1 to 7, in which 1 denoted extremely disabled/distressed/symptomatic and 7 denoted no disability/distress/symptoms. Other studies in chronic airflow limitation, asthma, and rhinoconjunctivitis have suggested that the MID is often approximately 0.5 per question.[41-43] A moderate difference may correspond to a change of approximately 1.0 per question, and changes greater than 1.5 can be considered to be large.[44]

USING THE GUIDE

Leucht et al[21] gained insight into the interpretation of the PANSS by comparing it against the Clinical Global Impression of Improvement, which is a global transition rating that classifies patients into 7 grades, from 1 (very much improved) to 7 (very much worse). They found that, to be rated as minimally improved, the PANSS scores needed to be reduced by about 19% to 28%. Because the baseline PANSS score in the data set was 94, this translates to about 18 to 26. Because the PANSS consists of 30 items for schizophrenic psychopathology, each rated on a 7-point Likert scale, ranging from 1 (no symptoms) to 7 (extreme), this MID roughly corresponds with the 0.5-per-question guideline mentioned above.

Distribution-Based Approaches to Establishing Interpretability

Distribution-based methods interpret results in terms of the relation between the magnitude of effect and some measure of variability in results. The magnitude of effect may be the difference in patients' scores before and after treatment or the difference in score between treatment and control groups. As a measure of variability, investigators may choose between-patient variability (for example, the standard deviation [SD] of patients at baseline) or within-patient variability (for example, the SD of change that patients experienced during a study).

The most frequently used of the distribution-based index is Cohen d, also often referred to as *effect size*, which is the difference in mean scores between the treatment and control groups divided by the SD of the scores in the control group (or the pooled SD of the treatment and control groups).

Consider a hypothetical trial in which the intervention group had a mean score of 50 (SD = 15) and the control group had a mean score of 40 (SD = 15) at the end of the trial. Cohen d will be $(50 - 40)/15 = 0.67$.

Cohen provided a rough rule of thumb to interpret the magnitude of the effect sizes. Changes in the range of 0.2 represent small changes, those in the range of 0.5 moderate changes, and those in the range of 0.8 large changes.[45] Thus, clinicians could anticipate moderate to large improvements in HRQL with this hypothetical intervention. Some recent empirical studies suggest that Cohen's guideline may in fact be generally applicable,[46] but other studies suggest that the MID as determined by the anchor-based approach roughly corresponds to an effect size of 0.5.[47,48]

Using the Number Needed to Treat to Enhance Interpretability

Using the strategies we have reviewed, we may, for instance, establish that a 4.0-point change on the Owestry Back-Disability Index signifies, on average, small but important differences for individuals. This still leaves problems in the interpretation of results from clinical trials. Presentation of mean changes in HRQL (for instance, the treatment group improved by 2.0 points more than the control group on the Owestry Back-Disability Index) can be misleading. Can we infer from the mean difference of 2.0 that the treatment is unimportant to patients? Because not everyone in the trial experiences the mean effect, this is not necessarily so. Although some patients may have experienced no benefit from treatment, treatment may have resulted in important improvement for others.

Investigators have gained insight into this issue by examining the distribution of change in HRQL in individual patients and by calculating the proportion of patients who achieved small, medium, and large gains from treatment.[44] The proportion of patients achieving a particular degree of benefit and the corresponding *number needed to treat (NNT)* to ensure that a single person obtains that benefit provide a more informative way of presenting results. For instance, trials of asthma medication have yielded NNTs of 2.8, 3.3, 4.5, and 21, corresponding to mean differences between treatments of 0.9, 0.5, 0.3, and 0.2, respectively, on a 1 to 7 scale whose MID is 0.5.[44] Note that the latter 2 mean differences are appreciably less than the MID, yet the NNT is appreciable.

What if, while adopting the anchor-based approach, the investigators fail to report the proportions of patients who got better, remained about the same, and got worse? For example, the investigators who conducted the trial of methotrexate for Crohn disease did not help clinicians interpret the magnitude of difference in HRQL.[39] The mean difference in IBDQ scores between the treatment and control groups at 16 weeks was 0.56 ($P < .002$). Thus, the mean difference between treated and control patients in the methotrexate study is likely to fall within the category of small but important change in HRQL.

Is there more we can do to enhance the interpretability of the results? One approach would be to calculate Cohen d. In this instance, the mean difference of 0.56 translates into an effect size of 0.43 ($= 0.56/1.3$, which is the SD of the control group).

Another approach is to further transform an effect size into NNT.[49] Table 10.5-3 presents the conversion from effect size into NNT for approximate effect sizes

TABLE 10.5-3

From Effect Size (ES) Into Number Needed to Treat

	Response Rate, %								
Control Group	**10**	**20**	**30**	**40**	**50**	**60**	**70**	**80**	**90**
Or Treatment Group	90	80	70	60	50	40	30	20	10
ES = 0.2	25.2	16.5	13.7	12.7	12.6	13.4	15.2	19.5	32.5
ES = 0.5	8.5	6.0	5.3	5.1	5.2	5.7	6.8	9.1	16.0
ES = 0.8	4.6	3.5	3.2	3.3	3.5	3.9	4.8	6.7	12.3
ES = 1.0	3.5	2.8	2.6	2.7	2.9	3.4	4.2	6.0	11.3

and event rates in the control group or treatment group. In the case of the methotrexate trial, if we assume that an incidence of important improvement in HRQL was about the same as the reported remission rates in terms of disease activity and was 20% in the placebo group, the mean difference of 0.43 SDs translates approximately into an NNT between 6.0 (corresponding to the intersection for control group response rate = 20% and effect size = 0.5) and 16.5 (corresponding to the same for control group response rate = 20% and effect size = 0.2).

An Excel spreadsheet to calculate NNT from effect size and response rate is available on the *Users' Guides* Web site (http://www.jamaevidence.com/). In the methotrexate case, you enter 0.20 in the response rate and 0.43 in the effect size, and the spreadsheet will give you an NNT of 16. Other methods for estimating NNT from continuous data and MID[47] provide similar results.

USING THE GUIDE

The CATIE trial showed that, by 3 months, olanzapine produced a reduction of about 7 points on the PANSS, whereas risperidone resulted in smaller reductions of around 3 points only (no table is given, and these numbers are derived from graphs, where the overall difference is *statistically significant* at $P = .002$).[1] Because the MID of the PANSS is approximately 18 to 26, we are tempted to conclude that no antipsychotic could produce tangible changes, but, as we discussed above, this can be a misleading conclusion.

The trial report provides no indication of the proportion of patients who got better, remained unchanged, or deteriorated, and we therefore use the distribution-based interpretation. The difference in the PANSS scores between olanzapine and risperidone is, on average, about 1 point at 1 month and 4 points at 3 months, and the SD of the PANSS at baseline is 18, which would then give a between-group effect size between $1/18 = 0.06$ and $4/18 = 0.22$. These between-group effect sizes can be characterized as small to very small, according to Cohen's guideline. Because the absolute percentage of patients achieving important improvement must be small, in the range of 10% to 20% (the average improvement was 7 for olanzapine, when the MID was around 20), cells in Table 10.5-3 corresponding with an effect size of 0.2 at 3 months and percentage improving in treatment group of 10% or 20% indicate an NNT of olanzapine over risperidone in the range of 20 to 30 to produce an additional patient with a small but important change. Or you can enter effect size $= 0.06$ at 1 month and response rates $= 10\%$ or 20% in the corresponding Excel calculator, available on the *Users' Guides* Web site (http://www.JAMAevidence.com), and obtain an NNT of approximately 60 to 100.

HOW CAN I APPLY THE RESULTS TO PATIENT CARE?

Has the Information From the Study Addressed Aspects of Life That Your Patient Considers Important?

Before answering the question about how the treatment would affect patients' lives, the clinician must be cognizant of the problems patients are experiencing, the importance they attach to those problems, and the value they might attach to having the problems ameliorated (see Chapter 22.2, Decision Making and the Patient). HRQL instruments that focus on specific aspects of patients' function and their symptoms may be of more use than global measures or measures that tell us simply about patients' satisfaction or well-being.

For instance, patients with chronic lung disease may find it more informative to know that their compatriots who accepted treatment became less dyspneic and fatigued in daily activity, rather than simply that they judged their quality of life to be improved. HRQL measures will be most useful when results facilitate their practical use by you and the patients in your practice.

USING THE GUIDE

The patient asked you 2 specific questions: what is the nature of the adverse effects he might experience, and how much better he will feel while taking alternative medications. Aside from his tremor, the patient is not terribly concerned about his current extrapyramidal adverse effects, but his family is.

The CATIE study showed that the neurologic effects of olanzapine and risperidone were very similar, with approximately 8% experiencing some extrapyramidal signs. The study also tells us about additional adverse effects—olanzapine will result in additional weight gain (body weight gain greater than 7% was observed in 30% who were taking olanzapine vs 14% taking risperidone; $P < .001$) and increase in glycosylated hemoglobin—but it does not tell us whether there were any patient-important consequences of the increased blood glucose level. The study also reported that there was a greater increase in plasma prolactin for patients taking risperidone than those taking other medications ($P < .001$), but again it does not tell us if it led to any patient-important consequences. The patient is concerned about his current symptoms of insomnia, fearfulness, and hearing voices. The study does not report changes in those particular symptoms separately but, given changes in the PANSS, one would anticipate small average effects and a low (but nonzero) likelihood of important improvement with olanzapine vs risperidone.

CLINICAL RESOLUTION

Returning to our opening clinical scenario, in light of the available information, you inform the patient that he is less likely to experience intolerable extrapyramidal adverse effects with newer antipsychotics, and given his concern about tremor and his family's concern about his looking ill, you strongly recommend a switch to one of the newer agents. The patient concurs. Among the newer antipsychotics, olanzapine produced greater a reduction in symptoms, but the probability that your patient will benefit is small: 1 in 20 to 100 patients experienced a small but important change in symptoms when taking olanzapine that he or she would not have experienced if taking risperidone. Therefore, considering the tradeoff between a small likelihood of benefit in terms of decreased symptoms with olanzapine and the probability of increased weight gain and an increase in blood glucose of uncertain significance, the patient decides to try olanzapine first while being ready to switch to risperidone soon if significant adverse effects (such as substantial weight gain or polydipsia or polyuria as a result of hyperglycemia) occur.

Conclusion

We encourage clinicians to consider the effect of their treatments on patients' HRQL and to look for information regarding this influence in clinical trials.

Responsive, valid, and interpretable instruments measuring experiences of importance to most patients should increasingly help guide our clinical decisions.

References

1. Lieberman JA, Stroup TS, McEvoy JP, et al. Effectiveness of antipsychotic drugs in patients with chronic schizophrenia. *N Engl J Med.* 2005;353(12):1209-1223.

2. Fletcher RH, Wagner EH. *Clinical Epidemiology*. Baltimore, MD: Williams & Wilkins; 1996.

3. Beck AT, Brown GK. *BDI-II: Beck Depression Inventory Manual*. 2nd ed. San Antonio, TX: Psychological Corporation; 1996.

4. Folstein MF, Folstein SE, McHugh PR. "Mini-mental state": a practical method for grading the cognitive state of patients for the clinician. *J Psychiatr Res.* 1975;12 (3):189-198.

5. Callahan CM, Unverzagt FW, Hui SL, Perkins AJ, Hendrie HC. Six-item screener to identify cognitive impairment among potential subjects for clinical research. *Med Care.* 2002;40(9):771-781.

6. Guyatt GH, Berman LB, Townsend M, Pugsley SO, Chambers LW. A measure of quality of life for clinical trials in chronic lung disease. *Thorax.* 1987;42(10):773-778.

7. Juniper EF, Guyatt GH, Epstein RS, Ferrie PJ, Jaeschke R, Hiller TK. Evaluation of impairment of health related quality of life in asthma: development of a questionnaire for use in clinical trials. *Thorax.* 1992;47(2):76-83.

8. Brazier JE, Harper R, Jones NM, et al. Validating the SF-36 health survey questionnaire: new outcome measure for primary care. *BMJ.* 1992;305(6846): 160-164.

9. Bergner M, Bobbitt RA, Carter WB, Gilson BS. The Sickness Impact Profile: development and final revision of a health status measure. *Med Care.* 1981; 19(8):787-805.

10. Williams JB. A structured interview guide for the Hamilton Depression Rating Scale. *Arch Gen Psychiatry.* 1988;45(8):742-747.

11. Kay SR, Fiszbein A, Opler LA. The Positive and Negative Syndrome Scale (PANSS) for schizophrenia. *Schizophr Bull.* 1987;13(2):261-276.

12. Guy W. *ECDEU Assessment Manual for Psychopharmacology*. Rockville, MD: US Dept of Health and Human Services; 1976.

13. Mahler DA, Weinberg DH, Wells CK, Feinstein AR. The measurement of dyspnea. Contents, interobserver agreement, and physiologic correlates of two new clinical indexes. *Chest.* 1984;85(6):751-758.

14. Nocturnal Oxygen Therapy Trial Group. Continuous or nocturnal oxygen therapy in hypoxemic chronic obstructive lung disease: a clinical trial. *Ann Intern Med.* 1980;93(3):391-398.

15. Heaton RK, Grant I, McSweeny AJ, Adams KM, Petty TL. Psychologic effects of continuous and nocturnal oxygen therapy in hypoxemic chronic obstructive pulmonary disease. *Arch Intern Med.* 1983;143(10):1941-1947.

16. Wu HS, McSweeney M. Assessing fatigue in persons with cancer: an instrument development and testing study. *Cancer.* 2004;101(7):1685-1695.

17. Dittner AJ, Wessely SC, Brown RG. The assessment of fatigue: a practical guide for clinicians and researchers. *J Psychosom Res.* 2004;56(2):157-170.

18. Juniper EF, Svensson K, O'Byrne PM, et al. Asthma quality of life during 1 year of treatment with budesonide with or without formoterol. *Eur Respir J.* 1999; 14(5):1038-1043.

19. Jaeschke R, Guyatt GH, Willan A, et al. Effect of increasing doses of beta agonists on spirometric parameters, exercise capacity, and quality of life in patients with chronic airflow limitation. *Thorax.* 1994;49(5):479-484.

20. Kay SR, Opler LA, Lindenmayer JP. Reliability and validity of the positive and negative syndrome scale for schizophrenics. *Psychiatry Res.* 1988;23(1):99-110.

21. Leucht S, Kane JM, Kissling W, Hamann J, Etschel E, Engel RR. What does the PANSS mean? *Schizophr Res.* 2005;79(2-3):231-238.

22. Goldstein RS, Gort EH, Stubbing D, Avendano MA, Guyatt GH. Randomised controlled trial of respiratory rehabilitation. *Lancet.* 1994;344(8934):1394-1397.

23. Wasson JH, Reda DJ, Bruskewitz RC, Elinson J, Keller AM, Henderson WG. A comparison of transurethral surgery with watchful waiting for moderate symptoms of benign prostatic hyperplasia: the Veterans Affairs Cooperative Study Group on Transurethral Resection of the Prostate. *N Engl J Med.* 1995;332(2):75-79.

24. Kirshner B, Guyatt G. A methodological framework for assessing health indices. *J Chronic Dis.* 1985;38(1):27-36.

25. Pitt B, Zannad F, Remme WJ, et al. The effect of spironolactone on morbidity and mortality in patients with severe heart failure: Randomized Aldactone Evaluation Study Investigators. *N Engl J Med.* 1999;341(10):709-717.

26. Guyatt GH, Kirshner B, Jaeschke R. Measuring health status: what are the necessary measurement properties? *J Clin Epidemiol.* 1992;45(12):1341-1345.

27. Wijkstra PJ, TenVergert EM, Van Altena R, et al. Reliability and validity of the chronic respiratory questionnaire (CRQ). *Thorax.* 1994;49(5):465-467.

28. de Weerdt I, Visser AP, Kok GJ, de Weerdt O, van der Veen EA. Randomized controlled multicentre evaluation of an education programme for insulin-treated diabetic patients: effects on metabolic control, quality of life, and costs of therapy. *Diabet Med.* 1991;8(4):338-345.

29. Guillemin F, Bombardier C, Beaton D. Cross-cultural adaptation of health-related quality of life measures: literature review and proposed guidelines. *J Clin Epidemiol.* 1993;46(12):1417-1432.

30. Mathew NT, Saper JR, Silberstein SD, et al. Migraine prophylaxis with divalproex. *Arch Neurol.* 1995;52(3):281-286.

31. Tyring S, Barbarash RA, Nahlik JE, et al. Famciclovir for the treatment of acute herpes zoster: effects on acute disease and postherpetic neuralgia: a randomized, double-blind, placebo-controlled trial: Collaborative Famciclovir Herpes Zoster Study Group. *Ann Intern Med.* 1995;123(2):89-96.

32. Kirwan JR. The effect of glucocorticoids on joint destruction in rheumatoid arthritis: the Arthritis and Rheumatism Council Low-Dose Glucocorticoid Study Group. *N Engl J Med.* 1995;333(3):142-146.

33. Malmivaara A, Hakkinen U, Aro T, et al. The treatment of acute low back pain: bed rest, exercises, or ordinary activity? *N Engl J Med.* 1995;332(6):351-355.

34. Felson DT, Anderson JJ, Boers M, et al. The American College of Rheumatology preliminary core set of disease activity measures for rheumatoid arthritis clinical trials: the Committee on Outcome Measures in Rheumatoid Arthritis Clinical Trials. *Arthritis Rheum.* 1993;36(6):729-740.

35. Wolfe F, Pincus T, O'Dell J. Evaluation and documentation of rheumatoid arthritis disease status in the clinic: which variables best predict change in therapy. *J Rheumatol.* 2001;28(7):1712-1717.

36. Tarlov AR, Ware JE Jr, Greenfield S, Nelson EC, Perrin E, Zubkoff M. The Medical Outcomes Study: an application of methods for monitoring the results of medical care. *JAMA.* 1989;262(7):925-930.

37. Ware JE Jr, Kosinski M, Bayliss MS, McHorney CA, Rogers WH, Raczek A. Comparison of methods for the scoring and statistical analysis of SF-36 health profile and summary measures: summary of results from the Medical Outcomes Study. *Med Care.* 1995;33(4 suppl):AS264-279.

38. Wiebe S, Guyatt G, Weaver B, Matijevic S, Sidwell C. Comparative responsiveness of generic and specific quality-of-life instruments. *J Clin Epidemiol.* 2003;56(1):52-60.

39. Feagan BG, Rochon J, Fedorak RN, et al. Methotrexate for the treatment of Crohn's disease: the North American Crohn's Study Group Investigators. *N Engl J Med.* 1995;332(5):292-297.

40. Tugwell P, Pincus T, Yocum D, et al. Combination therapy with cyclosporine and methotrexate in severe rheumatoid arthritis: the Methotrexate-Cyclosporine Combination Study Group. *N Engl J Med.* 1995;333(3):137-141.

41. Jaeschke R, Singer J, Guyatt GH. Measurement of health status: ascertaining the minimal clinically important difference. *Control Clin Trials.* 1989;10(4):407-415.

42. Juniper EF, Guyatt GH, Willan A, Griffith LE. Determining a minimal important change in a disease-specific Quality of Life Questionnaire. *J Clin Epidemiol.* 1994;47(1):81-87.

43. Juniper EF, Guyatt GH, Griffith LE, Ferrie PJ. Interpretation of rhinoconjunctivitis quality of life questionnaire data. *J Allergy Clin Immunol.* 1996;98(4):843-845.

44. Guyatt GH, Juniper EF, Walter SD, Griffith LE, Goldstein RS. Interpreting treatment effects in randomised trials. *BMJ.* 1998;316(7132):690-693.

45. Cohen J. *Statistical Power Analysis in the Behavioral Sciences*. Hillsdale, NJ: Erlbaum; 1988.

46. Samsa G, Edelman D, Rothman ML, Williams GR, Lipscomb J, Matchar D. Determining clinically important differences in health status measures: a general approach with illustration to the Health Utilities Index Mark II. *Pharmacoeconomics.* 1999;15(2):141-155.

47. Norman GR, Sridhar FG, Guyatt GH, Walter SD. Relation of distribution- and anchor-based approaches in interpretation of changes in health-related quality of life. *Med Care.* 2001;39(10):1039-1047.

48. Norman GR, Sloan JA, Wyrwich KW. Interpretation of changes in health-related quality of life: the remarkable universality of half a standard deviation. *Med Care.* 2003;41(5):582-592.

49. Furukawa TA. From effect size into number needed to treat. *Lancet.* 1999;353(9165):1680.

11.1

APPLYING
RESULTS TO
INDIVIDUAL
PATIENTS

Antonio L. Dans, Leonila F. Dans,
and Gordon Guyatt

IN THIS CHAPTER:

CLINICAL SCENARIO

For Which Myocardial Infarction Patients Is Thrombolytic Therapy Indicated in the Philippines?

You are the attending internist on duty when a 40-year-old history professor presents to the emergency department of a general hospital in the Philippines. He has experienced severe chest pain for 2 hours, associated with clammy perspiration. The pain is now settling, and the patient is not feeling dyspneic or otherwise in distress. Physical examination reveals a blood pressure of 110/70 mm Hg, a heart rate of 92/min, a normal first heart sound, and clear lungs. An electrocardiogram discloses 3-mm ST-segment elevation in leads II, II, and aVF, suggesting an acute inferior wall myocardial infarction (MI). As nurses place intravenous lines and prepare the patient for admission to the coronary care unit, you consider the possible benefits and *risks* of administering thrombolytic therapy. Because, to be fully prepared to advise just this sort of patient, you have recently examined the literature, you move quickly and confidently to the bedside.

FINDING THE EVIDENCE

Streptokinase is the only thrombolytic agent that most of your patients might afford. In your recent review of the *evidence*, you therefore confined your search to this drug, trying to locate the best evidence from an appropriate *randomized trial* or, if available, a *meta-analysis* of many trials. Launching PubMed from the Web site of the National Library of Medicine, you selected "myocardial infarction" from the list of Medical Subject Headings used to index articles. On the second subject line, you used the Medical Subject Headings term "streptokinase." Using the limit function, you restricted the publication type to "meta-analysis." You retrieved a meta-analysis that deals with effectiveness[1] but not with safety. Therefore, you also review a single *randomized controlled trial (RCT)*, the Second International Study of Infarct Survival (ISIS-2),[2] which you choose on the basis of its size (17 000 patients), strong design (which includes *blinding*), and the wide variety of centers that participated. The articles meet the *validity* criteria for *systematic reviews* and trials. You observe that, in the meta-analysis,[1] treatment reduced the *event rate* from 17.4% to 12.8%. For the average participant in these trials, this clearly outweighs the potential harm of bleeding requiring transfusion, which occurred in 0.5% of streptokinase-treated patients compared with 0.2% in the *placebo* group in the ISIS-2 trial.[2]

As you consider how to treat your patient, you notice that Asians compose only a minority of the patients in the trial and in the meta-analysis.

INTRODUCTION

Clinicians looking at RCTs to guide medical decisions must decide how to apply results to individual patients. Chapter 6, Therapy, suggested 2 criteria for deciding on applicability: (1) Can you apply the results of the study to the patient before you? (2) Are the benefits worth the risks and costs? In this chapter, we discuss these guides in greater detail.

Clinical trialists typically spend a lot of effort ensuring comparability of treatment and *control groups* (*internal validity*) through strategies such as randomization, blinding, and intention-to-treat analyses. They spend much less effort on ensuring comparability of trial patients to actual patients (external validity) through strategies such as population sampling[3] because the main focus of trials has been to answer the question, can the drug work at all, rather than the question, will it actually work in real life?

Nevertheless, published trials provide information that helps clinicians decide on the applicability of the results to individual patients. Inclusion and exclusion criteria, for example, help us decide whether our patients would have been eligible to participate. Similarly, subgroup analyses may elucidate the effects of treatment on specific populations that may be of interest as we try to apply the results (see Chapter 20.4, When to Believe a Subgroup Analysis). Unfortunately, in real life, we face myriad patient subtypes, but trials typically are underpowered to address more than a few subgroup hypotheses. Therefore, physicians need to become skilled in applying trial results to individual patients. Table 11.1-1 summarizes criteria that will help you compromise between hasty generalizations and imprudent hesitation in the application of trial results. Sometimes, the guides may lead to clear decisions about whether to apply the results. At other times, they will at least increase or decrease your level of confidence in using a treatment.

The *relative risk reductions* (*RRRs*) estimated in trials reflect the average response of a population to a treatment. Because biologic and socioeconomic characteristics of individual patients sometimes modulate the treatment effect, the average response may not always be the same in different patient subgroups. Here, we review these biologic and socioeconomic characteristics that may modify treatment response.

TABLE 11.1-1

Users' Guides for Applying Study Results to Individual Patients

A. Can I apply the results to my patients?

1. Have biologic factors that might modify the treatment response been excluded?
2. Can the patients comply with treatment requirements?
3. Can the health care providers comply with treatment requirements?

B. Are the benefits worth the risks and costs?

Have Biologic Factors That Might Modify the Treatment Response Been Excluded?

Table 11.1-2 lists 5 biologic factors that sometimes lead us to reject the idea of applying results to a particular patient. "SCRAP" is a mnemonic to remember these 5 factors, which include a patient's sex, presence of comorbidity, race or ethnicity, age, and pathology of the disease. The following examples illustrate how these factors may modify treatment effects in individual patients.

Sex

Cardiovascular disease prevention provides a setting in which treatment responses have differed between men and women.[5] For example, a meta-analysis of the use of aspirin in primary prevention detected significant differences in the treatment effect between men and women.[4] As Figure 11.1-1 shows, administration of aspirin to healthy women did not decrease the incidence of MI as it did in men. In contrast, aspirin reduced the incidence of stroke in women while seeming to increase it in men. Contrary to expectations, these findings suggest that, overall, women derive more benefit from treatment.

Another example of sex differences involves the use of stents after percutaneous transluminal coronary angioplasty for acute MI. Stent insertion in women has a

TABLE 11.1-2

Biologic Factors That May Modulate an Individual's Response to Therapy

Biologic Factor	Examples
Sex	Aspirin for prevention of atherosclerosis: the relative risk reduction for stroke and coronary disease is greater in women than in men[4]
	Use of stents after angioplasty: the risk reduction for bypass surgery is smaller among women[6,7]
Comorbidities	Measles vaccination: the degree of antibody response to vaccines has been observed to be lower in the presence of malnutrition[8,9]
	Treatment of hypertension: a target diastolic pressure of 80 mm Hg or less reduces events in diabetic patients but not in the general population[10]
Race	Diuretics for hypertension: better response in blacks compared with whites[11]
	Proton-pump inhibitors for peptic ulcer disease: more effective in Asians compared with non-Asians[12]
Age	Influenza vaccine for flu prevention: lower immune response in elderly patients[13]
	Dual therapy for peptic ulcer disease: higher *Helicobacter pylori* eradication rates in the elderly[14]
Pathology	Influenza vaccine for flu prevention: effectiveness depends on viral strain used[15]
	Breast cancer chemotherapy: response dependent on certain gene expressions[16]

FIGURE 11.1-1

Meta-analysis of Aspirin in the Primary Prevention of Myocardial Infarction and Stroke in Men and Women

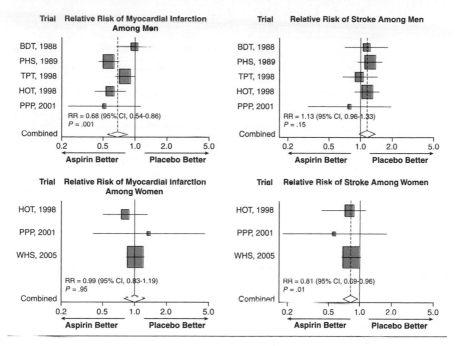

Abbreviations: BDT, British Doctor's Trial; CI, confidence interval; HOT, Hypertension Optimal Treatment study; PHS, Physician's Health Study; PPP, Primary Prevention Project; RR, relative risk; TPT, Thrombosis Prevention Trial; WHS, Women's Health Study.

lower RRR for coronary bypass grafting compared with that for men.[6] Although such observations on outcome differences are partially explained by body size and clinical risk factors, sex itself may be an important determinant of response to therapy.[7]

Comorbidity

Comorbidities can modify therapeutic effectiveness when, for instance, comorbidities render the administration of therapy dangerous (eg, one would ordinarily not consider warfarin in a patient with a recent gastrointestinal bleed). Comorbidity can also decrease or increase the magnitude of treatment effects.

In measles prevention, for example, malnutrition can reduce treatment response as measured by immunogenicity.[8,9] Table 11.1-3 summarizes the results of the Hypertension Optimal Treatment (HOT) study that showed that target diastolic blood pressures below 80 mm Hg reduced cardiovascular events in diabetic patients but not in the general population. Here, the presence of comorbidity (diabetes) enhanced treatment effectiveness (additional lowering of blood pressure reduced adverse outcomes in diabetic patients but not in nondiabetic patients). Because of these

TABLE 11.1-3

Effect of Various Levels of Target Blood Pressure on the Incidence of Major Cardiovascular Events, Comparing Diabetic Patients and the General Population[10]

Target DBP (mm Hg)	No. of Events	Events/1000 Patient-years	P for Trend	Comparison	RR (95% CI)
Diabetic Patients					
≤ 90	45	24.4		≤ 90 vs ≤ 85	1.32 (0.84-2.06)
≤ 85	34	18.6		≤ 85 vs ≤ 80	1.56 (0.91-2.67)
≤ 80	22	11.9	0.005	≤ 90 vs ≤ 80	2.06 (1.24-3.44)
General Population					
≤ 90	232	9.9		≤ 90 vs ≤ 85	0.99 (0.83-1.19)
≤ 85	234	10.0		≤ 85 vs ≤ 80	1.08 (0.89-1.29)
≤ 80	217	9.3	0.5	≤ 90 vs ≤ 80	1.07 (0.89-1.28)

Abbreviations: CI, confidence interval; DBP, diastolic blood pressure; RR, relative risk.

findings, most hypertension guidelines recommend lower target blood pressures for diabetic patients.[10]

Race
Racial or ethnic differences may sometimes modify an expected treatment response. In the treatment of hypertension, for example, blacks or black non-Americans have proved more responsive to diuretics and less responsive to β-blockers than whites.[11]

This selective response reflects a state of relative volume excess that investigators theorize may have served protective functions in hot and arid ancestral environments.[17]

In peptic ulcer disease, a recent meta-analysis of patients with acute gastrointestinal bleeding suggests that proton-pump inhibitors (PPIs) are more effective among Asians than whites in reducing mortality and preventing rebleeding and surgical intervention (Table 11.1-4).[12] This differential response may be the result of a lower parietal cell mass, a higher *Helicobacter pylori* infection rate, or a slower metabolism rate for PPIs among Asians.

Age
Age is a commonly recognized factor that affects the response to treatment. For example, after influenza vaccination, older patients show lower RRRs in the incidence of flu,[13] perhaps because of a diminished immune response to the antigenic stimulus (Table 11.1-5). Sometimes, age increases the therapeutic response. A recent study showed that the *H pylori* eradication rate with PPI and antibiotics was about 2.5 times higher among patients older than 50 years.[14] The mechanism for this difference is unclear, but investigators have

TABLE 11.1-4

Meta-analyses of PPIs for Ulcer Bleeding, Comparing RCTs on Asians and Non-Asians

	Rate With PPI (%)	Rate With Control (%)	OR (95% CI)	NNT (95% CI)
Mortality				
Asian	1.5	4.7	0.35 (0.16-0.74)	31 (20-100)
Non-Asian	4.8	3.6	1.36 (0.94-1.96)	Incalculable
Rebleeding				
Asian	6.8	22.5	0.24 (0.16-0.36)	6 (5-8)
Non-Asian	11.9	15.5	0.72 (0.58-0.89)	27 (17-100)
Surgery				
Asian	2.9	9.2	0.29 (0.16-0.53)	16 (11-33)
Non-Asian	7.5	9.8	0.74 (0.56-0.97)	43 (20-100)

Abbreviations: CI, confidence interval; NNT, number needed to treat; OR, odds ratio; PPI, proton-pump inhibitor; RCT, randomized controlled trial.

Reproduced from Leontiadis et al,[12] with permission from Wiley-Blackwell. Copyright © 2005.

theorized that, because *H pylori* infection has persisted longer in older patients, time-related alterations in the function or structure of the gastric mucosa might contribute to a more effective local drug action.

Pathology

Finally, diseases we refer to by the same name sometimes differ in the underlying pathology and, consequently, in response to treatment. In influenza vaccination, for example, effectiveness depends on whether the influenza strains in the coming year are the same as those contained in

TABLE 11.1-5

Influence of Age on Effect Size Estimates of Trials Evaluating the Efficacy of Vaccination in Preventing Influenza in Healthy Adults

Median Age of Patients, y	Clinically Confirmed Cases		Laboratory Confirmed Cases	
	No. of Trials	RR (95% CI)[a]	No. of Trials	RR (95% CI)[a]
<33	15	0.54 (0.44-0.67)	5	0.22 (0.13-0.37)
≥33	23	0.89 (0.85-0.94)	16	0.43 (0.33-0.57)

Abbreviations: CI, confidence interval; RR, relative risk.

[a]RR pooled estimate (random effects model and DerSimonian and Laird method).

Reproduced with permission from Belshe.[15]

the vaccine.[15] Another example of differences in disease pathology that can modify a treatment effect is breast cancer. Here, response to chemotherapy depends on certain gene expressions.[16]

A Caution Against Overcaution

You can sometimes find information regarding biologic factors affecting treatment response in reports of trials and systematic reviews, especially when investigators have explored subgroup differences. When such analyses are not available, clinicians must rely on biologic rationale as gleaned from in vitro and animal experiments, as well as pathologic studies on humans.

Although our examples illustrate instances in which treatment effect is modified by biologic factors, readers must be cautious in becoming overly restrictive in applying results of trials or systematic reviews that evaluate therapy. There are many instances in which treatments have been withheld unnecessarily because of perceived biologic problems that affect applicability.

Women, for example, have generally received inferior care in the treatment and prevention of cardiovascular disease.[5] Although recent findings do suggest sex differences in response to treatments, most of these differences do not warrant withholding therapy. As we have mentioned, in the case of stroke prevention, women seem to benefit even more than men from use of aspirin.

Another example of unjustified withholding of therapy was the use of diuretics for hypertension in diabetic patients. Because diuretics increased blood sugar, many specialty societies did not recommend them as first-line therapy for diabetic patients, despite convincing evidence that diuretics reduce cardiovascular events in the general population.[18] A long-term study has shown that despite the metabolic effects, diuretics reduced serious morbid and mortal events in diabetic patients.[19]

Similarly, because of peculiarities in their lipid profiles, statins were initially not recommended as first-line therapy for dyslipidemic diabetic patients despite overwhelming proof of reductions in cardiovascular events in the general population. Fibrates were recommended as the drug of choice until a systematic review showed that statins work as well in diabetic patients as in others.[20]

Deciding when to apply results to an individual patient can be tricky. In general, we would suggest you apply results to individuals unless there is strong evidence that biologic differences will significantly attenuate treatment response or cause harm. Such evidence sometimes comes from subgroups in a randomized trial (see Chapter 20.4, When to Believe a Subgroup Analysis). At other times, they will come from epidemiologic studies that support theories on the influence of sex, comorbidity, race, age, and pathology, as well as studies on patient and provider adherence.

USING THE GUIDE

Searching through your local database of medical literature, you retrieve a case series of autopsies performed on Filipino patients with MI.[21] This study showed that pathologic changes in the coronary arteries and myocardium were similar to those observed among North American patients. Nonatherosclerotic causes of coronary disease occurred rarely.[22] Furthermore, the subsequent INTER-HEART study showed that the effect of risk factors on the incidence of coronary artery disease was similar across countries around the world.[23] Finally, local postmarketing studies show that Filipinos experience the same reperfusion arrhythmias and bleeding complications as North Americans when given streptokinase at the same dose.[24] These studies provide some assurance that the biologic response to treatment will be similar among Filipino patients.

Can the Patients Comply With Treatment Requirements?

When satisfied that biologic differences do not compromise treatment applicability, clinicians must examine constraints related to the social environment that may modify the effectiveness and safety of treatment. This issue is important not just in disadvantaged populations but also in settings in which patients are privileged.

Because trials normally recruit patients with unusually high levels of adherence, trial patients tend to be systematically different from those in the general population. Investigators have documented these differences in situations such as management of hypertension[25] and asthma.[26] To the extent that groups of people exhibit different levels of adherence to treatment, clinicians may expect variation in treatment effectiveness.

Variability in adherence between populations may stem from obvious resource limitations or from less obvious attitudinal or behavioral characteristics.

As an example, both types of problems may affect the safety of outpatient administration of anticoagulant agents. Because of resource constraints, neither indigent patients nor their society may be able to afford repeated clinic visits and tests for prothrombin time monitoring that are essential for treatment safety. Similarly, persons with alcohol or drug addiction, regardless of their financial situation, may be less likely to comply with monitoring. Inadequate monitoring, whatever the reason, increases bleeding risk from overanticoagulation and may shift the balance between benefit and harm.

Although clinicians are often unable to predict patient adherence, a systematic examination of adherence in individual patients—or groups of patients—is likely to aid in identifying varying adherence patterns. Community studies give us a general idea of how different adherence may be from that reported in clinical trial settings.[25,26] Clinicians may also refer to more general sources of evidence, such as sociologic descriptions of attitudes of specific groups of people (see Chapter 11.5, Qualitative Research).

In the Philippines, for example, an attitude called *bahala na* connotes a lack of capacity or will to control one's fate.[27] In English, a near-equivalent statement would be "Let's just wait and see; there's really nothing much we can do about the situation." This external locus of control[28] may have an adverse effect on patient adherence.

USING THE GUIDE

Streptokinase is administered intravenously as a single dose. Thus, in our scenario, if the patient can afford the drug, patient adherence will not be a problem.

Can the Health Care Providers Comply With Treatment Requirements?

The term "provider adherence" or "compliance" refers to a host of diagnostic tests, monitoring equipment, interventional capabilities, skills, and other technical specifications needed to administer a treatment safely and effectively. The ability of health care providers to comply with these requirements may influence treatment effectiveness, which is especially true in trials of invasive interventions in which clinicians' skill becomes an important criterion for involvement in the clinical trial. When clinicians in the general population are not as skilled as those in a study, you should seriously question applicability of that study.

For example, in a meta-analysis of randomized trials of carotid endarterectomy for asymptomatic carotid stenosis patients at relatively low risk of stroke nevertheless showed benefit from surgery.[29] However, the surgery-associated stroke rate was low, probably because of the high level of experience and expertise of the surgical centers that participated in the trial. The net effect in other centers in the community may be an increase in adverse outcomes,[30] particularly worrisome because surgical teams with complication rates and operative volumes that would have rendered them ineligible for the trial do most endarterectomies.[31]

Even noninvasive interventions can pose challenges to provider adherence. For example, although rheumatic atrial fibrillation remains a common problem in Asian countries and some patients may be willing and able to comply with monitoring, few laboratories in rural areas perform the tests necessary for titration of warfarin dose. Like constraints in patient adherence that we just described, limitation in provider adherence is likely to influence the critical balance between effectiveness and safety, possibly leading to nonapplication of the results of an otherwise valid trial.

USING THE GUIDE

Administration of streptokinase carries potential hazards, foremost of which is catastrophic bleeding. Facilities for emergency administration of cryoprecipitate, fresh frozen plasma, or whole blood must be available.[32] In hospitals without efficient blood banking systems, coping with bleeding emergencies may be difficult. This increases the potential hazards of treatment and may tip the balance between benefit and harm. Fortunately, after reviewing hospital facilities and competence of medical and paramedical personnel, the tertiary hospital in the scenario was found to have sufficient safeguards for use of streptokinase.

ARE THE LIKELY BENEFITS WORTH THE POTENTIAL RISKS AND COSTS?

When you are satisfied that biologic and socioeconomic differences do not compromise applicability of the risks and benefits estimated in a trial, the next step in applying results is to estimate the patient-specific benefit. This is reflected, for instance, in the *number needed to treat (NNT)*. Using the example of hypothetical drug A that reduces the incidence of stroke by 25% (RRR), Table 11.1-6 shows 5 steps in making the calculation. Given varying baseline risks, the resulting risk difference or *absolute risk reduction (ARR)* and thus the NNT may vary.

Clinicians can derive estimates of the patient's baseline risk from various sources. First, they can use their intuition, which may sometimes be accurate—at least in terms of the extent to which risk is increased or decreased relative to the typical patient in a trial.[33] Second, if the randomized trials or meta-analyses report risks in patient subgroups, clinicians can choose the subgroup that best applies to the patient. Atrial fibrillation investigators pooled the individual patient data from all the randomized trials testing antithrombotic therapy in nonvalvular atrial fibrillation and were able to provide estimates of prognosis for patients in clinically important subgroups.[34] Unfortunately, most trials and meta-analyses fail to report estimates of baseline risk in all patient subgroups.

Third, clinicians can find information about baseline risks in subgroups of patients in studies on prognosis (see Chapter 18, Prognosis). For example, analysis of the Malmo Stroke Registry demonstrated that during the 3 years after a stroke, patients have a 6% risk of recurrent nonfatal stroke. These risks were higher in older patients and in those with diabetes mellitus or cardiac disease.[35]

TABLE 11.1-6

Effect of Baseline Risk of Stroke on the ARR and the NNT, Using Hypothetical Treatment A That Can Reduce Events by 25%[a]

Baseline Risk of Stroke Without Treatment (Rc), %	RRR, %	Risk of Stroke With Treatment (Rt), %	ARR, %	NNT
20	25	15	5	20
16	25	12	4	25
12	25	9	3	33
8	25	6	2	50
4	25	3	1	100

Abbreviations: ARR, absolute risk reduction; NNT, number needed to treat; RRR, relative risk reduction.

[a]Estimating NNT takes 5 easy steps: (1) estimate the baseline risk of your patient for the event (Rc); (2) estimate the RRR using the trial results; (3) calculate the new risk of an event with treatment (Rt) by reducing Rc by 25% (the RRR for treatment); (4) calculate the ARR by getting the difference between Rc and Rt; and (5) divide 100 by the ARR (expressed as a percentage) to estimate the patient-specific NNT.

Sometimes, investigators use data from prognostic studies to construct models that incorporate a large number of variables to create clinically helpful risk strata (see Chapter 17.4, Clinical Prediction Rules). When prospectively validated in new populations, these risk stratification systems can provide accurate patient-specific estimates of prognosis. A popular example is the Framingham risk calculator that estimates the risk of a coronary event for an individual according to age, sex, serum lipid levels, blood pressure, body mass index, use of tobacco, and blood glucose level.[36]

Epidemiologic Studies of the Incidence of Disease May Elucidate Baseline Risk

Keys[37] compared the 20-year incidence of deaths from coronary heart disease in the United States, 5 European countries, and Japan and found an extremely low incidence of death from coronary heart disease in the Japanese cohort, despite correction for differences in baseline characteristics representing recognized risk factors. The Multinational Monitoring of Cardiovascular Disease and Their Determinants project[38] has reported similar results. In this study involving 39 centers from 26 countries, east Asians showed a much lower incidence of death from coronary heart disease than their western counterparts. Age-standardized mortality rates for coronary heart disease were lowest in Japan (40/100000) and highest in north Ireland (414/100000).

Estimating Patient-Specific Number Needed to Treat: An Example

Let us now consider as an example the decision about whether to recommend carotid endarterectomy for a 65-year-old diabetic patient from Sweden with a previous mild ischemic stroke and high-grade carotid stenosis. To estimate the baseline risk of stroke (step 1), we use the Malmo Stroke Registry study, which tells us that such a patient faces an 8.4% probability of recurrent stroke within the next 3 years.[35] To estimate RRR (step 2), we use the results from a carotid endarterectomy study[39] that shows that the procedure will reduce the *relative risk* (*RR*) of stroke by approximately 44% (assuming we can find a surgical team that achieves the same low risk of perioperative stroke as did trial participants). The risk of stroke with treatment (step 3) will therefore decrease to approximately 5.4% (obtained by reducing the baseline 8.4% risk by 44%). In step 4, we calculate the difference between baseline risk and the risk with treatment to get an ARR of 3% (8.4% baseline risk minus the new risk of 5.4% with treatment). Finally, in step 5, we divide 100 by the ARR to estimate the patient-specific NNT of 100/3, or 33. Whether this is unacceptably high or suitably low will depend largely on the outcomes avoided, the risks involved, and the cost of treating each of these 33 individuals.

For those who prefer to avoid the arithmetic of the final step, a nomogram allows the clinician armed only with a ruler (or any other straightedge) to proceed from the patient's baseline risk, through the RRR (or RR increase), to the NNT or number needed to harm (NNH)[40] (see Figure 7-2 from Chapter 7, Does Treatment Lower Risk? Understanding the Results).

Whatever strategy one chooses, varying patient risk will affect benefit regardless of the environment in which you practice. Even if you work in a western tertiary-care environment in which investigators conducted their original studies, you will still face high- and low-risk patients. The critical tradeoff between risk and benefit may vary in these patient groups, mandating different treatment decisions (see Chapter 21, How to Use a Patient Management Recommendation).

USING THE GUIDE

Returning to our decision about the administration of thrombolytic agents to a patient in the Philippines, we use the same 5 steps to generate a patient-specific NNT.

Step 1: Estimating baseline risk. To estimate baseline risk for our patient, we use a cohort study conducted in 9 centers in metropolitan Manila. This study evaluated 424 Filipinos with MI who were eligible for streptokinase but for whom the drug was not administered. Cardiac death rates in patients younger than 60 years and with an inferior MI were 2%.[41]

Step 2: Estimating the treatment effect. According to the ISIS study, if streptokinase had been given, it would have reduced the risk of death by 25% (RRR).

Step 3: Calculating the posttreatment risk. Reducing the baseline risk of 2% (step 1) by 25% (step 2) would result in an event rate of 1.5% if streptokinase were administered.

Step 4: Calculating the ARR. Subtracting posttreatment risk from the baseline risk (2% − 1.5%) gives us an ARR of 0.5%. This means 0.5% of those otherwise destined to have events would have avoided it.

Step 5: Calculating the patient-specific NNT for this scenario. The NNT would be the mathematical inverse of ARR in percent (ie, 100/0.5, or approximately 200).

SUMMARY

Although the inspiration for these guides came from a predicament in developing countries, the guides are relevant to all situations in which clinicians must make decisions regarding applicability. By breaking down the problem into specific questions, we have provided guides for clinicians' daily attempts to strike a balance between making unjustifiably broad decisions about generalizability and being too conservative in their conclusions.[42]

To summarize (see Table 11.1-1), guide A1 (biologic factors) helps us answer the question, can the drug work at all under ideal conditions? Guides A2-3 (patient and provider adherence) help us consider whether the drug will actually work. Finally, guide B (risks and costs) helps us answer how efficiently this drug will work in particular patients. Guides A1-3 examine whether the RRR is the same in your patient as in the trial. At the very least, these guides allow us room for considering whether we may be overestimating or underestimating effectiveness. Guide B, on the other hand, helps us generate patient-specific ARRs and NNTs.

You should not consider these guides as absolute rules on whether to apply the results of a trial to a particular patient. In instances in which there is overwhelming proof of benefits in the general population, clinicians should insist on strong evidence of diminished response before deciding not to apply. When the evidence of benefit is less certain, however, doubt raised by considering these biologic factors may be enough to dissuade clinicians from recommending treatment.

When clinicians suspect limited applicability, what can they do? This will depend on whether the anticipated differences are important and, if they are important, whether they are remediable. Biologic differences (guide A1) can often be addressed by altering administration of a treatment (such as adjusting the dose of a drug). Patient and provider adherence problems (guides A2-3), on the other hand, can be remedied by strategies such as education, training, and provision of necessary equipment. Finally, as we have shown, differences in event rates (guide B) can be calculated to generate patient-specific estimates of NNT and NNH. This may then be used to provide patients with a reasonable estimate of the tradeoff between benefits, risks, and costs.

CLINICAL RESOLUTION

What should we recommend regarding use of thrombolytic agents for the Filipino patient admitted to the hospital with acute MI? In summary, there is no reason to believe that Filipinos will have a different response to treatment with thrombolytic agents under ideal conditions. Patient adherence will not be an important issue because the drug is given intravenously as a single dose. The technical requirements for administration are often (but not always) available, and when they are not, the risks of thrombolytic administration may outweigh the benefits. Fortunately, in this hospital, minimum technical requirements were met.

The baseline risk of cardiac death in Filipinos in general is 11.1%, and, using streptokinase, we can reduce this by 25%, resulting in an NNT of 36 for the overall population. For subgroups of patients, however, the NNT will range from 16 to 179, depending on the age and the size of the infarct. The 40-year-old man with an inferior MI has an expected mortality of only 2% during the course of the next 30 days, suggesting an NNT of 200.

Should we recommend streptokinase for this patient? Although we have confirmed the applicability of the thrombolytic data on the effectiveness of streptokinase for centers with adequate blood-banking facilities, we must also consider cost. The cost of the drug is approximately US $150 per treatment in a country in which the average annual per capita income is $1000.[43]

In the end, you approach the patient and explain that you could offer him a treatment that will reduce his risk of dying, which is already quite low, to slightly less. There will be a small bleeding risk and a charge of $150. The patient consults with his wife, and with some regret, they decline the intervention. You leave them looking slightly troubled, rationalizing their decision with each other. You reflect on how much more comfortable you would be if your country offered universal health care.

References

1. Midgette AS, O'Connor GT, Baron JA, Bell J. Effect of intravenous streptokinase on early mortality In patients with suspected acute myocardial infarction: a meta-analysis by anatomic location of infarction. *Ann Intern Med.* 1990;113(12):961-968.

2. ISIS-2 (Second International Study of Infarct Survival) Collaborative Group. Randomised trial of intravenous streptokinase, oral aspirin, both, or neither among 17,187 cases of suspected acute myocardial infarction: ISIS-2. *Lancet.* 1988;2(8607):349-360.

3. Rothwell PM. External validity of randomised controlled trials: "to whom do the results of this trial apply?" *Lancet.* 2005;365(9453):82-93.

4. Ridker PM, Cook NR, Lee IM, et al. A randomized trial of low-dose aspirin in the primary prevention of cardiovascular disease in women. *N Engl J Med.* 2005;352 (13):1293-1304.

5. Crawford BM, Meana M, Stewart D, Cheung AM. Treatment decision making in mature adults: gender differences. *Health Care Women Int.* 2000;21(2):91-104.

6. Watanabe CT, Maynard C, Ritchie JL. Comparison of short-term outcomes following coronary artery stenting in men versus women. *Am J Cardiol.* 2001; 88(8):848-852.

7. Lansky AJ, Pietras C, Costa RA, et al. Gender differences in outcomes after primary angioplasty versus primary stenting with and without abciximab for acute myocardial infarction: results of the Controlled Abciximab and Device Investigation to Lower Late Angioplasty Complications (CADILLAC) trial. *Circulation.* 2005;111(13):1611-1618.

8. Adu FD, Akinwolere OA, Tomori O, Uche LN. Low seroconversion rates to measles vaccine among children in Nigeria. *Bull World Health Organ.* 1992;70 (4):457-460.

9. Bautista-Lopez NL, Vaisberg A, Kanashiro R, Hernandez H, Ward BJ. Immune response to measles vaccine in Peruvian children. *Bull World Health Organ.* 2001;79(11):1038-1046.

10. Hansson L, Zanchetti A, Carruthers SG, et al. Effects of intensive blood-pressure lowering and low-dose aspirin in patients with hypertension: principal results of the Hypertension Optimal Treatment (HOT) randomised trial: HOT Study Group. *Lancet* 1998;351(9118):1755-1762.

11. Falkner B, Kushner H. Effect of chronic sodium loading on cardiovascular response in young blacks and whites. *Hypertension.* 1990;15(1):36-43.

12. Leontiadis GI, Sharma VK, Howden CW. Systematic review and meta-analysis: enhanced efficacy of proton-pump inhibitor therapy for peptic ulcer bleeding in Asia—a post hoc analysis from the Cochrane Collaboration. *Aliment Pharmacol Ther.* 2005;21(9):1055-1061.

13. Villari P, Manzoli L, Boccia A. Methodological quality of studies and patient age as major sources of variation in efficacy estimates of influenza vaccination in healthy adults: a meta-analysis. *Vaccine.* 2004;22(25-26):3475-3486.

14. Treiber G, Ammon S, Klotz U. Age-dependent eradication of *Helicobacter pylori* with dual therapy. *Aliment Pharmacol Ther*. 1997;11(4):711-718.

15. Belshe RB. Current status of live attenuated influenza virus vaccine in the US. *Virus Res*. 2004;103(1-2):177-185.

16. Trock BJ, Leonessa F, Clarke R. Multidrug resistance in breast cancer: a meta-analysis of MDR1/gp170 expression and its possible functional significance. *J Natl Cancer Inst*. 1997;89(13):917-931.

17. Wilson TW. History of salt supplies in West Africa and blood pressures today. *Lancet*. 1986;1(8484):784-786.

18. Staessen JA, Wang JG, Thijs L. Cardiovascular prevention and blood pressure reduction: a quantitative overview updated until 1 March 2003. *J Hypertens*. 2003;21(6):1055-1076.

19. Kostis JB, Wilson AC, Freudenberger RS, Cosgrove NM, Pressel SL, Davis BR. Long-term effect of diuretic-based therapy on fatal outcomes in subjects with isolated systolic hypertension with and without diabetes. *Am J Cardiol*. 2005;95(1):29-35.

20. Vijan S, Hayward RA. Pharmacologic lipid-lowering therapy in type 2 diabetes mellitus: background paper for the American College of Physicians. *Ann Intern Med*. 2004;140(8):650-658.

21. Canlas MM, Dominguez AE, Abarquez RF. Ten year review of the clinicopatho-logic findings of coronary artery disease at the University of the Philippines, Philippine General Hospital (1969-1978). *Phil J Int Med*. 1980;18:65-74.

22. Roberts WC, Potkin BN, Solus DE, Reddy SG. Mode of death, frequency of healed and acute myocardial infarction, number of major epicardial coronary arteries severely narrowed by atherosclerotic plaque, and heart weight in fatal athero-sclerotic coronary artery disease: analysis of 889 patients studied at necropsy. *J Am Coll Cardiol*. 1990;15(1):196-203.

23. Yusuf S, Hawken S, Ounpuu S, et al. Effect of potentially modifiable risk factors associated with myocardial infarction in 52 countries (the INTERHEART study): case-control study. *Lancet*. 2004;364(9438):937-952.

24. Dela Paz AG PN, Justinian RP. Thrombolysis in acute myocardial infarction. *Phil J Cardiol*. 1988;17:185-188.

25. Cardinal H, Monfared AA, Dorais M, LeLorier J. A comparison between persis-tence to therapy in ALLHAT and in everyday clinical practice: a generalizability issue. *Can J Cardiol*. 2004;20(4):417-421.

26. Kennedy WA, Laurier C, Malo JL, Ghezzo H, L'Archeveque J, Contandriopoulos AP. Does clinical trial subject selection restrict the ability to generalize use and cost of health services to "real life" subjects? *Int J Technol Assess Health Care*. 2003;19(1):8-16.

27. Bulatao J. *Split-Level Christianity.* Manila, Philippines: University of St. Tomas Press; 1966.

28. Raja SN, Williams S, McGee R. Multidimensional health locus of control beliefs and psychological health for a sample of mothers. *Soc Sci Med*. 1994;39(2):213-220.

29. Chambers BR, You RX, Donnan GA. Carotid endarterectomy for asymptomatic carotid stenosis. *Cochrane Database Syst Rev*. 2000;(2):CD001923.

30. Barnett HJ, Eliasziw M, Meldrum HF, Taylor DW. Do the facts and figures warrant a 10-fold increase in the performance of carotid endarterectomy on asymptomatic patients? *Neurology*. 1996;46(3):603-608.

31. Tu JV, Hannan EL, Anderson GM, et al. The fall and rise of carotid endarterectomy in the United States and Canada. *N Engl J Med*. 1998;339(20):1441-1447.

32. White HD, Gersh BJ, Opie LH. *Antithrombotic Agents: Platelet Inhibitors, Anticoagulants and Fibrinolytics*. 3rd ed. Philadelphia, PA: WB Saunders; 1991.

33. Grover SA, Lowensteyn I, Esrey KL, Steinert Y, Joseph L, Abrahamowicz M. Do doctors accurately assess coronary risk in their patients? preliminary results of the coronary health assessment study. *BMJ*. 1995;310(6985):975-978.

34. Atrial Fibrillation Investigators. Risk factors for stroke and efficacy of antithrombotic therapy in atrial fibrillation: analysis of pooled data from five randomized controlled trials. *Arch Intern Med*. 1994;154(13):1449-1457.

35. Elneihoum AM, Goransson M, Falke P, Janzon L. Three-year survival and recurrence after stroke in Malmo, Sweden: an analysis of stroke registry data. *Stroke*. 1998;29(10):2114-2117.

36. Sheridan S, Pignone M, Mulrow C. Framingham-based tools to calculate the global risk of coronary heart disease: a systematic review of tools for clinicians. *J Gen Intern Med*. 2003;18(12):1039-1052.

37. Keys A. *Seven Countries: A Multivariate Analysis of Death and Coronary Heart Disease*. Cambridge, MA: Harvard University Press; 1980.

38. Tuomilehto J, Kuulasmaa K. WHO MONICA Project: assessing CHD mortality and morbidity. *Int J Epidemiol*. 1989;18(3)(suppl 1):S38-S45.

39. European Carotid Surgery Trialists' Collaborative Group. Randomised trial of endarterectomy for recently symptomatic carotid stenosis: final results of the MRC European Carotid Surgery Trial (ECST). *Lancet*. 1998;351 (9113):1379-1387.

40. Chatellier G, Zapletal E, Lemaitre D, Menard J, Degoulet P. The number needed to treat: a clinically useful nomogram in its proper context. *BMJ*. 1996;312 (7028):426-429.

41. Dans AL; ISIP Study Group. Acute myocardial infarction in tertiary centres in Metro Manila: in-hospital survival and physicians practices. *ASEAN Heart J*. 1999;7(1):1-6.

42. Gottlieb SS, McCarter RJ, Vogel RA. Effect of beta-blockade on mortality among high-risk and low-risk patients after myocardial infarction. *N Engl J Med*. 1998;339(8):489-497.

43. World Bank. *World Development Report 2000/2001*. Washington, DC: World Bank; 2000.

EXAMPLE
NUMBERS
NEEDED TO
TREAT

Ignacio Ferreira-González, Christina Lacchetti,
Gordon Guyatt, and P. J. Devereaux

IN THIS CHAPTER:

HOW CAN WE SUMMARIZE BENEFITS AND RISKS?

Evidence-based practice requires that clinicians summarize the benefits and *risks* of treatment of patients. Furthermore, when called on, clinicians must incorporate patient values and preferences with benefit/risk *evidence* to determine which management strategies are in patients' best interests (see Chapter 22.2, Decision Making and the Patient).

These activities require clear and vivid summaries of the magnitude of treatment effect. The *relative risk reduction (RRR;* the *control group risk* minus the *experimental group risk* divided by the control group risk), the *absolute risk reduction (ARR;* the control group risk minus the experimental group risk), and the *number needed to treat (NNT)* represent alternative ways of summarizing the effect of treatment (see Chapter 7, Does Treatment Lower Risk? Understanding the Results). In this chapter, we provide a number of examples of the last of these, the NNT.

THE NUMBER NEEDED TO TREAT IN WEIGHING BENEFIT AND HARM

The NNT, the number of patients the clinician must treat for a particular period to prevent 1 adverse target event (such as a stroke) or to create a positive outcome (such as a patient free of dyspepsia), may be the most attractive single measure. Arithmetically, the NNT is the inverse of the ARR. Clinicians could therefore simply take the ARR from a *randomized controlled trial (RCT)*, calculate its inverse, and derive an NNT for their patients. Such an approach, however, can be profoundly misleading.

Consider, for instance, the Global Utilization of Streptokinase and Tissue Plasminogen Activator for Occluded Coronary Arteries trial, which reported the mortality in the 30 days after hospital admission of approximately 20 000 patients who received streptokinase and approximately 10 000 who received tissue plasminogen activator (TPA).[1] In the patients receiving TPA, the risk of dying was 6.3%; in those receiving streptokinase, the risk was 7.3%. The relative risk of dying of TPA is therefore 6.3 (86%) of 7.3; RRR, 100 − 86 (14%); ARR, 7.3 − 6.3 (1%); and NNT, 1/0.01 (100). When deciding about whether a patient required TPA, we could assume that we might treat 100 patients to prevent a single death.

Such an approach ignores the fact that in the acute phase of ST-elevation myocardial infarction, patients have very different risks of dying. The first row of the Table 11.2-1 tells us that in the next month after ST-elevation myocardial infarction, no more than 4.4% of patients aged 76 years with noncomplicated Killip I inferior-wall myocardial infarction and absence of other adverse prognostic factors will die. On the other hand, 36% of those aged 76 years and with anterior-wall myocardial infarction Killip III to IV will die.[2]

THE NUMBER NEEDED TO TREAT IN WEIGHING BENEFIT AND HARM—OTHER EXAMPLES

The TPA/streptokinase example also illustrates the usefulness of the NNT in helping clinicians judge the degree of benefit and the degree of harm patients can expect from therapy. One of the examples in Table 11.2-1 further illustrates this point.

As a result of taking aspirin, patients with hypertension without known coronary artery disease can expect a reduction of approximately 15% in their relative risk of cardiovascular-related events during the subsequent 4 years.[6] For an otherwise low-risk woman with hypertension and a baseline risk of cardiovascular-related events of between 2.5% and 5%,[28] this translates into an NNT of approximately 200 during a 5-year period. However, as presented in Table 11.2-1, for every 476 patients treated with aspirin each year, 1 would experience a major hemorrhage. Thus, in 1000 patients treated during 5 years, aspirin would be responsible for preventing 5 cardiovascular events, but it would also be responsible for causing approximately 10 serious bleeding episodes. Recommending aspirin to such low-risk patients would be questionable at best. For a patient at high risk for cardiovascular events (eg, a man with hypertension and diabetes who is older than 70 years), the NNT of approximately 44 (in 1000 patients, 22 cardiovascular events prevented by aspirin and 10 bleeding episodes caused by aspirin) suggests that recommending aspirin may be much more appropriate.

Another example from Table 11.2-1 emphasizes the importance of considering the time frame in evaluating the NNT. During a 1-year period, the NNT for prevention of stroke or myocardial infarction with angiotensin-converting enzyme inhibitors in low- and high-risk hypertensive patients is 303 and 151, respectively. However, if a period of 20 years is considered, the corresponding NNTs are 27 and 13. These figures help demonstrate that how one presents NNT data can determine the effect of the information on clinicians and patients.

A final point is that clinicians can also apply the NNT concept to adverse effects of interventions; it then becomes a *number needed to harm* (*NNH*). Clinicians can use the data from Table 11.2-1 in making treatment decisions with patients. More important, the results illustrate the importance of considering individual patients' *baseline risk* and the RRR associated with treatment before advising patients about the optimal management of their health problems.

TABLE 11.2-1

Example Number Needed to Treat

Condition or Disorder	Intervention vs Control	Outcome During 1 Year[a]	Risk Groups, %[a]	RRR (95% CI)[a]	ARR, %	NNT
Acute phase of ST-elevation myocardial infarction	Thrombolysis with TPA vs streptokinase	Total mortality at 1 mo	Low = 0.8-4.4[b]	14 (5.9-21.3)[1]	0.1-0.6	1000-166
			Medium = 4.5-16		0.6-2.25	166-44
			High = 16.1-36		2.25-5	44-20
Survivors of myocardial infarction[c]	ACE inhibitors therapy vs placebo	Total mortality	Low = 4[d]	17 (3-29)[3]	0.68	147
			Medium = 19.8		3.3	30
			High = 28.8		4.8	20
Persons without diagnosed cardiovascular disease[e]	Statin therapy vs placebo	Major cardiovascular event[f]	Low < 2[g]	10 (4-15)[4]	0.2	500
			Moderate = 6.5		0.65	154
			High = 12.5		1.25	80
			Very high = 20		2	50
Persons without diagnosed cardiovascular disease[e]	Aspirin vs placebo	Any important vascular event during 5 years[h]	Low < 2[g]	15 (0-28)[5]	0.3	333
			Moderate = 6.5		1	100
			High = 12.5		1.9	53
			Very high = 20		2.25	44
Persons without diagnosed cardiovascular disease[e]	Aspirin vs placebo	Major bleeding episodes (fatal and nonfatal)	Not available	RR increase = 75 (31-130)[6]	0.21	NNH = 476

Congestive heart failure	Spironolactone vs placebo	Total mortality	30 (18-40)[7]	Low = 8[i]	2.40	42
				Medium = 21	6.30	16
				High = 33	9.90	10
Congestive heart failure	ACE inhibitor vs placebo	Total mortality	23 (12-33)[8]	Low = 8[i]	1.84	54
				Medium = 21	4.83	21
				High = 33	7.59	13
Congestive heart failure	β-Blocker therapy vs placebo	Total mortality	35 (20-47)[9]	Low = 8[i]	2.8	36
				Medium = 21	7.35	14
				High = 33	11.55	9
People with history of coronary event	Implantation cardioverter defibrillator	Risk of sudden cardiac death	53 (48-74)[10]	Low = 5	2.65	38
				Medium = 20	10.6	9
				High = 27	14.3	7
				Very high = 35	18.5	5
Nonvalvular atrial fibrillation	Warfarin vs placebo	Stroke	62 (48-72)[11]	Low = 1.9[k]	1.1	85
				Low-medium = 2.8	1.7	58
				Medium = 3.6	2.2	45
				Medium-high = 6.4	4	25
				High = 8	5	20
				Very high = 44	27	4

(Continued)

TABLE 11.2-1

Example Number Needed to Treat (*Continued*)

Condition or Disorder	Intervention vs Control	Outcome During 1 Year[a]	Risk Groups, %[a]	RRR (95% CI)[a]	ARR, %	NNT
Nonvalvular atrial fibrillation	Oral anticoagulant therapy vs aspirin therapy	Stroke	Low = 1.9[k]	45 (29-57)[12]	0.85	117
			Low-medium = 2.8		1.26	79
			Medium = 3.6		1.62	62
			Medium-high = 6.4		2.9	35
			High = 8		3.6	28
			Very high = 44		19.8	5
Hypertension	ACE inhibitors vs placebo	Fatal or nonfatal stroke or fatal or nonfatal myocardial infarction	Low risk < 1.5[l]	22 (17-27)[13]	0.33	303
			High risk > 3		0.66	151
Hypertension	Calcium antagonist vs placebo	Fatal or nonfatal stroke or fatal or nonfatal myocardial infarction	Low risk < 1.5[l]	18 (5-29)[13]	0.27	370
			High risk > 3		0.54	185
HIV infection	Ritonavir vs placebo	AIDS-defining illness	Low = 0.7[m]	42 (29-52)[14]	0.29	340
			High = 2.1		0.9	113
HIV infection	Triple antiretroviral regimen vs dual regimen	AIDS-defining illness	Low = 0.7[m]	25 (19-48)[15]	0.17	571
			High = 2.1		0.52	190

Patients	Intervention	Outcome	Baseline risk	Relative measure	Absolute measure	NNT/NNH
Survivors of curative resection for colorectal cancer	Intensive follow-up vs usual care	Total mortality	Low = 2[n]	19 (6-30)[16]	0.38	263
			Medium = 6		1.1	88
			High = 11		2.1	48
Symptomatic carotid stenosis	Carotid endarterectomy vs optimal medical care, including antiplatelet therapy	Stroke	Low = 3.5[o]	RR increase[p] = 20 (range, 0-44)	ARI = 3.7	NNH = 27
			High = 6	RRR = 27 (range, 5-44)	ARR = 1.6	NNT = 62
				RRR = 48 (range, 27-73)	ARR = 2.9	NNT = 35
Rheumatoid arthritis treated with nonsteroidal anti-inflammatory drugs	Concurrent misoprostol vs placebo	Development of serious upper gastrointestinal complications	Low = 0.8[q]	40 (1.8-64)[17]	0.32	312
			Medium = 2.0		0.80	125
			High = 18		7.20	14
One or more unprovoked seizures	Immediate treatment with antiepileptic drugs vs treatment only after seizure recurrence	Recurrent seizures	Low = 13.5[r]	60 (40-70)[18]	8.1	12
			Medium = 30		18.3	6
			High = 34		20	5
Breast cancer	Radiotherapy plus tamoxifen vs tamoxifen alone	Any recurrence	Low = 4.3[s]	22 (13-29)[19]	0.95	100
			High = 7.8		1.7	59

(Continued)

Abbreviations: ACE, angiotensin converting enzyme; ARI, absolute risk increase; ARR, absolute risk reduction; NNH, number needed to harm; NNT, number needed to treat; RRI, relative risk increase; RRR, relative risk reduction; TPA, tissue plasminogen activator.

[a]Unless otherwise specified, all calculations performed have been standardized over 1 year, assuming both a constant baseline risk and a constant risk reduction through the period of the corresponding study.

[b]Risk according to the Thrombolysis In Myocardial Infarction (TIMI) risk scale for the ST-elevation myocardial infarction. Strata risk have been defined as follows: low risk, lower than 4 points; medium risk, 4 to 6 points; high risk, more than 6 points, where each point corresponds to the presence of any of the following 30-day mortality predictors in the acute phase of the event: age (<65 years = 1 point; 65-74 years = 2 points; >74 years = 3 points); systolic blood pressure (SBP) lower than 100 mm Hg (3 points); heart rate greater than 100/min (2 points); Killip II-IV (2 points); anterior ST-elevation or left bundle-branch block (1 point); diabetes (1 point); weight lower than 67 kg (1 point); time to treatment less than 4 hours (1 point).[2]

[c]After 1 week of the index episode.

[d]Low, 1 to 10 premature ventricular beats (PVBs) per hour and no congestive heart failure (CHF); medium, 1 to 10 PVBs/h and CHF; high, more than 10 PVBs/h and CHF. PVBs were analyzed from Holter recordings performed between the first week and the first month after the index episode.[20]

[e]More than 90% of study patients did not have diagnosed cardiovascular disease.

[f]Major cardiovascular event is defined as major coronary event (nonfatal myocardial infarction or death related to coronary artery disease), nonfatal or fatal stroke, or coronary revascularization.

[g]One-year risk of fatal cardiovascular disease. Risk varies according to a patient's sex, cholesterol levels, smoking status, and age. For example, low risk represents patients aged 40 to 49 years with SBP between 120 and 140 mm Hg, who do not smoke and with total cholesterol levels below 200 mg/dL; moderate risk, patients aged 50 years and older with SBP 140 to 160 mm Hg, who may have total cholesterol levels of more than 300 mg/dL, and who do not smoke; high risk, patients aged 60 years and older with SBP 160 to 180 mm Hg, who may have total cholesterol levels of more than 250 mg/dL, and who do not smoke; very high risk, patients aged 70 years and older with SBP 180 mm Hg, who may have total cholesterol level of more than 300 mg/dL, and who do not smoke. Modified from Conroy et al.[21] Refer to Conroy et al[21] to identify the various combinations of factors that determine a patient's risk category.

[h]Any important vascular event is the composite of vascular death, nonfatal myocardial infarction, or nonfatal stroke.[5]

[i]Low risk, New York Heart Association (NYHA) functional class II; medium risk, NYHA functional class III; high risk, NYHA functional class IV.[22]

[j]Risk of sudden cardiac death according to the following risk groups: low risk group, history of coronary event; medium risk subgroup, history of coronary event and ejection fraction of less than 30%; high-risk subgroup, out-of-hospital cardiac arrest survivor secondary to acute coronary event; very-high-risk subgroup, sustained ventricular tachycardia or ventricular fibrillation episodes in the convalescent phase after a coronary event (usually after the first 48 hours of the index episode). Modified from Myerburg and Castellanos.[23]

[k]Adjusted stroke rate. Every risk stratum is defined from a score scale risk, in which each of the following adds 1 point: recent CHF, hypertension, age at least 75 years, or diabetes mellitus. Previous stroke or transient ischemic attack adds 2 points. The score defines each stratum of risk as follows: low risk (0 points), low-medium risk (1 point), medium risk (3 points), high risk (4 points), very high risk (6 points).[24]

[l]Low risk: SBP 140 to 159 mm Hg or diastolic blood pressure (DBP) 90 to 99 mm Hg without any other cardiovascular risk factor. Medium risk: SBP 140 to 159 mm Hg with 1 to 2 additional risks factors; SBP 160 to 179 mm Hg or DBP 100 to 109 mm Hg with 0, 1, or 2 additional risk factors. High risk: SBP 140 to 159 mm Hg or DBP 90 to 99 mm Hg with 3 or more risk factors; SBP 160 to 179 mm Hg or DBP 100 to 109 mm Hg with 3 or more risk factors; SBP higher than 180 mm Hg or DBP higher than 110 mm Hg. Modified from Whitworth.[25]

[m]Baseline HIV-1 RNA level (copies/mL): low, 501 to 3000; medium, 3001 to 10 000; high, 10 001 to 30 000; very high, more than 30 000.[26]

[n]1,5 Years' mortality of colorectal cancer according to Duke stages.

[o]Low, lower than 50% stenosis; medium, 50% to 69% stenosis; high, more than 70%.[27]

[p]Because the effects of carotid endarterectomy vary with the degree of stenosis, 3 benefits or risks of surgery are presented.

[q]Low risk, patients with none of the following risk factors: 75 years or older, history of peptic ulcer, history of gastrointestinal bleeding, or history of cardiovascular disease; medium risk, patients with any single factor; high risk, patients with all 4 factors.[17]

[r]Low risk, first seizure; medium risk, second seizure; high risk, third seizure.[18]

[s]Low, no nodes affected; medium, 1 to 3 affected nodes; high, more than 3 nodes affected.[19]

References

1. GUSTO Investigators. An international randomized trial comparing four thrombolytic strategies for acute myocardial infarction. *N Engl J Med*. 1993;329(10):673-682.

2. Morrow DA, Antman EM, Charlesworth A, et al. TIMI risk score for ST-elevation myocardial infarction: a convenient, bedside, clinical score for risk assessment at presentation: an Intravenous nPA for Treatment of Infarcting Myocardium Early II Trial substudy. *Circulation*. 2000;102(17):2031-2037.

3. Domanski MJ, Exner DV, Borkowf CB, Geller NL, Rosenberg Y, Pfeffer MA. Effect of angiotensin converting enzyme inhibition on sudden cardiac death in patients following acute myocardial infarction: a meta-analysis of randomized clinical trials. *J Am Coll Cardiol*. 1999;33(3):598-604.

4. Baigent C, Keech A, Kearney PM, et al. Efficacy and safety of cholesterol-lowering treatment: prospective meta-analysis of data from 90,056 participants in 14 randomised trials of statins. *Lancet*. 2005;366(9493):1267-1278.

5. Eidelman RS, Hebert PR, Weisman SM, Hennekens CH. An update on aspirin in the primary prevention of cardiovascular disease. *Arch Intern Med*. 2003; 163(17):2006-2010.

6. Hansson L, Zanchetti A, Carruthers SG, et al. Effects of intensive blood-pressure lowering and low-dose aspirin in patients with hypertension: principal results of the Hypertension Optimal Treatment (HOT) randomised trial: HOT Study Group. *Lancet*. 1998;351(9118):1755-1762.

7. Pitt B, Zannad F, Remme WJ, et al. The effect of spironolactone on morbidity and mortality in patients with severe heart failure: Randomized Aldactone Evaluation Study Investigators. *N Engl J Med*. 1999;341(10):709-717.

8. Garg R, Yusuf S. Overview of randomized trials of angiotensin-converting enzyme inhibitors on mortality and morbidity in patients with heart failure: Collaborative Group on ACE Inhibitor Trials. *JAMA*. 1995;273(18):1450-1456.

9. Brophy JM, Joseph L, Rouleau JL. Beta-blockers in congestive heart failure: a Bayesian meta-analysis. *Ann Intern Med*. 2001;134(7):550-560.

10. Ezekowitz JA, Armstrong PW, McAlister FA. Implantable cardioverter defibrillators in primary and secondary prevention: a systematic review of randomized, controlled trials. *Ann Intern Med*. 2003;138(6):445-452.

11. Hart RG, Benavente O, McBride R, Pearce LA. Antithrombotic therapy to prevent stroke in patients with atrial fibrillation: a meta-analysis. *Ann Intern Med*. 1999;131(7):492-501.

12. van Walraven C, Hart RG, Singer DE, et al. Oral anticoagulants vs aspirin in nonvalvular atrial fibrillation: an individual patient meta-analysis. *JAMA*. 2002;288(19):2441-2448.

13. Turnbull F. Effects of different blood-pressure-lowering regimens on major cardiovascular events: results of prospectively-designed overviews of randomised trials. *Lancet*. 2003;362(9395):1527-1535.

14. Cameron DW, Heath-Chiozzi M, Danner S, et al. Randomised placebo-controlled trial of ritonavir in advanced HIV-1 disease: the Advanced HIV Disease Ritonavir Study Group. *Lancet*. 1998;351(9012):543-549.

15. Yazdanpanah Y, Sissoko D, Egger M, Mouton Y, Zwahlen M, Chene G. Clinical efficacy of antiretroviral combination therapy based on protease inhibitors or non-nucleoside analogue reverse transcriptase inhibitors: indirect comparison of controlled trials. *BMJ*. 2004;328(7434):249-253.

16. Renehan AG, Egger M, Saunders MP, O'Dwyer ST. Impact on survival of intensive follow up after curative resection for colorectal cancer: systematic review and meta-analysis of randomised trials. *BMJ*. 2002;324(7341):813-816.

17. Silverstein FE, Graham DY, Senior JR, et al. Misoprostol reduces serious gastrointestinal complications in patients with rheumatoid arthritis receiving nonsteroidal anti-inflammatory drugs: a randomized, double-blind, placebo-controlled trial. *Ann Intern Med*. 1995;123(4):241-249.

18. Hauser WA, Rich SS, Lee JR, Annegers JF, Anderson VE. Risk of recurrent seizures after two unprovoked seizures. *N Engl J Med*. 1998;338(7):429-434.

19. Overgaard M, Jensen MB, Overgaard J, et al. Postoperative radiotherapy in high-risk postmenopausal breast-cancer patients given adjuvant tamoxifen: Danish Breast Cancer Cooperative Group DBCG 82c randomised trial. *Lancet*. 1999;353(9165):1641-1648.

20. Maggioni AP, Zuanetti G, Franzosi MG, et al. Prevalence and prognostic significance of ventricular arrhythmias after acute myocardial infarction in the fibrinolytic era: GISSI-2 results. *Circulation*. 1993;87(2):312-322.

21. Conroy RM, Pyorala K, Fitzgerald AP, et al. Estimation of 10-year risk of fatal cardiovascular disease in Europe: the SCORE project. *Eur Heart J*. 2003;24(11):987-1003.

22. Matoba M, Matsui S, Hirakawa T, et al. Long-term prognosis of patients with congestive heart failure. *Jpn Circ J*. 1990;54(1):57-61.

23. Myerburg RJ, Castellanos A. Cardiac arrest and sudden death. Chapter 24. In: Saunders WB, ed. *Heart Disease: A Textbook of Cardiovascular Medicine*. Philadelphia, PA: WB Saunders; 1997:742-779.

24. Gage BF, Waterman AD, Shannon W, Boechler M, Rich MW, Radford MJ. Validation of clinical classification schemes for predicting stroke: results from the National Registry of Atrial Fibrillation. *JAMA*. 2001;285(22):2864-2870.

25. Whitworth JA. 2003 World Health Organization (WHO)/International Society of Hypertension (ISH) statement on management of hypertension. *J Hypertens*. 2003;21(11):1983-1992.

26. Mellors JW, Munoz A, Giorgi JV, et al. Plasma viral load and CD4$^+$ lymphocytes as prognostic markers of HIV-1 infection. *Ann Intern Med*. 1997;126(12):946-954.

27. Barnett HJ, Taylor DW, Eliasziw M, et al. Benefit of carotid endarterectomy in patients with symptomatic moderate or severe stenosis: North American Symptomatic Carotid Endarterectomy Trial Collaborators. *N Engl J Med*. 1998;339(20):1415-1425.

28. Jackson R. Updated New Zealand cardiovascular disease risk-benefit prediction guide. *BMJ*. 2000;320(7236):709-710.

DEALING WITH MISLEADING PRESENTATIONS OF CLINICAL TRIAL RESULTS

Victor Montori, John Ioannidis, Roman Jaeschke,
P. J. Devereaux, Holger Schünemann,
Mohit Bhandari, and Gordon Guyatt

IN THIS CHAPTER:

Beware Uneven Emphasis on Benefits and Harms

Wait for the Overall Results to Emerge; Do Not Rush

Conclusion

INTRODUCTION

Science is often not objective.[1] The choice of research questions, the methods to collect and analyze data, and the interpretation of results all reflect the *Weltan-schauung*, or worldview of the investigator.[2] Investigators' emotional investment in their own ideas, and their personal interest in academic success and advancement, may further compromise scientific objectivity. Investigators often overemphasize the importance of their findings and the quality of their work and choose interpretations that will enhance chances of success in obtaining funds from granting bodies. Scrutiny of the work of the current authors will demonstrate we are not immune to these lapses.

Other serious conflicts of interest arise when for-profit organizations, such as device, biotechnology, and pharmaceutical companies, provide funds for conduct of research, consulting, and attending scientific meetings. In the past 20 years, there has been an 8-fold increase in the number of trials for which authors declare industry affiliation.[3] Investigators accepting funds risk conflicts of interest. Even more problematic, they may cede their right to directly supervise data collection, participate in or supervise data analysis, and write the research reports to which their name is attached.[4-6] Finally, recent experience has shown that some authors deliberately engage in duplicate publication and distort the data, analysis, and presentation of reports to please their sponsors.

Extensive publicity highlighting these problems has caught the attention of many clinicians who are therefore well aware of their vulnerability to biased and potentially misleading presentations of *randomized controlled trial* (*RCT*) results. This book describes, in some detail, guides to help recognize methodologic weaknesses that may introduce *bias*. These criteria, however, do not protect readers against misleading interpretations of apparently methodologically sound studies. Indeed, all the studies we use as examples in this chapter satisfy minimal *validity* criteria, and most were exceptionally strong. In this chapter, we go beyond issues of validity to present a set of users' guides to biased presentation and interpretation of data that can aid clinicians in optimally applying research findings (Table 11.3-1). We illustrate our guides with actual examples, not to embarrass or adversely criticize individual publications, but to help raise awareness of the dangers that the medical literature currently presents to unwary clinicians.

There are some guides to avoid being misled that are at least as important as those we present here, so important that we have allocated them their own chapters (see

TABLE 11.3-1

Users' Guides to Avoid Being Misled by Biased Presentation and Interpretation of Data

1. Read methods and results; bypass the discussion section
2. Read the abstract reported in evidence-based secondary publications
3. Beware large effects in trials with only a few events
4. Beware faulty comparators
5. Beware misleading claims of equivalence
6. Beware small treatment effects and extrapolation to low-risk patients
7. Beware uneven emphasis on benefits and harms
8. Wait for the overall results to emerge; do not rush

BMJ. 2004;329(7474):1093-1096. Amended with permission from the BMJ Publishing Group.

Chapter 9.3, Randomized Trials Stopped Early for Benefit; Chapter 10.4, Composite Endpoints; Chapter 19, Summarizing the Evidence; Chapter 20.1, Reporting Bias; and Chapter 20.4, When to Believe a Subgroup Analysis). Attention to those issues, and the 8 guides below, will help you negotiate the minefield of sophisticated clinical trial reports with presentations that serve interests other than those of your patients.

EIGHT GUIDES TO AVOID BEING MISLED

Read Only Methods and Results; Bypass the Discussion Section
The discussion (and to some extent the abstracts, introduction, and the conclusion section of structured abstracts) often offers inferences that differ from those a dispassionate reader would draw from the methods and results.[7]

Consider, for example, 2 *systematic reviews* published in 2001 summarizing randomized trials assessing the effect of albumin use for fluid resuscitation. One review, funded by the Plasma Proteins Therapeutic Association, pooled 42 short-term trials reporting mortality and found no significant difference in mortality with albumin vs crystalloid solutions across all groups of patients (relative risk [RR], 1.11; 95% confidence interval [CI], 0.95-1.28) and in patients with burns (RR, 1.76; 95% CI, 0.97-3.17).[8] The other review, funded by the UK National Health Service, pooled 31 short-term trials reporting mortality and found a significantly higher mortality with albumin in all patient groups (RR, 1.52; 95% CI, 1.17-1.99) and in patients with burns (RR, 2.40; 95% CI, 1.11-5.19).[9]

Although these 2 reviews included a slightly different set of trials (eg, the former included an additional trial in patients with burns), both yield point estimates suggesting that albumin may increase mortality and CIs that include the possibility of a considerable increase in mortality. The trials were small, many were methodologically weak, and the results were heterogeneous. The authors of the first review concluded, in their discussion, that their results "should serve to allay concerns regarding the safety of albumin." In contrast, the discussion section of the second review recommended banning the use of albumin outside the context of a rigorously conducted RCT.

Authors of an editorial accompanying the first review[10] suggested that the funding source may have been, at least in part, responsible for the different interpretations. On one hand, the Plasma Proteins Therapeutic Association promotes access to and reimbursement for the use of albumin, an expensive intervention; on the other hand, the National Health Service pays for it in the United Kingdom.

Examples of potential conflict of interest apparently driving conclusions abound. Systematic examinations of the relationship between funding and conclusions have found that authors show greater enthusiasm for the experimental treatment when funded by for-profit than nonprofit interests.[11-14] Even after adjusting for magnitude of treatment effect and adverse events, for-profit organization funding results in a 5-fold increase in the odds of recommending an experimental drug as treatment of choice (odds ratio, 5.3; 95% CI, 2.0-14.4) compared with nonprofit funding.[11]

To apply this first guide and bypass the discussion, clinicians must be able to make sense of the methods and results. If you have gained familiarity with the content of this book, you achieved this happy state.

Read the Abstract Reported in Preappraised Resources

Secondary journals, such as the *ACP Journal Club*, *Evidence-Based Medicine*, and *Evidence-Based Mental Health*, publish *structured abstracts* produced by a team of clinicians and methodologists in collaboration with the authors of the original articles. These abstracts often include critical information about research conduct (allocation concealment; blinding of patients, health care providers, data collectors, data analysts, and outcome adjudicators; complete follow-up) omitted from the original reports.[15] The structured abstracts do not include the introduction or the discussion sections of the original report or the conclusions of the original study. The title and the conclusions of this secondary abstract are the product of critical appraisal by individuals for whom competing financial or personal interests will be minimum or absent in most instances.

Compare, for example, the *ACP Journal Club* abstract and the full publication of an important trial[16] addressing the prevention of stroke.[17] The title of the original publication describes the study as testing "a perindopril-based blood pressure lowering regimen" and reports that the perindopril-containing regimen resulted in a 28% relative risk reduction (RRR) in the risk of recurrent stroke (95% CI, 17%-38%).

The *ACP Journal Club* abstract and its commentary identified the publication as describing 2 parallel but separate randomized placebo-controlled trials including approximately 6100 patients with a history of stroke or transient ischemic attack. In 1 trial, patients were randomized to receive perindopril or placebo; active treatment had no appreciable effect on stroke (RRR, 5%; 95% CI, −19% to

23%). In the second trial, patients were allocated to receive perindopril plus indapamide or double placebo. Combined treatment resulted in a 43% RRR (95% CI, 30%-54%) in recurrent stroke. The *ACP Journal Club* commentary notes that the authors, in communication with the editors, refused to accept the interpretation of the publication as reporting 2 separate RCTs (which explains why it is difficult for even the knowledgeable reader to get a clear picture of the design from the original publication).

The objectivity and methodologic sophistication of those preparing the independent structured abstracts may provide additional value for clinicians. We suggest checking out the structured abstract of any article that appears in high-quality secondary publications. We do not claim perfection of this methodologic review: residual hidden bias or misleading presentation may elude the methodologists. Nevertheless, the resource is certain, on occasion, to help.

Beware Large Treatment Effects in Trials With Only a Few Events

Although you should be particularly skeptical of large treatment effects from trials with few events that are stopped early (see Chapter 9.3, Randomized Trials Stopped Early for Benefit), any time you see an unusually large effect (say, an RRR >50%) from a study with few events (say, <100) it is wise to be cautious. One reason to be cautious is that investigators may not have had a formal stopping rule but may have been taking repeated looks at their data and chose to stop early when they saw a large effect. If this is the case, neither the nominal P value nor the CI is valid.

Very large effects are implausible because multiple mechanisms underlie most diseases, and therapies typically address only one or two of those mechanisms. The complementary success of angiotensin-converting enzyme (ACE) inhibitors, antiplatelet agents, lipid-lowering agents, and β-blockers in reducing cardiac events in patients with myocardial infarction (MI) illustrates this multiplicity of disease mechanisms. Predictably, each agent offers only a modest magnitude of risk reduction (from 1/5 to 1/3).

These considerations should leave us unsurprised when subsequent trials suggest that initial large positive effects represent overly optimistic or even completely spurious findings. For example, an otherwise methodologically rigorous RCT randomized 103 patients with an acute MI to receive a 48-hour magnesium or placebo infusion. The trial reported 1 in-hospital death in the magnesium group and 9 in the placebo group (ie, an 88% RRR; $P < .001$).[18] However, a subsequent RCT of approximately 60 000 patients with more than 4300 deaths showed no benefit; in fact, there was a trend toward excess mortality with magnesium ($P = .07$).

The implication is clear: wait until a sufficient number of studies showing a sufficient number of events have been conducted before exposing your patients to inconvenient, costly, or potentially risky interventions (see Guide 8 in this chapter).

Beware Faulty Comparators

Industry-funded studies typically yield larger treatment effects than nonprofit origination–funded studies.[3,13,14,19] One major explanation is choice of comparators.[20] Table 11.3-2 lists the types of faulty comparators to which you should be alert.

TABLE 11.3-2

Faulty Comparators

- Comparison with placebo when effective agents are available
- Comparison with less effective agents when more effective comparators are available
- Comparison with more toxic agents when less toxic comparators are available
- Comparison with too low a dose (or inadequate dose titration) of an otherwise effective comparator, leading to misleading claims of effectiveness
- Comparison with a too high (and thus toxic) dose (or inadequate dose titration) of an otherwise safe comparator, leading to misleading claims of lower toxicity

Although placebos are often appropriate comparators, this is not always the case. Those invested in a positive trial result may choose a placebo comparator rather than an alternative agent with demonstrated effectiveness. For instance, in a study of 136 trials of new treatments for multiple myeloma, 60% of studies funded by for-profit organizations, but only 21% of trials funded by nonprofit organizations, compared their new interventions against placebo or no treatment.[19]

Three important trials of angiotensin-receptor blockers for patients with diabetic nephropathy used placebo, rather than drugs of demonstrated effectiveness, ACE inhibitors, as the control management strategy.[21-23] The accompanying editorial suggested that the economic interests of the sponsor dictated that choice of comparator. The sponsors may have avoided an ACE inhibitor control group because "...sales of angiotensin-receptor blockers would be lower if the 2 classes of drugs proved equally effective."[24]

Choice of dose and administration regimen can also result in misleading comparisons.[25] Typically, sponsors will choose less effective or more toxic agents than the best ones available or administer the best available agent in excessively small or excessively large doses.

For example, Safer[25] identified 8 trials sponsored by 3 drug companies that compared newer second-generation neuroleptic agents to a fixed high dose (20 mg/d; optimal dosing < 12 mg/d[26]) of haloperidol. Not surprisingly, these trials showed that patients using the new agents had fewer extrapyramidal adverse effects.

Safer[25] offers another example in which a study compared paroxetine against amitriptyline, a sedating tricyclic antidepressant. The trial administered amitriptyline twice daily, possibly leading to excessive daytime somnolence.[27] Johansen and Gotzsche[28] noted the use of an ineffective comparator (nystatin) and the use of an inadequate and unusual administration route (oral amphotericin B, poorly absorbed in the gastrointestinal tract) as comparators in RCTs of the efficacy of antifungals in patients with cancer and neutropenia.

When reading reports of RCTs with active comparators, clinicians should ask themselves whether the comparator should have been another active agent rather than placebo, and if so, whether the dose, formulation, and administration regimen was optimal.

Beware Misleading Claims of Equivalence

One strategy for getting a new drug on the market is to demonstrate its therapeutic equivalence to a currently widely used product and then to make the case for some (often marginal) nontherapeutic benefit (convenience, less frequent dosing, better adverse effect profile). For the clinician, this strategy involves a number of dangers.

The first problem in such trials is that they are likely to have relatively small sample sizes and thus have a relatively small number of outcome events. The result will be imprecise estimates of treatment effect (ie, wide CIs).

The sponsor is likely to make claims of equivalence on the basis of the correct statement that the difference between drugs was not significant, ignoring the fact that the wide CIs include the possibility that the new drug is indeed inferior to the standard therapy. In other words, the trial was not large enough to demonstrate equivalence. You may want to review the explanation of CIs and in particular the discussion of how to decide whether a *negative trial* is large enough in Chapter 8, Confidence Intervals, for a full understanding of this issue.

Second, the comparison agent, usually an older drug, may have only weak evidence supporting its benefit over no treatment or placebo. Thus, the underlying truth may be that the new and old drugs are indeed equivalent—they are both useless! Demonstration of equivalence under these circumstances results in a weak—but sadly enough, often marketable—case for the new agent.

Not infrequently, sample size will be small and evidence for the comparison older drug will be of low quality. Consider antibiotic trials for common mild infections, such as acute rhinosinusitis. Although antibiotics may benefit some patients with bacterial acute sinusitis, the majority of infections in the community are either nonbacterial or self-limited.[29] Investigations have failed to show convincingly that antibiotics have any patient-important benefit in this setting, whereas they will cause adverse events.[30] Nevertheless, there are more than 100 trials comparing antibiotics against each other for this common condition.[31] These trials circulate in medical meetings and medical journals and help maintain, with varying success in different countries, a large irrational market of antibiotic use.[32] This market gradually shifts toward adding big shares for newer agents, without the old antibiotics losing their absolute sales.[33]

A similar situation exists for trials of chemotherapy for some advanced-stage cancers for which chemotherapy is of limited benefit. For advanced-stage non-small-cell lung cancer, if chemotherapy offers any benefit at all, it is marginal.[34] Nevertheless, more than 250 RCTs have compared one chemotherapy regimen against another.[35] Over time, investigators have selected patients with progressively better prognosis for inclusion in these trials. The result has been longer median survival, although the regimens are uniformly ineffective. Investigators may focus on describing this artificial prolongation of median survival, to the detriment of patients who subsequently experience treatment toxicity.

Beware Small Treatment Effects and Extrapolation to Low-Risk Patients

Increasingly, pharmaceutical companies are conducting very large RCTs to be able to exclude chance as an explanation for small treatment effects. Results are consistent with small treatment effects when either the point estimate is very close to no effect (an RRR or absolute risk reduction [ARR] close to 0; an RR or odds ratio close to 1) or the CI includes values close to no effect.

> In one very large trial, investigators randomly allocated more than 6000 subjects to receive antihypertensive therapy based on ACE inhibitor therapy or to receive therapy based on diuretic agents and concluded "initiation of antihypertensive treatment involving ACE inhibitors in older subjects...appears to lead to better outcomes than treatment with diuretic agents...."[36] In absolute terms, however, the difference between the regimens was small: there were 4.2 events per 100 patient-years and 4.6 events per 100 patient-years in the ACE inhibitor and diuretic groups, respectively. The RRR corresponding to this absolute difference, 11%, had an associated 95% CI of −1% to 21%.
>
> Here, we have 2 reasons to doubt the importance of the apparent difference between treatment groups. First, the point estimate suggests a small absolute difference (0.4 events per 100 patient-years), and second, the CI suggests it may have been even smaller. Indeed, there may have been no true difference at all.

There is a variety of strategies investigators and sponsors use to create a spurious impression of a large treatment effect (Table 11.3-3). When the absolute risk of adverse events in untreated patients—the *baseline risk*—is low, you are likely to see a presentation that focuses on RRR and deemphasizes or ignores ARR. The focus on RR conveys a spurious sense of the importance of the result.

TABLE 11.3-3

Strategies for Making a Treatment Effect Appear Larger Than It Is

1. Use relative rather than absolute risk; a 50% relative risk reduction may mean a decrease in risk from 1% to 0.5%.

2. Express risk during a long period; the reduction in risk from 1% to 0.5% may occur during 10 years.

3. For visual presentations, make sure the x-axis intersects the y-axis well above 0; if the x-axis intersects the y-axis at 60%, you can make an improvement from 70% to 75% appear as a 33% increase in survival.

4. Include a minority of high-risk patients in a trial of predominantly low-risk patients; even though most events occur in high-risk individuals, claim important benefits for a large number of low-risk patients in the general population.

5. Ignore the lower boundary of the confidence interval; when the lower boundary of the confidence interval around the relative risk reduction approaches 0, declare significance and henceforth focus exclusively on the point estimate.

6. Focus on statistical significance; when a result achieves statistical significance but both relative and absolute effects are small, highlight the statistical significance and downplay or ignore the magnitude.

For instance, the European Trial on the Reduction of Cardiac Events with Perindopril in Stable Coronary Artery Disease (EUROPA) demonstrated a reduction in MI with perindopril in patients surviving a previous MI and was hailed as a breakthrough. The RRR in MI of 22% (95% CI, 10%-33%) translates into an ARR of 1.4% during 4 years. Thus, clinicians must treat approximately 70 patients for 4 years to prevent a single MI. In particular, when one considers that most of these patients may already be ingesting aspirin or warfarin, a statin, and a β-blocker to reduce their MI risk, one may question the characterization of the incremental benefit as a breakthrough.

Other techniques complement the use of RRRs in making treatment effects appear large. For visual presentations, beware of survival curves in which the x-axis intersects the y-axis much above the 0 level, giving the visual impression of a large effect.[37] Another technique relates to choice of period for presenting treatment effect: long periods for effects that investigators or sponsors wish to make appear large and short ones for those they wish to make appear small.

For instance, McCormack and Greenhalgh[38] pointed out that report 33 of the United Kingdom Prospective Diabetes Study trial[39] expressed the risk of severe hypoglycemia as percentage of participants per year (eg, 2.3% per year for patients receiving insulin). This contrasts with the expression of the benefits as percentage of participants during 10 years (eg, 3.2% absolute reduction in the risk of any diabetes-related endpoints). The presentation obscures the fact that the absolute increase in frequency of hypoglycemia with intensive glycemic control is approximately 7 times the absolute reduction in diabetes complications.

A shift of the target study population to include very-low-risk patients means a potentially major expansion in market size for the agent and a consequent larger effect on health care costs associated with small and possibly marginal gains in health. In the past few years, several professional societies have decreased the threshold for diagnosis and treatment of hypertension, diabetes, and hyperlipidemia, which has drastically increased the proportion of people eligible for treatment. Even if RCTs show benefits in populations that include such very-low-risk patients, the number of events in very-low-risk patients is typically few and the results of such trials are driven entirely by a minority of very-high-risk patients.[40]

Whenever relative or absolute benefits are small or the lower boundary of the CI approaches no effect, the treatment benefits and the potential *harm*, inconveniences, and costs are likely to be, at best, finely balanced. Judicious rather than routine administration of new drugs under these circumstances is unlikely to best serve patient needs or represent prudent allocation of health care resources.

Beware Uneven Emphasis on Benefits and Harms

Clinical decision making requires a balanced interpretation of both benefits and harms associated with any intervention. Unfortunately, many clinical trials neglect even the minimal reporting of harm.[41,42] In an analysis of trials from 7 areas, investigators found that the space allocated to harms in the results was slightly less than the space allocated to the names of authors and their affiliations.[41] Even when investigators report some information regarding harms, failure to present event rates in treatment and control groups, omission of severity of the events, or inappropriate combining of disparate events can compromise sensible interpretation.

> For example, a trial of intravenous immunoglobulin in advanced human immunodeficiency infection stopped early because of efficacy failed to mention any adverse events.[43] In this trial, omission of harm data compounds problems associated with early stopping (see Chapter 9.3, Randomized Trials Stopped Early for Benefit). One placebo-controlled trial of nabumetone for rheumatoid arthritis stated that "the adverse experience profiles were similar for both treatment groups," with no further information concerning the nature of the adverse effects.[44]

Wait for the Overall Results to Emerge; Do Not Rush

Many clinical specialties move at a high speed in terms of introducing new treatments, diagnostics, and other interventions in the market. Although this is exciting and may often improve patient outcomes, problems will arise if clinicians adopt the interventions prematurely. The most common problem is that early claims of efficacy or efficiency are exaggerated. As clinical studies accumulate, it is more common for effects to shrink than to increase.[45]

A first study may show a huge effect, and when the next study shows a negligible or even negative effect, the result is controversy. This scenario is most commonly observed in molecular medicine studies, in which turnaround of information can be fast and proposed hypotheses can be rejected rapidly. Subsequent studies of the same question may show intermediate results between these 2 extremes.[46,47]

> For example, an article in 1994 reported that a variant of the vitamin D receptor gene explains most of the population risk for having low bone-mineral density (ie, weak bones prone to fracture).[48] The finding made the cover page of *Nature* that heralded the "osteoporosis gene." Other subsequent studies showed an opposite effect with the same variant predisposing to stronger bones. A large-scale analysis of 100-fold more participants than the original *Nature* study showed that there is no effect at all.[49]

Another reason to wait is that RCTs do not enroll sufficient patients or follow them for a long enough period to permit detection of relatively uncommon, serious adverse events, particularly if those adverse events occur not uncommonly in the absence of the intervention (such as MIs that occur without exposure to cyclooxygenase-2 inhibitors). Within 25 years from licensing, approximately 20% of drugs that the US Food and Drug Administration licenses are either withdrawn or have major safety warnings added to the drug labels.[50]

A final reason to wait is that evidence of serious misrepresentation of results may emerge. For instance, the original published report of a trial investigating the toxicity of anti inflammatory drugs contained 6-month data and indicated that celecoxib caused fewer symptomatic ulcers and ulcer complications than diclofenac or ibuprofen.[51] However, when the Food and Drug Administration reviewed 12-month data combining both trials, the result was inconclusive: the RR for ulcer complications in patients receiving celecoxib and in patients receiving ibuprofen or diclofenac was 0.83 (95% CI, 0.46-1.50).[52] The authors explained their omission on the basis of large differential loss to follow-up, particularly of high-risk patients in the diclofenac arm, after 6 months.[53] Fortunately, such egregious instances of misleading presentations of evidence are rare.

Table 11.3-4 provides a number of reasons for caution in adopting new interventions, some drawn from other chapters of this book. In every case in which new promising interventions are available, the clinician should balance the risk of offering potentially suboptimal management by using the established intervention vs prematurely offering the new intervention that may be less effective than advertised or may be associated with yet undisclosed or unknown toxicity. The decision is not easy, particularly because clinicians face both marketing pressures and peer pressure to be up to date according to what circulates in recent meetings and medical journals. Indeed, many may perceive themselves as practicing evidence-based medicine when they adopt the newest therapy tested in a recently published RCT.

TABLE 11.3-4

Reasons for Being Cautious in Adopting New Interventions

1. Initial studies may be biased by inadequacies in concealment, blinding, loss to follow-up, or stopping early.

2. Initial studies are particularly susceptible to reporting bias.

3. Initial studies are particularly susceptible to dissemination bias; dramatically positive studies are likely to receive disproportionate attention.

4. Initial studies may overestimate effects by chance (particularly if effects are large and number of events is small).

5. There is a substantial probability (20%) that serious adverse effects will emerge subsequently (cyclooxygenase-2 inhibitors provide a dramatic recent example).

6. On rare occasions, research results will prove to have been misrepresented.

CONCLUSION

We have presented 8 guides for users that can help clinicians protect themselves and their patients from biased and potentially misleading presentations and interpretations of data in the medical literature. These strategies are unlikely to be foolproof. Decreasing the dependence of the research endeavor and regulatory agencies on pharmaceutical industry funding, implementing a requirement for mandatory registration of planned clinical trials and disclosure of research results, and instituting more structured approaches to the peer review and reporting of research[54,55] may decrease the magnitude of biased reporting to which clinicians must be alert. At the same time, potentially misleading reporting will always be with us, and wise clinicians need to stay armed with critical appraisal tools, including the 8 guides outlined in this chapter.

References

1. Horton R. The rhetoric of research. *BMJ*. 1995;310(6985):985-987.

2. Trotter G. Why were the benefits of tPA exaggerated? *West J Med*. 2002; 176(3):194-197.

3. Buchkowsky SS, Jewesson PJ. Industry sponsorship and authorship of clinical trials over 20 years. *Ann Pharmacother*. 2004;38(4):579-585.

4. LaRosa SP. Conflict of interest: authorship issues predominate. *Arch Intern Med*. 2002;162(14):1646; author reply 1646.

5. Davidoff F, DeAngelis CD, Drazen JM, et al. Sponsorship, authorship, and accountability. *N Engl J Med*. 2001;345(11):825-826.

6. Bodenheimer T. Uneasy alliance—clinical investigators and the pharmaceutical industry. *N Engl J Med*. 2000;342(20):1539-1544.

7. Bero LA, Rennie D. Influences on the quality of published drug studies. *Int J Technol Assess Health Care*. 1996;12(2):209-237.

8. Wilkes MM, Navickis RJ. Patient survival after human albumin administration: a meta-analysis of randomized, controlled trials. *Ann Intern Med*. 2001;135(3):149-164.

9. Alderson P, Bunn F, Lefebvre C, et al. Human albumin solution for resuscitation and volume expansion in critically ill patients. *Cochrane Database Syst Rev*. 2002;(1):CD001208.

10. Cook D, Guyatt G. Colloid use for fluid resuscitation: evidence and spin. *Ann Intern Med*. 2001;135(3):205-208.

11. Als-Nielsen B, Chen W, Gluud C, Kjaergard LL. Association of funding and conclusions in randomized drug trials: a reflection of treatment effect or adverse events? *JAMA*. 2003;290(7):921-928.

12. Bhandari M, Busse JW, Jackowski D, et al. Association between industry funding and statistically significant pro-industry findings in medical and surgical randomized trials. *CMAJ.* 2004;170(4):477-480.

13. Lexchin J, Bero LA, Djulbegovic B, Clark O. Pharmaceutical industry sponsorship and research outcome, and quality: systematic review. *BMJ.* 2003;326(7400): 1167-1170.

14. Bekelman JE, Li Y, Gross CP. Scope and impact of financial conflicts of interest in biomedical research: a systematic review. *JAMA.* 2003;289(4):454-465.

15. Devereaux PJ, Manns BJ, Ghali WA, Quan H, Guyatt GH. Reviewing the reviewers: the quality of reporting in three secondary journals. *CMAJ.* 2001;164(11):1573-1576.

16. Tirschwell D. Combined therapy with indapamide and perindopril but not perindopril alone reduced the risk of recurrent stroke. Commentary on: PROGRESS Collaborative Group. Randomised trial of perindopril-based blood pressure-lowering regimen among 6105 individuals with previous stroke or transient ischaemic attack. *Lancet.* 2001;358(9287):1033-1041. *ACP Journal Club.* 2002;136(2):51.

17. PROGRESS Collaborative Group. Randomised trial of a perindopril-based blood-pressure-lowering regimen among 6,105 individuals with previous stroke or transient ischaemic attack. *Lancet.* 2001;358(9287):1033-1041.

18. Shechter M, Hod H, Marks N, Behar S, Kaplinsky E, Rabinowitz B. Beneficial effect of magnesium sulfate in acute myocardial infarction. *Am J Cardiol.* 1990;66 (3):271-274.

19. Djulbegovic B, Lacevic M, Cantor A, et al. The uncertainty principle and industry-sponsored research. *Lancet.* 2000;356(9230):635-638.

20. Mann H, Djulbegovic B. *Biases Due to Differences in the Treatments Selected for Comparison (Comparator Bias).* Oxford, UK: James Lind Library: Library and Information Services Department of the Royal College of Physicians of Edinburgh; 2003.

21. Parving H-H, Lehnert H, Brochner-Mortensen J, et al. The effect of irbesartan on the development of diabetic nephropathy in patients with type 2 diabetes. *N Engl J Med.* 2001;345(12):870-878.

22. Brenner BM, Cooper ME, de Zeeuw D, et al. Effects of losartan on renal and cardiovascular outcomes in patients with type 2 diabetes and nephropathy. *N Engl J Med.* 2001;345(12):861-869.

23. Lewis EJ, Hunsicker LG, Clarke WR, et al. Renoprotective effect of the angiotensin-receptor antagonist irbesartan in patients with nephropathy due to type 2 diabetes. *N Engl J Med.* 2001;345(12):851-860.

24. Hostetter TH. Prevention of end-stage renal disease due to type 2 diabetes. *N Engl J Med.* 2001;345(12):910-912.

25. Safer DJ. Design and reporting modifications in industry-sponsored comparative psychopharmacology trials. *J Nerv Ment Dis.* 2002;190(9):583-592.

26. Geddes J, Freemantle N, Harrison P, Bebbington P. Atypical antipsychotics in the treatment of schizophrenia: systematic overview and meta-regression analysis. *BMJ.* 2000;321(7273):1371-1376.

27. Christiansen PE, Behnke K, Black CH, Ohrstrom JK, Bork-Rasmussen H, Nilsson J. Paroxetine and amitriptyline in the treatment of depression in general practice. *Acta Psychiatr Scand.* 1996;93(3):158-163.

28. Johansen HK, Gotzsche PC. Problems in the design and reporting of trials of antifungal agents encountered during meta-analysis. *JAMA.* 1999;282(18):1752-1759.

29. de Ferranti SD, Ioannidis JP, Lau J, Anninger WV, Barza M. Are amoxycillin and folate inhibitors as effective as other antibiotics for acute sinusitis? a meta-analysis. *BMJ.* 1998;317(7159):632-637.

30. Ioannidis JP, Chew P, Lau J. Standardized retrieval of side effects data for meta-analysis of safety outcomes: a feasibility study in acute sinusitis. *J Clin Epidemiol.* 2002;55(6):619-626.

31. Ioannidis JP, Lau J. State of the evidence: current status and prospects of meta-analysis in infectious diseases. *Clin Infect Dis.* 1999;29(5):1178-1185.

32. Cars O, Molstad S, Melander A. Variation in antibiotic use in the European Union. *Lancet.* 2001;357(9271):1851-1853.

33. Zintzaras E, Ioannidis JP. Modelling of escalating outpatient antibiotic expenditures. *J Antimicrob Chemother.* 2003;52(6):1001-1004.

34. Non-Small Cell Lung Cancer Collaborative Group. Chemotherapy in non-small cell lung cancer: a meta-analysis using updated data on individual patients from 52 randomised clinical trials. *BMJ.* 1995;311(7010):899-909.

35. Ioannidis JP, Polycarpou A, Ntais C, Pavlidis N. Randomised trials comparing chemotherapy regimens for advanced non-small cell lung cancer: biases and evolution over time. *Eur J Cancer.* 2003;39(16):2278-2287.

36. Wing LM, Reid CM, Ryan P, et al. A comparison of outcomes with angiotensin-converting–enzyme inhibitors, and diuretics for hypertension in the elderly. *N Engl J Med.* 2003;348(7):583-592.

37. Pocock SJ, Clayton TC, Altman DG. Survival plots of time-to-event outcomes in clinical trials: good practice and pitfalls. *Lancet.* 2002;359(9318):1686-1689.

38. McCormack J, Greenhalgh T. Seeing what you want to see in randomised controlled trials: versions and perversions of UKPDS data: United Kingdom Prospective Diabetes Study. *BMJ.* 2000;320(7251):1720-1723.

39. UK Prospective Diabetes Study (UKPDS) Group. Intensive blood-glucose control with sulphonylureas or insulin compared with conventional treatment and risk of complications in patients with type 2 diabetes (UKPDS 33). *Lancet.* 1998;352(9131):837-853.

40. Ioannidis JP, Lau J. The impact of high-risk patients on the results of clinical trials. *J Clin Epidemiol.* 1997;50(10):1089-1098.

41. Ioannidis JP, Lau J. Completeness of safety reporting in randomized trials: an evaluation of 7 medical areas. *JAMA.* 2001;285(4):437-443.

42. Ioannidis JP, Evans SJ, Gotzsche PC, et al. Better reporting of harms in randomized trials: an extension of the CONSORT statement. *Ann Intern Med.* 2004;141(10):781-788.

43. Kiehl MG, Stoll R, Broder M, Mueller C, Foerster EC, Domschke W. A controlled trial of intravenous immune globulin for the prevention of serious infections in adults with advanced human immunodeficiency virus infection. *Arch Intern Med.* 1996;156(22):2545-2550.

44. Lanier BG, Turner RA Jr, Collins RL, Senter RG Jr. Evaluation of nabumetone in the treatment of active adult rheumatoid arthritis. *Am J Med.* 1987;83(4B):40-43.

45. Ioannidis JP. Contradicted and initially stronger effects in highly cited clinical research. *JAMA.* 2005;294(2):218-228.

46. Ioannidis JP, Trikalinos TA. Early extreme contradictory estimates may appear in published research: the Proteus phenomenon in molecular genetics research and randomized trials. *J Clin Epidemiol.* 2005;58(6):543-549.

47. Ioannid is J, Lau J. Evolution of treatment effects over time: empirical insight from recursive cumulative metaanalyses. *Proc Natl Acad Sci U S A.* 2001;98(3):831-836.

48. Morrison NA, Qi JC, Tokita A, et al. Prediction of bone density from vitamin D receptor alleles. *Nature.* 1994;367(6460):284-287.

49. Uitterlinden AG, Weel AE, Burger H, et al. Interaction between the vitamin D receptor gene and collagen type Ialpha1 gene in susceptibility for fracture. *J Bone Miner Res.* 2001;16(2):379-385.

50. Lasser KE, Allen PD, Woolhandler SJ, Himmelstein DU, Wolfe SM, Bor DH. Timing of new black box warnings and withdrawals for prescription medications. *JAMA.* 2002;287(17):2215-2220.

51. Silverstein FE, Faich G, Goldstein JL, et al. Gastrointestinal toxicity with celecoxib vs nonsteroidal anti-inflammatory drugs for osteoarthritis and rheumatoid arthritis: the CLASS study: a randomized controlled trial: Celecoxib Long-term Arthritis Safety Study. *JAMA.* 2000;284(10):1247-1255.

52. Hrachovec JB, Mora M. Reporting of 6-month vs 12-month data in a clinical trial of celecoxib. *JAMA.* 2001;286(19):2398; author reply 2399-2400.

53. Silverstein F, Simon LS, Faich G. Reporting of 6-month vs 12-month data in a clinical trial of celecoxib. *JAMA.* 2001;286(19):2399-2400.

54. Docherty M, Smith R. The case for structuring the discussion of scientific papers. *BMJ.* 1999;318(7193):1224-1225.

55. Moher D, Schulz KF, Altman DG. The CONSORT statement: revised recommendations for improving the quality of reports of parallel-group randomised trials. *Lancet.* 2001;357(9263):1191-1194.

ADVANCED TOPICS IN APPLYING
THE RESULTS OF THERAPY TRIALS

SURROGATE OUTCOMES

Heiner C. Bucher, Regina Kunz, Deborah J. Cook,
Anne Holbrook, and Gordon Guyatt

IN THIS CHAPTER:

CLINICAL SCENARIO

Can We Confidently Offer an Angiotensin-Converting Enzyme Inhibitor to a Normotensive Woman With Type 2 Diabetes and Early Nephropathy?

You are an internist treating a 56-year-old woman with type 2 diabetes diagnosed about 5 years ago. The patient is obese (body mass index, 29.5 kg/m^2) and has difficulties adhering to a recommended diet. Her glycosylated hemoglobin (HbA1c) during the past 2 years has been reasonably well controlled (between 7.5% and 8.5%). She has repeatedly shown normal low-density lipoprotein (LDL) cholesterol levels and blood pressure (<135/80 mm Hg), but at the last 2 visits you found a microalbuminuria level of 200 mg per 24 hours. This raises your concern about the patient's risk of developing end-stage renal disease (ESRD) like her sister with diabetes, who is 8 years older.

You are aware that the newly detected microalbuminuria strengthens the case for 2 new therapies. Direct evidence from a large, well-designed *randomized controlled trial* (*RCT*) tells you that treatment with an angiotensin-converting enzyme (ACE) inhibitor will reduce the patient's risk of myocardial infarction and stroke[1] (Figure 11.4-1, column A). Three large, well-designed RCTs provide direct evidence that an angiotensin II (AT-II) receptor blocker will slow progression of albuminuria and the development of ESRD[2-4] (see Figure 11.4-1, column H).

Now you have a dilemma: Should you offer your patient an AT-II receptor blocker to reduce her renal risk, hoping that this will also reduce her cardiac risk? Although both ACE inhibitors and AT-II receptor blockers target the renin-angiotensin-aldosterone system, the 2 drugs act at different sites of the system,[5] and their biological activity may well differ. Indeed, available RCTs provide evidence that AT-II receptor blockers do not provide the same cardiovascular risk reduction in patients with type 2 diabetes as do ACE inhibitors.[3,6]

What about the other alternative, offering your patient an ACE inhibitor to reduce her cardiac risk, hoping that this will also slow the progression of her renal impairment? Ideally, you would like to have the same sort of direct evidence that ACE inhibitors reduce ESRD in patients with type 2 diabetes that you have for cardiovascular outcomes. Alternatively, a head-to-head comparison of an ACE inhibitor and an AT-II blocker demonstrating similar renal outcomes would be satisfactory. Unfortunately, neither alternative is available (Figure 11.4-1, column E).

Because ACE inhibitors and AT-II receptor blockers have a similar mechanism of action, you reason that if they have a similar effect on reducing diabetic albuminuria, they will have a similar effect on patient-important renal disease. Does this assumption hold? To give your patient sound information about the overall treatment benefits, you search for more information regarding the legitimacy of your assumption.

Finding the Evidence

You connect to the National Library of Medicine's PubMed site. Using the PubMed Medical Subject Headings (MeSH) database, you construct a search strategy that includes the terms "diabetes mellitus type 2," "diabetic nephropathies," and "angiotensin-converting enzyme inhibitors." You restrict your search by including only RCTs (from the "publication types" drop-down menu) and retrieve 41 trials. Browsing through the titles and abstracts, you search for a head-to-head-comparison between an ACE inhibitor and an AT-II blocker that assessed an important outcome such as doubling of creatinine level (which may result in patient-important outcomes such as initiation of low-protein diet or psychological guidance toward dialysis) or a clearly patient-important outcome such as ESRD. If such a study existed, you would not have to rely on the substitute of effect on albuminuria. As you suspect, no such trial exists.

The best available study is a randomized head-to-head comparison of the AT-II receptor blocker telmisartan and the ACE inhibitor enalapril in 250 patients with type 2 diabetes and nephropathy that measured change in glomerular filtration rate as the primary outcome and change in albuminuria as secondary outcome. This study failed to show any difference in glomerular filtration rate (treatment difference, -2.6 mL/min/1.73 m^2; 95% confidence interval [CI], -7.1 to 2.0 mL/min/1.73 m^2) or albuminuria (urinary albumin excretion ratio between groups, 1.04; 95% CI, 0.71-1.51) between the drugs after 5 years.[7] So now you confront your question: Can you use microalbuminuria in patients with type 2 diabetes as a substitute or surrogate for the long-term outcome of ESRD, allowing the substitution of the ACE inhibitor for the AT-II receptor blocker for prevention of progression to renal failure (see Figure 11.4-1, column E)?

What Is a Surrogate Outcome?

Ideally, clinicians making treatment decisions should refer to methodologically strong RCTs examining the effect of therapy on patient-important outcomes such as stroke, myocardial infarction, health-related quality of life, and death.[8] Often, however, conducting these trials requires such a large sample size or extended patient follow-up that researchers or drug companies look for alternatives. Substituting laboratory or physiologic measures (*surrogate endpoints*) for patient-important outcomes permits researchers to conduct shorter and smaller trials, thus offering an apparent solution to the dilemma.[9]

Surrogate endpoints—outcomes that substitute for direct measures of how a patient feels, functions, or survives[10]—include physiologic variables (such as urinary albumin excretion as a surrogate endpoint for ESRD, bone mineral density as a surrogate for long-bone fractures, blood pressure as a surrogate endpoint for stroke,

FIGURE 11.4-1

Renal Outcomes With Angiotensin-Converting Enzyme Inhibitors and Angiotensin II Blockers and Evidence Supporting the Use of a Surrogate (Proteinuria) for End-Stage Renal Failure

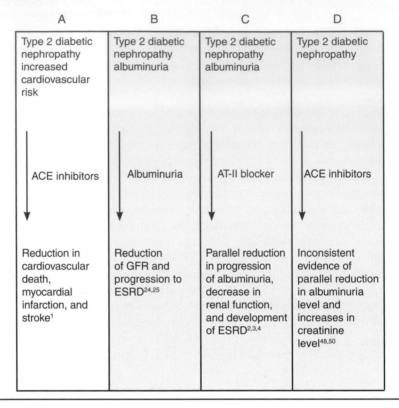

A	B	C	D
Type 2 diabetic nephropathy increased cardiovascular risk	Type 2 diabetic nephropathy albuminuria	Type 2 diabetic nephropathy albuminuria	Type 2 diabetic nephropathy
ACE inhibitors	Albuminuria	AT-II blocker	ACE inhibitors
Reduction in cardiovascular death, myocardial infarction, and stroke[1]	Reduction of GFR and progression to ESRD[24,25]	Parallel reduction in progression of albuminuria, decrease in renal function, and development of ESRD[2,3,4]	Inconsistent evidence of parallel reduction in albuminuria level and increases in creatinine level[48,50]

Abbreviations: ACE, angiotensin-converting enzyme; ACEI, angiotensin-converting enzyme inhibitor; AT-II, angiotensin II; ESRD, end-stage renal disease; GFR, glomerular filtration rate; RCT, randomized controlled trial.

Column A depicts the direct evidence that ACE inhibitors reduce cardiovascular adverse outcomes in patients with type 2 diabetes and cardiovascular risk. Column H depicts the evidence that AT-II inhibitors improve renal outcome

and CD4 cell count as a surrogate endpoint for AIDS and AIDS-related mortality) or measures of subclinical disease (such as degree of atherosclerosis on coronary angiography as surrogate endpoints for future myocardial infarction or coronary death). Such physiologic variables are also sometimes described as biomarkers, an indicator of normal biologic processes, pathogenic processes, or pharmacologic responses to a therapeutic intervention. The substitution of surrogate endpoints for patient-important outcomes is attractive when the surrogate can be measured earlier, more easily, more frequently, with higher precision, or with less confounding by competing risks or other therapies. To be valid, the marker not only has to be statistically correlated with the patient-important outcome but also must capture to the greatest possible extent the net effect of the intervention on the patient-important outcome.[9]

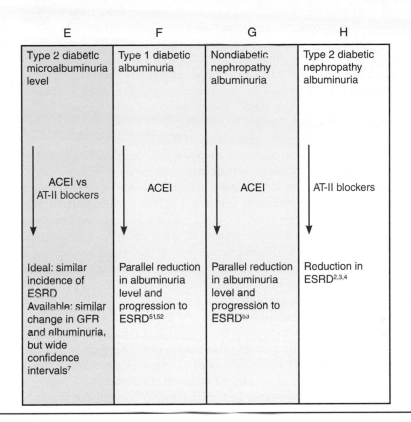

	E	F	G	H
	Type 2 diabetic microalbuminuria level	Type 1 diabetic albuminuria	Nondiabetic nephropathy albuminuria	Type 2 diabetic nephropathy albuminuria
	ACEI vs AT-II blockers	ACEI	ACEI	AT-II blockers
	Ideal: similar incidence of ESRD Available: similar change in GFR and albuminuria, but wide confidence intervals[7]	Parallel reduction in albuminuria level and progression to ESRD[51,52]	Parallel reduction in albuminuria level and progression to ESRD[53]	Reduction in ESRD[2,3,4]

in patients with type 2 diabetes with nephropathy. Column E (in dark blue) depicts the evidence we would like to have (RCT demonstrating similar apparent influence of ACE inhibitors and AT-II blockers on ESRD) in patients with type 2 diabetic nephropathy and albuminuria and the evidence we do have (similar apparent influence on glomerular filtration rate and albuminuria, the surrogate endpoint).

USE OF SURROGATE OUTCOMES: GOOD, BAD, OR INDIFFERENT?

The use of surrogate endpoints is indispensable for drug evaluation in phase II trials and early phase III trials geared to establish or verify a drug's promise of benefit. In many countries, companies may obtain a license to market the drug by demonstrating a positive effect on surrogate endpoints. The use of surrogate endpoints for regulatory purposes reflects drug-approval decisions that regulators must make in the face of public health exigencies and business pressures for faster decision making. Nevertheless, the debate continues about whether and under what circumstances the use of surrogate endpoints constitutes an appropriate shortcut for practice and for drug licensing.

Reliance on surrogate endpoints may be beneficial or harmful. On the one hand, use of the surrogate endpoint may lead to a rapid and appropriate access to new treatments.

> For example, the decision of the US Food and Drug Administration to approve new antiretroviral drugs according to information from trials using surrogate endpoints recognized the enormous continuous need for effective therapies for patients with human immunodeficiency virus (HIV) infection. The first generation of protease inhibitors proved effective in RCTs focusing on patient-important outcomes.[11] More recent trials of antiretroviral drugs from different classes have demonstrated effect on surrogate markers of HIV infection, whereas results from cohort studies suggest associated reduction of AIDS and AIDS-related morbidity.[12]

On the other hand, reliance on surrogate endpoints can be misleading and thus result in excess morbidity and mortality. For instance, flosequinan, milrinone, ibopamine, vesnarinone, and xamoterol all improve surrogate outcomes of hemodynamic function in ambulatory patients with heart failure, but RCTs have demonstrated that each of these agents leads to excess mortality (see Chapter 9.2, Surprising Results of Randomized Trials). Given that the underlying motivation for use of a surrogate is often to decrease the sample size and duration of follow-up that would be necessary if investigators were to measure a patient-important outcome, surrogates use may result in poorer estimation of toxicity, which further emphasizes the necessity for a high level of confidence in the validity of the surrogate.

How are clinicians to distinguish between valid and invalid surrogate markers? In this section, we present an approach to the critical appraisal of studies using surrogate endpoints and the application of their results to the management of individual patients. As our discussion will demonstrate, clinicians need to assess far more than a single study to decide on the adequacy of a surrogate endpoint. Evaluation may require a *systematic review* of observational studies of the relationship between the surrogate endpoint and the target endpoint, along with a review of some or all of the RCTs that have evaluated treatment effect on both endpoints. Although most clinicians will not have the time to conduct such an investigation, our guidelines will allow them to evaluate experts' arguments—or those of the pharmaceutical industry—for prescribing treatments according to their effect on surrogate endpoints.

ARE THE RESULTS VALID?

When we consider the validity of a surrogate endpoint, we must address 2 issues. First, a surrogate outcome will be consistently reliable only if there is a causal connection between change in surrogate and change in the patient-important outcome. Thus, the surrogate must be in the causal pathway of the disease process. For instance, LDL must be a cause of atherosclerotic cardiac and cerebral events to act as a valid surrogate for those events. Second, we must be confident that change in the surrogate captures all

TABLE 11.4-1

Users' Guide for a Surrogate Endpoint Trial

Are the results valid?

- Is there a strong, independent, consistent association between the surrogate outcome and the patient-important outcome?
- Have randomized trials of different drug classes shown that improvement in the surrogate endpoint has consistently led to improvement in patient-important outcome?[a]
- Have randomized trials of the same drug class shown that improvement in the surrogate endpoint has consistently led to improvement in the patient-important outcome?[a]

What are the results?

- How large, precise, and lasting was the treatment effect?

How can I apply the results to patient care?

- Are the likely treatment benefits worth the potential risks and costs?

[a]Answers to one or both of these questions should be yes for a surrogate trial to be an adequate guide for clinical action.

critical influences on patient-important outcomes.[9] For instance, if the treatment affects either positively or negatively (as turned out to be the case for fibrates[13]) the morbidity or mortality independent of its effect on LDL, the validity of the surrogate is threatened.

Our guides for validity, as presented in Table 11.4-1, directly affect these 2 issues.

Is There a Strong, Independent, Consistent Association Between the Surrogate Outcome and the Patient-important Outcome?

To function as a valid substitute for an important target outcome, the surrogate endpoint must be associated with that target outcome. Often, researchers choose surrogate endpoints because they have found a correlation between a surrogate outcome and a target outcome in observational studies. Their understanding of biologic characteristics gives them confidence that changes in the surrogate will invariably lead to changes in the important outcome. The stronger the association, the more likely the causal link between the surrogate and the target. The strength of an association is reflected in statistical measures such as the *relative risk* (*RR*) or the *odds ratio* (see Chapter 7, Does Treatment Lower Risk? Understanding the Results).

Many biologically plausible surrogates are only weakly associated with patient-important outcomes. For example, measures of respiratory function in patients with chronic lung disease—or conventional exercise tests in patients with heart and lung disease—are only weakly associated with capacity to undertake activities of daily living.[14,15] When correlations are low, the surrogate is likely to be a poor substitute for the target outcome.

In addition to the strength of the association, one's confidence in the validity of the association depends on whether it is consistent across different studies and after adjustment for known confounding variables.

For example, ecologic studies such as the Seven Countries Study[16] suggested a strong correlation between serum cholesterol levels and coronary heart disease mortality even after adjustment for other predictors such as age, smoking, and systolic blood pressure. When a surrogate is associated with an outcome after adjustment for multiple other potential prognostic factors, the association is an independent association (see Chapter 13, Advanced Topics in Harm Correlation and Regression). Subsequent large observational studies have confirmed this association in individuals from all continents.[17]

Similarly, cohort studies have consistently revealed that a single measurement of plasma viral load predicts the subsequent risk of AIDS or death in patients with HIV infection.[18-23] For example, in one study the proportion of patients that progressed to AIDS after 5 years in the lowest through the highest quartiles of viral load was 8%, 26%, 49%, and 62%.[23] Moreover, this association retained its predictive power after adjustment for other potential predictors such as CD4 cell count.[18-22]

USING THE GUIDE

Let us return to our patient with type 2 diabetes and your question about whether you can substitute albuminuria for the actual target outcome ESRD.

Ideally, to establish the association between progression of albuminuria and progression to ESRD in type 2 diabetes, one would want to have a large cohort in which patients with type 2 diabetes have been followed from the onset of diabetes through the different stages of renal involvement up to the development of ESRD. Unfortunately, nobody has ever initiated such a comprehensive long-term study, and given the treatment options available, it is unlikely that anyone ever will. Therefore, we have to collect the evidence from different sources to explore the development from one stage to the next. One prospective cohort study compared 78 patients with type 2 diabetes and initial microalbuminuria to those without. After 10 years of follow-up, patients with initial microalbuminuria were 4 times more likely to develop macroalbuminuria (>300-mg loss of albumin/24 h)[24] (see Figure 11.4-1, column B). A recently published cohort study of 227 patients with type 2 diabetes and a mean follow-up of 6.5 years found a strong association between macroalbuminuria and progression to renal failure[25] (see Figure 11.4-1, column B). Using a multivariable analysis, macroalbuminuria, diabetic retinopathy, age, HbA1c, baseline glomerular filtration rate (GFR), and systolic blood pressure (listed in the order of their effect) independently determined the decline in GFR. Macroalbuminuria proved the strongest predictor for "time to the composite endpoint of doubling of baseline creatinine/ESRD" with a hazard ratio (HR) of 7.4 (95% CI, 3.4-15.7) per log10 increase from baseline albumin, followed by HbA1c (HR, 1.5; 95% CI, 1.2-1.8) and systolic blood pressure (HR, 1.2; 95% CI, 1.1-1.4).

We can thus conclude that microalbuminuria is a strong, independent predictor of ESRD, and it fits our first criterion for an acceptable surrogate endpoint.

Meeting this first criterion is necessary, but it is not sufficient to support reliance on a surrogate outcome. Before offering an intervention on the basis of effects on a surrogate outcome, you should observe a consistent relationship between surrogate and target outcome in RCTs; the effect of the intervention on the surrogate must be large, precise, and lasting; and the benefit/risk tradeoff must be clear.

Have Randomized Trials of Different Drug Classes Shown That Improvement in the Surrogate Endpoint Has Consistently Led to Improvement in the Target Outcome?

Pathophysiologic studies, ecologic studies, and cohort studies are insufficient to definitely establish the link between surrogate and patient-important outcomes.

Consider the example of antiarrhythmic drugs. Class I antiarrhythmic agents[26] effectively prevented ventricular ectopic beats that were strongly associated with adverse prognosis in patients with myocardial infarction[27] and were therefore in widespread use. When finally—with considerable delay—an RCT was launched to evaluate the effect of the drugs on morbidity and mortality, the agents actually increased mortality.[28] Injudicious reliance on the surrogate endpoint of suppression of nonlethal arrhythmias led to the deaths of tens of thousands of patients.

The treatment of heart failure provides another instructive example. Trials of ACE inhibitors in patients with heart failure have revealed parallel increases in exercise capacity[29-32] and a decrease in mortality,[33] suggesting that clinicians may be able to rely on exercise capacity as a valid surrogate. Both milrinone, a phosphodiesterase inhibitor,[34] and epoprostenol, a prostaglandin,[35] have demonstrated improved exercise tolerance in patients with symptomatic heart failure. However, when these drugs were evaluated in RCTs, both showed an increase in cardiovascular mortality, which in one instance was statistically significant[36] and which in the second case led to the trial's stopping early.[37] Thus, exercise tolerance is inconsistent in predicting improved mortality and is therefore an invalid substitute.

Other suggested surrogate endpoints in patients with heart failure have included ejection fraction, heart rate variability, and markers of autonomic function.[38] The dopaminergic agent ibopamine positively influences all 3 surrogate endpoints, yet an RCT found that the drug increases mortality in patients with heart failure, mainly because of ibopamine-induced tachyarrhythmias.[39]

A trial of sodium fluoride as secondary prevention against osteoporosis in postmenopausal women provides further support for cautious use of surrogates. Although sodium fluoride increased bone mineral density at the lumbar spine by 35% during a 5-year period, more vertebral and nonvertebral fractures occurred in the intervention group than in the placebo group (163 vertebral and 72 nonvertebral fractures occurred in 101 women treated with sodium fluoride vs 136 vertebral and 24 nonvertebral fractures in 101 women receiving placebo).[40] A meta-analysis of 11 RCTs has confirmed that sodium fluoride failed to improve fracture rates despite large increases in bone density.[41]

Evidence from multiple trials of multiple agents further indicates that changes in bone density in RCTs are only weakly associated with reduction in nonvertebral fractures.[42] These findings attest to the wisdom of demanding that trials of therapies for osteoporosis be powered to show differences in incidence of fractures. Thus, for the safe use of zoledronate, a bisphosphonate now being licensed for the prevention of osteoporotic fractures in patients unable to take oral bisphosphonates, confident clinical use of the agent required the results from an RCT reporting fracture data. The Food and Drug Administration's policy for licensing drugs for the prevention of osteoporotic fractures also follows this line of argument.

There are, however, examples of appropriate surrogates. For instance, therapy trials in HIV patients have consistently shown that modification of CD4 cell count and complete suppression of HIV-1 RNA plasma viral are associated with change in important outcomes. Trials comparing different classes of antiretroviral therapies have demonstrated that patients randomized to more potent drug regimens had higher CD4 cell counts and higher rates of HIV-1 viral load suppression and were less likely to progress to AIDS or death.[11,43] Subsequently conducted large cohort studies investigating different new antiretroviral drugs have shown substantial reductions in AIDS and AIDS-related morbidity.[44]

Although there is no guarantee that the next trial using a different class of drugs will show the same pattern, these results greatly strengthen our confidence that, for example, a new protease inhibitor such as atazanavir for HIV infection that increases the CD4 cell count and effectively suppresses HIV-1 viral load will result in a reduction in AIDS-related morbidity and mortality. We must bear in mind, however, that convincing evidence of the validity of the surrogate does not obviate concern about initially inapparent long-term drug toxicity.

USING THE GUIDE

Let us return to our opening clinical scenario. Placebo-controlled trials of AT-II blockers in patients with type 2 diabetes and microalbuminuria have shown a decrease in the development of macroalbuminuria.[2] Similar placebo-controlled trials of AT-II receptor blockers losartan[3] and irbesartan in patients with macroalbuminuria have shown a decrease in the patient-relevant outcomes "doubling of serum creatinine level" (losartan: RR, 0.75; 95% CI, 0.61-0.92; irbesartan: RR, 0.71; 95% CI, 0.57-0.90) and "ESRD" (losartan: RR, 0.72; 95% CI, 0.58-0.89; irbesartan: RR, 0.79; 95% CI, 0.61-1.04). Thus, improvement in microalbuminuria in patients with type 2 diabetes shows a consistent relationship with improvement in target outcome (doubling of baseline serum creatinine level and ESRD) for AT-II blockers (see Figure 11.4-1, column C).

Have Randomized Trials of the Same Drug Class Shown That Improvement in the Surrogate Endpoint Has Consistently Led to Improvement In the Target Outcome?

Clinicians are in a stronger position to trust surrogate endpoints if a new drug belongs to a class of drugs in which RCTs have verified a strong relationship between surrogate endpoint and target outcome.

For example, several large trials of primary and secondary prevention of coronary heart disease with statins have consistently observed that these drugs reduce cardiovascular adverse outcomes.[13] We could therefore assume that a new statin such as rosuvastatin with a similar or even more potent LDL cholesterol–lowering potency may also reduce patient-important outcomes. Even so, the recent experience in observational studies of a 10-fold increase in severe rhabdomyolysis associated with another statin, cerivastatin, that had been approved solely on the basis of its lipid-lowering activities[45] reminds us that reliance on a surrogate for benefit still leaves the issue of toxicity open to serious question.

We would, for 2 reasons, be reluctant to easily generalize these results to another class of lipid-lowering agents. First, the biological relation between the surrogate the patient-important endpoint that exists with one class of agents may not exist with another. Second, there may be effects of an agent quite unrelated to those mediated by the surrogate that influence the patient-important outcome.

Consider, for instance, trials of how one class of anticholesterol agents (the fibrates) has shown a significant reduction of myocardial infarction but an increased risk of mortality from other causes that counteracted this benefit and led to no effect on overall mortality.[13] As we have pointed out, confidence in a surrogate outcome depends on the assumption that the surrogate captures the full relationship between the treatment and the outcome.[46,47]

This assumption can be violated 2 ways. First, treatment may have an additional beneficial mechanism of effect on the outcome independent of its effect on the surrogate.

For instance, neither AT-II receptor blockers nor calcium-channel blockers appear to have any favorable effect on cardiovascular or cerebrovascular events in patients with type 2 diabetes and overt nephropathy beyond what can be achieved by blood pressure control.[6] AT-II receptor blockers, however, have demonstrated a superior effect on renal outcome such as ESRD, an additional biological effect that calcium-channel blockers do not seem to share.[4]

Second, treatment may have deleterious effects on the outcome that are not mediated through the surrogate. Mortality-increasing effects of fibrates, rather than inability to lower morbidity and mortality through cholesterol reduction, probably explain the overall lack of effect of fibrates on mortality. That such additional deleterious effects are less likely to occur across rather than within drug classes is another reason to be more confident about within-class evidence from surrogate outcomes.

This criterion is complicated by various interpretations of the term "drug class." A manufacturer will naturally argue for a broad definition of "class" when its drug fits in a class of agents with a consistent positive association between surrogate and target endpoint (such as β-blockers in patients who have sustained a myocardial infarction). If substances are related to drugs with known or suspected adverse effects on target events (eg, clofibrate or some cyclooxygenase-2 inhibitors), manufacturers of agents are more likely to argue that the chemical or physiologic connection is not sufficiently close for the new drug to be relegated to the same class as the harmful agent (see Chapter 22.5, Drug Class Effects).

USING THE GUIDE

Returning to the opening scenario, we have established from observational studies that microalbuminuria holds the characteristics of a potentially reliable surrogate marker and from RCTs that AT-II receptor blockers consistently show a relationship between the decrease in albuminuria and ESRD in type 2 diabetic nephropathy.

For the effect of ACE inhibitors in patients with type 2 diabetes, however, the data are less clear. A small placebo-controlled RCT including 94 patients found a strong reduction in the progression from micro- to macroalbuminuria (RR, 0.08; 95% CI, 0.02-0.34), as well as a reduction in the doubling of serum creatinine level (RR, 0.15; 95% CI, 0.04-0.65).[48] In a subgroup analysis of a large RCT comparing ramipril with placebo for the prevention of cardiovascular diseases in patients at high risk for the target disease,[49] the investigators observed a reduction in the progression to macroalbuminuria that was independent from blood pressure reduction (RR, 0.87; 95% CI, 0.69-1.10), but there was no difference in doubling creatinine level or ESRD.[50] The short follow-up and the low event rate in the control group limit the inferences from this study. Thus, there is some inconsistency in the apparent relation between reduction in albuminuria and reduction in progression of renal failure with ACE inhibitors (see Figure 11.4-1, column D).

There is, however, additional evidence of a consistent relationship of improvement in the surrogate (microalbuminuria) and target outcomes in patients with type 1 diabetes treated with ACE inhibitors. In an individual patient data meta-analysis of RCTs in patients with type I diabetes, ACE inhibitors were associated with a strong and consistent reduction in the progression from micro- to macroalbuminuria (odds ratio, 0.38; 95% CI, 0.25-0.57)[51] (Figure 11.4-1, column F). In another trial of patients with type 1 diabetes and macroalbuminuria, ACE inhibitors were associated with a reduction in macroalbuminuria and in the composite endpoint of death, dialysis, or transplantation (RR, 0.50; 95% CI, 0.30-0.82)[52] (Figure 11.4-1, column F). Similar effects were observed in an individual patient data meta-analysis of patients with macroalbuminuria caused by nondiabetic renal disease (RR for doubling of baseline creatinine level, 0.64; 95% CI, 0.51-0.80; RR for ESRD, 0.63; 95% CI, 0.47-0.85)[53] (Figure 11.4-1, column G).

In summary, there is some evidence from RCTs that ACE inhibitors in type 2 diabetes reduce the development of macroalbuminuria. There is a compelling body of evidence in type 1 diabetes and nondiabetic renal disease that ACE inhibitors reduce the development of microalbuminuria and decrease albuminuria and reduce the development of ESRD.

In Table 11.4-2, we apply our validity criteria to a number of controversial examples of the use of surrogate endpoints.

TABLE 11.4-2

Selected Controversial Examples of Applied Validity Criteria for the Critical Evaluation of Studies Using Surrogate Endpoints

Types of Intervention	Surrogate Endpoint	Target Endpoint	Criterion 1	Criterion 2	Criterion 3
			Is there a strong, independent, consistent association between the surrogate endpoint and the clinical endpoint?	Is there evidence from randomized trials in other drug classes that improvement in the surrogate endpoint has consistently led to improvement in the target outcome?	Is there evidence from randomized trials in the same drug class that improvement in the surrogate endpoint has consistently led to improvement in the target outcome?
Bisphosphonate zoledronate[a,54]	Bone mineral density	Osteoporotic fractures	Yes[55]	No[40,41]	Yes[56]
Proteinase inhibitor[b] atazanavir[57]	HIV-1 viral plasma load	AIDS or death	Yes[18-22]	Yes[58]	Yes[11,43]
Proteinase inhibitor[b] atazanavir[57]	CD4 cell count	AIDS or death	Yes[18-22]	Yes[58]	Yes[11,43]
Antilipidemic drug rosuvastatin[59,60]	Cholesterol-level reduction or LDL-cholesterol-level reduction	Myocardial infarction or death from myocardial infarction	Yes[16,61]	No[13]	Yes[13]

Abbreviations: HIV, human immunodeficiency virus; LDL, low density lipoprotein.

[a]A trial[67] not completed at the time this chapter was written has provided evidence that zoledronate reduces the risk of recurrent fractures in patients having undergone repair of hip fractures.
[b]In combination therapy with 2 reverse-transcription inhibitors.

WHAT ARE THE RESULTS?

How Large, Precise, and Lasting Was the Treatment Effect?

When considering results, we are interested not only in whether an intervention alters a surrogate endpoint but also in the magnitude, precision, and duration of the effect. If an intervention results in large reductions in the surrogate endpoint, if the 95% CIs around those large reductions are narrow, and if the effect persists throughout a sufficiently long period, our confidence that the target outcome will be favorably affected increases. Positive effects that are smaller, with wider CIs and shorter duration of follow-up, leave us less confident.

We have already cited evidence suggesting that CD4 counts may be an acceptable surrogate endpoint for mortality in patients with HIV infection. Before the successful introduction of potent antiretroviral therapy, an RCT of immediate vs delayed zidovudine therapy in asymptomatic patients with HIV infection reported a positive result for immediate therapy, largely on the basis of the existence of a greater proportion of treated patients with CD4 cell counts exceeding 350/mL at a median follow-up of 1.7 years.[62] Subsequently, the Concorde study addressed the same question in an RCT with a median follow-up of 3.3 years.[63] The Concorde investigators found a continuous decline in CD4 cells in both the treatment and the control groups, but the median difference of 30 cells/mL in favor of treated patients at study termination was statistically significant. Nevertheless, the study showed no effect of zidovudine in terms of reduced progression to AIDS or death. The median CD4 cell difference was insufficient to affect patient-important outcomes. The Concorde authors concluded that the small but highly significant and persistent difference in CD4 count between the groups was not translated into a significant clinical benefit and it "called into question the uncritical use of CD4 cell counts as a surrogate end point."[63] Had the Concorde analysis that showed significantly shorter times to reach a CD4 count of 350/mL in the control group been regarded as fundamental, the trial might have been stopped early on the basis of a false-positive result.[64] The message here is that the effect of an intervention on a surrogate endpoint must be large, robust, and of sufficient duration even if the surrogate fulfilled the criteria we developed. Only then can inferences about patient-important effects become credible.

USING THE GUIDE

Returning to our scenario and the study we retrieved, the randomized trial of telmisartan vs enalapril in type 2 diabetic nephropathy[7] found no difference between the groups in the primary endpoint, the glomerular filtration rate (treatment difference, –2.6 mL/min/1.73 m^2; 95% CI, –7.1 to 2.0 mL/min/1.73 m^2). The similar reduction in albuminuria of AT-II receptor blockers and ACE inhibitors suggests that ACE inhibitors may be similarly effective in reducing the patient-important endpoint of ESRD, but to be certain in our conclusion we would prefer a much narrower CI than the one we observed in the study. Overall, there seems to be reasonable evidence that ACE inhibitors are similarly effective in reducing albuminuria in patients with type 2 diabetes compared with AT-II receptor blockers, providing an additional piece of evidence to support an inference that we can rely on the ACE inhibitor to delay progression of renal failure in our patient.

As we will illustrate when we consider weighing benefits and harms, the magnitude of the effect on the surrogate endpoint may or may not help us to estimate the magnitude of possible effect on the target outcome.

Are the Likely Treatment Benefits Worth the Potential Harm and Costs?

The 3 questions clinicians should ask themselves in applying the results are the same ones we have suggested for any issue of therapy or prevention (see Chapter 6, Therapy): Were the study patients similar to my patient? Were all patient-important outcomes considered? Are the likely benefits worth the potential harms and costs? The third criterion, balancing the benefits against the treatment risks, presents particular challenges when investigators have focused on surrogate endpoints only. We will therefore discuss this aspect in some detail.

Before offering a treatment to their patients, clinicians need to know the magnitude of the likely benefit. Estimating this magnitude becomes a challenging endeavor when our knowledge of benefit is limited to the effect of the intervention on a surrogate endpoint. One approach is to look for 1 or more RCTs in a similar patient population that assess a related intervention using both surrogate and target endpoints and extrapolate from those data. When this is unavailable, we must extrapolate from prognostic models that relate the surrogate marker to the target clinical outcome.

How can we ascertain the risk reduction of ACE inhibitors on ESRD in type 2 diabetes if all we know is the effect on albuminuria? Recognizing the limitations of this approach, we could use the results of the placebo-controlled trials that include both the effect on the surrogate albuminuria and the risk reduction on ESRD to approximate the risk reduction of ACE inhibitors for clinical outcome that has been assessed only for the surrogate albuminuria. Losartan reduced macroalbuminuria by 35% compared with baseline, whereas macroalbuminuria slightly increased in the placebo group ($P < .001$).[3] These changes translated into a 25% relative risk reduction of doubling serum creatinine level (95% CI, 8%-39%) and a 28% relative risk reduction (95% CI, 11%-42%) of ESRD. We would therefore need to treat 17 patients for 3.4 years to prevent 1 patient from developing ESRD. The similar reduction in albuminuria observed in the RCT comparing telmisartan with enalapril[7] allows us to extrapolate that the ACE inhibitor enalapril might lead to similar relative reductions of ESRD. Nevertheless, extrapolation and indirect comparisons of results from different RCTs are known to have inherent problems and may lead to seriously biased estimates.[65]

CLINICAL RESOLUTION

We have found a strong, more or less consistent, independent, and biologically plausible association between albuminuria and ESRD. Randomized trials in AT-II receptor blockers have shown a consistent relationship between decrease in albuminuria and ESRD in patients with type 2 diabetes. The evidence that ACE inhibitors reduce albuminuria and ESRD in patients with type 2 diabetes is less strong, but trials of ACE inhibitors in type 1 diabetes and nondiabetic renal disease provide additional evidence of the link between reduction of albuminuria and reduction of ESRD with ACE inhibitors. Although the case is not as strong as it could be, we might reasonably conclude that albuminuria is a surrogate marker that sufficiently fulfils our criteria, and we may therefore use evidence based on the surrogate marker to guide our decision whether to prescribe an ACE inhibitor in this patient with type 2 diabetes to lower the risk of ESRD. This evidence comes from the RCT that suggests that ACE inhibitors are not inferior to AT-II receptor blockers in reducing albuminuria but is limited by the wide CI.

Clinicians and patients must also consider potential harm and adverse effects when making treatment decisions. Most patients tolerate both drugs well. Adverse effects that do occur are primarily related to reduced AT-II formation and arise in both drugs at a comparable frequency. Troubling cough represents an additional adverse effect of ACE inhibitors, but the problem is reversible when the drug is discontinued.

What can we tell our patient? If he or she wishes to minimize risk of stroke or myocardial infarction, the strong RCT evidence suggests the patient should be taking an ACE inhibitor. For concern about renal disease, we must convey the data presented in Figure 11.4-2. The patient's risk of developing macroalbuminuria within the next 2 years is about 15%.[2] If that happens, he or she will have a 30% risk of doubling serum creatinine level and a 7% risk of having ESRD within the next 6.5 years.[25] According to the evidence from the irbesartan trial,[2] treating 14 patients like this one with an AT-II blocker during 2 years would prevent 1 patient from progressing from microalbuminuria to macroalbuminuria. In the presence of macroalbuminuria, AT-II receptor blockers would reduce the risk of doubling creatinine level and ESRD, in relative terms, by 20% to 30% and in absolute terms by approximately 1.3% (*number needed to treat*, 76) (Figure 11.4-2).[3,4] Because the patient is at low risk of developing ESRD (1%), treatment will reduce the absolute risk of ESRD by only 2 in 1000 (number needed to treat, 500) (Figure 11.4-2).

Will an ACE inhibitor result in a similar reduction in risk? The link between ACE-inhibitor-induced reduction in albuminuria in patients with type 2 diabetes and subsequent reduction in ESRD is substantial, but not as strong as we would like. The same is true for the evidence that ACE inhibitors achieve the same reduction in albuminuria level as AT-II inihibitors.[7]

This leaves us with 3 potential treatment options. First, we might suggest monotherapy with ACE inhibitors because there is good evidence for a reduction of cardiac risk and substantial but no optimal evidence that the patient will also benefit for the renal risk. Second, we might recommend monotherapy with AT-II receptor blockers. This would minimize renal risk but may fail to reduce cardiac risk. Third, we could suggest dual therapy with ACE inhibitors and AT-II blockers, thereby inhibiting the renin-angiotensin-aldosterone pathway at 2 sites, but little is known about the adverse-effects profile of combined therapy, and dual therapy for microalbuminuria seems to be inappropriately aggressive.[66]

According to the best available evidence, including the patient's low risk of developing ESRD in the next decade, you advise the patient to take an ACE inhibitor. You are more confident in your recommendation because of what, in discussing the choice with the patient, you find out about the patient's values and preferences. As it turns out, the patient is loath (in part because of cost) to take yet another medication and finds the prospect of the additional careful monitoring for hyperkalemia that combined therapy would require unappealing.

CONCLUSION

When we use surrogate endpoints to make inferences about expected benefit, we are making assumptions regarding the link between the surrogate endpoint and patient-important outcomes. In this section, we have outlined criteria that you can use to decide when these assumptions might be appropriate. Even if a surrogate endpoint meets all of these criteria, inferences about a treatment benefit may still prove to be misleading. Thus, treatment recommendations based on surrogate outcome effects can never be as strong as the results focused on a patient-important target outcome.

These considerations emphasize that waiting for results from RCTs investigating the effect of the intervention on outcomes of unequivocal importance to patients is the only definitive solution to the surrogate outcome dilemma. The large number of instances in which reliance on surrogate endpoints has led or might have led clinicians astray argues for the wisdom of this conservative approach (see Chapter 9.2, Surprising Results of Randomized Trials). On the other hand, when a patient's risk of serious morbidity or mortality is high, a wait-and-see strategy may pose problems for many patients and their physicians.

We encourage clinicians to critically question therapeutic interventions in which the only proof of efficacy is from surrogate endpoint data. When the surrogate endpoint meets all of our validity criteria, when the effect of the intervention on the surrogate endpoint is large, when the patient's risk of the target

FIGURE 11.4-2

Extrapolation of the Results From Cohort and Intervention Studies (Angiotensin II Receptor Blockers) to an Imaginary Cohort of 1000 Patients

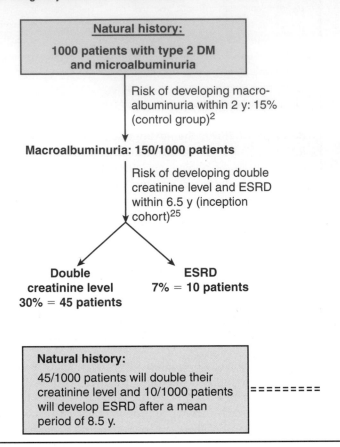

Natural history:

1000 patients with type 2 DM and microalbuminuria

Risk of developing macro-albuminuria within 2 y: 15% (control group)[2]

Macroalbuminuria: 150/1000 patients

Risk of developing double creatinine level and ESRD within 6.5 y (inception cohort)[25]

Double creatinine level 30% = 45 patients

ESRD 7% = 10 patients

Natural history:

45/1000 patients will double their creatinine level and 10/1000 patients will develop ESRD after a mean period of 8.5 y.

outcome is high, when the patient places a high value on avoiding the target outcome, and when there are no satisfactory alternative therapies, clinicians may choose to recommend therapy on the basis of RCTs evaluating only surrogate endpoints. In all situations, clinicians must carefully consider the known and potential adverse effects and the costs of therapy before recommending an intervention based solely on surrogate endpoints.

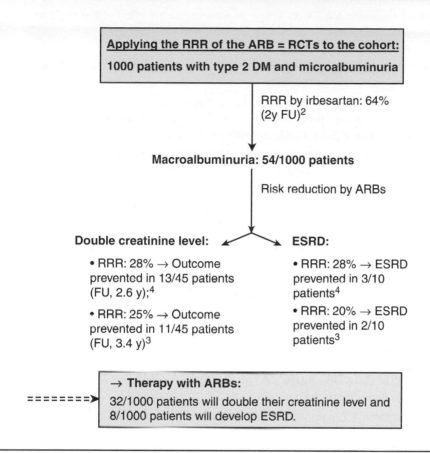

Applying the RRR of the ARB = RCTs to the cohort:
1000 patients with type 2 DM and microalbuminuria

RRR by irbesartan: 64%
(2y FU)[2]

Macroalbuminuria: 54/1000 patients

Risk reduction by ARBs

Double creatinine level:

- RRR: 28% → Outcome prevented in 13/45 patients (FU, 2.6 y);[4]
- RRR: 25% → Outcome prevented in 11/45 patients (FU, 3.4 y)[3]

ESRD:

- RRR: 28% → ESRD prevented in 3/10 patients[4]
- RRR: 20% → ESRD prevented in 2/10 patients[3]

→ **Therapy with ARBs:**
32/1000 patients will double their creatinine level and 8/1000 patients will develop ESRD.

Abbreviations: ARB, angiotensin II receptor blocker; DM, diabetes mellitus; ESRD, end-stage renal disease; FU, follow-up; RCT, randomized controlled trial; RRR, relative risk reduction.

References

1. Yusuf S, Sleight P, Pogue J, Bosch J, Davies R, Dagenais G. Effects of an angiotensin-converting-enzyme inhibitor, ramipril, on cardiovascular events in high-risk patients: the Heart Outcomes Prevention Evaluation Study Investigators. *N Engl J Med.* 2000;342(3):145-153.

2. Parving HH, Lehnert H, Brochner-Mortensen J, Gomis R, Andersen S, Arner P. The effect of irbesartan on the development of diabetic nephropathy in patients with type 2 diabetes. *N Engl J Med.* 2001;345(12):870-878.

3. Brenner BM, Cooper ME, de Zeeuw D, et al. Effects of losartan on renal and cardiovascular outcomes in patients with type 2 diabetes and nephropathy. *N Engl J Med.* 2001;345(12):861-869.

4. Lewis EJ, Hunsicker LG, Clarke WR, et al. Renoprotective effect of the angiotensin-receptor antagonist irbesartan in patients with nephropathy due to type 2 diabetes. *N Engl J Med.* 2001;345(12):851-860.

5. Burnier M. Angiotensin II type 1 receptor blockers. *Circulation.* 2001;103(6):904-912.

6. Berl T, Hunsicker LG, Lewis JB, et al. Cardiovascular outcomes in the Irbesartan Diabetic Nephropathy Trial of patients with type 2 diabetes and overt nephropathy. *Ann Intern Med.* 2003;138(7):542-549.

7. Barnett AH, Bain SC, Bouter P, et al. Angiotensin-receptor blockade vs converting-enzyme inhibition in type 2 diabetes and nephropathy. *N Engl J Med.* 2004;351(19):1952-1961.

8. Guyatt G, Montori V, Devereaux PJ, Schunemann H, Bhandari M. Patients at the center: in our practice and in our use of language. *ACP J Club.* 2004;140(1):A11-A12.

9. Biomarkers Definitions Working Group. Biomarkers and surrogate endpoints: preferred definitions and conceptual framework. *Clin Pharmacol Ther.* 2001; 69(3):89-95.

10. Temple R. *A Regulatory Authority's Opinion About Surrogate Endpoints.* New York, NY: John Wiley & Sons; 1995:3-22.

11. Hammer SM, Squires KE, Hughes MD, et al. A controlled trial of two nucleoside analogues plus indinavir in persons with human immunodeficiency virus infection and CD4 cell counts of 200 per cubic millimeter or less: AIDS Clinical Trials Group 320 Study Team. *N Engl J Med.* 1997;337(11):725-733.

12. Olsen CH, Gatell J, Ledergerber B, et al. Risk of AIDS and death at given HIV-RNA and CD4 cell count, in relation to specific antiretroviral drugs in the regimen. *AIDS.* 2005;19(3):319-330.

13. Studer M, Briel M, Leimenstoll B, Glass TR, Bucher HC. Effect of different antilipidemic agents and diets on mortality: a systematic review. *Arch Intern Med.* 2005;165(7):725-730.

14. Guyatt GH, Thompson PJ, Berman LB, et al. How should we measure function in patients with chronic heart and lung disease? *J Chronic Dis.* 1985;38(6):517-524.

15. Mahler DA, Weinberg DH, Wells CK, Feinstein AR. The measurement of dyspnea: contents, interobserver agreement, and physiologic correlates of two new clinical indexes. *Chest.* 1984;85(6):751-758.

16. Verschuren WM, Jacobs DR, Bloemberg BP, et al. Serum total cholesterol and long-term coronary heart disease mortality in different cultures: twenty-five-year follow-up of the Seven Countries Study. *JAMA.* 1995;274(2):131-136.

17. Yusuf S, Hawken S, Ounpuu S, et al. Effect of potentially modifiable risk factors associated with myocardial infarction in 52 countries (the INTERHEART Study): case-control study. *Lancet.* 2004;364(9438):937-952.

18. Mellors JW, Rinaldo CR Jr, Gupta P, White RM, Todd JA, Kingsley LA. Prognosis in HIV-1 infection predicted by the quantity of virus in plasma. *Science.* 1996;272(5265):1167-1170.

19. Mellors JW, Kingsley LA, Rinaldo CR Jr, et al. Quantitation of HIV-1 RNA in plasma predicts outcome after seroconversion. *Ann Intern Med.* 1995;122(8): 573-579.

20. Ruiz L, Romeu J, Clotet B, et al. Quantitative HIV-1 RNA as a marker of clinical stability and survival in a cohort of 302 patients with a mean CD4 cell count of 300 $\times 10^{(6)}$/l. *AIDS.* 1996;10(11):F39-F44.

21. O'Brien TR, Blattner WA, Waters D, et al. Serum HIV-1 RNA levels and time to development of AIDS in the Multicenter Hemophilia Cohort Study. *JAMA.* 1996;276(2):105-110.

22. Yerly S, Perneger TV, Hirschel B, et al. A critical assessment of the prognostic value of HIV-1 RNA levels and CD4+ cell counts in HIV-infected patients: the Swiss HIV Cohort Study. *Arch Intern Med.* 1998;158(3):247-252.

23. Ho DD. Viral counts count in HIV infection. *Science.* 1996;272(5265):1124-1125.

24. Mogensen CE. Microalbuminuria predicts clinical proteinuria and early mortality in maturity-onset diabetes. *N Engl J Med.* 1984;310(6):356-360.

25. Rossing K, Christensen PK, Hovind P, Tarnow L, Rossing P, Parving HH. Progression of nephropathy in type 2 diabetic patients. *Kidney Int.* 2004;66(4):1596-1605.

26. McAlister FA, Teo KK. Antiarrhythmic therapies for the prevention of sudden cardiac death. *Drugs.* 1997;54(2):235-252.

27. Bigger JT Jr, Fleiss JL, Kleiger R, Miller JP, Rolnitzky LM. The relationships among ventricular arrhythmias, left ventricular dysfunction, and mortality in the 2 years after myocardial infarction. *Circulation.* 1984;69(2):250-258.

28. Echt DS, Liebson PR, Mitchell LB, et al. Mortality and morbidity in patients receiving encainide, flecainide, or placebo: the Cardiac Arrhythmia Suppression Trial. *N Engl J Med.* 1991;324(12):781-788.

29. Drexler H, Banhardt U, Meinertz T, Wollschlager H, Lehmann M, Just H. Contrasting peripheral short-term and long-term effects of converting enzyme inhibition in patients with congestive heart failure: a double-blind, placebo-controlled trial. *Circulation.* 1989;79(3):491-502.

30. Lewis GR. Comparison of lisinopril vs placebo for congestive heart failure. *Am J Cardiol.* 1989;63(8):12D-16D.

31. Giles TD, Fisher MB, Rush JE. Lisinopril and captopril in the treatment of heart failure in older patients: comparison of a long- and short-acting angiotensin-converting enzyme inhibitor. *Am J Med.* 1988;85(3B):44-47.

32. Riegger GA. Effects of quinapril on exercise tolerance in patients with mild to moderate heart failure. *Eur Heart J.* 1991;12(6):705-711.

33. Garg R, Yusuf S; Collaborative Group on ACE Inhibitor Trials. Overview of randomized trials of angiotensin-converting enzyme inhibitors on mortality and morbidity in patients with heart failure. *JAMA.* 1995;273(18):1450-1456.

34. DiBianco R, Shabetai R, Kostuk W, Moran J, Schlant RC, Wright R. A comparison of oral milrinone, digoxin, and their combination in the treatment of patients with chronic heart failure. *N Engl J Med.* 1989;320(11):677-683.

35. Sueta CA, Gheorghiade M, Adams KF Jr, et al; Epoprostenol Multicenter Research Group. Safety and efficacy of epoprostenol in patients with severe congestive heart failure. *Am J Cardiol.* 1995;75(3):34A-43A.

36. Packer M, Carver JR, Rodeheffer RJ, et al; PROMISE Study Research Group. Effect of oral milrinone on mortality in severe chronic heart failure. *N Engl J Med.* 1991;325(21):1468-1475.

37. Califf RM, Adams KF, McKenna WJ, et al. A randomized controlled trial of epoprostenol therapy for severe congestive heart failure: the Flolan International Randomized Survival Trial (FIRST). *Am Heart J.* 1997;134(1):44-54.

38. Yee KM, Struthers AD. Can drug effects on mortality in heart failure be predicted by any surrogate measure? *Eur Heart J.* 1997;18(12):1860-1864.

39. Hampton JR, van Veldhuisen DJ, Kleber FX, et al; Second Prospective Randomised Study of Ibopamine on Mortality and Efficacy (PRIME II) Investigators. Randomised study of effect of ibopamine on survival in patients with advanced severe heart failure. *Lancet.* 1997;349(9057):971-977.

40. Riggs BL, Hodgson SF, O'Fallon WM, et al. Effect of fluoride treatment on the fracture rate in postmenopausal women with osteoporosis. *N Engl J Med.* 1990;322(12):802-809.

41. Haguenauer D, Welch V, Shea B, Tugwell P, Adachi JD, Wells G. Fluoride for the treatment of postmenopausal osteoporotic fractures: a meta-analysis. *Osteoporos Int.* 2000;11(9):727-738.

42. Guyatt GH, Cranney A, Griffith L, et al. Summary of meta-analyses of therapies for postmenopausal osteoporosis and the relationship between bone density and fractures. *Endocrinol Metab Clin North Am.* 2002;31(3):659-679, xii.

43. Cameron DW, Heath-Chiozzi M, Danner S, et al; Advanced HIV Disease Ritonavir Study Group. Randomised placebo-controlled trial of ritonavir in advanced HIV-1 disease. *Lancet.* 1998;351(9102):543-549.

44. Sterne JA, Hernan MA, Ledergerber B, et al. Long-term effectiveness of potent antiretroviral therapy in preventing AIDS and death: a prospective cohort study. *Lancet.* 2005;366(9483):378-384.

45. Furberg CD, Pitt B. Withdrawal of cerivastatin from the world market. *Curr Control Trials Cardiovasc Med.* 2001;2(5):205-207.

46. Prentice RL. Surrogate endpoints in clinical trials: definition and operational criteria. *Stat Med.* 1989;8(4):431-440.

47. Fleming TR. Surrogate markers in AIDS and cancer trials. *Stat Med.* 1994;13(13-14):1423-1435; discussion 1437-1440.

48. Ravid M, Savin H, Jutrin I, Bental T, Katz B, Lishner M. Long-term stabilizing effect of angiotensin-converting enzyme inhibition on plasma creatinine and on proteinuria in normotensive type II diabetic patients. *Ann Intern Med.* 1993;118(8):577-581.

49. Gerstein HC, Yusuf S, Mann JFE, Hoogwerf B; Heart Outcomes Prevention Evaluation Study Investigators. Effects of ramipril on cardiovascular and microvascular outcomes in people with diabetes mellitus: results of the HOPE study and MICRO-HOPE substudy. *Lancet.* 2000;355(9200):253-259.

50. Strippoli GF, Craig M, Deeks JJ, Schena FP, Craig JC. Effects of angiotensin converting enzyme inhibitors and angiotensin II receptor antagonists on mortality and renal outcomes in diabetic nephropathy: systematic review. *BMJ.* 2004; 329(7470):828.

51. ACE Inhibitors in Diabetic Nephropathy Trialist Group. Should all patients with type 1 diabetes mellitus and microalbuminuria receive angiotensin-converting enzyme inhibitors? a meta-analysis of individual patient data. *Ann Intern Med.* 2001;134(5):370-379.

52. Lewis EJ, Hunsicker LG, Bain RP, Rohde RD; Collaborative Study Group. The effect of angiotensin-converting-enzyme inhibition on diabetic nephropathy. *N Engl J Med.* 1993;329(20):1456-1462.

53. Jafar TH, Schmid CH, Landa M, et al. Angiotensin-converting enzyme inhibitors and progression of nondiabetic renal disease: a meta-analysis of patient-level data. *Ann Intern Med.* 2001;135(2):73-87.

54. Reid IR, Brown JP, Burckhardt P, et al. Intravenous zoledronic acid in postmenopausal women with low bone mineral density. *N Engl J Med.* 2002;346(9):653-661.

55. Huang C, Ross PD, Wasnich RD. Short-term and long-term fracture prediction by bone mass measurements: a prospective study. *J Bone Miner Res.* 1998; 13(1):107-113.

56. Karpf DB, Shapiro DR, Seeman E, et al; Alendronate Osteoporosis Treatment Study Groups. Prevention of nonvertebral fractures by alendronate: a meta-analysis. *JAMA.* 1997;277(14):1159-1164.

57. Johnson M, Grinsztejn B, Rodriguez C, et al. Atazanavir plus ritonavir or saquinavir, and lopinavir/ritonavir in patients experiencing multiple virological failures. *AIDS.* 2005;19(2):153-162.

58. Montaner JS, Reiss P, Cooper D, et al. A randomized, double-blind trial comparing combinations of nevirapine, didanosine, and zidovudine for HIV-infected patients: the INCAS Trial: Italy, The Netherlands, Canada and Australia Study. *JAMA.* 1998;279(12):930-937.

59. Jones PH, Davidson MH, Stein EA, et al. Comparison of the efficacy and safety of rosuvastatin vs atorvastatin, simvastatin, and pravastatin across doses (STELLAR* Trial). *Am J Cardiol.* 2003;92(2):152-160.

60. Brown WV, Bays HE, Hassman DR, et al. Efficacy and safety of rosuvastatin compared with pravastatin and simvastatin in patients with hypercholesterolemia: a randomized, double-blind, 52-week trial. *Am Heart J.* 2002;144(6):1036-1043.

61. Law MR, Wald NJ, Thompson SG. By how much and how quickly does reduction in serum cholesterol concentration lower risk of ischaemic heart disease? *BMJ.* 1994;308(6925):367-372.

62. Cooper DA, Gatell JM, Kroon S, et al; European-Australian Collaborative Group. Zidovudine in persons with asymptomatic HIV infection and CD4+ cell counts greater than 400 per cubic millimeter. *N Engl J Med.* 1993;329(5):297-303.

63. Aboulker JP, Babiker AG, Darbyshire JH, Dormont J; Concorde Coordinating Committee. MRC/ANRS randomised double-blind controlled trial of immediate and deferred zidovudine in symptom-free HIV infection. *Lancet.* 1994; 343(8902):871-881.

64. Montori VM, Devereaux PJ, Adhikari NK, et al. Randomized trials stopped early for benefit: a systematic review. *JAMA.* 2005;294(17):2203-2209.

65. Bucher HC, Guyatt GH, Griffith LE, Walter SD. The results of direct and indirect treatment comparisons in meta-analysis of randomized controlled trials. *J Clin Epidemiol.* 1997;50(6):683-691.

66. Kunz R, Friedrich C, Wolbers M, Mann JFE. Meta-analysis: effect of monotherapy and combination therapy with inhibitors of the renin–angiotensin system on proteinuria in renal disease. *Ann Intern Med*. 2008;148(1):30-48.

67. Lyles KW, Colón-Emeric CS, Magaziner JS, et al; HORIZON Recurrent Fracture Trial. Zoledronic acid and clinical fractures and mortality after hip fracture. *N Engl J Med*. 2007;357(18):1799-1809.

ADVANCED TOPICS IN APPLYING
THE RESULTS OF THERAPY TRIALS

QUALITATIVE
RESEARCH

Mita Giacomini and Deborah J. Cook

IN THIS CHAPTER:

CLINICAL SCENARIO

After a grand rounds presentation by a visiting speaker on polypharmacy in the elderly, you reflect on a patient under your care, a 77-year-old woman with chronic obstructive pulmonary disease (COPD), hypertension, and mild renal insufficiency who presented with community-acquired pneumonia. After 6 days of antibiotic treatment, she developed *Clostridium difficile* colitis. During rounds yesterday, the intern suggested that the antibiotic therapy contributed to the development of colitis. You pointed out that the proton-pump inhibitor the patient had taken for more than a year, and which you continued in hospital, increased her risk of developing both the original pneumonia[1] and the hospital-acquired *C difficile* infection.[2] The day she was admitted, you remember charging the intern with finding out why she had been taking a proton-pump inhibitor. The intern discovered that the drug was started 1 year ago, during an intensive care unit admission for an exacerbation of her COPD that required mechanical ventilation. The clinicians responsible for the patient's care administered the proton-pump inhibitor, instead of the more appropriate histamine-2 receptor antagonist, to prevent stress ulceration. Furthermore, there was no documentation in the chart about why the proton-pump inhibitor was subsequently continued. The patient remembers receiving a prescription for this new drug when she was discharged from the hospital but does not recall a conversation about why.

You are troubled at what you see as another example of suboptimal prescribing, and you want to find research evidence that might clarify how communication affects polypharmacy. Above all, you seek new ideas about what might be happening in your hospital and insight into the nature of poor inpatient prescribing and potential solutions. You reflect on how better access of medical records would help, as well as mandatory review of long-term medications. Walking back to the wards, a colleague laments that for her, the real problem is keeping abreast of information about drugs and their interactions in the elderly. You realize that the problem is complex, that it concerns behavior and not biomedicine, and that you lack a broad view of its contributing factors. Before you start seeking possible solutions, you want more systematic, evidence-based, robust information about the nature of the problem. Perhaps social science can help. You pledge to extend the grand rounds topic further by presenting and critically appraising an article on inappropriate drug prescribing at a noon conference, using your patient as an illustrative case. The agenda for the conference is adverse drug reactions, the unique challenges of caring for elderly persons receiving numerous medications, and an introduction to *qualitative research*.

FINDING THE EVIDENCE

Because you are interested in better understanding your hospital's culture of communication, you know that you are looking for descriptive evidence from social science, in particular, a qualitative research study. Although there are currently no Medical Subject Headings that indicate qualitative research methodology, there is a PubMed strategy with which few are familiar—but you are. So, back in your office, you enter PubMed and go to the "Special Queries" listed in the left-hand column of the initial screen under "PubMed Services." In the next screen, you choose "Health Services Research [HSR] Queries" and in the screen that follows choose "Qualitative Research" and "Narrow, specific search." You enter "communication decision making drug utilization" as a single string; the search yields 2 hits. One of these seems to be directly relevant to your inquiry: a qualitative study of appropriateness of medication use in elderly inpatients.[3]

The authors' description of their study objectives is directly relevant to your concern: "To explore the processes leading to inappropriate use of medicines for elderly patients admitted for acute care." You download the article, read it, and make copies for the noon conference. The methodology section of the article cites http://www.bmj.com for further details on the research methods, and you retrieve this supplementary appendix to aid with critical appraisal.

INTRODUCTION

Qualitative research has 2 qualities that distinguish it from traditional quantitative research in health care: (1) it focuses on social and interpreted, rather than quantifiable, phenomena; and (2) it aims to discover, describe, and understand, rather than to test and evaluate. Qualitative and quantitative studies address fundamentally different questions; they are not interchangeable with respect to either goals or methods.

What are social phenomena, and how are they different from the biomedical phenomena based in the natural sciences? Imagine you are attempting to understand what a wristwatch does, and you have never encountered one before. If you approach it as a natural phenomenon, you might make observations about its chemistry and mechanics and discover how, like all things (and people), the watch obeys immutable laws of physics. But can this approach discover the essential nature of a watch or describe the effect of the wristwatch on human life? No, and it overlooks powerful social forces that constitute what a watch is and does.

Understanding these aspects requires descriptive interpretation. What do the numbers on the face of the watch do? Their power lies in their symbolic nature. They represent agreed-on times of the day for which we have many social conventions (eg, lunch) and expectations (eg, an appointment). Those numbers move people even when the numbers are entirely missing from the face of a watch; they are present in our tacit understandings, our agreed-on social reality.

Whereas natural laws are inviolable, if someone violates a social rule (eg, shows up late for an appointment), this does not mean that the social rule does not exist. Social rules differ fundamentally from natural laws in the way in which they change with context and require interpretation both to detect and to understand.[4] This flux and subjectivity makes social rules and symbols no less real or powerful than physical phenomena, but studying them well requires different methods.

In quantitative research, *validity* refers to the likelihood that the study methods will yield an unbiased assessment of the underlying *intervention effect, prognosis*, or diagnostic test performance. In qualitative research, the social or personal truths we seek are naturally mutable and context-dependent. We also know that truthful descriptions will vary with the perspective of the researcher, and poor research is often not so much untrue as it is uninsightful, shallow, or unhelpful. Many qualitative researchers reject the term *validity* entirely in favor of terms such as *credibility* or *trustworthiness* that point to the element of investigator judgment, as well as procedures: we need to believe that much careful, sensitive work was done behind the scenes where methodology descriptions do not go. To keep meanings of words consistent, we use the word *credibility* instead of *validity* here.

By credibility, we mean not only whether findings correspond with facts but also whether the research report shows signs that investigators engaged thoroughly and sensitively with the material and whether the interpretations of the investigators are credible. For the same reasons, signs of methodologic excellence can be found not only in the procedural descriptions of methodology but also through an assessment of the coherence and depth of the findings as reported.

The wide breadth and varying purposes of qualitative research explain in part why there are no widely accepted standards for its critical appraisal. In addition, some qualitative researchers find critical appraisal or hierarchic criteria for valuing qualitative research philosophically objectionable. Despite debates within the field, most proposals for appraising qualitative studies in some way address the general issues outlined in Table 11.5-1. We focus here on the use of qualitative research information for clinical practice and policy and refer readers elsewhere for introductions to the design and conduct of qualitative research.[5-8]

WHEN IS QUALITATIVE RESEARCH RELEVANT?

To be relevant for clinicians, qualitative research must not only be on topic (eg, prescription drugs, care of the elderly) but also fulfill 2 other criteria. First, the clinical problem must concern social, not natural, phenomena. For example, a qualitative study will not tell you whether an intervention achieved benefit (a randomized trial is best for that question). However, it could help you discover how people experienced the intervention, how they reorganized to accommodate it and otherwise reacted to it, or what outcomes they most valued and why. Second, one must seek theoretical or conceptual understanding of the problem. Qualitative research makes inductive, descriptive inferences to theory concerning social experiences or settings, whereas quantitative research makes causal or *correlational* inferences to populations.[9]

TABLE 11.5-1

Users' Guides for an Article Reporting the Results of Qualitative Research in Health Care

Is qualitative research relevant?
- Is my question about social, rather than biomedical, phenomena?
- Do I seek theoretical or conceptual understanding of the problem?

Are the results credible?
- Was the choice of participants or observations explicit and comprehensive?
- Was research ethics approval obtained?
- Was data collection sufficiently comprehensive and detailed?
- Were the data analyzed appropriately and the findings corroborated adequately?

What are the results?

How can I apply the results to patient care?
- Does the study offer helpful theory?
- Does the study help me understand the context of my practice?
- Does the study help me understand social interactions in clinical care?

Qualitative studies may generate simple or elaborate theories. Findings may contribute to knowledge in the social sciences, or they may prove useful for lay, professional, or interdisciplinary audiences. For clinicians, qualitative findings may provide understanding and explanation of phenomena that are unrecognized, poorly understood, or unfamiliar. They may also provide new insight into familiar patterns and problems, such as communication barriers with patients. Although brainstorming and armchair hypothesizing have their places, qualitative research can offer a more rigorous and empirically grounded source of insight into what might be going on; that is, it can offer a useful theory. As the clinician seeking to understand dilemmas in prescribing in the elderly, you have a sense that this sort of theory might not only deepen your understanding of the problem but also develop sharper hypotheses about possible solutions to the problem.[10]

ARE THE RESULTS CREDIBLE?

The methods section of a qualitative study should describe several aspects of the research design, including the way study participants were selected, the methods used to generate data, the comprehensiveness of data collection, and procedures for analyzing the data and validating the findings. Below we describe some general guidelines to help clinical readers determine whether the findings of a qualitative study are credible.

Was the Choice of Participants or Observations Explicit and Comprehensive?

The exploratory and inductive nature of qualitative research requires investigators not to prespecify a study population or sample size in strict terms, lest they overlook important participants or social roles they do not yet understand. In contrast to the quantitative research imperative to select large numbers of representative participants, qualitative researchers aim for a small number of participants (or observations) selected deliberately to meet particular criteria. This process is called *purposive sampling*.

Sampling usually aims to cover the range of potentially relevant phenomena and perspectives from appropriately diverse data types. Selection criteria typically evolve during the course of analysis to explore emerging themes or perspectives. Depending on the topic, purposive sampling might aim to represent any of the following: typical cases, unusual cases, critical cases, cases that reflect important political issues, or cases with connections to other cases.[11,12] Least compelling would be merely convenient cases. Random sampling is usually inappropriate. Readers of qualitative studies should look for sound reasoning describing and justifying the participant selection strategies.

The *unit of analysis* for a qualitative study is not always the individual, and thus sampling issues extend beyond participants. It may be documents, observation periods in a setting involving many people, particular social roles (eg, patient, family member, clinician), events, interviews, rituals, routines, etc. Many studies use multiple units of analysis, calling for multiple data sources. To judge whether enough data were collected, relevance and meaningful diversity count (and there is no statistical method for assessing adequacy of the sample). The study must involve a sufficient number of observations to achieve an adequate breadth of perspective and to avoid capturing a misleading picture.

USING THE GUIDE

Spinewine et al[3] practiced purposive sampling and involved various units of analysis. The setting was acute hospital wards for the elderly, and the activity of interest was medication prescribing and use. Investigators involved 5 wards in 5 hospitals (teaching and some nonteaching, urban and some rural). They do not explain the rationale but use common distinctions among hospital types that may differ with respect to patients, processes of care, and organizational culture. Investigators involved participants with a variety of roles (5 physicians comprising 2 residents and 3 geriatricians, 4 nurses, 3 hospital pharmacists, and 17 patients from 2 wards).

They excluded cognitively impaired patients (although cognitively impaired individuals constitute about two-thirds of the elderly inpatient population in this setting). They did not state the rationale, although presumably it had to do with difficulties of communication and understanding. The exclusion means that the study may be limited in providing insight into special needs or problems of cognitively impaired patients, and readers must speculate about how the findings might apply to this type of patient.

The study was conducted in French-speaking Belgium. Readers need to consider whether clinician and patient attitudes and prescribing practices would differ from those in their own health care system. Health care delivery as it relates to drug prescribing in the elderly is likely similar to that in most developed countries. Given the international readership of this journal, it would have been helpful if discussion of the Belgian context in relation to other health care systems had been provided.

Was Research Ethics Approval Obtained?

The ethical treatment of human research participants is a fundamental feature of the quality of any health research, and in qualitative research, ethics approval also reflects favorably on the ability of the investigators to approach participants with due respect and sensitivity. It thus helps reflect favorably on—although does not alone determine—the credibility of the findings. Although qualitative studies typically take a noninterventionist approach from the perspective of quantitative research, qualitative studies require formal research ethics board approval to examine the protocol and consent process for potential risks to participants, including loss of confidentiality, interview burdens, incentives that may undermine voluntary consent, truthfulness in information provided to participants, researcher interference in care or other experiences, and the possibility of psychological trauma from participating. It is standard practice to secure voluntary informed consent from individuals or their substitute decision makers to protect the confidentiality of participants through discreet secure data collection and to guarantee anonymity. Qualitative reports should state that the study received formal ethics board approval.

USING THE GUIDE

Spinewine et al[3] provide a detailed account of the informed consent process and measures to protect confidentiality and ensure anonymity in the appendix at the http://www.bmj.com Web site. At the end of the article, authors state that their study was part of a global project approved by the local ethics committee. The overall project was approved by the Belgian National Foundation for Scientific Research and the University Research Committee.

Was Data Collection Sufficiently Comprehensive and Detailed?

Qualitative research strives to render a comprehensive, rich picture of participants' experiences and social dynamics. To achieve this, investigators must involve enough relevant people and situations and collect adequate volumes and quality of data from them. Qualitative researchers usually choose from among 3 basic data collection strategies (Figure 11.5-1). *Field observation* involves witnessing and recording events as they occur. *Interviews* engage participants in dialog, allowing them to interpret events and experiences in their own terms. *Document analysis* involves the interpretive review of written material.

Given each source, qualitative researchers have further methods from which to choose; these choices may influence the completeness of the study or the perspective of the results (Figure 11.5-1). Readers should consider whether the researchers have used multiple sources of information and, if not, whether they might have obtained a more complete or accurate picture if they had. The value of data collected will reflect not only the nature and breadth of sources but also the extent

FIGURE 11.5-1

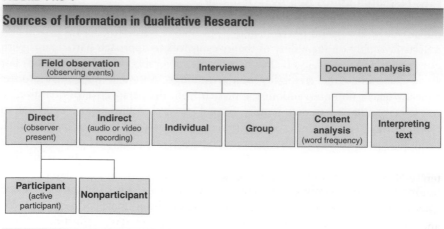

Sources of Information in Qualitative Research

to which each source generated adequate and detailed text for interpretive analysis. As we will see, all qualitative data eventually take the form of written words, and it is the interpretation of these words that generates the findings.

Field Observation

Field observation records social interactions prospectively and directly. For *direct observation*, investigators record detailed field notes from the milieu they are studying. In *nonparticipant observation*, the researcher participates relatively little in the interactions he or she is studying. Clinician readers should consider whether and how the presence of the researcher might influence the behavior of the participants. For example, a researcher in a crowded waiting room may go unnoticed and not much affect how events there unfold. By contrast, a researcher in a clinic examining room may be conspicuous and may substantially affect social interactions there.

In *participant observation*, the researcher assumes a role within the social setting beyond that of a researcher (eg, clinician, committee member). For both nonparticipant and participant observation, the question for readers of the report is whether the researchers' presence and role allow them access to candid and meaningful social interactions. Their involvement could allow extra insight, or it could obscure it, depending on the situation.[7]

Qualitative researchers sometimes use indirect observation through video or audio recordings, but the presence of surveillance itself can influence what participants say and do. Regardless of the observation method, the observer will always have some inevitable effect, small or large. This interaction of the observer with what is observed is called *reflexivity* in qualitative research. Whether it plays a positive or negative role in accessing social truths, the researcher must acknowledge and investigate reflexivity and account for it in the interpretation of the data.

Interviews

A second potential source of information is the interview. The most common interviews are semistructured, detailed interviews of individuals or discussion-based interviews of groups (focus groups). Standardized questionnaires are usually inappropriate for qualitative research because they presuppose responses (literally providing the words that respondents use) and are not structured to allow respondents to relate experiences in their own terms. Open-ended questions on questionnaires allow respondents to use their own words but are inferior to interviews because they yield relatively little text for analysis and researchers can miss the opportunity to probe for more information through dialog.

The appropriate interview method depends on the topic. Individual interviews tend to be more useful than group interviews for evoking personal experiences and perspectives, particularly on sensitive topics. Group interviews tend to be more useful than individual interviews for capturing interpersonal dynamics, language, and culture. Focus groups can be appropriate for emotionally sensitive topics if participants feel empowered speaking in the presence of peers; the public forum of a focus group can, however, also inhibit candid disclosure.[13,14] Critical readers should look for the researchers' rationale for choosing a particular approach and should assess its appropriateness for the specific topics addressed. Using more than 1 interview method may be helpful in capturing a wider range of perspectives, as well as assessing the influence of others on participants on responses.

Document Analysis

Finally, documents such as medical charts, journals, correspondence, and other material artifacts can provide qualitative data.[15] These are especially useful for policy, historical, or organizational studies of health care. There are different approaches to the analysis of documents. An approach from the quantitative research tradition involves simply counting specific content elements (eg, frequencies of particular words). This is not adequate for the interpretation of the meaning of either terms or documents. More appropriate qualitative approaches involve interpreting text as one would interpret any other form of communication (eg, seeking nuances of meaning and considering context).

Whatever the source of data, it must be adequate in quantity, quality, and diversity to address the research question. Several aspects of a qualitative report indicate how extensively the investigators collected data: the number of observations, interviews, or documents; the duration of the observations; the duration of the study period; the diversity of units of analysis and data collection techniques; the number or diversity of investigators involved in collecting and analyzing data; and the degree of involvement of individual investigators in data collection and analysis.[12,16-18]

The more text generated by each encounter, the better. Taped and transcribed interviews are superior to those recalled from memory or selective notes. Look for the investigator to note whether and where he or she wrote up field observations: ideally, this should be done in or on leaving the field. Memos on the reflections of investigators at any point in the research process help to identify personal biases, yet the investigators can use personal experiences as analytic information.[19]

USING THE GUIDE

The Spinewine et al[3] study drew on several sources of data, including direct participant field observation, individual interviews, and group interviews. The diversity of sources allowed researchers not only to investigate how participants describe and explain medication prescribing and use but also to observe actual prescribing behavior.

Although observation was intended to be unobtrusive, the observers were pharmacists and, to some degree, participants. The reflexivity of the research process is especially salient because the observing pharmacists discussed any inappropriate prescribing observed with the observed prescribers (regardless of its effect on the research, such intervention would be required by professional ethics). The authors acknowledge the possibility that observation and interviews by the researchers affected the behavior and statements of respondents. They inaccurately refer to this possibility as the Hawthorne effect (which is the apparent tendency for workers to increase productivity when they sense that someone is simply paying attention to them). The Hawthorne effect does not capture the breadth of possible researcher-participant influences in qualitative research. Reflexivity is a more appropriate term used in qualitative research methodology and has both positive and negative implications here. The feedback may have helped correct the problem of the presence of researchers affecting behavior and allowed less opportunity to observe and study it. On the other hand, to the extent that inappropriate prescribing persisted, this may suggest that feedback does not apparently correct the problem.

Was data collection extensive enough? Spinewine et al[3] interviewed health professionals from 5 hospitals, including 5 physicians, 4 nurses, and 3 pharmacists. They also interviewed and observed 17 patients from 2 included teaching hospitals, one of which was urban and one, rural. They interviewed 5 patients individually and 12 in 4 small focus groups. They made observations of prescribing behavior on the same 2 hospital wards during a 1-month period. They do not report total hours or days of observation, so we cannot determine how extensive these investigations were.

The authors note (at http://www.bmj.com) that patient data were insufficient to support a patient-focused analysis and were analyzed only in comparison to providers' data. Although this weakens our confidence that the analysis represents the patient perspective or experience well, the disclosure encourages further study. Clinician readers must judge whether the remaining data were adequate in part by the quality of the results they produced, which we address in the next section. Data collection appears sufficient for the narrower focus on clinician perspectives and behavior.

Did the Investigators Analyze the Data Appropriately and Corroborate the Findings Adequately?

Qualitative research is not a single method but a family of analytic approaches that rely on the description and interpretation of qualitative data. Specific methods include grounded theory, ethnography, phenomenology, case study, critical theory, historiography, and others. These originate in various social sciences and take distinctive approaches to building theories or narratives from qualitative data. We focus here on some general features of qualitative analysis that are relevant to most methods. However, readers should look for reference to a specific, named methodology (and preferably the relevant methodologic text). This orients the reader to more specific analytic goals and may also point to methodologic procedures and details not covered in the report.

Qualitative researchers begin with an exploratory question and preliminary concepts that help identify whom to study and how to approach the setting. They then collect relevant data, observe patterns in the data, and organize these into concepts. Next, they resume data collection to both explore and challenge this preliminary conceptual framework and revise or refine it. They may repeat this cycle several times. The iterations among data collection, analysis, and theory development continue until a conceptual framework is well developed and further observations yield no useful new information (a point variously referred to as theoretical saturation[20] or informational redundancy,[21] depending on the specific method). Such analysis-stopping criteria are so basic to qualitative analysis that authors seldom declare that they have reached this point.

In the course of analysis, investigators also corroborate key findings by using multiple sources of information, a process called *triangulation*. Triangulation is a metaphor and does not mean literally that 3 or more sources are required. The appropriate number of sources will depend on the importance of the findings, specific implications for theory, and the relevance and richness of the data sources. Because no 2 qualitative data sources will generate exactly the same information or interpretations, much of the qualitative interpretation involves exploring why and how different sources yield slightly (or profoundly) different information.[22]

For example, if a respondent reports in one interview that he or she is an intravenous drug user and in a subsequent interview reports not being one, the question for analysis becomes not only whether the respondent is in fact a user but also why the story changed. It could be that the respondent lost trust in the researcher, changed his or her own definitions, was boasting initially and telling the truth the second time, and so on. A close friend or the physician could also describe the person's habits to the researcher, but their accounts will lack the respondent's perspective. All of this requires further investigation by the researcher.

This example also shows how the concepts investigated by qualitative analysis are not fixed variables: the range of meanings given to intravenous drug use by the interviewee, interviewer, friend, and physician itself could become a key finding of the study and have important implications for clinician-patient communication. The task of corroborating a qualitative finding is different from, for example, establishing intra- or interrater reliability in a quantitative study in which we assume that there is a fixed fact of the matter and that any deviation from this fact is an error. Power[23] describes this type of methodologic issue in a detailed case study.

Readers may encounter several triangulation techniques for corroborating qualitative findings.[24,25] Investigator triangulation requires more than 1 investigator to collect and analyze the raw data, such that the findings emerge through consensus among a team of investigators. Sometimes interdisciplinary teams bring richer perspectives, but the difficulty of interdisciplinary communication can also tend to "dumb down" findings unless the investigators are sufficiently engaged with one another.[26]

Use of external investigators who are not involved in the study is controversial because they may have only superficial understanding to offer.[24] Member checking involves sharing draft study findings with the participants to inquire whether their viewpoints were faithfully interpreted, to determine whether there are gross errors of fact, and to ascertain whether the account makes sense to participants with different perspectives. Theory triangulation is a process whereby investigators corroborate emergent findings with existing social science theories.[12]

Some qualitative research reports describe the use of qualitative analysis software packages. Readers should not equate the use of computers with analytic rigor; software is merely a data management tool and these programs do not perform analysis. The investigators themselves conduct the analysis as they create the key words, categories, concepts, and logical relationships to organize and interpret the electronic data. The validity of qualitative study findings depends on these investigator judgments, which cannot be programmed into software packages.

We indicated earlier that qualitative data collection must be comprehensive: adequate in its breadth and depth to yield a meaningful description. The closely related criterion for judging whether the data were analyzed appropriately is whether this comprehensiveness was determined in part by research results themselves, with the aims of challenging, elaborating, and corroborating emerging findings. This is most apparent when researchers state that they alternated between data collection and analysis, collected data with the purpose of elucidating the analysis in progress and, if they corroborated key findings with multiple sources (triangulation), stopped collecting data when new data consistently failed to provide new information (redundancy), and continued with analysis until the central themes and categories were organized into a coherent theory or conceptual framework (saturation). We summarize these terms for easy reference in Table 11.5-2.

TABLE 11.5-2

Terms Commonly Used to Describe the Extent of Data Analysis in Qualitative Research

Triangulation—seeking and using multiple sources of evidence to corroborate key findings

Redundancy—the point in the analysis at which new data fail to generate new themes and new information becomes redundant (considered an appropriate stopping point for data collection in most methods and for analysis in some methods)

Saturation—the point in the analysis at which themes are well organized into a coherent theory or conceptual framework; new data fit easily without requiring revision to the theory (considered an appropriate stopping point for data analysis, especially in grounded theory methods)

Adapted from Glaser and Strauss,[20] Lincoln and Guba,[21] and Stake.[22]

USING THE GUIDE

Spinewine et al[3] reported systematic data analysis following appropriate conventions for grounded theory. The authors reported that they collected and analyzed data simultaneously, strengthening our confidence that they explored, corroborated, and developed their findings adequately.

Spinewine et al[3] took both conventional and unconventional approaches to triangulation. The study was designed well to capture a breadth of relevant perspectives: those of the patients, the physicians, the nurses, and the pharmacists (although not all were captured in equal depth, as noted above in the case of patients). Investigator triangulation was possible through the involvement of both a sociologist and pharmacists in data analysis. The investigators also presented the results in a member-checking step to the professional participants (although not to the patient participants) for their feedback.

They also used a more controversial method of triangulation (see http://www.bmj.com): a pharmacist uninvolved in the study checked 2 interview transcripts for reliability in coding. Authors calculated κ values to document chance-corrected agreement; codes with low interrater reliability were redefined and material was recoded. Qualitative researchers do not normally seek reliability of this sort because they believe in treating codes as interpretations rather than objective representations: if 2 people see the same thing differently, it does not mean that their perceptions are unreliable; it means that they see things differently, and this difference may become the focus of further qualitative inquiry (rather than quantitative measurement).

In qualitative research, investigators often seek, discuss, and reconcile differences in coding. This practice is a form of investigator triangulation and the dialog often helps enrich theory development. It is also controversial to recruit investigators from outside the study to judge coding. These individuals do not necessarily possess superior objectivity—they, too, must bring their subjective perspectives to interpretation—and their detachment from the study situation may be a liability for understanding it well. What is clearly valuable from this exercise, however, was that the discrepancies led to discussion and development of the coding scheme.

There is no mention of achieving data redundancy or theoretical saturation per se, but these stopping points often go unmentioned in qualitative reports because they are taken as given. The detailed description of grounded theorizing provided in the http://www.bmj.com supplement suggests that the researchers followed conventions of qualitative coding and data analysis.

WHAT ARE THE RESULTS?

The product of a qualitative study is a narrative that faithfully represents the social world that the investigators studied. Ideally, it will be meaningful to participants, researchers, and readers alike. This challenges the authors to translate between all 3 worlds. Although the research methodology focuses on translation between the views of participants and researchers, writing adds further consideration of the reader.

A good qualitative report provides enough descriptive detail to evoke a vivid picture of the interactions and experiences of those in the setting. Authors typically illustrate key findings with data excerpts from field notes, interview transcripts, or documents. These excerpts offer an excellent opportunity for the reader to examine and judge how the investigators interpreted the data. Illustrative data excerpts should clearly support the interpretation taken from them; if they do not, this may raise doubts about the interpretive skills of the investigators, the completeness of the analysis, or both. In addition, the report must be meaningful to the reader of the publication; here, we have focused on the needs of clinicians reading clinical journals.

USING THE GUIDE

Spinewine et al[3] described their result in major and minor categories, which they summarize in a table that we reproduce here (Table 11.5-3) and which they described in some detail, using illustrative excerpts from the data. For the purpose of informing practice, these findings may help clinicians reflect on prescribing and communication dynamics that affect patients and their health.

HOW CAN I APPLY THE RESULTS TO PATIENT CARE?

Does the Study Offer Helpful Theory?

Qualitative inquiry aims for descriptive theories about the way things are (as opposed answers to questions about the extent to which things work). The findings of qualitative research are concepts (often referred to as categories) and relationships. Categories are the building blocks of the theory. Sometimes their relationships are hierarchic (major categories containing minor subcategories), but categories potentially relate to each other in many other ways (eg, opposites of each other). For example, in a different study there might be not only a category of "paternalism" with various subordinate aspects, as Spinewine et al[3] portrayed in Table 11.5-3, but also a category of "empowering" to describe some clinicians' contrasting approach. These categories would relate as opposites.

TABLE 11.5-3

Categories Summarizing the Findings of Spinewine et al[3]

Categories Underlying Inappropriate Use of Medicines

Reliance on general acute care and short-term treatment

- Review of treatment driven by acute considerations; other considerations over-looked
- Limited transfer of information on medicines from primary to secondary care
- "One size fits all": prescribing behavior not tailored to the older patient

Passive attitude toward learning

- Anticipated inefficiency in searching for medicines information
- Reliance on being taught (teacher-centered) rather than self-directed learning

Paternalistic decision making

- Patients thought to be conservative
- Patients declared as unable to comprehend
- Ageism
- Difficulty in sharing decisions about treatment with other prescribers

Reproduced from Spinewine et al, with permission from the BMJ Publishing Group.[3]

One test of a theory may be its overall intuitive appeal: does the reader find it compelling? However, the reader may also gauge its usefulness by some more specific characteristics such as coherence, comprehensiveness, and relevance.[27] Coherence entails parsimony (invokes a minimal number of assumptions), consistency (accords with what is already known and explains the unexpected), clarity (expresses ideas evocatively and sensibly), and fertility (suggests directions for further investigation or action). Beyond this, much of the analysis emerges in the writing: sensible narratives and arguments, evocative metaphors and analogies, and meaningful terms and labels. These qualities are partly subjective, partly shared; ideally, participants, authors, and readers alike should find the account compelling. Similarly, illustrations such as diagrams should make sense overall and with respect to their component parts. An empirically developed theory need not agree with existing beliefs or social science theories. Whether it agrees or not, it is helpful especially to nonexpert users if the authors critically describe how their findings relate to prevailing knowledge.[28,29]

USING THE GUIDE

Table 11.5-3 summarizes the theory that Spinewine et al[3] advance. There are 3 major categories: reliance on general acute care and short-term treatment, clinicians' passive attitude toward learning, and paternalistic decision making. Each of these major categories also entails 2 to 4 subthemes.

Does this framework capture the spectrum of important phenomena? We can judge this by drawing on the author's own account, our own experience as clinicians, and knowledge of the relevant social science and biomedical literature. The account presented by the authors supports their finding well. However, there are 2 intriguing themes that might have been developed further. The first is under the category of a passive attitude by clinicians to learning. A lack of time is mentioned in 2 of the data excerpts, but time pressure is not highlighted in the findings. The investigators might have developed a category of anticipated inefficiency in searching for information as lack of time and inefficiency, which are not necessarily the same problem.

The second provocative finding is the reluctance of clinicians to question or challenge the decisions made by their colleagues, evidenced in 2 data excerpts. This may be important and is something distinct from paternalistic decision making, which refers to how clinicians approach patients. Some readers may also take issue with the term "paternalistic" because of its sex-related connotations ("parental" or "authoritarian" might be an alternative phrase, but what would be most useful perhaps is to label this in the participants' own terms).

Is the theoretical framework of Spinewine et al[3] coherent; that is, does it exhibit qualities of parsimony, consistency, clarity, and fertility as defined above? The categories seem generally parsimonious, clear, and believable, as well as consistent with recognized problems in hospital care continuity, communication, and continuing education. The findings are also fertile in that they point to potential solutions and directions for further investigation.

Does the Study Help Me Understand Social Interactions in Clinical Care?

Interpretive qualitative research offers clinicians an understanding of social roles, interactions, relationships, and experiences. Many qualitative studies of interest to clinicians focus on communication or behaviors among patients, families, and caregivers. They provide theory to aid understanding, not a definitive answer to a question. Qualitative findings must be applied with judgment to specific situations, which will always differ from the setting of the study. However, even when qualitative research findings do not reflect the readers' own experience, they may provide insight into what is really going on. For example, some readers may balk at the terms "paternalism" or "ageism" as used by Spinewine et al[3] and would not use these labels themselves. However, their own theorizing about this—why the labels do not apply, why they could be better labeled, and so on—aids their reflection on the clinical problem, its dynamic social nature, and its possible solution.

USING THE GUIDE

Most clinicians recognize that patients are vulnerable at transition points of care (eg, when patients move from curative to palliative care or from retirement home to hospital care). Spinewine et al[3] point out that clinicians can use transition points to clarify the goals of drug therapy and to review the rationale for each drug, in addition to dosing suitability in light of new medications. Interactions among caregivers are an important source of the problem of inappropriate prescribing, whether because of lack of dialog about the rationale for medications or disinclination to question the prescribing of colleagues. A paternalistic attitude among clinicians is not uncommon and could contribute to poor communication between clinicians and patients about drug prescribing.[30] This study gives further impetus to change this aspect of medical culture. Finally, we might reflect on the effects of these communication and prescribing dynamics on cognitively impaired patients. This study did not include this population, but such patients may be at even greater risk when clinicians do not communicate well, raising the possibility that interventions to address this problem should include such patients.

CLINICAL RESOLUTION

Returning to our 77-year-old patient with COPD, you observe that the problems associated with her medication regimen arose in the context of several transitions between acute and chronic care. You observe that the study you have appraised has identified overemphasis on acute treatment considerations as a potential source of inappropriate prescribing. Furthermore, the Spinewine et al[3] report describes errors of omission and commission. Reflecting on this, you realize that you might approach the problem of polypharmacy from a patient safety perspective. Although physicians have clear responsibility for drug prescribing, they may not be accountable for doing so optimally. As the authors mention, multidisciplinary care environments such as the hospital could minimize errors associated with polypharmacy by better organizing and eliciting the extensive professional knowledge and skills of ward pharmacists.[31] This model has been used to good effect in the intensive care unit,[31] where polypharmacy is the norm for vulnerable critically ill patients unable to speak for themselves, such as the cognitively impaired patients omitted from this report.

After the noon conference, the charge nurse decides to develop an inservice for ward nurses to alert them to the need for medication review with medical teams for each new admission and during weekly team meetings. The senior resident volunteers to create a case-based interactive noon conferenceon appropriate drug prescribing in the elderly every 2 months for the rotating residents. Acknowledging the important role of patient empowerment, you plan to explore the possibility of support and information groups for patients and family caregivers to help them learn about the risks and appropriate management of complex drug regimens. The pharmacist on your team is thinking of a pharmacy student project designed to understand the needs of patients and their families in this regard. You suggest that the pharmacist also involve a student with training in qualitative research methods, perhaps from the sociology department, who could study the issues raised in this report from the perspective of your institution.

References

1. Laheij R, Sturkenboom M, Hassing R, Dieleman J, Stricker B, Jansen J. Risk of community-acquired pneumonia and use of gastric acid-suppressive drugs. *JAMA.* 2004;292(16):1955-1960.

2. Dial S, Alrasadi K, Manoukian C, Huang A, Menzies D. Risk of *Clostridium difficile* diarrhea among hospital inpatients prescribed proton pump inhibitors: cohort and case-control studies. *CMAJ.* 2004;171(1):33-38.

3. Spinewine A, Swine C, Dhillon S, et al. Appropriateness of use of medicines in elderly inpatients: qualitative study. *BMJ.* 2005;331(7522):935.

4. Geertz C. Thick description: toward an interpretive theory of culture. In: *The Interpretation of Cultures.* New York, NY: Basic Books; 1973:3-30.

5. Creswell JW. *Research Design: Qualitative, Quantitative, and Mixed Methods Approaches.* Thousand Oaks, CA: Sage Publications; 2003.

6. Patton MQ. *Qualitative Evaluation and Research Methods.* 3rd ed. Thousand Oaks, CA: Sage Publications; 2002.

7. Lincoff MA, Topol EJ. Interventional catheterization techniques. In: Braunwald E, ed. *Heart Disease.* 5th ed. Philadelphia, PA: WB Saunders Co; 1997:1366-1391.

8. Denzin NK, Lincoln YS. *Handbook of Qualitative Research.* 2nd ed. Thousand Oaks, CA: Sage Publications; 2000.

9. Yin RK. The case study method as a tool for doing evaluation. *Curr Soc.* 1992;40(1):122-137.

10. Walker S, McGeer A, Simor AE, Armstrong-Evans M, Loeb M. Why are antibiotics prescribed for asymptomatic bacteriuria in institutionalized elderly people? a qualitative study of physicians' and nurses' perceptions. *CMAJ.* 2000;163(3):273-277.

11. Patton MQ. Designing qualitative studies. In: *Qualitative Evaluation and Research Methods.* 3rd ed. Thousand Oaks, CA: Sage Publications; 2002:209-257.

12. Lincoln YS, Guba EG. Is being value-free valuable? In: *Naturalistic Inquiry.* London, England: Sage Publications; 1985:160-186.

13. Kitzhaber J. A healthier approach to health care. *Issues Sci Technol.* 1991; 7(2):59-65.

14. Steward DW, Shamdasani PN. Group dynamics and focus group research. In: *Focus Groups: Theory and Practice.* London, England: Sage Publications; 1990:33-50.

15. Hodder I. The interpretation of documents and material culture. In: Denzin N, Lincoln Y, eds. *Handbook of Qualitative Research.* 2nd ed. London, England: Sage Publications; 2000:703-716.

16. Kirk J, Miller ML. *Reliability and Validity in Qualitative Research.* London, England: Sage Publications; 1986.

17. Schachter S, Rauscher F, Christenfeld N, Crone KT. The vocabularies of academia. *Psychol Sci.* 1994;5(1):37-41.

18. Patton MQ. Fieldwork strategies and observation methods. In: *Qualitative Evaluation and Research Methods.* Thousand Oaks, CA: Sage Publications; 2002:259-338.

19. Patton MQ. Qualitative analysis and interpretation. In: *Qualitative Evaluation and Research Methods.* 3rd ed. Thousand Oaks, CA: Sage Publications; 2002:431-540.

20. Glaser B, Strauss AL. The constant comparative methods of qualitative analysis. In: *Discovery of Grounded Theory.* New York, NY: Aldine de Gruyter; 1967:101-116.

21. Lincoln YS, Guba EG. Designing a naturalistic inquiry. In: *Naturalistic Inquiry.* London, England: Sage Publications; 1985:221-249.

22. Stake R. Triangulation. In: Stake R, ed. *The Art of Case Study Research.* London, England: Sage Publications; 1995:107-120.

23. Power E. Toward understanding in postmodern interview analysis: interpreting the contradictory remarks of a research participant. *Qual Health Res.* 2004;14(6):858-865.

24. Lincoln YS, Guba EG. Establishing trustworthiness. In: *Naturalistic Inquiry.* London, England: Sage Publications; 1985:289-331.

25. Patton MQ. Enhancing the quality and credibility of qualitative analysis. In: *Qualitative Evaluation and Research Methods.* 3rd ed. London, England: Sage Publications; 2002:541-598.

26. Giacomini M. Interdisciplinarity in health services research: dreams and nightmares, maladies and remedies. *J Health Serv Res Policy.* 2004;9(3):117-183.

27. Elder NC, Miller WL. Reading and evaluating qualitative research studies. *J Fam Pract.* 1995;41(3):279-285.

28. Hamberg K, Johansson E, Lindgren G, Westman G. Scientific rigour in qualitative research: examples from a study of women's health in family practice. *Fam Pract.* 1994;11(2):176-181.

29. Strauss A, Corbin J. *Basics of Qualitative Research: Grounded Theory Procedures and Techniques.* London, England: Sage Publications; 1990.

30. Stevenson F, Barry C, Britten N, Barber N, Bradley C. Doctor-patient communication about drugs: the evidence for shared decision making. *Soc Sci Med.* 2000;50(6):829-840.

31. Montazeri M, Cook D. The impact of a clinical pharmacist in a multi-disciplinary intensive care unit. *Crit Care Med.* 1994;22(6):1044-1048.

Part C

Harm (Observational Studies)

HARM (OBSERVATIONAL STUDIES)

Mitchell Levine, John Ioannidis, Ted Haines, and Gordon Guyatt

IN THIS CHAPTER:

Is the Exposure Similar to What Might Occur in My Patient?

What Is the Magnitude of the Risk?

Are There Any Benefits That Offset the Risks Associated With Exposure?

Clinical Resolution

CLINICAL SCENARIO

Does Soy Milk (or Soy Formula) Increase the Risk of Developing Peanut Allergy in Children?

You are a general practitioner with a 29-year-old patient who is 8 months pregnant with her second child. Her first child, who is now 3 years old, had demonstrated an intolerance to cow's milk as an infant. He was switched to soy formula, and then soy milk, which he subsequently tolerated very well. At age 2 years, cow's milk was reintroduced without any problems, and he has been receiving cow's milk since. She was planning to start feeding her next child soy formula at birth but heard from a neighbor that it can increase the risk of peanut allergy in her child, a potentially serious and lifelong disease. She asks for your advice on the topic. Because you are not particularly familiar with this issue, you inform your patient that you will examine the evidence and discuss your findings with her when she returns for her next prenatal visit in 1 week.

FINDING THE EVIDENCE

You formulate the relevant question: In infants, what is the association between *exposure* to soy milk and the subsequent development of peanut allergy? Searching Ovid (MEDLINE) with the terms "peanut" AND "soy" AND "allergy" AND "risk," you identify 12 articles. One article appears to be particularly relevant to your target: factors associated with the development of peanut allergy in childhood.[1] You print a copy of the abstract and then arrange to obtain a copy of the full-text article from your local hospital library.

The article describes a case-control study that used a geographically defined cohort of 13 971 preschool children. The investigators identified children with a convincing history of peanut allergy who reacted to a blinded peanut challenge. They collected detailed information from the children's parents and from 2 groups of control parents (a random sample from the geographically defined cohort and from a subgroup of children from the cohort who had eczema in the first 6 months of life and whose mothers had a history of eczema).

Table 12-1 presents our usual 3-step approach to using an article about harm from the medical literature to guide your practice. You will find these criteria useful for a variety of issues involving concerns of etiology or risk factors in which a potentially harmful exposure cannot be randomly assigned. These *observational studies* involve using either cohort or case-control designs.

TABLE 12-1

Users' Guides for an Article About Harm

Are the results valid?

In a cohort study, aside from the exposure of interest, did the exposed and control groups start and finish with the same risk for the outcome?

- Were patients similar for prognostic factors that are known to be associated with the outcome (or did statistical adjustment level the playing field)?
- Were the circumstances and methods for detecting the outcome similar?
- Was the follow-up sufficiently complete?

In a case-control study, did the cases and control group have the same risk (chance) for being exposed in the past?

- Were cases and controls similar with respect to the indication or circumstances that would lead to exposure?
- Were the circumstances and methods for determining exposure similar for cases and controls?

What are the results?

- How strong is the association between exposure and outcome?
- How precise was the estimate of the risk?

How can I apply the result to patient care?

- Were the study patients similar to the patient in my practice?
- Was follow-up sufficiently long?
- Is the exposure similar to what might occur in my patient?
- What is the magnitude of the risk?
- Are there any benefits that are known to be associated with exposure?

Are the Results Valid?

Clinicians often encounter patients who face potentially harmful exposures either to medical interventions or environmental agents. These circumstances give rise to important questions. Are pregnant women at increased risk of miscarriage if they work in front of video display terminals? Do vasectomies increase the risk of prostate cancer? Do changes in health care policies lead to harmful outcomes? When examining these questions, health care providers and administrators must evaluate the validity of the data, the strength of the association between the assumed cause and the adverse outcome, and the relevance to patients in their domain.

In answering any clinical question, our first goal should be to identify any existing *systematic review* of the topic that can provide a summary of the highest-quality available evidence (see Chapter 19, Summarizing the Evidence). Interpreting such a *review* requires an understanding of the rules of evidence for individual or *primary studies, randomized controlled trials (RCTs)*, and observational studies. The tests for judging the validity of observational study results will help you decide whether exposed and control groups (or cases and controls) began and finished the study with sufficient similarities that we obtain a minimally biased assessment of the influence of exposure on outcome (see Chapter 5, Why Study Results Mislead: Bias and Random Error).

RCTs provide less biased estimates of potentially harmful effects than other study designs because randomization is the best way to ensure that groups are balanced with respect to both known and unknown determinants of the outcome (see Chapter 6, Therapy). Although investigators conduct RCTs to determine whether therapeutic agents are beneficial, they should also look for harmful effects and may sometimes make surprising discoveries about the negative effects of the intervention on their primary outcomes (see Chapter 9.2, Surprising Results of Randomized Trials).

There are 3 reasons why RCTs may not be helpful for determining whether a putative harmful agent truly has deleterious effects. First, we would consider it unethical to randomize patients to exposures that we anticipate might result in harmful effects without benefit. Second, we are often concerned about rare and serious adverse effects that may become evident only after tens of thousands of patients have consumed a medication for a period of years. Even a very large RCT[2] failed to detect an association between clopidogrel and thrombotic thrombocytopenic purpura, which appeared in a subsequent observational study.[3] RCTs specifically addressing adverse effects may be feasible for adverse event rates as low as 1%.[4,5] But the RCTs that we need to explore harmful events occurring in less than 1 in 100 exposed patients are logistically difficult and often prohibitively expensive because of huge sample size and lengthy follow-up. Meta-analyses may be very helpful when the event rates are very low.[6] Across almost 2000 systematic reviews, however, only 25 reviews had large-scale data on 4000 or more randomized subjects regarding well-defined harms that might be associated with the assessed interventions.[7] Third, RCTs often fail to adequately report information on harm.[8]

Given that clinicians will not find RCTs to answer most questions about harm, they must understand the alternative strategies used to minimize *bias*. This requires a familiarity with observational study designs, which we will now describe (Table 12-2).

TABLE 12-2

Directions of Inquiry and Key Methodologic Strengths and Weaknesses for Different Study Designs

Design	Starting Point	Assessment	Strengths	Weaknesses
Randomized controlled trial	Exposure status	Outcome event status	Low susceptibility to bias	Feasibility and generalizability constraints
Cohort	Exposure status	Outcome event status	Feasible when randomization of exposure not possible, generalizability	Susceptible to bias
Case-control	Outcome event status	Exposure status	Overcomes temporal delays and the need for huge sample sizes to accumulate rare events	Susceptible to bias

There are 2 main types of observational studies, cohort and case-control. In a cohort study, the investigator identifies exposed and nonexposed groups of patients, each a cohort, and then follows them forward in time, monitoring the occurrence of the predicted outcome. The cohort design is similar to an RCT but without randomization; rather, the determination of whether a patient received the exposure of interest results from the patient or physician's preference or from happenstance.

Case-control studies also assess associations between exposures and outcomes. Rare outcomes or those that take a long time to develop can threaten the feasibility of cohort studies. The case-control study provides an alternative design that relies on the initial identification of cases—that is, patients who have already developed the target outcome—and the selection of controls—persons who do not have the outcome of interest. Using case-control designs, investigators assess the relative frequency of previous exposure to the putative harmful agent in the cases and the controls.

In a Cohort Study, Aside From the Exposure of Interest, Did the Exposed and Control Groups Start and Finish With the Same Risk for the Outcome? Were Patients Similar for Prognostic Factors That Are Known to Be Associated With the Outcome (or Did Statistical Adjustment Level the Playing Field)?

In a cohort study, the investigator identifies exposed and nonexposed groups of patients, each a cohort, and then traces their outcomes forward in time. Cohort studies may be either prospective or retrospective. In prospective studies, the investigator starts the follow-up and waits for the outcome (events of interest) to occur. Such studies may take many years to complete and thus they are difficult to conduct. On the other hand, an advantage is that the investigator may have a better idea of how patients are to be monitored and data are to be collected. In retrospective studies, the outcomes (events of interest) have already happened at some point in the past; the investigator simply goes back even farther in the past and selects exposed and unexposed people; then the question is whether these differ in the development of these outcomes of interest. These studies are easier to perform because they depend on the availability of data on exposures and outcomes that have already happened. On the other hand, the investigator has less control over the quality and relevance of the available data for the research question being addressed.

Cohort studies of potentially harmful exposures will yield biased results if the group exposed to the putative harmful agent and the unexposed group begin with different baseline characteristics that give them a different prognosis (and the analysis fails to deal with this imbalance). Investigators rely on cohort designs when exposure has little or no possible benefit and possible harm (making randomization unethical) or when harmful outcomes occur infrequently.

In an example of the latter situation, clinically apparent upper gastrointestinal hemorrhage in nonsteroidal anti-inflammatory drug (NSAID) users occurs approximately 1.5 times per 1000 person-years of exposure, in comparison with 1.0 per 1000 person-years in those not taking NSAIDs.[9] Because the event rate in unexposed patients is so low (0.1%), an RCT to study an increase in risk of 50% would require huge numbers of patients (sample size calculations suggest about 75000 patients per group) for adequate power to test the hypothesis that NSAIDs cause the additional bleeding.[10] Such an RCT would not be feasible, but a cohort study, in which the information comes from a large administrative database, would be possible.

One danger in using observational studies to assess a possible harmful exposure is that exposed and unexposed patients may begin with a different risk of the target outcome. For instance, in the association between NSAIDs and the increased risk of upper gastrointestinal bleeding, age may be associated with both exposure to NSAIDs and gastrointestinal bleeding. In other words, because patients taking NSAIDs will be older and because older patients are more likely to bleed, this confounding variable makes attribution of an increased risk of bleeding to NSAID exposure problematic.

There is no reason that patients who self-select (or who are selected by their physician) for exposure to a potentially harmful agent should be similar to the nonexposed patients with respect to other important determinants of that outcome. Indeed, there are many reasons to expect they will not be similar. Physicians are reluctant to prescribe medications they perceive will put their patients at risk and can selectively prescribe low-risk medications.

In one study, for instance, 24.1% of patients who were given a then-new NSAID, ketoprofen, had received peptic ulcer therapy during the previous 2 years in comparison with 15.7% of the control population.[11] The likely reason is that the ketoprofen manufacturer succeeded in persuading clinicians that ketoprofen was less likely to cause gastrointestinal bleeding than other agents. A comparison of ketoprofen to other agents would be subject to the risk of finding a spurious increase in bleeding with the new agent (compared with other therapies) because higher-risk patients would have been receiving the ketoprofen.

The prescription of benzodiazepines to elderly patients provides another example of the way that selective physician prescribing practices can lead to a different distribution of risk in patients receiving particular medications, sometimes referred to as the channeling bias.[12] Ray et al[13] found an association between long-acting benzodiazepines and risk of falls (relative risk [RR], 2.0; 95% confidence interval [CI], 1.6-2.5) in data from 1977 to 1979 but not in data from 1984 to 1985 (RR, 1.3; 95% CI, 0.9-1.8). The most plausible explanation for the change is that patients at high risk for falls (those with dementia) selectively received these benzodiazepines during the earlier period. Reports of associations between benzodiazepine use and falls led to greater caution, and the apparent association disappeared when physicians began to avoid using benzodiazepines in those at high risk of falling.

Therefore, investigators must document the characteristics of the exposed and nonexposed participants and either demonstrate their comparability or use statistical techniques to create a level playing field by adjusting for differences. Effective adjusted analyses for prognostic factors require the accurate measurement of those prognostic factors. For prospective cohorts, the investigators may take particular care of the quality of this information. For retrospective databases, however, one has to make use of what is available. Large administrative databases, although providing a sample size that allows ascertainment of rare events, sometimes have limited quality of data concerning relevant patient characteristics.

For example, Jollis et al[14] wondered about the accuracy of information about patient characteristics in an insurance claims database. To investigate this issue, they compared the insurance claims data with prospective data collection by a cardiology fellow. They found a high degree of chance-corrected agreement between the fellow and the administrative database for the presence of diabetes: the κ, a measure of chance-corrected agreement, was 0.83 (see Chapter 17.3, Measuring Agreement Beyond Chance). They also found a high degree of agreement for myocardial infarction (κ, 0.76) and moderate agreement for hypertension (κ, 0.56). However, agreement was poor for heart failure (κ, 0.39) and very poor for tobacco use (κ, 0.19).

Even if investigators document the comparability of potentially confounding variables in exposed and nonexposed cohorts and even if they use statistical techniques to adjust for differences, important prognostic factors that the investigators do not know about or have not measured may be unbalanced between the groups and thus may be responsible for differences in outcome. We call this residual confounding. Returning to our earlier example, for instance, it may be that the illnesses that require NSAIDs, rather than the NSAIDs themselves, can contribute to the increased risk of bleeding. Thus, the strength of inference from a cohort study will always be less than that of a rigorously conducted RCT.

Were the Circumstances and Methods for Detecting the Outcome Similar?

In RCTs and cohort studies, ascertainment of outcome is the key issue. For example, investigators have reported a 3-fold increase in the risk of malignant melanoma in individuals working with radioactive materials. One possible explanation for some of the increased risk might be that physicians, concerned about a possible risk, search more diligently and therefore detect disease that might otherwise go unnoticed (or they may detect disease at an earlier point in time). This could result in the exposed cohort having an apparent, but spurious, increase in risk—a situation we refer to as surveillance bias.[15]

The choice of outcome may partially address this problem. In one cohort study, for example, investigators assessed perinatal outcomes among infants of men exposed to lead and organic solvents in the printing industry by means of a cohort study assessing all the men who had been members of the printers' unions in Oslo.[16] The investigators used job classification to categorize the fathers as either being exposed to lead and organic solvents or not exposed to those substances. Investigators' awareness of whether the fathers had been exposed to the lead or solvents might bias their assessment of the baby's outcome for minor birth defects or for defects that required special investigative procedures. On the other hand, the outcome of preterm birth would be less susceptible to a detection bias. In the study, exposure was associated with an 8-fold increase in preterm births, but it was not linked with birth defects, so detection bias was unlikely.

Was the Follow-up Sufficiently Complete?

As we pointed out in Chapter 6, Therapy, loss to follow-up can introduce bias because the patients who are lost may have different outcomes from those patients still available for assessment. This is particularly problematic if there are differences in follow-up between the exposed and nonexposed groups.

In a well-executed study,[17] investigators determined the vital status of 1235 of 1261 white men (98%) employed in a chrysotile asbestos textile operation between 1940 and 1975. The RR for lung cancer death over time increased from 1.4 to 18.2 in direct proportion to the cumulative exposure among asbestos workers with at least 15 years since first exposure. In this study, where exposure was on a continuum (ie, not dichotomous), the 2% missing data were unlikely to affect the results, and the loss to follow-up did not threaten the validity of the inference that asbestos exposure caused lung cancer deaths.

In a Case-Control Study, Did the Cases and Control Group Have the Same Risk (Chance) for Being Exposed in the Past?

Were Cases and Controls Similar With Respect to the Indication or Circumstances That Would Lead to Exposure?

Investigators used a case-control design to demonstrate the association between diethylstilbestrol (DES) ingestion by pregnant women and the development of vaginal adenocarcinomas in their daughters many years later.[18] An RCT or prospective cohort study designed to test this cause-and-effect relationship would have required at least 20 years from the time when the association was first suspected until the completion of the study. Further, given the infrequency of the disease, either an RCT or a cohort study would have required hundreds of thousands of participants. By contrast, using the case-control strategy, the investigators delineated 2 relatively small groups of young women. Those who had the outcome of interest (vaginal adenocarcinoma) were designated as the cases (n = 8) and those who did not experience the outcome were designated as the controls (n = 32). Then working backward in time, they determined exposure rates to DES for the 2 groups. The investigators found a strong association between in utero DES exposure and vaginal adenocarcinoma, which was extremely unlikely to be attributable to the play of chance ($P < .001$) They found their answer without a delay of 20 years and by studying only 40 women.

A critical issue in that study would be whether the cases would have had any other special circumstances to be exposed to DES that controls would not. In this situation, DES had been prescribed to woman at risk for miscarriages or having premature births. It would be important in the assessment of this study to be confident that those risk factors on their own could not account for the subsequent high rate of vaginal pathology in the female offspring.

In another study, investigators used a case-control design relying on computer record linkages between health insurance data and a drug plan to investigate the possible relationship between use of β-adrenergic agonists and mortality rates in patients with asthma.[19] The database for the study included 95% of the population of the province of Saskatchewan in western Canada. The investigators used matching to choose 129 cases of fatal or near-fatal asthma attack with 655 controls that also had asthma but who had not had a fatal or near-fatal asthma attack.

The tendency of patients with more severe asthma to use more β-adrenergic medications could create a spurious association between drug use and mortality rate. The investigators attempted to control for the confounding effect of disease severity by measuring the number of hospitalizations in the 24 months before death (for the cases) or before the index date of entry into the study (for the control group) and by using an index of the aggregate use of medications. They found an association between the routine use of large doses of β-adrenergic agonist-metered dose inhalers and death from asthma (odds ratio [OR], 2.6 per canister per month; 95% CI, 1.7-3.9), even after correcting for their measures of disease severity.

As with cohort studies, case-control studies are susceptible to unmeasured confounding variables, particularly when exposure varies over time. For instance, previous hospitalization and medication use may not adequately capture all the variability in underlying disease severity in asthma. In addition, adverse lifestyle behaviors of asthmatic patients who use large amounts of β-agonists could be the real explanation for the association.

Were the Circumstances and Methods for Determining Exposure Similar for Cases and Controls?

In case-control studies, ascertainment of the exposure is a key issue. If case patients have a better memory for exposure than control patients, the result will be a spurious association.

For example, a case-control study found a 2-fold increase in risk of hip fracture associated with psychotropic drug use. In this study, investigators established drug exposure by examining computerized claims files of the Michigan Medicaid program, a strategy that avoided selective memory of exposure—recall bias—and differential probing of cases and controls by an interviewer—interviewer bias.[20]

Another example is a study that evaluated whether the use of cellular phones increases the risk of motor vehicle crash. Suppose the investigators had tried to ask people who had a motor vehicle crash and control patients (who were in no crash at the same day and time) whether they were using their cellular phone around the time of interest. People who were in a crash would have been more likely to recall such use because their memory might be heightened by the unfortunate circumstances. This would have led to a spurious relationship because of differential recall. Therefore, the investigators in this study instead used a computerized database of cellular phone use. Moreover, they used each person in a crash as his or her own control: the time of the crash was matched against corresponding times of the life of the same person when they were driving but when no crash occurred (eg, same time driving to work). This appropriate design established that use of cellular phones increases the risk of having a motor vehicle crash.[21]

Not all studies have access to unbiased information on exposure. In a case-control study looking at the association between coffee and pancreatic cancer, the patients with cancer may be more motivated to identify possible explanations for their problem and provide a greater recounting of coffee use.[22] Also, if the interviewers are not blinded to whether a patient is a case or a control patient, the interviewer may probe deeper for exposure information from cases. In this particular study, there were no objective sources of data regarding exposure. Recall or interviewer bias may explain the apparent association.

As it turns out, another bias provides an even more likely explanation for what turned out to be a spurious association. The investigators chose control patients from the practices of the physicians looking after the patients with pancreatic cancer. These control patients had a variety of gastrointestinal problems, some of which were exacerbated by coffee ingestion. The control patients had learned to avoid coffee, which explains the investigators' finding of an association between coffee (which the pancreatic cancer patients consumed at general population levels) and pancreatic cancer. Subsequent investigations, using more appropriate controls, refuted the association.[23]

The examples above relate to the biased assessment of exposure, but the inaccurate assessment of exposure may also be random. In other words, lots of exposed persons get classified as unexposed, and vice versa, but the rates of misclassification are similar in cases and controls. Such nondifferential misclassification tends to dilute the association (ie, the true association will be larger than the observed association). In the extreme case in which errors are very frequent, even associations that are very strong in reality may not be identified in the database.

Cross-sectional Studies

Like the cohort and the case-control study, the cross-sectional study is also an observational study design. Like a cohort study, a cross-sectional study is based on an assembled population of exposed and unexposed subjects. But in the cross-sectional study, the exposure and the existing or prevalent outcome are measured at the same time. Accordingly, the direction of association may be difficult to determine. Another important limitation is that the outcome, or the threat of getting it, may have led to a departure of cases, so that a measure of association may be biased against the association. However, cross-sectional studies are relatively inexpensive and quick to conduct and may be useful in generating and exploring hypotheses that will be subsequently investigated using other observational designs or RCTs.

Case Series and Case Reports

Case series (descriptions of a series of patients) and case reports (descriptions of individual patients) do not provide any comparison group, so it is impossible to determine whether the observed outcome would likely have occurred in the absence of the exposure. Although descriptive studies occasionally demonstrate dramatic findings mandating an immediate change in physician behavior as a precaution, before the availability of evidence from stronger study designs (eg, recall the consequences of case reports of specific birth defects occurring in association with thalidomide exposure),[24] there are potentially undesirable consequences when actions are taken in response to weak evidence.

Consider the case of the drug Bendectin (a combination of doxylamine, pyridoxine, and dicyclomine used as an antiemetic in pregnancy), whose manufacturer withdrew it from the market as a consequence of case reports suggesting that it was teratogenic.[25] Later, although a number of comparative studies demonstrated the drug's relative safety,[26] they could not eradicate the prevailing litigious atmosphere—which prevented the manufacturer from reintroducing Bendectin. Thus, many pregnant women who might have benefited from the drug's availability were denied the symptomatic relief it could have offered.

For some interventions, registries of adverse events may provide the best possible evidence initially. For example, there are vaccine registries that record adverse events among people who have received the vaccine. These registries may signal problems with a particular adverse event that would be very difficult to capture from prospective studies (too small sample size). Even retrospective studies might be too difficult to conduct if most people receive the vaccine or the people who do not receive the vaccine may be quite different from those who get it, and the differences cannot be accounted for adequately. In this case, a before/after comparison using the general population before the introduction of the new vaccine can be conducted. But such comparisons using historical controls are prone to bias because many other things may have changed in the same period. However, if changes in the incidence of an adverse event are very large, the signal may be real. An example is the clustering of intussusception cases among children receiving rotavirus vaccine,[27] resulting in a decision to withdraw the vaccine. The association was subsequently strengthened by a case-control study.[28]

In general, clinicians should not draw conclusions about cause-and-effect relationships from case series, but rather, they should recognize that the results may generate questions for regulatory agencies, which clinical investigators should address with valid studies. When the immediate risk of exposure outweighs the benefits (and outweighs the risk of stopping an exposure), the clinician may have to make a management decision with less than optimal data.

Design Issues: Summary

Just as it is true for the resolution of questions of therapeutic effectiveness, clinicians should first look to RCTs to resolve issues of harm. They will often be disappointed in the search and must make use of studies of weaker design. Regardless of the design, however, they should look for an appropriate control population before making a strong inference about a putative harmful agent. For RCTs and cohort studies, the control group should have a similar baseline risk of outcome, or investigators should use statistical techniques to adjust or correct for differences. In case-control studies, the cases and the controls should have had a similar opportunity to have been exposed, so that if a difference in exposure is observed one might legitimately conclude that the association could be due to a causal link between the exposure and the outcome and not due to a confounding factor. Alternatively, investigators should use statistical techniques to adjust for differences.

Even when investigators have taken all the appropriate steps to minimize bias, clinicians should bear in mind that residual differences between groups may still bias the results of observational studies.[29] Because evidence, provider preferences, and patient values and preferences determine the use of interventions in the real world, exposed and unexposed patients are likely to differ in prognostic factors.

The extent of bias in observational studies vs randomized trials remains uncertain. An empirical evaluation of 15 harms in which both types of evidence were available showed that observational studies might give either smaller or larger risk estimates compared with RCTs, but it is more common for observational studies to underestimate rather than overestimate the absolute risk of harm.[30] Therefore, evidence of harmful effects from well-designed observational studies should not be easily dismissed.

USING THE GUIDE

Returning to our earlier discussion, the study that we retrieved investigating the association between soy milk (or formula) and the development of peanut allergy used a case-control design.[1] Those with peanut allergy (cases) appear to be similar to the controls with respect to the indication or circumstances leading to soy exposure, but there were a few potentially important imbalances. In the peanut allergy group (cases), both a family history of peanut allergy and an older sibling with a history of milk intolerance were more common and could bias the likelihood of a subsequent child's being exposed to soy. To avoid confounding, these factors were adjusted in the analysis to provide an independent assessment of the association between soy and peanut allergy.

The methods for determining exposure were similar for cases and controls because the data were collected prospectively and both the interviewers and parents were unaware of the hypothesis relating soy exposure to peanut allergy (thus avoiding interviewer and perhaps recall bias). With regard to access to soy, all the children came from the same geographic region, although this does not ensure that cultural and economic factors that might determine soy access were balanced between cases and controls. Thus, from the initial assessment, the validity of the study appears adequate with the appropriate adjustments being done.

WHAT ARE THE RESULTS?

How Strong Is the Association Between Exposure and Outcome?

We describe the alternatives for expressing the association between the exposure and the outcome—the RR and the OR—in other chapters of this book (see Chapter 6, Therapy; Chapter 7, Does Treatment Lower Risk? Understanding the Results; and Chapter 10.2, Understanding the Results: More About Odds Ratios).

In a cohort study assessing in-hospital mortality after noncardiac surgery in male veterans, 23 of 289 patients with a history of hypertension died compared with 3 of 185 patients without the condition. The RR for mortality in hypertensive patients[31] (23/289 and 3/185) was 4.9. The RR tells us that death after noncardiac surgery occurs almost 5 times more often in patients with hypertension than in normotensive patients.

The estimate of RR depends on the availability of samples of exposed and unexposed patients, where the proportion of the patients with the outcome of interest can be determined. The RR is therefore not applicable to case-control studies in which the number of cases and controls—and, therefore, the proportion of individuals with the outcome—is chosen by the investigator. For case-control studies, instead of using a ratio of RR, we use OR, the odds of a case patient being exposed divided by the odds of a control patient being exposed (see Chapter 7, Does Treatment Lower Risk? Understanding the Results; and Chapter 10.2, Understanding the Results: More About Odds Ratios). In circumstances in which the outcome is rare in the population at large (< 1%), the OR of a case-control study represents the risk ratio in the whole population from which the cases and controls have been sampled. Even when event rates are as high as 10%, the OR and RR may still be quite close.

When considering both study design and strength of association, we may be ready to interpret a small increase in risk as representing a true harmful effect if the study design is strong (such as in an RCT). A much greater increase in risk might be required of weaker designs (such as cohort or case-control studies) because subtle findings are more likely to be caused by the inevitably higher chance of bias. Very large values of RR or OR represent strong associations that are less likely to be the result of bias.

In addition to showing a large magnitude of RR or OR, there is a second finding that can strengthen an inference that an exposure is truly associated with harmful effect. If, when the quantity or the duration of exposure to the putative harmful agent increases, the risk for the adverse outcome also increases (ie, the data suggest a dose-response gradient), then we are more likely to be dealing with a causal relationship between exposure and outcome. The fact that the risk of dying from lung cancer in male physician smokers increases by 50%, 132%, and 220% for 1 to 14, 15 to 24, and 25 or more cigarettes smoked per day, respectively, strengthens our inference that cigarette smoking causes lung cancer.[32]

How Precise Is the Estimate of the Risk?

Clinicians can evaluate the precision of the estimate of risk by examining the CI around that estimate (see Chapter 6, Therapy; see also Chapter 8, Confidence Intervals). In a study in which investigators have shown an association between an exposure and an adverse outcome, the lower limit of the estimate of RR associated with the adverse exposure provides an estimate of the lowest possible magnitude of the association. Alternatively, in a negative study (in which the results are not statistically significant) the upper boundary of the CI around the RR tells the clinician just how big an adverse effect may still be present, despite the failure to show a statistically significant association (see Chapter 8, Confidence Intervals).

USING THE GUIDE

The investigators calculated the OR for the risk of peanut allergy in those exposed to soy vs those not exposed to be 2.6 (95% CI, 1.3-5.2). These results were adjusted for skin manifestations of allergy (ie, atopy). The consumption of soy by the infants was independently associated with peanut allergy and could not be explained as a dietary response to other atopic conditions. It nevertheless remains possible that the association with soy was confounded by other, unknown factors.[1] Unfortunately, the investigators did not address the possibility of a dose-response relationship for soy exposure and the development of peanut allergy.

HOW CAN I APPLY THE RESULTS TO PATIENT CARE?

Were the Study Patients Similar to the Patient in My Practice?

If possible biases in a study are not sufficient to dismiss the study out of hand, you should consider the extent to which the results might apply to the patient in your practice. Could your patient have met the eligibility criteria? Is your patient similar to those described in the study with respect to potentially important factors, such as patient characteristics or medical history? If not, is the biology of the harmful exposure likely to be different for the patient for whom you are providing care (see Chapter 11.1, Applying Results to Individual Patients)?

Was Follow-up Sufficiently Long?

Studies can be pristine in terms of validity but of limited use if patients are not followed up for a sufficiently long period. That is, they may provide an unbiased estimate of the effect of an exposure during the short term, but the effect we are really interested in is during a longer period. For example, most cancers take a decade or longer to develop from the original assault at the biologic level to the clinically detected malignancy. For example, if the question is whether a specific exposure, say to an industrial chemical, causes cancer to develop, one would not expect cancers detected in the first few years to reflect any of the effect of the exposure under question.

Is the Exposure Similar to What Might Occur in My Patient?
Are There Important Differences in the Exposures, for Instance, Dose or Duration, Between Your Patients and the Patients in the Study?

As an illustration, the risk of thrombophlebitis associated with oral contraceptive use described in the 1970s may not be applicable to the patient in the 21st century because of the lower estrogen dose in oral contraceptives currently used. Another example comes from the study that showed that workers employed in chrysotile asbestos textile operation between 1940 and 1975 had an increased risk for lung cancer death, a risk that increased from 1.4 to 18.2 in direct relation to cumulative exposure among asbestos workers with at least 15 years since first exposure.[17] The study does not provide reliable information regarding what might be the risks associated with only brief or intermittent exposure to asbestos (eg, a person working for a few months in an office located in a building subsequently found to have abnormally high asbestos levels).

What Is the Magnitude of the Risk?
The RR and OR do not tell us how frequently the problem occurs; they tell us only that the observed effect occurs more or less often in the exposed group compared with the unexposed group. Thus, we need a method for assessing clinical importance. In our discussion of therapy (see Chapter 6, Therapy; and Chapter 7, Does Treatment Lower Risk? Understanding the Results), we described how to calculate the number of patients whom clinicians must treat to prevent an adverse event (number needed to treat). When the issue is harm, we can use data from a randomized trial or cohort study in a similar way, only this time to calculate the number of patients that would have to be exposed to result in 1 additional harmful event. We may even use data from case-control studies with OR, although the formula is a bit more complex, and we would need to know the event rate for the outcome in the unexposed population from which the cases and controls were drawn (see Chapter 10.2, Understanding the Results: More About Odds Ratios).

During an average of 10 months of follow-up, investigators conducting the Cardiac Arrhythmia Suppression Trial, an RCT of antiarrhythmic agents,[33] found that the mortality rate at approximately 10 months was 3.0% for placebo-treated patients and 7.7% for those treated with either encainide or flecainide. The absolute risk increase was 4.7%, the reciprocal of which tells us that, on average, for every 21 patients treated with encainide or flecainide for about a year, we would cause 1 excess death. This contrasts with our example of the association between NSAIDs and upper gastrointestinal bleeding. Of 2000 unexposed patients, 2 will have a bleeding episode each year. Of 2000 patients taking NSAIDs, 3 will have such an episode each year. Thus, if we treat 2000 patients with NSAIDs, we can expect a single additional bleeding event.[9]

Are There Any Benefits That Offset the Risks Associated With Exposure?

Even after evaluating the evidence that an exposure is harmful and establishing that the results are potentially applicable to the patient in your practice, determining subsequent actions may not be simple. In addition to considering the magnitude of the risk, one must consider what are the adverse consequences of reducing or eliminating exposure to the harmful agent; that is, the magnitude of any potential benefit that patients will no longer receive.

Clinical decision making is simple when harmful consequences are unacceptable and benefit is absent. Because the evidence of increased mortality from encainide and flecainide came from an RCT, we can be confident of the causal connection. Because treating only 21 people would result in an excess death, it is no wonder that clinicians quickly curtailed their use of these antiarrhythmic agents when the study results became available.

The clinical decision is also made easier when an acceptable alternative for avoiding the risk is available. Even if the evidence is relatively weak, the availability of an alternative substance can result in a clear decision.

For instance, the early case-control studies demonstrating the association between aspirin use and Reye syndrome were relatively weak and left considerable doubt about the causal relationship. Although the strength of the inference was not great, the availability of a safe, inexpensive, and well-tolerated alternative, acetaminophen, justified the preference for using this alternative agent in lieu of aspirin in children at risk for Reye syndrome.[34]

In contrast to the early studies regarding aspirin and Reye syndrome, multiple well-designed cohort and case-control studies have consistently demonstrated an association between NSAIDs and upper gastrointestinal bleeding; therefore, our inference about harm has been relatively strong. However, the risk of an upper gastrointestinal bleeding episode is quite low, and there may not be safer and equally efficacious anti-inflammatory alternatives available. We were therefore probably right in continuing to prescribe NSAIDs for the appropriate clinical conditions.

USING THE GUIDE

You determine that the patient's unborn child, once he or she reaches early childhood, would likely fulfill the eligibility criteria in the study. Also relevant to the clinical scenario, but perhaps unknown, is whether the soy products discussed in the study are similar to the ones that the patient is considering using. With regard to the magnitude of risk, we are told that the prevalence of peanut allergy is approximately 4 per 1000 children. An approximate calculation would suggest that with exposure to soy, 10 children per 1000 would be affected by peanut allergy. In other words, the number of children needed to be exposed to soy that would result in 1 additional case of peanut allergy is 167. (This estimate is crude and relies on a number of unverified assumptions regarding the true incidence of peanut allergy.) Finally, there are no data regarding the negative consequences of withholding soy formula or soy milk products, and this would clearly be dependent on how severe and sustained an intolerance to cow's milk was in a particular child.

CLINICAL RESOLUTION

To decide on your course of action, you proceed through the 3 steps of using the medical literature to guide your clinical practice. First, you consider the validity of the study before you. Adjustments of known confounders did not diminish the association between soy exposure as a neonate and the development of peanuts allergy. Also, the design of the study does not have any obvious problems with either recall or interviewer bias. Although you remain uncertain about unknown confounders, the study provides evidence of an association that one cannot easily dismiss.

Turning to the results, you note only a moderate association between soy exposure and the development of peanut allergy (2 < OR < 5). Although the results are statistically significant (ie, the 95% CI excludes 1), hidden biases and confounding could account for some or most of the magnitude of the observed OR.

You therefore proceed to the third step, with some reservations, and consider the implications of the study results for your patient. The study would appear to apply to a future child of your patient. Although the magnitude of the overall risk is small, perhaps about 1%, the consequences of peanut allergy can be a serious health threat to a patient and quite disruptive for a family because of the required precautions and food restrictions. Because the consequence of not using soy products may have minimal negative consequence and there appears to be some potential risk for increasing the likelihood of developing a peanut allergy in an infant exposed to soy, you may recommend to the mother not to use soy products unless the child is demonstrably intolerant to breast or cow's milk.

References

1. Lack G, Fox D, Northstone K, Golding J. Factors associated with the development of peanut allergy in childhood. *N Engl J Med.* 2003;348(11):977-985.

2. CAPRIE Steering Committee. A randomised, blinded, trial of clopidogrel versus aspirin in patients at risk of ischaemic events (CAPRIE). *Lancet.* 1996;348 (9038):1329-1339.

3. Bennett CL, Connors JM, Carwile JM, et al. Thrombotic thrombocytopenic purpura associated with clopidogrel. *N Engl J Med.* 2000;342(24):1773-1777.

4. Silverstein FE, Graham DY, Senior JR, et al. Misoprostol reduces serious gastrointestinal complications in patients with rheumatoid arthritis receiving nonsteroidal anti-inflammatory drugs: a randomized, double-blind, placebo-controlled trial. *Ann Intern Med.* 1995;123(4):241-249.

5. Bombardier C, Laine L, Reicin A, et al; VIGOR Study Group. Comparison of upper gastrointestinal toxicity of rofecoxib and naproxen in patients with rheumatoid arthritis. *N Engl J Med.* 2000;343(21):1520-1528.

6. Langman MJ, Jensen DM, Watson DJ, et al. Adverse upper gastrointestinal effects of rofecoxib compared with NSAIDs. *JAMA.* 1999;282(20):1929-1933.

7. Papanikolaou PN, Ioannidis JP. Availability of large-scale evidence on specific harms from systematic reviews of randomized trials. *Am J Med.* 2004;117(8):582-589.

8. Ioannidis JP, Haidich AB, Pappa M, et al. Comparison of evidence of treatment effects in randomized and nonrandomized studies. *JAMA.* 2001;286(7):821-830.

9. Carson JL, Strom BL, Soper KA, West SL, Morse ML. The association of nonsteroidal anti-inflammatory drugs with upper gastrointestinal tract bleeding. *Arch Intern Med.* 1987;147(1):85-88.

10. Walter SD. Determination of significant relative risks and optimal sampling procedures in prospective and retrospective comparative studies of various sizes. *Am J Epidemiol.* 1977;105(4):387-397.

11. Leufkens HG, Urquhart J, Stricker BH, Bakker A, Petri H. Channelling of controlled release formulation of ketoprofen (Oscorel) in patients with history of gastrointestinal problems. *J Epidemiol Community Health.* 1992;46(4):428-432.

12. Joseph KS. The evolution of clinical practice and time trends in drug effects. *J Clin Epidemiol.* 1994;47(6):593-598.

13. Ray WA, Griffin MR, Downey W. Benzodiazepines of long and short elimination half-life and the risk of hip fracture. *JAMA.* 1989;262(23):3303-3307.

14. Jollis JG, Ancukiewicz M, DeLong ER, Pryor DB, Muhlbaier LH, Mark DB. Discordance of databases designed for claims payment versus clinical information systems: implications for outcomes research. *Ann Intern Med.* 1993;119 (8):844-850.

15. Hiatt RA, Fireman B. The possible effect of increased surveillance on the incidence of malignant melanoma. *Prev Med.* 1986;15(6):652-660.

16. Kristensen P, Irgens LM, Daltveit AK, Andersen A. Perinatal outcome among children of men exposed to lead and organic solvents in the printing industry. *Am J Epidemiol.* 1993;37(2):134-144.

17. Dement JM, Harris RL Jr, Symons MJ, Shy CM. Exposures and mortality among chrysotile asbestos workers, part II: mortality. *Am J Ind Med.* 1983;4(3):421-433.

18. Herbst AL, Ulfelder H, Poskanzer DC. Adenocarcinoma of the vagina: association of maternal stilbestrol therapy with tumor appearance in young women. *N Engl J Med.* 1971;284(15):878-881.

19. Spitzer WO, Suissa S, Ernst P, et al. The use of beta-agonists and the risk of death and near death from asthma. *N Engl J Med.* 1992;326(8):501-506.

20. Ray WA, Griffin MR, Schaffner W, Baugh DK, Melton LJ 3rd. Psychotropic drug use and the risk of hip fracture. *N Engl J Med.* 1987;316(7):363-369.

21. Redelmeier DA, Tibshirani RJ. Association between cellular-telephone calls and motor vehicle collisions. *N Engl J Med.* 1997;336(7):453-458.

22. MacMahon B, Yen S, Trichopoulos D, Warren K, Nardi G. Coffee and cancer of the pancreas. *N Engl J Med.* 1981;304(11):630-633.

23. Baghurst PA, McMichael AJ, Slavotinek AH, Baghurst KI, Boyle P, Walker AM. A case-control study of diet and cancer of the pancreas. *Am J Epidemiol.* 1991;134(2):167-179.

24. Lenz W. Epidemiology of congenital malformations. *Ann N Y Acad Sci.* 1965;123:228-236.

25. Soverchia G, Perri PF. 2 Cases of malformations of a limb in infants of mothers treated with an antiemetic in a very early phase of pregnancy. *Pediatr Med Chir.* 1981;3(1):97-99.

26. Holmes LB. Teratogen update: Bendectin. *Teratology.* 1983;27(2):277-281.

27. Centers for Disease Control and Prevention. Intussusception among recipients of rotavirus vaccine—United States, 1998-1999. *Morb Mortal Wkly Rep CDC Surveill Summ.* 1999;48(27):577-581.

28. Murphy TV, Gargiullo PM, Massoudi MS, et al. Intussusception among infants given an oral rotavirus vaccine. *N Engl J Med.* 2001;344(8):564-572.

29. Kellermann AL, Rivara FP, Rushforth NB, et al. Gun ownership as a risk factor for homicide in the home. *N Engl J Med.* 1993;329(15):1084-1091.

30. Papanikolaou PN, Christidi GD, Ioannidis JP. Comparison of evidence on harms of medical interventions in randomized and nonrandomized studies. *CMAJ.* 2006;174(5):635-641.

31. Browner WS, Li J, Mangano DT. In-hospital and long-term mortality in male veterans following noncardiac surgery: the Study of Perioperative Ischemia Research Group. *JAMA.* 1992;268(2):228-232.

32. Doll R, Hill AB. Mortality in relation to smoking: ten years' observations of British doctors. *BMJ.* 1964;1(5395):1399-1410.

33. Echt DS, Liebson PR, Mitchell LB, et al. Mortality and morbidity in patients receiving encainide, flecainide, or placebo: the Cardiac Arrhythmia Suppression Trial. *N Engl J Med.* 1991;324(12):781-788.

34. Soumerai SB, Ross-Degnan D, Kahn JS. Effects of professional and media warnings about the association between aspirin use in children and Reye's syndrome. *Milbank Q.* 1992;70(1):155-182.

13

ADVANCED
TOPICS IN HARM

CORRELATION
AND REGRESSION

Gordon Guyatt, Stephen Walter, Deborah J. Cook,
and Roman Jaeschke

IN THIS CHAPTER:

Introduction

Investigators are sometimes interested in the relationship between different measures or variables. They pose questions related to the correlation of these variables. For example, they might ask, how well does the clinical impression of an asthmatic child's symptoms relate to the parents' perception? How strong is the relationship between a patient's physical and emotional function?

By contrast, other investigators are primarily interested in predicting individuals at high risk of having a subsequent event. For instance, can we identify individuals at high risk for myocardial infarction or cardiac death after noncardiac surgery?

Still other investigators seek the causal relations between biologic phenomena. For instance, they might ask, what determines the extent to which we feel dyspneic when we exercise or when we have a cardiac or respiratory illness? Finally, investigators may also pose causal questions that could directly inform patient management: Do cyclooxygenase 2 (COX-2) inhibitors really cause myocardial infarction?

Clinicians may be interested in the answers to all 3 sorts of questions—those of correlation, prediction, and causation. To the extent that the relationship between child and parental perceptions is weak, clinicians must obtain both perspectives. If physical and emotional functions are only weakly related, then clinicians must probe both areas thoroughly. We may target patients at high risk of subsequent adverse events with prophylactic interventions. If clinicians know that hypoxemia is strongly related to dyspnea, they may be more inclined to administer oxygen to patients with dyspnea. The clinical implications of the causal questions are more obvious. We may target high-risk surgical patients for preventive interventions, and we may withdraw dangerous COX-2 inhibitors from the market.

We refer to the magnitude of the relationship between different variables or phenomena as *correlation*. We call the statistical techniques for prediction, or for making a causal inference, *regression*. In this chapter, we will provide examples to illustrate the use of correlation and regression in the medical literature.

Correlation

Traditionally, we perform laboratory measurements of exercise capacity in patients with cardiac and respiratory illnesses by using a treadmill or cycle ergometer. About 30 years ago, investigators interested in respiratory disease began to use a simpler test that is related more closely to day-to-day activity.[1] In the walk test, patients are asked to cover as much ground as they can during a specified period (typically 6 minutes) walking in an enclosed corridor. For a number of reasons, we may be interested in the strength of the relationship between the walk test and conventional laboratory measures of exercise capacity. If the tests relate strongly enough to one another, we might be able to substitute one test for the other. In addition, the strength of the relationship might inform us as to the potential of laboratory tests of exercise capacity to predict patients' ability to undertake physically demanding activities of daily living.

What do we mean by the strength of the relationship between 2 measures? One finds a strong positive relationship between 2 measures when patients who obtain high scores on the first also obtain high scores on the second, when those in whom we find intermediate scores on the first also show intermediate values on the second, and when patients who score low on one measure score low on the other measure. One can also have strong negative relationships: those who score high on one measure score low on the other. If patients who score low on one measure are equally likely to score low or high on another measure, the relationship between the 2 variables is poor, weak, or nonexistent.

We can gain a sense of the strength of the correlation by examining a visual plot relating patients' scores on the 2 measures. Figure 13-1 presents such a plot relating walk test results (on the x-axis) to the results of cycle ergometer exercise test (on the y-axis). The data for this plot, and those for the subsequent analyses using walk test results, come from 3 studies of

FIGURE 13-1

Relationship Between Walk Test Results and Cycle Ergometer Exercise Test Results

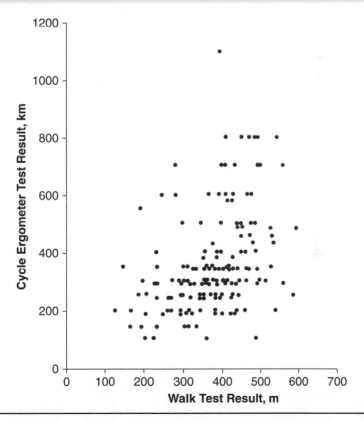

patients with chronic airflow limitation.[3-5] Each dot in Figure 13-1 represents an individual patient and presents 2 pieces of information: the patient's walk test score and cycle ergometer exercise time. Although the walk test results are truly continuous, the cycle ergometer results tend to take only certain values because patients usually stop the test at the end of a particular level, rather than partway through a level.

Examining Figure 13-1, you can see that, in general, patients who score well on the walk test also tend to score well on the cycle ergometer exercise test, and patients who score poorly on the cycle ergometer tend to score poorly on the walk test. Yet, you can find patients who represent exceptions, scoring better than most other patients on one test and not as well on the other test. These data, therefore, represent a moderate relationship between 2 variables, the walk test and the cycle ergometer exercise test.

One can summarize the strength of a relationship between 2 continuous (also called interval) variables in a single number, the correlation coefficient. The correlation coefficient, which is denoted by r, can range from −1.0 (representing the strongest possible negative relationship, in which the person who scores the highest on one test scores the lowest on the other test) to 1.0 (representing the strongest possible positive relationship, in which the person who scores the highest on one test also scores the highest on the other test). A correlation coefficient of 0 denotes no relationship between the 2 variables (ie, people who score high on test A have the same range of values on test B as those who score low on test A). The plot of data with a correlation of 0 shows no relationship.

The correlation coefficient assumes a linear relationship between the variables. There may be a relationship between the variables, but it may not take the form of a straight line when viewed visually. For example, even if scores on the variables rise together, one may rise more slowly than the other for low values but will rise more quickly than the other for high values. If there is a strong relationship but it is not a linear one, the correlation coefficient may be misleading.

In the example depicted in Figure 13-1, the relationship does appear to approximate a straight line, and the r value for the correlation between the walk test and the cycle ergometer is 0.50. Is this moderately strong correlation good or bad? It depends on how we wish to apply the information. If we were thinking of using the walk test value as a substitute for the cycle ergometer—after all, the walk test is much simpler to carry out—we would be disappointed. A correlation of 0.8 or higher (although the threshold is arbitrary) would be required for us to be confident in that kind of substitution. If the correlation were too low, there would be too much risk that a person with a high walk test score would have mediocre or low performance on the cycle ergometer test or that a person who did poorly on the walk test would do well on the cycle ergometer test. On the other hand, if we assume that the walk test gives a good indication of exercise capacity in daily life, the moderate correlation suggests that the cycle ergometer result tells us something (less than the walk test, but still something) about day-to-day exercise capacity.

In getting a sense of the magnitude of a correlation, in addition to the possibility of substituting one variable for another (requiring a very high correlation) or one variable giving us some indication of status on another (requiring a lower correlation), one can think of the proportion of variability or variance in one variable that is explained by another. The square of the correlation represents the proportion of variance explained (if the correlation is 0.4, one variable explains 16% of the variance in the other; if the correlation is 0.8, 64% of the variance is explained).

You will often see a *P* value in association with a correlation coefficient (see Chapter 10.1, Hypothesis Testing). When one considers correlation coefficients, the *P* value is associated with the null hypothesis that the true correlation between the 2 measures is 0. Thus, the *P* value represents the probability that, if the true correlation were 0, an apparently linear relationship as strong as or stronger than the one we actually observed would have occurred as a result of chance. The smaller the *P* value, the less likely it is that chance explains the apparent relationship between the 2 measures.

> The *P* value depends not only on the strength of the relationship but also on the sample size. In this case, we had data on both the walk test and the cycle ergometer from 179 patients, and with a correlation of 0.50, the associated *P* value is less than .001. A relationship can be very weak, but if the sample size is sufficiently large, the *P* value may be small. For instance, with a sample size of 500, we reach the conventional threshold *P* value of .05 at a correlation of only .10.

In evaluating treatment effects, the size of the effect and the confidence intervals around the effect tend to be much more informative than *P* values (see Chapter 8, Confidence Intervals).[6] The same is true of correlations, in which the magnitude of the correlation and the confidence interval around the correlation are the key parameters.

> The 95% confidence interval around the correlation between the walk test and laboratory exercise tests ranges from 0.38 to 0.60.

REGRESSION

As clinicians, we are often interested in prediction. We want to know which person will develop a disease (such as coronary artery disease) and which person will not and which patient will do well and which patient will do poorly. We are also interested in making causal inferences in situations in which randomized controlled trials are not possible. Regression techniques are useful in addressing both sorts of issues.[7]

Regression Modeling With Continuous Target Variables

In any regression, we have a target outcome or response variable that we call the dependent variable because it is influenced or determined by other variables or factors. When this dependent variable is a continuous variable such as a 6-minute walk test score that can take a large number of values, the appropriate tool is linear regression. Sometimes, statisticians treat target variables that take one of a number of discrete values, such as the 10 or so levels that a patient might achieve on a conventional exercise test, as if they were continuous.

Regressions also involve explanatory or predictor variables that we suspect may be associated with, or causally related to, the dependent variable. These independent variables can be binary (either/or)—such as sex (male or female), which we call dichotomous variables—or continuous, such as forced expiratory volume in 1 second (FEV_1).

When there is a single predictor variable, we call the regression univariable or simple regression (or less technically correct, but more often used, univariate).[8] When we are examining more than 1 independent variable, we call the regression multivariable or multiple regression (or multivariate). We often refer to regression approaches as producing statistical models.

Let us assume we are trying to predict patients' walk test scores using easily measured variables: sex, height, and a measure of lung function—FEV_1. Alternatively, we can think of the investigation as examining a causal hypothesis: To what extent are patients' walk test scores determined by sex, height, and pulmonary function? Either way, the dependent variable here is the walk test and the independent variables are sex, height, and FEV_1.

Figure 13-2, a histogram of the walk test scores of 219 patients with chronic lung disease, demonstrates that walk test scores vary widely among patients. If we had to predict an individual's walk test score without any other information, our best guess would be the mean score of all patients (394 m). For many patients, however, this prediction would be well off the mark.

Figure 13-3 shows the relationship between FEV_1 and the walk test. Note that there is a relationship between the 2 variables, although the relationship is not as strong as the relationship between the walk test and the exercise test

FIGURE 13-2

Distribution of Walk Test Results in the Total Sample of 219 Patients

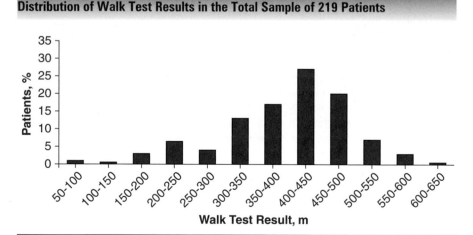

FIGURE 13-3

Relationship Between FEV₁ and Walk Test Results in 219 Patients

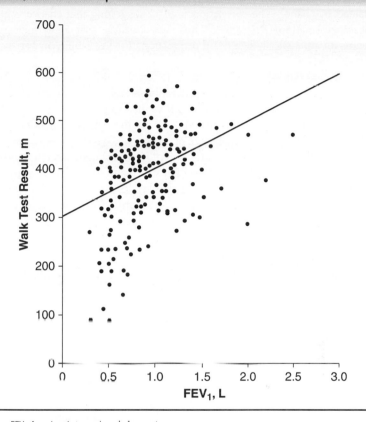

Abbreviation: FEV₁, forced expiratory volume in 1 second.

Adapted from Guyatt et al,[2] by permission of the publisher. Copyright © 1995, Canadian Medical Association.

depicted in Figure 13-1. Thus, some of the differences, or variation, in walk test scores seems to be explained by, or attributable to, the patient's FEV_1. We can construct an equation using FEV_1 to predict walk test scores.

Generally, when we construct regression equations, we refer to the predictor (independent) variable as x and the target (dependent) variable as y. The regression equation assumes a linear fit between the FEV_1 and the walk test data and specifies the point at which the straight line meets the y-axis (the intercept) and the steepness of the line (the slope). In this case, the regression is expressed as follows:

$$y = 298 + 108x$$

where y is the value of the walk test, 298 is the intercept, 108 is the slope of the line, and x is the value of the FEV_1 in liters. In this case, the intercept of 298 has little practical meaning; it predicts the walk test distance of a patient with an FEV_1 of 0. The slope of 108, however, does have some meaning: It predicts that for every increase in FEV_1 of 1 L, the patient will walk 108 m farther. We show the regression line corresponding to this formula in Figure 13-3.

Having constructed the regression equation, we can examine the correlation between the 2 variables, and we can determine whether the correlation can be explained by chance. The correlation is 0.40, suggesting that chance is a very unlikely explanation ($P < .001$). Thus, we conclude that FEV_1 explains or accounts for a statistically significant proportion of the variability, or variance, in walk test scores.

We can also examine the relationship between walk test score and patients' sex (Figure 13-4). Although there is considerable variability within the sexes, men tend to have higher scores than women. If we had to predict a man's score, we would choose the mean score of the men (410 m); to predict a woman's score, we would choose the women's mean score of 363 m.

We can ask the question, Does the apparent relationship between sex and walk test score result from chance? One way of answering this question is to construct another simple regression equation with walk test as the dependent variable and patient's sex as the independent variable. As it turns out, chance is an unlikely explanation of the relationship between sex and the walk test ($P < .001$).

FIGURE 13-4

Distribution of Walk Test Results in Men and in Women (Sample of 219 Patients)

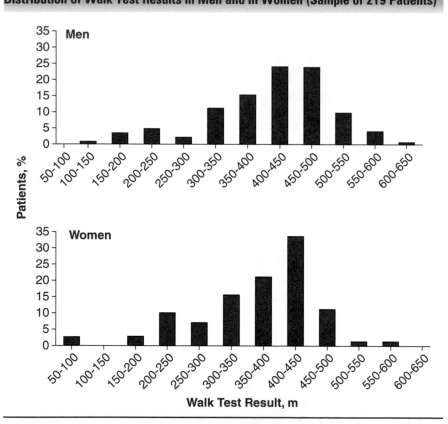

Adapted from Guyatt et al,[2] by permission of the publisher. Copyright © 1995, Canadian Medical Association.

In Figure 13-5, we have separated the men from the women, and for each sex, we have divided them into groups with high and low FEV_1 results. Although there is a range of scores within each of these groups, the range is narrower than among all women or all men and even more so than all patients, and when we use the mean of any group as our best guess of the walk test score of any member of that group, we will, on average, be closer to the true value than if we had used the mean for all patients.

Figure 13-5 illustrates how we can take more than 1 independent variable into account at the same time in explaining or predicting the dependent variable. We can construct a mathematical model that explains or predicts the walk test score by simultaneously considering all of the independent variables, thus creating a multivariable regression equation.

Multivariable regression equations allow us to determine whether each of the variables that were associated with the dependent variable in the univariable equations makes contributions to explaining the variation. Independent variables that are strongly associated with one another (such as age and year of birth) will not make strong separate contributions to predicting the dependent variable. Multivariable regression approaches leave us with models in which each variable makes its own independent contribution to the prediction.[9]

For example, FEV_1 and sex both make independent contributions to explaining walk test results ($P < .001$ for FEV_1 and $P = .03$ for sex in the multiple regression analysis), but height (which was significant at the $P = .02$ level when considered in a univariable regression) does not make a comparable contribution to the explanation.

If we had chosen both the FEV_1 and peak expiratory flow rates as independent variables, they would both show significant associations with walk test score. However, because FEV_1 and peak expiratory flow rates are associated very strongly with one another, they are unlikely to provide independent contributions to explaining the variation in walk test scores. In other words, once we take FEV_1 into account, peak flow rates are not likely to be of any help in predicting walk test scores, and if we first took peak flow rate into account, FEV_1 would not provide further explanatory power to our predictive model. Similarly, height was a significant predictor of walk test score when considered alone but was no longer significant in the multivariable regression because of its correlation with sex and FEV_1.

We have emphasized how the P value associated with a correlation provides little information about the strength of the relation between 2 values; the correlation coefficient itself is required. Similarly, knowing that a number of independent variables in a multivariable model explain some of the variation in the dependent variable tells us little about the power of our predictive model.

Regression equations can tell us much more: the proportion of the variation in the dependent variable that is explained by the model. If a model explains less than 10% of the variability, it is not very useful. If it explains more than 50% of the

FIGURE 13-5

Distribution of Walk Test Results in Men and Women With High and Low FEV₁ (Sample of 219 Patients)

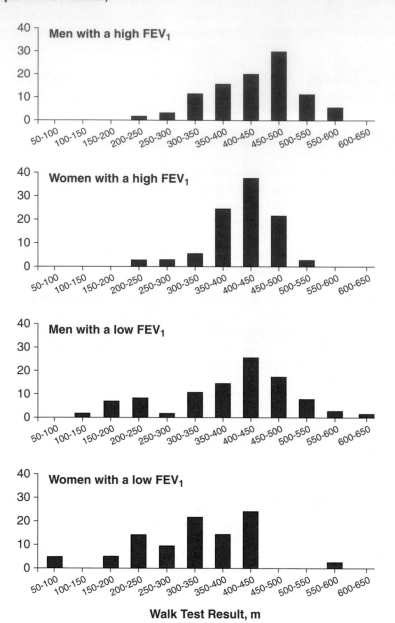

Walk Test Result, m

Abbreviation: FEV₁, forced expiratory volume in 1 second.

Adapted from Guyatt et al,[2] by permission of the publisher. Copyright © 1995, Canadian Medical Association.

variability, it will be extremely useful. Intermediate proportions of variability explained are of intermediate value.

Returning to our example, Figure 13-5 gives us some sense of the model's predictive power. Although the distributions of walk test scores in the 4 subgroups differ appreciably, considerable overlap remains. In this case, FEV_1 explains 15% of the variation when it is the first variable entered into the model, sex explains an additional 2% of the variation, and the total model explains 17% of the variation. We can therefore conclude that there are many other factors that we have not measured—and, perhaps, that we cannot measure—that determine how far people with chronic lung disease can walk in 6 minutes. Other investigations using regression techniques have found that patients' experience of the intensity of their exertion, as well as the perception of the severity of their illness, may be more powerful determinants of walk test distance than is their FEV_1.[10]

Another Example of Regression: Predicting Clinically Important Bleeding (Regression Modeling With Dichotomous Target Variables)

Frequently, we are interested in predicting a patient's status on a dichotomous variable such as death or myocardial infarction in which the outcome is either present or absent. We use the term *logistic regression* to refer to such models.

Some time ago, we addressed the question of whether we could predict which critically ill patients are at risk of clinically important upper gastrointestinal bleeding.[11] The dependent variable was whether patients had a clinically important bleeding episode. The independent variables included whether patients were breathing independently or required mechanical ventilation and the presence of coagulopathy, sepsis, hypotension, hepatic failure, or renal failure.

Table 13-1 shows some of the results from this study, in which we documented the frequency of major bleeding episodes in 2252 critically ill patients. The table shows that in univariable logistic regression equations, many independent variables (respiratory failure, coagulopathy, hypotension, sepsis, hepatic failure, renal failure, enteral feeding, steroid administration, organ transplantation, anticoagulant therapy) were significantly associated with clinically important bleeding. For a number of variables, the odds ratio (see Chapter 6, Therapy), which indicates the strength of the association, is quite large.

When we constructed a multiple logistic regression equation, however, only 2 of the independent variables, mechanical ventilation and coagulopathy, were significantly and independently associated with risk of bleeding. All of the other variables that predicted bleeding in the univariate analysis were correlated either with mechanical ventilation or with coagulopathy and, therefore, did not reach conventional levels of statistical significance in the multiple regression model. Of those who were not requiring mechanical ventilation, 3 (0.2%) of 1597 experienced a bleeding episode; of those who were ventilated, 30 (4.6%) of 655 experienced a bleeding episode. Of those with no coagulopathy, 10 (0.6%) of 1792 bled; of those with coagulopathy, 23 (5.1%) of 455 experienced a bleeding episode.

TABLE 13-1

Odds Ratios and *P* Values According to Simple (Univariable) and Multiple (Multivariable) Logistic Regression Analysis for Risk Factors for Clinically Important Gastrointestinal Bleeding in Critically Ill Patients

Risk Factors	Simple Regression		Multiple Regression	
	OR	*P* Value	OR	*P* Value
Mechanical ventilation	25.5	<.001	15.6	<.001
Coagulopathy	9.5	<.001	4.3	<.001
Hypotension	5.0	.03	2.1	.08
Sepsis	7.3	<.001	NS	
Hepatic failure	6.5	<.001	NS	
Renal failure	4.6	<.001	NS	
Enteral feeding	3.8	<.001	NS	
Steroid administration	3.7	<.001	NS	
Organ transplant	3.6	.006	NS	
Anticoagulant therapy	3.3	.004	NS	

Abbreviations: OR, odds ratio; NS, not significant.

Adapted from Guyatt et al,[2] by permission of the publisher. Copyright © 1995, Canadian Medical Association.

Our primary clinical interest was to identify a subgroup with a sufficiently low bleeding risk that prophylaxis might be withheld. Separate from the regression analysis but suggested by its results, we divided the patients into 2 groups, those who were neither mechanically ventilated nor had a coagulopathy and in whom the incidence of bleeding was only 2 (0.14%) of 1405 and those who were either ventilated or had a coagulopathy and of whom 31 (3.7%) of 847 had a bleeding episode. We concluded that prophylaxis may reasonably be withheld in the former low-risk group.

CONCLUSION

Correlation is a statistical tool that permits researchers to examine the strength of the relationship between 2 variables when neither one is necessarily considered the target variable. Regression, by contrast, examines the strength of relationship between 1 or more predictor variables and a target variable. Regression can be very useful in formulating predictive models to assess risks; for example, the risk of subsequent death in patients presenting with acute coronary syndrome,[12] the risk of cardiac events in patients undergoing noncardiac surgery,[13] or the risk of bleeding in critically ill patients.[11] Such predictive models can help us make better clinical decisions. Such models are also vital for examining causal associations, particularly with rare harmful events, in observational studies when randomization is not possible. Regardless of whether you are considering an issue of correlation or regression, you should note not only whether the relationship between variables is statistically significant but also the magnitude or strength of the relationship in terms of the proportion of variation explained, the extent to which groups with very different risks of the target event can be specified, or the odds ratio associated with a putative harmful *exposure*.

References

1. McGavin CR, Gupta SP, McHardy GJ. Twelve-minute walking test for assessing disability in chronic bronchitis. *BMJ.* 1976;1(6013):822-823.

2. Guyatt G, Walter S, Shannon H, Cook D, Jaeschke R, Heddle N. Basic statistics for clinicians, 4: correlation and regression. *CMAJ* 1995;152(4):497-504.

3. Guyatt GH, Berman LB, Townsend M. Long-term outcome after respiratory rehabilitation. *CMAJ.* 1987;137(12):1089-1095.

4. Guyatt G, Keller J, Singer J, Halcrow S, Newhouse M. Controlled trial of respiratory muscle training in chronic airflow limitation. *Thorax.* 1992;47(8):598-602.

5. Goldstein RS, Gort EH, Stubbing D, Avendano MA, Guyatt GH. Randomised controlled trial of respiratory rehabilitation. *Lancet.* 1994;344(8934);1394-1397.

6. Guyatt G, Jaeschke R, Heddle N, Cook D, Shannon H, Walter S. Basic statistics for clinicians, 2: interpreting study results: confidence intervals. *CMAJ.* 1995;152(2): 169-173.

7. Katz MH. Multivariable analysis: a primer for readers of medical research. *Ann Intern Med.* 2003;138(8):644-650.

8. Godfrey K. Simple linear regression in medical research. *N Engl J Med.* 1985;313(26):1629-1636.

9. Babyak MA. What you see may not be what you get: a brief, nontechnical introduction to overfitting in regression-type models. *Psychosom Med.* 2004; 66(3):411-421.

10. Morgan AD, Peck DF, Buchanan DR, McHardy GJ. Effect of attitudes and beliefs on exercise tolerance in chronic bronchitis. *Br Med J (Clin Res Ed).* 1983;286 (6360):171-173.

11. Cook DJ, Fuller HD, Guyatt GH, et al. Risk factors for gastrointestinal bleeding in critically ill patients: Canadian Critical Care Trials Group. *N Engl J Med.* 1994; 330(6):377-381.

12. Eagle KA, Lim MJ, Dabbous OH, et al. A validated prediction model for all forms of acute coronary syndrome: estimating the risk of 6-month postdischarge death in an international registry. *JAMA.* 2004;291(22):2727-2733.

13. Detsky AS, Abrams HB, McLaughlin JR, et al. Predicting cardiac complications in patients undergoing non-cardiac surgery. *J Gen Intern Med.* 1986;1(4):211-219.

Part D

Diagnosis

14

THE PROCESS OF DIAGNOSIS

W. Scott Richardson and Mark C. Wilson

IN THIS CHAPTER:

CLINICAL SCENARIOS

Consider the following diagnostic situations:

1. A 43-year-old woman presents with a painful cluster of vesicles grouped in the T3 dermatome of her left thorax, which you recognize as shingles from reactivation of herpes zoster.

2. A 78-year-old man returns to the office for follow-up of hypertension. He has lost 10 kg since his last visit 4 months ago. He describes reduced appetite, but otherwise, there are no localizing symptoms. You recall that his wife died a year ago and consider depression as a likely explanation, yet his age and exposure history (ie, smoking) suggest other possibilities.

TWO COMPLEMENTARY APPROACHES TO DIAGNOSIS

The probabilistic approach to clinical diagnosis that uses *evidence* from clinical research—the focus of this chapter—complements the pattern recognition that expert clinicians use as a powerful tool (see Figure 14-1).[1-8] The first case in the opening scenario illustrates how rapidly this recognition can occur.

For more challenging or less familiar circumstances in which pattern recognition fails, clinicians can use a probabilistic mode of diagnostic thinking. Here, they generate a list of potential diagnoses, estimate the probability associated with each, and conduct investigations, the results of which increase or decrease the probabilities, until they believe they have found the answer.[9-14] The second case scenario

FIGURE 14-1

Pattern Recognition vs Probabilistic Diagnostic Reasoning

Pattern recognition	Probabilistic diagnostic reasoning
See it and recognize disorder	Clinical assessment generates pretest probability
↓	↓
Compare posttest probability with thresholds	New information generates posttest probability
(usually pattern recognition implies probability near 100% and so above threshold)	(may be iterative)
	↓
	Compare posttest probability with thresholds

illustrates a situation in which the clinician requires this probabilistic approach for accurate diagnosis.

Applying the probabilistic mode requires knowledge of human anatomy, pathophysiology, and the taxonomy of disease.[11,12,14] Evidence from clinical research represents another form of knowledge required for optimal diagnostic reasoning.[15-17] The remainder of this chapter will describe how evidence from clinical research can facilitate the probabilistic mode of diagnosis.

CLUSTERS OF FINDINGS DEFINE CLINICAL PROBLEMS

Using the probabilistic mode, clinicians begin with the medical interview and physical examination, which they use to identify individual findings as potential clues. For instance, in the second scenario, the clinician noted a 10-kg weight loss in 4 months that is associated with anorexia but without localizing symptoms. Experienced clinicians often group findings into meaningful clusters, summarized in brief phrases about the symptom, body location, or organ system involved, such as "involuntary weight loss with anorexia." These clusters, often termed *clinical problems*, represent the starting point for the probabilistic approach to differential diagnosis.[11,18]

CLINICIANS SELECT A SMALL LIST OF DIAGNOSTIC POSSIBILITIES

When considering a patient's differential diagnosis, clinicians must decide which disorders to pursue. If they considered all known causes to be equally likely and tested for them all simultaneously (the "possibilistic" list), unnecessary testing would result. Instead, experienced clinicians are selective, considering first those disorders that are more likely (a probabilistic list), more serious if left undiagnosed and untreated (a prognostic list), or more responsive to treatment (a pragmatic list). Wisely selecting an individual patient's prioritized differential diagnosis involves all 3 of these considerations (probabilistic, prognostic, and pragmatic).

One might label the single best explanation for the patient's problem as the leading hypothesis or working diagnosis. In the second scenario, the clinician suspected depression as the most likely cause of the patient's anorexia and weight loss. A few (usually 1-5) other diagnoses may be worth considering at the initial evaluation because of their likelihood, seriousness if undiagnosed and untreated, or responsiveness to treatment. In the case of unexplained weight loss, the man's age raises the specter of neoplasm, and in particular, his past smoking suggests the possibility of lung cancer.

Additional causes of the problem may be too unlikely to consider at the initial diagnostic evaluation but could arise subsequently if the initial hypotheses are later disproved. Most clinicians considering the 78-year-old man with weight loss would not select a disease that causes malabsorption as their initial differential diagnosis but might turn to this hypothesis if investigation ultimately excludes depression and cancer.

ESTIMATING THE PRETEST PROBABILITY FACILITATES THE DIAGNOSTIC PROCESS

Having assembled a short list of plausible target disorders to be investigated—the differential diagnosis for this patient—clinicians rank-order these conditions. The probabilistic approach to diagnosis encourages clinicians to estimate the probability of each target condition on the short list, the *pretest probability* (Figure 14-1).[18,19] The sum of the probabilities for all candidate diagnoses should equal 1.

How can the clinician estimate these pretest probabilities? One method is implicit, drawing on memories of previous cases with the same clinical problem(s) and using the frequency of disorders found in those previous patients to guide estimates of pretest probability for the current patient. Often, though, memory is imperfect and we are excessively influenced by particular vivid or recent experiences and by previous inferences, and we put insufficient weight on new evidence. Further, our experience with a given clinical problem may be limited. All these factors leave the probabilities arising from clinicians' intuition subject to *bias* and *random error*.[20-22]

A complementary approach uses evidence from research to guide pretest probability estimates. In one type of relevant research, patients with the same clinical problem undergo thorough diagnostic evaluation, yielding a set of frequencies of the underlying diagnoses made, which clinicians can use to estimate the initial pretest probability (see Chapter 15, Differential Diagnosis). A second category of relevant research generates clinical decision rules or prediction rules. Patients with a defined clinical problem undergo diagnostic evaluation, and investigators use statistical methods to identify clinical and diagnostic test features that segregate patients into subgroups with different probabilities of a target condition (see Chapter 17.4, Clinical Prediction Rules).

NEW INFORMATION GENERATES POSTTEST PROBABILITIES

Clinical diagnosis is a dynamic process. As new information arrives, it may increase or decrease the probability of a target condition or diagnosis. For instance, in the older man with involuntary weight loss, the presence of a recent major life event (his wife's death) raises the likelihood that depression is the cause, whereas the absence of localizing gut symptoms decreases the probability of an intestinal disorder. Likelihood ratios capture the extent to which new pieces of information revise probabilities (see Chapter 16, Diagnostic Tests).

Although intuitive estimates based on experience may, at times, serve clinicians well in interpreting test results, confidence in the extent to which a result increased or decreased probabilities requires systematic research. This research can take several forms, most notably individual *primary studies* of test accuracy (see Chapter 16, Diagnostic Tests) and *systematic reviews* of these test accuracy studies (see Chapter 19, Summarizing the Evidence). Once these research results have been appraised for validity and applicability, the discriminatory power of the findings or test results can be collected into reference resources useful for each clinical discipline (see for example, Chapter 17.2, Examples of Likelihood Ratios).[23,24]

THE RELATION BETWEEN POSTTEST PROBABILITIES AND THRESHOLD PROBABILITIES DETERMINES CLINICAL ACTION

After the test result generates the posttest probability, one can compare this new probability to 2 thresholds (Figure 14-2).[25-27] If the posttest probability is equal to 1, the diagnosis would be absolutely certain. Short of certainty, as the posttest probability approaches 1, the diagnosis becomes more and more likely and reaches a threshold of probability above which the clinician would recommend starting treatment for the disorder (the *treatment threshold*) (Figure 14-2). These thresholds apply to both pattern recognition and probabilistic or *bayesian diagnostic reasoning* (Figure 14-1). For instance, consider the first scenario, the patient who presents with a painful eruption of grouped vesicles in the distribution of a single derma-

FIGURE 14-2

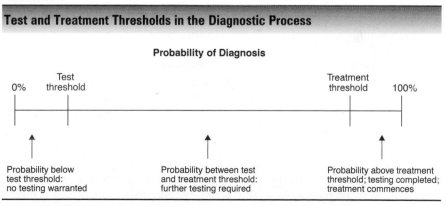

Test and Treatment Thresholds in the Diagnostic Process

Probability of Diagnosis

0% Test threshold Treatment threshold 100%

Probability below test threshold: no testing warranted

Probability between test and treatment threshold: further testing required

Probability above treatment threshold; testing completed; treatment commences

tome. In an instant, an experienced clinician would make a diagnosis of herpes zoster and consider whether to offer the patient therapy. In other words, the probability of herpes zoster is so high (near 1.0, or 100%) that it is above a threshold (the *treatment threshold*) that requires no further testing.

Alternatively, if the posttest probability equaled 0, the diagnosis would be disproved. Short of this certainty, as the posttest probability nears 0, the diagnosis becomes less and less likely, until a probability threshold is reached, below which the clinician would consider the diagnosis excluded (the test threshold).[25] Between the test and treatment thresholds are intermediate probabilities that mandate further testing. For instance, consider a previously healthy athlete who presents with lateral rib cage pain after being accidentally struck by an errant baseball pitch. Again, an experienced clinician would recognize the clinical problem (posttraumatic lateral chest pain), identify a leading hypothesis (rib contusion) and an active alternative (rib fracture), and plan a test (radiograph) to investigate the latter. If asked, the clinician could also list disorders that are too unlikely to consider further (such as myocardial infarction). In other words, although not as likely as rib contusion, the probability of a rib fracture is above a threshold for testing, whereas the probability of myocardial infarction is below the threshold for testing.

What determines these test and treatment thresholds? They are a function of the properties of the test, the disease prognosis, and the nature of the treatment. For the test threshold, the safer and less costly the testing strategy, the more serious the condition if left undiagnosed, and the more effective and safe the available treatment is, the lower we would place the test threshold. On the other hand, the less safe or more costly the test strategy, the less serious the condition if undiagnosed, and the less secure we are about the effectiveness and safety of treatment, the higher we would place the test threshold.

Consider, for instance, ordering troponin for suspected acute coronary syndrome. The condition, if present, can lead to serious consequences (such as fatal arrhythmias), and the test is inexpensive and noninvasive. This is the reason one sees emergency department physicians ordering the test for patients with even a very low probability of acute coronary syndrome; they have set a very low diagnostic threshold.

Contrast this with a pulmonary angiogram for suspected pulmonary embolism. Although the condition is serious, the test is invasive and may be complicated. As a result, if after tests such as Doppler compression ultrasonography and ventilation-perfusion scanning or helical computed tomography they are left with a low probability of pulmonary embolism, clinicians may choose to monitor closely. The test threshold is higher because of the invasiveness and risks of the test.

For the treatment threshold, the safer and the less expensive our next test, the more benign the prognosis of the illness, and the higher the costs or greater the adverse effects of the treatment options, the higher we would place the threshold, requiring greater diagnostic certainty before exposing our patients to treatment. On the other hand, the more invasive and less safe the next test needed, the more ominous the prognosis, and the safer and less costly the proposed treatment, the lower we would place the treatment threshold, as proceeding with treatment may be preferable to increasing diagnostic certainty. For instance, consider patients presenting with suspected malignancy. In general, clinicians are ready to subject such patients to invasive diagnostic tests associated with possible serious complications before treating. The reason is that the treatment—surgery, radiation, or chemotherapy—is itself associated with morbidity or even mortality. Thus, clinicians set the treatment threshold very high.

Contrast this with a patient presenting with symptoms of heartburn and acid reflux. Even if symptoms are atypical, clinicians may be ready to prescribe a proton-pump inhibitor for symptom relief rather than subject the patient to endoscopy. The lower treatment threshold is a function of the relatively benign nature of the treatment in relation to the invasiveness of the next test.

Conclusion

In this chapter, we outlined the probabilistic tradition of diagnostic reasoning and identified how different types of clinical research evidence can inform our diagnostic decisions and actions. The next chapters highlight particular aspects of the diagnostic process.

References

1. Elstein AS, Shulman L, Sprafka S. *Medical Problem Solving: An Analysis of Clinical Reasoning.* Cambridge, MA: Harvard University Press; 1978.

2. Schmidt HG, Norman GR, Boshuizen HP. A cognitive perspective on medical expertise: theory and implication. *Acad Med.* 1990;65(10):611-621.

3. Regehr G, Norman GR. Issues in cognitive psychology: implications for professional education. *Acad Med.* 1996;71(10 suppl):988-1001.

4. Redelmeier DA, Ferris LE, Tu JV, Hux JE, Schull MJ. Problems for clinical judgment: introducing cognitive psychology as one more basic science. *CMAJ.* 2001;164(3):358-360.

5. Eva KW. What every teacher needs to know about clinical reasoning. *Med Educ.* 2004;39(1):98-106.

6. Norman G. Research in clinical reasoning: past history and current trends. *Med Educ.* 2005;39(4):418-427.

7. Norman GR, Brooks LR. The non-analytical basis of clinical reasoning. *Adv Health Sci Educ.* 1997;2(2):173-184.

8. Norman GR. The epistemology of clinical reasoning: perspectives from philosophy, psychology, and neuroscience. *Acad Med.* 2000;75(10 suppl):S127-S135.

9. Barrows HS, Pickell GC. *Developing Clinical Problem Solving Skills: A Guide to More Effective Diagnosis and Treatment.* New York, NY: WW Norton; 1991.

10. Kassirer JP, Kopelman RI. *Learning Clinical Reasoning.* Baltimore, MD: Williams & Wilkins; 1991.

11. Barondess JA, Carpenter CCJ, eds. *Differential Diagnosis.* Philadelphia, PA: Lea & Febiger; 1994.

12. Bordage G. Elaborated knowledge: a key to successful diagnostic thinking. *Acad Med.* 1994;69(11):883-885.

13. Glass RD. *Diagnosis: A Brief Introduction.* Melbourne, Australia: Oxford University Press; 1996.

14. Cox K. *Doctor and Patient: Exploring Clinical Thinking.* Sydney, Australia: UNSW Press; 1999.

15. Kassirer JP. Diagnostic reasoning. *Ann Intern Med.* 1989;110(11):893-900.

16. Richardson WS. Integrating evidence into clinical diagnosis. In: Montori VM, ed. *Evidence-Based Endocrinology.* Totowa, NJ: Humana Press; 2006:69-89.

17. Richardson WS. We should overcome the barriers to evidence-based clinical diagnosis. *J Clin Epidemiol.* 2007;60(3):217-227.

18. Richardson WS, Wilson MC, Guyatt GH, Cook DJ, Nishikawa J; Evidence-Based Medicine Working Group. Users' guides to the medical literature, XV: how to use an article about disease probability for differential diagnosis. *JAMA.* 1999; 281(13):1214-1219.

19. Sox HC Jr, Blatt MA, Higgins MC, Marton KI, eds. *Medical Decision Making.* Boston, MA: Butterworth-Heinemann; 1988.

20. Richardson WS. Where do pretest probabilities come from [editorial, EBM Note]? *Evidence Based Med.* 1999;4:68-69.

21. Richardson WS, Glasziou P, Polashenski WA, Wilson MC. A new arrival—evidence about differential diagnosis [editorial]. *ACP J Club.* 2000;133(3):A11-A12.

22. Richardson WS. Five uneasy pieces about pre-test probability [editorial]. *J Gen Intern Med.* 2002;17(11):882-883.

23. Fletcher RH, Fletcher SW. *Clinical Epidemiology: The Essentials.* 4th ed. Baltimore, MD: Lippincott Williams & Wilkins; 2005.

24. Straus SE, Richardson WS, Glasziou P, Haynes RB, eds. *Evidence-Based Medicine: How to Practice and Teach EBM.* 3rd ed. Edinburgh, Scotland: Churchill-Livingstone; 2005.

25. Pauker SG, Kassirer JP. The threshold approach to clinical decision making. *N Engl J Med.* 1980;302(20):1109-1117.

26. Gross R. *Making Medical Decisions: An Approach to Clinical Decision Making for Practicing Physicians.* Philadelphia, PA: ACP Publications; 1999.

27. Hunink M, Glasziou P, eds. *Decision Making in Health and Medicine: Integrating Evidence and Values.* Cambridge, England: Cambridge University Press; 2001.

DIFFERENTIAL DIAGNOSIS

W. Scott Richardson, Mark C. Wilson,
and Thomas G. McGinn

IN THIS CHAPTER:

FINDING THE EVIDENCE

You begin by framing your knowledge gap as a question: In adults presenting with involuntary weight loss who undergo a diagnostic evaluation, how frequent are the important categories of underlying disease such as neoplasms, gastrointestinal conditions, and psychiatric disorders? As you sit in front of your computer to search for an answer, you notice your nearby files that store your article reprint collection. On a whim, you open the file for involuntary weight loss and find 1 article about the frequency of diseases in patients with involuntary weight loss that was published more than 25 years ago.[1] Hoping to find some newer evidence, you access PubMed and locate this older citation in the database. Clicking the "Related Articles" link yields 102 citations, of which the second new listing by Hernandez et al,[2] published in 2003, looks promising because it also explicitly addresses the frequency of underlying disorders in patients with weight loss.[2] Farther down the list, you find a recent narrative review article on unintentional weight loss,[3] which cites the Hernandez et al[2] article as the most recent study of causes of weight loss. To double check, you scan the chapter on weight loss in an electronic text and find that no newer study is mentioned. With some confidence that you have found the most recent evidence, you retrieve its full text to appraise critically.

Using the Guide

Table 15-1 summarizes the guides for an article about disease probabilities for differential diagnosis.

TABLE 15-1

Users' Guide for Articles About Disease Probability for Differential Diagnosis

Are the results valid?

Did the study patients represent the full spectrum of those with this clinical problem?

Was the diagnostic evaluation definitive?

What are the results?

What were the diagnoses and their probabilities?

How precise are the estimates of disease probability?

How can I apply the results to patient care?

Are the study patients and clinical setting similar to mine?

Is it unlikely that the disease possibilities or probabilities have changed since this evidence was gathered?

ARE THE RESULTS VALID?

Did the Study Patients Represent the Full Spectrum of Those With This Clinical Problem?

The patients in a study are drawn or sampled from an underlying target population of persons who seek care for the clinical problem being investigated. Ideally, this sample mirrors the target population in all important ways, so that the frequency of underlying diseases found in the sample reflects the frequency in the whole population. A patient sample that mirrors the target population well is termed "representative." The more representative the sample, the more accurate the resulting disease probabilities. As shown in Table 15-2, we suggest 4 ways to examine how well the study patients represent the entire target population.

First, find the investigators' definition of the presenting clinical problem because this determines the target population from which the study patients should be drawn. For instance, for a study of chest discomfort, you would want to find whether the investigators' definition included patients with chest discomfort who deny pain (like many patients with angina do), whether "chest" means discomfort only in the anterior thorax (vs also posterior), and whether patients with obvious recent trauma

TABLE 15-2

Ensuring a Representative Patient Sample

Did the investigators define the clinical problem clearly?

Were study patients collected from all relevant clinical settings?

Were study patients recruited consecutively from the clinical settings?

Did the study patients exhibit the full clinical spectrum of this presenting problem?

are excluded. In addition, investigators may specify the level of care or amount of previous evaluation; for example, "fatigue in primary care,"[4] or "referred for persistent unexplained cough."[5] Differing definitions would define differing target populations that would yield differing disease probabilities. A detailed, specific definition of the clinical problem allows you to recognize clearly the target population to which you will compare the patient sample assembled for the study. The less clear the definition is, the less certain you can be of the intended population, and the less confident you can be in judging how well the sample patients represent the whole and in the validity of the resulting disease probabilities.

Second, examine the settings from which patients are recruited. Patients with the same clinical problem could present to any of the different clinical settings, whether primary care offices, emergency departments, or referral clinics. The choice of where to seek care can involve several factors, including the severity of illness, the availability of various settings, the referral habits of one's clinician, or patient preferences. These influences mean that different clinical settings will treat patient groups with different disease frequencies. Typically, patients in secondary or tertiary care settings have higher proportions of more serious or less common diseases than patients treated in primary care settings. For instance, in a study of patients presenting with chest pain, a higher proportion of referral practice patients had coronary artery disease than the primary care practice patients, even among patients with similar clinical histories.[6]

Investigators should avoid restricting recruitment to idiosyncratic settings that are likely to treat an unrepresentative patient sample. For instance, for the "fatigue in primary care" problem, although only primary care settings would be relevant, the investigators would ideally recruit from a broad spectrum of primary care settings (eg, those serving patients of varying socioeconomic status). In general, the fewer the relevant sites used for patient recruitment, the greater the risk that the setting will be idiosyncratic or unrepresentative.

Third, note the investigators' methods for identifying patients at each site and how carefully they avoided missing patients. Ideally, they would recruit a consecutive sample of all patients who seek care at the study sites for the clinical problem during a specified period. If patients are not included consecutively, then unequal inclusion of patients with different underlying disorders may occur, which would reduce the representativeness of the sample and reduce confidence in the validity of the resulting disease probabilities.

Fourth, examine the spectrum of severity and clinical features exhibited by the patients in the study sample. Are mild, moderate, and severely symptomatic patients included? Are all the important variations of this presenting clinical problem found in the sample? For instance, for a study of chest discomfort, you would want to determine whether patients with chest discomfort of any degree of severity were included and whether patients were included whether they did or did not have important associated symptoms such as dyspnea, diaphoresis, or pain radiation. The fuller the clinical spectrum of patients in the sample is, the more representative the sample should be of the target population. Conversely, the narrower the clinical spectrum is, the less representative you would rate the sample and the less confidence you would have in the validity of the resulting disease probabilities.

USING THE GUIDE

Hernandez et al[2] defined the clinical problem for their study as "isolated involuntary weight loss," meaning that a verified, unintentional loss of more than 5% of body weight during 6 months occurred without localizing signs or symptoms and with no diagnosis made on initial testing. From January 1991 through December 1996, there were 1211 patients referred consecutively from a defined geographic area to their general internal medicine outpatient and inpatient settings for involuntary weight loss, of whom 306 met their definition of "isolated." Men and women are included, and ages ranged from 15 to 97 years. The sample patients' races, cultures, and socioeconomic status are not described. Patients were excluded from the sample if they lost less than 5 kg, if they had a previous diagnosis that could explain involuntary weight loss, if the initial evaluation identified the cause (eg, diuretic use in the last 3 months), or if weight loss was intentional. Thus, their study sample represents fairly well the target population of patients who are referred for the evaluation of involuntary weight loss and who are most difficult diagnostically, with only a modest restriction of the clinical spectrum.

Was the Diagnostic Evaluation Definitive?

Articles about disease probability for differential diagnosis will provide valid evidence only if the investigators arrive at correct final diagnoses for the study patients. To judge the accuracy of the final diagnoses, you should examine the diagnostic evaluation used to reach them. The more definitive this diagnostic evaluation is, the more likely it is that the frequencies of the diagnoses made in the sample are accurate estimates of the disease frequencies in the target population. As shown in Table 15-3, we suggest 6 ways to examine how definitive the diagnostic evaluation is.

First, how comprehensive is the investigators' diagnostic evaluation? Ideally, the diagnostic evaluation would be able to detect all possible causes of the clinical problem, if

TABLE 15-3

Ensuring a Definitive Diagnostic Evaluation

Was the diagnostic evaluation sufficiently comprehensive?

Was the diagnostic evaluation consistently applied to all patients?

Were the criteria for all candidate diagnoses explicit and credible?

Were the diagnostic labels assigned reproducibly?

Were there few patients left undiagnosed?

For undiagnosed patients, was follow-up sufficiently long and complete?

any are present. Within reason, the more comprehensive the set of investigations is, the smaller the chance that investigators will reach invalid conclusions about disease frequency. For example, a retrospective study of stroke in 127 patients with mental status changes failed to include a comprehensive search for all causes of delirium, and 118 cases remained unexplained.[7] Because the investigators did not describe a complete and systematic search for causes of delirium, the disease probabilities appear less credible.

Second, examine how consistently the diagnostic evaluation was carried out in the study patients. This does not mean that every patient must undergo every test. Instead, for many clinical problems, the clinician takes a detailed yet focused medical history and performs a problem-oriented physical examination of the involved organ systems, along with a few initial tests. Then, depending on the diagnostic clues from this information, further inquiry proceeds down one of multiple branching pathways. Ideally, investigators would evaluate all patients with the same initial evaluation and then follow the resulting clues using prespecified multiple branching pathways of testing. Once a definitive test result confirms a final diagnosis, further testing is unnecessary.

You may find it relatively easy to decide whether the patients' illnesses have been thoroughly and consistently investigated if they were evaluated prospectively with a predetermined diagnostic approach. When clinicians do not standardize their investigation, this becomes harder to judge. For example, in a study of precipitating factors in 101 patients with decompensated heart failure, although all patients underwent a medical history-taking and physical examination, the lack of standardization of subsequent testing makes it difficult to judge the accuracy of the disease probabilities.[8]

Third, examine the sets of criteria for each disorder used in assigning patients' final diagnoses. Ideally, investigators will develop or adapt a set of explicit criteria for each underlying candidate disorder that could be diagnosed and then apply these criteria consistently when assigning each patient a final diagnosis. When possible, these criteria should include not only the findings needed to confirm each diagnosis but also those findings useful for rejecting each diagnosis. For example, published diagnostic criteria for infective endocarditis include criteria for verifying the infection and criteria for rejecting it.[9,10] Investigators can then classify study patients into diagnostic groups that are mutually exclusive, with the exception of patients whose symptoms stem from more than 1 etiologic factor. Because a complete, explicit, referenced, and credible set of diagnostic criteria can be long, it may appear as an appendix to the printed article, such as in a study of patients with palpitations,[11] or as an electronic appendix for a Web-based publication.

While reviewing the diagnostic criteria, keep in mind that "lesion finding" is not necessarily the same thing as "illness explaining." In other words, when using credible diagnostic criteria, investigators may find that patients have 2 or more disorders that might explain the clinical problem, causing some doubt as to which disorder is the culprit. Better studies of disease probability will include some assurance that the disorders found actually did account for the patients' illnesses.

For example, in a sequence of studies of syncope, investigators required that the symptoms occur simultaneously with an arrhythmia before that arrhythmia was judged to be the cause.[12] In a study of chronic cough, investigators gave cause-specific therapy and used positive responses to this to strengthen the case for these disorders actually causing the chronic cough.[5]

Fourth, consider whether the assignments of the patients' final diagnoses were reproducible. Ensuring reproducibility begins with the use of explicit criteria and a comprehensive and consistent evaluation, as described above. Also, investigators can use a formal test of reproducibility, as was done in a study of causes of dizziness.[13] The greater the investigators' agreement beyond chance on the final diagnoses assigned to their patients, the more confident you can be in the validity of the resulting disease probabilities.

Fifth, look at how many patients remain undiagnosed despite the study evaluation. Ideally, a comprehensive diagnostic evaluation would leave no patient's illness unexplained, yet even the best evaluation may fall short of this goal. The higher the proportion of undiagnosed patients, the greater the chance of error in the estimates of disease probability.

> For example, in a retrospective study of various causes of dizziness in 1194 patients in an otolaryngology clinic, about 27% remained undiagnosed.[14] With more than a quarter of patients' illnesses unexplained, the disease frequencies for the overall sample might be inaccurate.

Sixth, if the study evaluation leaves some patients undiagnosed, look at the length and completeness of their follow-up and whether additional diagnoses are made and the clinical outcomes are known. The longer and more complete the follow-up, the greater our confidence in the benign nature of the conditions in patients who remain undiagnosed yet unharmed at the end of the study. How long is long enough? No single answer would satisfy all clinical problems, but we suggest 1 to 6 months for symptoms that are acute and self-limited and 1 to 5 years for chronically recurring or progressive symptoms.

USING THE GUIDE

Hernandez et al[2] described the consistent use of a standardized initial evaluation of medical history, physical examination, blood tests (blood cell counts, sedimentation rate, blood chemistries, protein electrophoresis, thyroid hormone levels), urine analysis, and radiographs (chest and abdomen), after which further testing was done at the discretion of the attending physician. The set of diagnostic criteria for each disorder is not listed. For the patients' final diagnosis, the investigators required not only finding a disorder recognized in the literature to cause weight loss but also a correlation of weight loss with the clinical outcome of the disorder (recovery or progression). Diagnostic assignments were done independently by 2 investigators, and disagreements (<5%) were resolved by consensus. An underlying disorder explaining involuntary weight loss was diagnosed for 221 (72%) patients, so 85 (28%) were initially undiagnosed. During follow-up and repeated evaluations at 3, 6, and 12 months, 55 of these 85 patients were seen, and diagnoses were made for 41, leaving 14 unexplained diagnoses at 1 year and 30 patients lost to follow-up. Thus, the reported diagnostic evaluation appears fairly credible overall, although some uncertainty exists because of unspecified criteria and the 10% loss to follow-up.

WHAT ARE THE RESULTS?

What Were the Diagnoses and Their Probabilities?

In many studies of disease probability, the authors display the main results in a table listing the diagnoses made, along with the numbers and percentages of patients found with those disorders. For some symptoms, patients may have more than 1 underlying disease coexisting with and presumably contributing to the clinical problem. In these situations, authors often identify the major diagnosis for such patients and separately tabulate contributing causes. Alternatively, authors could identify a separate multiple-etiology group.

USING THE GUIDE

Hernandez et al[2] show in a table the diagnoses made by the end of the study follow-up in 276 (90%) of their 306 patients. For instance, neoplasms were found in 104 (34%) and psychiatric diseases in 63 (21%), whereas no known cause was identified in 14 (5%).

How Precise Are the Estimates of Disease Probability?

Even when valid, these disease frequencies found in the study sample are only estimates of the true disease probabilities in the target population. You can examine the precision of these estimates with the *confidence intervals (CIs)* presented by the authors. If the authors do not provide them for you, you can calculate them yourself with the following formula:

$$95\% \, CI = P \pm 1.96 \times \sqrt{(P(1-P))/N}$$

where P is the proportion of patients with the etiology of interest and N is the number of patients in the sample. This formula becomes inaccurate when the number of cases is 5 or fewer, and approximations are available for this situation. For instance, consider the category of psychiatric causes of involuntary weight loss in the Hernandez et al[2] study. Using the above formula, we would start with $P = 0.23$, $(1 - P) = 0.77$, and N = 276. Working through the arithmetic, we find the CI to be 0.23 ± 0.049. Thus, although the measured proportion is 23%, it may range between 18.1% and 27.9%.

Whether you will deem the CIs sufficiently precise depends on where the estimated proportion and CIs fall in relation to your *test* or *treatment thresholds*. If both the estimated proportion and the entire 95% CI are on the same side of your threshold, then the result is precise enough to permit firm conclusions about disease probability for use in planning tests or treatments. Conversely, if the confidence limit around the estimate crosses your threshold, the result may not be precise enough for definitive conclusions about disease probability. A valid but imprecise probability result might still be used, keeping in mind the uncertainty and what it might mean for testing or treatment.

USING THE GUIDE

Hernandez et al[2] do not provide the 95% CIs for the probabilities they found. As we illustrate, if you were concerned about how close the probabilities were to your thresholds, you could calculate the 95% CIs yourself. In this situation, even the lower boundary of the CI appears high enough for you to pursue an underlying psychiatric disease as the cause of involuntary weight loss.

How Can I Apply the Results to Patient Care?

Are the Study Patients and Clinical Setting Similar to Mine?

Earlier, we urged you to examine how the study patient sample was selected from the target population to judge the sample's representativeness and thus the validity of the results. You should now reexamine the study sample to make a different judgment—its applicability to your patients and your practice. Try asking this question framed both ways (Are the study patients and clinical setting similar enough to mine that I can use the evidence? Or, are the patients and settings so different from mine that I should disregard the results?) and compare your answers. For instance, if patients who present with this problem in your practice come from areas in which one of the underlying disorders is endemic, the probability of that condition would be much higher than its frequency found in a study done in a nonendemic area, limiting the applicability of the study results to your practice.

USING THE GUIDE

For the 76-year-old man referred to you for evaluation of involuntary weight loss, the clinical setting described by Hernandez et al[2] appears to fit fairly well. The partial description of the sample patients sounds similar enough to this man in age and sex, so that although some uncertainty may remain, they are probably not so dissimilar that this evidence cannot be used.

Is It Unlikely That the Disease Possibilities or Probabilities Have Changed Since This Evidence Was Gathered?

As time passes, evidence about disease frequency can become obsolete. Old diseases can be controlled or, as in the case of smallpox, eliminated.[15] New diseases or new epidemics of disease can arise. Such events can so alter the list of possible diseases or their likelihood that previously valid and applicable studies may lose their relevance. For example, consider how dramatically the arrival of human immuno-deficiency virus transformed the possibilities and the probabilities for clinical problems such as generalized lymphadenopathy, chronic diarrhea, and involuntary weight loss.

Similar changes can occur as the result of progress in medical science or public health. For instance, in studies of fever of unknown origin, new diagnostic technologies have substantially altered the proportions of patients who are found to have malignancy or whose fevers remain unexplained.[16-18] Treatment advances that improve survival, such as chemotherapy for childhood leukemia, can bring about shifts in disease likelihood because the treatment might cause complications such as secondary malignancy years after cure of the disease. Public health measures that control diseases such as cholera can alter the likelihood of occurrence of the remaining etiologies of the clinical problems that the prevented disease would have caused; in this example, acute diarrhea.

USING THE GUIDE

The Hernandez et al[2] study was published in 2003, and the study period was 1991 to 1997. In this instance, you know of no new developments likely to change the causes or probabilities of disease in patients with involuntary weight loss since this evidence was gathered.

CLINICAL RESOLUTION

Let us return to the 76-year-old man being evaluated for involuntary weight loss. After an initial evaluation yielded no leads, a detailed interview turns up strong clues to a depressed mood with anorexia and reduced appetite after his wife died a year ago. Your leading hypothesis becomes that major depressive disorder is causing your patient's involuntary weight loss, yet this diagnosis is not sufficiently certain to stop testing to exclude other conditions. From the Hernandez et al[2] study, you decide to include in your active alternatives selected neoplasms (common, serious, and treatable) and hyperthyroidism (less common yet serious and treatable), and you arrange testing to exclude these disorders (ie, these alternatives are above your test threshold). Finally, given that few of the study patients had a malabsorption syndrome, and because your patient has no other features of this disorder besides involuntary weight loss, you place it into your "other hypotheses" category (ie, below your test threshold) and decide to delay testing for this condition. You use the disease frequencies from the study as starting estimates for pretest probability and then raise the probability for depression, given the clues, which lowers the probabilities for the other conditions.

References

1. Marton KI, Sox HC Jr, Krupp JR. Involuntary weight loss: diagnostic and prognostic significance. *Ann Intern Med.* 1981;95(5):568-574.

2. Hernandez JL, Riancho JA, Matorras P, Gonzalez-Macias J. Clinical evaluation for cancer in patients with involuntary weight loss without specific symptoms. *Am J Med.* 2003;114(8):631-637.

3. Alibhai SMH, Greenwood C, Payette H. An approach to the management of unintentional weight loss in elderly people. *CMAJ.* 2005;172(6):773-780.

4. Elnicki DM, Shockcor WT, Brick JE, Beynon D. Evaluating the complaint of fatigue in primary care: diagnoses and outcomes. *Am J Med.* 1992;93(3):303-306.

5. Pratter MR, Bartter T, Akers S, et al. An algorithmic approach to chronic cough. *Ann Intern Med.* 1993;119(10):977-983.

6. Sox HC, Hickam DH, Marton KI, et al. Using the patient's history to estimate the probability of coronary artery disease: a comparison of primary care and referral practices. *Am J Med.* 1990;89(1):7-14.

7. Benbadis SR, Sila CA, Cristea RL. Mental status changes and stroke. *J Gen Intern Med.* 1994;9(9):485-487.

8. Ghali JK, Kadakia S, Cooper R, Ferlinz J. Precipitating factors leading to decompensation of heart failure: traits among urban blacks. *Arch Intern Med.* 1988;148(9):2013-2016.

9. von Reyn CF, Levy BS, Arbeit RD, Friedland G, Crumpacker CS. Infective endocarditis: an analysis based on strict case definitions. *Ann Intern Med.* 1981;94(4 pt 1):505-517.

10. Durack DT, Lukes AS, Bright DK; Duke Endocarditis Service. New criteria for diagnosis of infective endocarditis: utilization of specific echocardiographic findings. *Am J Med.* 1994;96(3):200-209.

11. Weber BE, Kapoor WN. Evaluation and outcomes of patients with palpitations. *Am J Med.* 1996;100(2):138-148.

12. Kapoor WN. Evaluation and outcome of patients with syncope. *Medicine.* 1990;69(3):160-175.

13. Kroenke K, Lucas CA, Rosenberg ML, et al. Causes of persistent dizziness: a prospective study of 100 patients in ambulatory care. *Ann Intern Med.* 1992;117(11):898-904.

14. Katsarkas A. Dizziness in aging—a retrospective study of 1194 cases. *Otolaryngol Head Neck Surg.* 1994;110(3):296-301.

15. Barquet N, Domingo P. Smallpox: the triumph over the most terrible of the ministers of death. *Ann Intern Med.* 1997;127(8 pt 1):635-642.

16. Petersdorf RG, Beeson PB. Fever of unexplained origin: report on 100 cases. *Medicine.* 1961;40:1-30.

17. Larson EB, Featherstone HJ, Petersdorf RG. Fever of undetermined origin: diagnosis and follow up of 105 cases, 1970-1980. *Medicine.* 1982;61(5):269-292.

18. Knockaert DC, Vanneste LJ, Vanneste SB, Bobbaers HJ. Fever of unknown origin in the 1980s: an update of the diagnostic spectrum. *Arch Intern Med.* 1992;152(1):51-55.

16

DIAGNOSTIC TESTS

Toshi A. Furukawa, Sharon Strauss,
Heiner C. Bucher, and Gordon Guyatt

IN THIS CHAPTER:

INTRODUCTION

In the previous 2 chapters (Chapter 14, The Process of Diagnosis, and Chapter 15, Differential Diagnosis), we explained the process of diagnosis, the way diagnostic test results move clinicians across the test threshold and the therapeutic threshold, and how to use studies to help obtain an accurate *pretest probability*. In this chapter, we show you how to use an article addressing the ability of a diagnostic test to move clinicians toward the extremely high (ruling in) and extremely low (ruling out) *posttest probabilities* they seek. Later in this book, we will show you how to use articles that integrate a number of test results into a clinical prediction rule (Chapter 17.4, Clinical Prediction Rules).

CLINICAL SCENARIO

How Can We Identify Dementia Quickly and Accurately?

You are a busy primary care practitioner with a large proportion of elderly patients in your practice. Earlier in the day, you treated a 70-year-old woman who lives alone and has been managing well. On this visit, she complained about a longstanding problem, joint pain in her lower extremities. During the visit, you have the impression that, as you put it to yourself, "she isn't quite all there," although you find it hard to specify further. On specific questioning about memory and function, she acknowledges that her memory is not what it used to be but otherwise denies problems. Pressed for time, you deal with the osteoarthritis and move on to the next patient.

That evening, you ponder the problem of making a quick assessment of your elderly patients when the possibility of cognitive impairment occurs to you. The Mini-Mental Status Examination (MMSE), with which you are familiar, takes too long. You wonder whether there are any brief instruments that allow a reasonably accurate rapid diagnosis of cognitive impairment to help you identify patients who need more extensive investigation.

FINDING THE EVIDENCE

You formulate the clinical question: In older patients with suspected cognitive impairment, what is the accuracy of a brief screening tool for diagnosing dementia (or for identifying those who need more extensive investigation)? You select "diagnosis" and "narrow, specific search" from the PubMed Clinical Queries page. Using search terms "dementia AND screen* AND brief," the search yields 48 citations. Limiting to English-language studies of humans in the last 5 years cuts the list to 21.

You survey the abstracts, looking for articles that focus on patients with suspected dementia and report accuracy similar to your previous standard, the MMSE. An article reporting results for an instrument named Six-Item Screener (SIS) meets both criteria.[1] You retrieve the full-text article electronically and start to read it, hoping its methods and results will justify using the instrument in your office.

ARE THE RESULTS VALID?

Table 16-1 summarizes our Users' Guides for assessing the validity, examining the results, and determining the applicability of a study reporting on the accuracy of a diagnostic test.

Did Participating Patients Present a Diagnostic Dilemma?

A diagnostic test is useful only if it distinguishes between conditions and disorders that might otherwise be confusing. Although most tests can differentiate healthy persons from severely affected ones, this ability will not help us in clinical practice. Studies that confine themselves to florid cases vs asymptomatic healthy volunteers are unhelpful because, when the diagnosis is obvious, we do not need a diagnostic test. Only a study that closely resembles clinical practice and includes patients with mild, early manifestations of the target condition can establish a test's true value.

TABLE 16-1

Users' Guide for an Article About Interpreting Diagnostic Test Results

Are the results valid?

- Did participating patients present a diagnostic dilemma?
- Did investigators compare the test to an appropriate, independent reference standard?
- Were those interpreting the test and reference standard blind to the other results?
- Did investigators perform the same reference standard to all patients regardless of the results of the test under investigation?

What are the results?

- What likelihood ratios were associated with the range of possible test results?

How can I apply the results to patient care?

- Will the reproducibility of the test result and its interpretation be satisfactory in my clinical setting?
- Are the study results applicable to the patients in my practice?
- Will the test results change my management strategy?
- Will patients be better off as a result of the test?

The story of carcinoembryonic antigen (CEA) testing in patients with colorectal cancer shows how choosing the wrong spectrum of patients can dash the hopes raised with the introduction of a diagnostic test. A study found that CEA was elevated in 35 of 36 people with known advanced cancer of the colon or rectum. The investigators found much lower levels in normal people, pregnant women, or in patients with a variety of other conditions.[2] The results suggested that CEA might be useful in diagnosing colorectal cancer or even in screening for the disease. In subsequent studies of patients with less advanced stages of colorectal cancer (and therefore lower disease severity) and patients with other cancers or other gastrointestinal disorders (and therefore different but potentially confused disorders), the accuracy of CEA testing as a diagnostic tool plummeted. Clinicians appropriately abandoned CEA measurement for new cancer diagnosis and screening.

There have been 3 systematic, empirical examinations of design-related *bias* in studies of diagnostic tests. Lijmer et al[3] and Rutjes et al[4] collected meta-analyses of diagnostic tests and examined what aspects of study design influenced the apparent diagnostic power of the tests. Whiting et al[5] systematically collected and reviewed *primary studies* that investigated the effects of bias on estimates of diagnostic test performances.

All 3 studies documented substantial bias associated with unrepresentative patient selection. Enrolling target-positive (those with the underlying condition of interest—in our scenario, people with dementia) and target-negative patients (those without the target condition) from separate populations results in overestimates of the test's power (*relative diagnostic odds ratio* [RDOR], 3.0; 95% confidence interval [CI], 2.0-4.5; and RDOR, 4.9; 95% CI, 0.6-37.3).[3,4] Even if investigators enroll target-positive and target-negative patients from the same population, nonconsecutive patient sampling and retrospective data collection may inflate estimates of diagnostic test performances (RDOR, 1.5; 95% CI, 1.0-2.1; and RDOR, 1.6; 95% CI, 1.1-2.2, respectively).[2,3] We label studies with unrepresentative patient selection as having spectrum bias (see Chapter 17.1, Spectrum Bias). Table 16-2 summarizes the empirically supported sources of bias in studies of diagnostic tests.

Did the Investigators Compare the Test to an Appropriate, Independent Reference Standard?

The accuracy of a diagnostic test is best determined by comparing it to the "truth." Readers must assure themselves that investigators have applied an appropriate *reference, criterion,* or *gold standard* (such as biopsy, surgery, autopsy, or long-term follow-up without treatment) to every patient who undergoes the test under investigation.

One way a study can go wrong is if the test that is being evaluated is part of the reference standard. The incorporation of the test into the reference standard is likely to inflate the estimate of the test's diagnostic power. Thus, clinicians should insist on the independence as one criterion for a satisfactory reference standard.

TABLE 16-2

Empirical Evidence of Sources of Bias in Diagnostic Accuracy Studies[a]

	Lijmer et al[3] (RDOR; 95% CI)	Whiting et al[5]	Rutjes et al[4] (RDOR; 95% CI)
Did participating patients present a diagnostic dilemma?	Case-control design (3.0; 2.0-4.5)	Distorted selection of participants (some empirical support)	Case-control design (4.9; 0.6-37.3)
	Nonconsecutive patient selection (0.9; 0.7-1.1)		Nonconsecutive sampling (1.5; 1.0-2.1)
	Retrospective data collection (1.0; 0.7-1.4)		Retrospective data collection (1.6; 1.1-2.2)
Did investigators compare the test to an appropriate, independent reference standard?		Inappropriate reference standard (some empirical support)	
		Incorporation bias (using test as part of reference standard) (no empirical support)	Incorporation (1.4; 0.7-2.8)
Were those interpreting the test and reference standard blind to the other result?	Not blinded (1.3; 1.0-1.9)	Review bias (some empirical support)	Single or non-blinded reading (1.1; 0.8-1.6)
Did investigators perform the same reference standard to all patients regardless of the results of the test under investigation?	Different reference tests (2.2; 1.5-3.3)	Differential verification bias (some empirical support)	Differential verification (1.6; 0.9-2.9)
	Partial verification (1.0; 0.8-1.3)	Partial verification bias (strong empirical support)	Partial verification (1.1; 0.7-1.7)

Abbreviations: CI, confidence interval; RDOR, relative diagnostic odds ratio.

[a]RDOR, point estimates, and 95% CIs are shown.

For instance, consider a study that evaluated the utility of abdominojugular reflux for the diagnosis of congestive heart failure. This study used, however, clinical and radiographic criteria, including abdominojugular reflex, as the reference test.[6] Another example comes from a study evaluating screening instruments for depression in terminally ill people. The authors claimed perfect performance (sensitivity = 1.0, specificity = 1.0) for a single question (Are you depressed?) to detect depression. Their diagnostic criteria included 9 questions, of which 1 was "Are you depressed?"[7]

In reading articles about diagnostic tests, if you cannot accept the reference standard (within reason, that is; after all, nothing is perfect), then the article is unlikely to provide valid results (Table 16-2).[4]

Were Those Interpreting the Test and Reference Standard Blind to the Other Results?

If you accept the reference standard, the next question is whether the interpreters of the test and reference standard were aware of the results of the other investigation (blind assessment).

Consider how, once clinicians see a pulmonary nodule on a computed tomographic (CT) scan, they can see the previously undetected lesion on the chest radiograph, or, once they learn the results of an echocardiogram, they hear a previously inaudible cardiac murmur.

The more likely that knowledge of the reference standard result can influence the interpretation of a test, the greater the importance of the blinded interpretation. Similarly, the more susceptible the reference standard is to changes in interpretation as a result of knowledge of the test being evaluated, the more important the blinding of the reference standard interpreter. The empirical study by Lijmer et al[3] demonstrated bias associated with unblinding, although the magnitude was small (RDOR, 1.3; 95% CI, 1.0-1.9), whereas Rutjes et al[4] found a compatible although statistically nonsignificant RDOR (RDOR, 1.1; 95% CI, 0.8-1.6) (Table 16-2).

Did Investigators Perform the Same Reference Standard to All Patients Regardless of the Results of the Test Under Investigation?

The properties of a diagnostic test will be distorted if its results influence whether patients undergo confirmation by the reference standard (verification[8,9] or work-up[10,11] bias). This can occur in 2 ways. First, only a selected sample of patients who underwent the index test may be verified by the reference standard. For example, patients with suspected coronary artery disease whose exercise test results are positive may be more likely to undergo coronary angiography (the reference standard) than those whose exercise test results are negative. Whiting et al[5] reviewed several documented instances of this type of verification bias, known as partial verification bias.

Second, results of the index test may be verified by different reference standards. Lijmer et al[3] and Rutjes et al[4] found a large magnitude of bias associated with the use of different reference tests for positive and negative results. The RDOR for this type of bias, also known as differential verification bias, was 2.2; 95% CI, 1.5-3.3[3] and 1.6; 95% CI, 0.9-2.9,[4] respectively, in these 2 *systematic reviews* (Table 16-2).

Verification bias proved a problem for the Prospective Investigation of Pulmonary Embolism Diagnosis (PIOPED) study that evaluated the utility of ventilation perfusion scanning in the diagnosis of pulmonary embolism. Patients whose ventilation perfusion scan results were interpreted as "normal/near normal" and "low probability" were less likely to undergo pulmonary angiography (69%) than those with more positive ventilation perfusion scan results (92%), which is not surprising because clinicians might be reluctant to subject patients with a low probability of pulmonary embolism to the risks of angiography.[12]

Most articles would stop here, and readers would have to conclude that the magnitude of the bias resulting from different proportions of patients with high- and low-probability ventilation perfusion scans undergoing adequate angiography is uncertain but perhaps large. The PIOPED investigators, however, applied a second reference standard to the 150 patients with low-probability or normal/near-normal scan results who failed to undergo angiography (136 patients) or for whom angiogram interpretation was uncertain (14 patients). They judged such patients to be free of pulmonary embolism if they did well without treatment. Accordingly, they followed all such patients for 1 year without treating them with anticoagulant drugs. No patient developed clinically evident pulmonary embolism during follow-up, allowing us to conclude that patient-important pulmonary embolism (if we define patient-important pulmonary embolism as requiring anticoagulation therapy to prevent subsequent adverse events) was not present when they underwent ventilation perfusion scanning. Thus, the PIOPED study achieved the goal of applying a reference standard assessment to all patients but failed to apply the same standard to all.

USING THE GUIDE

The study of a brief diagnostic test for cognitive impairment included 2 cohorts. One was a stratified random sample of community-dwelling black persons aged 65 years and older; the other was a consecutive sample of nonselected nonscreened patients referred by family, caregivers, or providers for cognitive evaluation at the Alzheimer Disease Center. In the former group, the authors included all patients with a high suspicion of dementia on a detailed screening test and a random sample of those with moderate and low suspicion. The investigators faced diagnostic uncertainty in both populations. The populations are not perfect: the former included individuals without any suspicion of dementia, and the latter had already passed an initial screen at the primary care level (indeed, whether to refer for full geriatric assessment is one of the questions you are trying to resolve for the patient who triggered your literature search). Fortunately, test properties proved similar in the 2 populations, considerably lessening your concern.

All patients received the SIS, which asks the patient to remember 3 words (apple, table, penny); then to say the day of the week, month, and year; and finally to recall the 3 words without prompts. The number of errors provides a result with a range of 0 to 6.

For the reference standard diagnosis of dementia, patients had to satisfy both *Diagnostic and Statistical Manual of Mental Disorders* (Third Edition Revised) (*DSM-III-R*) and the *International Classification of Diseases, Tenth Revision* (*ICD-10*) criteria, according to an assessment by a geriatric psychiatrist or a neurologist that included medical history and physical and neurologic examination; a complete neuropsychological test battery, including MMSE and 5 other tests; and interview with a relative of the participant.

Although you are satisfied with this reference standard, the published article leaves you unsure whether those making the SIS and the reference diagnosis were blind to the other results. To resolve the question, you e-mail the first author and ask for clarification. A couple of e-mails later, you have learned that "research assistants who had been trained and tested" administered the neuropsychological battery. On the other hand, "a consensus team composed of a geriatric psychiatrist, social psychologist, a geriatrician, and a neuropsychologist" made the reference standard diagnoses. The author reports that "there were open discussions of the case, and they had access to the entire medical record, including results of neuropsychological testing, at their disposal." The 6 items included in the SIS are derived from the MMSE but "were not pulled out as a separate instrument in the consensus team conference."

Thus, although there was no blinding, you suspect that this did not create important bias and are therefore ready to consider its results.

WHAT ARE THE RESULTS?

What Likelihood Ratios Were Associated With the Range of Possible Test Results?

In deciding how to interpret diagnostic tests results, we will consider its ability to change our estimate of the likelihood the patient has the target condition (we call this the pretest probability) to a more accurate estimate (we call this the posttest probability of the target disorder). The *likelihood ratio* (*LR*) for a particular test result moves us from the pretest probability to a posttest probability.

Put yourself in the place of the primary care physician in the scenario and consider 2 patients with suspected cognitive impairment with clear consciousness. The first is the 70-year-old woman in the clinical scenario who seems to be managing rather well but has a specific complaint that her memory is not what it used to be. The other is an 85-year-old woman, another longstanding patient, who arrives accompanied, for the first time, by her son. The concerned son tells you that she has, on one of her usual morning walks, lost her way. A neighbor happened to catch her a few miles away from home and notified him of the incident. On visiting his mother's house, he was surprised to find her room in a mess. Yet in your office, she greets you politely and protests that she was just having a bad day and does not think the incident warrants any fuss (at which point the son looks to the ceiling in frustrated disbelief). Your clinical hunches about the probability of dementia for these 2 people—that is, their pretest probabilities—are different. For the first woman, the probability is relatively low, perhaps 20%; for the second, it is relatively high, perhaps 70%.

The results of a formal screening test, the SIS in our example, will not tell us definitively whether dementia is present; rather, the results modify the pretest probability of that condition, yielding a new posttest probability. The direction and magnitude of this change from pretest to posttest probability are determined by the test's properties, and the property of most value is the LR.

We will use the results of the study by Callahan et al[1] to illustrate LRs. Table 16-3 presents the distribution of SIS scores in cohort of patients in the study by Callahan et al.[1]

How likely is a test result of 6 among people who do have dementia? Table 16-3 shows that 105 of 345 (or 30.4%) people with the condition made 6 errors. We can also see that of 306 people without dementia, 2 (or 0.65%) made 6 errors. How likely is this test result (ie, making 6 errors) in someone with dementia as opposed to someone without? Determining this requires us to look at the ratio of the 2 likelihoods that we have just calculated (30.4/0.65) and equals 47. In other words, the test result of 6 is 47 times as likely to occur in a patient with, as opposed to without, dementia.

In a similar fashion, we can calculate the LR associated with a test result of each score. For example, the LR for the test score of 5 is (64/345)/(2/306) − 28. Table 16-3 provides the LR for each possible SIS score.

How can we interpret LRs? LRs indicate the extent to which a given diagnostic test result will increase or decrease the pretest probability of the target disorder. An LR of

TABLE 16-3

Six-Item Screener Scores in Patients With and Without Dementia, and Corresponding Likelihood Ratios

	Dementia (+)	Dementia (−)	Likelihood Ratio
SIS = 6	105	2	47
SIS = 5	64	2	28
SIS = 4	64	8	7.1
SIS = 3	45	16	2.5
SIS = 2	31	35	0.79
SIS = 1	25	80	0.28
SIS = 0	11	163	0.06
Sum	345	306	

Abbreviation: SIS, Six-Item Screener.

Data from Callahan et al.[1]

1 tells us that the posttest probability is exactly the same as the pretest probability. LRs greater than 1.0 increase the probability that the target disorder is present; the higher the LR, the greater this increase. Conversely, LRs less than 1.0 decrease the probability of the target disorder, and the smaller the LR, the greater the decrease in probability.

How big is a "big" LR, and how small is a "small" one? Using LRs in your day-to-day practice will lead to your own sense of their interpretation, but consider the following a rough guide:

- LRs of greater than 10 or less than 0.1 generate large and often conclusive changes from pretest to posttest probability;

- LRs of 5 to 10 and 0.1 to 0.2 generate moderate shifts in pretest to posttest probability;

- LRs of 2 to 5 and 0.5 to 0.2 generate small (but sometimes important) changes in probability; and

- LRs of 1 to 2 and 0.5 to 1 alter probability to a small (and rarely important) degree.

Having determined the magnitude and significance of LRs, how do we use them to go from pretest to posttest probability? One way is to convert pretest probability to odds, multiply the result by the LR, and convert the consequent posttest odds into a posttest probability. A much easier strategy uses a nomogram proposed by Fagan[13] (Figure 16-1) that does all the conversions and allows an easy transition from pretest to posttest probability.

The left-hand column of this nomogram represents the pretest probability, the middle column represents the LR, and the right-hand column shows the posttest probability. You obtain the posttest probability by anchoring a ruler at the pretest probability and rotating it until it lines up with the LR for the observed test result. There is also a Web-based interactive program (http://www.JAMAevidence.com) that will do this for you. You can enter exact numbers for a pretest probability and an LR to obtain the exact posttest probability.

Recall the elderly woman from the opening scenario, who has suspected dementia. We have decided that the probability of this patient's having the condition is about 20%. Let us suppose that the patient made 5 errors on the SIS. Anchoring a ruler at her pretest probability of 20% and aligning it with the LR of 28 associated with the test result of 5, you can obtain her posttest probability, around 90%.

The pretest probability is an estimate. Although the literature dealing with differential diagnosis can sometimes help us in establishing the pretest probability (see Chapter 15, Differential Diagnosis), we know of no such study that will complement our intuition in arriving at a pretest probability when the suspicion of dementia arises. Although our intuition makes precise estimates of pretest probability difficult, we can deal with residual uncertainty by examining the implications of a plausible range of pretest probabilities.

For example, if the pretest probability in this case is as low as 10% or as high as 30%, using the nomogram, we will obtain the posttest probability of about 80% and above 90%. Table 16-4 tabulates the posttest probabilities corresponding with each possible SIS score for the 70-year-old woman in the clinical scenario.

FIGURE 16-1

Likelihood Ratio Nomogram

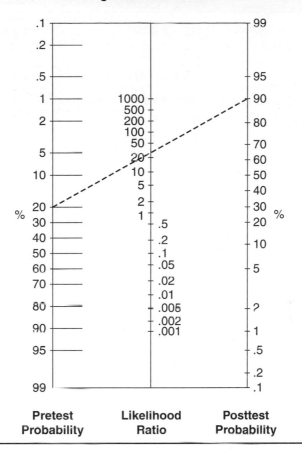

Interpreting
Diagnostic Test Results

Pretest Probability | Likelihood Ratio | Posttest Probability

We can repeat this exercise for our second patient, the 85-year-old woman who had lost her way. You estimate that her medical history and presentation are compatible with a 70% probability of dementia. With our nomogram (Figure 16-1), the posttest probability with an SIS score of 6 or 5 is almost 100%; with an SIS score of 4, it is 94%; with an SIS score of 3, it is 85% and so on. The pretest probability (with a range of possible pretest probabilities from 60% to 80%), LRs, and posttest probabilities associated with each of these possible SIS scores are presented in Table 16-5.

Having learned to use LRs, you may be curious about where to find easy access to the LRs of the tests you use regularly in your own practice. The

TABLE 16-4

Pretest Probabilities, Likelihood Ratios of the Six-Item Screener, and Posttest Probabilities in the 70-Year-Old Woman With Moderate Suspicion of Dementia

Pretest Probability, % (Range)[a]	SIS Result (LR)	Posttest Probability, % (Range)[a]
20 (10-30)	SIS = 6 (47)	92 (84-95)
	SIS = 5 (28)	88 (76-92)
	SIS = 4 (7.1)	64 (44-75)
	SIS = 3 (2.5)	38 (22-52)
	SIS = 2 (0.79)	16 (8-25)
	SIS = 1 (0.28)	7 (3-11)
	SIS = 0 (0.06)	1 (1-3)

Abbreviations: LR, likelihood ratio; SIS, Six-Item Screener.

[a]The values in parentheses represent a plausible range of *pretest probabilities*; that is, although the best guess as to the pretest probability is 20%, values of 10% to 30% would also be reasonable estimates.

Rational Clinical Examination[14] is a series of *systematic reviews* of the diagnostic properties of the medical history and physical examination that have been published in *JAMA*. Chapter 17.2, Examples of Likelihood Ratios, lists some examples of LRs. Further examples are accumulated on the *Users' Guides* Web site (http://www.JAMAevidence.com).

TABLE 16-5

Pretest Probabilities, Likelihood Ratios[a] of the Six-Item Screener, and Posttest Probabilities in the 85-Year-Old Woman With High Suspicion of Dementia

Pretest Probability, % (Range)[a]	SIS Result (LR)	Posttest Probability % (Range)[a]
70 (60-80)	SIS = 6 (47)	99 (99-99)
	SIS = 5 (28)	98 (98-99)
	SIS = 4 (7.1)	94 (91-97)
	SIS = 3 (2.5)	85 (79-76)
	SIS = 2 (0.79)	65 (54-76)
	SIS = 1 (0.28)	40 (30-53)
	SIS = 0 (0.06)	12 (8-19)

Abbreviations: LR, likelihood ratio; SIS, Six-Item Screener.

[a]The values in parentheses represent a plausible range of *pretest probabilities*. That is, although the best guess as to the pretest probability is 70%, values of 60% to 80% would also be reasonable estimates.

Dichotomizing Continuous Test Scores, Sensitivity and Specificity, and LR+ and LR−

Readers who have followed the discussion to this point will understand the essentials of interpretation of diagnostic tests. In part because they remain in wide use, it is also helpful to understand 2 other terms in the lexicon of diagnostic testing: *sensitivity* and *specificity*. Many articles on diagnostic tests report a 2 × 2 table and its associated sensitivity and specificity, as in Table 16-6, and to go along with it a figure that depicts the overall power of the diagnostic test (called a *receiver operating characteristic [ROC] curve*).

The study by Callahan et al[1] recommends a cutoff of 3 or more errors for the diagnosis of dementia. Table 16-7 provides the breakdown of the cohort of referred patients according to this cutoff.

When we set the cutoff of 3 or more, SIS has a sensitivity of 0.81 (278/345) and a specificity of 0.91 (278/306). We can also calculate the LRs, exactly as we did in Table 16-3. The LR for SIS greater than or equal to 3 is therefore (278/345)/(28/306) = 8.8, and the LR for SIS less than 3 is (67/345)/(278/306) = 0.21. LR for a positive test result is often denoted as LR+, and that for a negative test result is denoted as LR−.

Let us now try to resolve our clinical scenario using this dichotomized 2 × 2 table. We had supposed that the pretest probability for the woman in the opening scenario was 20%, and she had made 5 errors. Because the SIS score of 5 is associated here with an LR+ of 8.8, using Fagan's nomogram,[13] we arrive at the posttest probability of around 70%, a figure considerably lower than the 90% that we had arrived at when we had a specific LR for 5 errors. This is because the

TABLE 16-6

Comparison of the Results of a Diagnostic Test With the Results of Reference Standard Using a 2 × 2 Table

Test Results	Reference Standard	
	Disease Present	**Disease Absent**
Test positive	TP	FP
Test negative	FN	TN
Sensitivity (Sens) = $\dfrac{TP}{TP+FN}$		
Specificity (Spec) = $\dfrac{TN}{FP+TN}$		
Likelihood ratio for positive test (LR+) =	$\dfrac{Sens}{1-Spec}=\dfrac{True\ positive\ rate}{False\ positive\ rate}=\dfrac{TP/(TP+FN)}{FP/(FP+TN)}$	
Likelihood ratio for negative test (LR−) =	$\dfrac{1-Sens}{Spec}=\dfrac{False\ negative\ rate}{True\ negative\ rate}=\dfrac{FN/(TP+FN)}{TN/(FP+TN)}$	

Abbreviations: FN, false negative; FP, false positive; TN, true negative; TP, true positive.

Sensitivity is the proportion of people with a positive test result among those with the target condition. Specificity is the proportion of people with a negative test result among those without the target condition.

TABLE 16-7

Comparison of the Results of a Diagnostic Test (Six-Item Screener) With the Results of Reference Standard (Consensus *DSM-IV* and *ICD-10* Diagnosis) Using the Recommended Cutoff

	Dementia (+)	Dementia (−)
SIS ≥ 3	278	28
SIS < 3	67	278
Sum	345	306

Abbreviations: *DSM-IV, Diagnostic and Statistical Manual of Mental Disorders*, (Fourth Edition); *ICD-10, International Classification of Diseases, Tenth Revision*; SIS, Six-Item Screener.

dichotomized LR+ for SIS scores of 3 or more pooled strata for SIS scores of 3, 4, 5, and 6, and the resultant LR is thus diluted by the adjacent strata.

Although the difference between 70% and 90% may not dictate change in management strategies for the case in the clinical scenario, this will not always be the case. Consider a third patient, an elderly man with a pretest probability of 50% of dementia who has surprised us by making not a single error on the SIS. With the dichotomous LR+/LR− approach (or, for that matter, with the sensitivity/specificity approach, because these are mathematically equivalent and interchangeable), you combine the pretest probability of 50% with the LR− of 0.21 and arrive at the posttest probability of about 20%, likely necessitating further neuropsychological and other examinations. The true posttest probability for this man when we apply the LR associated with a score of 0 from Table 16-3 (0.06) is only about 5%. With this posttest probability, you (and the patient and his family) can feel relieved and be spared of further testing and further distress.

In summary, using multiple cuts or thresholds (sometimes referred to as multilevel LRs or stratum-specific LRs) has 2 key advantages over the sensitivity/specificity approach. First, for a test that produces continuous scores or a number of categories (which many tests in medicine do), using multiple thresholds retains as much information as possible. Second, knowing the LR of a particular test result, you can use a simple nomogram to move from the pretest to the posttest probability that is linked to your patient.

USING THE GUIDE

Thus far, we have established that the results are likely true for the people who were included in the study, and we have calculated the multilevel LRs associated with each possible score of the test. We have shown how the results could be applied to our patient (though we do not yet know the patient's score and have not decided how to proceed when we do).

HOW CAN I APPLY THE RESULTS TO PATIENT CARE?

Will the Reproducibility of the Test Result and Its Interpretation Be Satisfactory in My Clinical Setting?

The value of any test depends on its ability to yield the same result when reapplied to stable patients. Poor reproducibility can result from problems with the test itself (eg, variations in reagents in radioimmunoassay kits for determining hormone levels) or from its interpretation (eg, the extent of ST-segment elevation on an electrocardiogram). You can easily confirm this when you recall the clinical disagreements that arise when you and 1 or more colleagues examine the same electrocardiogram, ultrasonograph, or CT scan (even when all of you are experts).

Ideally, an article about a diagnostic test will address the reproducibility of the test results using a measure that corrects for agreement by chance (see Chapter 17.3, Measuring Agreement Beyond Chance), especially for issues of interpretation.

If the reported reproducibility of a test in the study setting is mediocre and disagreement between observers is common, and yet the test still discriminates well between those with and without the target condition, the test is likely to be useful. Under these circumstances, the likelihood is good that the test can be readily applied to your clinical setting.

If, on the other hand, reproducibility of a diagnostic test is high, either the test is simple and unambiguous or those interpreting it are highly skilled. If the latter applies, less skilled interpreters in your own clinical setting may not do as well. You will either need to obtain appropriate training (or ensure that those interpreting the test in your setting have that training) or look for an easier and more robust test.

Are the Study Results Applicable to the Patients in My Practice?

Test properties may change with a different mix of disease severity or with a different distribution of competing conditions. When patients with the target disorder all have severe disease, LRs will move away from a value of 1.0 (ie, sensitivity increases). If patients are all mildly affected, LRs move toward a value of 1.0 (ie, sensitivity decreases). If patients without the target disorder have competing conditions that mimic the test results observed for patients who do have the target disorder, the LRs will move closer to 1.0 and the test will appear less useful (ie, specificity decreases). In a different clinical setting in which fewer of the disease-free patients have these competing conditions, the LRs will move away from 1.0 and the test will appear more useful (ie, specificity increases).

Investigators have demonstrated the phenomenon of differing test properties in different subpopulations for exercise electrocardiography in the diagnosis of coronary artery disease. The more extensive the severity of coronary artery disease, the larger the LRs of abnormal exercise electrocardiography for angiographic narrowing of the coronary arteries.[15] Another example comes from the diagnosis of venous thromboembolism, in which compression ultrasonography for proximal-vein thrombosis has proved more accurate in symptomatic outpatients than in asymptomatic postoperative patients.[16]

Sometimes, a test fails in just the patients one hopes it will best serve. The LR of a negative dipstick test result for the rapid diagnosis of urinary tract infection is approximately 0.2 in patients with clear symptoms and thus a high probability of urinary tract infection but is more than 0.5 in those with low probability,[17] rendering it of little help in ruling out infection in the latter situation.

If you practice in a setting similar to that of the study, and if the patient under consideration meets all the study eligibility criteria, you can be confident that the results are applicable. If not, you must make a judgment. As with therapeutic interventions, you should ask whether there are compelling reasons why the results should not be applied to the patients in your practice, either because of the severity of disease in those patients or because the mix of competing conditions is so different that generalization is unwarranted. You may resolve the issue of generalizability if you can find an overview that summarizes the results of a number of studies.[18]

Will the Test Results Change My Management Strategy?

It is useful, when making and communicating management decisions, to link them explicitly to the probability of the target disorder. For any target disorder, there are probabilities below which a clinician would dismiss a diagnosis and order no further tests—the test threshold. Similarly, there are probabilities above which a clinician would consider the diagnosis confirmed and would stop testing and initiate treatment—the treatment threshold. When the probability of the target disorder lies between the test and treatment thresholds, further testing is mandated (see Chapter 14, The Process of Diagnosis).

If most patients have test results with LRs near 1.0, test results will seldom move us across the test or treatment threshold. Thus, the usefulness of a diagnostic test is strongly influenced by the proportion of patients suspected of having the target disorder whose test results have very high or very low LRs. Among the patients suspected of having dementia, a review of Table 16-3 allows us to determine the proportion of patients with extreme results (either LR > 10 or LR < 0.1). The proportion can be calculated as $(105 + 2 + 64 + 2 + 11 + 163)/(345 + 306)$ or $347/651 = 53\%$. The SIS is likely to move the posttest probability in a decisive manner in half of the patients suspected of having dementia and examined, an impressive proportion and better than for most of our diagnostic tests.

A final comment has to do with the use of sequential tests. A new test can be integrated into the existing diagnostic pathway in 3 main ways—as replacement, triage, or add-on (Figure 16-2). That is, a new test can replace an existing test in the existing diagnostic pathway, can be performed before the old test so that only patients with particular results on this triage test continue the testing pathway, or can be placed after the old test so that only patients with a particular result on the old test may need this add-on new test.[19]

The LR approach fits in particularly well in thinking about the diagnostic pathway. Each item of the medical history, or each finding on physical examination, represents a diagnostic test. We can use one test to obtain a certain posttest probability that can be further increased or decreased by using another subsequent test. In general, we can also use laboratory tests or imaging procedures in the same way. If 2 tests are closely related, however, application of the second test may provide little or no information, and the

FIGURE 16-2

Three Roles of a New Test in the Existing Diagnostic Pathway

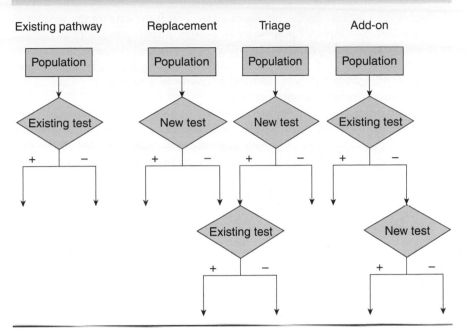

Adapted from Bossuyt et al,[19] with permission from the BMJ Publishing Group.

sequential application of LRs will yield misleading results. For example, once one has the results of the most powerful laboratory test for iron deficiency, serum ferritin, additional tests such as serum iron or transferrin saturation add no further useful information.[20]

Clinical prediction rules deal with the lack of independence of a series of tests and provide the clinician with a way of combining their results (see Chapter 17.4, Clinical Prediction Rules). For instance, for patients with suspected pulmonary embolism, one could use a rule that incorporates respiratory symptoms, heart rate, leg symptoms, oxygen saturation, electrocardiographic findings, and other aspects of medical history and physical examination to accurately classify patients with suspected pulmonary embolism as being characterized by high, medium, and low probability.[21]

Will Patients Be Better Off as a Result of the Test?

The ultimate criterion for the usefulness of a diagnostic test is whether the benefits that accrue to patients are greater than the associated risks.[22] How can we establish the benefits and risks of applying a diagnostic test? The answer lies in thinking of a diagnostic test as a therapeutic maneuver (see Chapter 6, Therapy). Establishing whether a test does more good than harm will involve randomizing patients to a diagnostic strategy that includes the test under investigation, creating a management schedule linked to the diagnostic strategy or to one in which the test is not available, and following up patients in both groups to determine the frequency of patient-important outcomes.

When is demonstrating accuracy sufficient to mandate the use of a test, and when does one require a randomized controlled trial? The value of an accurate test will be undisputed when the target disorder is dangerous if left undiagnosed, if the test has acceptable risks, and if effective treatment exists. This is the case for the ventilation perfusion scan for suspected pulmonary embolism. A high-probability or normal/near-normal result of a ventilation perfusion scan may well eliminate the need for further investigation and may result in anticoagulant agents being appropriately given or appropriately withheld (with either course of action having a substantial positive influence on patient outcome).

Sometimes, a test may be completely benign, represent a low resource investment, be evidently accurate, and clearly lead to useful changes in management. Such is the case for use of the SIS in patients with suspected dementia, when test results may dictate reassurance or extensive investigation and ultimately planning for a deteriorating course.

In other clinical situations, tests may be accurate, and management may even change as a result of their application, but their effect on patient outcome may be far less certain. Consider one of the issues we raised in our discussion of framing clinical questions (see Chapter 3, What Is the Question). There, we considered a patient with apparently resectable non–small-cell carcinoma of the lung and wondered whether the clinician should order a CT scan and base further management on the results or whether an immediate mediastinoscopy should be undertaken. For this question, knowledge of the accuracy of CT scanning is insufficient. A randomized trial of CT-directed management or mediastinoscopy for all patients is warranted, and indeed, investigators have conducted such a trial.[23] Other examples include catheterization of the right side of the heart for critically ill patients with uncertain hemodynamic status and bronchoalveolar lavage for critically ill patients with possible pulmonary infection. For these tests, randomized trials have helped elucidate optimal management strategies.

USING THE GUIDE

Although the study itself does not report reproducibility, its scoring is simple and straightforward because you need only count the number of errors made to 6 questions. It does not require any props or visual cues and is therefore unobtrusive and easy to administer. The SIS takes only 1 to 2 minutes to complete (compared with 5 to 10 minutes for the MMSE). The appendix of the published article gives a detailed word-by-word instruction on how to administer the SIS. You believe that you too can administer this scale reliably.

The patient in the clinical scenario is an older woman who was able to come to your clinic by herself but appeared no longer as lucid as she used to be. The Alzheimer Disease Center cohort in the study we had been examining in this chapter consists of people suspected of having dementia by their caregivers and brought to a tertiary care center directly. Their test characteristics were reported to be similar to those observed in the general population cohort, that is, in a sample with less severe presentations. You decide that there is no compelling reason that the study results would not apply to your patient.

You invite your patient back to the office for a follow-up visit and administer the SIS. The result is a score of 4, which, given your pretest probability of 20%, increases the probability to more than 60%. After hearing that you are concerned about her memory and possibly about her function, she agrees to a referral to a geriatrician for more extensive investigation.

References

1. Callahan CM, Unverzagt FW, Hui SL, Perkins AJ, Hendrie HC. Six-Item Screener to identify cognitive impairment among potential subjects for clinical research. *Med Care*. 2002;40(9):771-781.

2. Thomson DM, Krupey J, Freedman SO, Gold P. The radioimmunoassay of circulating carcinoembryonic antigen of the human digestive system. *Proc Natl Acad Sci U S A*. 1969;64(1):161-167.

3. Lijmer JG, Mol BW, Heisterkamp S, et al. Empirical evidence of design-related bias in studies of diagnostic tests. *JAMA*. 1999;282(11):1061-1066.

4. Rutjes AW, Reitsma JB, Di Nisio M, Smidt N, van Rijn JC, Bossuyt PM. Evidence of bias and variation in diagnostic accuracy studies. *CMAJ*. 2006;174(4):469-476.

5. Whiting P, Rutjes AW, Reitsma JB, Glas AS, Bossuyt PM, Kleijnen J. Sources of variation and bias in studies of diagnostic accuracy: a systematic review. *Ann Intern Med*. 2004;140(3):189-202.

6. Marantz PR, Kaplan MC, Alderman MH. Clinical diagnosis of congestive heart failure in patients with acute dyspnea. *Chest*. 1990;97(4):776-781.

7. Chochinov HM, Wilson KG, Enns M, Lander S. Are you depressed? screening for depression in the terminally Ill. *Am J Psychiatry*. 1997;154(5):674-676.

8. Begg CB, Greenes RA. Assessment of diagnostic tests when disease verification is subject to selection bias. *Biometrics*. 1983;39(1):207-215.

9. Gray R, Begg CB, Greenes RA. Construction of receiver operating characteristic curves when disease verification is subject to selection bias. *Med Decis Making*. 1984;4(2):151-164.

10. Ransohoff DF, Feinstein AR. Problems of spectrum and bias in evaluating the efficacy of diagnostic tests. *N Engl J Med*. 1978;299(17):926-930.

11. Choi BC. Sensitivity and specificity of a single diagnostic test in the presence of work-up bias. *J Clin Epidemiol*. 1992;45(6):581-586.

12. PIOPED Investigators. Value of the ventilation/perfusion scan in acute pulmonary embolism: results of the Prospective Investigation of Pulmonary Embolism Diagnosis (PIOPED). *JAMA*. 1990;263(20):2753-2759.

13. Fagan TJ. Letter: nomogram for Bayes theorem. *N Engl J Med*. 1975;293(5):257.

14. Sackett DL, Rennie D. The science of the art of the clinical examination. *JAMA*. 1992;267(19):2650-2652.

15. Hlatky MA, Pryor DB, Harrell FE Jr, Califf RM, Mark DB, Rosati RA. Factors affecting sensitivity and specificity of exercise electrocardiography: multivariable analysis. *Am J Med*. 1984;77(1):64-71.

16. Ginsberg JS, Caco CC, Brill-Edwards PA, et al. Venous thrombosis in patients who have undergone major hip or knee surgery: detection with compression US and impedance plethysmography. *Radiology*. 1991;181(3):651-654.

17. Lachs MS, Nachamkin I, Edelstein PH, Goldman J, Feinstein AR, Schwartz JS. Spectrum bias in the evaluation of diagnostic tests: lessons from the rapid dipstick test for urinary tract infection. *Ann Intern Med*. 1992;117(2):135-140.

18. Irwig L, Tosteson AN, Gatsonis C, et al. Guidelines for meta-analyses evaluating diagnostic tests. *Ann Intern Med*. 1994;120(8):667-676.

19. Bossuyt PM, Irwig L, Craig J, Glasziou P. Comparative accuracy: assessing new tests against existing diagnostic pathways. *BMJ*. 2006;332(7549):1089-1092.

20. Guyatt GH, Oxman AD, Ali M, Willan A, McIlroy W, Patterson C. Laboratory diagnosis of iron-deficiency anemia: an overview. *J Gen Intern Med*. 1992;7(2):145-153.

21. Wells PS, Ginsberg JS, Anderson DR, et al. Use of a clinical model for safe management of patients with suspected pulmonary embolism. *Ann Intern Med*. 1998;129(12):997-1005.

22. Guyatt GH, Tugwell PX, Feeny DH, Haynes RB, Drummond M. A framework for clinical evaluation of diagnostic technologies. *CMAJ*. 1986;134(6):587-594.

23. Canadian Lung Oncology Group. Investigation for mediastinal disease in patients with apparently operable lung cancer. *Ann Thorac Surg*. 1995;60(5):1382-1389.

ADVANCED TOPICS IN DIAGNOSIS

SPECTRUM BIAS

Gordon Guyatt, Victor Montori, Peter Wyer,
Thomas Newman, and Sheri Keitz

IN THIS CHAPTER:

CHOOSING THE WRONG PATIENTS WILL BIAS ESTIMATES OF THE USEFULNESS OF A DIAGNOSTIC TEST

For clinicians to appropriately use diagnostic tests in clinical practice, they need to know the tests' *power* to distinguish between those who have the *target condition* and those who do not. As we pointed out in Chapter 16, Diagnostic Tests, if investigators choose clinically inappropriate populations for their study of a diagnostic test (introducing what is sometimes called *spectrum bias*), the results may seriously mislead clinicians.

In this chapter, we present a series of examples that expand on the points related to spectrum bias in Chapter 16, Diagnostic Tests. Working through these examples, you will gain a deeper understanding of which characteristics of a study population are and are not likely to result in misleading results. Readers will find an elaborated version of this demonstration, intended to assist teachers in interactive sessions with small groups, in another publication.[1]

TARGET-POSITIVE PATIENTS WITH SEVERE DISEASE AND TARGET-NEGATIVE WITHOUT SUSPECTED DISEASE ARE THE WRONG PATIENTS

Ideally, the ability of a test to correctly identify patients with a particular disease, condition, or *outcome* (*target-positive* patients) and those without (*target-negative* patients) would not vary from patient to patient. A test may, however, perform better when used to evaluate patients with more severe disease than it would in patients whose disease is less advanced and less obvious. Moreover, clinicians do not need diagnostic tests when the disease is either clinically manifest or sufficiently unlikely that they need not seriously consider it.

A study of the performance of a diagnostic test involves performing the test of interest, together with a second test or investigation (which we will call the *reference standard*, *criterion standard*, or *gold standard*) on patients with and without the disease or condition of interest. We accept the results of the reference standard as the criterion by which the results of the test under investigation are assessed.

In designing such a study, investigators sometimes choose patients with unequivocally far-advanced disease together with unequivocally disease-free people, such as healthy asymptomatic volunteers. This approach ensures the *validity* of the criterion standard and may be appropriate in the early stages of developing a test. Any study done on a population lacking diagnostic uncertainty may, however, produce a biased estimate of a test's performance relative to a study restricted to patients for whom the test would be clinically indicated.

Distributions of Test Results Illustrate the Spectrum Problem

A crucial issue in the design of a diagnostic test study is the distribution of illness or abnormality among the patients who were enrolled. We refer to this distribution as the spectrum of disease, illness, or abnormality.

Brain natriuretic peptide (BNP) is a hormone that the ventricles of the heart secrete in response to expansion. Plasma levels of BNP increase in congestive heart failure (CHF). Consequently, investigators have suggested BNP as a test to distinguish between CHF and other causes of acute dyspnea among patients presenting to emergency departments.[2]

One highly publicized study reported promising results using a BNP cutoff of 100 pg/mL.[3,4] In thinking about the use of BNP as a test for CHF among patients with acute dyspnea, consider Figure 17.1-1. The horizontal axis corresponds to increasing values of BNP. The 2 bell curves constitute hypothetical probability density plots of the distribution of BNP values among patients with and without CHF. The height of the vertical axis at any point in either curve reflects the proportion of emergency department patients having the corresponding BNP result. Aside from the choice of cutoff value, this figure is an illustration that does not directly reflect the results of any actual study.

The bell curve on the left of Figure 17.1-1 represents a schematic of the distribution of BNP values in a group of young individuals with known asthma and no risk factors for CHF. They will tend to have very low levels of circulating BNP. The bell curve on the right represents the distribution of BNP values in older patients with

FIGURE 17.1-1

Distribution of Brain Natriuretic Peptide Values Among Patients With and Without Congestive Heart Failure: Patients With Asthma and Those With Severe Heart Failure

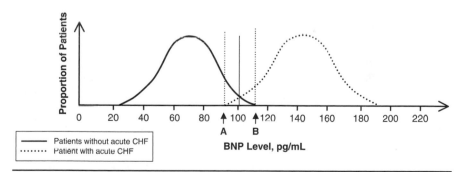

The height of the bell curve at each point reflects the proportion of the patient subgroup having the corresponding BNP value. Patients without CHF (left hand curve) are made up of younger patients with known asthma and no risk factors for CHF. The patients with CHF are older and are clinically severe and unequivocal. Treating clinicians in the emergency department have little uncertainty regarding the etiology of dyspnea in any of these patients. Abbreviations: BNP, brain natriuretic peptide; CHF, congestive heart failure.

unequivocal and severe acute CHF. Such patients will have test results clustered on the high end of the scale.

If Figure 17.1-1 accurately represented the performance of BNP in distinguishing between patients with and without CHF as the cause of their symptoms, BNP would be a very good test. The 2 curves demonstrate very little overlap. For BNP values above 110 pg/mL (point B), all patients have CHF, and for BNP values below 85 pg/mL (point A), no patients have CHF. This means that you can be completely certain about the diagnosis for all individuals with BNP values above 110 pg/mL or below 85 pg/mL. Only for patients whose BNP values are within the narrow range of 85 to 110 pg/mL is there residual uncertainty after the test has been performed regarding their likelihood of CHF.

Before you embrace a test according to its performance in clinically unequivocal patients, however, you need to consider the likely distribution of test results in a population of patients for whom you would be less certain. In Figure 17.1-2, imagine that the entire population is made up of middle-aged patients, all of whom have a history of chronic CHF and also of asthma episodes.

The distributions of BNP values among the subgroups with and without acute CHF are both closer to the middle. The extent of the overlap of the curves between points A and B is much greater. This means that even after the BNP test has been performed, residual uncertainty regarding the disease status of a large proportion of the tested patients remains.

In the cited study of performance of BNP, the sensitivity and specificity of the test, using the 100 pg/mL cutoff, were 90% and 76%, respectively, when all patients were included.[3] Only about 25% of the study population, however, comprised patients judged by the treating physicians to be in the intermediate range of probability of acute CHF.[3] When only patients in the latter range were considered in a number of studies, the specificity of BNP at a cutoff of 100 pg/mL decreased to 55%.[5]

FIGURE 17.1-2

Distribution of Brain Natriuretic Peptide Values Among Patients With and Without Congestive Heart Failure

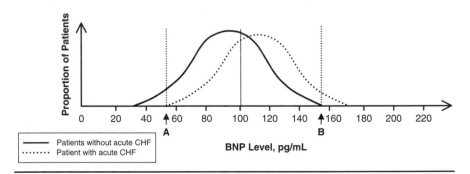

Individuals with a history of CHF and asthma, some of whom have CHF and some of whom do not. The probability density distributions now reflect a study population of middle-aged patients who all have recurrent asthma and chronic CHF. The patients whose dyspnea is due to asthma exacerbations manifest test results similar to those whose symptoms are being caused by acute CHF. Abbreviations: BNP, brain natriuretic peptide; CHF, congestive heart failure.

Adapted from Montori et al,[1] by permission of the the publisher. Copyright © 2005, Canadian Medical Association.

As it turns out, BNP test performance appears adequate to aid clinicians in treating emergency department patients with suspected heart failure.[6-8] Randomized controlled trials in which patients with acute dyspnea and possible heart failure were randomized to BNP testing or no BNP testing have demonstrated that access to BNP results decreases hospital admission rates and length of stay in those admitted to the hospital.[6-8]

The Right Population Includes Only Patients With Diagnostic Uncertainty

The message here is that clinicians do not need new tests to differentiate normal from severely diseased patients; rather, additional testing must differentiate between those who appear as if they might have the target condition and do from those who appear as if they might have the target condition and do not. Table 17.1-1 presents various ways of expressing the right population for a diagnostic test study.

Distribution of Test Results Helps Understanding of Likelihood Ratios

As Chapter 16, Diagnostic Tests, describes at length, *likelihood ratios* are the best way of expressing and using diagnostic test results. As it turns out, the likelihood ratio for any given test value is represented by the ratio of respective heights of the curves at that point on the x-axis (Figure 17.1-3). The point on the x-axis below the intersection of the 2 curves is the test result with a likelihood ratio of 1. As the proportion of those in the target-positive and target-negative populations with particular test results diverges, likelihood ratios move farther and farther from 1.

TABLE 17.1-1

Three Valid Ways of Characterizing the Right Population for a Diagnostic Test Study

Those in whom we are uncertain of the diagnosis

Those in whom we will use the test in clinical practice to resolve our uncertainty

Patients with the disease who suffer from a wide spectrum of severity and patients without the disease who suffer from a representative sample of the conditions commonly confused with the target disease

FIGURE 17.1-3

Distribution of Brain Natriuretic Peptide Values Among Patients With and Without Congestive Heart Failure

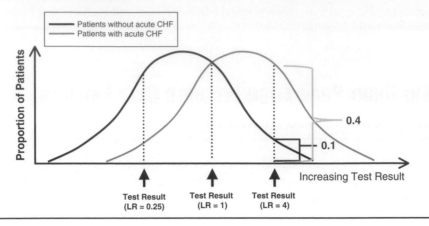

Note how the height of the curves relates to the LRs. The LR of a test result represented by a point on the horizontal line is the height of the right-hand distribution curve (patients with the disease of interest) divided by the height of the left-hand distribution curve (patients without the disease of interest) at that point. Abbreviations: CHF, congestive heart failure; LR, likelihood ratio.

Adapted from Montori et al,[1] by permission of the the publisher. Copyright © 2005, Canadian Medical Association.

SPECTRUM, NOT DISEASE PREVALENCE, DETERMINES TEST PROPERTIES

You may have learned that whereas *posttest probabilities* vary with disease prevalence, likelihood ratios do not. Is this true? The answer is yes, provided that disease spectrum remains the same in high- and low-prevalence populations, which is admittedly, as we will note below, a strong assumption.

Referring once again to Figure 17.1-1, let us consider 3 cases. In the first, we will assume that there were 2000 patients in whom CHF was unequivocally the cause of their dyspnea and 1000 in whom asthma was almost certainly the cause. The prevalence of CHF is 67%. Each bell curve corresponds to the distribution of BNP values within the respective subgroup.

Now consider a second case in which there are 1000 patients with severe CHF and 1000 patients with recurrent asthma and no risk factors for CHF. The prevalence of CHF is 50%.

Finally, consider a third case in which investigators study 1000 patients with CHF and 2000 with asthma. The prevalence of CHF is 33%.

In each case, regardless of the prevalence of CHF, the shapes of the 2 bell curves in Figure 17.1-1 do not change because the vertical axis represents the proportion, not the absolute number, of patients with that test value in that group. Changes in the total number of patients will therefore not alter the performance of the test, as measured by likelihood ratios. Hence, when the spectrum remains the same, the prevalence of CHF within the study population is irrelevant to the estimation of test characteristics.

> Let us take a different clinical example. The ICON urine test for pregnancy has a very high sensitivity and specificity when done within 2 weeks of conception.[9] It is a qualitative and inherently dichotomized test.
>
> Let us assume that the ICON is positive in 95% of women who are pregnant and is negative in 99% of women who are not. Tables 17.1-2A, B, and C show the sensitivity and specificity of the test when it is administered in 3 geographic locations with high, moderate, and low population growth and where the proportion of women presenting within 2 weeks of conception is constant. Again, for simplicity, we are considering only the prevalence of pregnancy in the population being studied; in other words, the percentage of women tested who are pregnant. A practitioner might estimate the probability of pregnancy in an individual patient to be higher or lower than this on the basis of clinical features such as use of birth control methods or history of recent sexual activity. As Tables 17.1-2A-C show, the prevalence of pregnancy in the population has no effect on the estimation of test characteristics.

There are many other examples of conditions that may present with equal severity in people with different demographics (age, sex, ethnic origin) but that are much more prevalent in a certain group than in another. Mild osteoarthritis of the knee is rare in young but common in older patients. Asymptomatic thyroid abnormalities are rare in men but common in women. In both examples, as long as the spectrum of disease and of competing conditions is similar, diagnostic tests will have the same likelihood ratios in young and old and in men and women.

TABLE 17.1-2A

Women Attending a Screening Clinic Located in a Community Center Serving a Moderately Growing Population Are Tested for Pregnancy

	Pregnant	Not Pregnant	Total
ICON+	A	B	A + B
	95	1	96
ICON−	C	D	C + D
	5	99	104
Total	A + C	B + D	A + B + C + D
	100	100	200

The urine pregnancy test has a sensitivity of 95% and a specificity of 99%. The sensitivity takes into account women who present fewer than 2 weeks after conception; 50% of the women are pregnant.

Adapted from Montori et al,[1] by permission of the the publisher. Copyright © 2005, Canadian Medical Association.

TABLE 17.1-2B

The Same Test Used in Table 17.1-2A Performed in a Similar Clinic Located in a Geographic Area Characterized by High Population Growth

	Pregnant	Not Pregnant	Total
ICON+	A × 4	B	4A + B
	380	1	381
ICON−	C × 4	D	4C + D
	20	99	119
Total	4A + 4C	B + D	4A + B + 4C + D
	400	100	500

The same proportion of women presents within 2 weeks of conception; 80% of the women are pregnant.

Adapted from Montori et al,[1] by permission of the the publisher. Copyright © 2005, Canadian Medical Association.

TABLE 17.1-2C

The Same Pregnancy Test Used in Tables 17.1-2A and B Is Now Used in a Similar Clinic Servicing a Population Characterized by Low Population Growth

	Pregnant	Not Pregnant	Total
ICON+	A	B × 4	A + 4B
	95	4	99
ICON−	C	D × 4	C + 4D
	5	396	401
Total	A + C	4B + 4D	A + 4B + C + 4D
	100	400	500

The same proportion of women presents within 2 weeks of conception; only 20% of them are pregnant.

Adapted from Montori et al,[1] by permission of the the publisher. Copyright © 2005, Canadian Medical Association.

PREVALENCE (OR PRETEST PROBABILITY) DOES INFLUENCE POSTTEST PROBABILITY

Higher prevalence will, however, result in a higher proportion of those with either normal or abnormal results who are in fact target positive. Referring to Table 17.1-2B, in population B, of whom 80% are pregnant, 380 of 381 (99.7%) test-positive women are pregnant, as are 20 of 119 (17%) test-negative women. In population C (Table 17.1-2C), of whom 20% are pregnant, 95 of 99 (96%) test-positive women are pregnant, but only 5 of 401 (1.2%) test-negative women.

The results show how test properties can remain the same across populations of varying prevalence but posttest probabilities may differ substantially.

LIKELIHOOD RATIOS SHOULD REFLECT APPROPRIATE SPECTRUMS OF TARGET-POSITIVE AND TARGET-NEGATIVE PATIENTS

Although differences in prevalence alone should not affect the sensitivity or specificity of a test, in many clinical settings, disease prevalence and disease spectrum may be related. For instance, rheumatoid arthritis observed in a family physician's office will be relatively uncommon, and most patients will have relatively mild disease. In contrast, rheumatoid arthritis will be common in a rheumatologist's office, and the patients will tend to have relatively severe disease. Tests to diagnose rheumatoid arthritis in the rheumatologist's waiting area (ie, hand inspection for joint deformity) are likely to be relatively more sensitive not because of the increased prevalence, but because of the spectrum of disease present (ie, degree and extent of joint deformity) in this setting.

As long as the clinicians are facing diagnostic uncertainties, both are valid disease spectrums, which therefore yield different but valid likelihood ratios.

References

1. Montori VM, Wyer P, Newman TB, Keitz S, Guyatt G. Tips for learners of evidence-based medicine, 5: the effect of spectrum of disease on the performance of diagnostic tests. *CMAJ.* 2005;173(4):385-390 and online appendix.

2. Dao Q, Krishnaswamy P, Kazanegra R, et al. Utility of B type natriuretic peptide in the diagnosis of congestive heart failure in an urgent-care setting. *J Am Coll Cardiol.* 2001;37(2):379-385.

3. Maisel AS, Krishnaswamy P, Nowak RM, et al. Rapid measurement of B-type natriuretic peptide in the emergency diagnosis of heart failure. *N Engl J Med.* 2002;347(3):161-167.

4. McCullough PA, Nowak RM, McCord J, et al. B-type natriuretic peptide and clinical judgement in emergency diagnosis of heart failure: analysis from Breathing Not Properly (BNP) Multinational Study. *Circulation.* 2002;106(4):416-422.

5. Schwam E. B-type natriuretic peptide for diagnosis of heart failure in emergency department patients: a critical appraisal. *Acad Emerg Med.* 2004;11(6):686-691.

6. Mueller C, Scholer A, Laule-Kilian K, et al. Use of B-type natriuretic peptide in the evaluation and management of acute dyspnea. *N Engl J Med.* 2004;350(7): 647-654.

7. Mueller C, Laule-Kilian K, Scholer A, et al. Use of B-type natriuretic peptide for the management of women with dyspnea. *Am J Cardiol.* 2004;94(12):1510-1514.

8. Mueller C, Laule-Kilian K, Frana B, et al. The use of B-type natriuretic peptide in the management of elderly patients with acute dyspnoea. *J Intern Med.* 2005;258(1):77-85.

9. ICON 25 hCG Test [package insert]. Fullerton, CA: Beckman Coulter, Inc; 2001. http://www.beckman.com/literature/ClinDiag/08109.D.pdf. Accessed July 13, 2005.

ADVANCED TOPICS IN DIAGNOSIS

EXAMPLES OF LIKELIHOOD RATIOS

Luz Maria Letelier, Gabriel Rada, Daniel Capurro, Solange Rivera, and Victor Montori

IN THIS CHAPTER:

INTRODUCTION

Previous chapters of this book have made the case for the usefulness of *likelihood ratios (LRs)* in the process of diagnosis (see Chapter 14, The Process of Diagnosis; and Chapter 16, Diagnostic Tests). In this chapter, we present some examples of LRs, along with their associated 95% *confidence intervals*. For each test, we describe the population to whom the test was applied and the range of *prevalence (pretest probability)* found for each *target condition* (disease). Our choice of conditions has been idiosyncratic and has represented the interests of the leading authors who are secondary-care general internists (L.M.L., G.R., D.C., V.M.) and a family physician (S.R.). We restricted ourselves to tests in current use and so do not offer a technical description of the tests. The authors conducted all searches and summaries, without duplicate adjudication of eligibility or data extraction.

METHODS FOR SUMMARIZING THE INFORMATION ON LIKELIHOOD RATIOS

Eligibility Criteria

For each test and target condition under consideration, we included studies that met each of the following criteria:

- The authors presented LRs or sufficient data to allow their calculation.

- The investigators compared the test to a *criterion standard* (*reference standard* or *gold standard*) that was defined in advance and that met the following criteria: (1) at the study it was in wide use and no better standard was available; (2) when the decision to apply the criterion standard was unrelated to the results of the test, it was applied to at least 50% of eligible patients; and (3) when the decision to apply the criterion standard may have been influenced by test results, it was applied to 90% of eligible patients or it was blindly applied.

- The investigators enrolled patients similar to those treated in clinical practice for whom the test might be reasonably applied.

- Publications were in English or Spanish.

We excluded studies that met the following criteria:

- The study was concerned with predicting long-term outcomes.

- The study evaluated diagnostic models, including multiple tests such as decision trees, diagnostic algorithms, neural networks, or computer-based pattern recognition systems.

Literature Search

For the first edition, we searched the electronic databases Best Evidence (1991-2000), and MEDLINE (1966-2000); we hand-searched the *JAMA* series entitled "The Rational Clinical Examination" (1992-2000) and references from a diagnostic textbook.[1] We also reviewed the citations of articles we found for additional potentially eligible studies. For tests included in the first edition, we have updated the MEDLINE search from 2000 to 2005 and reviewed the *JAMA* series from 2000 to 2005.

For every pair of target condition and test, we searched the databases with the following search strategy template, using both Medical Subject Headings (MeSH) and text words (Figure 17.2-1). An example of typical search strategy is shown in Figure 17.2-2.

Selection Process

Whenever we found a good-quality *systematic review*,[2] we used it as our only data source, although we sometimes reviewed the original studies to obtain the data required for our own statistical analysis and searched for more recent studies on the topic. When we identified more than 1 systematic review, we either selected the better-quality and more comprehensive one or presented the range of possible LRs.

Statistical Analysis

For topics without a systematic review and formal *meta-analysis*, LRs and 95% confidence intervals for individual 2×2 and $2 \times J$ (ie, 2 outcomes—*target positive* and *target negative*—but J levels of test result) tables were computed using methods described by Simel et al.[3] We computed *random-effect* pooled estimates of the LRs (with $\Delta = 0.25$ added to each cell count) using the general meta-analytic method advanced by Fleiss.[4]

FIGURE17.2-1

Search Strategy Template

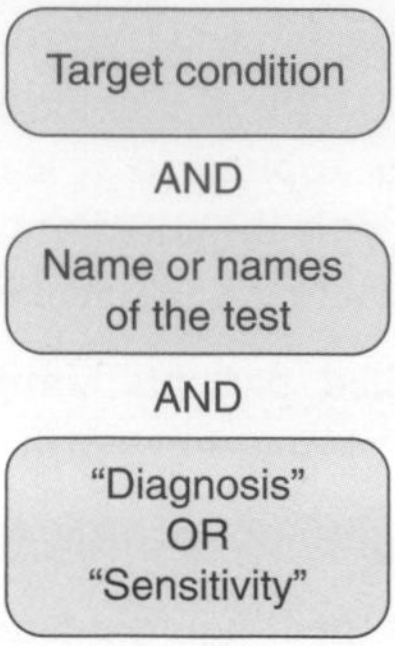

In calculating summary LRs, we did not take into account study quality, differences in calibration between centers, or differences in study population beyond those of our eligibility criteria, so these results are not considered to qualify as a formal meta-analysis.

EXAMPLES

Abdominal Aortic Aneurysm

In the following study, investigators enrolled asymptomatic people with risk factors for abdominal aortic aneurysm (AAA). Their criterion standard was abdominal ultrasonography. We found the results in 1 systematic review (Table 17.2-1).

FIGURE 17.2-2

Sample Search Strategy

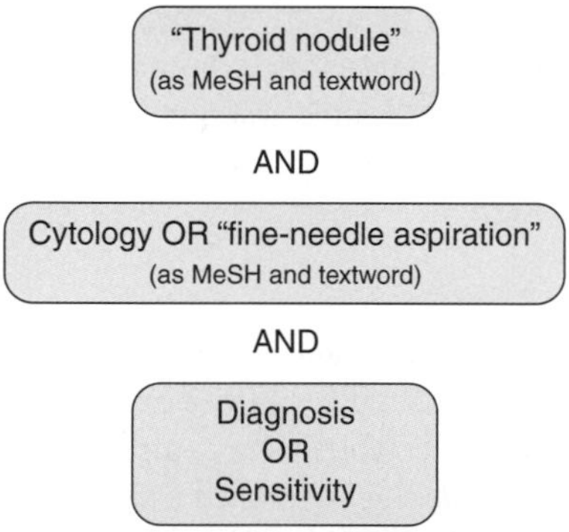

TABLE 17.2-1

Likelihood Ratios for Detection of Abdominal Aortic Aneurysm in Asymptomatic People

Prevalence, Pretest Probability, %	Patients, No.	Test	Test Result	Likelihood Ratio (95% CI)	Reference
Target Condition: AAA ≥ 3 cm					
1-28	2955	Abdominal palpation directed toward AAA detection	Positive	12 (7.4-20)	5
			Negative	0.72 (0.65-0.81)	
Target Condition: AAA ≥ 4 cm					
1-28	2955	Abdominal palpation directed toward AAA detection	Positive	6 (8.6-29)	5
			Negative	0.51 (0.38-0.67)	

Abbreviations: AAA, abdominal aortic aneurysm; CI, confidence interval.

Acute Appendicitis

In 8 studies assessing medical history and physical examination, investigators enrolled patients with right lower quadrant pain or acute abdominal pain (<1 week), including children older than 2 years. For assessing ultrasonographic and computed tomography scan, we found a recent and good-quality systematic review including patients older than 14 years and suspected of having acute appendicitis. The reference standard for diagnosing acute appendicitis was surgery and histopathology or clinical follow-up in all included studies (Table 17.2-2).

Acute Cholecystitis

This review included adult patients with abdominal pain or suspected acute cholecystitis. The reference standard used to confirm that diagnosis was surgery with histopathology or clinical follow-up (Table 17.2-3).

Acute Myocardial Infarction

We found a recent systematic review assessing several symptoms, signs, and electrocardiographic (ECG) changes in patients with acute chest pain for the diagnosis of acute myocardial infarction (MI). The criterion standard was the combination of clinical findings and ECG changes and cardiac biomarkers. Twenty-one studies were included to assess clinical findings and 53 for assessing ECG. Although the tests are not

TABLE 17.2-2

Likelihood Ratios of Tests for the Diagnosis of Acute Appendicitis

Prevalence, Pretest Probability, %	Patients, No.	Test	Test Result	Likelihood Ratio (95% CI)	Reference
12-26	2447	Medical history or physical examination			6-13
		Rigidity	Present	3.8 (3.0-4.8)	
			Absent	0.82 (0.79-0.85)	
		Psoas sign[a]	Present	2.7 (1.5-4.7)	
			Absent	0.82 (0.76-0.99)	
		Pain migration from periumbilical area or epigastrium to the RLQ	Present	2.4 (1.4-4.2)	
			Absent	0.55 (0.38-0.78)	
		Guarding	Present	2.2 (1.6-3.0)	
			Absent	0.34 (0.22-0.53)	
		Pain located in the RLQ	Present	2.2 (0.77-6.1)	
			Absent	0.29 (0.11-0.77)	
		Rebound sign[b]	Present	1.9 (1.6-2.2)	
			Absent	0.36 (0.25-0.52)	
		Radiologic tests			
50	1516	US by radiologist or trained surgeon with or without graded compression technique	Positive	5.8 (3.5-9.5)	14
			Negative	0.19 (0.13-0.27)	
45	1172	High-resolution helical CT: abdominal and pelvic or just focused to the appendix; with intravenous, oral or colonic contrast media, or without intestinal contrast.[c]	Positive	13.3 (9.9-17.9)	14
			Negative	0.09 (0.07-0.12)	

Abbreviations: CI, confidence interval; CT, computed tomography; RLQ, right lower quadrant; US, ultrasonography.

[a]Psoas sign: A sign of irritation of the psoas muscle, which is elicited by having the patient extend the leg (ipsilateral to the location of abdominal pain) at the hip against resistance (by the examiner) while lying on the unaffected side. If abdominal pain appears or is exacerbated with this maneuver, the sign is considered positive. In acute appendicitis, this sign may be positive on the right side.

[b]Rebound sign: A sign of peritoneal inflammation, which is elicited by first palpating deeply and slowly an area of the abdomen distant from the location of abdominal pain, followed by quick removal of the palpating hand. If abdominal pain appears or is exacerbated with removal of the palpating hand, the sign is considered positive.

[c]No differences were found among different CT scan techniques.

TABLE 17.2-3

Likelihood Ratios of Tests for Diagnosing Cholecystitis in Patients With Abdominal Pain or Suspected Acute Cholecystitis

Prevalence, Pretest Probability, %	Patients, No.	Test	Test Result	Likelihood Ratio (95% CI)	Reference
41-80		History			15
	1135	Anorexia	Present	1.1-1.7	
			Absent	0.5-0.9	
	669	Nausea	Present	1.0-1.2	
			Absent	0.6-1.0	
	1338	Emesis	Present	1.5 (1.1-2.1)	
			Absent	0.6 (0.3-0.9)	
41-80		Physical examination			15
	1292	Fever (temperature > 35°C)	Present	1.5 (1.0-2.3)	
			Absent	0.9 (0.8-1.0)	
	1170	Guarding	Present	1.1-2.8	
			Absent	0.5-1.0	
	565	Murphy sign	Present	2.8 (0.8-8.6)	
			Absent	0.5 (0.2-1.0)	
	1381	Rebound	Present	1.0 (0.6-1.7)	
			Absent	1.0 (0.8-1.4)	
	1170	Rectal tenderness	Present	0.3-0.7	
			Absent	1.0-1.3	
	1140	Rigidity	Present	0.5-2.32	
			Absent	1.0-1.2	
	408	Right upper abdominal quadrant mass	Present	0.8 (0.5-1.2)	
			Absent	1.0 (0.9-1.1)	
	949	Right upper abdominal quadrant pain	Present	1.5 (0.9-1.1)	
			Absent	0.7 (0.3-1.6)	
	1001	Right upper abdominal quadrant tenderness	Present	1.6 (1.0-2.5)	
			Absent	0.4 (0.2-1.1)	

(Continued)

TABLE 17.2-3

Likelihood Ratios of Tests for Diagnosing Cholecystitis in Patients With Abdominal Pain or Suspected Acute Cholecystitis (*Continued*)

Prevalence, Pretest Probability, %	Patients, No.	Test	Test Result	Likelihood Ratio (95% CI)	Reference
41-80		Laboratory			15
	556	Alkaline phosphatase >120 U/L	Present	0.8 (0.4-1.6)	
			Absent	1.1 (0.6-2.0)	
	592	Elevated ALT or AST[a]	Present	1.0 (0.5-2.0)	
			Absent	1.0 (0.8-1.4)	
	674	Total bilirubin >2 mg/dL	Present	1.3 (0.7-2.3)	
			Absent	0.9 (0.7-1.2)	
	270	Total bilirubin, AST, or alkaline phosphatase. All elevated	Present	1.6 (1.0-2.8)	
			Absent	0.8 (0.8-0.9)	
	270	Total bilirubin, AST, or alkaline phosphatase. Any one elevated	Present	1.2 (1.0-1.5)	
			Absent	0.7 (0.6-0.9)	
	1197	Leukocytosis[b]	Present	1.5 (1.2-1.9)	
			Absent	0.6 (0.5-1.8)	

Abbreviations: ALT, alanine aminotransferase; AST, aspartate aminotransferase; CI, confidence interval.

[a]Greater than upper limit of normal (ALT: 40 U/L; AST: 48 U/L).
[b]White blood cell count >10000/μL.

independent from the criterion standard, we included the results, considering that this criterion standard is the most widely used (Table 17.2-4).

Airflow Limitation
In the following study of the diagnosis of chronic or acute airflow limitation, investigators enrolled patients with current respiratory symptoms and used spirometry as their reference standard (Table 17.2-5).

Alcohol Abuse or Dependence
For the diagnosis of alcohol abuse or dependence with the CAGE (Cut down, Annoyed, Guilty, Eye opener) score (see Table 17.2-6 for a description of the CAGE score), 1 systematic review involving a general population (excluding psychiatric facilities and emergency department) is presented. The criterion standard used was *Diagnostic and Statistical Manual of Mental Disorders* (Third Edition Revised or Fourth Edition) (*DSM-III-R* or *DSM-IV*) criteria (Table 17.2-6).

TABLE 17.2-4

Likelihood Ratios of Tests for the Diagnosis of Myocardial Infarction in Patients Admitted for Suspected Myocardial Infarction or Consulting Emergency Departments for Chest Pain

Prevalence, Pretest Probability, %	Patients, No.	Test	Test Result	Likelihood Ratio (95% CI)	Reference
9	38 638	Medical history			16
		Left-sided radiation of pain	Present	1.45 (1.36-1.55)	
		Right-sided radiation of pain	Present	2.59 (1.85-3.70)	
		Any radiation of pain	Present	1.43 (1.33-1.55)	
		Central pain	Present	1.24 (1.20-1.27)	
		Pleuritic pain	Present	0.19 (0.14-0.25)	
		Sharp pain	Present	0.32 (0.21-0.50)	
		Positional pain	Present	0.27 (0.21-0.36)	
		Crushing pain	Present	1.44 (0.39-1.49)	
		Pain duration >1 h	Present	1.30 (1.15-1.47)	
		Previous MI/angina	Present	1.29 (1.22-1.36)	
		Nausea/vomiting	Present	1.88 (1.58-2.23)	
		Sweating	Present	2.06 (1.96-2.16)	
9	38 638	Physical examination			16
		Pain on palpation	Present	0.23 (0.08-0.30)	
		Third heart sound	Present	3.21 (1.60-6.45)	
		Pulmonary crackles	Present	2.08 (1.42-3.05)	
		SBP <80 mm Hg	Present	3.06 (1.80-5.22)	
9	78 515	Electrocardiogram			16
		Normal ECG	Present	0.14 (0.11-0.20)	
		ST-segment elevation	Present	13.1 (8.28-20.6)	
		ST-segment depression	Present	3.13 (2.50-3.92)	
		Abnormal T waves	Present	1.87 (1.41-2.48)	

(Continued)

TABLE 17.2-4

Likelihood Ratios of Tests for the Diagnosis of Myocardial Infarction in Patients Admitted for Suspected Myocardial Infarction or Consulting Emergency Departments for Chest Pain (*Continued*)

Prevalence, Pretest Probability, %	Patients, No.	Test	Test Result	Likelihood Ratio (95% CI)	Reference
		Q waves	Present	5.01 (3.56-7.06)	
		Left BBB	Present	0.49 (0.15-1.60)	
		Right BBB	Present	0.28 (0.04-2.12)	

Abbreviations: BBB, bundle branch block; CI, confidence interval; ECG, electrocardiograph; MI, myocardial infarction; SBP, systolic blood pressure.

TABLE 17.2-5

Likelihood Ratios of Tests for Diagnosis of Acute or Chronic Airflow Limitation in Symptomatic Patients

Prevalence, Pretest Probability, %	Patients, No.	Test	Test Result	Likelihood Ratio (95% CI)[a]	Reference
Not reported	Not reported	History			17
		Smoking pack-year	>70	8.0	
			<70	0.63	
		Smoking	Ever	1.8	
			Never	0.16	
		Sputum production (>$1/4$ cup)	Present	4.0	
			Absent	0.84	
		Wheezing	Present	3.8	
			Absent	0.66	
		Exertional dyspnea (grade 4)	Present	3.0	
			Absent	0.98	
		Exertional dyspnea (any grade)	Present	2.2	
			Absent	0.83	
		Physical examination			
		Wheezing	Present	36	
			Absent	0.85	
		Decreased heart dullness	Present	10	
			Absent	0.88	

(*Continued*)

TABLE 17.2-5

Likelihood Ratios of Tests for Diagnosis of Acute or Chronic Airflow Limitation in Symptomatic Patients (*Continued*)

Prevalence, Pretest Probability, %	Patients, No.	Test	Test Result	Likelihood Ratio (95% CI)[a]	Reference
		Match test[b]	Positive	7.1	
			Negative	0.43	
		Chest hyperresonance on percussion	Present	4.8	
			Absent	0.73	
		Subxiphoid palpation of cardiac apex impulse	Present	4.6	
			Absent	0.94	
		Forced expiratory time (s)	>9	4.8	
			9-6	2.7	
			<6	0.45	

Abbreviation: CI, confidence interval.

[a]Not enough data for 95% CI.
[b]Match test: inability to extinguish a lighted match held 10 cm from the mouth.

Ascites

In the following study of the diagnosis of ascites, investigators enrolled patients suspected of having liver disease or ascites, using abdominal ultrasonography as their reference standard (Table 17.2-7).

TABLE 17.2-6

Likelihood Ratios for Tests for the Diagnosis of Alcohol Abuse or Dependence

Prevalence, Pretest Probability, %	Patients, No.	Test	Test Result[a]	Likelihood Ratio (95% CI)	Reference
10-53	4562	CAGE questionnaire	4	25.18 (14.6-43.43)	18
			3	15.33 (8.22-28.6)	
			2	6.86 (4.17-11.31)	
			1	3.44 (2.31-5.11)	
			0	0.18 (0.11-0.29)	

Abbreviation: CI, confidence interval.

[a]The CAGE questionnaire score results from adding 1 point for each question answered affirmatively. CAGE: C, have you ever felt you ought to *Cut* down on your drinking? A, Have people *A*nnoyed you by criticizing your drinking? G, Have you ever felt bad or *G*uilty about your drinking? E, Have you ever had a drink first thing in the morning to steady your nerves or get rid of a hangover (*E*ye opener)?

TABLE 17.2-7

Likelihood Ratios of Tests for Diagnosing Ascites in Patients Suspected of Having Liver Disease or Ascites

Prevalence, Pretest Probability, %	Patients, No.	Test	Test Result	Likelihood Ratio (95% CI)	Reference
29-33	Not reported	Increased girth	Present	4.6[a]	19
			Absent	0.17[a]	
		Recent weight gain	Present	3.2[a]	
			Absent	0.42[a]	
		Hepatitis	Present	3.2[a]	
			Absent	0.80[a]	
		Ankle swelling	Present	2.8[a]	
			Absent	0.10[a]	
		Fluid wave	Present	6.0 (3.3-11)	
			Absent	0.4 (0.3-0.6)	
		Shifting dullness	Present	2.7 (1.9-3.9)	
			Absent	0.3 (0.2-0.6)	
		Flank dullness	Present	2.0 (1.5-2.9)	
			Absent	0.3 (0.1-0.7)	
		Bulging flanks	Present	2.0 (1.5-2.6)	
			Absent	0.3 (0.2-0.6)	

Abbreviation: CI, confidence interval.

[a]Insufficient data to determine 95% CI.

Carotid Artery Stenosis

In the following studies of the diagnosis of carotid artery stenosis (defined as stenosis of more than 50% of the arterial lumen), investigators enrolled patients undergoing angiography for transient ischemic attacks or other neurologic conditions, using the results of carotid angiography as their reference standard (Table 17.2-8).

Community-Acquired Pneumonia

In the following studies of the diagnosis of community-acquired pneumonia, investigators enrolled patients with fever, cough, or other respiratory symptoms or those suspected of having pneumonia, excluding those with nosocomial infections and immunosuppression. Their reference standard was defined as the presence of definite or suspicious new infiltrates on chest radiograph. We found the results in 1 overview and use the necessary data from 4 of its included studies (Table 17.2-9).

TABLE 17.2-8

Likelihood Ratios for Tests for Diagnosis of Carotid Artery Stenosis (>50%) in Symptomatic Patients Undergoing Cerebral Angiography

Prevalence, Pretest Probability, %	Patients, No.	Test	Test Result	Likelihood Ratio (95% CI)	Reference
8.2-38	2011	Carotid bruit	Present	4.4 (2.9-6.8)	20-23
			Absent	0.62 (0.45-0.86)	

Abbreviation: CI, confidence interval.

TABLE 17.2-9

Likelihood Ratios of Tests for the Diagnosis of Community-Acquired Pneumonia in Symptomatic Patients Suspected of Having Pneumonia

Prevalence, Pretest Probability, %	Patients, No.	Test	Test Result	Likelihood Ratio (95% CI)	Reference
3-38		Medical history			24-28
	1118	Dementia[a]	Present	3.4 (1.6-6.5)	
			Absent	0.94 (0.90-0.99)	
	1118	History of asthma	Present	0.30 (0.16-0.54)	
			Absent	1.2 (1.2-1.3)	
3-38		Physical Examination			24-28
	483	Asymmetric respiration	Present	80 (1.3-5,003)	
			Absent	0.96 (0.90-1.0)	
	1909	Egophony	Present	4.0 (2.0-8.1)	
			Absent	0.93 (0.88-0.99)	
	1118	Bronchial breath sounds	Present	3.5 (2.0-5.6)	
			Absent	0.90 (0.83-0.96)	
	1426	Dullness to percussion	Present	3.0 (1.6-5.8)	
			Absent	0.86 (0.74-1.0)	
	308	Respiration rate >30/min	Present	2.6 (1.6-4.1)	
			Absent	0.80 (0.70-0.90)	
	1426	Decreased breath sounds	Present	2.4 (2.0-2.9)	
			Absent	0.71 (0.59-0.86)	

(*Continued*)

TABLE 17.2-9

Likelihood Ratios of Tests for the Diagnosis of Community-Acquired Pneumonia in Symptomatic Patients Suspected of Having Pneumonia (*Continued*)

Prevalence, Pretest Probability, %	Patients, No.	Test	Test Result	Likelihood Ratio (95% CI)	Reference
	2164	Temperature >37.8°C (>100°F)	Present	2.3 (1.5-3.5)	
			Absent	0.67 (0.58-0.77)	
	1601	Respiration rate >25/min	Present	2.2 (1.0-5.0)	
			Absent	0.80 (0.71-0.90)	
	2164	Crackles on chest auscultation	Present	2.1 (1.5-2.9)	
			Absent	0.77 (0.65-0.91)	
	308	Any abnormal vital sign	Present	1.2 (1.1-1.3)	
			Absent	0.18 (0.07-0.46)	

Abbreviation: CI, confidence interval.

[a]Significant cognitive impairment with ineffective airway protection mechanisms.

Deep Venous Thrombosis

For deep venous thrombosis (DVT), we found 2 systematic reviews, one concerning ultrasonography and plethysmography–enrolled symptomatic hospitalized or ambulatory patients suspected of having a first episode of DVT. Their reference standard was venography.

The systematic review assessing D-dimer included 49 studies enrolling any patient with suspected DVT. The cutoff for most studies was 500. For reference standard, they used any "objective tests" (Table 17.2-10).

Hypovolemia

For the diagnosis of hypovolemia, we found 1 systematic review involving patients aged 60 years or older with acute conditions associated with vomiting, diarrhea, or decreased oral intake. Their criterion standard included chemical measures such as serum sodium level, blood urea nitrogen level, the blood urea nitrogen-to-creatinine ratio, and osmolality (Table 17.2-11).

Influenza

In the following studies about the diagnostic accuracy of clinical findings for the diagnosis of influenza, the investigators enrolled patients who presented with acute respiratory symptoms during influenza seasons. The reference standards used were cultures, polymerase chain reaction for influenza A, enzyme-linked immunosorbent assay, immunofluorescence, or a 4-fold increase in influenza titers (Table 17.2-12).

TABLE 17.2-10

Likelihood Ratios for Tests for Diagnosis of Deep Venous Thrombosis (DVT) in Symptomatic Patients

Prevalence, Pretest Probability, %	Patients, No.	Test	Test Result	Likelihood Ratio (95% CI)	Reference
Target Condition: All DVT, Including Distal (Isolated Calf DVT) and Proximal DVT					
Not reported	2658	Ultrasonography	Positive	15[a]	29
			Negative	0.12[a]	
	1156	Impedance plethysmography	Abnormal	10[a]	29
			Normal	0.18[a]	
36	Not reported	D-dimer (Assay)			30
		ELISA	Positive	1.60 (1.39-1.83)	
			Negative	0.12 (0.03-0.36)	
		Quantitative rapid ELISA	Positive	1.71 (1.43-2.05)	
			Negative	0.10 (0.03-0.36)	
		Semiquantitative rapid ELISA	Positive	1.48 (1.24-1.78)	
			Negative	0.25 (0.12-0.55)	
		Qualitative rapid ELISA	Positive	1.73 (1.40-2.13)	
			Negative	0.15 (0.07-0.37)	
		Quantitative latex	Positive	2.20 (1.70-2.84)	
			Negative	0.23 (0.13-0.41)	
		Semiquantitative latex	Positive	2.33 (1.75-3.11)	
			Negative	0.32 (0.20-0.51)	
		Whole blood	Positive	2.62 (2.17-3.16)	
			Negative	0.20 (0.13-0.32)	
Target Condition: Proximal DVT (Popliteal or More Proximal Veins)					
	2658	Ultrasonography	Positive	49[a]	29
			Negative	0.03[a]	
	1156	Impedance plethysmography	Abnormal	8.4[a]	29
			Normal	0.09[a]	

Abbreviations: CI, confidence interval; DVT, deep venous thrombosis; ELISA, enzyme-linked immunosorbent assay.

[a]Insufficient data available to determine CI.

TABLE 17.2-11

Likelihood Ratios for Diagnosis of Hypovolemia in Patients Aged 60 Years or Older Experiencing Acute Conditions Associated With Volume Loss[31]

Prevalence, Pretest Probability, %	Patients, No.	Test	Test Result	Likelihood Ratio (95% CI)	Reference
Not available	38	Sunken eyes	Present	3.4 (1.0-12)	31
			Absent	0.50 (0.3-0.7)	
	86	Dry axilla	Present	2.8 (1.4-5.4)	31
			Absent	0.6 (0.4-1.0)	
	38	Dry tongue	Present	2.1 (0.8-5.8)	31
			Absent	0.6 (0.3-1.0)	
	38	Dry mouth and nose mucosa	Present	2.0 (1.0-4.0)	31
			Absent	0.3 (0.1-0.6)	
	38	Longitudinal furrows on tongue	Present	2.0 (1.0-4.0)	31
			Absent	0.3 (0.1-0.6)	
	38	Unclear speech	Present	3.1 (0.9-11)	31
			Absent	0.5 (0.4-0.8)	
	38	Weak upper or lower extremities	Present	2.3 (0.6-8.6)	31
			Absent	0.7 (0.5-1.0)	
	38	Confusion	Present	2.1 (0.8-5.7)	31
			Absent	0.6 (0.4-1.0)	

Abbreviation: CI, confidence interval.

TABLE 17.2-12

Likelihood Ratios of Clinical Tests for the Diagnosis of Influenza

Prevalence, Pretest Probability, %	Patients, No.	Test	Test Result	Likelihood Ratio (95% CI)	Reference
28-67	4712	Fever any age	Present	1.8 (1.1-2.9)	32
			Absent	0.40 (0.25-0.66)	
7	1838	Fever >60 y	Present	3.8 (2.8-5.0)	32
			Absent	0.72 (0.64-0.82)	
66-67	3825	Feverishness any age	Present	1.0 (0.86-1.2)	32
			Absent	0.70 (0.27-2.5)	
8	614	Feverishness >60 y	Present	2.1 (1.2-3.7)	32
			Absent	0.68 (0.45-1.0)	
28-67	4793	Cough any age	Present	1.1 (1.1-1.2)	32
			Absent	0.42 (0.31-0.57)	
7-8	2371	Cough >60 y	Present	2.0 (1.1-3.5)	32
			Absent	0.57 (0.37-0.87)	
50-67	4183	Myalgia any age	Present	0.93 (0.83-1.0)	32
			Absent	1.2 (0.90-1.16)	
7-8	2371	Myalgia >60 y	Present	2.4 (1.9-2.9)	32
			Absent	0.68 (0.58-0.79)	
67	81	Malaise any age	Present	0.98 (0.75-1.3)	32
			Absent	1.1 (0.51-2.2)	
50	1838	Malaise >60 y	Present	2.6 (2.2-3.1)	32
			Absent	0.55 (0.44-0.67)	
28-68	4793	Headache any age	Present	1.0 (1.0-1.1)	32
			Absent	0.75 (0.63-0.89)	
7-8	2371	Headache >60 y	Present	1.9 (1.6-2.3)	32
			Absent	0.70 (0.60-0.82)	

Abbreviation: CI, confidence interval.

Iron Deficiency Anemia

For studies on the diagnosis of iron deficiency anemia, investigators enrolled patients with hemoglobin levels less than 11.7 g/dL and less than 13.0 g/dL for women and men, respectively. Their reference standard was a bone marrow aspirate stained for iron (Table 17.2-13).

TABLE 17.2-13

Likelihood Ratios of Tests for Diagnosis of Iron Deficiency Anemia in Patients With Anemia

Prevalence, Pretest Probability, %	Patients, No.	Test	Test Result	Likelihood Ratio (95% CI)	Reference
21-50	2798	Serum ferritin, µg/L	<15	55 (35-84)	33, 34
			15-25	9.3 (6.3-14)	
			25-35	2.5 (2.1-3.0)	
			35-45	1.8 (1.5-2.2)	
			45-100	0.54 (0.48-0.60)	
			>100	0.08 (0.06-0.11)	
21-50	536	Mean cell volume, µm³	<70	13 (6.1-19)	33
			70-75	3.3 (2.0-4.7)	
			75-85	1.0 (0.69-1.31)	
			85-90	0.76 (0.56-0.96)	
			>90	0.29 (0.21-0.37)	
21-50	764	Transferrin saturation, %	<5	11 (6.4-15)	33
			5-10	2.5 (2.0-3.1)	
			10-20	0.81 (0.70-0.92)	
			20-30	0.52 (0.41-0.63)	
			30-50	0.43 (0.31-0.55)	
			>50	0.15 (0.06-0.24)	
21-50	278	Red cell protoporphyrin, µg/dL	>350	8.3 (2.6-14)	33
			350-250	6.1 (2.8-9.3)	
			250-150	2.0 (1.4-2.6)	
			150-50	0.56 (0.48-0.64)	
			<50	0.12 (0.0-0.25)	

(Continued)

TABLE 17.2-13

Likelihood Ratios of Tests for Diagnosis of Iron Deficiency Anemia in Patients With Anemia (*Continued*)

Prevalence, Pretest Probability, %	Patients, No.	Test	Test Result	Likelihood Ratio (95% CI)	Reference
Patients With Anemia and Chronic Renal Failure Receiving Hemodialysis or Peritoneal Dialysis					
9-50	190	Serum ferritin, µg/L	<50	12 (4.4-32)	35-39
			50-100	2.3 (0.70-7.3)	
			100-300	0.64 (0.32-1.2)	
			>300	0.27 (0.12-0.61)	
Patients With Anemia and Cirrhosis					
40	72	Serum ferritin, µg/L	<50	22[a]	40
			50-400	1.0-1.8[a]	
			400-1000	0.13[a]	
			1000-2200	0.19[a]	

Abbreviation: CI, confidence interval.

[a]Insufficient data to determine confidence intervals.

Melanoma

In the following study of the diagnosis of melanoma, investigators enrolled patients with pigmented skin lesions and used biopsy of the lesions as their reference standard (Table 17.2-14).

Osteoporosis

This systematic review included patients older than 50 years (mostly women). The reference standard used was bone densitometry or documented vertebral fracture using either a semiquantitative technique or vertebral morphometry (Table 17.2-15).

TABLE 17.2-14

Likelihood Ratios of Tests for Diagnosis of Melanoma in Patients With Pigmented Skin Lesions

Prevalence, Pretest Probability, %	Patients, No.	Test	Result	Likelihood Ratio (95% CI)	Reference
3	192	ABCD(E) checklist	BCD positive	62 (19-170)	41
			BCD negative	0 (0-0.5)	

Abbreviation: ABCD(E) checklist: A, asymmetry; B, border irregularity; C, color variegation; D, diameter >6 mm; E, elevation.

TABLE 17.2-15

Likelihood Ratios of Tests for Diagnosis of Osteoporosis

Prevalence, Pretest Probability, %	Patients, No.	Test	Test Result	Likelihood Ratio (95% CI)	Reference
Patients With Clinical Signs and Symptoms of Osteoporosis					
50	4638	Height loss >3 cm	Present	1.1 (1.0-1.1)	42
			Absent	0.60 (0.4-0.9)	
50	4638	Weight <60 kg	Present	1.9 (1.8-2.0)	42
			Absent	0.3 (0.3-0.4)	
50	4638	Grip strength <59 kPa	Present	1.2 (1.1-1.2)	42
			Absent	0.6 (0.5-0.7)	
50	4638	Grip strength <44 kPa	Present	1.7 (1.5-1.9)	42
			Absent	0.8 (0.7-0.9)	
8	1873	Weight <51 kg	Present	7.3 (5.0-10.8)	42
			Absent	0.8 (0.7-0.9)	
10	610	Kyphosis	Present	3.1 (1.8-5.3)	42
			Absent	0.8 (0.7-1.0)	
63	225	Hand skinfold	Present	1.2 (1.0-1.3)	42
			Absent	0.40 (0.2-0.8)	
33	1365	Tooth count <22 teeth	Present	1.0 (0.8-1.2)	42
			Absent	1.0 (0.9-1.1)	
11.5	190	Tooth count <20 teeth	Present	3.4 (1.4-8.0)	42
			Absent	0.8 (0.6-1.0)	
Patients With Clinical Signs and Symptoms of Spinal Fracture					
3.4 (55-59 y) / 21.9 (80-84 y)	449	Arm-span height difference >5 cm	Present	1.6 (1.1-2. 5)	42
			Absent	0.8 (0.6-1.0)	
14	781	Rib-pelvis distance <2 fingerbreadths	Present	3.8 (2.9-5.1)	42
			Absent	0.6 (0.5-0.7)	

Abbreviation: CI, confidence interval.

Peripheral Arterial Disease or Peripheral Vascular Insufficiency

In the following studies of the diagnosis of peripheral artery disease or peripheral vascular insufficiency, investigators used the ankle to arm (brachial) systolic pressure index (AAI) as a reference standard. We found the results in 1 systematic review and its included studies (Table 17.2-16).

TABLE 17.2-16

Likelihood Ratios of Tests for Diagnosis of Peripheral Artery Disease

Prevalence, Pretest Probability, %	Patient Legs, No.	Test	Test Result	Likelihood Ratio (95% CI)	Reference
Patients: Asymptomatic/Symptomatic With Risk Factors for Atherosclerosis or Classical PAD History					
Target Outcome: Severe PAD (AAI <0.5)					
Symptomatic or asymptomatic with risk factors[a]: 10-12	605	Venous filling time	>20 s	3.6 (1.9-6.8)	43,44, 46,47
			<20 s	0.8 (0.7-1.0)	
With classic PAD history: 71	854	Tibial or dorsalis pedis pulse	Weak/ absent	3.2 (2.7-3.9)	43-44
			Present	0.19 (0.03-1.15)	
	605	Absent lower limb hair; atrophic skin; cool skin; blue/ purple skin; capillary refilling time >5 s	Any of them	0.5-2.0	45
Patients: Asymptomatic or Symptomatic With Risk Factors for Atherosclerosis or With Any Leg Complaint on Walking With or Without Risk Factors					
Target Outcome: Moderate PAD (AAI <0.9)					
10-12	4597	Tibial or dorsalis pedis pulse, or both	Weak/ absent	8.9 (7.1-11)	44, 46, 47
			Present	0.33 (0.28-0.40)	
10-12	4910	Wound or sores on foot or toes	Present	6.9 (2.9-16)	47
			Absent	0.98 (0.97-1.0)	
10-12	5418	Femoral pulse	Weak/ absent	6.7 (4.3-10)	46, 47
			Present	0.94 (0.91-0.96)	
10-12	4910	Unilateral cooler skin	Present	5.8 (4.0-8.4)	47
			Absent	0.92 (0.89-0.95)	
10-12	5418	Femoral bruit	Present	5.4 (4.5-6.5)	46, 47
			Absent	0.78 (0.70-0.86)	
10-12	4910	Abnormal color on feet or leg	Present	2.8 (2.4-3.2)	47
			Absent	0.74 (0.69-0.80)	

(Continued)

TABLE 17.2-16

Likelihood Ratios of Tests for Diagnosis of Peripheral Artery Disease (*Continued*)

Prevalence, Pretest Probability, %	Patient Legs, No.	Test	Test Result	Likelihood Ratio (95% CI)	Reference
Patients: Classic PAD History					
Target Outcome: Moderate PAD (AAI <0.9)					
71	4597	Tibial or dorsalis pedis pulse, or both	Weak/ absent	8.9 (7.1-11)	44, 46, 47
			Present	0.33 (0.28-0.40)	

Abbreviations: AAI, ankle to arm (brachial) systolic pressure index; CI, confidence interval; PAD, peripheral artery disease.

[a]Risk factors include dyslipidemia, diabetes mellitus, smoking, hypertension, and cardiovascular disease.

Renovascular Hypertension

In the following study of the diagnosis of renovascular hypertension, investigators enrolled patients with hypertension referred to arteriography by using renal arteriography as the reference standard (Table 17.2-17).

Stroke

In the following systematic review about the diagnostic accuracy of clinical findings for the diagnosis of stroke, the investigators enrolled patients who presented to the emergency department or were given prehospital attention for neurologic symptoms. The prehospital patients had to be older than 45 years, to have had symptoms less than 24 hours, to not be wheelchair bound or bedridden, and to have a blood glucose level between 60 and 400 mg/dL. The reference standards used were neuroimaging studies (Table 17.2-18).

TABLE 17.2-17

Likelihood Ratios for Tests for Diagnosis of Renovascular Hypertension

Prevalence, Pretest Probability, %	Patients, No.	Test	Test Result	Likelihood Ratio (95% CI)	Reference
24	263	Systolic and diastolic abdominal bruit	Present	39 (9.4-160)	48
			Absent	0.62 (0.51-0.75)	
23	118	Any epigastric or flank systolic bruit	Present	6.4 (3.2-12.6)	48
			Absent	0.42 (0.25-0.68)	

Abbreviation: CI, confidence interval.

TABLE 17.2-18

Likelihood Ratios of Clinical Findings for the Diagnosis of Stroke

Prevalence, Pretest Probability, %	Patient, No.	Test	Test Result	Likelihood Ratio (95% CI)	Reference
Assessment (Physical Examination) by Emergency Physicians					
24	161	Facial paresis or arm drift or abnormal speech	3 Findings (+)	14 (1.6-121)	49
			2 Findings (+)	4.2 (1.4-13)	
			1 Finding (+)	5.2 (2.6-11)	
			>1 Finding (+)	5.5 (3.3-9.1)	
			0 Findings (+)	0.39 (0.25-0.61)	
Assessment (Physical Examination) by Emergency Medical Personnel					
24	161	Facial paresis or arm drift or abnormal speech	3 Findings (+)	7.0 (3.3-14)	49
			2 Findings (+)	7.6 (3.7-16)	
			1 Finding (+)	4.4 (3.0-6.4)	
			≥ 1 Finding (+)	5.4 (4.1-7.0)	
			0 Findings (+)	0.46 (0.38-0.56)	
Prehospital Assessment (Physical Examination) by Paramedics					
16.5	206	One of 3 unilateral deficits (arm drift, altered handgrip strength, or facial paresis)	Present	31 (13-75)	49
			Absent	0.09 (0.03-0.027)	

Abbreviation: CI, confidence interval.

Thromboembolism or Acute Pulmonary Embolism

In studies on diagnosis of acute pulmonary embolism (PE), using clinical assessment or ECG or chest radiograph or V/Q scan (scintigraphy), investigators used angiography or clinical follow-up for more than 1 year as their reference standard. Normal ventilation-perfusion scan was used to rule out PE on those trials using "clinical assessment," ECG, or chest radiograph.

For D-dimer assessment, we found 1 recent systematic review including 31 studies enrolling patients with suspected PE. D-Dimer cutoff point was 500 for most studies. The criterion standard was any "objective test."

Another systematic review including 48 studies (11004 patients) assessed different images in patients suspected of having PE. The criterion standard was angiography for individuals with positive results and angiography or follow-up for those individuals negative results (Table 17.2-19).

TABLE 17.2-19

Likelihood Ratios of Tests for the Diagnosis of Pulmonary Embolism

Prevalence, Pretest Probability, %	Patients, No.	Test	Test Result	Likelihood Ratio (95% CI)	Reference
		Patients Suspected of Having Acute Pulmonary Embolism With Symptoms for the Past 24 h			
32-44		Medical history/ physical exami- nation		[a]	
	78	Blood pressure	<100/70	3.1	50
			>100/70	0.8	
	78	Ventricular dia- stolic gallop	Present	3.0	50
			Absent	0.9	
	78	Congestive heart failure	Present	0.3	50
			Absent	1.2	
	403	Risk factors[b]		0.5-2.0[c]	50-52
		Symptoms[b]			
		Signs[b]			
41-44		Electrocardio- gram		[a]	
	78	S-I/Q-III/T-III	Present	2.4	50
			Absent	0.88	
	78	Inverted T waves V1→V3	Present	2.3	50
			Absent	0.94	
	78	Normal	Present	0.82	50
			Absent	2.2	
	78	Right bundle- branch block		0.5-2.0[c]	50
		Right ventricular hypertrophy			
27-44	1203	Chest radiograph	Any sign	0.5-2.0[c]	53, 54
		• Normal			
		• Pulmonary edema			
		• Enlarged hilum or mediastinum			

(Continued)

TABLE 17.2-19

Likelihood Ratios of Tests for the Diagnosis of Pulmonary Embolism (*Continued*)

Prevalence, Pretest Probability, %	Patients, No.	Test	Test Result	Likelihood Ratio (95% CI)	Reference
		• Prominent central artery			
		• Atelectasis			
		• Pleural effusion			
25	Not reported	D-Dimer (Assay)			30
		ELISA	Positive	1.97 (1.72- 2.26)	
			Negative	0.08 (0.01-0.43)	
		Quantitative rapid ELISA	Positive	1.64 (1.40-1.91)	
			Negative	0.07 (0.00-1.55)	
		Semiquantitative rapid ELISA	Positive	1.55 (1.25-1.93)	
			Negative	0.18 (0.04-0.94)	
		Qualitative rapid ELISA	Positive	3.01 (1.52-5.96)	
			Negative	0.13 (0.01-1.28)	
		Quantitative latex	Positive	1.69 (1.44-1.99)	
			Negative	0.23 (0.11-0.48)	
		Semiquantitative latex	Positive	1.81 (1.35-2.42)	
			Negative	0.36 (0.20-0.67)	
		Whole blood	Positive	2.32 (1.87-2.88)	
			Negative	0.27 (0.17-0.42)	
30	378	Leg vein ultra-sonography	Positive	16.2 (5.6-46.7)	55
			Negative	0.67 (0.50-0.89)	
30	431 (+) CT[d]	Spiral CT	Positive	24.1 (12.4-46.7)	55
	1197 (+) CT[d]		Negative	0.11 (0.06-0.19)	
30		Ultrasonography and spiral tomog-raphy	Negative	0.04 (0.03-0.06)	55

(*Continued*)

TABLE 17.2-19

Likelihood Ratios of Tests for the Diagnosis of Pulmonary Embolism (*Continued*)

Prevalence, Pretest Probability, %	Patients, No.	Test	Test Result	Likelihood Ratio (95% CI)	Reference
29	881	Ventilation-perfusion scintigram (V/Q scan)	High probability	18 (11-31)	56
			Intermediate probability	1.2 (1.0-1.5)	
			Low probability	0.36 (0.26-0.49)	
			Normal	0.10 (0.04-0.25)	
30	148	Echocardiography	Positive	5 (2.3-10.6)	55
			Negative	0.59 (0.41-0.86)	
30	221	Magnetic resonance angiography	Positive	11.7 (3.6-37.8)	55
			Negative	0.20 (0.12-0.34)	
Patients With Suspected PE and Normal Chest Radiograph Result[a]					
15	133	V/Q scan	High probability	10	57
			Intermediate probability	1.7	
			Low probability	1.1	
			Normal	0.2	
15	110	Dyspnea and PaO_2	<70	2.8	57
			>70	0.58	
15	110	PaO_2	<70	2.2	57
			>70	0.62	
Patients With Suspected PE and Normal Chest Radiograph Result and No Previous Cardiopulmonary Disease[a]					
15	110	Dyspnea and PaO_2	<60	6	57
			>60	0.84	
			<70	3.6	
			>70	0.77	

Abbreviations: CI, confidence interval; CT, computed tomography; ELISA, enzyme-linked immunosorbent assay; PE, pulmonary embolism.

[a]Insufficient data to determine 95% CI.
[b]Risk factors: immobilization, surgery, trauma, malignancy, previous deep venous thrombosis, estrogen, postpartum, and stroke. Symptoms: dyspnea, hemoptysis, any type of chest pain, cough, leg pain, or swelling. Signs: fever, heart rate >100/min, respiratory rate >20/min, crackles, wheezes, third or fourth heart sounds, increased pulmonic component of second heart sound, Homan sign, actual deep venous thrombosis, edema, and varices.
[c]Range of possible LRs.
[d]More studies assessed CT to exclude PE than to confirm PE.

TABLE 17.2-20

Likelihood Ratios for the Diagnosis of Malignancy in Euthyroid Patients With a Single or Dominant Thyroid Nodule

Prevalence, Pretest Probability, %	Patients, No.	Test	Test Result	Likelihood Ratio (95% CI)	Reference
20	132	Fine-needle aspiration cytology guided with ultrasonography	Malignant	226 (4.4-11739)	58
			Suspicious	1.3 (0.52-3.2)	
			Insufficient	2.7 (0.52-15)	
			Benign	0.24 (0.11-0.52)	
7-22	868	Fine-needle aspiration cytology not guided	Malignant	34 (15-74)	59-64
			Suspicious	1.7 (0.94-3.0)	
			Insufficient	0.5 (0.27-0.76)	
			Benign	0.23 (0.13-0.42)	

Abbreviation: CI, confidence interval.

Thyroid Cancer

In the following studies on the diagnosis of malignancy in thyroid nodules (primary or metastatic cancer or lymphoma), investigators enrolled patients with normal thyroid function and palpable thyroid nodules. The nodules could be solid or cystic and solitary or dominant if multiple nodules were present. Their reference standard was histopathologic examination after surgical excision or clinical follow-up (Table 17.2-20).

CONCLUSION

In this chapter, we have described a series of LRs supported by high-quality evidence for historical clues, physical examination signs, and laboratory or radiologic tests to aid in the diagnosis of common medical problems.

References

1. Black ER, Bordely DR, Tape TG, Panzer RJ, eds. *Diagnostic Strategies for Common Medical Problems*. 2nd ed. Philadelphia, PA: American College of Physicians; 1999.

2. Oxman AD, Cook DJ, Guyatt GH. Users' guides to the medical literature, VI: how to use an overview. *JAMA*. 1994;272(17):1367-1371.

3. Simel DL, Samsa GP, Matchar DB. Likelihood ratios with confidence: sample size estimation for diagnostic test studies. *J Clin Epidemiol*. 1991;44(8):763-770.

4. Fleiss JL. The statistical basis of meta-analysis. *Stat Methods Med Res*. 1993;2(2):121-145.

5. Lederle FA, Simel DL. Does this patient have abdominal aortic aneurysm? *JAMA*. 1999;281(1):77-82.

6. Nauta RJ, Magnant C. Observation versus operation for abdominal pain in the right lower quadrant: roles of the clinical examination and the leukocyte count. *Am J Surg*. 1986;151(6):746-748.

7. Dixon JM, Elton RA, Rainey JB, Macleod DA. Rectal examination in patients with pain in the right lower quadrant of the abdomen. *BMJ*. 1991;302(6773):386-388.

8. Liddington MI, Thomson WH. Rebound tenderness test. *Br J Surg*. 1991;78(7):795-796.

9. Izbicki JR, Knoefel WT, Wilker DK, et al. Accurate diagnosis of acute appendicitis: a retrospective and prospective analysis of 686 patients. *Eur J Surg*. 1992;158(4):227-231.

10. John H, Neff U, Kelemen M. Appendicitis diagnosis today: clinical and ultrasonic deductions. *World J Surg*. 1993;17(2):243-249.

11. Eskelinen M, Ikonen J, Lipponen P. The value of history-taking, physical examination, and computer assistance in the diagnosis of acute appendicitis in patients more than 50 years old. *Scand J Gastroenterol*. 1995;30(4):349-355.

12. Wagner JM, McKinney WP, Carpenter JL. Does this patient have appendicitis? *JAMA*. 1996;276(19):1589-1594.

13. Andersson RE, Hugander AP, Ghazi SH, et al. Diagnostic value of disease history, clinical presentation, and inflammatory parameters of appendicitis. *World J Surg*. 1999;23(2):133-140.

14. Terasawa T, Blackmore C, Bent S, Kohlwes J. Systematic review: computed tomography and ultrasonography to detect acute appendicitis in adults and adolescents. *Ann Intern Med*. 2004;141(7):537-546.

15. Trowbridge RL, Rutkowski NK, Shojania KG. Does this patient have acute cholecystitis? *JAMA*. 2003;289(1):80-86.

16. Mant J, McManus RJ, Oakes RA, et al. Systematic review and modeling of the investigation of acute and chronic chest pain presenting in primary care. *Health Technol Assess*. 2004;8(2):iii, 1-158.

17. Holleman DR Jr, Simel DL. Does the clinical examination predict airflow limitation? *JAMA*. 1995;273(4):313-319.

18. Aertgeerts B, Buntinx F, Kester A. The value of the CAGE in screening for alcohol abuse and alcohol dependence in general clinical populations: a diagnostic meta-analysis. *J Clin Epidemiol*. 2004;57(1):30-39.

19. Williams JW Jr, Simel DL. Does this patient have ascites? how to divine fluid in the abdomen. *JAMA*. 1992;267(19):2645-2648.

20. Ziegler DK, Zileli T, Dick A, Sebaugh JL. Correlation of bruits over the carotid artery with angiographically demonstrated lesions. *Neurology*. 1971;21(8):860-865.

21. Ingall TJ, Homer D, Whisnant JP, Baker HL Jr, O'Fallon WM. Predictive value of carotid bruit for carotid atherosclerosis. *Arch Neurol*. 1989;46(4):418-422.

22. Hankey GJ, Warlow CP. Symptomatic carotid ischaemic events: safest and most cost effective way of selecting patients for angiography, before carotid endarterectomy. *BMJ*. 1990;300(6738):1485-1491.

23. Sauve JS, Laupacis A, Ostbye T, Feagan B, Sackett DL. Does this patient have a clinically important carotid bruit? *JAMA*. 1993;270(23):2843-2845.

24. Metlay JP, Kapoor WN, Fine MJ. Does this patient have community-acquired pneumonia? diagnosing pneumonia by history and physical examination. *JAMA*. 1997;278(17):1440-1445.

25. Diehr P, Wood RW, Bushyhead J, Krueger L, Wolcott B, Tompkins RK. Prediction of pneumonia in outpatients with acute cough—a statistical approach. *J Chronic Dis*. 1984;37(3):215-225.

26. Gennis P, Gallagher J, Falvo C, Baker S, Than W. Clinical criteria for the detection of pneumonia in adults: guidelines for ordering chest roentgenograms in the emergency department. *J Emerg Med*. 1989;7(3):263-268.

27. Singal BM, Hedges JR, Radack KL. Decision rules and clinical prediction of pneumonia: evaluation of low-yield criteria. *Ann Emerg Med*. 1989;18(1):13-20.

28. Heckerling PS, Tape TG, Wigton RS, et al. Clinical prediction rule for pulmonary infiltrates. *Ann Intern Med*. 1990;113(9):664-670.

29. Kearon C, Julian JA, Newman TE, Ginsberg JS. Noninvasive diagnosis of deep venous thrombosis: McMaster Diagnostic Imaging Practice Guidelines Initiative. *Ann Intern Med*. 1998;128(8):663-677.

30. Stein P, Russell H, Kalpesh P, et al. D-Dimer for the exclusion of acute venous thrombosis and pulmonary embolism. *Ann Intern Med*. 2004;140(8):589-602.

31. McGee S, Abernethy WB 3rd, Simel DL. Is this patient hypovolemic? *JAMA*. 1999;281(11):1022-1029.

32. Call SA, Vollenweider MA, Hornung CA, Simel DL, McKinney WP. Does this patient have influenza? *JAMA*. 2005;293(8):987-997.

33. Guyatt GH, Oxman AD, Ali M, Willan A, McIlroy W, Patterson C. Laboratory diagnosis of iron-deficiency anemia: an overview. *J Gen Intern Med*. 1992;7(2):145-153.

34. Punnonen K, Irjala K, Rajamaki A. Serum transferrin receptor and its ratio to serum ferritin in the diagnosis of iron deficiency. *Blood*. 1997;89(3):1052-1057.

35. Hussein S, Prieto J, O'Shea M, Hoffbrand AV, Baillod RA, Moorhead JF. Serum ferritin assay and iron status in chronic renal failure and haemodialysis. *BMJ*. 1975;1(5957):546-548.

36. Milman N, Christensen TE, Pedersen NS, Visfeldt J. Serum ferritin and bone marrow iron in non-dialysis, peritoneal dialysis and hemodialysis patients with chronic renal failure. *Acta Med Scand*. 1980;207(3):201-205.

37. Blumberg AB, Marti HR, Graber CG. Serum ferritin and bone marrow iron in patients undergoing continuous ambulatory peritoneal dialysis. *JAMA*. 1983;250(24):3317-3319.

38. Kalantar-Zadeh K, Hoffken B, Wunsch H, Fink H, Kleiner M, Luft FC. Diagnosis of iron deficiency anemia in renal failure patients during the post-erythropoietin era. *Am J Kidney Dis*. 1995;26(2):292-299.

39. Fernandez-Rodriguez AM, Guindeo-Casasus MC, Molero-Labarta T, et al. Diagnosis of iron deficiency in chronic renal failure. *Am J Kidney Dis*. 1999;34(3):508-513.

40. Intragumtornchai T, Rojnukkarin P, Swasdikul D, Israsena S. The role of serum ferritin in the diagnosis of iron deficiency anaemia in patients with liver cirrhosis. *J Intern Med*. 1998;243(3):233-241.

41. Whited JD, Grichnik JM. Does this patient have a mole or a melanoma? *JAMA*. 1998;279(9):696-701.

42. Green AD, Colon-Emeric CS, Bastian L, Drake MT, Lyles KW. Does this woman have osteoporosis? *JAMA*. 2004;292(23):2890-2900.

43. Boyko EJ, Ahroni JH, Davignon D, Stensel V, Prigeon RL, Smith DG. Diagnostic utility of the history and physical examination for peripheral vascular disease among patients with diabetes mellitus. *J Clin Epidemiol*. 1997;50(6):659-668.

44. Christensen JH, Freundlich M, Jacobsen BA, Falstie-Jensen N. Clinical relevance of pedal pulse palpation in patients suspected of peripheral arterial insufficiency. *J Intern Med*. 1989;226(2):95-99.

45. McGee SR, Boyko EJ. Physical examination and chronic lower-extremity ischemia: a critical review. *Arch Intern Med*. 1998;158(12):1357-1364.

46. Criqui MH, Fronek A, Klauber MR, Barrett-Connor E, Gabriel S. The sensitivity, specificity, and predictive value of traditional clinical evaluation of peripheral arterial disease: results from noninvasive testing in a defined population. *Circulation*. 1985;71(3):516-522.

47. Stoffers HE, Kester AD, Kaiser V, Rinkens PE, Knottnerus JA. Diagnostic value of signs and symptoms associated with peripheral arterial occlusive disease seen in general practice: a multivariable approach. *Med Decis Making*. 1997;17(1):61-70.

48. Turnbull JM. Is listening for abdominal bruits useful in the evaluation of hypertension? *JAMA*. 1995;274(16):1299-1301.

49. Goldstein LB, Simel DL. Is this patient having a stroke? *JAMA*. 2005;293(19):2391-2402.

50. Hildner FJ, Ormond RS. Accuracy of the clinical diagnosis of pulmonary embolism. *JAMA*. 1967;202(7):567-570.

51. Stein PD, Terrin ML, Hales CA, et al. Clinical, laboratory, roentgenographic, and electrocardiographic findings in patients with acute pulmonary embolism and no pre-existing cardiac or pulmonary disease. *Chest*. 1991;100(3):598-603.

52. Nazeyrollas P, Metz D, Jolly D, et al. Use of transthoracic Doppler echocardiography combined with clinical and electrocardiographic data to predict acute pulmonary embolism. *Eur Heart J*. 1996;17(5):779-786.

53. Worsley DF, Alavi A, Aronchick JM, Chen JT, Greenspan RH, Ravin CE. Chest radiographic findings in patients with acute pulmonary embolism: observations from the PIOPED Study. *Radiology*. 1993;189(1):133-136.

54. Moons KG, van Es GA, Michel BC, Buller HR, Habbema JD, Grobbee DE. Redundancy of single diagnostic test evaluation. *Epidemiology*. 1999;10(3):276-281.

55. Roy PM, Colombet I, Durieux P, Chatellier G, Sors H, Meyer G. Systematic review and meta-analysis of strategies for the diagnosis of suspected pulmonary embolism. *BMJ*. 2005;331(7511):259.

56. PIOPED Investigators. Value of the ventilation/perfusion scan in acute pulmonary embolism: results of the Prospective Investigation of Pulmonary Embolism Diagnosis (PIOPED). *JAMA*. 1990;263(20):2753-2759.

57. Stein PD, Alavi A, Gottschalk A, et al. Usefulness of noninvasive diagnostic tools for diagnosis of acute pulmonary embolism in patients with a normal chest radiograph. *Am J Cardiol*. 1991;67(13):1117-1120.

58. Cochand-Priollet B, Guillausseau PJ, Chagnon S, et al. The diagnostic value of fine-needle aspiration biopsy under ultrasonography in nonfunctional thyroid nodules: a prospective study comparing cytologic and histologic findings. *Am J Med*. 1994;97(2):152-157.

59. Walfish PG, Hazani E, Strawbridge HT, Miskin M, Rosen IB. A prospective study of combined ultrasonography and needle aspiration biopsy in the assessment of the hypofunctioning thyroid nodule. *Surgery*. 1977;82(4):474-482.

60. Prinz RA, O'Morchoe PJ, Barbato AL, et al. Fine needle aspiration biopsy of thyroid nodules. *Ann Surg*. 1983;198(1):70-73.

61. Jones AJ, Aitman TJ, Edmonds CJ, Burke M, Hudson E, Tellez M. Comparison of fine needle aspiration cytology, radioisotopic and ultrasound scanning in the management of thyroid nodules. *Postgrad Med J*. 1990;66(781):914-917.

62. Cusick EL, MacIntosh CA, Krukowski ZH, Williams VM, Ewen SW, Matheson NA. Management of isolated thyroid swellings: a prospective six year study of fine needle aspiration cytology in diagnosis. *BMJ*. 1990;301(6747):318-321.

63. Perez JA, Pisano R, Kinast C, Valencia V, Araneda M, Mera ME. Needle aspiration cytology in euthyroid uninodular goiter. *Rev Med Chil*. 1991;119(2):158-163.

64. Piromalli D, Martelli G, Del Prato I, Collini P, Pilotti S. The role of fine needle aspiration in the diagnosis of thyroid nodules: analysis of 795 consecutive cases. *J Surg Oncol*. 1992;50(4):247-250.

MEASURING AGREEMENT BEYOND CHANCE

Thomas McGinn, Gordon Guyatt, Richard Cook, Deborah Korenstein, and Maureen O. Meade

IN THIS CHAPTER:

CLINICIANS OFTEN DISAGREE

Clinicians often disagree in their assessment of patients. When 2 clinicians reach different conclusions regarding the presence of a particular physical sign, either different approaches to the examination or different interpretation of the findings may be responsible for the disagreement. Similarly, disagreement between repeated applications of a diagnostic test may result from different application of the test or different interpretation of the results.

Researchers may also face difficulties in agreeing on issues such as whether patients meet the eligibility requirements for a *randomized trial*, whether patients in a trial have experienced the outcome of interest (eg, they may disagree about whether a patient has had a transient ischemic attack or a stroke or about whether a death should be classified as a cardiovascular death), or whether a study meets the eligibility criteria for a *systematic review*.

CHANCE WILL ALWAYS BE RESPONSIBLE FOR SOME OF THE APPARENT AGREEMENT BETWEEN OBSERVERS

Any 2 people judging the presence or absence of an attribute will agree some of the time simply by chance. Similarly, even inexperienced and uninformed clinicians may agree on a physical finding on occasion purely as a result of chance. This chance agreement is more likely to occur when the prevalence of a target finding (a physical finding, a disease, an eligibility criterion) is high. When investigators present agreement as raw agreement (or crude agreement)—that is, by simply counting the number of times agreement has occurred—this chance agreement gives a misleading impression.

ALTERNATIVES FOR DEALING WITH THE PROBLEM OF AGREEMENT BY CHANCE

This chapter describes approaches to addressing the problem of misleading results based on chance agreement. When we are dealing with categorical data (ie, placing patients in discrete categories such as mild, moderate, or severe or stage 1, 2, 3, or 4), the most popular approach to dealing with chance agreement is with *chance-corrected agreement*. Chance-corrected agreement is quantitated as κ, or *weighted* κ. Another option is the use of *chance-independent agreement*, or φ. One can use these 3 statistics to measure nonrandom agreement between observers, investigators, or measurements.

One Solution to Agreement by Chance: Chance-Corrected Agreement, or κ

κ removes most of the agreement by chance and informs clinicians of the extent of the possible agreement over and above chance. The total possible agreement on any judgment is always 100%. Figure 17.3-1 depicts a situation in which agreement by chance is 50%, leaving possible agreement above and beyond chance of 50%. As depicted in the figure, the raters have achieved an agreement of 75%. Of this 75%, 50% was achieved by chance alone. Of the remaining possible 50% agreement, the raters have achieved half, resulting in a κ value of 0.25/0.50, or 0.50.

Calculating κ

How is κ calculated? Assume that 2 observers are assessing the presence of Murphy sign, which may help clinicians detect an inflamed gallbladder. Unfortunately, they have no skill at detecting the presence or absence of Murphy sign, and their evaluations are no better than blind guesses. Let us say they are both guessing in a ratio of 50:50; they guess that Murphy sign is present half of the time and that it is absent half of the time. On average, if both raters were evaluating the same 100 patients, they would achieve the results presented in Figure 17.3-2. Referring to that figure, you observe that these results demonstrate that the 2 cells that tally the raw agreement, A and D, include 50% of the observations. Thus, simply by guessing (and thus by chance), the raters have achieved 50% agreement.

FIGURE 17.3-1

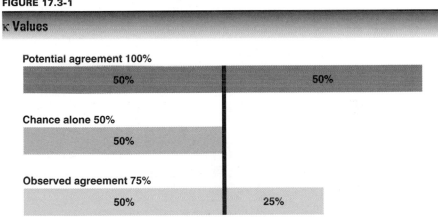

κ Values

Potential agreement 100%

| 50% | 50% |

Chance alone 50%

| 50% |

Observed agreement 75%

| 50% | 25% |

κ = 0.25/0.50 = 0.50 (good agreement)

FIGURE 17.3-2

Agreement by Chance When Both Reviewers Are Guessing in a Ratio of 50% Target Positive and 50% Target Negative

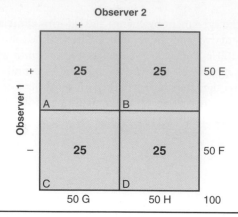

+ Refers to target positive and – to target negative; in this case, + is Murphy sign present and – is Murphy sign absent. A, Patients in which both observers find the sign present. B, Patients in which observer 1 finds the sign present and observer 2 finds the sign absent. C, Patients in which observer 1 finds the sign absent and observer 2 finds the sign present. D, Patients in which both observers find the sign absent.

Reprinted from McGinn et al,[1] by permission of the publisher. Copyright © 2005, Canadian Medical Association.

What happens if the raters repeat the exercise of rating 100 patients, but this time, each guesses in a ratio of 80% positive and 20% negative? Figure 17.3-3 depicts what, on average, will occur. Now, the agreement (the sum of cells A and D) has increased to 68%.

What is the arithmetic involved in filling in the table to determine the level of agreement that occurs by chance? The procedure involves, for each cell, multiplying the total number of observations in the row of which that cell is a part by the number

FIGURE 17.3-3

Agreement by Chance When Both Reviewers Are Guessing in a Ratio of 80% Target Positive and 20% Target Negative

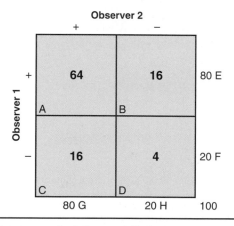

+ Refers to target positive and – to target negative; in this case, + is Murphy sign present and – is Murphy sign absent.

of observations in the column of which that cell is a part and dividing by the total number of patients. In the example in Figure 17.3-2, for instance, we can calculate how many observations we expect by chance to fall in cell A, which represents the number of positives agreed on by both reviewers. First, we multiply the number of times observer 1 finds a Murphy sign (50) by the number of times observer 2 detects a Murphy sign (also 50), and we divide by 100 the total number of patients evaluated. Similarly, to calculate the number of observations we expect in cell D, we again multiply 50 by 50 (the 2 numbers of expected negatives) and divide by 100. Readers can find a more detailed demonstration of the rationale behind this and other calculations presented here in the Evidence-Based Medicine Tips series.[1]

Were we to repeat this arithmetic exercise with different marginal totals, we would find that as the proportion of observations classified as positive becomes progressively more extreme (ie, as it moves away from 50%), the agreement by chance increases. The average chance agreement changes are shown in Table 17.3-1, as 2 observers classify an increasingly higher proportion of patients in one category or the other (such as positive and negative; sign present or absent).

Figure 17.3-4 illustrates the calculation of κ with a hypothetical data set. First, we calculate the agreement observed: In 40 patients, the 2 observers agreed that Murphy sign was positive (cell A) and they further agreed that in another 40 patients, it was negative (cell D). Thus, the total agreement is 40 + 40, or 80.

Next we calculate the agreement by chance by multiplying the proportions of tests read as positive by the 2 observers (0.5 × 0.5) and adding that to the product of the proportions of tests read as negative by the 2 observers (0.5 × 0.5). The total agreement by chance is 0.25 + 0.25, or 0.50, 50%.

We can then calculate κ using the principle illustrated in Figure 17.3-1.

$$\frac{(\text{agreement observed} - \text{agreement by chance})}{(\text{agreement possible} - \text{agreement by chance})}$$

or in this case:

$$\frac{80 - 50}{100 - 50} = \frac{30}{50} = 0.6$$

TABLE 17.3-1

Relationship Between the Proportion Positive and the Expected Agreement by Chance

Proportion Positive	Agreement by Chance (%)
0.5	0.5 (50)
0.6	0.52 (52)
0.7	0.58 (58)
0.8	0.68 (68)
0.9	0.82 (82)

Reprinted from McGinn et al,[1] by permission of the publisher. Copyright © 2005, Canadian Medical Association.

FIGURE 17.3-4

Observed and Expected Agreement

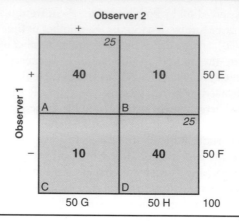

+ Refers to target positive and − to target negative; in this case, + is Murphy sign present and − is Murphy sign absent. Expected agreement by chance appears in italics in cells A and D.

Reprinted from McGinn et al,[1] by permission of the publisher. Copyright © 2005, Canadian Medical Association.

κ WITH 3 OR MORE RATERS, OR 3 OR MORE CATEGORIES

Using similar principles, one can calculate chance-corrected agreement when there are more than 2 raters.[2] Furthermore, one can calculate κ when raters place patients into more than 2 categories (eg, patients with heart failure may be rated as New York Heart Association class I, II, III, or IV). In these situations, one may give partial credit for intermediate levels of agreement (for instance, one observer may classify a patient as class II, whereas another may observe the same patient as class III) by adopting a so-called weighted κ statistic. Weighting refers to calculations that give full credit to full agreement and partial credit to partial agreement (according to distance from the diagonal on an agreement table).[3]

There are a number of approaches to valuing the κ levels raters achieve. One option is the following: 0 = poor agreement; 0 to 0.2 = slight agreement; 0.21 to 0.4 = fair agreement; 0.41 to 0.6 = moderate agreement; 0.61 to 0.8 = substantial agreement; and 0.81 to 1.0 = almost perfect agreement.[4]

Examples of chance-corrected agreement that investigators have calculated in clinical studies are as follows: exercise stress test cardiac T-wave changes, κ = 0.25; jugular venous distention, κ = 0.50; arterial stenosis on cardiac catheterization, κ = 0.70; CAGE questionnaire score for alcoholism (Cut down, Annoyed, Guilty, Eye opener), κ = 0.82; tenderness on abdominal examination in the emergency department, κ = 0.42; and presence of retinopathy on examination, κ = 0.72-0.75.

A Limitation of κ

Despite its intuitive appeal and widespread use, the κ statistic has one important disadvantage: As a result of the high level of chance agreement when distributions become more extreme, the possible agreement above chance agreement becomes small, and even moderate values of κ are difficult to achieve. Thus, using the same raters in a variety of settings, as the proportion of positive ratings becomes extreme, κ will decrease even if the raters' skill at interpretation does not.[5-7]

An Alternative to κ: Chance-Independent Agreement, or φ

One solution to this problem is chance-independent agreement using the φ statistic.[8] Here, one begins by estimating the *odds ratio (OR)* from a 2 × 2 table displaying the agreement between 2 observers. Figure 17.3-5 contrasts the formulas for raw agreement, κ, and φ.

The OR (*ad/bc*) in Figure 17.3-5 provides the basis for calculating φ. The OR is the odds of a positive classification by rater B when rater A gives a positive classification divided by the odds of a positive classification by rater B when rater A gives a negative classification (see Chapter 10.2, Understanding the Results: More About Odds Ratios). The OR would not change if we were to reverse the rows and columns. Thus, it does not matter which observer we identify as observer A and which one we identify as observer B. The OR provides a natural measure of agreement. This agreement can be made more easily interpretable by converting it into a form that takes values from −1.0 (representing extreme disagreement) to 1.0 (representing extreme agreement). The φ statistic makes this conversion using the following formula:

$$\varphi = \frac{\sqrt{OR} - 1}{\sqrt{OR} + 1} = \frac{\sqrt{ad} - \sqrt{bc}}{\sqrt{ad} + \sqrt{bc}}$$

When both margins are 0.5 (ie, when both raters conclude that 50% of the patients are positive and 50% are negative for the trait of interest), φ is equal to κ.

Advantages of φ Over Other Approaches

The use of φ has 4 important advantages over other approaches. First, it is independent of the level of chance agreement. Thus, investigators could expect to find similar levels of φ whether the distribution of results is 50% positive and 50%

FIGURE 17.3-5

Calculations of Agreement

		Rater B	
		Observation present	Observation absent
Rater A	Observation present	A	B
	Observation absent	C	D

Raw agreement $= \dfrac{a+d}{a+b+c+d}$

$\kappa = \dfrac{\text{Observed agreement} - \text{Expected agreement}}{1 - \text{Expected agreement}}$

where observed agreement $= \dfrac{a+d}{a+b+c+d}$

and expected agreement $= \dfrac{(a+b)(a+c)}{a+b+c+d} + \dfrac{(c+d)(b+d)}{a+b+c+d}$

Odds ratio (OR) $= \dfrac{ad}{bc}$

$\phi = \dfrac{\sqrt{OR}-1}{\sqrt{OR}+1} = \dfrac{\sqrt{ad}-\sqrt{bc}}{\sqrt{ad}+\sqrt{bc}}$

negative or whether it is 90% positive and 10% negative. As we have pointed out, this is not true for κ.

Second, φ allows statistical modeling approaches that the κ statistic does not offer. For instance, such flexibility allows investigators to take advantage of all ratings when observers assess patients, radiographs, or other study outcomes on multiple occasions.[8]

Third, φ allows testing of whether differences in agreement between pairings of raters are statistically significant, an option that is not available with κ.[8]

Fourth, because φ is based on the OR, one can carry out exact analyses. This feature is particularly attractive when the sample is small or if there is a zero cell among the observations.[9]

Statisticians may disagree about the relative usefulness of κ and φ. Most important, from a clinician's point of view, is that either approach provides a major improvement over raw agreement.

References

1. McGinn T, Wyer P, Newman T, Keitz S, Leipzig R, Guyatt G; Evidence-Based Medicine Teaching Tips Working Group. Tips for the teachers of evidence-based medicine, 3: measures of observer variability (kappa statistic). *CMAJ.* 2004;171(11):online-1 to online-9. http://www.cmaj.ca/cgi/data/171/111/1369/DC1361/1361.

2. Cohen J. Weighted kappa: nominal scale agreement with provision for scaled disagreement or partial credit. *Psychol Bull.* 1968;70:213-220.

3. Landis J, Koch G. The measurement of observer agreement for categorical data. *Biometrics.* 1977;33(1):159-174.

4. Sackett D, Hayes R, Guyatt G, Tugwell P. *Clinical Epidemiology: A Basic Science for Clinical Medicine.* 2nd ed. Boston, MA: Brown & Co; 1991:30.

5. Thompson W, Walter S. A reappraisal of the kappa coefficient. *J Clin Epidemiol.* 1988;41(10):949-958.

6. Feinstein A, Cicchetti D. High agreement but low kappa, I: the problems of two paradoxes. *J Clin Epidemiol.* 1990;43(6):543-549.

7. Cook R, Farewell V. Conditional inference for subject-specific and marginal agreement: two families of agreement measures. *Can J Stat.* 1995;23:333-344.

8. Meade M, Cook R, Guyatt G, et al. Interobserver variation in interpreting chest radiographs for the diagnosis of acute respiratory distress syndrome. *Am J Respir Crit Care Med.* 2000;161(1):85-90.

9. Armitage P, Colton T, eds. *Encyclopedia of Biostatistics.* Chichester, NY: John Wiley & Sons; 1998.

CLINICAL PREDICTION RULES

Thomas McGinn, Peter Wyer, Juan Wisnivesky, P. J. Devereaux, Ian Stiell, Scott Richardson, and Gordon Guyatt

IN THIS CHAPTER:

Can a Clinical Prediction Rule Reduce Unnecessary Ankle Radiographs?

You are the medical director of a busy inner-city emergency department. Faced with a limited budget and pressure to improve efficiency, you have conducted an audit of radiologic procedures ordered for minor trauma and have found that the rate of radiographs ordered for ankle and knee trauma is high. You are aware of the Ottawa Ankle Rules, which are guidelines that identify patients for whom it is safe to omit ankle radiographs without adverse consequences (Figure 17.4-1).[1,2] In addition, you are aware that only a small number of faculty and residents currently rely on these guidelines to make quick frontline decisions in the emergency department.

You are interested in knowing the accuracy of the Ottawa Ankle Rules, whether they are applicable to the population of patients in your hospital, and whether you should implement them in your own practice. Furthermore, you wonder whether implementing the guidelines can change clinical behavior and reduce costs without compromising quality of care. You decide to consult the original medical literature and assess the evidence for yourself.

FIGURE 17.4-1

Ottawa Ankle Rules

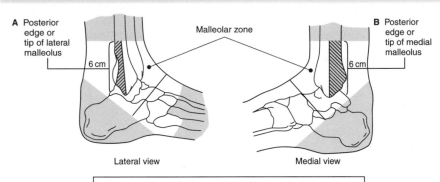

A Posterior edge or tip of lateral malleolus

Malleolar zone

B Posterior edge or tip of medial malleolus

6 cm

6 cm

Lateral view   Medial view

An ankle radiograph series is required only if
there is any pain in the malleolar zone and any of these findings:
1. Bone tenderness at **A**
    or
2. Bone tenderness at **B**
    or
3. Inability to bear weight both
    immediately and in
    emergency department

Reproduced from Stiell et al,[3] with permission from *JAMA*.

FINDING THE EVIDENCE

Currently, *prediction rules* or *decision rules* have no separate Medical Subject Headings (MeSH) in the National Library of Medicine MEDLINE database. Logging onto the Internet, you search PubMed "ankle injuries decision rules." This search yields 40 citations, several of which deal with the derivation and validation of the Ottawa *clinical prediction rules* (*CPRs*) for ankle fractures. A search filter for CPRs is now available as part of the PubMed Clinical Queries package. Searching with the narrow clinical query (http://www.ncbi.nlm.nih.gov/entrez/query/static/clinical.shtml) using the term "ankle fracture" gave 17 citations but not the original derivation.

In reviewing these articles and deciding whether to implement changes in your emergency department, you require criteria for deciding on the strength of the inference you can make about the accuracy and influence of the Ottawa Ankle Rules. This chapter provides the tools required to answer those questions.

WHAT IS A CLINICAL PREDICTION RULE?

Establishing a patient's diagnosis and prognosis is central to every physician's practice. The diagnoses we make—and our assessment of patients' prognoses—generally determine the recommendations we make to patients. Clinical experience provides us with an intuitive sense of which findings on medical history, physical examination, and laboratory or radiologic investigation are critical in making an accurate diagnosis or an accurate assessment of a patient's likely fate. Although a clinician's intuition is sometimes extraordinarily accurate, at times this intuition may be misleading. CPRs attempt to increase the accuracy of clinicians' diagnostic and prognostic assessments.

We define a CPR as a clinical tool that quantifies the individual contributions that various components of the medical history, physical examination, and basic laboratory results make toward the diagnosis, prognosis, or likely response to treatment in an individual patient. This definition is equally applicable to what have been called "clinical prediction guides" and "clinical decision rules."

Prediction implies helping the clinician to better decide on a future clinical event. Decision implies directing a clinician to a specific course of action. Application of CPRs sometimes results in a decision and other times in a prediction but may also lead to a probability or a *likelihood ratio* (*LR*) that a clinician applies to a current diagnostic problem. The abbreviation CPR is used in this chapter regardless of whether the output of the "rule" is a suggested clinical course of action, the probability of a future event, or an increase or decrease in the likelihood of a particular diagnosis.

Whatever the CPR is generating, a decision, a prediction, or a change in diagnostic probability, clinicians are most likely to find it useful in situations in which decision making is complex, when the clinical stakes are high, or when opportunities exist to achieve cost savings without compromising patient care.

USERS' GUIDES TO CLINICAL PREDICTION RULES

Our usual approach to users' guides—validity, results, and applicability—does not work well for CPRs because developing and testing a CPR involves 3 steps: the creation or derivation of the rule, the testing or validation of the rule, and the assessment of the effect of the rule on clinical behavior—the impact analysis. The validation process may require several studies at different clinical sites to fully test the accuracy of the rule (Figure 17.4-2). Different authors may publish separately each step in the evolution of a CPR or, rarely, they may publish multiple steps in 1 article. Authors frequently report a "derivation and validation" of a prediction rule when the "validation" is limited to the use of statistical techniques on a single data set. Under most circumstances, a statistical validation of this type would not qualify as an independent step beyond the derivation process. Table 17.4-1 presents a hierarchy of evidence that can guide clinicians in assessing the full range of evidence supporting use of a CPR in their practice. We will now review the steps in the development and testing of a CPR, relating each stage of the process to the users' guides presented in Table 17.4-1.

DEVELOPING A CLINICAL PREDICTION RULE

Our search revealed 3 articles related to the Ottawa Ankle Rules[1,2,4]; the first described the rules' derivation.[1] CPR developers begin by constructing a list of potential predictors of the outcome of interest—in this case, ankle fractures demonstrated on ankle radiograph. The list typically includes items from the medical history, physical examination, and basic laboratory tests. The investigators then examine a group of patients and determine (1) whether the candidate clinical

FIGURE 17.4-2

Development and Testing of a Clinical Prediction Rule

Step 1. Derivation	Step 2. Validation		Step 3. Impact analysis
Identification of factors with predictive power	Evidence of reproducible accuracy		Evidence that rule changes physician behavior and improves patient outcomes or reduces costs
	Narrow validation	Broad validation	
	Application of rule in a similar clinical setting and population as in step 1	Application of rule in multiple clinical settings with varying prevalence and outcomes of disease	

Level of evidence

| 4 | 3 | 2 | 1 |

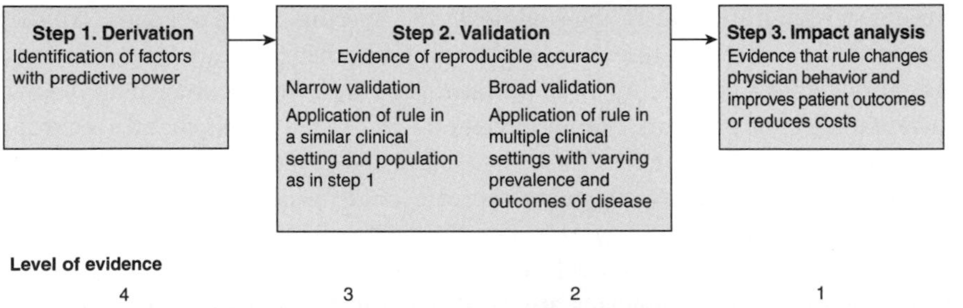

TABLE 17.4-1

Users' Guide to Clinical Prediction Rules

Level I

Has the rule undergone at least 1 prospective validation in a population separate from the derivation set, plus 1 impact analysis that demonstrates a change in clinician behavior with beneficial consequences? If yes, clinicians can use the rule in a wide variety of settings with confidence that they can change clinician behavior, facilitate patient decision making, improve patient outcomes, or reduce costs.

Level II

Has the rule shown accuracy either in 1 large prospective multicenter study including a broad spectrum of patients and clinicians or validation in several smaller settings that differ from one another? If so, but if there is no impact analysis, clinicians can use it in various settings with confidence in their accuracy but with no certainty that patient outcomes will improve.

Level III

Has the rule been validated in only 1 narrow prospective sample? If so, clinicians may consider using the CPR with caution and only if patients in the study are similar to those in their clinical setting.

Level IV

Has the rule been derived but not validated or validated only in split samples, large retrospective databases, or through statistical techniques? If so, this is a CPR that needs further validation before it can be applied clinically.

Abbreviation: CPR, clinical prediction rule.

predictors are present and (2) each patient's status on the outcome of interest; in this case, the result of the ankle radiograph.[5] Statistical analysis reveals which predictors are most powerful and which predictors can be omitted from the rule by researchers without loss of predictive power. Typically, the statistical techniques used in this process are based on logistic regression (see Chapter 13, Advanced Topics in Harm: Correlation and Regression). Other techniques that investigators sometimes use include discriminant analysis, which produces equations similar to regression analysis[6]; recursive partitioning analysis, which divides the patient population into smaller and smaller groups according to discriminating risk factors[7]; and neural networks.[8] Standards for the development of a CPR are available beyond the scope of what is required for a clinician who is interested in using a CPR and needs to focus on the extent of CPR validation.

CPRs that are not validated are usually not ready for clinical application (see Table 17.4-1). Despite this major limitation, clinicians can still extract clinically relevant messages from an article describing the development of a CPR. They may wish to note the most important predictors and to consider them more carefully in their own practice. They may also consider giving less importance to variables that failed to show predictive power.

For instance, in developing a CPR to predict mortality from pneumonia, investigators found that the white blood cell count had no bearing on subsequent mortality.[9,10] Hence, clinicians may wish to put less weight on the white blood cell count when making decisions about admitting pneumonia patients to the hospital.

DERIVATION—EVEN WHEN RIGOROUS— IS SELDOM SUFFICIENT

There are 3 reasons why even rigorously derived CPRs are generally not ready for application in clinical practice without further validation. First, the prediction rules derived from one set of patients may reflect associations between given predictors and outcomes that occur primarily because of the play of chance. If that is so, a different set of predictors will emerge in a different group of patients, even if they come from the same setting. Second, predictors may be idiosyncratic to the population, to the clinicians using the rule, or to other aspects of the design of individual studies. If that is so, the rule may fail in a new setting. Finally, because of problems in the feasibility of rule application in the clinical setting, clinicians may fail to implement a rule comprehensively or accurately, which would result in a rule that succeeds in theory but fails in practice.

Statistical methods can deal with the first of these problems. For instance, investigators may split their population into 2 groups, using one to develop the rule and the other to test it. Alternatively, they may use more sophisticated statistical methods built on the same logic. Conceptually, these approaches involve removing 1 patient from the sample, generating the rule using the remainder of the patients, and testing it on the patient who was removed from the sample. One repeats this procedure, sometimes referred to as a bootstrap technique, in sequence for every patient under study.

Although statistical validations within the same setting or group of patients reduce the likelihood that the rule reflects the play of chance rather than true associations, they fail to address the other 2 threats to validity. Because of the risk that a CPR will provide misleading information when applied in an actual clinical setting, a CPR that has undergone development without validation is situated as level IV in the hierarchy (see Table 17.4-1). To ascend from level IV in our hierarchy of evidence, studies must assess the use of the rule by clinicians in clinical practice.

Authors frequently entitle their pilot reports of development of a prediction rule as "derivation and validation," implying that they have performed the first 2 steps in our developmental hierarchy. More often than not, the validation phase involves the equivalent of a split-sample statistical control within a single developmental trial, rather than an independent clinical application of the derived rule on a noncontiguous sample of patients. Readers should regard such reports in their entirety as conforming to the level IV phase of development within our scheme.

As an example, a recent study designed to develop a rule to identify a low-risk group of children presenting to emergency departments with signs and symptoms suggestive of acute appendicitis enrolled patients during a 16-month period.[11] Without altering any other aspect of the study protocol, the authors chose to define patients enrolled during the final 5 months of the study period as a "validation" group. The authors presented the resulting instrument as a prediction rule that had already undergone validation and therefore was ready for clinical application. This rule, although promising, is classified as class IV within our hierarchy.

A CPR developed to predict a serious outcome (including heart failure or ventricular arrhythmia) in syncope patients further highlights the importance of clinical validation. Investigators derived the rule using data from 252 patients who presented to the emergency department; subsequently, they attempted to prospectively validate it in a sample of 374 patients.[12] The prediction rule gave individuals a score from 0 to 4, depending on the number of clinical predictors present. Unfortunately, if one used results from the derivation patients, one would estimate that patients had almost twice the risk of a poor outcome than was the case for patients in the validation set! For example, in the derivation set, the risk of a poor outcome among patients with a score of 3 was 52%; by contrast, patients with the same score in the validation set had a much lower probability of a poor outcome, 27%. This variation in results may have occurred as a result of differences in the severity of the syncope cases entered into the 2 studies— or different criteria for generating a score of 3.

There are instances in which rigid application of this hierarchy could mislead. For example, Eagle et al[13] performed a large multicenter study in more than 90 hospitals with 15000 patients. The study evaluated predictors of mortality in patients who were discharged after an acute coronary syndrome. The prediction rule was developed with a prospective data set including more than 15000 patients and then validated in a second cohort of more than 7000 patients. Some would argue that although this study was not a formal prospective validation and clinicians never actually used the rule, the sheer size of the validation makes the rule ready for clinical application (Figure 17.4-1). Given that the authors identified 9 variables predictive of 6-month mortality (older age, history of myocardial infarction, history of heart failure, increased pulse rate at presentation, lower systolic blood pressure at presentation, elevated initial serum creatinine level, elevated initial serum cardiac biomarker levels, ST-segment depression on presenting electrocardiogram, and not having a percutaneous coronary intervention performed in hospital) and clinicians are unlikely to be able to remember this number of predictors, one might question the feasibility of application in clinical practice. Thus, a compelling argument remains for further study to ensure feasibility and accuracy in actual clinical use.

MOVING UP THE HIERARCHY—VALIDATION OF A CLINICAL PREDICTION RULE

To move up the hierarchy, CPRs must provide additional evidence of validity. The second article in our search described the refinement and prospective validation of the Ottawa Ankle Rules. Validation of a CPR involves demonstrating that its repeated application as part of the process of clinical care leads to the same results. Ideally, validation entails application of the rule prospectively in a new population (with dissimilar prevalence and spectrum of disease from the derivation population) and by a variety of clinicians in a variety of institutions. Also important is whether it works well when clinicians are consciously applying it as a rule, rather than as a statistical derivation from a large number of potential predictors gathered by, for instance, medical-record review or data collection by research personnel.

If the setting in which the prediction rule was originally developed was limited and its validation was confined to this setting, application by clinicians working in other settings is less secure. Validation in a similar setting can take a number of forms. Most simply, after developing the prediction rule, the investigators return to their population, draw a new sample of patients, and then test the rule's performance as actually implemented by physicians. Thus, we classify rules that have been validated in the same—or very similar—limited or narrow populations as the sample used in the development phase as level III on our hierarchy, and we recommend that clinicians use the result cautiously (see Table 17.4-1).

In the derivation phase, if investigators draw patients from a sufficiently heterogenous population across a variety of institutions, testing the rule in the same population provides strong validation. Validation in a new population by physicians in that setting provides the clinician with strong inferences about the usefulness of the rule, corresponding to level II in our hierarchy (see Table 17.4-1). The more numerous and diverse the settings in which the rule is tested and found accurate, the more likely it is that it will generalize to an untested setting.[14]

The Ottawa Ankle Rules were derived in 2 large, university-based emergency departments in Ottawa and then prospectively validated in a large sample of patients from the same emergency departments.[2] At this stage, the rule would be classified as level II in our hierarchy because of the large number and diversity of patients and physicians involved in the study. Since that initial validation, other studies[15-18] have validated the rule in several clinical settings, with relatively consistent results. This evidence further strengthens our inference about its predictive power when applied in actual clinical settings.

To demonstrate the importance of the progression from level III to level II, consider a rule that was derived to predict preserved left ventricular (LV) function after MI.[19] The initial derivation and validation were performed on 314 patients who were admitted to a tertiary care center. The prediction rule was first derived by using 162 patients and then was validated with 152 patients in the same setting. The prediction rule demonstrated that, of patients in whom the rule suggested LV function was preserved, this was, in fact, true in 99%.

At this stage in the rule development, one would consider the rule as level III, to be used only in settings similar to that of the validation study, that is, in similar cardiac care units. The rule was further validated in 2 larger trials, one trial using 213 patients from a single site and a larger trial using 1891 patients from several institutions.[20,21] In both settings, 11% of patients in whom the rule suggested that LV function had been preserved had abnormal LV function. This decrease in accuracy changes the potential use and implications of the rule in clinical practice. At this point in development, we would consider the rule to fall within the category of level II, meaning that clinicians can use the rule in clinical settings with a high degree of confidence to identify patients with approximately a 90% probability of preserved LV function.

STRONG METHODOLOGY INCREASES CONFIDENCE IN VALIDATION STUDIES

Regardless of whether investigators have conducted their validation study in a similar, narrow (level III) or broad, heterogeneous, or different (level II) population,

TABLE 17.4-2

Methodologic Standards for Validation of a Clinical Prediction Rule

- Were the patients chosen in an unbiased fashion and do they represent a wide spectrum of severity of disease?
- Was there a blinded assessment of the criterion standard for all patients?
- Was there an explicit and accurate interpretation of the predictor variables and the actual rule without knowledge of the outcome?
- Was there 100% follow-up of those enrolled?

their results allow stronger inferences if they have adhered to a number of methodologic standards (Table 17.4-2). Interested readers can find a complete discussion on the validation process and these criteria in an article by Laupacis et al.[5]

If those evaluating predictor status of study patients are aware of the outcome, or if those assessing the outcome are aware of patients' status with respect to the predictors, their assessments may be biased. For instance, in a CPR developed to predict the presence of pneumonia in patients presenting with cough, the authors make no mention of blinding during either the derivation process or the validation process.[22] Knowledge of medical history or physical examination findings may have influenced the judgments of the unblinded radiologists.

The investigators testing the Ottawa Ankle Rules enrolled consecutive patients, obtained radiographs for all of them, and ensured that not only were the clinicians assessing the clinical predictors unaware of the radiologic results but also the radiologists had no knowledge of the clinical data.

How to Decide on the Power of the Rule

Regardless of the level of evidence associated with a CPR, its usefulness will depend on its predictive power. Investigators may report their results in a variety of ways. First, the results may dictate a specific course of action. For instance, the ankle component of the Ottawa Ankle Rules states that ankle radiographs are indicated only for patients with pain near the malleoli plus either inability to bear weight or localized bone tenderness at the posterior edge or tip of either malleolus (Figure 17.4-1).[2] Underlying this decision are the LRs associated with the rule as a diagnostic test (see Chapter 16, Diagnostic Tests). In the development process, all patients with fractures had a positive result (sensitivity of 100%), but only 40% of those without fractures had a negative result (specificity of 40%). These results suggest that if clinicians order radiographs only for those patients with a positive result, they will not miss any fractures and will avoid the test in 40% of those without a fracture.

The validation study confirmed these results. The test maintained a sensitivity of 100%, with a 95% confidence interval (CI) around this estimate of 93% to 100%.[2] Some clinicians might remain uncomfortable committing themselves to the use of the rule were the true value of the sensitivity as low as 93%, the lower limit of this interval. Clinicians adopting the rule would nevertheless miss few, if any, fractures.

Another way of reporting CPR results is in terms of probability of the target condition or outcome, given a particular result. When investigators report prediction rule results in this fashion, they are implicitly incorporating all clinical information. In doing so, they remove any need for clinicians to consider independent information in deciding about the likelihood of the diagnosis or about a patient's prognosis. For example, a recent prediction rule for pulmonary embolus derived and validated by Wells et al[23] accurately placed inpatients and outpatients presenting to tertiary care hospitals into low (3.4%; 95% CI, 2.2%-5.0%), intermediate (28%; 95% CI, 23.4%-32.2%), or high (78%; 95% CI, 69.2%-89.6%) probability categories.

Finally, investigators may report their findings about the accuracy of prediction rules as LRs or as absolute risks or relative risks. Using LRs, investigators are implicitly suggesting that clinicians should use other, independent information to generate a pretest probability (or prerule probability). Clinicians can then use the LRs generated from the rule to establish a posttest probability. (For approaches to using LRs, see Chapter 16, Diagnostic Tests.) For example, accuracy of the CAGE (Cut down, Annoyed, Guilty, Eye-opener) prediction rule for detecting alcoholism has been reported using LRs (eg, for CAGE scores of 0/4, LR = 0.14; for scores of 1/4, LR = 1.5; for scores of 2/4, LR = 4.5; for scores of 3/4, LR = 13; and for scores of 4/4, LR = 100).[24] In this example, the probability of disease, alcoholism, depends on the combination of the prevalence of disease in the community and the score on the CAGE prediction rule.

TESTING THE CLINICAL IMPACT OF A CLINICAL PREDICTION RULE

Use of CPRs involves remembering the relevant predictor variables and often entails making calculations to determine a patient's probability of having the target outcome. Pocket cards and computer algorithms can facilitate the use of complex CPRs. Nonetheless, they demand clinician time and energy, and their use is warranted only if they change physician behavior in a manner that improves patient outcomes or reduces costs while maintaining quality.

Even an accurate prediction rule may fail to produce a change in behavior or an improvement in outcomes. First, clinicians' intuitive estimation of probabilities may be as good as, if not better than, the rule. Second, the calculations involved may be cumbersome, and as a result, clinicians may not use the rule. Even worse, they may miscalculate. Third, there may be practical barriers to acting on the results of the CPR. For instance, in the case of the Ottawa Ankle Rules, clinicians may be sufficiently concerned about protecting themselves against litigation that they may order radiographs despite a prediction rule result suggesting a negligible probability of fracture.

These are the considerations that lead us to classify a CPR with evidence of accuracy in diverse populations as level II and insist on a positive result from a study of impact before a CPR ascends to level I.

Ideally, an impact study would randomize patients—or larger administrative units—to either apply or not to apply the CPR and follow patients for all relevant outcomes (including quality of life, morbidity, and resource use). Randomization of individual patients is unlikely to be appropriate because one would expect the participating clinicians to incorporate the rule into the care of all patients. A suitable alternative is to randomize institutions or practice settings and to conduct analyses appropriate to these larger units of randomization. Another potential design is to look at a single group before and after clinicians began to use the CPR, but choice of a before-after study will substantially reduce the strength of inference.

Investigators examining the impact of the Ottawa Ankle Rules conducted 1 nonrandomized study in which they compared one hospital in which the rule was implemented to a control hospital in which it was not.[3] Results suggested an impact of rule implementation. Subsequently, they randomized 6 emergency departments to use or not use their prediction rule.[4] Just before initiating the study, one center dropped out, leaving a total of 5 emergency departments, 2 in the intervention group and 3 in the usual-care group. The intervention consisted of introducing the prediction rule at a general meeting, distributing pocket cards summarizing the rule, posting the rule throughout the emergency department, and applying pre-printed data collection forms to each patient chart. In the control group, the only intervention was the introduction of preprinted data collection forms without the Ottawa Ankle Rules attached to each chart. A total of 1911 eligible patients were entered into the study, 1005 in the control group and 906 in the intervention group. There were 691 radiographs requested in the intervention group and 996 requested in the control group. In an analysis that focused on the ordering physician, the investigators found that the mean proportion of patients referred for radiography was 99.6% in the control group and 78.9% in the intervention group ($P = .03$). The investigators noted 3 missed fractures in the intervention group, none of which led to adverse outcomes. Thus, the investigators demonstrated a positive resource utilization impact of the Ottawa Ankle Rules (decreased test ordering) without increase in adverse outcomes, moving the CPR to level I in the hierarchy (see Table 17.4-1).

Some prediction rules require, by their very nature, evidence of clinical impact as a precondition of use. The Pneumonia Outcomes Research Team's (PORT) instrument for stratifying mortality risk in patients with community-acquired pneumonia does not itself prescribe a course of action for clinicians.[25] The authors of the original study included recommendations regarding appropriate assignment of patients in different risk classes to management as outpatients or inpatients or in intensive care units. However, it is ultimately up to the treating physicians to make the site of care decision for each patient, and the PORT severity score is only 1 factor that they must consider in the process. A before-after study[26] incorporated the PORT score as part of an emergency department–based clinical pathway and demonstrated that clinicians were more inclined to manage low-risk patients outside of the hospital when the scores were made available to them. More recently, Yealy et al[27] published a sound proposal for a randomized controlled trial studying the clinical impact of the PORT rule, and preliminary results of their study confirm its clinical value.

META-ANALYSIS OF CLINICAL PREDICTION RULES

As CPRs become more common, it is not unusual to encounter several rules to predict the same event or an individual rule that has been derived and validated in multiple populations and different settings. Systematic reviews and, if appropriate, meta-analyses are the preferred tools to assess the quality of prediction and the level of evidence. Researchers have used meta-analysis to generate best estimates of a CPR's predictive power the same way they use meta-analysis to generate best estimates of the properties of a diagnostic test.[28] Although performing systematic reviews and meta-analyses of diagnostic tests can be challenging, this is especially challenging with CPRs because of the various numbers of predictors that make up a CPR.[29]

Evidence regarding the accuracy of the Ottawa knee rule was summarized in a recently published meta-analyis.[30] The authors systematically reviewed the literature and identified 6 studies involving 4249 adult patients who were included in the analysis. Using these data, the pooled sensitivity of the decision rule was 98.5% (95% CI, 93.2%-100%) and the pooled specificity was 48.6% (95% CI, 43.4%-51.0%). Thus, combined evidence from these studies suggests that the Ottawa rule accurately excludes knee fractures after acute knee injury.

CLINICAL RESOLUTION

You have found level I evidence supporting the use of the Ottawa decision rule in reducing unnecessary ankle radiographs in patients presenting to the emergency department with ankle injuries. You therefore feel confident that you can use the rule in your own practice. Another study makes you aware that changing the behavior of your colleagues to realize the possible reductions in cost may be a challenge. Cameron and Naylor[31] reported on an initiative in which clinicians who are expert in the use of the Ottawa Ankle Rules trained 16 other individuals to teach the use of the rule. These individuals returned to their emergency departments armed with slides, overheads, a 13-minute instructional video, and a mandate to train their colleagues locally and regionally in the use of the rule. Unfortunately, this program led to no change in the use of ankle radiography.

Graham et al[32] conducted a structured survey of emergency practitioners in 5 countries to determine their awareness of and use of the ankle and foot rules. Awareness of the rule by respondents in Canada, the United Kingdom, and the United States ranged from 91% to 99%. However, only 32% of practitioners in the United States who were aware of the rule stated that they actually used it all or most of the time. This contrasted dramatically with their counterparts in Canada and the United Kingdom, more than 80% of whom consistently used the instrument (the difference may be related to differing risk of malpractice lawsuits). In a similar survey of only Canadian emergency department providers, approximately 90% stated that they used the rule in practice and believed strongly that it was an important tool. A large percentage, however, more than 50% of respondents, stated that the Ottawa Ankle Rules were not the primary determinant in making decisions of whether or not to order an ankle radiograph.

The results demonstrate that even the availability of a level I CPR may require local implementation strategies with known effectiveness in changing provider behavior to ensure implementation. The need to find ways of changing physician behavior in the direction of consistent use of validated guidelines and therapies is considered the principal agenda of the emerging field of knowledge translation.

CPRs inform our clinical judgment and have the potential to change clinical behavior and reduce unnecessary costs while maintaining quality of care and patient satisfaction. The challenge for clinicians is to evaluate the strength of the rule and its likely effect and to find ways of efficiently incorporating level I rules into their daily practice.

The importance of CPRs is likely to increase as they are built into systems providing probability estimates, LRs, and recommended actions. In the interval, clinicians can access a summary of CPRs that highlights their level of evidence on the Internet (http://med.mssm.edu/ebm).

References

1. Stiell IG, Greenberg GH, McKnight RD, Nair RC, McDowell I, Worthington JR. A study to develop clinical decision rules for the use of radiography in acute ankle injuries. *Ann Emerg Med*. 1992;21(4):384-390.

2. Stiell IG, Greenberg GH, McKnight RD, et al. Decision rules for the use of radiography in acute ankle injuries: refinement and prospective validation. *JAMA*. 1993;269(9):1127-1132.

3. Stiell IG, McKnight RD, Greenberg GH. Implementation of the Ottawa ankle rules. *JAMA*. 1994;271(11):827-832.

4. Auleley GR, Ravaud P, Giraudeau B, et al. Implementation of the Ottawa ankle rules in France: a multicenter randomized controlled trial. *JAMA*. 1997;277(24): 1935-1939.

5. Laupacis A, Sekar N, Stiell IG. Clinical prediction rules: a review and suggested modifications of methodological standards. *JAMA*. 1997;277(6):488-494.

6. Rudy TE, Kubinski JA, Boston JR. Multivariate analysis and repeated measurements: a primer. *J Crit Care*. 1992;7(5):30-41.

7. Cook EF, Goldman L. Empiric comparison of multivariate analytic techniques: advantages and disadvantages of recursive partitioning analysis. *J Chronic Dis*. 1984;37(9-10):721-731.

8. Baxt WG. Application of artificial neural networks to clinical medicine. *Lancet*. 1995;346(8983):1135-1138.

9. Fine MJ, Auble TE, Yealy DM, et al. A prediction rule to identify low-risk patients with community-acquired pneumonia. *N Engl J Med*. 1997;336(4):243-250.

10. Fine MJ, Hanusa BH, Lave JR, et al. Comparison of a disease-specific and a generic severity of illness measure for patients with community-acquired pneumonia. *J Gen Intern Med*. 1995;10(7):359-368.

11. Kharbanda AB, Taylor GA, Fishman SJ, Bachur RG. A clinical decision rule to identify children at low risk for appendicitis. *Pediatrics*. 2005;116(3):709-716.

12. Martin TP, Hanusa BH, Kapoor WN. Risk stratification of patients with syncope. *Ann Emerg Med*. 1997;29(4):459-466.

13. Eagle KA, Lim MJ, Dabbous OH, et al. A validated prediction model for all forms of acute coronary syndrome: estimating the risk of 6-month postdischarge death in an international registry. *JAMA*. 2004;291(22):2727-2733.

14. Justice AC, Covinsky KE, Berlin JA. Assessing the generalizability of prognostic information. *Ann Intern Med*. 1999;130(6):515-524.

15. Lucchesi GM, Jackson RE, Peacock WF, Cerasani C, Swor RA. Sensitivity of the Ottawa rules. *Ann Emerg Med*. 1995;26(1):1-5.

16. Kelly AM, Richards D, Kerr L, et al. Failed validation of a clinical decision rule for the use of radiography in acute ankle injury. *N Z Med J*. 1994;107(982):294-295.

17. Stiell I, Wells G, Laupacis A, et al. Multicentre trial to introduce the Ottawa ankle rules for use of radiography in acute ankle injuries: Multicentre Ankle Rule Study Group. *BMJ*. 1995;311(7005):594-597.

18. Auleley GR, Kerboull L, Durieux P, Cosquer M, Courpied JP, Ravaud P. Validation of the Ottawa ankle rules in France: a study in the surgical emergency department of a teaching hospital. *Ann Emerg Med*. 1998;32(1):14-18.

19. Silver MT, Rose GA, Paul SD, O'Donnell CJ, O'Gara PT, Eagle KA. A clinical rule to predict preserved left ventricular ejection fraction in patients after myocardial infarction. *Ann Intern Med*. 1994;121(10):750-756.

20. Tobin K, Stomel R, Harber D, Karavite D, Sievers J, Eagle K. Validation in a community hospital setting of a clinical rule to predict preserved left ventricular

ejection fraction in patients after myocardial infarction. *Arch Intern Med.* 1999;159(4):353-357.

21. Krumholz HM, Howes CJ, Murillo JE, Vaccarino LV, Radford MJ, Ellerbeck EF. Validation of a clinical prediction rule for left ventricular ejection fraction after myocardial infarction in patients > or = 65 years old. *Am J Cardiol.* 1997; 80(1):11-15.

22. Heckerling PS, Tape TG, Wigton RS, et al. Clinical prediction rule for pulmonary infiltrates. *Ann Intern Med.* 1990;113(9):664-670.

23. Wells PS, Ginsberg JS, Anderson DR, et al. Use of a clinical model for safe management of patients with suspected pulmonary embolism. *Ann Intern Med.* 1998;129(12):997-1005.

24. Buchsbaum DG, Buchanan RG, Centor RM, Schnoll SH, Lawton MJ. Screening for alcohol abuse using CAGE scores and likelihood ratios. *Ann Intern Med.* 1991;115(10):774-777.

25. Atlas SJ, Benzer TI, Borowsky LH. Safely increasing the proportion of patients with community-acquired pneumonia treated as outpatients: an interventional trial. *Arch Intern Med.* 1998;158(12):1350-1356.

26. Yealy DM, Fine MJ, Auble TE. Translating the pneumonia severity index into practice: a trial to influence the admission decision [abstract]. *Ann Emerg Med.* 2002;9:361.

27. Yealy DM, Auble TE, Stone RA, et al. The emergency department community-acquired pneumonia trial: methodology of a quality improvement intervention. *Ann Emerg Med.* 2004;43(6):770-782.

28. Irwig L, Macaskill P, Glasziou P, Fahey M. Meta-analytic methods for diagnostic test accuracy. *J Clin Epidemiol.* 1995;48(1):119-130; discussion 131-132.

29. Wisnivesky JP, Serebrisky D, Moore C, Sacks HS, Iannuzzi MC, McGinn T. Validity of clinical prediction rules for isolating inpatients with suspected tuberculosis: a systematic review. *J Gen Intern Med.* 2005;20(10):947-952.

30. Bachmann LM, Haberzeth S, Steurer J, ter Riet G. The accuracy of the Ottawa knee rule to rule out knee fractures: a systematic review. *Ann Intern Med.* 2004;140(2):121-124.

31. Cameron C, Naylor CD. No impact from active dissemination of the Ottawa Ankle Rules: further evidence of the need for logical implementation of practice guidelines. *CMAJ.* 1999;160(8):1165-1168.

32. Graham ID, Stiell IG, Laupacis A, et al. Awareness and use of the Ottawa ankle and knee rules in 5 countries: can publication alone be enough to change practice? *Ann Emerg Med.* 2001;37(3):259-266.

Part E

Prognosis

PROGNOSIS

Adrienne Randolph, Deborah J. Cook,
and Gordon Guyatt

IN THIS CHAPTER:

CLINICAL SCENARIO

What Is the Prognosis of a Patient Aged 364 Days With Newly Diagnosed Neuroblastoma?

Three months into pediatric internship, you saw a clinic patient for her 12-month routine health checkup. Although she was healthy except for her big stomach, you felt something in the abdomen that you thought could be a tumor. During the next several weeks, the infant undergoes abdominal ultrasonography and magnetic resonance imaging, bone scintigraphy, a skeletal survey, and finally a bone marrow and tumor biopsy. The day after tomorrow is your patient's first birthday. You sat with the oncologist as she told the patient's family that their infant daughter has neuroblastoma, the most common intra-abdominal malignancy of infancy. The parents learn that, because the infant was younger than 365 days on the initial diagnosis and because her tumor markers and bone marrow involvement were consistent with stage IV-S disease and a favorable prognosis, she has at least an 85% chance of cure with surgical resection. The oncologist also told the parents that children older than 1 year with different tumor markers and extent of disease usually need additional chemotherapy and sometimes a bone marrow transplant. Still numb and trying to take it all in, the parents have no questions for the oncologist. Later, when you are following up with them in the family waiting area, they express worry that their infant daughter was diagnosed so close to the 365-day age cutoff. They ask you what would have happened if her checkup had been 3 weeks later, when it was originally scheduled. Would her prognosis then be worse? You see their point. Their doubt makes you wonder where the oncologist got the estimate of an 85% or higher cure. You decide to check out the *evidence* for yourself.

FINDING THE EVIDENCE

You use your hospital's free Internet connection to access MEDLINE at the National Library of Medicine Web site via PubMed. You click on the "Clinical Queries" section under PubMed services. Under the "Search by Clinical Study Category" section, you enter the terms "neuroblastoma" and "age" and click on "prognosis" and "narrow, specific search." You see an article titled "Evidence for an Age Cutoff Greater Than 365 Days for Neuroblastoma Risk Group Stratification in the Children's Oncology Group [COG]."[1] The librarian helps you to obtain a copy from the hospital library. This data analysis from multiple pediatric neuroblastoma clinical trials and *observational studies*, including 3666 children with neuroblastoma, examined the effect of age on the likelihood of recurrence.[1]

WHY AND HOW WE MEASURE PROGNOSIS

Clinicians help patients in 3 broad ways: by diagnosing what is wrong with them, by administering treatment that does more good than *harm*, and by giving them an indication of what the future is likely to hold. Clinicians require studies of *prognosis*—those examining the possible *outcomes* of a disease and the probability with which they can be expected to occur—to achieve the second and third goals.

Knowledge of a patient's prognosis can help clinicians make the right treatment decisions. If a patient will get well anyway, clinicians should not recommend expensive or potentially toxic treatments. If a patient is at low risk of adverse outcomes, even beneficial treatments may not be worthwhile. On the other hand, patients may be destined to have poor outcomes despite whatever treatment we offer. Aggressive therapy in such individuals may only prolong suffering and waste resources. Whatever the treatment possibilities, by under- standing prognosis and presenting the expected future course of a patient's illness, clinicians also offer reassurance and hope, or preparation for death or long-term disability.

To estimate a patient's prognosis, we examine outcomes in groups of patients with a similar clinical presentation. We may then refine our prognosis by looking at subgroups defined by demographic variables such as age and by *comorbidity* and decide which subgroup the patient belongs in. When these variables or factors really do predict which patients do better or worse, we call them *prognostic factors*.

Authors may distinguish between prognostic factors and *risk factors*, those patient characteristics associated with the development of the disease in the first place. For example, smoking is an important risk factor for the development of lung cancer, but it is not an important prognostic factor in someone who has lung cancer. The issues in studies of prognostic factors and risk factors are identical for assessing *validity* and for using the results in patient care.

In this chapter, we focus on how to use articles that may contain valid prognostic information that physicians will find useful for counseling patients (Table 18-1).

Using the same observational study (*cohort* and *case-control*) designs as investigators addressing issues of harm (see Chapter 12, Harm), investigators addressing issues of prognosis conduct studies to explore the determinants of outcome. Implicitly, *randomized controlled trials* also address issues of prognosis. The results reported for the treatment group and the *control group* both provide prognostic information: The control group results tell us about the prognosis in patients who did not receive the *experimental therapy*, whereas the experimental group results tell us about the prognosis in patients receiving the investigational intervention. In this sense, each arm of a randomized trial represents a cohort study. If the randomized trial meets the criteria we describe later in this chapter, it can provide useful information about patients' likely fate.

TABLE 18-1

Users' Guides to an Article About Prognosis

Are the results valid?

- Was the sample of patients representative?
- Were the patients sufficiently homogeneous with respect to prognostic risk?
- Was follow-up sufficiently complete?
- Were outcome criteria objective and unbiased?

What are the results?

- How likely are the outcomes over time?
- How precise are the estimates of likelihood?

How can I apply the results to patient care?

- Were the study patients and their management similar to those in my practice?
- Was the follow-up sufficiently long?
- Can I use the results in the management of patients in my practice?

ARE THE RESULTS VALID?

Was the Sample of Patients Representative?

Bias has to do with systematic differences from the truth. A prognostic study is biased if it yields a systematic overestimate or underestimate of the likelihood of adverse outcomes in the patients under study. When a sample is systematically different from the population of interest and is therefore likely biased because patients will have a better or worse prognosis than those in the population of interest, we label the sample as unrepresentative.

How can you recognize an unrepresentative sample? First, determine whether patients pass through some sort of filter before entering the study. If they do, the result is likely a sample that is systematically different from the underlying population of interest. One such filter is the sequence of referrals that leads patients from primary to tertiary centers. Tertiary centers often care for patients with rare and unusual disorders or increased illness severity. Research describing the outcomes of patients in tertiary centers may not be applicable to the general patient with the disorder in the community (sometimes referred to as *referral bias*).

As an example, when children are admitted to the hospital with febrile seizures, parents want to know the risk of their child having more seizures. This risk is much lower in population-based studies (reported risks range from 1.5% to 4.6%) than in clinic-based studies (reported risks are 2.6% to 76.9%).[2] Those in clinic-based studies may have other neurologic problems predisposing them to have higher rates of recurrence.

Were the Patients Sufficiently Homogeneous With Respect to Prognostic Risk?

Prognostic studies are most useful if individual members of the entire group of patients being considered are similar enough that the outcome of the group is applicable to each group member. This will be true only if patients are at a similar well-described point in their disease process. The point in the clinical course need not be early, but it does need to be consistent. For instance, in a study of the prognosis of children with acquired brain injury, researchers examined not the entire population but a subpopulation that remained unconscious after 90 days.[3]

After ensuring that patients were at the same disease stage, you must consider other factors that might influence patient outcome. If factors such as age or severity influence prognosis, then providing a single prognosis for young and old, mild and severe, will be misleading for each of these subgroups. For instance, a study examining neurologic outcome in children with acquired brain injury that pooled patients with and without head trauma would mislead if these 2 groups have different prognoses. Indeed, the authors of a study addressing the issue[3] found that patients with posttraumatic injuries fared much better than those with anoxic injuries. Of 36 patients with closed head injury, 23 (64%) regained enough social function to express their wants and needs and 9 (25%) eventually regained the capacity to walk independently. Of 13 children with anoxic injuries, none regained important social or cognitive function. Providing an overall intermediate prognosis for both groups would profoundly mislead the parents of these children.

Not only must investigators consider all important prognostic factors but also they must consider them in relation to one another. If sickness but not age truly determines outcome, and sicker patients tend to be older, investigators who fail to simultaneously consider age and severity of illness may mistakenly conclude that age is an important prognostic factor. For example, investigators in the Framingham study examined risk factors for stroke.[4] They reported that the rate of stroke in patients with atrial fibrillation and rheumatic heart disease was 41 per 1000 person-years, which was similar to the rate for patients with atrial fibrillation but without rheumatic heart disease. Patients with rheumatic heart disease were, however, much younger than those who did not have rheumatic heart disease. To properly understand the influence of rheumatic heart disease, investigators in these circumstances must consider separately the relative risk of stroke in young people with and without rheumatic disease and the risk of stroke in elderly people with and without rheumatic disease. We call this separate consideration an *adjusted analysis*. Once adjustments were made for age, the investigators found that the rate of stroke was 6-fold greater in patients with rheumatic heart disease and atrial fibrillation than in patients with atrial fibrillation who did not have rheumatic heart disease.

If a large number of variables have a major effect on prognosis, investigators should use sophisticated statistical techniques to determine the most powerful predictors (see Chapter 13, Advanced Topics in Harm: Correlation and Regression). Such an analysis may lead to a *clinical decision rule* that guides clinicians in simultaneously considering all of the important prognostic factors (see Chapter 17.4, Clinical Prediction Rules).

How can you decide whether the groups are sufficiently homogeneous with respect to their risk? On the basis of your clinical experience and your understanding of the biology of the condition under study, can you think of factors that the investigators have neglected that are likely to define subgroups with very different prognoses? To the extent that the answer is yes, the validity of the study results may be compromised.

Was Follow-up Sufficiently Complete?

Investigators who lose track of a large number of patients compromise the validity of their prognostic study. The reason is that those who are followed may be at systematically higher or lower risk than those not followed. As the number of patients who do not return for *follow-up* increases, the likelihood of bias also increases.

How many patients lost to follow-up is too many? The answer depends on the relationship between the proportion of patients who are lost and the proportion of patients who have had the adverse outcome of interest. The larger the number of patients whose fate is unknown relative to the number who have had the adverse event, the greater the threat to the study's validity. For instance, let us assume that 30% of a particularly high-risk group (such as elderly patients with diabetes) have had an adverse outcome (such as cardiovascular death) during long-term follow-up. If 10% of the patients have been lost to follow-up, the true rate of patients who had died may be as low as approximately 27% or as high as 37%. Across this range, the clinical implications would not change appreciably, and the loss to follow-up does not threaten the validity of the study. However, in a much lower-risk patient sample (otherwise healthy middle-aged patients, for instance), the observed event rate may be 1%. In this case, if we assumed that all 10% of the patients lost to follow-up had died, the event rate of 11% might have very different implications.

A large loss to follow-up constitutes a more serious threat to validity when the patients who are lost may be different from those who are easier to find. In one study, for example, after much effort, the investigators managed to follow 180 of 186 patients treated for neurosis.[5] The death rate was 3% among the 60% who were easily traced. Among those who were more difficult to find, however, the death rate was 27%.

If a differential fate for those followed and those lost is plausible (and in most prognostic studies, it will be), loss to follow-up that is large in relation to the proportion of patients having an adverse outcome of interest constitutes an important threat to validity.

Were Outcome Criteria Objective and Unbiased?

Outcome events may be objective and easily measured (eg, death), require some judgment (eg, myocardial infarction), or require considerable judgment and effort to measure (eg, disability, quality of life). Investigators should clearly specify and define their *target outcomes* and, whenever possible, they should base their criteria on objective measures.

The study of children with acquired brain injury provides a good example of the issues involved in measuring outcome.[3] The examiners found that patients' families frequently optimistically interpreted interactions with the patients. The investigators therefore required that development of a social response in the affected children be verified by study personnel.

USING THE GUIDE

Returning to our opening clinical scenario, the investigators in the COG neuroblastoma prognosis study used data from 3666 children younger than 21 years with a pathologically confirmed diagnosis of neuroblastoma who partici-pated in 1 of 11 therapeutic trials or observational studies.[1] Because more than 60% of all children treated for cancer participate in clinical trials vs less than 2% of adult patients with cancer,[6] this cohort is likely to represent most of the children with neuroblastoma. The investigators considered whether sub-groups defined by age, disease stage, and cancer stage and tumor marker (*MYCN*) amplification (a tumor marker that is either amplified or nonamplified) differed in their prognosis. The investigators do not report the number of patients lost to follow-up, and this is problematic. A review of the 5 references that included data from the 13 study reports reveals that some patients were registered for multiple studies with different follow-up requirements. It is not possible to determine the rate of loss to follow-up in the 3666 children from review of the referenced reports. Finally, the authors defined *event-free survival* as patients who were free of relapse of the cancer, disease progres-sion, secondary malignancy, and death. Although death is an objective, straightforward outcome, identification of disease progression, secondary malignancy, and cancer relapse may have differed across the numerous studies. Although you have some reservations about completeness of long-term follow-up, you conclude that the study is still likely to provide a good estimate of the prognosis of the child under your care and should help you to address the parents' question.

WHAT ARE THE RESULTS?

How Likely Are the Outcomes Over Time?

Results from studies of prognosis or risk are the number of events that occur over time. An informative way to depict these results is a *survival curve*, which is a graph of the number of events over time (or conversely, the chance of being free of these events over time) (see Chapter 7, Does Treatment Lower Risk? Understanding the Results). The events must be yes/no (eg, death, stroke, recurrence of cancer), and investigators must know the time at which they occur. Figure 18-1 shows 2 survival curves, one of survival after a myocardial infarction[7]; the other, need for revision surgery after hip replacement surgery.[8]

The chance of dying after a myocardial infarction is highest shortly after the event (reflected by an initially steep downward slope of the curve, which then becomes flat), whereas few hip replacements require revision until much later (this curve, by contrast, starts out flat and then steepens).

How Precise Are the Estimates of Likelihood?

The more precise the estimate of prognosis a study provides, the less we need be uncertain about the estimated prognosis and the more useful it is to us. Usually,

FIGURE 18-1

Survival Curves

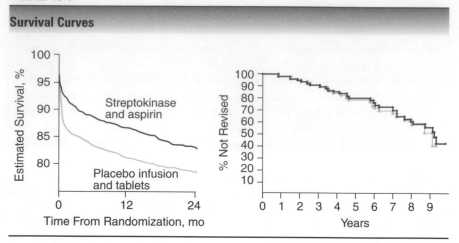

Left, Survival after myocardial infarction. Right, Results of hip replacement surgery: percentage of patients who survived without needing a new procedure (revision) after their initial hip replacement.

Reprinted from *The Lancet*,[7] Copyright © 1988, with permission from Elsevier (left). Reprinted from Dorey and Amstutz,[8] with permission from the *Journal of Bone and Joint Surgery* (right).

authors report the risks of adverse outcomes with their associated 95% *confidence intervals (CIs)*. If the study is valid, the 95% CI defines the range of risks within which it is highly likely that the true risk lies (see Chapter 8, Confidence Intervals). For example, a study of the prognosis of patients with dementia provided a 95% CI around the 49% estimate of survival at 5 years after presentation (ie, 39%-58%).[9]

In most survival curves, the earlier follow-up periods usually include results from more patients than do the later periods (owing to losses to follow-up and because patients are not enrolled in the study at the same time), which means that the survival curves are more precise in the earlier periods, indicated by narrower confidence bands around the lefthand parts of the curve (Figure 18-2).

USING THE GUIDE

The COG neuroblastoma study[1] evaluated the relative risk for an event in younger and older children before and after adjusting for *MYCN* status. You are concerned that, because your patient was diagnosed at about 365 days of age, she might be in a higher-risk group. Figure 18-3 shows the relevant results. Figure 18-3A shows that, before adjustment for stage and *MYCN* status, older age appears to have a large negative effect on prognosis. This is misleading, however, because older children also tend to have worse stage and marker status. Figure 18-3B shows a much more modest influence of age after adjustment. Note that the CIs are narrower in the younger age groups because most patients are diagnosed before 20 months of age. Figure 18-3B shows that risk begins to increase appreciably after 600, not 365, days.

FIGURE 18-2

Risk for an Event by Age Group in Children With Neuroblastoma

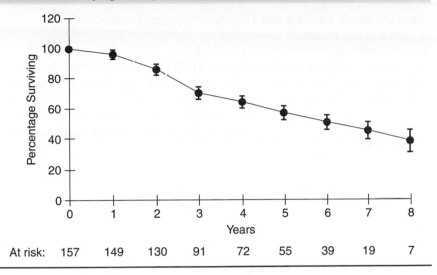

| At risk: | 157 | 149 | 130 | 91 | 72 | 55 | 39 | 19 | 7 |

Reproduced from Wood et al,[10] with permission of Wiley-Liss, Inc, a subsidary of John Wiley & Sons, Inc. Copyright © 1999, American Cancer Society.

FIGURE 18-3

Relative Risk for an Event, With 95% Confidence Intervals, by Age Group in Children With Neuroblastoma

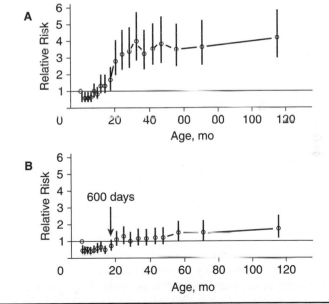

A, Univariate Cox proportional hazards model with age group. B, Multivariate Cox proportional model with International Neuroblastoma Staging System stage, MYCN status, and age group. There is neither increased nor decreased risk for an event where the curve crosses relative risk = 1 at roughly 600 days (19.7 months) of age.

Reprinted from London et al,[1] with permission of the American Society of Clinical Oncology.

HOW CAN I APPLY THE RESULTS TO PATIENT CARE?

Were the Study Patients and Their Management Similar to Those in My Practice?

Authors should describe the study patients explicitly and in enough detail that you can make a comparison with your patients. One factor sometimes neglected in prognostic studies that could strongly influence outcome is therapy. Therapeutic strategies often vary markedly among institutions and change over time as new treatments become available or old treatments regain popularity. To the extent that treatments are beneficial or detrimental, overall patient outcome might improve or become worse.

Was Follow-up Sufficiently Long?

Because the presence of illness often precedes the development of an outcome event by a long period, investigators must follow patients for a period long enough to detect the outcomes of interest. For example, recurrence in some women with early breast cancer can occur many years after initial diagnosis and treatment.[11] A prognostic study may provide an unbiased assessment of outcome during a short period if it meets the validity criteria in Table 18-1, but it may be of little use if a patient is interested in her prognosis during a long period.

Can I Use the Results in the Management of Patients in My Practice?

Prognostic data often provide the basis for sensible decisions about therapy (see Chapter 11.1, Applying Results to Individual Patients). Even if the prognostic result does not help with selection of appropriate therapy, it can help you in counseling a concerned patient or relative. Some conditions, such as asymptomatic hiatal hernia or asymptomatic colonic diverticulae, have such a good overall prognosis that they have been termed *nondisease*.[12] On the other hand, a result of uniformly bad prognosis could provide a clinician with a starting place for a discussion with the patient and family, leading to counseling about end-of-life care.

CLINICAL RESOLUTION

Your patient resembles those in the favorable risk subgroup of children in the study[1] in age, stage, and tumor markers, and you can readily generalize the results to her care. Therapeutic management for patients with this risk profile across the studies is similar to what your patient will receive. The minimal follow-up in the study was 3 years, and half of the patients were followed up to 5.8 years, allowing investigators to provide estimates for patients up to 5 years after diagnosis, which you consider adequate for advising the parents.

Although the parents are still upset abut the diagnosis of neuroblastoma in their infant and have to come to grips with any associated mortality risk, you have gleaned some reassuring information from the study.[1] All of your patient's findings suggest the most favorable prognosis. The study tells us that the 4-year event-free survival of patients 365 to 460 days old, excluding those with stage 4 disease and *MYCN*-amplified tumors, is 92% ± 3% standard error. Table 18-2 shows how to calculate CIs from standard errors of a proportion, which for the study under consideration, with 135 patients in that subgroup, gives a CI of 91.6% to 92.4%. Given the narrow CIs, you are secure using these estimates. Although your patient is at the 365-day mark at presentation, it is clear that risk does not increase appreciably with age until after 600 days. Your patient is still in the most favorable risk group, and you can reassure the parents that toxic chemotherapy is not necessary at this point.

TABLE 18-2

Calculating 95% Confidence Intervals From a Proportion

I. The rule of 3s[13]

Used when the numerator is 0 or 1 and there are at least 30 patients in the sample

= 100 × 3/number of patients = upper limit of the 95% CI

Example: 50 of 50 patients die; the upper limit of the 95% CI for survival = 100 × 3/50 = 6% or given a sample size of 50, the survival rate could still be as high as 6%.

II. Calculating the 95% CI from the standard error of a proportion[14]

Used when 2 or more patients have the outcome of interest

p = proportion = number of patients with the outcome/total number of patients

sep = standard error of the proportion = square root of $[p \times (1 - p)]/n$.

95% CI = 100 × $[p - (1.96 \times sep)]$, 100 × $[p + (1.96 \times sep)]$

Example from our scenario: 124 of 135 survive, p = 0.92, sep = square root of $(0.92 \times 0.08)/135 = 0.002$, 1.96 × sep = 1.96 × 0.002 = 0.004, 95% CI = 100 × (0.92 − 0.004), 100 × (0.92 + 0.004) = 91.6% to 92.4%, which is the 95% CI.

Abbreviation: CI, confidence interval.

References

1. London WB, Castleberry RP, Matthay KK, et al. Evidence for an age cutoff greater than 365 days for neuroblastoma risk group stratification in the Children's Oncology Group. *J Clin Oncol.* 2005;23(27):6459-6465.

2. Ellenberg JH, Nelson KB. Sample selection and the natural history of disease: studies of febrile seizures. *JAMA.* 1980;243(13):1337-1340.

3. Kriel RL, Krach LE, Jones-Saete C. Outcome of children with prolonged unconsciousness and vegetative states. *Pediatr Neurol.* 1993;9(5):362-368.

4. Wolf PA, Dawber TR, Thomas HE Jr, et al. Epidemiologic assessment of chronic atrial fibrillation and risk of stroke: the Framingham study. *Neurology.* 1978;28 (10):973-977.

5. Sims AC. Importance of a high tracing-rate in long-term medical follow-up studies. *Lancet.* 1973;2(7826):433-435.

6. Murthy VH, Krumholz HM, Gross CP. Participation in cancer clinical trials: race-, sex-, and age-based disparities. *JAMA.* 2004;291(22):2720-2726.

7. ISIS-2 (Second International Study of Infarct Survival) Collaborative Group. Randomised trial of intravenous streptokinase, oral aspirin, both, or neither among 17,187 cases of suspected acute myocardial infarction: ISIS-2. *Lancet.* 1988;2(8607):349-360.

8. Dorey F, Amstutz HC. The validity of survivorship analysis in total joint arthroplasty. *J Bone Joint Surg Am.* 1989;71(4):544-548.

9. Walsh JS, Welch HG, Larson EB. Survival of outpatients with Alzheimer-type dementia. *Ann Intern Med.* 1990;113(6):429-434.

10. Wood LA, Coupland RW, North SA, Palmer MC. Outcome of advanced stage low grade follicular lymphomas in a population-based retrospective cohort. *Cancer.* 1999;85(6):1361-1368.

11. Early Breast Cancer Trialists' Collaborative Group. Systemic treatment of early breast cancer by hormonal, cytotoxic, or immune therapy: 133 randomised trials involving 31,000 recurrences and 24,000 deaths among 75,000 women. *Lancet.* 1992;339(8784):1-15.

12. Meador CK. The art and science of nondisease. *N Engl J Med.* 1965 Jan 14;272:92-95.

13. Hanley JA, Lippman-Hand A. If nothing goes wrong, is everything all right? interpreting zero numerators. *JAMA.* 1983;249(13):1743-1745.

14. Sackett DL, Haynes RB, Guyatt GH, Tugwell P, eds. Making a prognosis. In: *Clinical Epidemiology: A Basic Science for Clinical Medicine.* 2nd ed. Toronto, Ontario, Canada: Little, Brown & Company; 1991.

Part F

Summarizing the Evidence

SUMMARIZING THE EVIDENCE

Gordon Guyatt, Roman Jaeschke, Kameshwar Prasad, and Deborah J. Cook

IN THIS CHAPTER:

Are the Benefits Worth the Costs and Potential Risks?

Clinical Resolution

CLINICAL SCENARIO

Should We Administer Intravenous Magnesium to Patients Presenting With Acute Severe Asthma?

On call for general internal medicine, you receive a referral of a 26-year-old woman with asthma exacerbation. She was in the emergency department 2 weeks earlier and was discharged after treatment with brochodilators and prescription for a short course of oral steroids. Despite advice to do so, she has not been able to give up her new cat. Her forced expired volume in 1 second (FEV_1), 78% predicted when she departed the emergency department 2 weeks ago, is now 41% of predicted, and her peak expiratory flow rate (PEFR) is 13% of predicted. Arterial blood gases show pH 7.37, PaO_2 69 mm Hg, and $PaCO_2$ 44 mm Hg. You start treatment with bronchodilators and corticosteroids and are considering whether the patient would be best treated in an intermediate care unit when one of your junior colleagues suggests treatment with intravenous magnesium sulfate. You are altogether uncertain about this suggestion and so offer nothing more than a polite acknowledgement, but she returns 15 minutes later with a printout of Cochrane Library review dealing with the topic.[1]

FINDING THE EVIDENCE

In this scenario, a colleague provided the relevant article from the Cochrane Library. Were you searching "asthma and magnesium," you could have found this article by entering the Cochrane Library and by typing "magnesium and asthma." You could also find it quickly in ACP Journal Club by typing the same terms and in UpToDate by looking in their asthma section, narrowing it by magnesium and looking into "alternative agents for treatment of asthma."

Traditional Narrative and Systematic Reviews

The large number of studies addressing many clinical questions makes *review articles* an efficient way to learn about relevant *evidence*. In the same way that it is important to use rigorous methods in primary research to protect against *bias* and *random error*, it is also important to use rigorous methods when summarizing the results of several studies. Traditional literature reviews, commonly found in journals and textbooks, typically provide *narrative reviews* of a disease or condition. Traditional narrative reviews often include a discussion of 1 or more aspects of disease etiology, diagnosis, *prognosis*, or management and address a number of *background questions*, *foreground questions*, and theoretical questions.

Typically, authors of traditional reviews make little or no attempt to be systematic in their formulation of the questions they are addressing, their search for and selection of evidence, their assessment of the quality of *primary studies*, and their summary of the results of the primary studies. Medical students and clinicians looking for background information often find narrative reviews useful for obtaining a broad overview of a clinical condition (see Chapter 3, What Is the Question?, and Chapter 4, Finding the Evidence).

Unfortunately, expert reviewers often make conflicting recommendations, and their advice has frequently lagged behind or has been inconsistent with the best available evidence.[2] One important reason for this phenomenon is the use of unsystematic approaches to collecting and summarizing the evidence. Indeed, in one study, self-rated expertise was inversely related to the methodologic rigor of the review.[3]

Although most *systematic reviews* focus on issues of the effect of interventions, they can also address issues of diagnosis and prognosis and even questions of how and why addressed by qualitative research studies (sometimes called *meta-synthesis*). In this chapter, although we focus on systematic reviews that address discrete patient management issues, the principles for other types of questions are similar.

Authors sometimes erroneously use the terms *systematic review* and *meta-analysis* interchangeably. We use the term *systematic review* for any summary of research that attempts to address a focused clinical question in a systematic, reproducible manner and *meta-analysis* for the quantitative synthesis that yields a single best estimate of, for instance, *treatment effect*. Most articles labeled as meta-analyses published in the biomedical literature are actually systematic reviews that statistically pool the results of 2 or more primary studies. Features distinguishing narrative reviews from systematic reviews and meta-analyses are shown in Table 19-1.[4]

TABLE 19-1

Differences Between Narrative and Systematic Reviews

Characteristic	Narrative Review	Systematic Review
Clinical question	Seldom reported, or addresses several general questions	Focused question specifying population, intervention or exposure, and outcome
Search for primary articles	Seldom reported; if reported, not comprehensive	Comprehensive search of several evidence sources
Selection of primary articles	Seldom reported; if reported, often biased sample of studies	Explicit inclusion and exclusion criteria for primary studies
Evaluation of quality of primary articles	Seldom reported; if reported, not usually systematic	Methodologic quality of primary articles is assessed
Summary of results of primary studies	Usually qualitative nonsystematic summary	Synthesis is systematic (qualitative or quantitative; if quantitative, this is often referred to as meta-analysis)

Reproduced from Cook et al.[4]

During the past decade, the literature describing the optimal methods for systematic reviews has grown enormously and now includes studies that provide an empirical basis for guiding decisions about the methods used in summarizing evidence.[5,6] Here, we emphasize key points from the perspective of a clinician needing to make a decision about patient care.

A Roadmap for Systematic Reviews

In applying the Users' Guides, you will find it useful to have a clear understanding of the process of conducting a systematic review. Figure 19-1 demonstrates how the process begins with the definition of the question, which is synonymous with specifying eligibility criteria for deciding which studies to include in a review. These criteria define the population, the *exposures* or interventions, and the outcomes of

FIGURE 19-1

The Process of Conducting a Systematic Review

Define the question
- Specify inclusion and exclusion criteria
  - Population
  - Intervention or exposure
  - Outcome
  - Methodology (including time, language, publication restrictions)

Conduct literature search
- Decide on information sources: databases, experts, funding agencies, pharmaceutical companies, hand-searching, personal files, trial registries, Cochrane Database of randomized controlled trials, citation lists of retrieved articles
- Identify titles and abstracts

Apply inclusion and exclusion criteria
- Apply inclusion and exclusion criteria to titles and abstracts
- Obtain full articles for eligible titles and abstracts
- Apply inclusion and exclusion criteria to full articles
- Select final eligible articles
- Assess agreement on study selection

Create data abstraction
- Data abstraction: participants, interventions, comparison interventions, study design
- Results
- Methodologic quality
- Assess agreement on validity assessment

Conduct analysis
- Determine method of generating pooled estimates across studies
- Generate pooled estimates (if appropriate)
- Explore heterogeneity, conduct subgroup analysis if appropriate
- Explore possibility of publications bias

TABLE 19-2

Users' Guides for How to Use Review Articles

Are the results valid?

- Did the review include explicit and appropriate eligibility criteria?
- Was biased selection and reporting of studies unlikely?
- Were the primary studies of high methodologic quality?
- Were assessments of studies reproducible?

What are the results?

- Were the results similar from study to study?
- What are the overall results of the review?
- How precise were the results?

How can I apply the results to patient care?

- Were all patient-important outcomes considered?
- Are any postulated subgroup effects credible?
- What is the overall quality of the evidence?
- Are the benefits worth the costs and potential risks?

interest. Depending on the scope of their review, authors may need to decide at this stage which *outcome* measures will be crucial for clinical decision makers and ensure they summarize the evidence for each of these outcomes. A systematic review will also restrict the included studies to those that meet minimal methodologic standards. For example, systematic reviews that address a question of therapy will often include only *randomized controlled trials (RCTs)*.

Having specified their selection criteria, reviewers must conduct a comprehensive search that yields a large number of potentially relevant titles and abstracts. They then apply the selection criteria to the titles and abstracts, arriving at a smaller number of articles that they can retrieve. Once again, the reviewers apply the selection criteria, this time to the complete reports. Having completed the culling process, they assess the methodologic quality of the articles and abstract data from each study. Finally, they summarize the data, including, if appropriate, a quantitative synthesis or meta-analysis. The analysis includes an examination of differences among the included studies, an attempt to explain differences in results (exploring *heterogeneity*), a summary of the overall results, and an overall assessment of methodologic quality. Guidelines for assessing the validity of reviews and using the results correspond to this process (Table 19-2).

ARE THE RESULTS VALID?

Did the Review Explicitly Address a Sensible Clinical Question?

Consider a systematic review that pooled results from all cancer therapeutic modalities for all types of cancer to generate a single estimate of the effect on mortality. Next, consider a review that pooled the results of the effects of all doses of all antiplatelet agents (including aspirin, sulfinpyrazone, dipyridamole, ticlodipine, and clopidogrel) on major thrombotic events (including myocardial infarctions, strokes, and acute arterial insufficiency in the leg) and mortality in patients with clinically manifest atherosclerosis (whether in the heart, head, or lower extremities). Finally, reflect on a review that addressed the influence of a wide range of aspirin doses to prevent thrombotic stroke in patients who had experienced a transient ischemic attack (TIA) in the carotid circulation.

Clinicians would not find the first of these reviews useful; they would conclude it is too broad. Most clinicians are uncomfortable with the second question, still considering it excessively broad. For this second question, however, a highly credible and experienced group of investigators found the question reasonable and published the results of their meta-analysis in a leading journal.[7-10] Most clinicians are comfortable with the third question, although they may express concerns about pooling across a wide range of aspirin doses.

What makes a systematic review too broad or too narrow? When deciding whether the question posed in the review is sensible, clinicians need to ask themselves whether the underlying biology is what they would more or less expect; that is, the same treatment effect across the range of patients (Table 19-3). They should ask the parallel question about the other components of the study question: Is the underlying biology such that, across the range of interventions and outcomes included, they expect more or less the same treatment effect? Clinicians can also construct a similar set of questions for other areas of clinical inquiry. For example, across the range of patients, ways of testing, and *reference* or *gold standard* for diagnosis, does one expect more or less the same *likelihood ratios* associated with studies examining a diagnostic test (see Chapter 16, Diagnostic Tests)?[11]

Clinicians reject a systematic review that pools data across all modes of cancer therapy for all types of cancer because they know that some cancer treatments are effective in certain cancers, whereas others are harmful. Combining the results of these studies would yield an estimate of effect that would be misleading for most of the interventions. Clinicians who reject the second review would argue that the biologic variation in antiplatelet agents is likely to lead to important differences in treatment effect. Furthermore, they may contend that there are important differ-

TABLE 19-3

Were Eligibility Criteria Appropriate?

Are results likely to be similar across the range of patients included (eg, older and younger, sicker and less sick)?

Are results likely to be similar across the range of interventions or exposures studied (eg, higher dose, lower dose; test interpreted by expert or nonexpert)?

Are results likely to be similar across the range of ways the outcome was measured (eg, shorter or longer follow-up)?

Did it turn out that results were indeed similar across the range of patients, interventions, and outcomes (ie, studies all showed similar results)?

ences in the biology of atherosclerosis in the vessels of the heart, head, and legs. Those who would endorse the second review would argue the similar underlying biology of antiplatelet agents—and atherosclerosis in different parts of the body—and thus anticipate a similar magnitude of treatment effects.

For the third question, most clinicians would accept that the biology of aspirin action is likely to be similar in patients whose TIA reflected right-sided or left-sided brain ischemia, in patients older than 75 years and in younger patients, in men and women, across doses, during periods of *follow-up* ranging from 1 to 5 years, and in patients with stroke who have been identified by the attending physician and those identified by a team of expert reviewers. The similar biology is likely to result in a similar magnitude of treatment effect, which explains the reviewers' comfort with combining studies of aspirin in patients who have had a TIA.

The clinician's task is to decide whether, across the range of patients, interventions or exposures, and outcomes, it is plausible that the intervention will have a similar effect. This judgment is possible only if the reviewers have provided a precise statement of what range of patients, exposures, and outcomes they decided to include; in other words, explicit eligibility criteria for their review.

In addition, reviewers must specify methodologic criteria for inclusion in their review. Generally, these should be similar to the most important *validity* criteria for primary studies (Table 19-4). Explicit eligibility criteria not only facilitate the decision regarding whether the question was sensible but also make it less likely that the authors will preferentially include studies that support their own previous conclusions.

Clinicians may legitimately ask, even within a relatively narrowly defined question, whether they can be confident that results will be similar across patients, interventions, and outcome measurement. Referring to the question of aspirin in patients with a TIA, the effect could conceivably differ in those with more or less

TABLE 19-4

Guides for Selecting Articles That Are Most Likely to Provide Valid Results[3]

Therapy	• Were patients randomized?
	• Was follow-up complete?
Diagnosis	• Was the patient sample representative of those with the disorder?
	• Was the diagnosis verified using credible criteria that were independent of the items of medical history, physical examination, laboratory tests, or imaging procedures under study?
Harm	• Did the investigators demonstrate similarity in all known determinants of outcome or adjust for differences in the analysis?
	• Was follow-up sufficiently complete?
Prognosis	• Was there a representative sample of patients?
	• Was follow-up sufficiently complete?

severe underlying atherosclerosis, across aspirin doses, or during short-term and long-term follow-up. Thus, this validity criterion cannot be fully resolved until one examines the results. Anticipating possible variability in results, reviewers should generate a priori hypotheses of features of population, intervention, outcome, and methodology that might explain such variability (Figure 19-1). As we describe in the "Results" section of this chapter, if there is large variation in results across studies that reviewers' a priori hypotheses cannot explain, our confidence in the estimates of effect is compromised.

Was the Search for Relevant Studies Detailed and Exhaustive?

Systematic reviews are at risk of presenting misleading results if they fail to secure a complete, or at least a representative, sample of the available eligible studies. To achieve this objective, reviewers search bibliographic databases, such as MEDLINE and EMBASE and the Cochrane Central Register of Controlled Trials (containing more than 450 000 RCTs), and databases of current research.[12] They check the reference lists of the articles they retrieve and seek personal contact with experts in the area. It may also be important to examine recently published abstracts presented at scientific meetings and to look at less frequently used databases, including those that summarize doctoral theses and databases of ongoing trials held by pharmaceutical companies. Unless the authors tell us what they did to locate relevant studies, it is difficult to know how likely it is that relevant studies were missed.

Reporting bias occurs in a number of forms, the most familiar of which is the failure to report or publish studies with negative results (see Chapter 20.1, Reporting Bias). This publication *bias* may result in misleading results of systematic reviews that fail to include unpublished studies.[13-18]

If investigators include unpublished studies in a review, they should obtain full written reports and they should use the same criteria to appraise the validity of both published and unpublished studies. There is a variety of techniques available to explore the possibility of publication bias, none of them fully satisfactory (see Chapter 20.1, Reporting Bias). Systematic reviews based on a number of small studies with limited total sample sizes are particularly susceptible to publication bias, especially if most or all of the studies have been sponsored by a commercial entity with a vested interest in the results. Findings that seem too good to be true may well not be true.

Another increasingly recognized form of reporting bias occurs when investigators measure a number of outcomes but report only those that favor the experimental intervention or those that favor the intervention most strongly (this is sometimes referred to as *selective outcome reporting bias*). If reviewers report that they have successfully contacted authors of primary studies who ensure full disclosure of results, concern about reporting bias decreases.

Reviewers may go even farther than simply contacting the authors of primary studies. They may recruit these investigators as collaborators in their review, and in the process, they may obtain individual patient records. Such *individual patient-data meta-analysis* can facilitate powerful analyses (addressing issues such as true *intention-to-treat* analyses, informed subgroup analyses), which may strengthen the inferences from a systematic review.

Were the Primary Studies of High Methodologic Quality?

Even if a systematic review includes only RCTs, knowing whether they were of good quality is important. Unfortunately, peer review does not guarantee the validity of published research.[19] Differences in study methods might explain important differences among the results.[20-22] For example, less rigorous studies tend to overestimate the effectiveness of therapeutic and preventive interventions.[23] Even if the results of different studies are consistent, determining their validity still is important. Consistent results are less compelling if they come from weak studies than if they come from strong studies.

Consistent results from *observational studies* putatively addressing treatment issues are particularly suspect. Physicians may systematically select patients with a good prognosis to receive therapy; and this pattern of practice may be consistent over time and geographic setting. Observational studies summarized in a systematic review,[24] for instance, have consistently shown average *relative risk reductions* in major cardiovascular events with hormone replacement therapy. The first large RCT addressing this issue found no effect of hormone replacement therapy on cardiovascular risk,[25] and the subsequent large RCT suggested possibly detrimental effect.[26-28] Hormone replacement therapy is one of many examples of misleading results of observational studies (see Chapter 9.2, Surprising Results of Randomized Trials).

All we have said about validity applies to the focus of this chapter: systematic reviews assessing questions of therapy. Investigators may also undertake systematic reviews of issues concerning diagnosis or prognosis. Different validity criteria (corresponding to the validity criteria of the prognosis and diagnosis chapters of this book) are appropriate for such systematic reviews.

There is no one correct way to assess the quality of studies, and clinicians should be cautious about the use of scales to assess the quality of studies.[29,30] Some reviewers use long checklists to evaluate methodologic quality, whereas others focus on 3 or 4 key aspects of the study. When considering whether to trust the results of a review, check to see whether the authors examined criteria similar to those we have presented in other chapters of this book (see Chapter 6, Therapy; Chapter 12, Harm; Chapter 16, Diagnostic Tests; and Chapter 18, Prognosis). Reviewers should apply these criteria with a relatively low threshold (such as restricting eligibility to RCTs) in selecting studies (Table 19-4) and more comprehensively (such as considering *concealment, blinding, stopping early* for benefit) in assessing the validity of the included studies (Figure 19-1).

Were Selection and Assessments of Studies Reproducible?

As we have seen, authors of review articles must decide which studies to include, how valid they are, and what data to abstract. These decisions require judgment by the reviewers and are subject to both mistakes (ie, random errors) and bias (ie, systematic errors). Having 2 or more people participate in each decision guards against errors; and if there is good agreement beyond chance between the reviewers, the clinician can have more confidence in the results of the systematic review (see Chapter 17.3, Measuring Agreement Beyond Chance).

USING THE GUIDE

Returning to our opening scenario, the Cochrane review you located included 7 trials enrolling patients who have asthma and present to the emergency department with an asthma attack, 5 of which addressed the investigators' designated primary outcome, hospitalization.[1] These patients were randomized to receive or not receive intravenous magnesium sulfate, on average 2 g during 20 minutes. The reviewers searched the Cochrane Airway Review Group asthma register and reference lists of all available primary studies and review articles, and they contacted authors of primary studies. It is likely they obtained all the relevant trials, although the relatively small number of small trials leaves some uncertainty regarding publication bias.

The authors of the review addressed concealment of randomization and also used the Jadad score that rates randomization, blinding, and loss to follow-up.[31] Of the 7 trials, 6 were randomized and placebo controlled and included some blinding; loss to follow-up was generally small. The seventh was quasi-randomized and described as "single blind." Of the 7 studies included, 6 were rated as strong and 1 as weak, according to the Jadad score.

Two of the review's authors decided whether potentially eligible trials met eligibility criteria, with disagreement resolved by consensus or third-party adjudication. The investigators report no measures of agreement for either the eligibility or quality rating decisions.

Both adults and children with varying severity of asthma were included, and authors planned a priori appropriate subgroup analyses based on age and severity. In addition to their primary outcome of need for admission to the hospital, they also considered pulmonary function tests (PEFR and FEV_1), vital signs (heart rate, respiratory rate, blood pressure), and adverse effects.

Overall, we conclude that the methods of the systematic review and the methodologic quality of the trials included in the systematic review were strong.

WHAT ARE THE RESULTS?

Were the Results Similar From Study to Study?

Most systematic reviews document important differences in patients, exposures, outcome measures, and research methods from study to study. As a result, the most common answer to whether eligibility criteria were appropriate—that is, whether we can expect similar results across the range of patients, interventions, and outcomes—is perhaps.

Fortunately, one can resolve this unsatisfactory situation. Having completed the review, investigators should present the results in a way that allows clinicians to check whether results proved similar from study to study. There are 4 elements to consider when deciding whether the results are sufficiently similar to warrant comfort with a single estimate of treatment effects that applies across the populations, interventions, and outcomes studied (Table 19-5, which also appears as Table 20.3-1 in Chapter 20.3, Making Sense of Variability in Study Results). First, how similar are the study-specific estimates of the treatment effect (that is, the *point estimates*) from the individual studies? The more different they are, the more clinicians should question the decision to pool results across studies.

Second, to what extent are differences among the results of individual studies greater than you would expect by chance? Users can make an initial assessment by examining the extent to which the *confidence intervals* (*CIs*) overlap. The greater the overlap, the more comfortable one is with pooling results. Widely separated CIs flag the presence of important variability in results that requires explanation.

Clinicians can also look to formal statistical analyses called *tests for heterogeneity*, which address the null hypothesis that underlying effects are in fact similar across studies and the observed differences in the size of effect between studies are due to chance. When the P value associated with the test of heterogeneity is small (for instance, $P < .05$), chance becomes an unlikely explanation for the observed differences in the size of the effect (see Chapter 10.1, Hypothesis Testing).

A fourth criterion is another statistic, the I^2, which describes the percentage of the variability in effect estimates that is due to underlying differences in effect rather than chance.[32] Rough guides for the interpretation of I^2 suggest that a value of less than 20% represents minimal variability, 20% to 50% variability raises concern, and values greater than 50% represent substantial heterogeneity that raises serious concern about a single pooled estimate. If you wish to more deeply understand these approaches to assessing heterogeneity, consult Chapter 20.3, Making Sense of Variability in Study Results.

Reviewers should try to explain between-study variability in findings by examining differences in patients, interventions, outcome measurement, and methodology.

TABLE 19-5

Evaluating Variability in Study Results

Visual evaluation of variability

    How similar are the point estimates?

    To what extent do the confidence intervals overlap?

Statistical tests evaluating variability

    Yes-or-no tests for heterogeneity that generate a P value

    I^2 test that quantifies the variability explained by between-study differences in results

Although appropriate and, indeed, necessary, this search for explanations of heterogeneity in study results may be misleading (see Chapter 20.4, When to Believe a Subgroup Analysis). Furthermore, how is the clinician to deal with residual heterogeneity in study results that remains unexplained? We will deal with this issue in the next section concerning the applicability of the study results.

What Are the Overall Results of the Review?

If the investigators decide that pooling results to generate a single estimate of effect is inappropriate, a systematic review will likely end with a table or tables describing results of individual studies. Often, however, reviewers present a meta-analysis with a single best estimate of effect from the weighted averages of the results of the individual studies. The weighting process depends on the sample size of the studies or, more specifically, the number of events (see Chapter 10.3, What Determines the Width of the Confidence Interval? and Chapter 20.2, Fixed-Effects and Random-Effects Models).

You should look to the overall results of a systematic review the same way you look to the results of primary studies. In a systematic review of a therapeutic question looking at dichotomous (yes/no) outcomes, you should look for the *relative risk (RR)* and *relative risk reduction* or the *odds ratio* and *odds reduction* (see Chapter 7, Does Treatment Lower Risk? Understanding the Results; and Chapter 10.2, Understanding the Results: More About Odds Ratios). In systematic reviews regarding diagnosis, you should look for summary estimates of the likelihood ratios (see Chapter 16, Diagnostic Tests).

In the setting of continuous rather than *dichotomous outcomes*, investigators typically use one of 2 options to aggregate data across studies. If the outcome is measured the same way in each study (eg, percentage of improvement in FEV_1 or difference in liters in PEFR), the results from each study are averaged, taking into account each study's precision to calculate what is called a *weighted mean difference*.

Sometimes the outcome measures used in the primary studies are similar but not identical. For example, one trial might measure exercise capacity by using a treadmill; a second, a cycle ergometer; and a third, a 6-minute walk test. If the patients and the interventions are reasonably similar, estimating the average effect of the intervention on exercise capacity still might be worthwhile. One way of doing this is to standardize the measures by looking at the mean difference between treatment and control and dividing this by the standard deviation.[33] The *effect size* that results from this calculation provides a pooled estimate of the treatment effect expressed in standard deviation units (eg, an effect size of one-half means that the average effect of treatment across studies is one-half of a standard deviation unit).

You may find it difficult to interpret the clinical importance of an effect size. Effect sizes of approximately 0.2 SD represent small effects; 0.5 SD, moderate; and 0.8, large.[34] Reviewers may help you interpret the results by translating the summary effect size back into natural units.[35] For instance, clinicians may have become familiar with the significance of differences in walk test scores in patients with chronic lung disease. Investigators can then convert the effect size of a treatment on a number of measures of functional status (eg, the walk test and stair climbing) back into differences in walk test scores.[36]

How Precise Were the Results?

In the same way that it is possible to estimate the average effect across studies, it is possible to estimate a CI around that estimate; that is, a range of values with a specified *probability* (typically 95%) of including the true effect (see Chapter 8, Confidence Intervals).

USING THE GUIDE

Returning to our opening scenario, the primary outcome, admission to the hospital, showed a trend in favor of magnesium sulfate that just reaches the threshold for *statistical significance* (RR, 0.70; 95% CI, 0.51-0.98). The results, however, are variable between studies (Figure 19-2) (the *P* value for the test of heterogeneity = .04, and the I^2 is 56%). In the severe asthma group, in contrast, the pooled difference between magnesium and *placebo* was clearly statistically significant and important (RR, 0.59; 95% CI, 0.43-0.80) and the results more consistent across studies (Figure 19-2). Four studies that enrolled patients with severe asthma included a total of 70 patients who received magnesium sulfate and 63 who received placebo; there were 56 admissions among placebo patients and 34 among active treatment patients (Figure 19-2). There were no differences in vital signs or measured adverse effects, although the authors indicate that an insufficient number of studies were available to draw firm conclusions about adverse effects and adverse events.

HOW CAN I APPLY THE RESULTS TO PATIENT CARE?

Were All Patient-Important Outcomes Considered?

Although it is a good idea to look for focused systematic review articles because they are more likely to provide accurate results, this does not mean that you should ignore outcomes that are not included in a review. For example, the potential benefits of hormone replacement therapy include a reduced risk of fractures and a reduced risk of colon cancer, and potential downsides include an increased risk of breast cancer and, surprisingly, possibly of adverse cardiovascular outcomes. Focused reviews of the evidence are more likely to provide accurate results of the impact of hormone replacement therapy on each of these 4 outcomes, but a clinical decision requires considering all of them. The best systematic review is a series of such reviews, one for each *patient-important outcome*.

FIGURE 19-2

Results of Randomized Trials of Magnesium Sulphate in Asthmatic Patients Presenting to the Emergency Department

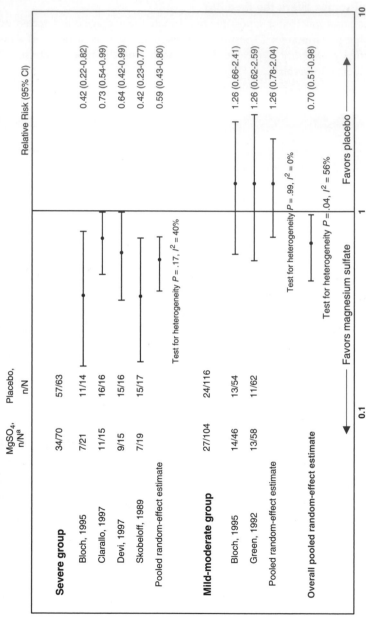

Systematic reviews frequently do not report the adverse effects of therapy. One reason is that the individual studies often measure these adverse effects either in different ways or not at all, making pooling, or even effective summarization, difficult. Costs are an additional outcome that you will often find absent from systematic reviews.

Are Any Postulated Subgroup Effects Credible?

The extent to which one finds subgroup analyses credible is often pivotal in interpreting the results of systematic reviews. Even if the true underlying effect is identical in each of a set of studies, chance will ensure that the observed results differ (see Chapter 5, Why Study Results Mislead: Bias and Random Error). As a result, systematic reviews risk capitalizing on the play of chance. Perhaps the studies with sicker patients happened, by chance, to be those with the larger treatment effects. The reviewer may erroneously conclude that the treatment is more effective in sicker patients. The more subgroup analyses the reviewer undertakes, the greater the risk of a spurious conclusion.

The clinician can apply a number of criteria to distinguish subgroup analyses that are credible from those that are not (see Table 19-6, which also appears as Table 20.4-1 in Chapter 20.4, When to Believe a Subgroup Analysis). If these criteria are not met, the results of a subgroup analysis are less likely to be credible and you should assume that the overall effect across all patients and all treatments, rather than the subgroup effect, applies to the patient at hand and to the treatment under consideration.

What are clinicians to do if subgroup analyses fail to provide an adequate explanation for unexplained heterogeneity in study results? Although a number of reasonable possibilities exist, including not to pool findings at all, we suggest that, pending further trials that may explain the differences, clinicians use a summary measure from all of the best available studies for the best estimate of the effect of the intervention or exposure.[37-39]

TABLE 19-6

Guidelines for Deciding Whether Apparent Differences in Subgroup Response Are Real

- Did the hypothesis precede rather than follow the analysis?
- Was the subgroup difference one of a small number of hypothesized effects tested?
- Is the subgroup difference suggested by comparisons within rather than between studies?
- Is the magnitude of the subgroup difference large?
- Is the subgroup difference consistent across studies?
- Was the subgroup difference statistically significant?
- Does external evidence support the hypothesized subgroup difference?

USING THE GUIDE

Your confidence in the benefit of magnesium depends on the extent to which you find the subgroup analysis focusing on severely ill patients credible. Applying the 7 criteria, we find that the investigators generated the hypothesis before they began the analysis, and it was one of only 2 subgroup hypotheses they explored. Comparisons are based on between- and, in one case, within-study comparisons (Bloch; Figure 19-2). The magnitude of the difference in effect between the severe and mild or moderate asthma is large (RRs of 0.59 and 1.26), and the difference is reasonably consistent across studies (you observe an I^2 of 40%, suggesting appreciable residual variability in results in the studies of severe patients) and is unlikely to occur by chance ($P = .006$) (Figure 19-2). The plausibility is less certain, but because severe asthma was usually described as a condition unresponsive to initial β-agonist treatment, one may speculate that persistent bronchospasm was required to demonstrate an effect of magnesium. Thus, the postulated subgroup effect that magnesium is effective in severe but not mild to moderate asthma meets 4 criteria completely and 3 partially. You conclude that you are ready to believe in the subgroup effect.

What Is the Overall Quality of the Evidence?

For systematic reviews that focus on alternative patient management strategies—in most instances, treatment decisions for individual patients—it may be helpful to consider the overall quality of the evidence for each patient-important outcome for each subgroup of patients (if one finds 1 or more subgroup analyses credible). An international group of clinician-methodologists and guideline developers have suggested a framework for making this assessment[40] (see Chapter 22.4, Grading Recommendations). The system provides a definition of quality of evidence: the extent to which we can be confident in the estimates of intervention effects.

In this 4-category rating system (high, moderate, low, and very low), observational studies provide only low quality of evidence unless the magnitude of effect is large (eg, hip replacement in patients with severe hip osteoarthritis). RCTs start as high-quality evidence, but a number of concerns may lead us to lower our assessment of the quality of the evidence (Table 19-7). Observational studies begin as low quality but, if the magnitude of the effect is large enough, can move up to moderate or even high quality. Some applications of this approach (eg, UpToDate) combine the 2 lowest categories of evidence, low quality and very low quality, into a single category and report their recommendations accordingly.

Are the Benefits Worth the Costs and Potential Risks?

Finally, either explicitly or implicitly, the clinician and patient must weigh the expected benefits against the costs and potential *risks* (see Chapter 21, How to Use a Patient Management Recommendation). A valid set of systematic reviews comparing the effect of alternative management strategies on all patient-important outcomes provides the best possible basis for decision making, but clinicians must still consider the

TABLE 19-7

Simplified GRADE Rating of Quality of Evidence

Randomized trials start high but move down because:
- They constitute only indirect evidence regarding the question at hand
- Of poor design and implementation
- Of imprecision (wide confidence intervals)
- Of inconsistent results (variability in effect)
- Of high likelihood of publication bias

Observational studies start low but can move up because of:
- Large treatment effect

Abbreviation: GRADE, grades of recommendation, assessment, development, and evaluation.

results in the context of patients' *values and preferences* and in the context of your health care system's ability to deliver (see Chapter 21, How to Use a Patient Management Recommendation, and Chapter 22.2, Decision Making and the Patient).

USING THE GUIDE

The available data come from RCTs of patients with severe asthma focusing on a patient-important outcome (admission to the hospital), including methodologically strong studies, with reasonably narrow CIs, reasonably consistent results (Figure 19-2), and no strong suggestion of publication bias. On this basis, you rate the evidence as high quality. You are left, however, with 1 nagging doubt: the total number of patients with asthma is only 133 and the total number of events only 100. The authors examined adverse effects but, consistent with studies of magnesium for other conditions, they found no important adverse effects.

CLINICAL RESOLUTION

You have decided (despite the nagging doubt about the small number of patients included in the studies) that you have high-quality evidence of a large effect of magnesium in reducing the need for hospitalization in patients with asthma. You therefore administer 2 g of magnesium sulfate intravenously, in addition to bronchodilators and corticosteroids. Three hours later, the patient is feeling a little better, and you admit her to a well-monitored unit. During the next 48 hours, the patient improves and is discharged home on the third hospital day, with the strongest possible counsel to find a new home for her cat.

References

1. Rowe BH, Bretzlaff JA, Bourdon C, Bota GW, Camargo CA Jr. Magnesium sulfate for treating exacerbations of acute asthma in emergency department. *Cochrane Database Syst Rev*. 2000;(1):CD001490.

2. Antman EM, Lau J, Kupelnick B, Mosteller F, Chalmers TC. A comparison of results of meta-analyses of randomized control trials and recommendations of clinical experts: treatments for myocardial infarction. *JAMA*. 1992;268(2):240-248.

3. Oxman AD, Guyatt GH. The science of reviewing research. *Ann N Y Acad Sci*. 1993;703:125-133; discussion 133-124.

4. Cook DJ, Mulrow CD, Haynes RB. Systematic reviews: synthesis of best evidence for clinical decisions. *Ann Intern Med*. 1997;126(5):376-380.

5. Higgins JPGS, ed. Cochrane handbook for systematic review of interventions 425 (updated May 2005). Chichester, UK: John Wiley & Sons, Ltd: Cochrane Library; 2005; issue 3.

6. *Systematic Reviews in Health Care: Meta-Analysis in Context*. 2nd ed. London, England: BMJ Books; 2000.

7. Antiplatelet Trialists' Collaboration. Collaborative overview of randomised trials of antiplatelet therapy, I: prevention of death, myocardial infarction, and stroke by prolonged antiplatelet therapy in various categories of patients. *BMJ*. 1994;308(6921):81-106.

8. Antiplatelet Trialists' Collaboration. Collaborative overview of randomised trials of antiplatelet therapy, II: maintenance of vascular graft or arterial patency by antiplatelet therapy. *BMJ*. 1994;308(6922):159-168.

9. Antiplatelet Trialists' Collaboration. Collaborative overview of randomised trials of antiplatelet therapy, III: reduction in venous thrombosis and pulmonary embolism by antiplatelet prophylaxis among surgical and medical patients. *BMJ*. 1994;308(6923):235-246.

10. Antithrombotic Trialists' Collaboration. Collaborative meta-analysis of randomised trials of antiplatelet therapy for prevention of death, myocardial infarction, and stroke in high risk patients. *BMJ*. 2002;324(7329):71-86.

11. Irwig L, Tosteson AN, Gatsonis C, et al. Guidelines for meta-analyses evaluating diagnostic tests. *Ann Intern Med*. 1994;120(8):667-676.

12. Antithrombotic Trialists' Collaboration. The *meta*Register of Controlled Trials (*m*RCT). Current controlled trials. http://www.controlled-trials.com. Accessed March 20, 2008.

13. Dickersin K. The existence of publication bias and risk factors for its occurrence. *JAMA*. 1990;263(10):1385-1389.

14. Dickersin K, Min YI, Meinert CL. Factors influencing publication of research results: follow-up of applications submitted to two institutional review boards. *JAMA*. 1992;267(3):374-378.

15. Dickersin K. How important is publication bias? a synthesis of available data. *AIDS Educ Prev*. 1997;9(1 suppl):15-21.

16. Stern JM, Simes RJ. Publication bias: evidence of delayed publication in a cohort study of clinical research projects. *BMJ*. 1997;315(7109):640-645.

17. Ioannidis JP. Effect of the statistical significance of results on the time to completion and publication of randomized efficacy trials. *JAMA*. 1998;279(4):281-286.

18. Eysenbach G. Tackling publication bias and selective reporting in health informatics research: register your eHealth trials in the International eHealth Studies Registry. *J Med Internet Res*. 2004;6(3):e35.

19. Williamson JW, Goldschmidt PG, Colton T. The quality of medical literature: an analysis of validation assessments. In: Bailar JC, Mosteller F. *Medical Uses of Statistics*. 2nd ed. Waltham, MA: NEJM Books; 1992.

20. Horwitz RI. Complexity and contradiction in clinical trial research. *Am J Med*. 1987;82(3):498-510.

21. Detsky AS, Naylor CD, O'Rourke K, McGeer AJ, L'Abbe KA. Incorporating variations in the quality of individual randomized trials into meta-analysis. *J Clin Epidemiol*. 1992;45(3):255-265.

22. Moher D, Pham B, Jones A, et al. Does quality of reports of randomised trials affect estimates of intervention efficacy reported in meta-analyses? *Lancet*. 1998;352(9128):609-613.

23. Kunz R, Oxman AD. The unpredictability paradox: review of empirical comparisons of randomised and non-randomised clinical trials. *BMJ*. 1998;317(7167):1185-1190.

24. Stampfer MJ, Colditz GA. Estrogen replacement therapy and coronary heart disease: a quantitative assessment of the epidemiologic evidence. *Prev Med*. 1991;20(1):47-63.

25. Hulley S, Grady D, Bush T, et al. Randomized trial of estrogen plus progestin for secondary prevention of coronary heart disease in postmenopausal women: Heart and Estrogen/progestin Replacement Study (HERS) Research Group. *JAMA*. 1998;280(7):605-613.

26. Nelson HD, Humphrey LL, Nygren P, Teutsch SM, Allan JD. Postmenopausal hormone replacement therapy: scientific review. *JAMA*. 2002;288(7):872-881.

27. Manson JE, Hsia J, Johnson KC, et al. Estrogen plus progestin and the risk of coronary heart disease. *N Engl J Med*. 2003;349(6):523-534.

28. Anderson GL, Limacher M, Assaf AR, et al. Effects of conjugated equine estrogen in postmenopausal women with hysterectomy: the Women's Health Initiative randomized controlled trial. *JAMA*. 2004;291(14):1701-1712.

29. Moher D, Jadad AR, Nichol G, Penman M, Tugwell P, Walsh S. Assessing the quality of randomized controlled trials: an annotated bibliography of scales and checklists. *Control Clin Trials*. 1995;16(1):62-73.

30. Juni P, Witschi A, Bloch R, Egger M. The hazards of scoring the quality of clinical trials for meta-analysis. *JAMA*. 1999;282(11):1054-1060.

31. Jadad AR, Moore RA, Carroll D, et al. Assessing the quality of reports of randomized clinical trials: is blinding necessary? *Control Clin Trials*. 1996;17(1):1-12.

32. Higgins JP, Thompson SG, Deeks JJ, Altman DG. Measuring inconsistency in meta-analyses. *BMJ*. 2003;327(7414):557-560.

33. Rosenthal R. *Meta-analytic Procedures for Social Research*. 2nd ed. Newbury Park, CA: Sage Publications; 1991.

34. Cohen J. *Statistical Power Analysis for the Behavioral Sciences*. 2nd ed. Hillsdale, NJ: Lawrence Earlbaum Associates; 1988.

35. Smith K, Cook D, Guyatt GH, Madhavan J, Oxman AD. Respiratory muscle training in chronic airflow limitation: a meta-analysis. *Am Rev Respir Dis*. 1992;145(3):533-539.

36. Lacasse Y, Wong E, Guyatt GH, King D, Cook DJ, Goldstein RS. Meta-analysis of respiratory rehabilitation in chronic obstructive pulmonary disease. *Lancet*. 1996;348(9035):1115-1119.

37. Peto R. Why do we need systematic overviews of randomized trials? *Stat Med*. 1987;6(3):233-244.

38. Oxman AD, Guyatt GH. A consumer's guide to subgroup analyses. *Ann Intern Med*. 1992;116(1):78-84.

39. Yusuf S, Wittes J, Probstfield J, Tyroler HA. Analysis and interpretation of treatment effects in subgroups of patients in randomized clinical trials. *JAMA*. 1991;266(1):93-98.

40. Guyatt G, Gutterman D, Baumann MH, et al. Grading strength of recommendations and quality of evidence in clinical guidelines: report from an American College of Chest Physicians Task Force. *Chest*. 2006;129(1):174-181.

ADVANCED TOPICS IN
SYSTEMATIC REVIEWS

REPORTING BIAS

Victor Montori, John Ioannidis,
and Gordon Guyatt

IN THIS CHAPTER:

The Many Sources of Reporting Bias

Bigger Dangers in Reviews With Small Studies

Large Studies Are Not Immune

Dissemination Bias

Strategies to Address Reporting Bias

Prospective Registration Can Reduce Reporting Bias

A Final Warning

A *systematic review* follows a protocol describing the scope of the researcher's question, inclusion and exclusion criteria for *primary studies*, a search strategy, data extraction, quality assessment procedures, and data analysis. *Systematic error* can intrude at any of these steps. Perhaps the most difficult types of *bias* for reviewers to overcome relates to authors' inclination to publish material, either entire studies or specific *outcomes*, based on the magnitude, direction, or *statistical significance* of the results. We call the systematic error in the body of evidence that results from this inclination *reporting bias*.

THE MANY SOURCES OF REPORTING BIAS

Authors have used other terms to refer to specific types of reporting bias. When an entire study remains unreported, the standard term is *publication bias*. When authors or study sponsors selectively manipulate and report specific outcomes and analyses, critics have used the label *selective outcome reporting bias*.[1-3] When material is published later according to the results, authors have used the term *time lag bias*.[4] All these biases tend to distort and usually exaggerate estimates of magnitude of *treatment effect*.

Excluding unpublished studies from a systematic review will not bias the results of the review if the unpublished studies show, on average, the same magnitude of effect as the published reports. Unfortunately, studies without statistically significant results (*negative studies*) are less likely to be published than studies that show apparent differences (*positive studies*). The magnitude and direction of a study's results may be more important determinants of publication than study design, relevance, or quality.[5,6] Positive studies may be as much as 3 times more likely to be published than negative studies.[7,8] Although large randomized trials will usually appear in publications irrespective of whether they are positive or negative, positive studies tend to appear sooner.[4,9] This time lag bias may create spurious clinical impressions (usually that interventions are more effective than is truly the case) that subsequent publications fail to remedy. Finally, with selective outcome reporting, the overall impression of the data may be misleading. This will be true even in rigorous *systematic reviews* because reviewers will be unaware how the authors or sponsors have selectively manipulated and reported their data.[1-3]

Reporting bias can intrude at virtually all stages of the planning, implementation, and dissemination of research (Table 20.1-1).

BIGGER DANGERS IN REVIEWS WITH SMALL STUDIES

Systematic reviews that fail to identify and include unpublished studies face a risk of presenting overly sanguine estimates of treatment effectiveness (Figure 20.1-1).

TABLE 20.1-1

Reporting Bias

Phases of Research Publication	Actions Contributing to or Resulting in Bias
Preliminary and pilot studies	Small studies more likely to have negative results (eg, those with discarded failed hypotheses) remain unpublished; companies classify some as proprietary information.[5]
Trial design, organization, and funding	Proposal selectively cites studies with positive results.
Institutional/ethics review board approval	Review boards do not typically keep registries of approved trials.[10]
Study completion	Interim analysis shows that a study is likely to have negative results and project is dropped or stopped early, possibly obscuring demonstration of adverse effects.[11]
Report completion	Authors decide that reporting a study with negative results is uninteresting and do not invest the time and effort required for submission.[12]
Report submission	Authors decide to forgo or delay submission of the study with negative results.[12]
Selective analysis and outcome reporting	Authors decide to manipulate analyses and outcomes and to report information selectively according to the most impressive results.[1-3,13] Journal editors request that the manuscript be made briefer; authors delete mention of outcomes the intervention did not significantly affect.
Journal selection	Authors decide to submit the negative report results to a nonindexed, non-English, or limited-circulation journal.[13]
Editorial consideration	Editor decides that the negative study results do not warrant peer review and rejects manuscript. If editor decides it is worth reviewing, manuscript moves to lower-priority list.
Peer review	Peer reviewers conclude that the negative study results do not contribute to the field and recommend rejecting the manuscript.[4]
Author revision and resubmission	Author of rejected manuscript decides to forgo the submission of the negative study results or to submit the study results again at a later time to another journal (see "Journal Selection" above).
Report publication	Journal delays the publication of the negative study results.[4]

FIGURE 20.1-1

Treatment Effectiveness and Publication Bias

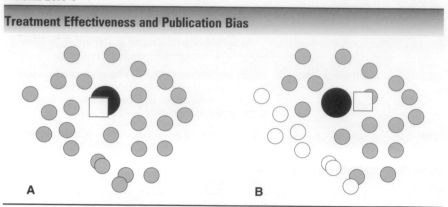

A
B

A, The black circle represents the underlying truth. The white square represents the pooled estimate from a systematic review of all the *evidence*. The small shaded circles represent the results of individual studies. B, The white circles represent the results of studies that the reviewers failed to identify because the studies were not published. Note the error in the pooled estimate represented by the gap between the pooled estimate (white square) and the underlying truth (black circle).

The risk is probably higher for *reviews* that are based on small studies.[14] Small studies are more likely than large studies to yield *false-positive* results, other things (eg, *study quality*) being equal.[15] Studies including large numbers of patients are less likely to remain unpublished or ignored and tend to provide more precise estimates of the treatment effect, whether positive or negative. Egger et al[16] offered a number of examples of *meta-analyses* of small trials that showed a larger treatment effect than a subsequent large trial. Discrepancies between results of meta-analysis and subsequent large trials may occur as often as 20% of the time,[17] and reporting bias may be a major a contributor to the discrepancies.[18]

LARGE STUDIES ARE NOT IMMUNE

Although large studies are more likely to be published, sponsors who are not pleased with the results may succeed in delaying publication.[4] Furthermore, they may publish in specialty journals with limited readership studies that, by their size and importance, warrant publication in the highest-profile general medical journals. They may also succeed in selective reporting of results using strategies that are scientifically unsound. The following example illustrates all these phenomena.

The Salmeterol Multicenter Asthma Research Trial (SMART) was a randomized trial designed to examine the effect of salmeterol or placebo on a composite endpoint of respiratory-related deaths and life-threatening experiences. In September 2002, after a data safety and monitoring board (DSMB) review of 25858 randomized patients that showed a nearly significant increase in the primary outcome in salmeterol-treated patients, the sponsor, GlaxoSmithKline, terminated the study. In a significant deviation from the original protocol, GlaxoSmithKline submitted to the Food and Drug Administration an analysis, including events in the 6 months after the termination of the trial, that produced an apparent diminution of the dangers associated with salmeterol. The Food and Drug Administration, through specific inquiry, eventually obtained the correct analysis.[19]

The SMART results finally found their way into print in January 2006, in a specialty journal, *Chest*, reporting the correct analysis.[20]

DISSEMINATION BIAS

Even if studies with negative results avoid every one of the reporting bias risks in Table 20.1-1, they may still experience a different fate than studies with positive results (Table 20.1-2). Although published, they may be published in less prominent journals and, as a result, they may not receive the same attention from fellow

TABLE 20.1-2

Dissemination Bias: The Fate of Published Studies With Negative Results

Phase of Dissemination	Actions Contributing to or Resulting in Publication Bias
Lay press report	Negative study results are not considered newsworthy.
Electronic database indexing	MEDLINE, EMBASE, and *ACP Journal Club* do not scan or index articles in the journal/language of publication of the study.
Decision-maker retrieval	Health managers and policy makers do not retrieve the study to dictate policy.
Further trial evidence	New trial reports discuss their findings but do not cite the findings of the study.
Narrative review	Experts draft a review, but study is never cited.
Systematic review	Reviewer goes to extremes to identify negative reports but misses the study with negative results. Industry-associated reviewer uses arbitrarily selected unpublished data on file; this further discredits incorporation of unpublished reports in systematic reviews. Systematic reviewer inadvertently includes duplicate publication.
Systematic review submission	Journal editors reject meta-analysis because it included unpublished reports not exposed to the rigor of peer review.[21] Review then follows the same path described here for the study with negative results.
Practice guidelines	Evidence-based guidelines are produced according to a systematic review that missed the study.
Funding opportunities	Further funding opportunities are identified without consideration of the study.

scientists, let alone the lay press. They may not receive adequate attention from policy makers, may be discarded in narrative reviews, omitted (if unidentified) even from systematic reviews, and have minimal or no effect in formulation of policy guidelines. Further funding decisions may also be made in the absence of evidence from these trials. The SMART study described in the previous section provides a compelling example of dissemination bias.

On the other hand, studies with positive results receive disproportionate attention. For instance, they are more likely to appear in secondary publications that summarize prominent results.[22] They may also be published more than once. This duplicate publication may be difficult to detect because of different authors, altered presentation, and variability in the exact numbers of patients and events presented.[23]

STRATEGIES TO ADDRESS REPORTING BIAS

Because even such comprehensive efforts may fail to identify all unpublished studies, methodologists have generated a number of tests that may be used for detecting publication bias. These tests are interesting, but unfortunately, they do not seem to work very well. In theory, they are appropriate only if there are more than 30 studies (an unusual situation). Many reviewers, however, use them in reviews with few studies. Moreover, none of these tests has been validated against a *criterion standard* (or *gold standard*) of real data in which we know whether publication or other biases existed or not.[24]

Despite the limitations of these strategies, we will tell you about them because they are all we have and because you will encounter them when you use systematic reviews and meta-analyses to guide your practice. Table 20.1-3 describes 4 categories of diagnostic tests for reporting bias that we describe in the text below. Hybrid tests combine features across these categories.

TABLE 20.1-3

Four Strategies to Address Reporting Bias

1. Examine whether the smaller studies show bigger effects
    a. Funnel plots, visually assessed
    b. Funnel plots, statistical analysis
2. Reconstruct evidence by restoring the picture after accounting for postulated publication bias
    a. Trim and fill
    b. Fail-safe N
3. Estimate the chances of publication according to the statistical significance level
4. Examine the evolution of effect size over time as more data appear

Several popular tests examine whether small studies differ from larger ones in their results. In a figure that relates the precision (as measured by sample size, inverse of *standard error* or *variance*) of studies included in a meta-analysis to the magnitude of treatment effect (as measured by *effect size, relative risk reduction,* or *odds ratio*), the resulting display should resemble an inverted funnel (Figure 20.1-2). Such *funnel plots* should be symmetric, around the *point estimate* (dominated by the largest trials) or the results of the largest trials themselves.

Unfortunately, funnel plots seldom provide such clear testimony about the absence (Figure 20.1-2A) or presence (Figure 20.1-2B) of publication bias. As a result, restricting testing for asymmetry to a visual look at the plot, although a common practice, is distressingly error prone.[25] Even if one can convincingly detect an apparent difference between studies with positive results and small studies with negative results on the funnel plot, there are other explanations for the asymmetry. For instance, because of a more restrictive (and thus responsive) population, or a more careful administration of the intervention, the effect may actually be larger in the small studies.

Statisticians have developed quantitative methods relying on the same principles,[14,26] although some have questioned their appropriateness.[27-29] When these tests suggest bias, explanations include true publication bias, chance, poor design of small studies, and true larger effects in small studies (eg, if compliance with the experimental intervention is higher or the intervention is more consistently delivered).[16]

A second set of tests tries to impute and correct for missing information and address its effect (*trim and fill*). Such tests begin by removing or trimming small

FIGURE 20.1-2A

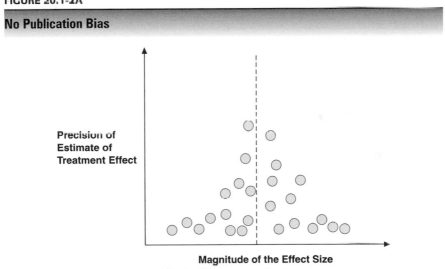

The circles represent the point estimates of the trials. The pattern of distribution resembles an inverted funnel. Larger studies tend to be closer to the pooled estimate (the dashed line). In this case, the effect sizes of the smaller studies are more or less symmetrically distributed around the pooled estimate.

FIGURE 20.1-2B

Possible Publication Bias

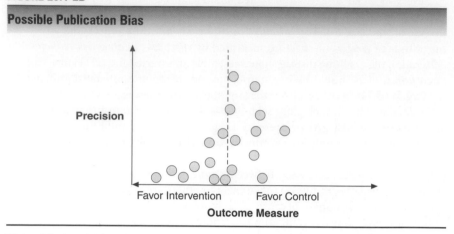

This funnel plot shows that the smaller studies are not symmetrically distributed around either the point estimate (dominated by the larger trials) or the results of the larger trials themselves. The trials expected in the bottom right quadrant are missing. This suggests publication bias and an overestimate of the treatment effect relative to the underlying truth.

studies with positive results that do not have a negative study counterpart. This leaves a symmetric funnel plot from which the investigators calculate a putative true effect. The investigators then replace the positive-result studies they have removed, and hypothetical studies that mirror these positive-result studies are imputed or filled to create a symmetric funnel plot that retains the new pooled effect estimate. This trim-and-fill method allows the calculation of an adjusted *confidence interval* and an estimate of the number of missing trials.[18]

The *fail-safe N* (an estimation of the number of undetected negative-result studies that would be needed to change the conclusions of a meta-analysis[30]) is another test in the same family. Again, the availability of few studies and the presence of heterogeneity make this second strategy inappropriate for most meta-analyses.

A third set of tests tries to estimate whether there are differential chances of publication according to the level of statistical significance.[31,32] These tests are the most directly linked to the usual driver of publication bias, and they are well established in the educational and psychology literature but are uncommonly used in the medical sciences, probably because of their computational difficulty and complex assumptions.

Finally, a set of tests aims to examine whether evidence changes over time as more data accumulate. Recursive cumulative meta-analysis[33] involves performing a meta-analysis every time a new trial is published or at the end of each year for trials ordered chronologically and noting the direction and magnitude of the change in the summary effect. Continuously diminishing effects are characteristic of time lag bias. Another test examines whether the number of statistically significant results is larger than what would be expected under plausible assumptions.[34]

In addition to these approaches, if authors have obtained the results of some unpublished studies and if published and unpublished data show different results, the possibility of publication bias is great.[35,36]

The most powerful test of publication bias would come from a comparison of prospectively registered trials with published study results.[37] Because registration of trials is completed before the results are available, the results do not influence study registration. Indeed, prospective registration of all trials represents the ultimate solution to the problem of publication bias. Registries could also address selective reporting if the registered protocols included detailed information about the outcomes and the analysis plan. Alternative suggestions include amnesty for unpublished trials or electronic publishing of all studies[38] regardless of previous or future journal publication.

PROSPECTIVE REGISTRATION CAN REDUCE REPORTING BIAS

This discussion makes evident that prospective study registration with accessible results represents the best solution to reporting bias. Proposals have long existed to link prospective registration to the work of institutional review boards or ethics review boards[39] or to the editorial process of medical journals and publishing societies.[40] The editors of most high-impact medical journals have implemented a policy whereby they do not publish randomized trials unless these are registered in advance in a clinical trials registry that satisfies minimal standards (as set forth by the World Health Organization International Clinical Trials Registry Platform, http://www.who.int/ictrp), such as http://www.clinicaltrials.gov.[41] Some pharmaceutical companies have made their research information available online,[42] but it is uncertain whether compliance will be high. Some journals, such as *Lancet* and some open-access medical journals on the internet, have established Web sites for posting study protocols and reports of completed studies undergoing peer review.[43] Until prospective registration and complete reporting become a reality, clinicians using research reports to guide their practice must remain cognizant of the dangers of reporting biases.

A FINAL WARNING

We have one more note of caution: Readers must be alert for the potentially unscrupulous use of unpublished data. For instance, a meta-analysis based on published data showed that selective serotonin reuptake inhibitor (SSRI) antidepressant medications have the same rate of discontinuation resulting from adverse effects as tricyclic antidepressants. A meta-analysis sponsored by an SSRI producer used unpublished data on file with the company to show that SSRIs are better tolerated than tricyclic antidepressants.[44] Two questions arise: Was the choice of unpublished data selective, and what was the *validity* of the studies? Use of unpublished data becomes more credible if access is open to other investigators.

References

1. Chan AW, Altman DG. Identifying outcome reporting bias in randomised trials on PubMed: review of publications and survey of authors. *BMJ*. 2005;330(7494): 753.

2. Chan AW, Krleza-Jeric K, Schmid I, Altman DG. Outcome reporting bias in randomized trials funded by the Canadian Institutes of Health Research. *CMAJ*. 2004;17 1(7):735-740.

3. Chan AW, Hrobjartsson A, Haahr MT, Gotzsche PC, Altman DG. Empirical evidence for selective reporting of outcomes in randomized trials: comparison of protocols to published articles. *JAMA*. 2004;291(20):2457-2465.

4. Ioannidis JP. Effect of the statistical significance of results on the time to completion and publication of randomized efficacy trials. *JAMA*. 1998;279(4):281-286.

5. Easterbrook P, Berlin J, Gopalan R, Matthews D. Publication bias in clinical research. *Lancet*. 1991;337(8746):867-872.

6. Misakian A, Bero L. Publication bias and research on passive smoking: comparison of published and unpublished studies. *JAMA*. 1998;280(3):250-253.

7. Egger M, Smith G. Bias in location and selection of studies. *BMJ*. 1998;316(7124):61-66.

8. Stern J, Simes R. Publication bias: evidence of delayed publication in a cohort study of clinical research projects. *BMJ*. 1997;315(7109):640-645.

9. Hopewell S, Clarke M, Stewart L, Tierney J. Time to publication for results of clinical trials (Cochrane methodology review). *Cochrane Database Syst Rev*. 2003;4:MR000011. doi:10.1002/14651858.MR000011.pub2.

10. Simes R. Publication bias: the case for an international registry of clinical trials. *J Clin Oncol*. 1986;4(10):1529-1541.

11. Meade M. Pro/con clinical debate: it is acceptable to stop large multicentre randomized controlled trials at interim analysis for futility: con: the hazards of stopping for futility. *Crit Care*. 2005;9(1):34-36; discussion 34-36.

12. Dickersin K. The existence of publication bias and risk factors for its occurrence. *JAMA*. 1990;263(10):1385-1390.

13. Kyzas P, Loizou K, Ioannidis J. Selective reporting biases in cancer prognostic factor studies. *J Natl Cancer Inst*. 2005;97(14):1043-1055.

14. Begg C, Berlin J. Publication bias: a problem in interpreting medical data. *J R Stat Soc A*. 1988;151(3):419-463.

15. Ioannidis JP. Why most published research findings are false. *PLoS Med*. 2005; 2(8):e124.

16. Egger M, Davey Smith G, Schneider M, Minder C. Bias in meta-analysis detected by a simple, graphical test. *BMJ*. 1997;315(7109):629-634.

17. Cappelleri J, Ioannidis J, Schmidt C, et al. Large trials vs meta-analysis of smaller trials: how do their results compare? *JAMA*. 1996;276(16):1332-1338.

18. Sutton A, Duval S, Tweedie R, Abrams K, Jones D. Empirical assessment of effect of publication bias on meta-analyses. *BMJ*. 2000;320(7249):1574-1577.

19. Lurie P, Wolfe S. Misleading data analyses in salmeterol (SMART) study. *Lancet*. 2005;366(9493):1261-1262.

20. Nelson HS, Weiss ST, Bleecker ER, Yancey SW, Dorinsky PM. The Salmeterol Multicenter Asthma Research Trial: a comparison of usual pharmacotherapy for asthma or usual pharmacotherapy plus salmeterol. *Chest*. 2006;129(1):15-26.

21. Cook D, Guyatt G, Ryan G, et al. Should unpublished data be included in meta-analyses? *JAMA*. 1993;269(21):2749-2753.

22. Carter AO, Griffin GH, Carter TP. A survey identified publication bias in the secondary literature. *J Clin Epidemiol*. 2006;59(3):241-245.

23. Rennie D. Fair conduct and fair reporting of clinical trials. *JAMA*. 1999;282(18): 1766-1768.

24. Lau J, Ioannidis JP, Terrin N, Schmid CH, Olkin I. The case of the misleading funnel plot. *BMJ*. 2006;333(7568):597-600.

25. Terrin N, Schmid CH, Lau J. In an empirical evaluation of the funnel plot, researchers could not visually identify publication bias. *J Clin Epidemiol*. 2005; 58(9):894-901.

26. Begg C, Mazumdar M. Operating characteristics of a rank correlation test for publication bias. *Biometrics*. 1994;50(4):1088-1101.

27. Irwig L, Macaskill P, Berry G, Glasziou P. Bias in meta-analysis detected by a simple, graphical test: graphical test is itself biased. *BMJ*. 1998;316(7129):470; discussion 470-471.

28. Stuck A, Rubenstein L, Wieland D. Bias in meta-analysis detected by a simple, graphical test: asymmetry: asymmetry detected in funnel plot was probably due to true heterogeneity. *BMJ*. 1998;316(7129):469.

29. Seagroatt V, Stratton I. Bias in meta-analysis detected by a simple, graphical test: test had 10% positive rate. *BMJ*. 1998;316(7129):470; discussion 470-471.

30. Gleser L, Olkin L. Models for estimating the number of unpublished studies. *Stat Med*. 1996;15(23):2493-2507.

31. Hedges L, Vevea J. Estimating effect size under publication bias: small sample properties and robustness of a random effects selection model. *J Educ Behav Stat*. 1996;21(4):299-333.

32. Vevea J, Hedges L. A general linear model for estimating effect size in the presence of publication bias. *Psychometrika*. 1995;60(3):419-435.

33. Ioannidis JP, Contopoulos-Ioannidis DG, Lau J. Recursive cumulative meta-analysis: a diagnostic for the evolution of total randomized evidence from group and individual patient data. *J Clin Epidemiol*. 1999;52(4):281-291.

34. Pan Z, Trikalinos T, Kavvoura F, Lau J, Ioannidis J. Local literature bias in genetic epidemiology: an empirical evaluation of the Chinese literature. *PLoS Med*. 2005;2(12):e334. doi:10.1371/journal.pmed.0020334.

35. Man-Son-Hing M, Wells G, Lau A. Quinine for nocturnal leg cramps: a meta-analysis including unpublished data. *J Gen Intern Med*. 1998;13(9):600-606.

36. Simes R. Confronting publication bias: a cohort design for meta-analysis. *Stat Med*. 1987;6(1):11-29.

37. Langhorne P. Bias in meta-analysis detected by a simple, graphical test: prospectively identified trials could be used for comparison with meta-analyses. *BMJ*. 1998;316(7129):471.

38. Varmus H. E-Biomed: a proposal for electronic publications in the biomedical sciences [PubMed Central Web site]. http://www.nih.gov/welcome/director/ebiomed/ebi.htm. Accessed August 8, 2000.

39. Boissel J, Haugh M. Clinical trial registries and ethics review boards: the results of a survey by the FICHTRE project. *Fundam Clin Pharmacol*. 1997;11(3):281-284.

40. Horton R, Smith R. Time to register randomised trials: the case is now unanswerable. *BMJ*. 1999;319(7214):865-866.

41. DeAngelis C, Drazen J, Frizelle F, et al. Clinical trial registration: a statement from the International Committee of Medical Journal Editors. *JAMA*. 2004;292(11):1363-1364.

42. Levy M. A new register for clinical trial information. *CMAJ*. 2000;162(7):970-971.

43. McConnell J, Horton R. Lancet electronic research archive in international health and eprint server. *Lancet*. 1999;354(9172):2-3.

44. Davey Smith G, Egger M. Meta-analysis: unresolved issues and future developments. *BMJ*. 1998;316(7126):221-225.

ADVANCED TOPICS IN
SYSTEMATIC REVIEWS

FIXED-EFFECTS AND RANDOM-EFFECTS MODELS

Victor Montori, John Ioannidis, Deborah J. Cook, and Gordon Guyatt

IN THIS CHAPTER:

Models for Combining Data for Meta-Analysis

In a *meta-analysis*, results from 2 or more *primary studies* are combined statistically. The meta-analyst seeking a method to combine primary study results can do so by using either a *fixed-effects model* or a *random-effects model*.[1]

A *fixed-effects model* considers the set of studies included in the meta-analysis and assumes that there is a single true value underlying all the study results.[2] That is, the assumption is that if all studies were infinitely large, they would yield identical estimates of the effect. Thus, the observed estimates of effect differ from one another only because of *random error*.[3] The error term for a fixed-effects model comes only from within-study variation (study *variance*); the model does not consider between-study variability in results (known as *heterogeneity*) (see Chapter 19, Summarizing the Evidence). A fixed-effects model aims to estimate this common-truth effect and the uncertainty about it.

By contrast, a *random-effects model* assumes that the studies included are a random sample of a population of studies addressing the question posed in the meta-analysis.[4] Each study estimates a different underlying true effect, and these effects are assumed to have a specific distribution. In the usual situation, this distribution is assumed to be normal and to have some mean value.[3] The random-effects model takes into account both within-study variability and variability in results beyond what is attributable to within-study variability (ie, between-study variability). It aims to estimate the mean effect across the distribution of effects, as well as the uncertainty about this mean effect.

There is a variety of statistical models to implement fixed-effects and random-effects methods. One typical application of a fixed-effects model is the Mantel-Haenszel method.[5] Although the DerSimonian and Laird method exemplifies the application of random-effects models,[4] there are a number of alternatives.[6,7] Fortunately, they usually give essentially the same result. One also frequently finds reference to "inverse variance method," which means that studies are combined and weighted by the inverse of the variance. If this is only the variance of the results of each study (within-study variance), this is a fixed-effects model. If this includes an estimate of the between-study variance, this is a random-effects model.

Differences in Results From Fixed-Effects and Random-Effects Models

Fixed-effects and random-effects models usually give either identical or similar results.[8] If the between-study variance is estimated to be zero (this does not mean that the results are all the same; there is always some between-study variability, but the statistical estimate will be zero when that variability is easily explained by chance), then the fixed-effects and random-effects calculations give identical results. This occurs in about 40% of meta-analyses of *randomized trials*[9] and in a smaller percentage of meta-analyses of epidemiologic studies.[10] In another 40% or so of meta-analyses of randomized trials, the estimated between-study variance is not that large; thus, fixed effects and random effects provide similar results. There is, however, an appreciable proportion of instances in which between-study variability may be large, and fixed-effects and random-effects calculations disagreements may then show important differences.

Provided that there is some between-study variability, compared with a fixed-effects model, a random-effects model gives smaller studies proportionally greater weight in the pooled estimate. Consequently, the direction and magnitude of the pooled estimate are influenced relatively more by smaller studies. Random-effects models therefore generate summary estimates closer to the *null result* (ie, no *treatment effect*) than the fixed-effects summary estimates if smaller study results are closer to the null result than those from larger studies. If the smaller studies are farther from the null than large studies, a random-effects model will produce larger estimates of beneficial or harmful effects than will a fixed-effects model.

Thus, with one important caveat, we can conclude that random-effects estimates may provide either a more conservative or less conservative estimate of the treatment effect than fixed-effects estimates.[11] The reservation is that the summary estimate derived from the random-effects model may be more susceptible to exaggerated results from the available small studies; this is not an uncommon phenomenon (see Chapter 20.1, Reporting Bias).

Between-study variability increases the random-effects estimate of random error. Thus, the random-effects model generally produces wider *confidence intervals (CIs)* around the summary estimates than the fixed-effects model. In this sense, the random-effects model generally produces a more conservative assessment of the precision of the pooled estimate than the fixed-effects model.

EXAMPLES OF DIFFERENCES IN POINT ESTIMATES AND CONFIDENCE INTERVALS FROM META-ANALYSES

Which model is preferred to conduct meta-analyses? The good news is that in most cases, the choice will not make an important difference.[8] However, exceptions do occur. Let us consider Figure 20.2-1. This figure shows 9 *randomized controlled trials* of alendronate in a dose of 5 mg to prevent fractures in sites not traditionally associated with osteoporosis. Examining the *point estimates* for each study, we see that 3 studies suggest alendronate is beneficial,[12-14] 1 shows no difference between treatments,[15] and 5 studies suggest that a control treatment is better than alendronate.[16-19] The smaller studies tend to favor the control intervention. There are large differences between the point estimates and several of the CIs show little or no overlap; consider the studies by Bone et al[13] and Hosking et al[18] or the

FIGURE 20.2-1

Impact of the Meta-analysis Model Chosen on the Pooled Estimate of Efficacy

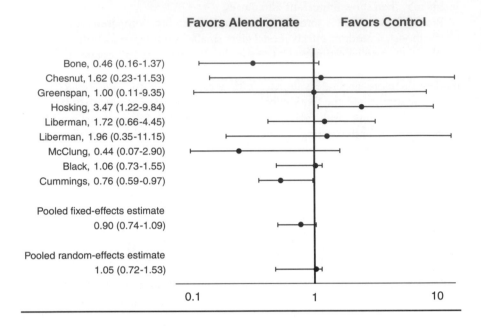

Relative Risk With 95% Confidence Interval for Low-Risk Fractures
After Treatment With Alendronate

studies by Hosking et al[18] and Cummings et al.[14] Despite these appreciable differences in study results, the formal test of heterogeneity barely crossed the 0.10 threshold ($P = .08$) (see Chapter 20.3, Making Sense of Variability in Study Results).

This meta-analysis includes 7 small studies and 2 larger studies, with point estimates at both sides of the line showing no difference at 1.0 and some CIs (in brackets) with little or no overlap (ie, CIs around estimates in different studies do not have any shared values). Using the fixed-effects model, we notice that the CI is narrow, underestimating the uncertainty about the magnitude of the effect. The random-effects model provides a more conservative estimate of the level of uncertainty about the treatment effect.

Consider the pooled estimate derived using the fixed-effects model. This summary estimate reflects the results of the larger studies included and it favors alendronate. Because the smaller studies have a greater effect on the random-effects model results, the summary estimate favors the *control group*. Neither summary effect approaches *statistical significance*.

Now, examine the CIs around these summary estimates. Which CI better reflects the level of uncertainty we have about the true effect of the intervention? We suggest that the narrower CI provided by the fixed-effects model may overestimate the strength of inference we can make about the true effect of the intervention. On the other hand, the CI obtained using the random-effects model may provide a more realistic estimate of the range of plausible true values (see Chapter 8, Confidence Intervals).

In most circumstances in which random effects and fixed effects disagree, it is a matter of the width of the CIs. In a few situations, however, the estimates of effect may also differ greatly. Let us consider magnesium in acute myocardial infarction (Figure 20.2-2), in which a series of small trials conducted in the 1980s suggested that magnesium may halve the risk of death.[20] A relatively large trial of 2316 patients published in 1992 also showed a significant reduction in mortality (odds ratio [OR], 0.74; 95% CI, 0.56-0.99), albeit not as large.[21] Then, ISIS-4 (Fourth International Study of Infarct Survival), a megatrial of 58 050 patients (a randomized factorial trial assessing early oral captopril, oral mononitrate, and intravenous magnesium sulfate in 58 050 patients with suspected acute myocardial infarction), was published. ISIS-4[22] provided a different estimate: a trend toward increasing the risk of death (OR, 1.06; 95% CI, 1.00-1.13; $P = .06$).

Figure 20.2-2 presents a meta-analysis of these, which are heterogeneous ($P < .001$; $I^2 = 67.9\%$). The fixed-effects summary OR suggests no benefit

FIGURE 20.2-2

Impact of the Meta-analysis Model Chosen on the Pooled Estimate of Efficacy

Odds Ratios With 95% Confidence Interval for Mortality After Treatment With Intravenous Magnesium in Acute Myocardial Infarction

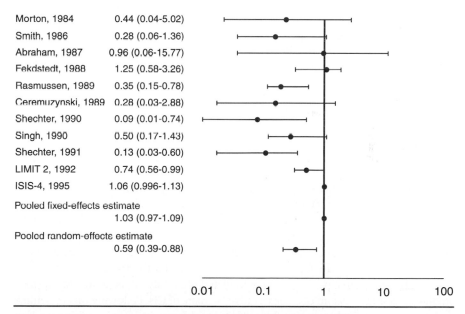

Morton, 1984	0.44 (0.04-5.02)
Smith, 1986	0.28 (0.06-1.36)
Abraham, 1987	0.96 (0.06-15.77)
Fekdstedt, 1988	1.25 (0.58-3.26)
Rasmussen, 1989	0.35 (0.15-0.78)
Ceremuzynski, 1989	0.28 (0.03-2.88)
Shechter, 1990	0.09 (0.01-0.74)
Singh, 1990	0.50 (0.17-1.43)
Shechter, 1991	0.13 (0.03-0.60)
LIMIT 2, 1992	0.74 (0.56-0.99)
ISIS-4, 1995	1.06 (0.996-1.13)
Pooled fixed-effects estimate	1.03 (0.97-1.09)
Pooled random-effects estimate	0.59 (0.39-0.88)

Abbreviations: ISIS-4, Fourth International Study of Infarct Survival; LIMIT 2, the Second Leicester Intravenous Magnesium Intervention Trial.

Adapted from Teo and Yusef.[20]

(OR, 1.03; 95% CI, 0.97-1.09), but using fixed effects is not strictly appropriate: the data clearly violate the assumption of common truth across the studies. The random-effects estimate suggests a large benefit from magnesium (OR, 0.59; 95% CI, 0.39-0.88), driven by the results of the small trials.

At first sight, it makes no sense to believe trials of a few few hundred patients when a trial of more than 50 000 patients is available. The credibility of the ISIS-4 result increased further with the publication, some years later, of another large trial[23] that showed no benefit of magnesium among 6213 randomized patients. Putting one's faith in the larger trials,[24] one would conclude that the random-effects estimate is profoundly misleading.

It is curious, however, that even a trial as large as the Second Leicester Intravenous Magnesium Intervention Trial suggested a benefit of magnesium.[25] Another interpretation would suggest that in the management setting in the 1980s, magnesium was in fact effective, but this was no longer the case with the additional drugs, more prompt mobilization, and decreased overall mortality in later years. This illustrates the concept of random-effects models: they focus on a mean effect across a population of effects representing a wide variety of populations and settings. Even so, if we believe we have an explanation of heterogeneity—the era in which the study was conducted—clinicians should look for separate meta-analyses for the earlier and more recent trials (see Chapter 19, Summarizing the Evidence; Chapter 20.3, Making Sense of Variability in Study Results; and Chapter 20.4, When to Believe a Subgroup Analysis).

This meta-analysis pools results from studies on magnesium salts in the management of acute myocardial infarction, and the outcome is mortality. In this case, the fixed-effects model is driven by the results of the largest study and shows no benefit at all (3% excess in the odds of death), whereas the random-effects model is driven by the results of the many small studies with positive results and suggests a highly statistically significant 41% reduction in the odds of death.

CONCLUSION

Overall, how should readers judge whether the appropriate model was used in a given meta-analysis? It is unlikely that true effects are exactly identical in various populations. Furthermore, we are always interested in extrapolating results beyond the study sample to patients in our own practice. These considerations draw us toward the random-effects model. Furthermore, when large between-study heterogeneity is documented, the assumptions of fixed-effects models are untenable. Furthermore, the instances in which subsequent large studies have contradicted the results of meta-analysis of small studies suggest the wisdom of a conservative estimate of CIs. Following this reasoning, authors are increasingly using random-effects models routinely and selecting variants of such models that yield maximal estimates of uncertainty.[26] On the other hand, the increased susceptibility of the random-effects model to publication *bias* as a result of its increased weighting of small trials is a disadvantage.

We do not think it is appropriate to be dogmatic about the choice of an analytic model. Although it usually makes little difference which model data analysts choose, understanding the implications associated with the choice of the model will help clinicians make sense of situations when large variability in study results exists.

References

1. Fleiss JL. The statistical basis of meta-analysis. *Stat Methods Med Res*. 1993; 2(2):121-145.

2. Anello C, Fleiss JL. Exploratory or analytic meta-analysis: should we distinguish between them? *J Clin Epidemiol*. 1995;48(1):109-116; discussion 117-118.

3. Lau J, Ioannidis JP, Schmid CH. Summing up evidence: one answer is not always enough. *Lancet*. 1998;351(9096):123-127.

4. DerSimonian R, Laird N. Meta-analysis in clinical trials. *Control Clin Trials*. 1986; 7(3):177-188.

5. Mantel N, Haenszel W. Statistical aspects of the analysis of data from retrospective studies of disease. *J Natl Cancer Inst*. 1959;22(4):719-748.

6. Smith TC, Spiegelhalter DJ, Thomas A. Bayesian approaches to random-effects meta-analysis: a comparative study. *Stat Med*. 1995;14(24):2685-2699.

7. Warn DE, Thompson SG, Spiegelhalter DJ. Bayesian random effects meta-analysis of trials with binary outcomes: methods for the absolute risk difference and relative risk scales. *Stat Med*. 2002;21(11):1601-1623.

8. Engels EA, Schmid CH, Terrin N, Olkin I, Lau J. Heterogeneity and statistical significance in meta-analysis: an empirical study of 125 meta-analyses. *Stat Med*. 2000;19(13):1707-1728.

9. Higgins JP, Thompson SG, Deeks JJ, Altman DG. Measuring inconsistency in meta-analyses. *BMJ*. 2003;327(7414):557-560.

10. Ioannidis JP, Trikalinos T, Ntzani E, Contopoulos-Ioannidis D. Genetic associations in large versus small studies: an empirical assessment. *Lancet*. 2003;361 (9357):567-571.

11. Poole C, Greenland S. Random-effects meta-analyses are not always conservative. *Am J Epidemiol*. 1999;150(5):469-475.

12. McClung M, Clemmesen B, Daifotis A, et al. Alendronate prevents postmenopausal bone loss in women without osteoporosis: a double-blind, randomized, controlled trial: Alendronate Osteoporosis Prevention Study Group. *Ann Intern Med*. 1998;128(4):253-261.

13. Bone HG, Downs RW, Tucci JR, et al. Dose-response relationships for alendronate treatment in osteoporotic elderly women: Alendronate Elderly Osteoporosis Study Centers. *J Clin Endocrinol Metab*. 1997;82(1):265-274.

14. Cummings SR, Black DM, Thompson DE, et al. Effect of alendronate on risk of fracture in women with low bone density but without vertebral fractures: results from the Fracture Intervention Trial. *JAMA*. 1998;280(24):2077-2082.

15. Greenspan SL, Parker RA, Ferguson L, et al. Early changes in biochemical markers of bone turnover predict the long-term response to alendronate therapy in representative elderly women: a randomized clinical trial. *J Bone Miner Res*. 1998;13(9):1431-1438.

16. Liberman UA, Weiss SR, Broll J, et al. Effect of oral alendronate on bone mineral density and the incidence of fractures in postmenopausal osteoporosis: the Alendronate Phase III Osteoporosis Treatment Study Group. *N Engl J Med*. 1995;333(22):1437-1443.

17. Black DM, Cummings SR, Karpf DB, et al. Randomised trial of effect of alendronate on risk of fracture in women with existing vertebral fractures: Fracture Intervention Trial Research Group. *Lancet*. 1996;348(9041):1535-1541.

18. Hosking D, Chilvers CED, Christiansen C, et al. Prevention of bone loss with alendronate in postmenopausal women under 60 years of age: Early Postmeno-pausal Intervention Cohort Study Group. *N Engl J Med*. 1998;338(8):485-492.

19. Chesnut CH III, McClung MR, Ensrud KE, et al. Alendronate treatment of the postmenopausal osteoporotic woman: effect of multiple dosages on bone mass and bone remodeling. *Am J Med*. 1995;99(2):144-152.

20. Teo KK, Yusuf S. Role of magnesium in reducing mortality in acute myocardial infarction: a review of the evidence. *Drugs*. 1993;46(3):347-359.

21. Woods KL, Fletcher S, Roffe C, Haider Y. Intravenous magnesium sulphate in suspected acute myocardial infarction: results of the Second Leicester Intrave-nous Magnesium Intervention Trial (LIMIT-2). *Lancet*. 1992;339(8809):1553-1558.

22. ISIS-4 (Fourth International Study of Infarct Survival) Collaborative Group. ISIS-4: a randomised factorial trial assessing early oral captopril, oral mononitrate, and intravenous magnesium sulphate in 58,050 patients with suspected acute myo-cardial infarction. *Lancet*. 1995;345(8951):669-685.

23. Early administration of intravenous magnesium to high-risk patients with acute myocardial infarction in the Magnesium in Coronaries (MAGIC) Trial: a ran-domised controlled trial. *Lancet*. 2002;360(9341):1189-1196.

24. Ioannidis JP, Cappelleri JC, Lau J. Issues in comparisons between meta-analyses and large trials. *JAMA*. 1998;279(14):1089-1093.

25. Woods KL. Mega-trials and management of acute myocardial infarction. *Lancet*. 1995;346(8975):611-614.

26. Babapulle MN, Joseph L, Belisle P, et al. A hierarchical bayesian meta-analysis of randomised clinical trials of drug-eluting stents. *Lancet*. 2004;364(9434):583-591.

ADVANCED TOPICS IN
SYSTEMATIC REVIEWS

MAKING SENSE
OF VARIABILITY
IN STUDY
RESULTS

Victor Montori, Rose Hatala, John Ioannidis,
Maureen O. Meade, Peter Wyer,
and Gordon Guyatt

IN THIS CHAPTER:

ARRIVING AT A SINGLE SUMMARY ESTIMATE OF EFFECT

Clinicians often approach the medical literature to find a single key piece of information. This information may be the effect of a treatment, the effect of a potentially harmful exposure, the information provided by a diagnostic test, or the association between a particular patient characteristic and the patient's *prognosis*. Each study provides a *point estimate* of that effect. However, point estimates from related studies inevitably vary to some extent. The primary goal of a quantitative *systematic review*, also called a *meta-analysis*, is to provide a single, best summary estimate of effect. To provide such an estimate, reviewers will statistically combine results across studies in a meta-analysis.

Another important goal of a systematic review is to make sense of the variability in point estimates from related studies. This chapter is devoted to making sense of variability in study results. Whether the focus is an effect of treatment, harmful *exposure*, diagnostic testing, or a prognostic variable, the principles are the same. We will focus on the issue of *treatment effects* in this chapter.

THE DILEMMA OF VARIABILITY: HETEROGENEITY IN STUDY RESULTS

The starting assumption of a systematic review that provides a summary estimate of an effect of treatment is that across the range of study patients, interventions, and *outcomes* included in the review, the effect of interest is more or less the same. In Chapter 19, Summarizing the Evidence, we framed the dilemma that clinicians must confront in evaluating such a review. On the one hand, a review question framed to include a broad range of patients, interventions, and ways of measuring outcome helps avoid spurious subgroup effects (see Chapter 20.4, When to Believe a Subgroup Analysis), leads to narrower confidence intervals, and increases applicability across a broad range of patients. On the other hand, combining the results of diverse studies may violate the starting assumption of the analysis: that the magnitude of effect is more or less the same across varying patient populations, interventions or exposures, and outcomes.

The solution to this dilemma is to evaluate the extent to which results differ from study to study; that is, the variability or *heterogeneity* of study results. Table 20.3-1 summarizes approaches to evaluating variability in study results, and the subsequent discussion expands on these principles.

VISUAL ASSESSMENT OF VARIABILITY

Because 2 studies seldom yield point estimates that are extremely close to one another, and they virtually never yield identical point estimates, any meta-analysis

TABLE 20.3-1

Evaluating Variability in Study Results

Visual evaluation of variability

   How similar are the point estimates?

   To what extent do the confidence intervals overlap?

Statistical tests evaluating variability

   Yes-or-no tests for heterogeneity that generate a P value

   I^2 test that quantifies the variability explained by between-study differences in results

that combines a number of studies will inevitably demonstrate some heterogeneity of results. The question is whether that heterogeneity is sufficiently great to make us uncomfortable with combining results from a group of related studies to generate a single summary effect.[1]

Consider the results of 2 meta-analyses shown in Figure 20.3-1 and Figure 20.3-2 (meta-analysis A and meta-analysis B, respectively). Reviewing the results of these studies, would clinicians be comfortable with a single summary result in either meta-analysis or in both meta-analyses? A single effect representing all studies in A seems implausible, although clinicians may easily accept a single summary effect for B.

Comfort with a single summary effect increases when all studies suggest benefit or all studies suggest harm, and thus when the point estimates of all studies are on the same side of the line of no effect. This condition holds in the case of meta-analysis B, but not in meta-analysis A, in which 2 studies suggest benefit and 2 suggest harm. Figure 20.3-3, however, highlights the limitation of this simple rule

FIGURE 20.3-1

Results of Meta-analysis A

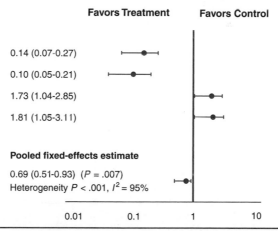

FIGURE 20.3-2

Results of Meta-analysis B

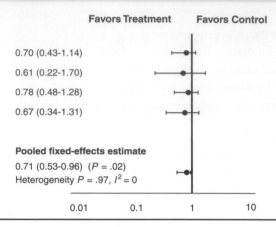

of thumb. This hypothetical meta-analysis C also shows point estimates on both sides of the line of no effect, but here most clinicians would be comfortable pooling the results.

A better approach to assessing heterogeneity focuses on the magnitude of the differences in the point estimates of the studies. Large differences in point estimates make clinicians less comfortable with pooling (as in meta-analysis A). In contrast, small differences in the magnitude of point estimates (as in meta-analyses B and C) support the underlying assumption that, across the range of study patients, interventions, and outcomes included in the review, the effect of interest is more or less the same.

FIGURE 20.3-3

Results of Meta-analysis C

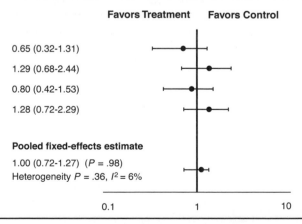

There is a second, equally important criterion that clinicians should apply when judging whether pooling is appropriate. If confidence intervals overlap widely (as in meta-analyses B and C), *random error* remains a plausible explanation for the differences in the point estimates. When confidence intervals do not overlap (as in meta-analysis A), random error becomes an unlikely explanation for differences in apparent treatment effect across studies.

YES-OR-NO STATISTICAL TESTS OF HETEROGENEITY

The subjective nature of visual assessments of heterogeneity risks makes them vulnerable to misinterpretation. Thus, formal statistical analysis provides a useful complement to visual inspection.

The *null hypothesis* of the *test for heterogeneity* is that the underlying effect is the same in each of the studies (eg, the underlying *relative risk* associated with study 1 is the same as the underlying relative risk associated with studies 2, 3, and 4) (see Chapter 10.1, Hypothesis Testing). There are several tests for heterogeneity that provide a *P* value representing how often one would obtain differences in study results as great as or greater than those observed if the null hypothesis were true and if we repeated the studies over and over.[2] A low *P* value means that random error is an unlikely explanation of the differences in results from study to study. Thus, a low *P* value in a test for heterogeneity should raise doubts about relying on a single summary estimate representing the treatment effect for all patients and all variations in the administration of a treatment. A high *P* value, on the other hand, increases our confidence that the underlying assumption of pooling holds true, and thus our confidence in an overall summary estimate. Because, in many meta-analyses, this test is underpowered to detect heterogeneity, investigators often choose a threshold *P* value of .10, rather than the .05 value used for most statistical tests.

TECHNICAL NOTE 20.3-1

Cochran *Q*, the most commonly used test for heterogeneity, assumes the null hypothesis that all the apparent variability between individual study results is due to chance. Cochran *Q* generates a probability, based on a χ^2 distribution, that between-study differences in results equal to or greater than those observed are likely to occur simply by chance.

In Figure 20.3-1, the *P* value associated with the test for heterogeneity is small ($P \le .001$), indicating that it is unlikely that we would observe results this disparate if all studies had the same underlying effect. The corresponding *P* value in Figure

20.3-2 is .97, approaching the maximum possible P value of 1.0. This means that if the null hypothesis were true, we would, on almost all repetitions of the experiments, observe differences in effect as great as or greater than we observe in these 4 studies. The P value for Figure 20.3-3 is also relatively large, .36.

Because the yes/no test of heterogeneity is underpowered when a meta-analysis is limited by a relatively small number of small studies, a nonsignificant result under these circumstances fails to rule out important underlying heterogeneity of treatment effect. In such situations, we might be unable to exclude chance as an explanation of differences, but we would remain suspicious that factors such as differences in populations, intervention, or measurement of outcome are responsible for differences in study results (see Chapter 20.4, When to Believe a Subgroup Analysis).

When a meta-analysis includes studies with large sample sizes and a correspondingly large number of events, the test for heterogeneity may also provide potentially misleading results. Under these circumstances, one may see small and unimportant differences in point estimates but, because of narrow confidence intervals, a positive statistical test result of heterogeneity. This is another reason why clinicians need to use their own visual assessments of heterogeneity and the results of formal statistical tests.

MAGNITUDE OF HETEROGENEITY STATISTICAL TESTS

Given the limitations of the yes/no P value approach, it is useful to use an alternative test that focuses on the magnitude of variability rather than the statistical significance of between-study variability. The I^2 statistic[3,4] provides an estimate of the percentage of variability in results across studies that is likely due to true differences in treatment effect as opposed to chance. When the I^2 is 0%, chance provides a satisfactory explanation for the variability in the individual study point estimates, and clinicians can be comfortable with a single pooled estimate of treatment effect. As the I^2 increases, we become progressively less comfortable with a single pooled estimate, and the need to look for explanations of variability other than chance becomes more compelling. One rule of thumb characterizes an I^2 of less than 0.25 as small heterogeneity, 0.25 to 0.5 as moderate, and more than 0.5 as large heterogeneity.[5]

TECHNICAL NOTE 20.3-2

One can calculate I^2 from Cochran Q (the most commonly used heterogeneity statistic) according to the formula: $I^2 = 100\% \times$ (Cochran Q – degrees of freedom). Any negative values of I^2 are considered equal to 0, so that the range of I^2 values is between 0% and 100%.

The results in Figure 20.3-1 generate an I^2 of more than 75%, whereas the results in Figures 20.3-2 and 20.3-3 yield I^2 values of less than 10%.

WHAT TO DO WHEN BETWEEN-STUDY VARIABILITY IN RESULTS IS LARGE

What should clinicians do when there is *evidence* for large or significant study-to-study differences in results? When chance becomes an unlikely explanation for differences, clinicians should make sure that meta-analysts have sought other explanations. Differences in study participants, interventions, outcomes, and study methodology may explain the variation in treatment effect.

Ideally, reviewers should specify candidate explanations for heterogeneity before analyzing data in a meta-analysis. When they do, apparent explanations of heterogeneity gain credibility; when investigators fail to provide a priori hypotheses, credibility diminishes. When apparent explanations for heterogeneity emerge from post hoc *data dredging*, we should view these apparent subgroup differences as hypothesis-generating insights. (For a deeper understanding of the principles by which clinicians should evaluate the exploration of the sources of heterogeneity, see Chapter 20.4, When to Believe a Subgroup Analysis. For a discussion of additional issues in statistical analysis related to heterogeneity of study results, see Chapter 20.2, Fixed-Effects and Random-Effects Models.)

What if, in the end, we are left with a large degree of unexplained between-study heterogeneity for which chance does not provide an adequate explanation? This is not an uncommon situation. Some argue that, in this situation, investigators should not combine the results. Nonetheless, clinicians still need a best estimate of the treatment effect to inform their decisions. Pending further studies that may explain the differences between results, the summary estimate remains the best explanation of the treatment effect. Clinicians should, however, exercise caution in recommending treatments based on summary estimates associated with large unexplained heterogeneity.

Acknowledgment

This chapter is based on an article previously published by Hatala et al.[5]

References

1. Lau J, Ioannidis JP, Schmid CH. Summing up evidence: one answer is not always enough. *Lancet*. 1998;351(9096):123-127.

2. Lau J, Ioannidis JP, Schmid CH. Quantitative synthesis in systematic reviews. *Ann Intern Med*. 1997;127(9):820-826.

3. Higgins J, Thompson S, Deeks J, Altman D. Measuring inconsistency in meta-analyses. *BMJ*. 2003;327(7414):557-560.

4. Higgins J, Thompson S, Deeks J, Altman D. Statistical heterogeneity in systematic reviews of clinical trials: a critical appraisal of guidelines and practice. *J Health Serv Res Policy*. 2002;7(1):51-61.

5. Hatala R, Keitz S, Wyer P, Guyatt G; for the Evidence-Based Medicine Teaching Tips Working Group. Tips for learners of evidence-based medicine, 4: assessing heterogeneity of primary studies in systematic reviews and whether to combine their results. *CMAJ*. 2005;172(5):661-665.

ADVANCED TOPICS IN
SYSTEMATIC REVIEWS

WHEN TO BELIEVE A SUBGROUP ANALYSIS

Gordon Guyatt, Peter Wyer, and John Ioannidis

IN THIS CHAPTER:

Is the Subgroup Difference Consistent Across Studies?

Is the Subgroup Difference Statistically Significant?

Is There External Evidence That Supports the Hypothesized Subgroup Difference?

Conclusion

Clinical Resolution

CLINICAL SCENARIO

You are the medical director of the emergency medical service in your region. The chair of your resuscitation training committee observes that your protocols for cardiac arrest do not include vasopressin. He points to a study in the *New England Journal of Medicine* that suggested that vasopressin, relative to epinephrine, saved lives in patients presenting in asystole[1] and that its use was supported by an editorial in the same issue.[2] He also mentions that the American Heart Association has released an update of their well-known Advanced Cardiac Life Support guidelines[3] and observes that they list vasopressin as a valid alternative to epinephrine, at the same time acknowledging that this recommendation is controversial.[4]

Spurred by your colleague's urgency, you review the new guideline document and observe that the findings regarding effectiveness of vasopressin for cardiac arrest patients in asystole come from a subgroup analysis of data from the *New England Journal of Medicine* trial that included patients presenting in different arrest rhythms.[1] You also find a recent meta-analysis of similar trials[5] in the relevant guidelines documents. The apparent contention is that vasopressin is effective relative to epinephrine for asystole, but not for other rhythms, particularly for ventricular fibrillation. You wonder about the credibility of the subgroup analysis and whether this kind of analysis can provide a basis for changing clinical practice. Faced with the conflicting evidence and controversy, you perform an additional search with PubMed Clinical Queries and locate an analysis of the vasopressin *evidence* based on published criteria for validity of a subgroup analysis.[6] Armed with this material, you set to work reviewing the evidence.

THE CHALLENGE OF SUBGROUP ANALYSIS

Clinicians faced with a treatment decision in a particular patient are interested in the evidence that pertains most directly to that individual. In a survey of 45 clinical trials reported in 3 leading medical journals, Pocock et al[7] found at least 1 subgroup analysis that compared the response to treatment in different categories of patients in 51% of the reports. Although the investigators conducting these analyses were trying to meet clinicians' need for information specific to their individual patients, they risked misleading physicians more than enlightening them.

In this chapter, we present guidelines for interpreting the results of *subgroup analyses*. Although our discussion focuses on *randomized controlled trials* (*RCTs*) and *systematic reviews* and *meta-analyses* of RCTs, the same principles apply to other research designs. Our discussion assumes that the underlying design of the studies is sound. For treatment trials, sound design involves randomization, blinding, completeness of follow-up, and avoiding premature termination (see Chapter 6, Therapy). If the study designs are not sound, the overall conclusions are suspect, let alone conclusions based on subgroup analyses.

WHY DO INVESTIGATORS CONDUCT SUBGROUP ANALYSES?

A subgroup analysis seeks important differences in treatment effect. These differences may be across types of patients (eg, older or younger patients, sicker or less sick ones) or across treatments (eg, low-dose or high-dose treatments, treatment with different drugs in the same class). When the magnitude of the difference between subgroups is real and sufficiently large, it may influence patient treatment.

Determining which subgroup analyses clinicians should believe remains controversial. Critics of subgroup analysis decry fishing expeditions and data-dredging exercises[8-11] that result in spurious inferences concerning subgroup effects. Advocates of subgroup analysis are alarmed at the risks of missing important differences in effect,[12,13] particularly with cavalier pooling of results[14] that they claim can result in meaningless conclusions about average effects[15] or failure to detect important treatment effects as a result of overly heterogeneous study populations.[16]

Clinicians need practical advice for when to believe an analysis that shows an apparent difference in treatment effects across subgroups. In considering this issue, clinicians need to bear in mind the different possible measures of effect and how the choice of measure of effect can influence inferences about subgroup differences.

USUALLY WE ANTICIPATE SIMILAR RELATIVE, NOT ABSOLUTE, RISK REDUCTIONS ACROSS SUBGROUPS

Consider a 40-year-old nonsmoking woman without diabetes and without a family history of heart disease, a blood pressure of 110/70 mm Hg, and an elevated serum cholesterol level with a total cholesterol to high-density-lipoprotein ratio of 6. Her risk of cardiovascular death in the next decade is 2% or less. Contrast this woman with a 70-year-old male smoker with diabetes who has a family history of heart disease, a blood pressure of 140/85 mm Hg, and an identical serum cholesterol level and cholesterol to high-density-lipoprotein ratio. His risk of a cardiovascular death in the next decade is 30% or more.

These 2 individuals represent extremes of high-risk and low-risk subgroups of candidates for lipid-lowering therapy. If one considers the absolute risk reduction these patients may achieve by taking a statin for the next decade, a subgroup effect is almost certain. The greatest absolute benefit the young woman could expect would be a risk reduction of 1% (from 2% to 1%), whereas the older man might have his risk reduced by 10% or more (from 30% to 20%). We would thus conclude there is a difference between high-risk and low-risk patients and the magnitude of treatment effect (ie, the biggest effects are observed in the higher-risk group).

On the other hand, the *relative risk reduction (RRR)*—in meta-analyses of statin drugs, about 30%[17]—may well be similar in high-risk and low-risk patients. Indeed, meta-analyses of randomized trials of statins suggest that RRRs vary little across higher-risk and lower-risk groups. In general, considering a wide variety of interventions, RRRs tend to be similar across risk groups, whereas absolute risk reductions show greater variability[18-20] (see Chapter 7, Does Treatment Lower Risk? Understanding the Results). In our discussion of subgroup analyses, we will be referring to RRRs unless we state otherwise.

SUBGROUP HYPOTHESES MUST FOCUS ON DIFFERENCES IDENTIFIABLE AT THE START OF A STUDY

A final issue is that subgroup analyses must focus on variables that one can define as patients begin a study. These can be characteristics of the patients (eg, older or younger, more or less sick), the intervention (eg, dose of drug, particular drug within a class), or outcome (eg, long-term vs short-term follow-up). Focusing on these variables will ensure that the prognostic balance created by randomization is maintained.

Analyses focusing on differences that arise after randomization are far less secure. For instance, a randomized trial of intensive glucose control vs standard glucose control in a medical intensive care unit found no difference in mortality between groups but a statistically significant difference among patients who stayed more than 3 days in the intensive care unit.[21] Because patients with a favorable prognosis may have been more likely to achieve early discharge in the control rather than the experimental group, the apparent effect is at least as likely to be due to prognostic imbalance as to the treatment. We restrict the subsequent discussion to variables identifiable at the start of a trial and suggest that clinicians pay little heed to analyses that focus on subgroup differences arising during its conduct.

AVOIDING MISLEADING CHANCE FINDINGS

In formulating guides for whether to believe a subgroup analysis, we will build on criteria that other authors have suggested.[22-25] Table 20.4-1 summarizes the approach that we will describe in detail below. Because we believe that investigators are more likely to commit serious errors when they present spurious subgroup analyses as real than when they fail to identify true subgroup differences, we will focus on the dangers of misleading analyses that suggest different treatment effects across subgroups. We present the criteria in an order that reflects the logic of thinking through a subgroup issue, rather than the importance of the criteria, which might differ in individual circumstances.

Chance is the explanation for spurious subgroup analyses. Clinicians and investigators tend to underestimate the effect of chance on the results of experiments.

In an imaginative investigation titled "The Miracle of DICE Therapy for Acute Stroke," Counsell et al[26] directed students in a practical class in statistics to roll different-colored dice numerous times to simulate 44 clinical trials of fictitious therapies. Participants received the dice in pairs and were told that one die in each pair was an ordinary die representing control patients, whereas the other die was loaded to roll either more or fewer sixes than the control. Rolling a 6 represented a patient death, and all other numbers represented a survival. Some pairs of dice were red, some white, and some green, each color representing a different medication (for instance, a different member of a common class of drugs). The investigators simulated trials of different size (various numbers of rolls of the paired dice) and methodologic rigor, along with the peer review and publication process.

Subgroup analysis suggested that "red" dice represented a therapy with a nonsignificant trend toward excess mortality; and when the inferior red drug was excluded, along with methodologically inferior and unpublished trials

TABLE 20.4-1

Guidelines for Deciding Whether Apparent Differences in Subgroup Response Are Real

Did the hypothesis precede rather than follow the analysis?

Was the subgroup difference one of a small number of hypothesized effects tested?

Is the subgroup difference suggested by comparisons within rather than between studies?

Is the magnitude of the subgroup difference large?

Is the subgroup difference consistent across studies?

Was the subgroup difference statistically significant?

Does external evidence support the hypothesized subgroup difference?

and data from inexperienced centers, roll-of-the-dice therapy offered an impressive 39% RRR for mortality.

The participants, however, had been deliberately misled: the dice were not loaded. The observed effects, which closely mimicked the patterns reported in actual medical literature, resulted entirely from chance. The impressive, statistically significant effect of properly administered DICE therapy resulted entirely from selective subgroup analyses and exclusions.

It remains true that when *sample sizes* are low and the *power* of analyses is limited, investigators may fail to detect true important underlying differences in treatment effect across subgroups. Most trials are underpowered to detect overall effects[27] and have negligible power to detect subgroup differences, even if they are large and patient-important. Meta-analyses combining the results of many trials may have improved power to document subgroup effects,[28] but published data do not usually provide sufficient information to allow consistent synthesis and analysis of subgroup-related data. Subgroup analyses may be more feasible with meta-analyses of individual-level data, but this is seldom an easy enterprise.[29]

All things considered, the power of chance to mislead suggests that clinicians should exercise great caution in interpreting apparent subgroup differences. Table 20.4-2 presents a number of claims of subgroup differences that ultimately proved false. We will now expand on the criteria in Table 20.4-1, explaining how you can differentiate such situations from real subgroup differences.

GUIDELINES FOR INTERPRETING SUBGROUP ANALYSES

Does the Hypothesis Precede Rather Than Follow the Analysis?

Embedded within any large data set are a certain number of apparent but, in fact, spurious subgroup differences. As a result, the credibility of any apparent subgroup difference that arises out of *post hoc* rather than *a priori* hypotheses is questionable.

Table 20.4-2 presents a number of examples of such spurious subgroup effects. One of these was the apparent finding that aspirin had a beneficial effect in the prevention of stroke in men with cerebrovascular disease but lacked the same effect in women.[31] For a considerable period, the finding led many physicians to withhold aspirin for women with cerebrovascular disease. This subgroup difference, which was discovered (ie, the investigators stumbled across the finding in exploring the data rather than suspecting it beforehand) in the first large trial of aspirin in patients with transient ischemic attacks, was subsequently found, in other studies and in a meta-analysis summarizing these studies,[33] to be false.

TABLE 20.4-2

Examples of Subgroup Analyses Subsequently Shown to be False

Observation (Citation)	Refutation Citation
Aspirin is ineffective in secondary prevention of stroke in women[31,32]	33
Antihypertensive treatment for primary prevention is ineffective in women[34,35]	36
Antihypertensive treatment is ineffective or harmful in elderly people[37]	38
ACE inhibitors do not reduce mortality and hospital admission in patients with heart failure who are also taking aspirin[39]	40
β-Blockers are ineffective after acute myocardial infarction in elderly people[41] and in patients with inferior MI[42]	43
Thrombolysis is ineffective > 6 h after acute MI[44]	45
Thrombolysis for acute MI is ineffective or harmful in patients with a previous MI[44]	46
Tamoxifen citrate is ineffective in women who have breast cancer and are aged < 50 y[47]	48
Benefit from carotid endarterectomy for symptomatic stenosis is reduced in patients taking only low-dose aspirin because of an increased operative risk[49]	50
Amlodipine reduces mortality in patients with chronic heart failure caused by nonischemic cardiomyopathy but not in patients with ischemic cardiomyopathy[51]	52
Platelet-activating factor receptor antagonist reduces mortality in patients with gram-negative sepsis but not in other patients with sepsis[53]	54
Ticlopidine is superior to aspirin for preventing recurrent stroke, MI, or vascular death in blacks but not in whites[55]	56
Angiotensin-receptor blockers increase mortality in patients with New York Heart Association functional class II-IV heart failure who also take both ACE inhibitors and β-blockers but lower mortality in patients not already taking drugs in both of these classes[57]	58
Lamifiban lowers 6-mo mortality and nonfatal MI at 6 mo in patients whose plasma concentrations are between 18 and 42 ng/mL but not in patients whose plasma concentrations are outside of this range[59,60]	61

Abbreviations: ACE, angiotensin-converting enzyme; MI, myocardial infarction.

Reprinted from Rothwell.[30] Copyright © 2005, with permission from Elsevier.

Whether a hypothesis preceded analysis of a data set is not necessarily a black-or-white issue. At one extreme, unexpected results might be clearly responsible for generating a new hypothesis; the results are discovered by a post hoc analysis. At the other extreme, a subgroup analysis to test a hypothesis suggested by previous research might be documented in a protocol, a study, or a systematic review. In between these 2 extremes is a range of possibilities, and the extent to which a hypothesis arose before, during, or after the data were collected and analyzed is frequently not clear in study reports. The situation may be further complicated by investigators' reluctance to acknowledge that a specific hypothesis was post hoc. Nevertheless, if a hypothesis has been clearly and unequivocally suggested by a different data set, one has moved from a hypothesis-generating framework to a hypothesis-testing framework.

USING THE GUIDE

Of the 2 trials that considered different presenting rhythm subgroups,[1,62] only 1 reported these subgroups as part of an a priori protocol.[62]

Is the Subgroup Difference One of a Small Number of Hypothesized Effects Tested?

Post hoc hypotheses based on subgroup analysis often arise from exploration of a data set in which many such hypotheses are considered. The greater the number of hypotheses tested, the greater the number of subgroup effects one will discover by chance. Even if investigators have clearly specified their hypotheses in advance, the strength of inference associated with the apparent confirmation of any single hypothesis will decrease if it is one of a large number they have tested.

For example, investigators conducted a study of platelet-activating factor receptor antagonist (PAFra) in septic patients. The result for all 262 patients showed a weak, nonsignificant trend in favor of active therapy. A subgroup analysis of 110 patients with gram-negative bacterial infection showed a large, statistically significant advantage for PAFra.[53] A subsequent larger study of 444 patients with gram-negative bacterial infection showed a small, nonsignificant trend in favor of PAFra almost identical to that of the previous trial analysis, which included all randomized patients.[54] The disappointed investigators might have been less surprised at the result of the second trial had they fully appreciated the limitations of their first subgroup analysis: The possible differential effect of PAFra in gram-negative bacterial infection was one of 15 subgroup hypotheses they tested.[63]

In another example, the Beta-Blocker Heart Attack Trial investigators conducted 146 subgroup comparisons.[64] Although the estimated effects of the treatment, propranolol, clustered around the overall effect, the effect in some small subgroups appeared to be either much greater or smaller.

> Nevertheless, the overall pattern was completely consistent with the observed difference in effect among the various subgroups because of sampling error rather than true differences.

Unfortunately, clinicians may not always be sure about the number of possible subgroup hypotheses that the investigators tested. If the investigators choose to withhold this information, reporting only hypotheses that were statistically significant, the reader is likely to be misled.

Moreover, with the advent of the molecular medicine era, the number of candidate subgroup analyses that can be performed according to molecular variables has increased greatly. Although this gene-based information is often biologically fascinating, databases may include data on many thousands or even millions of genetic or other molecular factors that are difficult to interpret. Testing large numbers of subgroup hypotheses can create misleading results.[65]

USING THE GUIDE

Of the 2 trials that considered presenting rhythm subgroups, Stiell et al[62] reported a large number of subgroup hypotheses as part of their protocol. Wenzel et al[1] did not report the number of subgroup analyses they conducted.

Is the Subgroup Difference Suggested by Comparisons Within Rather Than Between Studies?

Making inferences about different effect sizes in different groups according to between-study differences entails a high risk in comparison with inferences made according to within-study differences. For instance, one would be reluctant to conclude that treatment with propranolol results in a different magnitude of risk reduction for death after myocardial infarction than does administration of metoprolol according to data from 2 studies, one comparing propranolol with placebo and the other comparing metoprolol with placebo. Drawing inferences about these 2 drugs from 2 different placebo-controlled studies would be making an indirect comparison of their effect. A direct comparison would involve, in a single study, patients randomized to receive placebo, propranolol, or metoprolol. If, in such a direct comparison in a single high-quality study, investigators demonstrated patient-important and statistically significant differences in magnitude of effect between the 2 active treatments, the inference may be strong.

> In a systematic review examining the effectiveness of prophylaxis for gastrointestinal bleeding in critically ill patients,[66] histamine$_2$-receptor antagonists (H$_2$RAs) and antacids, when individually compared with placebo,

showed apparently similar effects in reducing overt bleeding, with odds ratios (ORs) of 0.29 (95% confidence interval [CI], 0.17-0.45) and 0.40 (95% CI, 0.20-0.79), respectively. Direct comparison from studies in which patients were randomized to receive H$_2$RAs or antacids demonstrated an important reduction in bleeding with the H$_2$RAs (common OR, 0.56; 95% CI, 0.33-0.97).

Inference based on between-study differences is potentially misleading because the apparent differentiating factor between studies will always be only one of many differences. For instance, aside from differences in the specific drugs used, different populations (varying in risk of adverse outcomes, for example), varying degrees of cointervention, or varying criteria for gastrointestinal bleeding all could explain the results. Explanations for these differences would not be plausible if the inference were based on within-study differences from randomized trials in which populations studied, control of cointervention, and outcome criteria were all identical. In this latter situation, 2 prime possible explanations of the difference in effect across subgroups exist: it is either true or it is a chance phenomenon.

Although direct comparisons are stronger, indirect comparisons are often all that exist. For many medical fields, conflicts of interest or other priorities mean investigators never undertake head-to-head comparisons of key therapeutic regimens.[67] Recently, investigators have refined statistical methods that respect the randomization and account for the much larger uncertainty that results from indirect comparisons.[68,69] Using such approaches, between-trial comparisons may be correct more often than they are misleading.[70] They are still, however, considerably less credible than are within-trial comparisons.

USING THE GUIDE

Returning to our opening scenario, Figure 20.4-1 presents the evidence from the relevant trials.[6] Both Wenzel et al[1] and Stiell et al[62] included patients with asystole and patients with ventricular fibrillation. Thus, the evidence of the subgroup differences comes from within-trial comparisons.

Is the Magnitude of the Subgroup Difference Large?

As a rule, the larger the difference between the observed effects in particular subgroups (or with particular drugs or dosages), the more plausible that the difference is real. At the same time, as the difference in effect size between the anomalous subgroup and the remainder of the patients becomes larger, the importance of the difference increases.

FIGURE 20.4-1

Predischarge Mortality: Subgroup Analyses Exact Inference Model

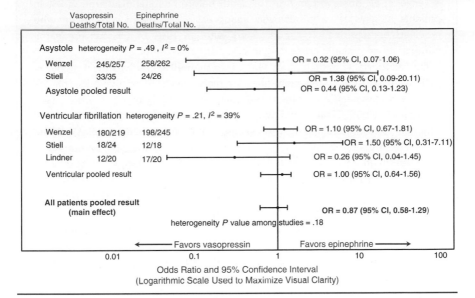

Abbreviations: CI, confidence interval; OR, odds ratio.

Forest plot illustrating the pooled subgroup effects from an analysis of 3 trials comparing vasopressin to epinephrine in patients with cardiac arrest. The analysis used an exact inference model and was restricted to subgroups of patients presenting with asystole or ventricular fibrillation. ORs for the effect on mortality of vasopressin compared with with epinephrine are pooled within each subgroup. The difference between the ORs for asystole and ventricular fibrillation subgroups is large but not statistically significant (P = .18).

Reprinted from Wyer et al.[6] Copyright © 2006, with permission from Elsevier. (Acknowledgment to Qi Zhou, PhD.)

When sample sizes are small, however, one will see large differences in apparent effect simply by chance. Were one to conclude that a subgroup difference is real just because it is large, one would be wrong more often than right.

For instance, a meta-analysis of 24 randomized trials compared the effect of sucralfate vs histamine receptor antagonists or antacids on the incidence of nosocomial pneumonia in critically ill patients. The pooled estimate showed a relative risk of 0.86 (95% CI, 0.75-0.97), suggesting a possible reduction of pneumonia with sucralfate.[71] The results of the individual studies varied, however, between a relative risk of 0.33 (a reduction of pneumonia with sucralfate of 2/3) to 1.84 (a > 80% increase in the incidence of pneumonia). These differences occurred despite that the results were entirely consistent with a single underlying magnitude of treatment effect for all these studies (heterogeneity P = .03) (see Chapter 19, Summarizing the Evidence; see also Chapter 20.3, Making Sense of Variability in Study Results). Thus, clinicians would be mistaken if they deduced that studies with different apparent effects represented underlying subgroup differences.

USING THE GUIDE

Wenzel et al[1] observed an RRR for death before hospital discharge of 3% in patients in asystole who received vasopressin compared with those who received epinephrine. This contrasted with an RRR of 0% for the same comparison in patients presenting in other arrest rhythms.

Overall mortality in their study was more than 90% and was even higher in patients in asystole. When event rates are high, the OR or relative odds may be a preferable measure of effect and may give a different impression (see Chapter 7, Does Treatment Lower Risk? Understanding the Results; and Chapter 10.2, Understanding the Results: More About Odds Ratios). When odds are substituted for risk in the Wenzel et al[1] study, the difference in vasopressin effect in patients with asystole appears much larger (OR of 0.32 for asystole compared with 1.0 for all patients).

Two other relevant RCTs deal with this issue.[62,72] Combining data from all 3 trials reporting results from presenting rhythm subgroups yields an OR for effect on predischarge mortality of vasopressin compared with epinephrine of 0.44 for the asystole subgroup compared with 1.0 for the ventricular fibrillation subgroup (Figure 20.4-1).[6] These comparisons suggest a substantial difference in effect between subgroups.

Is the Subgroup Difference Consistent Across Studies?

One may generate a hypothesis concerning differential response in a subgroup of patients by examination of data from a single study. Replication of the subgroup differences in other studies increases its credibility. The extent to which a rigorous systematic review of the relevant literature finds a subgroup difference to be consistently present is probably the best single index of its credibility. Readers of trial reports should look carefully in the discussion sections for reference to subgroup results in similar trials or in systematic reviews of such trials. Ideally, these replications should involve exactly the same subgroups and outcomes rather than having *bias* because of "moving the goalpost." For example, one trial may find a postulated subgroup benefit in patients younger than 50 years, whereas another may find a postulated subgroup benefit in patients younger than 60 years (but not in particular among those <50 years of age). It is possible that if the data are combined, neither patients younger than 50 years nor those 50 to 60 years old may be experiencing a benefit.

Investigators in one randomized trial believed that their subgroup analysis suggested that heart failure patients with a third heart sound benefited from digoxin, whereas those without a third heart sound did not.[73] A subsequent crossover trial tested the hypothesis concerning a third heart sound defining a subgroup with a different effect.[74] The presence of a third heart sound proved less powerful in defining subgroups with various response to digoxin than in the initial study, although its association with response to digoxin did reach conventional levels of statistical significance. A number of factors, which, like a third heart sound, reflect greater severity of heart failure, were associated with response to digoxin. Thus, the second study provided support for a more general hypothesis, that response may be related to severity of heart failure. However, this is a new hypothesis that must still be replicated in subsequent trials with the same definitions of severity.

USING THE GUIDE

Among the randomized trials comparing vasopressin to epinephrine for patients in cardiac arrest, only 3 report data for patients presenting in different arrest rhythms (Figure 20.4-1).[5] Of these, only Wenzel et al[1] observed an apparent mortality benefit in patients presenting in asystole. Stiell et al[62] reported a slightly greater mortality rate before hospital discharge in patients receiving vasopressin than in those receiving epinephrine in all presenting rhythms. Lindner et al[72] studied only patients presenting in ventricular arrest rhythms and observed a lower mortality rate in those receiving vasopressin compared with epinephrine. The finding that vasopressin benefits patients in asystole but not those in ventricular fibrillation is, therefore, inconsistent across studies.

Is the Subgroup Difference Statistically Significant?

A key question that investigators must address when examining apparent subgroup differences is, if the true underlying effect were the same in all patients, how likely is it that the differences between subgroups that we observed would have occurred by chance (see Chapter 10.1, Hypothesis Testing)?

For instance, in a trial of angiotensin-converting enzyme (ACE) inhibitor–based vs diuretic-based antihypertensive therapy, the conclusion reads "initiation of antihypertensive treatment involving ACE inhibitors in older subjects, particularly men, appears to lead to better outcomes than treatment with diuretic agents."[75] The investigators base their conclusion on the RRRs of 17% (95% CI, 3%-29%) they observed in men and the 0% (95% CI, -20% to 17%) RRR in women.

How would one go about determining whether the difference between the magnitude of the apparent effects in 2 subgroups was a real phenomenon or whether it was an artifact of chance? The wrong way would be to test whether the effect was significant in men and then, separately, to test whether the effect was significant in women. Figure 20.4-2 illustrates just how misleading such an analysis could be. Figure 20.4-2 depicts a treatment effect in 2 hypothetical subgroups, plus a pooled estimate combining the subgroups. The dashed line represents a relative risk of 1.0, indicating neither a

FIGURE 20.4-2

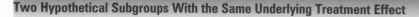

Two Hypothetical Subgroups With the Same Underlying Treatment Effect

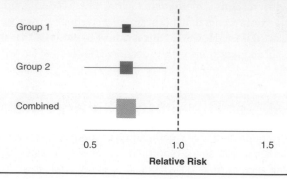

beneficial nor a harmful treatment effect. The underlying truth, reflected in the results, is that the treatment effect is identical in the 2 subgroups. If one looks only at subgroup 2, the effect is statistically significant. In subgroup 1, because of a smaller sample size, the effect does not reach statistical significance (reflected in the CI, which overlaps the line representing a treatment effect of zero). It would clearly be a mistake to conclude that treatment works in subgroup 2 but not in subgroup 1.

How should one handle this situation? Rather than asking separately, Is the treatment effective in subgroup 1? or Is it effective in subgroup 2? one should ask, Is the effect different in subgroup 1 vs in subgroup 2? In Figure 20.4-2, the answer to that question is a resounding no!

Using the correct structure for the subgroup difference question in the formal framework of hypothesis testing, one asks (see Chapter 10.1, Hypothesis Testing), how often, if no difference exists between the true underlying treatment effect in the 2 subgroups, would one observe differences in apparent effect as large as or larger than those we have observed?

Returning to the example of the antihypertensive trial, the question would be, how often, if no true difference exists in the gradient of effect between the ACE inhibitor and the thiazide, would investigators find differences as large as or larger than the difference between the 17% RRR in men and the 0% difference in women? Although the difference between the ACE inhibitor–based and diuretic-based therapies was statistically significant in men but not women, chance is sufficient to explain the difference in effect in the 2 subgroups. The *P* value associated with the null hypothesis that the underlying RRR is identical in men and women is .15, meaning that, if there were no true difference, we would see apparent differences of this magnitude or greater 15% of the time. Thus, the data provide support for the hypothesis that the effect of ACE inhibitor differs across sexes.

Contrast this with a meta-analysis examining the effect of alendronate on nonvertebral fractures.[76] The investigators used regression methods to discover that a model in which they pooled all doses of alendronate did not fit the data as well as a model that separated doses of less than 10 and 10 mg or more in explaining differences in results across studies ($P = .002$). The investigators therefore gained confidence that the apparently greater effect of doses of greater than 10 mg (RRR, 0.51; 95% CI, 0.38-0.69) compared with lower doses (RRR, 0.87; 95% CI, 0.73-1.02) was a real, rather than chance, phenomenon. In this case, the 95% CIs for the RRR estimates with the 2 doses do not even overlap.

Investigators can use a variety of statistical techniques to explore whether chance can explain apparent subgroup differences.[15,22,77-80] What readers should look for are the results of a statistical test that addresses the possibility that the apparent difference in magnitude of effect between subgroups is a chance finding.

USING THE GUIDE

Wenzel et al[1] emphasized that the effect on death before hospital discharge of vasopressin compared with epinephrine in patients presenting in asystole was statistically significant when analyzed by itself (OR, 0.32; 95% CI, 0.1-1.0; corresponding to a P value of .04; the different analytic approach in Figure 20.4-1[6] yields a CI just overlapping no effect), whereas the effect in patients with ventricular fibrillation was clearly not. However, as we have pointed out, the issue is not whether the finding is significant in one group and not the other, but rather whether the differences between treatment effect in the 2 groups can be explained by chance. The pooled OR for predischarge mortality across the 3 trials that considered presenting rhythm was 0.44 for patients in asystole compared with 1.0 for patients in ventricular fibrillation. A comparison of these 2 ORs yields a ratio of 0.44, with a 95% CI of 0.12 to 1.37. The P value for this comparison is .18.[6] Therefore, there is no statistical support for the hypothesis that the treatment effect differs in the 2 subgroups.

Is There External Evidence That Supports the Hypothesized Subgroup Difference?

We are generally more ready to believe a hypothesized interaction if additional, external evidence (such as from animal studies or analogous situations in human biology) makes the presence of a subgroup difference more plausible. That is, to the extent that a hypothesis is consistent with our current understanding of the biologic mechanisms of disease, we are more likely to believe it. Such understanding comes from 3 types of external evidence: studies of different populations (including animal studies), observations of subgroup differences for similar interventions, and results of studies of other related outcomes, particularly intermediary or surrogate outcomes.

The extent to which this external evidence strengthens an inference about a hypothesized interaction varies substantially. In general, evidence from intermediary outcomes is the strongest type of such evidence; for example, evidence of differences in immune response that support a conclusion that there is an important difference in the clinical effectiveness of a vaccine, depending on age.[81] Conversely, evidence from related interventions is generally the weakest type of external evidence; for example, evidence of a similar subgroup effect with other vaccines.

The human mind is sufficiently fertile that there is no shortage of biologically plausible explanations in support of almost any observation. One ironic example of biologic evidence supporting a possible interaction mentioned earlier in this chapter comes from an early trial suggesting that aspirin reduced stroke in men but not in women.[73] This finding stimulated animal research, which provided a biologic basis for the interaction.[82] Ultimately, however, it turned out that aspirin for stroke reduction was as effective in women as in men.[64]

USING THE GUIDE

Although investigators have advanced pathophysiologic explanations of why vasopressin might be superior to epinephrine in the setting of cardiac arrest, there is no clear physiologic rationale why it might have a greater effect in patients in asystole than in those with other arrest rhythms.[6]

CONCLUSION

The criteria suggested here can be useful in deciding when to believe an analysis that suggests a differential response to treatment in a definable subgroup of patients or with a particular drug or drug dose. At the one extreme are relatively small, marginally significant interactions based on between-study differences or generated for the first time by post hoc exploration of a single data set. At the other extreme are large, important interactions originally suggested by both indirect and direct evidence and independently tested either in a new trial or in a meta-analysis in which the possibility of the interaction resulting from chance is low. The former should be viewed with great skepticism; the latter can form the basis of clinical decision making. The strength of inference can range from one end of this spectrum to the other. When criteria are partially satisfied, strengthening the inference to the point at which clinicians can confidently use it to guide practice will require further information in the form of new *primary studies* or meta-analysis.

Decisions regarding how much effort to put into accumulating more evidence, and what clinical action to take, will depend on the potential benefits, risks, and costs involved. Decision thresholds, both for undertaking further research and for taking a clinical action, vary greatly. For problems with large potential benefits and small risks and costs, we are generally willing to accept lower standards of evidence than for problems with smaller potential benefits or larger risks or costs.

Deciding whether to base clinical practice on the average estimate of effect from an overall analysis (one that is more robust) or on a subgroup analysis (one that more closely reflects the specific clinical situation at hand) hinges on the criteria described above. It is tempting to take one extreme position or the other; that is, to always base decisions on the overall estimate of effect or to always base decisions on the most applicable subgroup analysis. A thoughtful approach based on the criteria we have suggested is more likely to result in the most benefit and the least harm for patients.

CLINICAL RESOLUTION

You now consider the answers you have generated to the issue of whether to believe the apparent subgroup effect of vasopressin vs epinephrine in asystolic vs ventricular fibrillation cardiac arrests:

- Is the subgroup difference suggested by comparisons within rather than between studies?
- Yes, the key comparisons are within study.
- Is the magnitude of the subgroup difference large?
- Yes, the apparent differences between the effect of vasopressin vs epinephrine of asystolic cardiac arrest are much greater than the apparent effects on arrest caused by ventricular fibrillation, when one uses the OR as a measure of association.
- Is the subgroup difference consistent across studies?
- No, the difference is inconsistent.
- Was the subgroup difference statistically significant?
- No, the difference did not approach statistical significance.
- Did the hypothesis precede rather than follow the analysis?
- It is unclear whether the hypothesis preceded or followed the analysis.
- Was the subgroup difference one of a small number of hypothesized effects tested?
- It is unclear how many hypotheses the investigators tested.

- Is there external evidence that supports the hypothesized subgroup difference?
- There is no external evidence to support the hypothesis.

Looking over the individual criteria, you conclude that the evidence suggesting a specific subgroup effect of vasopressin in patients with asystole is unconvincing. You report your conclusions to your colleague and decline to modify your protocols.

References

1. Wenzel V, Krismer AC, Arntz HR, et al. A comparison of vasopressin and epinephrine for out-of-hospital cardiopulmonary resuscitation. *N Engl J Med.* 2004;350(2):105-113.

2. McIntyre KM. Vasopressin in asystolic cardiac arrest [editorial]. *N Engl J Med.* 2004;350(2):179-181.

3. American Heart Association/International Liaison Committee on Resuscitation. Part 4: advanced life support. *Circulation.* 2005;112(22):III-25-III-54.

4. Hazinski MF, Nolan JP, Becker LB, Steen PA. Controversial topics from the 2005 International Consensus Conference on Cardiopulmonary Resuscitation and Emergency Cardiovascular Care Science With Treatment Recommendations [editorial]. *Circulation.* 2005;112(22):III-133-III-136.

5. Aung K, Htay T. Vasopressin for cardiac arrest. *Arch Intern Med.* 2005;165(1):17-24.

6. Wyer PC, Perera P, Jin Z, et al. Vasopressin or epinephrine for out-of-hospital cardiac arrest. *Ann Emerg Med.* 2006;48(1):86-97.

7. Pocock SJ, Hughes MD, Lee RJ. Statistical problems in the reporting of clinical trials: a survey of three medical journals. *N Engl J Med.* 1987;317(7):426-432.

8. Fletcher RH, Fletcher SW, Wagner EH. *Clinical Epidemiology: The Essentials.* 2nd ed. Baltimore, MD: Williams & Wilkins; 1988:185-186.

9. Feinstein AR. *Clinical Epidemiology: The Architecture of Clinical Research.* Philadelphia, PA: WB Saunders Co; 1985:306-307, 516-517.

10. Altman DG. Within trial variation—a false trail? *J Clin Epidemiol.* 1998(4);51(4):301-303.

11. Senn S, Harrell F. On wisdom after the event. *J Clin Epidemiol.* 1997;50(7):749-751.

12. Horwitz RI, Singer BH, Makuch RW, Viscoli CM. On reaching the tunnel at the end of the light. *J Clin Epidemiol.* 1997;50(7):753-755.

13. Feinstein AR. The problem of cogent subgroups: a clinicostatistical tragedy. *J Clin Epidemiol.* 1998;51(4):297-299.

14. Goldman L, Feinstein AR. Anticoagulants and myocardial infarction: the problems of pooling, drowning, and floating. *Ann Intern Med.* 1979;90(1):92-94.

15. Furberg CD, Morgan TM. Lessons from overviews of cardiovascular trials. *Stat Med.* 1987;6(3):295-306.

16. Horwitz RI. Complexity and contradiction in clinical trial research. *Am J Med.* 1987;82(3):498-510.

17. Bucher HC, Griffith LE, Guyatt GH. Systematic review on the risk and benefit of different cholesterol-lowering interventions. *Arterioscler Thromb Vasc Biol.* 1999;19(2):187-195.

18. Schmid CH, Lau J, McIntosh MW, Cappelleri JC. An empirical study of the effect of the control rate as a predictor of treatment efficacy in meta-analysis of clinical trials. *Stat Med.* 1998;17(17):1923-1942.

19. Furukawa TA, Guyatt GH, Griffith LE. Can we individualize the "number needed to treat"? an empirical study of summary effect measures in meta-analyses. *Int J Epidemiol.* 2002;31(1):72-76.

20. Deeks JJ. Issues in the selection of a summary statistic for meta-analysis of clinical trials with binary outcomes. *Stat Med.* 2002;21(11):1575-1600.

21. Van den Berghe G, Wilmer A, Hermans G, et al. Intensive insulin therapy in the medical ICU. *N Engl J Med.* 2006;354(5):449-461.

22. Buyse ME. Analysis of clinical trial outcomes: some comments on subgroup analyses. *Control Clin Trials.* 1989;10(suppl 4):187S-194S.

23. Bulpitt CJ. Subgroup analysis. *Lancet.* 1988;2(8601):31-34.

24. Byar DP. Assessing apparent treatment—covariate interactions in randomized clinical trials. *Stat Med.* 1985;4(3):255-263.

25. Shuster J, van Eys J. Interaction between prognostic factors and treatment. *Control Clin Trials.* 1983;4(3):209-214.

26. Counsell CE, Clarke MJ, Slattery J, Sandercock PA. The miracle of DICE therapy for acute stroke: fact or fictional product of subgroup analysis? *BMJ.* 1994; 309(6970):1677-1681.

27. Chan A, Altman DG. Epidemiology and reporting of randomised trials published in PubMed journals. *Lancet.* 2005;365(9465):1159-1162.

28. Lau J, Ioannidis JPA, Schmid CH. Summing up evidence: one answer is not always enough. *Lancet.* 1998;351(9096):123-127.

29. Stewart LA, Tierney JF. To IPD or not to IPD? advantages and disadvantages of systematic reviews using individual patient data. *Eval Health Prof.* 2002;25(1):76-97.

30. Rothwell PM. Subgroup analysis in randomised controlled trials: importance, indications, and interpretation. *Lancet.* 2005;365(9454):176-186.

31. The Canadian Cooperative Study Group. A randomized trial of aspirin and sulfinpyrazone in threatened stroke. *N Engl J Med.* 1978;299(2):53-59.

32. Fields WS, Lemak NA, Frankowski RF, Hardy RJ. Controlled trial of aspirin in cerebral ischaemia. *Stroke.* 1977;8(3):301-314.

33. Antiplatelet Trialists' Collaboration. Collaborative overview of randomised trials of antiplatelet therapy, I: prevention of death, myocardial infarction, and stroke by prolonged antiplatelet therapy in various categories of patients. *BMJ.* 1994; 308(6921):81-106.

34. Anastos K, Charney P, Charon RA, et al. Hypertension in women: what is really known? *Ann Intern Med.* 1991;115(4):287-293.

35. Medical Research Council Working Party. MRC trial of treatment of mild hypertension: principal results. *BMJ.* 1985;291(6488):97-104.

36. Gueyffier F, Boutitie F, Boissel JP, et al. Effect of antihypertensive drug treatment on cardiovascular outcomes in men and women. *Ann Intern Med.* 1997;126 (10):761-767.

37. Amery A, Birkenhäger W, Brixko P, et al. Influence of antihypertensive drug treatment on morbidity and mortality in patients over the age of 60 years: European Working Party on High Blood Pressure in the Elderly (EWPHE) results: sub-group analysis on entry stratification. *J Hypertens.* 1986;4(6 suppl):S642-S647.

38. Gueyffier F, Christopher Bulpitt C, Boissel J-P, et al. Antihypertensive drugs in very old people: a subgroup meta-analysis of randomised controlled trials. *Lancet.* 1999;353(9155):793-796.

39. Cleland JGF, Bulpitt CJ, Falk RH, et al. Is aspirin safe for patients with heart failure? *Br Heart J.* 1995;74(3):215-219.

40. Flather MD, Yusuf S, Køber L, et al. Long-term ACE-inhibitor therapy in patients with heart failure or left-ventricular dysfunction: a systematic overview of data from individual patients. *Lancet.* 2000;355(9215):1575-1581.

41. Andersen MP, Bechsgaard P, Frederiksen J, et al. Effects of alprenolol on mortality among patients with definite or suspected acute myocardial infarction: preliminary results. *Lancet.* 1979;2(8148):865-868.

42. Multicenter International Study. Supplemental report: reduction in mortality after myocardial infarction with long-term β-adrenoreceptor blockade. *BMJ.* 1977; 2(6084):419-421.

43. Yusuf S, Peto R, Lewis J, Collins R, Sleight P. Beta blockade during and after acute myocardial infarction: an overview of the randomized trials. *Prog Cardiovasc Dis.* 1985;27(5):335-371.

44. Gruppo Italiano perlo Studio della Streptochinasi nell'Infarto Myocardico (GISSI). Effectiveness of intravenous thrombolytic treatment in acute myocardial infarction. *Lancet.* 1986;1(8478):397-402.

45. ISIS-2 Collaborative Group. Randomised trial of IV streptokinase, oral aspirin, both, or neither among 17187 cases of suspected acute myocardial infarction: ISIS-2. *Lancet.* 1988;2(8607):349-360.

46. Fibrinolytic Therapy Trialists' (FTT) Collaborative Group. Indications for fibrinolytic therapy in suspected acute myocardial infarction: collaborative overview of early mortality and major morbidity results from all randomised trials of more than 1000 patients. *Lancet.* 1994;343(8893):311-322.

47. Early Breast Cancer Trialists' Collaborative Group. Effects of adjuvant tamoxifen and of cytotoxic therapy on mortality in early breast cancer: an overview of 61 randomized trials among 28,896 women. *N Engl J Med.* 1988;319(26):1681-1692.

48. Early Breast Cancer Trialists' Collaborative Group. Tamoxifen for early breast cancer. *Cochrane Database Syst Rev.* 2001;(1):CD000486.

49. Barnett HJM, Taylor DW, Eliasziw M, et al. Benefit of carotid endarterectomy in patients with symptomatic moderate or severe stenosis. *N Engl J Med.* 1998; 339(20):1415-1425.

50. Taylor W, Barnett HJM, Haynes RB, et al. Low-dose and high-dose acetylsalicylic acid for patients undergoing carotid endarterectomy: a randomised controlled trial. *Lancet.* 1999;353(9171):2179-2184.

51. Packer M, O'Connor CM, Ghali JK, et al. Effect of amlodipine on morbidity and mortality in severe chronic heart failure. *N Engl J Med.* 1996;335(15):1107-1114.

52. Wijeysundera HC, Hansen MS, Stanton E, et al. Neurohormones and oxidative stress in nonischemic cardiomyopathy: relationship to survival and the effect of treatment with amlodipine. *Am Heart J.* 2003;146(2):291-297.

53. Dhainaut JF, Tenaillon A, Le Tulzo Y, et al. Platelet-activating factor receptor antagonist BN 52021 in the treatment of severe sepsis: a randomized, double-blind, placebo-controlled, multicenter clinical trial. *Crit Care Med.* 1994;22(11): 1720-1728.

54. Dhainaut JF, Tenaillon A, Hemmer M, et al. Confirmatory platelet-activating factor receptor antagonist trial in patients with severe gram-negative bacterial sepsis: a phase III, randomized, double-blind, placebo-controlled, multicenter trial. *Crit Care Med.* 1998;26(12):1963-1971.

55. Weisberg LA. The efficacy and safety of ticlopidine and aspirin in non-whites: analysis of a patient subgroup from the Ticlopidine Aspirin Stroke Study. *Neurol.* 1993;43(1):27-31.

56. Gorelick PB, Richardson D, Kelly M, et al. Aspirin and ticlopidine for prevention of recurrent stroke in black patients: a randomized trial. *JAMA.* 2003;289(22):2947-2957.

57. Cohn JN, Tognoni GT; Valsartan Heart Failure Trial Investigators. A randomized trial of the angiotensin-receptor blocker valsartan in chronic heart failure. *N Engl J Med.* 2001;345(23):1667-1675.

58. McMurray JJV, Östergren J, Swedberg K, et al. Effects of candesartan in patients with chronic heart failure and reduced left-ventricular systolic function taking angiotensin-converting-enzyme inhibitors: the CHARM-Added trial. *Lancet.* 2003;362(9386):767-771.

59. Moliterno DJ; PARAGON B International Steering Committee. Patient-specific dosing of IIb/IIIa antagonists during acute coronary syndromes: rationale and design of the PARAGON B Study. *Am Heart J.* 2000;139(4):563-566.

60. PARAGON Investigators. International, randomized, controlled trial of lamifiban (a platelet glycoprotein IIb/IIIa Inhibitor), heparin, or both in unstable angina. *Circulation.* 1998;97(24):2386-2395.

61. Platelet IIb/IIIa Antagonist for the Reduction of Acute Coronary Syndrome Events in a Global Organization Network (PARAGON)-B Investigators. Randomized, placebo-controlled trial of titrated intravenous lamifiban for acute coronary syndromes. *Circulation.* 2002;105(3):316-321.

62. Stiell IG, Hebert PC, Wells GA, et al. Vasopressin versus epinephrine for in-hospital cardiac arrest: a randomised controlled trial. *Lancet.* 2001;358(9276):105-109.

63. Natanson C, Esposito CJ, Banks SM. The sirens' songs of confirmatory sepsis trials: selection bias and sampling error. *Crit Care Med.* 1998;26(12):1927-1931.

64. Furberg CD, Byington RP; Beta-Blocker Heart Attack Trial Experience. What do subgroup analyses reveal about differential response to beta-blocker therapy? *Circulation.* 1983;67(6 pt 2):I98-I101.

65. Ioannidis JPA. Microarrays and molecular research: noise discovery? *Lancet.* 2005;365(9458):454-455.

66. Cook DJ, Witt LG, Cook RJ, Guyatt GH. Stress ulcer prophylaxis in the critically ill: a meta-analysis. *Am J Med.* 1991;91(5):519-527.

67. Djulbegovic B, Lacevic M, Cantor A, et al. The uncertainty principle and industry-sponsored research. *Lancet.* 2000;356(9230):635-638.

68. Sterne JA, Hernan MA, Ledergerber B, et al. Long-term effectiveness of potent antiretroviral therapy in preventing AIDS and death: a prospective cohort study. *Lancet.* 2005;366(9483):378-384.

69. Glenny AM, Altman DG, Song F, et al. Indirect comparisons of competing interventions. *Health Technol Assess.* 2005;9(26):1-134, iii-iv.

70. Song F, Altman DG, Glenny AM, Deeks JJ. Validity of indirect comparison for estimating efficacy of competing interventions: empirical evidence from published meta-analyses. *BMJ.* 2003;326(7387):472.

71. Cook DJ, Reeve BK, Guyatt GH, et al. Stress ulcer prophylaxis in critically ill patients: resolving discordant meta-analyses. *JAMA.* 1996;275(4):308-314.

72. Lindner KH, Dirks B, Strohmenger HU, Prengel AW, Lindner IM, Lurie KG. Randomised comparison of epinephrine and vasopressin in patients with out-of-hospital ventricular fibrillation. *Lancet.* 1997;349(9051):535-537.

73. Lee DC, Johnson RA, Bingham JB, et al. Heart failure in outpatients: a randomized trial of digoxin versus placebo. *N Engl J Med.* 1982;306(12):699-705.

74. Guyatt GH, Sullivan MJ, Fallen EL, et al. A controlled trial of digoxin in congestive heart failure. *Am J Cardiol.* 1988;61(4):371-375.

75. Wing LM, Reid CM, Ryan P, et al. A comparison of outcomes with angiotensin-converting-enzyme inhibitors and diuretics for hypertension in the elderly. *N Engl J Med.* 2003;348(7):583-592.

76. Cranney A, Wells GA, Willan A, et al. Meta-analysis of alendronate for the treatment of osteoporosis in postmenopausal women. *Endocr Rev.* 2002;23(4):508-516.

77. Schneider B. Analysis of clinical trial outcomes: alternative approaches to subgroup analysis. *Control Clin Trials.* 1989;10(suppl 4):176S-186S.

78. Breslow NE, Day NE. Classical methods of analysis of grouped data. In: *Statistical Methods in Cancer Research, Vol 1: The Analysis of Case-Control Studies.* Lyon, France: International Agency for Research on Cancer; 1980:122-159.

79. Breslow NE, Day NE. Unconditional logistic regression for large strata. In: *Statistical Methods In Cancer Research. Vol 1. The Analysis of Case-Control Studies.* Lyon: International Agency for Research on Cancer; 1980:192-246.

80. Beach ML, Meier P. Choosing covariates in the analysis of clinical trials. *Control Clin Trials.* 1989;10(suppl 4):161S-175S.

81. Stieb DM, Frayha HH, Oxman AD, Shannon HS, Hutchison BG, Crombie FS. Effectiveness of *Haemophilus influenzae* type b vaccines. *CMAJ.* 1990;142(7): 719-733.

82. Kelton JG, Hirsh J, Carter CJ, Buchanan MR. Sex differences in the antithrombotic effects of aspirin. *Blood.* 1978;52(5):1073-1076.

Part G

Moving From Evidence to Action

HOW TO USE
A PATIENT
MANAGEMENT
RECOMMENDATION

Gordon Guyatt, Kameshwar Prasad,
Holger Schunemann, Roman Jaeschke,
and Deborah J. Cook

IN THIS CHAPTER:

CLINICAL SCENARIO

Warfarin in Atrial Fibrillation: Is It the Best Choice for This Patient?

You are a primary care practitioner considering the possibility of warfarin therapy in a 76-year-old woman with congestive heart failure and chronic atrial fibrillation who has just entered your practice. Aspirin is the only antithrombotic agent that the patient has received during the 10 years she has had atrial fibrillation. Her other medical problems include hypertension, which she has had since sometime in her fifth decade and for which she has been taking hydrochlorothiazide and metoprolol, which also serves to control her heart rate. The patient does not have valvular disease, diabetes, or other comorbidity, and she does not smoke.

You are concerned that the patient might have difficulties complying with regular monitoring of her international normalized ratio and that warfarin would present a risk of serious gastrointestinal bleeding that would prove to be greater than its benefit in terms of stroke prevention. During discussion, you learn that she places a high value on avoiding a stroke and a somewhat lower value on avoiding a major bleeding episode and would accept the inconvenience associated with monitoring anticoagulant therapy.

You consider this a good opportunity to review the *evidence* and so make no change to the patient's medication regimen today, but you make a note to yourself to reconsider when she returns for her regular visit in a month's time.

FINDING THE EVIDENCE

Reviewing the voluminous original literature relating to anticoagulant therapy in atrial fibrillation would take far more time than you have available, but you hope to find an evidence-based recommendation to guide you. You decide to search for 2 sources of such a recommendation: a *practice guideline* and a *decision analysis*.

You bring up your Web browser and go to your favorite search engine, http://www.Google.com. Entering the term "practice guidelines," you see that one of the first items on the results list is "National Guideline Clearinghouse," at http://www.guideline.gov. You note that the site contains "evidence-based clinical practice guidelines" and is an initiative of the US Agency for Healthcare Research and Quality, formerly known as the Agency for Health Care Policy and Research, which supports the production of reputable evidence summaries.

You observe on the left side of the screen that you can "browse" the site, and after clicking on this option, you find the first page includes a number of directly relevant guidelines. You choose the most recent of these, revised in September

2004: "Antithrombotic Therapy in Atrial Fibrillation: Seventh ACCP Consensus Conference on Antithrombotic and Thrombolytic Therapy," from the American College of Chest Physicians. Clicking on the guideline, you find that it has been published in the peer-reviewed literature,[1] and clicking on Go to Complete Summary, you print the text that appears. You also send an e-mail message to the hospital librarian, asking for a copy of the published article.

Returning to http://www.google.com, you enter the phrase "atrial fibrillation decision analysis" in the search text box, and then, clicking on the first item, you find a decision analysis published in *Lancet*[2] that appears highly suitable and that you also order from the library.

TREATMENT RECOMMENDATIONS REQUIRE A STRUCTURED PROCESS

Each day, clinicians face dozens of patient management decisions. These decisions involve weighing benefits against harms, burden, and cost—which we will refer to as downsides of treatment—and recommending or instituting a course of action consistent with the patient's best interest. Each decision involves a consideration of the relevant evidence and a weighing of the likely benefits and downsides in light of the patient's values and preferences. When considering choices, clinicians may benefit from structured enumeration of the options and outcomes, systematic reviews of the evidence regarding the relationship between options and outcomes, and recommendations regarding the best choices. This chapter explores the process of developing recommendations, suggests how that process may be conducted systematically, and provides a guide for differentiating recommendations that are more rigorous (and thus more trustworthy) from those that are less rigorous (and thus are more likely to be misleading).

Failure to follow a rigorous process may lead to variability in recommendations. For example, various recommendations emerged from different meta-analyses of selective decontamination of the gut using antibiotic prophylaxis for pneumonia in critically ill patients despite similar results. The recommendations varied from suggesting implementation, to equivocation, to rejecting implementation.[3-6] Historically, expert recommendations regarding therapy for patients with myocardial infarction have often been contradictory, lagged behind the evidence, and been inconsistent with the evidence.[7]

This chapter outlines the steps involved in developing a recommendation and introduces 2 formal processes that experts and authoritative bodies use in developing recommendations: clinical practice guidelines and decision analysis. We will offer criteria for deciding when the process is done well and when it is done poorly, along with a hierarchy of treatment recommendations that clinicians may find useful.

DEVELOPING RECOMMENDATIONS

Figure 21-1 presents the steps involved in developing a recommendation, along with formal strategies for doing so. The first step in clinical decision making is to define the decision. This involves specifying the alternative courses of action and the possible outcomes. Often, treatments are designed to delay or prevent an adverse outcome such as stroke, death, or myocardial infarction. As usual, we will refer to the outcomes that treatment is designed to prevent as *target outcomes*. Treatments are associated with their own adverse outcomes: adverse effects, toxicity, and inconvenience. In addition, new treatments may markedly increase or decrease costs. Ideally, the formulation of the question will be comprehensive, including all reasonable alternatives and all important beneficial and adverse outcomes.

> In patients such as the woman with nonvalvular atrial fibrillation described in the opening scenario, options for stroke prophylaxis include no intervention, giving aspirin, or administering anticoagulant therapy with warfarin. Outcomes include minor and major embolic stroke, intracranial hemorrhage, gastrointestinal hemorrhage, minor bleeding, the inconvenience associated with taking and monitoring medication, and costs to the patient, the health care system, and society.

Having identified the options and outcomes, decision makers must evaluate the links between the two. What will the alternative management strategies yield in terms of benefit and harm?[7,8] How are potential benefits and downsides likely to

FIGURE 21-1

A Schematic View of the Process of Developing a Treatment Recommendation

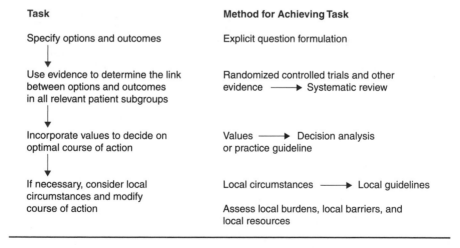

Task	Method for Achieving Task
Specify options and outcomes	Explicit question formulation
Use evidence to determine the link between options and outcomes in all relevant patient subgroups	Randomized controlled trials and other evidence ⟶ Systematic review
Incorporate values to decide on optimal course of action	Values ⟶ Decision analysis or practice guideline
If necessary, consider local circumstances and modify course of action	Local circumstances ⟶ Local guidelines Assess local burdens, local barriers, and local resources

vary in different groups of patients?[8,9] Once these questions are answered, making treatment recommendations involves judgments about the relative desirability or undesirability of possible outcomes, issues of values and preferences.

We will now discuss how one can apply scientific principles to the identification, selection, and summarization of evidence and to the valuing of outcomes that are involved in creating practice guidelines and decision analyses.

Practice Guidelines

Practice guidelines, systematically developed statements to assist practitioner and patient decisions about appropriate health care for specific clinical circumstances,[10] provide an alternative structure for integrating evidence and applying values to reach treatment recommendations.[1,11-16] Instead of precise quantitation, practice guidelines rely on the consensus of a group of decision makers who consider the evidence and decide on its implications. Guideline developers' mandate may be to adduce recommendations for a large part of the world, a country, a region, a city, a hospital, or a clinic. Depending on whether the country is the Philippines or the United States, whether the region is urban or rural, whether the institution is a large teaching hospital or a small community hospital, and whether the clinic serves a poor community or an affluent one, guidelines based on the same evidence may differ. For example, guideline developers may recommend against the administration of warfarin to even high-risk patients with atrial fibrillation if their recommendation is designed for rural parts of countries without resources to monitor anticoagulant intensity.

Decision Analysis

Rigorous decision analysis provides a formal structure for integrating the evidence about the beneficial and harmful effects of treatment options with the values or preferences associated with those beneficial and harmful effects. Decision analysis applies explicit, quantitative methods to analyze decisions under conditions of uncertainty; it allows clinicians to compare the expected consequences of pursuing different strategies. The process of decision analysis makes fully explicit all of the elements of the decision, so that they are open for debate and modification.[17-19]

Although clinicians may undertake such analyses to inform a decision for an individual patient (Should I recommend warfarin to this 76-year-old woman with atrial fibrillation?), most decision analyses help inform clinical policy[20] (Should I routinely recommend warfarin to patients in my practice with atrial fibrillation?).

Most clinical decision analyses are built as decision trees, and authors will usually include 1 or more diagrams showing the structure of the decision trees used for the analysis. Reviewing such diagrams will help you understand the model. Figure 21-2 shows a diagram of a simplified decision tree for the atrial fibrillation problem presented at the beginning of this chapter. The clinician has 3 options for such patients: to offer no prophylaxis, recommend aspirin, or recommend warfarin. Regardless of the choice, patients may or may not develop embolic events and, in particular, stroke. Prophylaxis decreases the chance of embolism but can

FIGURE 21-2

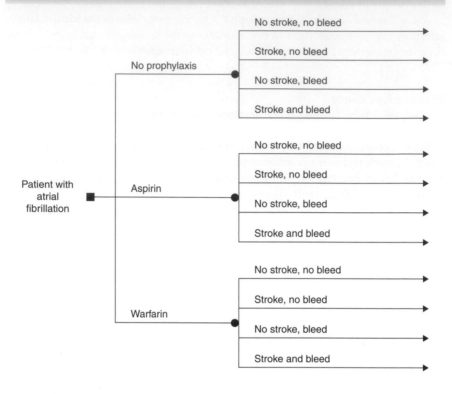

Simplified Decision Tree for a Patient With Atrial Fibrillation

cause bleeding in some patients. This simplified model excludes a number of important consequences, including the inconvenience of warfarin monitoring and the unpleasantness of minor bleeding.

As seen in Figure 21-2, decision trees are displayed graphically, oriented from left to right, with the decision to be analyzed on the left, the compared strategies in the center, and the clinical outcomes on the right. The decision is represented by a square, termed a "decision node." The lines emanating from the decision node represent the clinical strategies under consideration. Circles, called "chance nodes," symbolize chance events, and triangles or rectangles identify outcome states (Figure 21-2). When a decision analysis includes costs among the outcomes, it becomes an economic analysis and summarizes tradeoffs between health changes and resource expenditure[21,22] (see Chapter 22.1, Economic Analysis).

Once a decision analyst has constructed the tree, he or she must generate quantitative estimates of the likelihood of events, or *probabilities*. As usual for any event, probabilities may range from 0 (impossible) to 1.0 or 100% (certainty). The analyst must assign probabilities to each branch emanating from a chance node, and for each chance node, the sum of probabilities must add up to 1.0.

For example, returning to Figure 21-2, consider the no-prophylaxis strategy (the upper branch emanating from the decision node). This arm has 1 chance node at which 4 possible events could occur (the 4 possible combinations arising from bleeding or not bleeding and from having a stroke or not having a stroke). Figure 21-3 depicts the probabilities associated with one arm of the decision, the no-prophylaxis strategy (generated by assuming a 1% chance of bleeding and a 10% probability of stroke, with the 2 events being independent): Patients given no prophylaxis would have a 0.1% chance (a probability of .001) of bleeding and having a stroke, a 0.9% chance (a probability of .009) of bleeding and not having a stroke, a 9.9% chance (a probability of .099) of not bleeding but having a stroke, and an 89.1% chance (a probability of .891) of not bleeding and not having a stroke.

FIGURE 21-3

Decision Tree With Probabilities: No-Prophylaxis Option

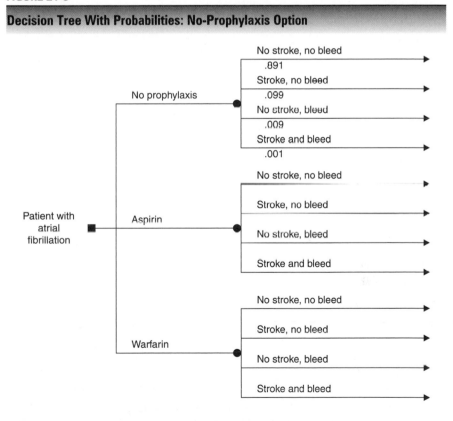

The decision analyst would generate similar probabilities for the other 2 branches. Presumably, the aspirin branch would have a higher risk of bleeding and a lower risk of stroke. The warfarin branch would have the highest risk of bleeding and the lowest risk of stroke.

These probabilities would not suggest a clear course of action, because the alternative with the lowest risk of bleeding has the highest risk of stroke, and vice versa. Thus, the right choice would depend on the relative value or utility one placed on bleeding and stroke.

Decision analysts typically place a utility on each of the final possible outcomes that varies from 0 (death) to 1.0 (full health). Figure 21-4 presents one possible set of utilities associated with the 4 outcomes and applied to the no-prophylaxis arm of the decision tree: 1.0 for no stroke or bleeding, 0.8 for no stroke and bleeding, 0.5 for stroke but no bleeding, and 0.4 for stroke and bleeding.

FIGURE 21-4

Decision Tree With Probabilities and Utilities Included in the No-Prophylaxis Arm of the Tree

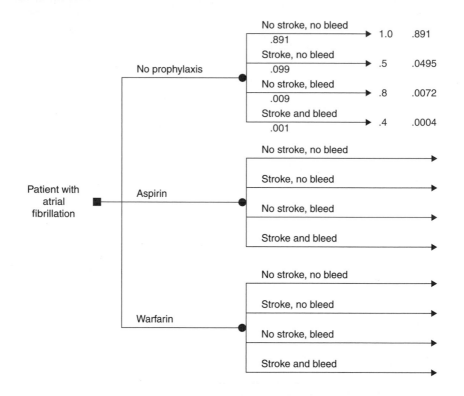

The final step in the decision analysis is to calculate the total expected value—the sum of the probabilities and utilities associated with each outcome—for each possible course of action. Given the particular set of probabilities and utilities we have presented, the value of the no-prophylaxis branch would be $(.891 \times 1.0) + (.009 \times .8) + (.099 \times .5) + (.001 \times .4)$, or .948. Depending on the probabilities attached to the aspirin and warfarin branches, they would be judged superior or inferior to the no-prophylaxis branch. If the total value of each of these branches were greater than .948, they would be judged preferable to the no-prophylaxis branch; if the total value were less than .948, they would be judged less desirable.

The model presented in Figures 21-2 to 21-4 is oversimplified in a number of ways, among which are its omission of the period of events and the possibility of a patient experiencing multiple events. Decision analysts can make use of software programs that model what might happen to a hypothetical cohort of patients during a series of time cycles (say, periods of 1 year's duration). The model allows for the possibility that patients might move from one health state to another. For instance, one unfortunate patient may have a mild stroke in one cycle, continue with minimal functional limitation for a number of cycles, experience a gastrointestinal bleeding episode in a subsequent cycle, and finally experience a major stroke. These *multistate transition models* or *Markov models* permit more sophisticated and true-to-life depictions.

Both decision analyses and practice guidelines can be methodologically strong or weak and thus may yield either valid or invalid recommendations. In Table 21-1, we offer 4 guidelines to assess the validity of a treatment recommendation, one for each step depicted in Figure 21-1.

ASSESSING RECOMMENDATIONS

Do the Recommendations Consider All Relevant Patient Groups, Management Options, and Possible Outcomes?

Regardless of whether recommendations apply to diagnosis, prevention, therapy, or rehabilitation, they should specify all relevant patient groups, the interventions of interest, and sensible alternative practices (Table 21-2).

TABLE 21-1

Users' Guides for the Validity of Treatment Recommendations

- Do the recommendations consider all relevant patient groups, management options, and possible outcomes?
- Are there systematic reviews of evidence that estimate the relative effect of management options on relevant outcomes?
- Is there an appropriate specification of values and preferences associated with outcomes?
- Do the authors grade the strength of their recommendations?

TABLE 21-2

Did the Recommendations Consider All Patient Groups, Management Options, and Outcomes?

Did the recommendation consider all relevant patient groups?
- Low risk and high risk
- More and less susceptible to adverse effects

Did the recommendation consider all relevant management options?
- Surgical and medical
- No-treatment option

Did the recommendation consider all patient-important outcomes?
- Morbidity and mortality
- Quality of life
- Toxicity and adverse effects
- Inconvenience
- Psychological burden
- Cost to the patient or to society

For example, a guideline based on a careful systematic literature review[23] offered recommendations for medical therapeutic options for preventing strokes.[24] Although the authors mention carotid endarterectomy as an alternative in their practice guidelines, the procedure is not included in the recommendations themselves. These guidelines would have been more useful if medical management for transient ischemic attacks had been placed in the context of this surgical procedure, which is effective in the hands of surgeons, with low complication rates.[25]

Treatment recommendations often vary for different subgroups of patients. In particular, those at lower risk of target outcomes that treatment is designed to prevent are less likely to benefit from therapy than those who are at higher risk (see Chapter 11.1, Applying Results to Individual Patients). The appropriateness of lipid-lowering therapy, for instance, depends very much on the presence of risk factors such as family history, hypertension, and smoking that determine a patient's risk of adverse cardiovascular events.[26] Recommendations may also differ according to patients' susceptibility to adverse events. For our patient with atrial fibrillation, for instance, we must consider her likelihood of a traumatic fall.

Recommendations must consider not only all relevant patient groups and management options but also all important consequences of the options. Evidence concerning the effects on morbidity, mortality, and quality of life is relevant to patients, and efficient use of resources dictates attention to costs. If recommendations consider costs, regardless of whether authors use the perspective of patients, insurers, or the health care system or consider broader issues such as the consequences of time lost from work, they can further affect the conclusions (see Chapter 22.1, Economic Analysis).

> In a decision analysis concerning anticoagulant therapy for patients with dilated cardiomyopathy,[27] the authors' decision model included all of the clinical events of interest to patients (stroke, other emboli, hemorrhage, etc). The analysts measured outcomes with "quality-adjusted life expectancy," a measure that combines information about both the quantity and the quality of life. This metric fits the clinical decision well, for one can expect that warfarin might affect both the quantity and quality of life.

Are There Systematic Reviews of Evidence That Estimate the Relative Effect of Management Options on Relevant Outcomes?

Having specified options and outcomes, decision makers must then estimate the relative effect of the management options on the occurrence of each outcome. In effect, decision makers have a series of specific questions. Consider hormone replacement therapy, in which the outcomes include the incidence of hip fracture, breast cancer, endometrial cancer, myocardial infarction, stroke, and dementia, as well as quality of life. For each of these outcomes, decisions makers must have access to, or conduct, a systematic review of the evidence. Chapter 19, Summarizing the Evidence, provides Users' Guides for deciding how likely it is that collection and summarization of the evidence are free from *bias*.

Although the authors of a systematic review may reasonably abandon their project if there are no high-quality studies to summarize, those making recommendations do not have this luxury. For important but ethically, technically, or economically difficult questions, high-quality evidence may never become available. Because recommendations must deal with the best (often low-quality) evidence available, they may need to consider a variety of studies (published and unpublished). Because the quality of the evidence in support of the recommendations can vary widely, even when grounded in rigorous collection and summarization of evidence, recommendations will usually be weak recommendations if the quality of the evidence is low. The guideline developers' systematic review must summarize the quality of the evidence on which they base their recommendations.

Is There an Appropriate Specification of Values and Preferences Associated With Outcomes?

Linking treatment options with outcomes is largely a question of fact and a matter of science. Assigning preferences to outcomes is a matter of values. Consider, for example, the relative importance of small incremental risks of developing breast cancer and possibly cardiovascular disease compared with decrease in perimenopausal hot flashes. Perimenopausal women considering hormone replacement therapy must consider these tradeoffs. Consequently, it is important that authors of guidelines or decision analyses report the principal sources of such judgments and the method of seeking consensus.

Clinicians should look for information about who was involved in assigning values to outcomes or who, by influencing recommendations, was implicitly involved in assigning values. Guideline panels are often populated largely or exclusively by clinical experts. Such expert panels may be subject to intellectual, territorial, and financial biases. Although the optimal composition of a guideline panel remains uncertain, it may be that the greater participation by methodologists, frontline clinicians, and members of the general public would lead to guidelines more in keeping with the public interest. There is no composition, however, than ensures that recommendations will be consistent with the values and preferences of your patients. As a result, for recommendations in which preferences are crucial, guidelines should state the underlying value judgments on which they are based.[28-30]

For instance, 2 chapters of the 2004 American College of Chest Physicians antithrombotic guidelines made conflicting recommendations on the basis of the same evidence. A large, well-conducted, *randomized controlled trial (RCT)* that included patients with cerebrovascular disease and peripheral vascular disease demonstrated a small—some might say marginal—benefit of clopidogrel over aspirin in decreasing vascular events.[31] The stroke chapter authors, in explaining their recommendation, commented on the underlying values and preferences: "This recommendation to use clopidogrel over aspirin places a relatively high value on a small absolute risk reduction in stroke rates, and a relatively low value on minimizing drug expenditures."[32] The authors of the peripheral vascular disease chapter, as a result of differing values and preferences, recommended aspirin over clopidogrel: "This recommendation places a relatively high value on avoiding large expenditures to achieve small reductions in vascular events."[33] Unfortunately, such explicit statements are, by far, the exception rather than the rule.

Clinicians using a decision analysis will not face the huge problem of implicit and hidden value judgments that affect practice guidelines. The reason, as Figure 21-4 demonstrates, is that decision analysis requires explicit and quantitative specification of values. These values, expressed as utilities, represent measurements of the value to the decision maker of the various outcomes of the decision. Several methods are available to measure these values directly[2,4,10,11]; the issue of which of these methods is best remains controversial.

Regardless of the measurement method used, the authors should report the source of the ratings. In a decision analysis built for an individual patient, the most (and probably only) credible ratings are those measured directly from that patient. For analyses built to inform clinical policy, credible ratings could come from 3 sources. First, they may come from direct measurements from a large group of patients with the disorder in question and to whom results of the decision analysis could be applied. Second, ratings may come from other published studies of quality-of-life judgments by such patients, as was done in an analysis of strategies for chronic atrial fibrillation.[12] Third, they may come from ratings made by an equally large group of people representing the general public. Whoever provides the rating must understand the outcomes they are asked to rate; the more the raters know about the condition, the more credible are their utility ratings.

Do the Authors Indicate the Strength of Their Recommendations?

Multiple considerations should inform the strength or grade of recommendations: the quality of the evidence, the magnitude of the intervention effects in different studies, the magnitude of adverse effects, the burden to the patient and the health care system, the costs, and the relative value placed on different outcomes. Thus, recommendations may vary from those that rely on evidence from a systematic review of RCTs that show large treatment effects on patient-important outcomes with minimal adverse effects, inconvenience, and costs (yielding a strong recommendation) to those that rely on evidence from observational studies showing a small magnitude of treatment effect with appreciable adverse effects and costs (yielding a weak recommendation).

There are 2 ways that those developing recommendations can indicate their strength. One, most appropriate for practice guidelines, is to formally grade the strength of a recommendation. The other, most appropriate for decision analyses, is to vary the assumptions about the effect of the management options on the outcomes of interest. In this latter approach, a sensitivity analysis, investigators explore the extent to which various assumptions might affect the ultimate recommendation. We will discuss the 2 approaches in turn.

Grades of Recommendation

The Canadian Task Force on the Periodic Health Examination proposed the first formal taxonomy of "levels of evidence"[34-36] focusing on individual studies. There has since been a gradual evolution of rating systems, which has included a tremendous proliferation in their number and variety.[37] An international group of methodologists and guideline developers, a number of whom also participated in producing this book, have created a framework for rating quality of evidence and strength of recommendations[38,39] that is being widely adopted.[37]

The grades of recommendation, assessment, development, and evaluation (GRADE) system, which we describe in detail in Chapter 22.4, Grading Recommendations, classifies recommendations in one of 2 levels, strong and weak, and quality of evidence into one of 4 categories, high, moderate, low, and very low. Evidence based on RCTs begins with a top rating on GRADE's 4-category quality of evidence classification (Table 21-3). GRADE takes into account, however, that not all RCTs are alike and that limitations of individual RCTs may compromise the quality of their evidence, as may other factors, including inconsistency of results, indirect evidence, and a high likelihood of reporting bias (Table 21-4). Evidence based on observational studies begins with a low-quality rating but may move up to moderate or high if the effect size is large enough, the evident biases all favor conventional rather than experimental therapy, or a dose-response gradient is evident (Table 21-4).

The GRADE system offers a strong recommendation when an intervention's benefits clearly outweigh its risks and burden or clearly do not. On the other hand, when the tradeoff between benefits and downsides is less certain, either because of low-quality

TABLE 21-3

Quality of Evidence and Its Definitions

Grade	Definition
High	Further research is unlikely to change our confidence in the estimate of effect.
Moderate	Further research is likely to have an important influence on our confidence in the estimate of effect and may change the estimate.
Low	Further research is very likely to have an important influence on our confidence in the estimate of effect and is likely to change the estimate.
Very low	Any estimate of effect is uncertain.

evidence or because high-quality evidence suggests benefits and downsides are closely balanced, weak recommendations become appropriate. Table 21-5 provides a structure for applying the results of the GRADE system of presenting recommendations.

Sensitivity Analysis

Decision analysts use the systematic exploration of the uncertainty in the data, known as *sensitivity analysis*, to see what effects varying estimates for downsides, benefits, and values have on expected clinical outcomes and, therefore, on the choice of clinical strategies. Sensitivity analysis asks the question, is the conclusion generated by the decision analysis affected by the uncertainties in the estimates of the likelihood or value of the outcomes? Estimates can be varied one at a time, termed "1-way" sensitivity analyses, or can be varied 2 or more at a time, known as "multiway" sensitivity analyses. For instance, investigators conducting a decision analysis of the administration of antibiotic agents for prevention of *Mycobacterium*

TABLE 21-4

Factors in Deciding on Confidence in Estimates of Benefits, Risks, Burden, and Costs

Factors that may decrease the quality of evidence
1. Poor quality of planning or implementation of the available studies, suggesting high likelihood of bias
2. Inconsistency of results
3. Indirectness of evidence
4. Imprecise estimates
5. Publication bias

Factors that may increase the quality of evidence
1. Large magnitude of effect
2. All plausible confounding would reduce a demonstrated effect
3. Dose-response gradient

TABLE 21-5

GRADE Recommendations

Grade of Recommendation	Benefit vs Risk and Burdens	Methodologic Quality of Supporting Evidence	Implications
Strong recommendation, high-quality evidence	Benefits clearly outweigh risk and burdens, or vice versa	RCTs without important limitations or overwhelming evidence from observational studies	Strong recommendation; can apply to most patients in most circumstances without reservation
Strong recommendation, moderate-quality evidence	Benefits clearly outweigh risk and burdens, or vice versa	RCTs with important limitations (inconsistent results; methodologic flaws; indirect, imprecise, or high likelihood of reporting bias) or exceptionally strong evidence from observational studies	
Strong recommendation, low- or very-low-quality evidence	Benefits clearly outweigh risk and burdens, or vice versa	Observational studies or case series	Strong recommendation but may change when higher-quality evidence becomes available
Weak recommendation, high-quality evidence	Benefits closely balanced with risks and burden	RCTs without important limitations	Weak recommendation; best action may differ, depending on circumstances or patients' or societal values
Weak recommendation, moderate-quality evidence	Benefits closely balanced with risks and burden	RCTs with important limitations (inconsistent results; methodologic flaws; indirect, imprecise, or high likelihood of reporting bias)	
Weak recommendation, low- or very-low-quality evidence	Uncertainty in the estimates of benefits, risks, and burden; benefits, risk, and burden may be closely balanced	Observational studies or case series	Very weak recommendations; other alternatives may be equally reasonable

Abbreviations: GRADE, grades of recommendation, assessment, development, and evaluation; RCT, randomized controlled trial.

avium intracellulare in patients with human immunodeficiency virus found that the cost-effectiveness of prophylaxis decreased if they assumed either a longer lifespan for patients or made a less sanguine estimate of the drugs' effectiveness.[40] If they simultaneously assumed a longer lifespan and decreased drug effectiveness (a 2-way sensitivity analysis), the cost-effectiveness decreased substantially. Clinicians should look for a table that lists which variables the analysts included in their sensitivity analyses, what range of values they used for each variable, and which variables, if any, altered the choice of strategies.

Ideally, decision analysts will subject all of their probability estimates to a sensitivity analysis. The range over which they will test should depend on the source of the data. If the estimates come from large, high-quality, randomized trials with narrow confidence limits, the range of estimates tested can be narrow. When methods are less valid or estimates of benefits and downsides less precise, sensitivity analyses testing a wide range of values become appropriate.

Decision analysts should also test utility values with sensitivity analyses, with the range of values again determined by the source of the data. If large numbers of patients or knowledgeable and representative members of the general public gave similar ratings to the outcome states, investigators can use a narrow range of utility values in the sensitivity analyses. If the ratings came from a small group of raters, or if the values for individuals varied widely, then investigators should use a wider range of utility values in the sensitivity analyses.

To the extent that the result of the decision analysis does not change with varying probability estimates and varying values, clinicians can consider the recommendation a strong one. When the final decision shifts with different plausible values of probabilities or values, the recommendation becomes much weaker.

We have suggested 4 criteria that affect the validity of a recommendation (Table 21-1). Table 21-6 presents a scheme for classifying the methodologic quality of treatment recommendations, emphasizing the 3 key components: consideration of all relevant options and outcomes, a systematic summary of the evidence, and an explicit or quantitative consideration, or both, of societal or patient preferences.

Are Treatment Recommendations Desirable at All?

The approaches we have described highlight the view that patient management decisions are always a function of both evidence and values and preferences. Values may differ substantially among settings. For example, monitoring of anticoagulant therapy might take on a much stronger negative value in a rural setting in which travel distances are large or in a more severely resource-constrained environment in which there is a direct inverse relationship between the resources available for purchase of antibiotic drugs and those allocated to monitoring levels of anticoagulation.

Patient-to-patient differences in values are equally important. The magnitude of the negative value of anticoagulant monitoring or the relative negative value associated with a stroke vs a gastrointestinal bleeding episode will vary widely among individual patients, even in the same setting.

If decisions are so dependent on preferences, what is the point of recommendations? Perhaps, rather than making recommendations, investigators should systematically search for, accumulate, and summarize information for presentation to

TABLE 21-6

A Hierarchy of Rigor in Making Treatment Recommendations

Level of Rigor	Systematic Summary of Evidence	Considers All Relevant Options and Outcomes	Explicit Statement of Values	Sample Methodologies
High	Yes	Yes	Yes	Practice guideline or decision analysis[a]
Intermediate	Yes	Yes or no	No	Systematic review[a]
Low	No	Yes or no	No	Traditional review; article reporting primary research

[a]Sample methodologies may not reflect the level of rigor shown. Exceptions may occur in either direction. For example, if the author of a practice guideline or decision analysis neither systematically collects nor summarizes information and it neither societal nor patient values are explicitly considered, recommendations will be produced that are of low rigor. Conversely, if the author of a systematic review does consider all relevant options and at least qualitatively considers values, the recommendations from the review may be rigorous.

clinicians. In addition, they may highlight the implications of different sets of values for clinical action. The dependence of any decision on patients' underlying values—and the variability of values—would suggest that such a presentation would be more useful than a recommendation.

Although this approach might be work in an ideal world, it is not well suited to the one in which we live. Its implementation depends on investigators using standard, rigorous methods of summarizing and presenting information and on clinicians having the time, energy, and skills to both interpret the summaries and integrate them with patient values and preferences. These requirements are unlikely to be met in the foreseeable future. Recommendations help clinicians practice efficiently, and applying the concepts of this chapter will allow clinicians to restrict their use of recommendations to those of high methodologic quality.

CLINICAL RESOLUTION

Returning to our opening clinical scenario,[26] you begin by considering whether the guideline developers have addressed all important patient groups, treatment options, and outcomes. You observe that they make separate recommendations for patients with various risk of stroke but not for patients with different risk of bleeding. The latter omission may occur because studies of prognosis have been inconsistent in the apparent risk factors for bleeding they identified. The guideline addresses the options you are seriously considering (full- and fixed-dose warfarin and aspirin) and major outcomes of interest (occlusive [embolic] stroke, hemorrhagic stroke, gastrointestinal bleeding, and other major bleeding events) but does not deal specifically with the need for regular blood testing or the frequent minor bruising and worries about bleeding associated with warfarin therapy.

Moving to the selection and synthesis of the evidence, you find the guideline's eligibility criteria to be appropriate and the supportive literature search to be comprehensive. The synthesis method, although not explicit, clearly relies on systematic reviews and meta-analyses.

The authors of the guideline make it clear that they believe patient values are crucial to the decision and do a good job of articulating the tradeoff.

Underlying values and preferences: Anticoagulation with warfarin has far greater efficacy than aspirin in preventing stroke, and particularly in preventing severe ischemic stroke, in atrial fibrillation. We recommend the option of aspirin therapy for lower-risk groups, estimating that the absolute expected benefit of anticoagulant therapy may not be worth the increased hemorrhagic risk and burden of anticoagulation. Individual lower-risk patients may rationally choose anticoagulation over aspirin therapy to gain greater protection against ischemic stroke if they value protection against stroke much more highly than reducing risk of hemorrhage and burden of managing anticoagulation.

The guideline developers present approaches for determining stroke risk: for this patient, the risk is approximately 4%. They use a grading system that is a predecessor to the one presented earlier in this chapter (Table 21-5) and is similar. For patients such as those in the scenario, the guideline developers provide a strong recommendation, based on high-quality evidence, for use of warfarin. Given that the guideline meets all the criteria of Table 21-2, you are inclined to take this recommendation seriously.

The decision analysis that you identified[2] restricts its comparison to warfarin therapy vs no treatment. Its rationale for omitting aspirin is that its efficacy is not proven (although the aspirin effect in other meta-analyses has achieved statistical significance, it has always been borderline). The investigators do not mention any other antiplatelet treatment. They include outcomes of the inconvenience associated with monitoring of anticoagulant therapy, major bleeding episodes, mild stroke, severe stroke, and cost. They omit minor bleeding.

The investigators present their search strategies clearly. They restrict themselves to the results of computer searches of the published literature but, given this limitation, their searches appear comprehensive. With great clarity, they also describe their rationale for selecting evidence, and their criteria appear rigorous. They note the limitations of one key decision: to choose data from the Framingham study, rather than from RCTs of therapy for patients with atrial fibrillation, from which to derive their risk estimates.

To generate values, the authors interviewed 57 community-dwelling elderly people with a mean age of 73 years. They used standard gamble methodology to generate utility values. Their key values include utilities, on a 0 to 1.0 scale in which 0 is death and 1.0 is full health, of 0.986 for warfarin managed by a general practitioner, 0.880 for a major bleeding episode, 0.675 for a mild stroke, and 0 for a severe stroke.

The investigators conducted a sensitivity analysis that indicated their model was sensitive to variation in patients' utility for taking warfarin. If they assumed utility values for taking warfarin in the upper quartile (1.0; that is, no disutility is suggested for taking warfarin), their analysis suggests that virtually all patients should be receiving warfarin treatment. If they assumed the lower quartile utility (0.92), the analysis suggests that most patients should not be taking warfarin.

This decision analysis rates high with respect to the validity criteria in Table 21-2. The utilities in the investigators' core analysis using best estimates of risk and risk reduction (their *base case* analysis) match those of the patient in the scenario well. The investigators provided tables that suggest the best decision for different patients; when we add the characteristics of the patient being considered in the opening scenario, we find that this patient fits into a cell near the boundary between "no benefit" and "clear benefit," and the investigators' sensitivity analysis suggests that if she places the same value on life while taking warfarin than life while not taking warfarin, she would benefit from using the drug.

Having reviewed what turns out to be a rigorous guideline and a rigorous decision analysis, you are in a much stronger position to help the patient with her decision. It is clear to you that you need to explore her feelings about how she would tolerate the inconvenience and bleeding risk associated with taking warfarin. Your preference is for a shared decision-making style (see Chapter 22.2, Decision Making and the Patient), and in preparation for the discussion with the patient, you note the high value you place on stroke prevention and your assessment that it would be in the patient's best interests to be taking warfarin.

References

1. Singer DE, Albers GW, Dalen JE, Go AS, Halperin JL, Manning WJ. Antithrombotic therapy in atrial fibrillation: the Seventh ACCP Conference on Antithrombotic and Thrombolytic Therapy. *Chest.* 2004;126(3)(suppl):429S-456S.

2. Thomson R, Parkin D, Eccles M, Sudlow M, Robinson A. Decision analysis and guidelines for anticoagulant therapy to prevent stroke in patients with atrial fibrillation. *Lancet.* 2000;355(9208):956-962.

3. Vandenbroucke-Grauls CM, Vandenbroucke JP. Effect of selective decontamination of the digestive tract on respiratory tract infections and mortality in the intensive care unit. *Lancet.* 1991;338(8771):859-862.

4. Selective Decontamination of the Digestive Tract Trialists' Collaborative Group. Meta-analysis of randomised controlled trials of selective decontamination of the digestive tract. *BMJ.* 1993;307(6903):525-532.

5. Heyland DK, Cook DJ, Jaeschke R, Griffith L, Lee HN, Guyatt GH. Selective decontamination of the digestive tract: an overview. *Chest.* 1994;105(4):1221-1229.

6. Kollef MH. The role of selective digestive tract decontamination on mortality and respiratory tract infections: a meta-analysis. *Chest.* 1994;105(4):1101-1108.

7. Glasziou PP, Irwig LM. An evidence based approach to individualising treatment. *BMJ.* 1995;311(7016):1356-1359.

8. Sinclair JC, Cook RJ, Guyatt GH, Pauker SG, Cook DJ. When should an effective treatment be used? derivation of the threshold number needed to treat and the minimum event rate for treatment. *J Clin Epidemiol.* 2006;54(3):217-324.

9. Smith GD, Egger M. Who benefits from medical interventions? *BMJ.* 1994; 308(6921):72-74.

10. Field MJ, Lohr KN, eds. *Clinical Practice Guidelines: Directions for a New Program*. Washington, DC: National Academy Press; 1990.

11. American Medical Association Specialty Society Practice Parameters Partnership and Practice Parameters Forum. *Attributes to Guide the Development of Practice Parameters*. Chicago, IL: American Medical Association; 1990.

12. American College of Physicians. *Clinical Efficacy Assessment Project: Procedural Manual*. Philadelphia, PA: American College of Physicians; 1986.

13. Gottlieb LK, Margolis CZ, Schoenbaum SC. Clinical practice guidelines at an HMO: development and implementation in a quality improvement model. *QRB Qual Rev Bull.* 1990;16(2):80-86.

14. Lohr KN, Field MJ. A provisional instrument for assessing clinical practice guidelines. In: Field MJ, Lohr KN, eds. *Guidelines for Clinical Practice: From Development to Use.* Washington, DC: National Academy Press; 1992:346-410.

15. Harris RP, Helfand M, Woolf SH, et al; Methods Work Group, Third US Preventive Services Task Force. Current methods of the US Preventive Services Task Force: a review of the process. *Am J Prev Med.* 2001;20(3 suppl):21-35.

16. Park RE, Fink A, Brook RH, et al. Physician ratings of appropriate indications for six medical and surgical procedures. *Am J Public Health.* 1986;76(7):766-772.

17. Keeney RL. Decision analysis: an overview. *Oper Res.* 1982;30(5):803-838.

18. Eckman MH, Levine HJ, Pauker SG. Decision analytic and cost-effectiveness issues concerning anticoagulant prophylaxis in heart disease. *Chest.* 1992;102(4)(suppl): 538S-549S.

19. Kassirer JP, Moskowitz AJ, Lau J, Pauker SG. Decision analysis: a progress report. *Ann Intern Med.* 1987;106(2):275-291.

20. Eddy DM. Clinical decision making: from theory to practice: designing a practice policy: standards, guidelines, and options. *JAMA.* 1990;263(22):3077, 3081, 3084.

21. Drummond MF, Richardson WS, O'Brien BJ, Levine M, Heyland D. Users' guides to the medical literature, XIII: how to use an article on economic analysis of clinical practice, A: are the results of the study valid? Evidence-Based Medicine Working Group. *JAMA.* 1997;277(19):1552-1557.

22. O'Brien BJ, Heyland D, Richardson WS, Levine M, Drummond MF. Users' guides to the medical literature, XIII: how to use an article on economic analysis of clinical practice, B: what are the results and will they help me in caring for my patients? Evidence-Based Medicine Working Group. *JAMA.* 1997;277(22):1802-1806.

23. Matchar DB, McCrory DC, Barnett HJ, Feussner JR. Medical treatment for stroke prevention. *Ann Intern Med.* 1994;121(1):41-53.

24. American College of Physicians. Guidelines for medical treatment for stroke prevention. *Ann Intern Med.* 1994;121(1):54-55.

25. North American Symptomatic Carotid Endarterectomy Trial Collaborators. Beneficial effect of carotid endarterectomy in symptomatic patients with high-grade carotid stenosis. *N Engl J Med.* 1991;325(7):445-453.

26. Jackson R, Lawes CM, Bennett DA, Milne RJ, Rodgers A. Treatment with drugs to lower blood pressure and blood cholesterol based on an individual's absolute cardiovascular risk. *Lancet.* 2005;365(9457):434-441.

27. Tsevat J, Eckman MH, McNutt RA, Pauker SG. Warfarin for dilated cardiomyopathy: a bloody tough pill to swallow? *Med Decis Making.* 1989;9(3):162-169.

28. Taylor R, Giles J. Cash interests taint drug advice. *Nature.* 2005;437(7062):1070-1071.

29. Laupacis A. On bias and transparency in the development of influential recommendations. *CMAJ.* 2006;174(3):335-336.

30. *CMAJ.* Clinical practice guidelines and conflict of interest. *CMAJ.* 2005;173(11):1297, 1299.

31. CAPRIE Steering Committee. A randomised, blinded, trial of clopidogrel versus aspirin in patients at risk of ischaemic events (CAPRIE). *Lancet.* 1996;348(9038):1329-1339.

32. Albers GW, Amarenco P, Easton JD, Sacco RL, Teal P. Antithrombotic and thrombolytic therapy for ischemic stroke: the Seventh ACCP Conference on Antithrombotic and Thrombolytic Therapy. *Chest.* 2004;126(3)(suppl):483S-512S.

33. Clagett GP, Sobel M, Jackson MR, Lip GY, Tangelder M, Verhaeghe R. Antithrombotic therapy in peripheral arterial occlusive disease: the Seventh ACCP Conference on Antithrombotic and Thrombolytic Therapy. *Chest.* 2004;126(3)(suppl): 609S-626S.

34. Canadian Task Force on the Periodic Health Examination. The periodic health examination. *CMAJ.* 1979;121(9):1193-1254.

35. Woolf SH, Battista RN, Anderson GM, Logan AG, Wang E. Assessing the clinical effectiveness of preventive maneuvers: analytic principles and systematic methods in reviewing evidence and developing clinical practice recommendations: a report by the Canadian Task Force on the Periodic Health Examination. *J Clin Epidemiol.* 1990;43(9):891-905.

36. Sackett DL. Rules of evidence and clinical recommendations on the use of antithrombotic agents. *Chest.* 1986;89(2 suppl):2S-4S.

37. Guyatt G, Vist G, Falck-Ytter Y, Kunz R, Magrini N, Schunemann H. An emerging consensus on grading recommendations? *ACP J Club.* 2006;144(1):A8-A9.

38. Atkins D, Best D, Briss PA, et al. Grading quality of evidence and strength of recommendations. *BMJ.* 2004;328(7454):1490.

39. Guyatt G, Gutterman D, Baumann MH, et al. Grading strength of recommendations and quality of evidence in clinical guidelines: report from an American College of Chest Physicians task force. *Chest.* 2006;129(1):174-181.

40. Bayoumi AM, Redelmeier DA. Preventing *Mycobacterium avium* complex in patients who are using protease inhibitors: a cost-effectiveness analysis. *AIDS.* 1998;12(12):1503-1512.

ADVANCED TOPICS IN MOVING
FROM EVIDENCE TO ACTION

ECONOMIC
ANALYSIS

Michael Drummond, Ron Goeree,
Paul Moayyedi, and Mitch Levine

IN THIS CHAPTER:

Are Results Reported Separately for Relevant Patient Subgroups?

Were Costs Measured Accurately?

Did Investigators Consider the Timing of Costs and Consequences?

What Are the Results?

What Were the Incremental Costs and Effects of Each Strategy?

Do Incremental Costs and Effects Differ Between Subgroups?

How Much Does Allowance for Uncertainty Change the Results?

How Can I Apply the Results to Patient Care?

Are the Treatment Benefits Worth the Risks and Costs?

Can I Expect Similar Costs in My Setting?

Clinical Resolution

CLINICAL SCENARIO

Is *Helicobacter pylori* "Test and Treat" More Cost-effective Than Prompt Endoscopy for the Management of Young Dyspeptic Patients Without Alarm Symptoms?

You are a gastroenterologist on the staff of a large community hospital. Your chief of medicine knows your interest in *evidence-based medicine*, and she asks you to help her solve a problem. There is considerable pressure on the endoscopy service to provide more colonoscopy screening to reduce colorectal cancer mortality, but no funds are available to increase endoscopy facilities. Approximately 50% of the workload is devoted to upper gastrointestinal endoscopy for patients with dyspepsia. One possibility is to reduce upper gastrointestinal endoscopy demand by providing a *Helicobacter pylori* test and treat service as the preferential management strategy for patients younger than 55 years with dyspepsia without alarm symptoms. This strategy involves giving patients a noninvasive test for *H pylori* (eg, a serology test or urea breath test), treating patients with positive results with antibiotic therapy, and reassuring patients with negative results that they are unlikely to have peptic ulcer disease.

You are hesitant to recommend the new approach. Some physicians believe that prompt endoscopy for all helps select the most effective treatment. Moreover, the *H pylori* test-and-treat strategy will save no resources if patients all undergo endoscopy anyway. Before providing your advice, you decide to seek a formal economic analysis of the *H pylori* test and treat compared with prompt endoscopy.

Finding the Evidence

Having recently attended a short workshop on economic evaluation, you are aware that a good source of information is the National Health Service Economic Evaluation Database (NHS EED) in the United Kingdom. This database contains structured abstracts of full economic evaluations, plus references to methodology articles and cost studies, and is available through the Cochrane Library (http://www3.interscience.wiley.com/cgi-bin/mrwhome/106568753/HOME). However, your hospital does not subscribe, so you decide to access this database free through the Web site of the Centre for Reviews and Dissemination of the University of York (http://www.york.ac.uk/inst/crd).

You click on the option "All These Words" and then enter the search terms of interest: "dyspepsia, endoscopy, helicobacter." This generates 42 hits in the NHS EED database. You click on the NHS EED tab and find that the structured abstract of the very first citation on the list, an article by Ford et al,[1] shows that the economic analysis is based directly on an individual patient data *meta-analysis* of 5 *randomized controlled trials* (*RCTs*), including 1924 patients, comparing test and treat with prompt endoscopy. This strikes you as the highest quality *evidence* you are likely to find, and you retrieve the article.

Why Economic Analysis?

Clinicians not only make decisions about the care of individual patients but also help establish clinical policy for an institution (addressing such questions as, should *H pylori* test and treat or prompt endoscopy be recommended for young dyspeptic patients without alarm symptoms?). Some clinicians also help set health policy at a broader level (addressing such questions as, should more resources be made available for the treatment of peptic ulcer disease?).

When making decisions for patient groups, clinicians need to not only weigh the benefits and risks but also consider whether these benefits will be worth the health care costs. More and more, clinicians must persuade colleagues and health policy makers that the benefits of their interventions justify the resources consumed.

When outcomes are equivalent between 2 or more management strategies, economic analysis will help us choose the less expensive option (cost-minimization analysis). In general, economic analysis can help justify allocation of scarce resources by providing a set of formal, quantitative methods to compare 2 or more treatments, programs, or strategies with respect to their resource use and their expected outcomes.[2-4] A comparison of 2 strategies that considers only costs informs only the resource-use half of the decision and is termed a cost analysis. Comparing only the consequences of 2 or more strategies (such as in an RCT of treatment efficacy) informs only the health benefit portion of the decision. A full economic comparison addresses both the costs and consequences of the strategies being compared.

Economic evaluations seek to inform resource allocation decisions, rather than to make them. Economic analyses, widely applied in the health care field, have informed decisions at different levels, including managing major institutions such as hospitals and determining regional or national policy.[4]

COST: JUST ANOTHER OUTCOME?

In one sense, cost is, like physiologic function, quality of life, morbid events such as stroke and myocardial infarction, and death, simply another outcome for clinicians to consider when assessing the effects of therapy. Although there are fundamental similarities between cost and other outcomes, there are also important differences that we will now describe.

The Role of Costs in Clinical Decision Making Remains Controversial

Although few would deny the importance of cost considerations in setting health care policy, the relevance of costs in individual patient decision making remains controversial. Some would argue—taking an extreme of what can be called a deontologic approach to distributive justice—that clinicians' only responsibility should be to best meet the needs of the individual under their care. An alternate view—philosophically consequentialist or utilitarian—would contend that even in individual decision making, clinicians should take a broader social view. In this broader view, the effect on others of allocating resources to a particular patient's care would bear on the decision.

As health care technologies proliferate, their potential benefits and their costs increase, but their marginal benefits over less resource-intensive approaches are often small. In such a world, the arguments for bedside rationing become more compelling.[5] Our own belief is that although individual clinicians should attend primarily to the needs of the patients under their care, they should not neglect the resource implications of the advice they offer their patients. Neglect of resource issues in one patient may, after all, affect resource availability for other patients under their care. For those who disagree, this section remains relevant for consideration of health policy decisions.

Costs Are More Variable Than Other Outcomes

Whether clinicians administer *H pylori* test and treat to a patient with dyspepsia in Toronto or Singapore, the relative effect on dyspepsia is likely to be similar. Indeed, treatment effects on conventional outcomes of quality of life, morbidity, and mortality have proved on most occasions to be similar across not only geographic location but also patient groups and ways of administering the intervention (see Chapter 20.4, When to Believe a Subgroup Analysis).

In contrast to clinical endpoints, costs vary hugely across jurisdictions, not only in absolute terms but also in the relative costs of different components of care, including physicians, other health workers, drugs, services, and technologic devices.

For example, outpatient treatment of deep venous thrombosis (DVT) with low-molecular-weight heparin (LMWH) compared with inpatient treatment with unfractionated heparin is more cost-effective in the United States than in Canada, although LMWH is more than double the price in the United States, because the price of reduced hospital days relative to the price of LMWH is much greater in the United States than in Canada.[6]

One need not move across international—or even national, or regional, or state—boundaries to see large cost differences. Adjacent hospitals may have different success in negotiating a contract with a drug company to purchase a large volume of a drug at a low price. Drug prices in adjacent hospitals may therefore vary by a factor of 2 or more, and the resource implications of use of alternative agents may therefore differ substantially in the 2 institutions.

Costs also depend on how care is organized, and organization of care varies widely across jurisdictions. The same service may be delivered by a physician or a nurse practitioner, in the outpatient setting or in the hospital, and with or without administrative costs related to adjudication of patient eligibility to receive the service. If it is delivered by a physician, in the hospital, with maximal administrative costs, as our example of inpatient DVT treatment in the United States suggests, the expense will be greater than if the service is delivered on an outpatient basis or in an institution with lower administrative costs.

The substantial dependence of resource consumption on local costs and local organization of health care delivery means that most cost data are specific to a particular jurisdiction and have limited transferability. An additional problem with RCTs is that their conduct may alter practice patterns in ways that further limit generalizability to other settings, or even to their own setting, outside the RCT context. For example, in an economic evaluation of misoprostol, a drug for prophylaxis against gastric ulcer in patients receiving high doses of nonsteroidal anti-inflammatory drugs, Hillman and Bloom[7] used data from an RCT undertaken by Graham et al.[8] This blinded RCT of 3 months' duration compared misoprostol (400 and 800 mg daily) with placebo. An important issue for economic analysis was that prevention of ulcers by misoprostol may generate savings in health care expenditure, savings that could balance the cost of adding the drug. In this study, however, endoscopy was performed monthly. In regular clinical practice, endoscopy would be undertaken in response to symptoms. An analysis of the results from this trial would have told clinicians of the cost implications of misoprostol administration when patients undergo routine monthly endoscopy, information that would be useless, given how different such circumstances are from regular clinical practice.

Using Cost Information Raises Questions of Distributive Justice

In health care policy decisions, we must use cost information to allocate scarce resources efficiently. Let us assume that 2 treatments both cost, in comparison to conventional treatment and after consideration of all their consequences, $1 000 000 for each 1000 patients treated for 1 year. For treatment A, the benefits achieved by this expenditure are the prevention of 200 patients from having symptoms of dyspepsia. For treatment B, the benefit is avoiding a single case of gastric cancer. If, in a resource-constrained environment, one had to choose between A and B, what would be the better choice?

If the choice makes you feel uncomfortable, you are in good company. Choosing between competing beneficial treatments presents daunting logistic, ethical, and political challenges. The example demonstrates how, in economic analysis, we must trade off costs against benefits and how we must deal with very different outcomes that accrue to very different people—in this case, prevention of dyspepsia in one patient group and prevention of a case of gastric cancer in another—in deciding on allocation of resources.

ECONOMIC ANALYSIS OFFERS SOLUTIONS TO ITS SPECIAL CHALLENGES

Problems of Cost Variability

As for other outcomes, there are 2 fundamental strategies for discovering the effect of alternative management strategies on resource consumption. One is to conduct a single study, ideally an RCT, comparing 2 or more interventions. Such an approach asks what happens (on average and limited by the precision of the estimate) when clinicians choose management strategy A vs strategy B.

The second approach is to construct a decision tree of events that flow from a clinical decision, using all the available evidence to estimate the probabilities of all possible outcomes, including the costs generated. This second approach asks what might happen if clinicians choose management strategy A vs strategy B. The what-might-happen modeling approach of *decision analysis* allows investigators to deal with problems such as the idiosyncrasies of care delivered in the RCT context and the variability in costs across jurisdictions.

Refer to the example of the unnecessary endoscopies conducted in the Graham et al[8] RCT of misoprostol for prevention of gastric ulcers in patients taking high doses of nonsteroidal anti-inflammatory drugs. In the subsequent analysis, Hillman and Bloom[7] adjusted observed ulcer rates to reflect the fact that 40% of endoscopically determined lesions did not produce any symptoms. Observing that compliance of patients in the trial was greater than one might expect in clinical practice, they also adjusted for lower compliance by using the ulcer rates in the evaluable cohort and assuming that only 60% of this efficacy would be achieved in practice.

The modeling approaches of decision analysis allow investigators to deal with other problems such as inadequate length of follow-up by using available data to estimate what will happen in the long term. Decision analysts can also examine a variety of cost assumptions and ways of organizing care and calculate the sensitivity of their results to these alternate assumptions (see Chapter 21, How to Use a Patient Management Recommendation).

The key limitation of the decision analytic approach is that if its assumptions are flawed, it will not give us an accurate picture. In one review of 326 pharmacoeconomic analyses submitted to the Australian Department of Health by the pharmaceutical industry, 218 (67%) included significant problems, many of which required a detailed review to detect.[9]

Even rigorous economic analyses without conflict of interest will yield misleading results if the underlying assumptions are inaccurate. A *cost-effectiveness analysis* using pristine *decision analysis* methodology concluded that trying to achieve rhythm control in older patients with atrial fibrillation was more cost-effective than a strategy based on controlling only the heart rate.[10] Unfortunately, subsequent RCTs demonstrated that the assumptions the authors made about the benefits of rhythm control were inaccurate.[11] A subsequent economic analysis based on more valid assumptions demonstrated the unequivocal superiority of the rate control approach.[12]

The ideal, then, may be a melding of the 2 approaches, in which the analysis rests on data from RCTs, with adjunctive analytic decision-based modeling to adapt the results to the actual situations in which they will be applied.[13] Even the melding approach, however, must use average patient values. These averages may be different from values or preferences of the individual patient, and different values may lead to different decisions (see Chapter 22.2, Decision Making and the Patient). Looking at the underlying assumptions of an economic analysis may provide clinicians insight into application of results to their patients. Thus, the extent to which the authors make their assumptions transparent will add to the credibility of any economic analysis.

There is another aspect to solving one component of the cost variability problem. If authors present resources used by the alternative management strategies, users of the research can consider how much those resources would cost in their own setting. Indeed, cost is really shorthand for resource consumption, a point that clinicians can usefully bear in mind when considering economic issues.

Trading Off Benefits, Risks, and Costs

As we have mentioned, economic analysis must deal with the problem of the relative value of different outcomes and the tradeoff of dollar values against health, issues of distributive justice. Typically, health economists use 3 strategies. One is to report patient-important outcomes in physical or natural units such as "life-years gained" or "patients symptom free" or "gastric cancers prevented" (cost-effectiveness analysis).

In a second approach, they weight different types of outcomes to produce a composite index of outcome, such as the *quality-adjusted life-year* (QALY) (we call this cost-utility analysis, sometimes classified as a subcategory of cost-effectiveness analysis). Quality adjustment involves placing a lower value on time spent with impaired physical and emotional function than time spent in full health. On a scale in which 0 represents death and 1.0 represents full health, the greater the impairment, the lower the value of a particular health state.

Finally, investigators may put a dollar value on additional life gained, cases of dyspepsia prevented, or gastric cancers prevented. In these cost-benefit analyses, health care consumers consider what they would be willing to pay for programs or products that achieve particular outcomes, such as prolonging life or preventing adverse events.

In the study from our scenario, Ford et al[1] chose cost-effectiveness as their primary analysis, using the outcome "patients symptom free of dyspepsia." The strength of this approach is that the outcome data are generated directly from the individual patient data meta-analysis that they conduct. The main disadvantage is that the outcome measure relates to dyspepsia only. Therefore, it is difficult to make any comparisons of cost-effectiveness, or value for money, with other interventions in gastroenterology or health care more generally.

A more generic outcome measure, such as QALYs gained, would have facilitated these comparisons. Small changes in dyspepsia symptoms may, however, not even register on a metric such as a QALY. Therefore, it may not be a good approach for detecting small differences in benefits between 2 treatment strategies for dyspepsia. It may also fail to represent adequately large differences in benefits that are limited to a brief period, such as the value of a local anesthetic when having root canal dental treatment. However, when it comes to the broader aspects of resource allocation in health care, we need a measure such as the QALY to compare the benefits of improvements in dyspepsia symptoms with outcomes in other fields of health care.

Using an Economic Analysis

Having outlined some of the challenges of economic analysis, we offer our usual structure for guides to the medical literature: Are the results valid? What are the results? How can I apply results to patient care? Our key criteria from Chapter 21, How to Use a Patient Management Recommendation (Do the recommendations consider all relevant patient groups, management options, and possible outcomes? Is there a *systematic review* of evidence linking options to each relevant outcome? Is there an appropriate specification of values and preferences associated with outcomes?), apply to economic analyses. The issues we present in Table 22.1-1 are those specific to economic analysis.

ARE THE RESULTS VALID?

Did Investigators Adopt a Sufficiently Broad Viewpoint?

Investigators can evaluate costs and consequences from a number of viewpoints: the patient, a health care institution such as a hospital, the third-party payer (insurer, drug benefit program, or national or local government in some countries), or society at large. Each viewpoint may be relevant, depending on the question being asked, but broader viewpoints are most relevant to those allocating

TABLE 22.1-1

Users' Guides for an Article About Economic Analyses

Are the results valid?

Did the recommendations consider all relevant patient groups, management options, and possible outcomes?

- Are the results valid?
- Did investigators adopt a sufficiently broad viewpoint?
- Are results reported separately for relevant patient subgroups?

Is there a systematic review and summary of evidence linking options to outcomes for each relevant question?

- Were costs measured accurately?
- Did investigators consider the timing of costs and consequences?

What are the results?

- What were the incremental costs and effects of each strategy?
- Do incremental costs and effects differ between subgroups?
- How much does allowance for uncertainty change the results?

How can I apply the results to patient care?

- Are the treatment benefits worth the risks and costs?
- Can I expect similar costs in my setting?

---

health care resources. For example, an evaluation adopting the viewpoint of the hospital will be useful in estimating the budgetary effect of alternative therapies for that institution. However, economic evaluation is usually directed at informing policy from a broader societal perspective. For example, in an evaluation of an early-discharge program, reporting only hospital costs is insufficient because patients discharged early may consume substantial community resources. One of the main reasons for considering narrower viewpoints in conducting an economic analysis is to assess the influence of change on the main budget holders because budgets may need to be adjusted before a new therapy can be adopted, often termed the *silo effect*. For instance, Feldman et al[14] reported that donepezil therapy in moderate to severe Alzheimer disease was worthwhile from the perspective of society as a whole because of the reduced demands on caregivers. Nevertheless, it would be more costly to the organization responsible for paying for the medication. Even within the same institution, narrow budgetary viewpoints can prevail. In an economic analysis comparing 2 drug regimens, it would be wrong to focus exclusively on the relative costs of the drugs, which are included in the pharmacy budget, if there are also effects on other hospital resource use. In the DVT example we used earlier, use of outpatient LMWH will decrease hospital cost, but whoever pays the drug budget will find their costs increasing. The patient's perspective may also merit specific consideration if costs (eg, travel-related ones) reduce access to care. Also, some patients may not be able to participate in community care programs if these impose major costs in terms of informal nursing support in the home. In general, however, economic analyses integrate the patient's perspective by measuring the consequences of therapy, such as effect on quality of life.

From a societal viewpoint, determination of costs should include the therapy's effect on the patients' ability to work and hence their contribution to the nation's productivity. The issue of inclusion or exclusion of productivity changes (sometimes known as indirect costs and benefits) remains a frequent topic of debate. On one hand, productivity changes represent resource-use changes such as those occurring in the health care system. On the other hand, production may not actually be lost if a worker is absent for a short period. Also, for longer periods of absence, employers may hire a previously unemployed worker. Furthermore, inclusion of productivity changes biases evaluations in favor of programs for individuals who are in full-time employment. Therefore, clinicians should be skeptical about any economic analysis that includes productivity changes without clearly presenting the implications.

Table 22.1-2, which outlines the costs used by Ford et al[1] in calculating the total cost per patient for the 2 alternative treatment strategies, shows that the costs span both primary and secondary care. If you work in health care, depending on your setting, some of the costs might strike you as unrealistic. This emphasizes the important issue of the lack of portability of unit costs across jurisdictions. Table 22.1-2 reflects the authors' decision to adopt the perspective of someone making decisions for the whole health care system. In publicly funded systems, this would be the government or national

TABLE 22.1-2

Costs Used in Obtaining a Total Cost per Patient

	Cost, $ (2003)
General practitioner visit	170
Outpatient visit	232
Inpatient day	550
PPI (1-mo single dose)	99.99
H_2RA (1 mo)	112.29
Prokinetic (1 mo)	70
Antacid (1 mo)	8.49
Eradication therapy	152
Urea breath test	80
Endoscopy	450
Barium meal	99.69
Abdominal ultrasonographic scan	118

Abbreviations: H_2RA, histamine$_2$-receptor antagonist; PPI, proton-pump inhibitors.

This article was published in *Gastroenterology*, Vol. 128, Ford AC et al. *Helicobacter pylori* "test and treat" or endoscopy for managing dyspepsia: An individual patient data meta-analysis, Pp 1838–1844.[1] Copyright Elsevier 2005.

health insurance agency. In privately funded systems, the relevant perspective would be that of an insurer providing coverage for health care costs.

Of course, in many health care systems, it is likely that there would be some element of patient copayments, in particular for drugs. Therefore, to the extent that the size of copayment differs between therapies, this may affect patient choice. The authors did not consider other patient costs or productivity losses. These are likely to be minor and restricted to the costs involved in visiting the general practitioner or hospital to undergo endoscopy.

Are Results Reported Separately for Relevant Patient Subgroups?

Costs and consequences may differ among patients of different age, sex, or illness severity. The most likely differences are those related to the *baseline risk* of the adverse outcome that the treatment is designed to prevent. For example, the cost-effectiveness of drug therapy for elevated cholesterol level will improve compared with no drug intervention as patient risk increases (the cost per unit effect, eg, a reduction in cardiovascular events, will be lower in higher-risk patients). Cost-effectiveness will be superior for men than women; older than younger patients; and those with higher cholesterol level, hypertension, diabetes, and family history of heart disease than in those without these risk factors.[15] Secondary prevention in those who have already had a cardiovascular event will be substantially more cost-effective than primary prevention in those who have not. Division of patients into risk categories is common in clinical practice. For instance, in a study of the cost-effectiveness of screening for proteinuria to slow progression of chronic renal disease, Boulware et al[16] found that the cost per QALY gained was $283 000 for all subjects older than 50 years but was only $19 000 for those with hypertension. The differences in the cost-effectiveness ratios were driven primarily by the patient's risk of developing chronic renal disease (ie, if you are unlikely to develop chronic renal disease, you have a limited capacity to benefit).

Were Costs Measured Accurately?

Although the viewpoint determines the relevant range of costs and consequences in an economic evaluation, there are many issues relating to their measurement and evaluation. First, clinicians should look for the physical quantities of resources consumed or released by the treatments separately from their prices or unit costs. Not only does this allow them to scrutinize the method of assigning monetary values to resources but also it helps to extrapolate the results of a study from one setting to another because prices vary by location.

Second, there are different approaches to valuing costs or cost savings. One approach is to use published charges. Charges, however, may differ from real costs, depending on the sophistication of accounting systems and the relative bargaining power of health care institutions and third-party payers.[17] Where there is a systematic deviation between costs and charges, the analyst may adjust the latter by a cost-to-charge ratio. The relationship between charges and costs may, however, vary markedly by institution, so simple adjustments may not suffice. From the third-party payer's perspective, charges will bear some relation to the amounts actually paid, although in some settings payments vary by payer. From a societal perspective, we would like the real costs because these reflect what society is forgoing in benefits elsewhere to provide a given treatment.

For example, Taira et al[18] compared the costs and charges for 2 methods of percutaneous coronary revascularization. When hospital charges were used, the difference in the mean cost between the 2 methods was $21 311. When itemized procedures costs and departmental cost-to-charge ratios were used, however, the difference was only $5454. Thus, clinicians may have been dissuaded from using one of the therapies because of the high "cost," when the apparent cost difference may have been an artifact of hospital accounting systems or bargaining power, rather than a reflection of the real value to society of the resources consumed by those procedures.

Ford et al[1] presented costs for the US setting for each of the 2 treatment strategies. Drug costs were obtained from the average retail prices for pharmaceuticals. Physician costs, including procedures, were obtained from the American Medical Association procedural code book and the 2003 Medicare fee schedule. The quantities of resources used (eg, number of outpatient visits, number of barium meals) were obtained from 1771 of 1924 patients enrolled in the 5 RCTs that were included in the individual patient data meta-analysis. Therefore, the accuracy of the cost estimates is likely to be more dependent on the accuracy of the unit costs than the resource use data. There are a number of reasons why published prices (eg, those of drugs) may differ from those actually paid. One can resolve this issue only through considering the relevance of study results to a particular setting, an issue to which we shall return.

Did Investigators Consider the Timing of Costs and Consequences?

A final issue in the measurement and valuation of costs and consequences relates to the adjustment for differences in their timing. Generally, people prefer benefits sooner and prefer to postpone costs because of uncertainty about the future and because resources, if invested, usually yield a positive return. The accepted way of allowing for this in economic evaluations is to discount costs and consequences occurring in the future to present values by assigning a lower weight to future costs and benefits. The US Panel on Cost-Effectiveness in Health and Medicine[16] proposed a 3% discount rate based on the inflation-adjusted rate of return on US government bonds, and this rate is the one most often used in studies undertaken in North America. There remain debates about whether health outcomes should be discounted at the same rate as costs.[19-22] Ford et al[1] did not discount because the period of the analysis was only 12 months, and making adjustments for differential timing of costs and benefits within this period would have minimally affected the results. The authors point out that there are few data on the effects of the 2 strategies on the long-term history of dyspepsia, although one study with 6-year follow-up showed that the difference in resource use at 12 months appears to continue thereafter, with no difference in the symptom status. The other longer-term issue is whether the choice of strategy has any effect on the costs of, or the rate of, survival from gastric carcinoma. In the absence of long-term clinical trials, the rates of gastric cancer would have to be estimated by the use of models. If there were such an influence, the costs and effects would need to be considered formally and, being mainly in the future, they would be discounted.

What Are the Results?

What Were the Incremental Costs and Effects of Each Strategy?

Consider the costs for each treatment option, remembering that costs are the product of the quantity of a resource used and its unit cost or price. These should include the costs incurred to "produce" the treatment, such as the physician's time, nurses' time, diagnostic tests, drugs, and so forth, which we might term the up-front costs, as well as the downstream costs because of resources consumed in the future and associated with clinical events that are attributable to the therapy.

Ford et al[1] state that they considered both primary and secondary care costs (including primary care and outpatient consultations with dyspepsia and inpatient admissions as a consequence of dyspepsia), costs of prescribed drugs for dyspepsia (using total defined doses of acid suppression drugs and number of courses of eradication therapy), and investigation rates (number of barium meals, upper gastrointestinal endoscopies, abdominal ultrasonographic scans, and breath tests). Resource use was tracked during a 1-year period, which was the follow-up time for the clinical trials included in the analysis.

The authors presented results as weighted mean difference, with a 95% *confidence interval (CI)*. Endoscopy was more expensive than test and treat by $389 (95% CI, $276-$502). The authors observed that most of this increased burden resulted from the cost of investigations in the prompt endoscopy group (weighted mean difference, $318; 95% CI, $285-$350).

The difference in the effectiveness of the 2 strategies was measured in 2 ways: total dyspepsia symptoms score and absence of dyspepsia at 12 months (expressed as a relative risk). Overall, 82% of the endoscopy group still had dyspepsia at 12 months compared with 86% of the test-and-treat group, corresponding to a *relative risk* of 0.95 (95% CI, 0.92-0.99).

A visual representation of the relationship between costs and effects, the cost-effectiveness (CE) plane, can highlight implications of the results (Figure 22.1-1). The horizontal axis in the plane represents the difference in effect between the experimental intervention (ie, endoscopy) and the control management strategy (ie, test and treat), and this points to the right of control, indicating superior effectiveness of the intervention. The vertical axis, the difference in costs, points above control, indicating the intervention is more costly than control. We can designate the point estimates of the effect and cost of our intervention as point A on this plane (the CE plane).

If point A is in quadrant 2, the intervention of interest is both more effective and less costly than the control strategy and therefore dominates the alternative. In quadrant 4, the opposite is true; the control is both more effective and less costly and dominates the experimental intervention. In quadrant 1, the choice depends on the maximum incremental costs (per unit of effect) one is willing to accept. In quadrant 3, the choice depends on the decrease in effectiveness one is willing to accept, given less resource consumption with the experimental intervention.

When (as is the case with endoscopy vs test and treat) the experimental intervention is both more effective and more costly (ie, in quadrant 1), one can calculate the incremental cost-effectiveness ratio (ICER; ie, the cost per unit benefit

FIGURE 22.1-1

The Cost-effectiveness Plane

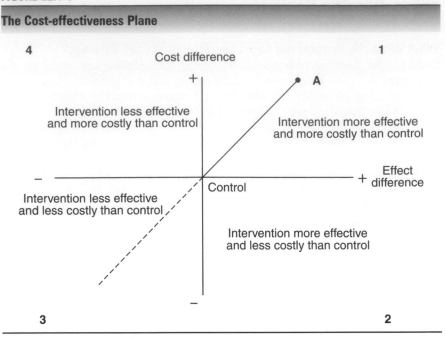

gained with the experimental intervention; in this case, the incremental cost per additional patient symptom free at 12 months). In Figure 22.1-1, the slope of the line from the origin to point A represents the ICER. Choice of a threshold (the maximum one is willing to pay to gain a single unit of benefit; in this case, how much one would be willing to pay to have a single patient symptom-free at 12 months) allows one to designate the experimental intervention as cost-effective (costs do not cross the threshold) or not cost-effective (costs greater than the threshold). In this case, the authors point out that even if one were willing to pay $1000 per patient symptom free (which the authors consider quite a high threshold), endoscopy would still not be the preferred strategy.

Do Incremental Costs and Effects Differ Between Subgroups?

One of our validity criteria for an economic analysis is to consider the possibility that cost-effectiveness differs across subgroups of patients. As we have observed, of particular relevance are patient groups that vary, to a large degree, in their risk of the adverse outcome that the experimental intervention is designed to prevent.

Ford et al[1] conducted prespecified subgroup analyses, examining symptom status at 12 months for patients according to sex, age (younger than 50 years or 50 years and older), predominant symptom at trial entry (epigastric pain or heartburn), and initial *H pylori* status. The analyses showed that there was a small but statistically significant effect on symptoms in favor of prompt endoscopy in patients 50 years and older compared with no difference in effect in those younger than 50 years. There appeared to be no overall difference in effect between the 2 strategies for patients with predominant epigastric pain, predominant heartburn, or initial *H pylori* status. The investigators failed to report differences in cost or cost-effectiveness by subgroup, so we do not know, for example, whether the higher effectiveness of the prompt endoscopy strategy in patients older than 50 years would make this strategy cost-effective. In the other subgroups, it is unlikely that there would be differences in cost-effectiveness, given the similarities in effectiveness.

How Much Does Allowance for Uncertainty Change the Results?

The primary output of an economic analysis uses the investigators' best estimates of each of the key variables that bear on the costs and effects of the alternative management strategies (often referred to as the base case). Inevitably, however, there is uncertainty that arises from choices concerning the data used in the analysis, the main methodologic assumptions used in the analysis, and the desire to generalize the results to other settings. Exploring the effect of these sources of uncertainty complements consideration of possible heterogeneity of cost-effectiveness across patient subgroups that we dealt with in the previous section.

The conventional approach for handling uncertainty in economic analyses is to undertake sensitivity analyses in which investigators vary estimates of key variables one at a time (1-way sensitivity analysis) or together (multiway sensitivity analysis) to assess the effect on study results. Investigators continue to use conventional sensitivity analysis, in which variables are altered one at a time or in combination with other variables, to explore uncertainty related to methodologic uncertainty (eg, the way of estimating the cost of a test/procedure), for transferability (eg, applying results to another geographic location with different practice patterns or unit costs), and for structural assumptions in a decision analytic model (eg, the number of dyspeptic episodes permitted per year in a model). To illustrate how investigators address uncertainty in economic evaluations, we will draw on another economic evaluation of alternative approaches for treating patients with gastro-esophageal reflux disease (GERD). GERD is a chronic relapsing-remitting–type disease and thus has both initial treatment and secondary prevention (ie, mainte-nance) components. There are different drugs (eg, histamine$_2$-receptor antagonists [H$_2$RAs], proton-pump inhibitors [PPIs]), doses of drugs, and combinations of drugs that a clinician can use for long-term patient treatment. For example, although PPIs are more effective in relieving symptoms and preventing recurrence, they are considerably more expensive than H$_2$RAs. As a result, experts often advocate strategies such as step-up therapy for relapses and step-down therapy for maintenance treatment. In this study, the authors estimated the costs and effects of 6 alternative management strategies.[23] The primary measure of effectiveness in this study was the number of weeks free of GERD symptoms during the year. An advantage of this type of outcome measure for chronic relapsing-remitting–type diseases is that it combines the probability of treatment success, the speed of treatment success, and the probability of recurrence of GERD in one single

TABLE 22.1-3

Base Case Cost, Effectiveness, and Cost-effectiveness Results for Alternative Strategies for Treating Patients With GERD

Strategy	Expected 1-Year Cost per Patient	Expected Weeks With (Without) GERD per Patient in 1 Year	Incremental Cost, $ (ΔC)	Incremental Effects (ΔE, No. of Weeks GERD Averted)	$\Delta C/\Delta E$
C, Maintenance H$_2$RA[a]	657	10.41 (41.59)	–	–	–
A, Intermittent PPI	678	7.778 (44.22)	21	2.63	
E, Step-down maintenance H$_2$RA	748	6.17 (45.83)	70[b]	1.61[b]	44[b]
B, Maintenance PPI	1093	4.82 (47.18)	345[c]	1.35[c]	256[c]
D, Step-down maintenance PA	805	12.60 (39.40)			Dominated
F, Step-down maintenance PPI	955	5.54 (46.46)			Dominated

Abbreviations: GERD, gastroesophageal reflux disease; H$_2$RA, histamine$_2$-receptor antagonist; PA, prokinetic agent; PPI, proton-pump inhibitor. –, data not available.

[a]Dashes indicate data not available.
[b]Relative to strategy A.
[c]Relative to strategy E.

measure. Table 22.1-3 presents a summary of the cost, effects, and cost-effectiveness from this analysis.

When comparing multiple alternatives in economic evaluations, investigators begin by making their base case estimates of the costs and effects for each alternative and determining whether any of the alternatives are dominated by another or if any combination of alternatives dominates another. As shown in Table 22.1-3, in this example, one alternative (D) was dominated by C, A, and E, and another (F) was dominated by a combination of E and B. The next step is to rank-order the nondominated strategies according to effectiveness and then calculate the ICERs of moving from one strategy to the next (see last column of Table 22.1-3). Authors can display these cost and effectiveness results graphically on the CE plane (Figure 22.1-2) and also display the ICERs (shown as the sloped line segments joining strategies C, A, E, and B). Taken together, the line segments in Figure 22.1-2 are referred to as the efficiency frontier for treating patients with GERD. Any treatment or strategy that has a

FIGURE 22.1-2

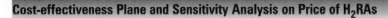

Cost-effectiveness Plane and Sensitivity Analysis on Price of H₂RAs

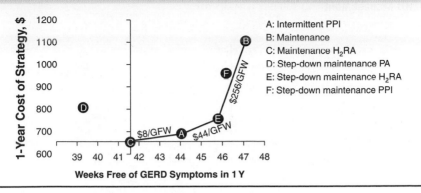

A: Intermittent PPI
B: Maintenance
C: Maintenance H₂RA
D: Step-down maintenance PA
E: Step-down maintenance H₂RA
F: Step-down maintenance PPI

Abbreviations: GERD, gastroesophageal reflux disease; GFW, GERD-free week; H₂RA, histamine₂-receptor agonist; PA, prokinetic agent; PPI, proton-pump inhibitor.

base-case cost-effectiveness that is above the efficiency frontier would be considered dominated.

To explore uncertainty related to methodologic uncertainty or for structural assumptions in a decision analytic model, conventional sensitivity analyses are used, and the results from these analyses are compared with the base case results (ie, Table 22.1-3 and Figure 22.1-2) to observe how sensitive the results are to changes in these analysis assumptions. For other types of uncertainty (eg, sensitivity of a diagnostic test, effectiveness of treatment, probability of adverse effects, recurrence of symptoms), current approaches to sensitivity analysis involve generating a distribution of the possible underlying true values associated with each key variable. The investigators then allow all these variables to vary simultaneously in the analysis. Computer random generators repeatedly draw a random point from each distribution and for each draw generate a single cost-and-effect pair for each treatment alternative. Repeated simulations (Monte Carlo simulations) generate a large number of cost-and-effect pairs that provide estimates of the underlying uncertainty.[24] The term applied to this approach is "probabilistic sensitivity analysis" (PSA). Patient-level trial data from RCTs usually provide the source for the distributions defined in a PSA model, although investigators can also use registries, administrative databases, surveys, and even expert opinion. Validity quality decreases progressively as investigators move away from RCTs to lower-quality sources of evidence.

The results of the PSA for the GERD example by Goeree et al[23] are shown in Figure 22.1-3A. Although the representation of uncertainty in Figure 22.1-3A provides a visual image of the sampling variation in a trial-based analysis or the parameter uncertainty in a decision analytic model, this method of display is difficult to interpret for public-policy decision making. To overcome the problem for summarizing all uncertainty on a single cost-effectiveness plane, the effect of sampling variation (trials) or parameter uncertainty (models) can be expressed

FIGURE 22.1-3

Probabilistic Sensitivity Analysis and Cost-effectiveness Acceptability Curves for GERD Management

A

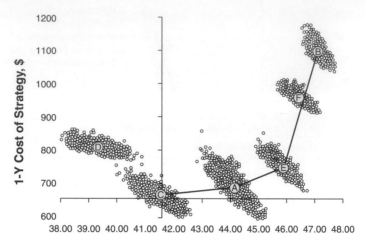

B

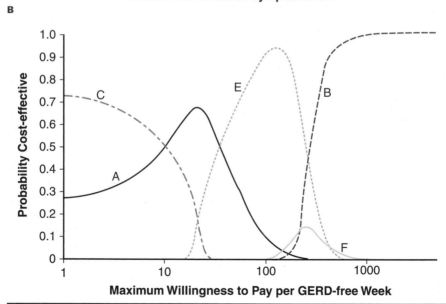

A, Probabilistic sensitivity analysis for GERD management. B, Cost-effectiveness acceptability curves for GERD management. The line segments in A represent the base case cost-effectiveness of alternative ways of treating patients with heartburn using best estimates of treatment success rates, event rates, and costs. The dots represent possible underlying true values of cost-effectiveness when fully accounting for uncertainty in these costs and outcomes. In both A and B, inset graph labels A-F represent the following test groups: A, intermittent PPI; B, maintenance; C, maintenance H_2RA; D, step-down maintenance PA; E, step-down maintenance H_2RA; F, step-down maintenance PPI. Abbreviations: GERD, gastroesophageal reflux disease; H_2RA, histamine$_2$-receptor agonist; PA, prokinetic agent; PPI, proton-pump inhibitor.

using *cost-effectiveness acceptability curves* (*CEACs*). The formula for the ICER can be rearranged into incremental net benefits (INBs) (INB = $\lambda \Delta E - \Delta C$), where λ (ceiling ratio) is the maximum amount a third-party payer or patient would be willing to pay per GERD week averted. INB can be applied to the sampling variation in trials or simulation results in models to estimate the probability a treatment or strategy is cost-effective for any given ceiling ratio (λ).

Figure 22.1-3B shows the CEACs for the GERD example. CEACs are useful because all the sampling variation or parameter uncertainty is simultaneously expressed in a single diagram, and decision makers can use their own criteria for how much they would be willing to pay to avoid a week of GERD symptoms. For example in Figure 22.1-3B, if decision makers were willing to pay only up to $10 per GERD-free week, the preferred option would be strategy C. Between $10 and $80, the preferred option would be strategy A; between $80 and $250, strategy E; and above $250, strategy B.

How Can I Apply the Results to Patient Care?

Having established the results of the economic study and the precision of the estimates, we now turn to 2 important issues of interpretation. The first is how clinicians can interpret ICERs to help in decision making; the second is the extent to which they can apply the cost or effects from the study in their practice settings.

Are the Treatment Benefits Worth the Risks and Costs?

Having estimated the incremental effectiveness of the endoscopy strategy (in terms of dyspepsia status at 1 year) and the incremental costs and assuming for the moment that these data apply to your practice setting, how do you decide whether the extra benefits are worth the extra costs? One approach would be to compare the ICER for endoscopy vs test and treat to other funded health care interventions. However, the specificity of the outcome, proportion of patients free of dyspeptic symptoms at 12 months, precludes such a comparison.

Another approach would be to explore what level of willingness to pay, per patient symptom-free of dyspepsia, would make the endoscopy strategy potentially cost-effective. The authors conduct this analysis and find the required willingness to pay to be approximately $180000. They argue that this is not a reasonable amount and so conclude that the extra costs of the endoscopy strategy are not worth the small additional effect.

When results are not available in units that can be applied across different diseases and conditions (such as QALYs) and investigators fall back on willingness-to-pay approaches and choose a willingness-to-pay threshold (such as the amount one is willing to pay for a single patient to be symptom free), one may disagree with the authors' threshold. In such instances, plotting of the CEAC allows one to apply one's own threshold value for willingness to pay. The decision maker can see immediately the probability that a given treatment strategy is cost-effective for different values of the willingness-to-pay threshold, as shown in Figure 22.1-3B.

Investigators have debated the validity of such interpretive strategies for ICERs and CEACs at both theoretical[25,26] and practical levels.[27] Although some health economists[25] maintain that prioritizing resource allocations based on rank-orderings of interventions by incremental cost-effectiveness does lead to an efficient allocation of resources, many—citing practical problems that include different methods, data, and underlying assumptions—disagree.

Clinicians should therefore exercise caution when drawing conclusions from ICERs. The ultimate criterion is one of local *opportunity cost*: If the money for a new program will result in decreased ability to deliver other health care interventions, what other services will be compromised and what are the consequences? For instance, what other programs' quality (such as screening colonoscopy) will decrease to use the prompt endoscopy strategy for all? One practical difficulty in choosing between alternative local programs is that many existing programs or services may not have been evaluated; therefore, the opportunity cost of reducing or removing them is unknown or speculative.

Can I Expect Similar Costs in My Setting?

If costs or consequences differ in your setting, the cost-effectiveness/utility/benefit ratios from the study will not apply. We deal with issues of whether you can anticipate the same consequences of treatment in detail in Chapter 11.1, Applying Results to Individual Patients, and we focus here on costs.

In the Ford et al[1] endoscopy study, the investigators used data from 5 pragmatic clinical trials in which the inclusion and exclusion criteria were sufficiently broad that patients likely reflect the mix of those with dyspepsia in many clinical settings. Further, given that the unit costs are presented, you should be able to judge their applicability to your own setting. Relevant prices that may vary from place to place include drugs and endoscopy (prices for which will be higher in the United States than in other jurisdictions). The authors recognize this and undertake a sensitivity analysis in which the unit cost of endoscopy is reduced from \$450 to \$80, a price more typical of European countries. They found that even in this situation, prompt endoscopy became cost-effective only when the willingness to pay per patient symptom free of dyspepsia at 12 months reached \$40000. An assessment of whether the resource use in this study applies in your own setting is more difficult. The 5 trials were conducted in England, Scotland, Wales, Denmark, and the Netherlands. Patterns of resource use might vary from country to country because of various clinical practice patterns, the availability of resources, the financial incentives faced by health care providers and institutions, and the relative prices of resources (if one item is particularly inexpensive in a given country, it might more often be used). Ford et al[1] recognize the potential for such cross-country differences, but they argue that it is unlikely to be substantial. Reporting similar resource use across the 5 country settings would have bolstered this argument, although this would still leave doubts about applicability to the United States. At the same time, if clinicians were to follow the same management protocols tested in the trials, the result is likely to be similar resource use.

CLINICAL RESOLUTION

The economic analysis of an individual patient data meta-analysis suggests upper gastrointestinal endoscopy is more effective than *H pylori* test and treat in curing dyspepsia symptoms at 1 year but is also more expensive. You decide that the costs and effects found in this article are likely to be applicable to your institution. All committee members agree that $180 000 per patient free of symptoms at 1 year is too expensive for the local hospital to fund (in fact, likely for anybody). This committee finds the practical choice they confront even more compelling: adopting the test-and-treat approach will permit more screening colonoscopies, which studies suggest will provide greater health benefits and superior cost-effectiveness to screening endoscopy.[28]

The committee decides to endorse the *H pylori* test-and-treat service for patients younger than 55 years with dyspepsia in the absence of alarm symptoms. The local hospital agrees to provide funds for ^{13}C-urea breath test kits and analysis so that *H pylori* can be diagnosed noninvasively.

References

1. Ford AC, Qume M, Moayyedi P, et al. *Helicobacter pylori* "test and treat" or endoscopy for managing dyspepsia: an individual patient data meta-analysis. *Gastroenterology.* 2005;128(7):1838-1844.

2. Eisenberg JM. Clinical economics: a guide to the economic analysis of clinical practices. *JAMA.* 1989;262(20):2879-2886.

3. Detsky AS, Naglie IG. A clinician's guide to cost-effectiveness analysis. *Ann Intern Med.* 1990;113(2):147-154.

4. Elixhauser A, Luce BR, Taylor WR, Reblando J. Health care CBA/CEA: an update on the growth and composition of the literature. *Med Care.* 1993;31(7)(suppl):JS1-JS11, JS18-JS149.

5. Ubel P. *Pricing Life: Why It's Time for Health Care Rationing.* Cambridge, MA: MIT Press; 2000.

6. O'Brien B, Levine M, Willan A, et al. Economic evaluation of outpatient treatment with low-molecular-weight heparin for proximal vein thrombosis. *Arch Intern Med.* 1999;159(19):2298-2304.

7. Hillman AL, Bloom BS. Economic effects of prophylactic use of misoprostol to prevent gastric ulcer in patients taking nonsteroidal anti-inflammatory drugs. *Arch Intern Med.* 1989;149(9):2061-2065.

8. Graham DY, Agrawal NM, Roth SH. Prevention of NSAID-induced gastric ulcer with misoprostol: multicentre, double-blind, placebo-controlled trial. *Lancet.* 1988;2(8623):1277-1280.

9. Hill SR, Mitchell AS, Henry DA. Problems with the interpretation of pharmacoeconomic analyses: a review of submissions to the Australian Pharmaceutical Benefits Scheme. *JAMA.* 2000;283(16):2116-2121.

10. Catherwood E, Fitzpatrick WD, Greenberg ML, et al. Cost-effectiveness of cardioversion and antiarrhythmic therapy in nonvalvular atrial fibrillation. *Ann Intern Med.* 1999;130(8):625-636.

11. de Denus S, Sanoski CA, Carlsson J, Opolski G, Spinler SA. Rate vs rhythm control in patients with atrial fibrillation: a meta-analysis. *Arch Intern Med.* 2005;165(3):258-262.

12. Marshall DA, Levy AR, Vidaillet H, et al. Cost-effectiveness of rhythm versus rate control in atrial fibrillation. *Ann Intern Med.* 2004;141(9):653-661.

13. O'Brien B. Economic evaluation of pharmaceuticals: Frankenstein's monster or vampire of trials? *Med Care.* 1996;34(12)(suppl):DS99-DS108.

14. Feldman H, Gauthier S, Hecker J, et al. Economic evaluation of donepezil in moderate to severe Alzheimer disease. *Neurology.* 2004;63(4):644-650.

15. Mihaylova B, Briggs A, Armitage J, Parish S, Gray A, Collins R. Cost-effectiveness of simvastatin in people at different levels of vascular disease risk: economic analysis of a randomised trial in 20,536 individuals. *Lancet.* 2005;365(9473):1779-1785.

16. Boulware LE, Jaar BG, Tarver-Carr ME, Brancati FL, Powe NR. Screening for proteinuria in US adults: a cost-effectiveness analysis. *JAMA.* 2003;290(23):3101-3114.

17. Finkler SA. The distinction between cost and charges. *Ann Intern Med.* 1982;96(1):102-109.

18. Taira DA, Seto TB, Siegrist R, Cosgrove R, Berezin R, Cohen DJ. Comparison of analytic approaches for the economic evaluation of new technologies alongside multicenter clinical trials. *Am Heart J.* 2003;145(3):452-458.

19. Parsonage M, Neuburger H. Discounting and health benefits. *Health Econ.* 1992;1(1):71-76.

20. Cairns J. Discounting and health benefits: another perspective. *Health Econ.* 1992;1(1):76-79.

21. van Hout BA. Discounting costs and effects: a reconsideration. *Health Econ.* 1998;7(7):581-594.

22. Smith DH, Gravelle H. The practice of discounting in economic evaluations of healthcare interventions. *Int J Technol Assess Health Care.* 2001;17(2):236-243.

23. Goeree R, O'Brien BJ, Blackhouse G, Marshall J, Briggs A, Lad R. Cost-effectiveness and cost-utility of long-term management strategies for heartburn. *Value Health.* 2002;5(4):312-328.

24. Briggs A. Handling uncertainty in economic evaluation. In: Drummond M, McGuire A, eds. *Economic Evaluation in Healthcare: Merging Theory With Practice.* Oxford, England: Oxford University Press; 2001:172-214.

25. Johannesson M, Weinstein MC. On the decision rules of cost-effectiveness analysis. *J Health Econ.* 1993;12(4):459-467.

26. Birch S, Gafni A. Changing the problem to fit the solution: Johannesson and Weinstein's (mis)application of economics to real world problems. *J Health Econ.* 1993;12(4):469-476.

27. Drummond M, Torrance G, Mason J. Cost-effectiveness league tables: more harm than good? *Soc Sci Med.* 1993;37(1):33-40.

28. Sonnenberg A, Delco F, Inadomi JM. Cost-effectiveness of colonoscopy in screening for colorectal cancer. *Ann Intern Med.* 2000;133(8):573-584.

22.2

ADVANCED TOPICS IN MOVING
FROM EVIDENCE TO ACTION

DECISION
MAKING AND
THE PATIENT

Victor M. Montori, P. J. Devereaux, Sharon Straus,
Brian Haynes, and Gordon Guyatt

IN THIS CHAPTER:

INTRODUCTION

One of the 2 key principles of *evidence-based medicine* (*EBM*) is that the *evidence* alone is never sufficient to make a clinical decision (see Chapter 2, The Philosophy of Evidence-Based Medicine). Clinicians require expertise in interpreting the patient dilemma (in its clinical, social, and economic contexts) and in identifying the evidence that bears on optimal patient treatment. These considerations, however, are not enough. EBM requires the incorporation of the patient's values and preferences into decision making.

We use values and preferences as an overarching term that includes patients' perspectives, beliefs, expectations, and goals for health and life. We also use this phrase, more precisely, to mean the processes that individuals use in considering the potential benefits, harms, costs, and inconveniences of the management options in relation to one another.

Consideration of values and preferences often enables clinicians to understand the patient who declines lifesaving treatment and the patient who seeks the same lifesaving treatment even after all hope seems lost. Differences in values and preferences may also explain policy decisions and *practice guidelines* that, despite relying on the same evidence, differ. Values and preferences become more crucial when quality of evidence is low and when the balance is close between important benefits and similarly important downsides.

USING THE GUIDE

What Approach to Decision Making With This Patient Should I Use Now?

Table 22.2-1 summarizes decision-making approaches theoretically available to the clinician and patient facing an important decision.

Parental or Paternalistic Approach

When clinicians offer patients minimal information about the options and make the decision without patient input, a style commonly referred as parental or paternalistic, they are not considering patient values and preferences. This does not mean that patients do not have an opportunity to express their wishes, but they may do so in a delayed fashion and through actions. For instance, if the choice was not consistent with their values and preferences, then patients may not act on the decision or may quickly abandon the plan shortly after the visit with the clinician. To the extent that EBM requires the incorporation of patient values and preferences in decision making, a parental approach to clinical decisions is inconsistent with the practice of EBM.

Clinician-as-Perfect-Agent Approach

In theory, one can ensure that decisions are consistent with patient values without actively involving the patient in the decision. To do so, clinicians must assess the values and preferences of the patient and then place these in the context of the evidence about the benefits and risks of alternative courses of action.

TABLE 22.2-1

Decision-Making Approaches

Minimal or no attempt to ensure decision consistent with patient values and preferences

Parental or paternalistic approaches

- Clinician makes minimal effort to establish patient values and preferences, makes decision on behalf of patient

Approaches that attempt to ensure decision consistent with patient values and preferences

Clinician-as-perfect-agent approach

- Clinician ascertains patient's values and preferences, makes decision on behalf of patient

- Informed decision making

- Physician provides patient with the information; patient makes the decision

Shared decision making

- Patient and clinician both bring information/evidence and values and preferences to the decision

Some experts consider this approach, sometimes called the clinician-as-perfect-agent model, impossible to implement.[1] Their position is based on the absence of approaches that would confidently yield a deep understanding of the processes that patients use in considering the potential benefits, harms, costs, and inconveniences of the options in relation to one another.

Other experts offer tools for eliciting patient values and preferences. Along with these tools, they offer models—*decision analysis*—for putting those values in the context of evidence about the outcomes of alternative management strategies (see Chapter 21, How to Use a Patient Management Recommendation). We will return to these tools later in the chapter. These models are limited in that decision psychologists have shown that patients do not consistently follow the underlying assumptions of decision analyses.[2,3] Moreover, there is limited empirical support for the assumptions supporting these tools,[4] and decisions from these analyses may not be the ones rational patients would make even after understanding the issues (Box 22.2-1).

BOX 22.2-1

Do Decision Analyses Predict Patient Preferences?

Heyland et al[b] asked 120 at-risk patients to consider whether they would prefer streptokinase or tissue plasminogen activator (TPA) if they were to have a myocardial infarction. To obtain their informed preference, they used a decision tool that described the outcomes (myocardial infarctions, death, and thrombolytic-associated stroke) and the likelihood of death and stroke when using TPA and streptokinase (ie, TPA use was associated with 9 fewer deaths and 4 more strokes per 1000 patients treated compared with streptokinase) derived from the Global Use of Strategies to Open Occluded Coronary Arteries (GUSTO) trial.[6] The tool worked insofar as all patients chose TPA when the difference in stroke risk was reduced to 0, and all patients chose streptokinase when the difference in mortality risk was reduced to 0. Decision analyses under the expected utility theory assumptions found TPA to be the dominant option. In the study, only half of the patients, however, chose TPA. The other half might have considered the additional 1% mortality benefit TPA afforded to not be worth the 0.33% additional stroke risk and therefore opted for streptokinase.

Informed Decision-Making Approach

In a very different decision-making style, empowered patients may obtain all the information pertinent to the decision, consider the options, and make a decision with minimal clinician input. This approach, often referred to as the informed decision-making style, recognizes that patients and physicians each have their own expertise. Patients are expert in their values and preferences and in their personal context (personal and social enablers and barriers that may affect their adherence to or tolerance of treatment or that may affect the effectiveness of treatment). Clinicians are expert in the technical aspects of the decision (ie, the evidence base informing the pros and cons of each of the options and experience concerning implementation). The clinician's role with such patients is primarily to present information with completeness and clarity.[7]

Shared Decision-Making Approach

In this approach, patients and clinicians engage in a bidirectional exchange. The clinician shares the evidence from clinical research, and the patient shares the evidence accessible in the "patient space" acquired through personal experience, social interaction, and consultation of lay sources, technical references, or the Internet. The bidirectional interaction also includes personal information (ie, sharing the basis for their values and preferences). Both patient and clinician deliberate about the options (ie, patients and clinicians consider the options together, explicitly acknowledging the values and preferences they are using) and together arrive at an agreement about the best course of action. The label offered for this model is the shared decision-making process.[7,8]

Shared decision making requires clinicians to present their own values and preferences that may then influence the decision. Evidence-based practitioners may find this undesirable for 2 reasons. The first one is philosophical: although clinicians may experience consequences of these choices through empathy, by having negative feelings and thoughts about their judgment when patients experience bad outcomes, or by getting sued, it is patients who endure the treatments and bear the burdens of the outcomes of the choices made. The second one is empirical: there is evidence, particularly in preventive care decisions, that values and preference differ systematically between patients and clinicians (Box 22.2-2).

BOX 22.2-2

Do Patients and Their Clinicians Share Similar Values and Preferences?

Devereaux et al[9] used a technique called probability tradeoff (including clear descriptions of the outcomes of interest and iterative testing of preferences with changing likelihood of competing outcomes) to determine the strength of preference for anticoagulation to prevent stroke in 61 at-risk patients and 63 physicians who treated patients with atrial fibrillation. The figure in this box shows the maximum number of excess upper gastrointestinal bleeding episodes per 100 patients treated to prevent 8 additional strokes (4 major and 4 minor) that patients and physicians found acceptable. The figure shows the following: (1) there is variability in stroke aversion among patients and among physicians; (2) patients seem more stroke averse than physicians; (3) physicians seem more averse to adverse outcomes that they "cause" with their prescription (eg, bleeding) than to adverse outcomes that result from clinical course (eg, strokes). If one believes that patient preferences should guide treatment, these data suggest the following: if clinicians fail to incorporate patient values and preferences in the decision-making process, they will recommend against anticoagulation more often than is appropriate and, depending on which physician patients see, they will or will not get the treatment they would prefer.

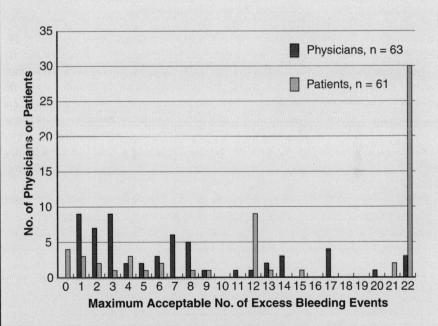

Reprinted from Devereaux et al,[9] with permission from the BMJ Publishing Group.

On the other hand, one might argue that all decision-making approaches incorporate clinician preferences if only to the extent that it is the clinician who decides the range of options that he or she is willing to implement and thus offer to the patient. If one takes this position, then shared decision making has the merit of explicitly considering clinicians' values and preferences rather than doing so implicitly. Furthermore, patients appear to be interested in the physicians' values and preferences. Our guess is that every clinician who has tried to encourage patient autonomy has faced some form of the question, What would you do? Finally, because shared decision making incorporates patient values and preferences into the decision-making process, it responds to patients' desires to be cared for by their clinician.

These considerations suggest that for shared decision making to work well, the power gradient between clinicians and patients needs to decrease substantially. Only a minimal gradient will ensure that informed patients can confidently choose an option inconsistent with the clinician's preferences (indeed, many patients report that physician's opinion was the most important factor driving their decision to undergo an invasive procedure[10]). A reduced power gradient implies that clinicians will act according to informed patients' preferences even when the decisions are not those they would have made for themselves (or what will enhance their income).

Figure 22.2-1 describes our current understanding of decision-making approaches. According to this understanding, clinicians can be aware of clues that patients give during the encounter about their preferences for involvement in a decision at a particular point. All forms of shared decision making, including its extremes of patient and clinician participation, involve clinicians offering patients evidence-based information about the available options.

FIGURE 22.2-1

Decision-Making Approaches and Evidence-Based Medicine

Approaches	Parental	Clinician as Perfect Agent	Shared Decision Making	Informed
Direction and amount of information flow about options	Clinician ▶ Patient	Clinician ▶ Patient	Clinician ◀▶ Patient	Clinician ▶ Patient
Direction of information flow about values and preferences	Clinician ▶ Patient	Clinician ◀ Patient	Clinician ◀▶ Patient	Clinician ◀ Patient
Deliberation	Clinician	Clinician	Clinician, patient	Patient
Decider	Clinician	Clinician	Clinician, patient	Patient
Consistent with EBM principles	No when decision is not purely technical and there are options	Yes	Yes	Yes

Abbreviation: EBM, evidence-based medicine. Modified from Charles et al.[11]

What Decision-Making Approach Should I Choose With This Patient?

Although surveys consistently reflect patients' willingness to receive information relevant to the decision at hand,[12] many patients prefer clinicians to take decisional responsibility.[13,14] Reasons include their intense emotions around the decision, lack of understanding, impaired physical or cognitive function, or lack of self-confidence. More problematic reasons, however, exist: patients may not participate in decision making because clinicians do not communicate information in ways that are accessible to the patient (ie, use of technical language that requires health literacy and numeracy[15]) or because they have no experience or expectation of participating.

These considerations suggest an approach in which clinicians present information about the options and then adapt to the decision approach patients prefer. Further, they suggest the need to exercise a high degree of empathy in determining what approach best accommodates the patient at this time with this decision and the need to remain flexible as the patient's wishes change because participation may change over time (even within the same visit) and with each decision considered.

Given the variation in patient preferences regarding the extent to which they wish to take responsibility for management decisions, an empathic approach within the range of shared decision making offers advantages. The extent to which physicians' values and preferences enter the discussion and the extent to which the physician vs the patient plays the most active role in the final decision-making process can reflect the patient's preferred decision-making approach. Many physicians have the impression that poorer or less-educated patients, particularly those in countries with a lower gross domestic product, are less inclined to participate in decision making. This may be so. It is also possible, however, that if physicians practice optimal information sharing, listening, and empathy, they will find such patients capable of and interested in participating in making decisions about their care.

In summary, EBM practitioners seeking to incorporate patient values and preferences into clinical decisions should be able to effectively communicate to patients the nature of each of the options (an action common to some extent to all approaches to decision making discussed above), empathically identify and enable the maximum extent of participation that the informed patient wants to have in the decision-making process, and identify and explicitly acknowledge when their own values and preferences are affecting the process of arriving at a decision.

What Tools Can I Use in Making Difficult Decisions With This Patient?
Decision Aids

To effectively communicate the nature of the options, researchers have devised and tested tools called *decision aids*. These tools are an alternative to the use of intuitive approaches to communicating concepts of risk and risk reduction that clinicians may have developed through clinical experience. Decision aids present, in a patient-friendly manner, descriptive and probabilistic information about the disease, treatment options, and potential outcomes.[16-18] A well-constructed decision aid is valuable in that someone has performed a *systematic review* of the literature and produced a rigorous summary of the outcomes and their probabilities. Clinicians who doubt that the summary of probabilities is rigorous can review the *primary studies* on which those probabilities are based and, using the principles of this book, determine their accuracy. Furthermore, a well-constructed decision aid offers a pretested and effective way of communicating information to patients who may have little background in quantitative decision making. Most commonly, decision aids use visual props to present the proportion of people who experience the outcomes of importance with and without the intervention (Figure 22.2-2A and B).

What influence do decision aids have on clinical practice? O'Connor et al[17] conducted a systematic review, finding 34 randomized trials that used 30 different decision aids. Compared with usual care, decision aids increased patient participation in decision making (relative risk, 1.4; 95% confidence interval [CI], 1.0-2.3), improved patient knowledge (19/100 points in knowledge surveys; 95% CI, 13-24), and reduced decisional conflict (−9.1/100; 95% CI, −12 to −6). The systematic reviewers concluded that decision aids did not, however, improve satisfaction with the decision-making process and were not associated with better health outcomes.

The effect of decision aids on the final decision has been inconsistent. For example, patients offered decision aids have proved less likely to choose coronary revascularization or mastectomy, yet more likely to accept hepatitis B vaccine.[17] Decision aids have had no effect on the proportion of parents choosing circumcision for their newborn boys, women choosing to undergo amniocentesis, or women electing to begin hormone replacement therapy.[17] One might argue that to the extent that they ensure decisions that are consistent with patients' values and preferences, the effect of decision aids on the final decision (ie, the proportion of patients choosing one alternative) is unimportant. The same proportion may be choosing to have their newborn boys undergo circumcision with or without decision aids, but with decision aids, the decisions are better aligned with patients' underlying values and preferences (ie, more or less equal numbers change decisions they otherwise would have made in opposite directions).

In summary, decision aids increase patient knowledge and decrease discomfort with decision making, as reflected in decisional conflict scores. The importance of the reduction in decisional conflict remains uncertain. Simple decision aids that clinicians can integrate into regular patient care could increase the extent of patient participation in decision making and in turn affect the extent to which informed patients' values truly determine health care decisions.

Tools Related to Decision Analysis

We have briefly discussed the controversy related to the use of decision analysis–based tools to determine patient values and preferences and to the practical (in)feasibility of the physician-as-perfect-agent approach that would require the use of these tools. For clinicians interested in quantitative decision making and who find seeking a qualitative understanding of the patient values and preferences at best vague, tools that characterize and quantify patient values and preferences represent an attractive solution. For others, these tools can assist patients and clinicians in exploring the options and their relative effect on the patient.

These tools were designed to, at minimum, establish the relative value the patient places on the target outcomes. Doing so requires that the patient under-

FIGURE 22.2-2A

Sample Decision Aid Developed to Help Patients With Diabetes Decide Whether to Take a Statin to Reduce Their Coronary Risk

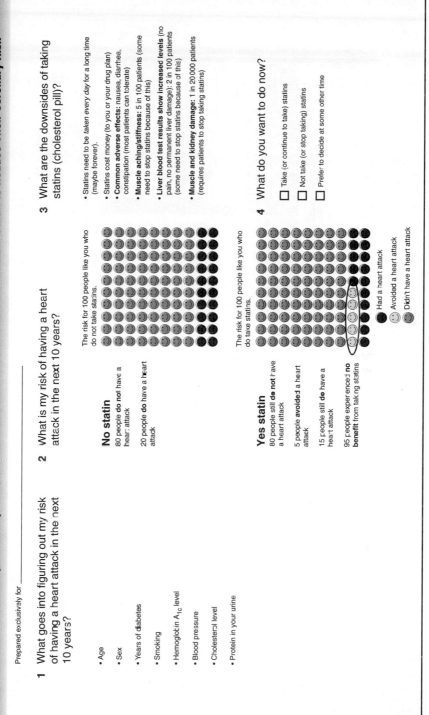

Prepared exclusively for _____

1 What goes into figuring out my risk of having a heart attack in the next 10 years?

- Age
- Sex
- Years of diabetes
- Smoking
- Hemoglobin A_{1c} level
- Blood pressure
- Cholesterol level
- Protein in your urine

2 What is my risk of having a heart attack in the next 10 years?

The risk for 100 people like you who do not take statins.

No statin

80 people **do not** have a heart attack

20 people **do** have a heart attack

The risk for 100 people like you who do take statins.

Yes statin

80 people still **do not** have a heart attack

5 people **avoided** a heart attack

15 people still **do** have a heart attack

95 people experienced **no benefit** from taking statins

● Had a heart attack
☺ Avoided a heart attack
☺ Didn't have a heart attack

3 What are the downsides of taking statins (cholesterol pill)?

- Statins need to be _taken every day_ for a long time (maybe forever).
- Statins cost money (to you or your drug plan)
- **Common adverse effects:** nausea, diarrhea, constipation (most patients can tolerate)
- **Muscle aching/stiffness:** 5 in 100 patients (some need to stop statins because of this)
- **Liver blood test results show increased levels** (no pain, no permanent liver damage): 2 in 100 patients (some need to stop statins because of this)
- **Muscle and kidney damage:** 1 in 20 000 patients (requires patients to stop taking statins)

4 What do you want to do now?

☐ Take (or continue to take) statins

☐ Not take (or stop taking) statins

☐ Prefer to decide at some other time

FIGURE 22.2-2B

Sample Decision Aid Developed to Help Patients With Tennis Elbow Decide Whether to Take a Steroid Injection

Step 1: Be clear about the choice
What are the options?

Should you have a steroid injection for tennis elbow?

When does this choice have to be made? Check ☑ one

☐ Within days ☐ Within weeks ☐ Within months

How far along are you with a choice? Check ☑ one

☐ You have not thought about it yet ☐ You are thinking about the choices
☐ You are close to making a choice ☐ You have made a choice

Step 2: Think about the pros and cons of the options

What does the research show?
Blocks of 100 faces show the "best guess" for what happens to 100 people with tennis elbow 6 weeks after a steroid injection. Each face ☺ stands for 1 person.

🎗 No Treatment	🎗 With a Steroid Injection

24 people may improve on the whole

76 people may not improve at all

92 people may improve overall (68 more people than with no treatment)

8 people may not improve at all

Ribbons show the strength of results from research studies

🎗 Platinum: **Research results from a well-done review of 2 or more randomized controlled studies.** Each study was well done and had at least 100 people in it.

🎗 Gold: **Research results from at least 1 well-done randomized controlled study** that had at least 100 people in the study.

🎗 Silver: **Research results from studies that were not as strong.** There may have been too few people in the study or the study was not well done.

🎗 Bronze: **Expert views and experiences,** or cases of what happened to someone taking a treatment.

What do you think of the pros and cons?

What do you think of the pros and cons of steroid injections?
The information below is from a review of 13 studies that tested steroid injections in people with tennis elbow. The studies lasted up to 4 years.

1. Review the common pros and cons.
2. Add any other pros and cons that matter to you.
3. Show how much each pro and con matters to you. Circle one (*) star if it matters a little to you and up to five (*****) stars if it matters a lot to you.

Pros and Cons of Steroids and Immunosuppressive Agents

Pros	How Much Does It Matter To You?	Cons	How Much Does It Matter To You?
Pain and overall well-being may improve in the short term (up to 6 weeks after injection)	*****	Pain may go away on its own	*****
Quicker relief compared with waiting	*****	Improved pain and overall well-being may not last long	*****
Avoid the risk of major stomach adverse affects if NSAIDs are not taken	*****	Short-term adverse effects: social flushing, pain, and hardening of the skin where injection occurred	*****
		Personal cost of medicine:	*****
Other pros:	*****	Other cons:	*****

What do you think about taking steroid injections? Check ☑ one

☐	☐	☐
You are willing to take this treatment Pros matter more to you than the cons	Unsure	You are not willing to take this treatment Cons matter more to you than the pros

Step 3: What role do you want to have in choosing your treatment? Check ☑ one

☐ You prefer to choose on your own after listening to the opinions of others.

☐ You prefer to share the choice with: _____

☐ You prefer someone else to choose for you, namely: _____

Abbreviation: NSAID, non-steroidal anti-inflammatory drug.

Excerpt from an Ottawa Decision Aid, http://decisionaid.ohri.ca/docs/Rheumatology/TennisElb_Steroid.pdf.

stand the nature of the outcomes. How, for instance, would the patient imagine living with a stroke or the experience of having a gastrointestinal bleeding episode? Patients may find a written description of the health states (such as the description of a mild and a severe stroke and a gastrointestinal bleeding episode in Box 22.2-3) useful in the process of describing their preferences.

BOX 22.2-3

Sample Descriptions of Mild Stroke, Severe Stroke, and Gastrointestinal Bleeding

Mild Stroke

Having a mild stroke causes you to slur your words. After a mild stroke, you are able to fully understand what is being said to you. Your thoughts remain clear and you can carry out a conversation without much trouble, but sometimes you cannot find the right word to use. Your thinking ability is otherwise normal. There is some weakness and numbness in your right arm and your face has a slight droop. You are able to feed, dress, and bathe yourself. However, you cannot grip objects as tightly as you could before the stroke, objects sometimes fall from your hands, and you have difficulty writing. Your condition will not get better.

Severe Stroke

After having a severe stroke, your speech is impaired, to the extent that others cannot understand your words. You can understand simple communication but have great difficulty with more complex communication. You are not confused, but your thinking is impaired to the point that you are unable to attend to your financial matters and you cannot work. You can feed and dress yourself, but you need assistance to bathe. Your right arm and right leg are weak. You can walk with the aid of a cane. Your condition will not get better.

Gastrointestinal Bleeding

You are vomiting bright-red blood, and there is blood in your stool, which is black. You experience dizziness and are feeling unwell enough to go to the emergency department. You feel as if you are going to die. You are admitted to the hospital, where the physicians insert a tube into your stomach. You require an urgent operation, followed by several blood transfusions. You are hospitalized for 10 days. You will need to take medication for the next 6 months to prevent further bleeding and to raise your blood count after the bleeding. Your blood will be checked monthly. You feel extremely tired to the point of exhaustion. Your energy will gradually improve until, at 4 months after discharge from hospital, you will be back to normal.

Having made their best effort to ensure that patients understand the outcomes, clinicians can choose from among a number of ways of obtaining patients' values for those outcomes. They can invite patients to directly compare outcomes. For instance, with only 2 outcomes, the patient can make a direct comparative rating. The questions may be, How much worse would it be to have a stroke vs a gastrointestinal bleeding episode? Would it be equally bad? Twice as bad to have a stroke? Three times as bad?

Using a somewhat more complex strategy, the clinician can ask the patient to place a mark on a visual analogue scale or feeling thermometer (Figure 22.2-3), in which the extremes are anchored at death and full health, to represent how the patient feels about the health states in question. When, as in the case of a gastrointestinal bleeding episode and a stroke, some health states are temporary and others are permanent, the clinician must ensure that patients incorporate the duration of the health state in their rating.

More sophisticated approaches include the time tradeoff and the standard gamble,[19] but these approaches, although theoretically superior, have inferior measurement properties to the feeling thermometer.[20-22]

Regardless of the strategy clinicians use to quantify patient values, they must somehow integrate these values with the likely outcomes of the alternative management strategies. Under certain assumptions, formal decision analysis provides the most rigorous method for making this integration (see Chapter 19, Summarizing the Evidence). A simplified and synthetic version of a decision analytic tree is the likelihood of being helped vs harmed.[23] The clinician begins by calculating the *number needed to treat* and *number needed to harm* for the average patients in the study or studies from which the data about treatment effectiveness and harm come (see Chapter 7, Does Treatment Lower Risk? Understanding the Results). The clinician then adjusts the average number needed to treat and number needed to harm for the individual patient according to that patient's likelihood of experiencing the target event that treatment is intended to prevent and the risks it may precipitate, relative to the average patient. Having established the relative likelihood of help vs harm, the clinician explores the patient's values about the severity of adverse events that might be caused by the treatment relative to the severity of the target event that treatment helps prevent. The final adjustment of the likelihood of being helped vs harmed incorporates the patient's values.

Given the limitations of valuation tools and decision analytic models in the context of individual patient decision making, the true virtue of tools that elicit values and preferences may not be to enable the clinician to capture patients' values and preferences to incorporate in a formal decision analysis. Rather, their value may be to help patients further understand the nature of the decision and help the physician gain insight into patient values and preferences. The true virtue of decision models in the context of individual decision making may not be to crank through the numbers to generate a final decision. Rather, their value may be in helping clinicians and patients understand all the choices available, the ramifications of those choices, and what factors may have the most influence on the decision.

FIGURE 22.2-3

Visual Analogue Scale as a "Feeling Thermometer"

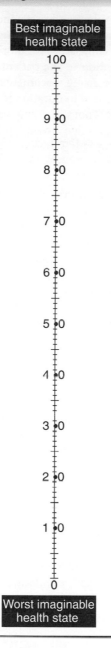

Should I Use More Time and Effort in Decision Making With This Patient Now?

Time as a Barrier

Should clinicians interested in practicing EBM and expecting to make clinical decisions that incorporate the values and preferences of the informed patient use one or more of the above approaches for all decisions? The ultimate constraint of clinical practice is time. Many clinicians have more to do in each encounter than they did in the past.[24-26] Attention to the patient's agenda competes with other activities that clinicians ought to do (eg, documentation, routine preventive care[27]) during visits that have not increased in duration to accommodate these additional activities and demands. Thus, it is not surprising that clinicians frequently cite time as a key barrier to patient education about options and to enhanced patient participation in decision making.[28-32] Table 22.2-2 provides some suggestions for what to do when time is limited.

Important vs Unimportant Decisions

Many of the decisions that patients face are not crucial. Even if the patient-clinician team makes the wrong choice (ie, they do not make the choice that would result from a full discussion), the adverse consequences are minimal, or at least limited. Rather than devoting time to these situations, busy clinicians may choose to focus their efforts to ensure that decisions are consistent with patients' values and preferences for choices associated with the most important consequences.

What may be unimportant for one patient, however, may be critical for another. Consider a farmer with an irritating but benign lesion on his hand and the rapidity with which the dermatologist would decide to freeze the lesion after obtaining patient consent. Now consider how the same dermatologist would consider treatment approaches for a similar skin lesion, this time in a woman working as a hand model. The dermatologist will have to engage in much more than a cursory consent procedure to care for this patient who is likely to place a much greater value on avoiding a visible scar than on avoiding costly cosmetic procedures compared with almost all other patients with the same lesion.

TABLE 22.2-2

Solutions to the Time Problem

Make time for discussion of key decisions
- Reserve special follow-up appointments for discussion

Restrict time-consuming approaches to key decisions

Reserve time-consuming approaches for important problems

Reserve time-consuming approaches for difficult decisions

Get help
- If possible, refer patient to colleagues with time and expertise for decision-making discussions

Use decision aid

Straightforward vs Difficult Decisions

When the decision is straightforward (ie, there is an option that almost all informed patients would choose because it is highly effective in achieving patient-important outcomes, easy to administer, inexpensive, and safe), decision making can be expeditious. This is the case for aspirin use in a patient in the emergency department who has an acute coronary syndrome. Under these circumstances, a single sentence explaining the rationale and plan can suffice.

In other situations, the benefits and downsides of an intervention are more closely balanced. For instance, clinicians should have a discussion with patients at moderate or low risk of coronary events considering using low-dose aspirin daily. The case for a detailed discussion about long-term aspirin prophylaxis becomes progressively stronger as the patient's risk decreases.

These 2 situations—a clear decision that virtually all informed patients would endorse vs a close call—should correspond to strong and weak recommendations that guideline panels offer (see Chapter 22.4, Grading Recommendations). If guideline panels function appropriately, clinicians can interpret a strong recommendation as "just do it" and a weak recommendation as an invitation to engage patients in shared decision making. Sometimes clinicians and patients need to spend more time making decisions that, when initially considered, appear straightforward. These decisions, however, require patients to revisit and reaffirm them over time. This is the case for lifestyle and pharmacologic treatments for chronic conditions. Patients who have decided to use these treatments may need to reevaluate their decision every time they learn about or experience a potential adverse effect, renew the prescription and pay for it, or learn about an alternative solution. Perhaps additional time and resources spent exploring these decisions during the encounter will help patients to remember why they started using these interventions in the first place and enhance their adherence to these treatments (this was the motivation behind the decision aid about statin use in patients with diabetes described in Figure 22.2-2).

Misinformed Participants

Clinicians may have a distorted perception of the evidence. Distortions can be the result of misleading marketing messages that reach clinicians informally through colleagues or formally through industry-funded continuing medical education and office detailing. Misleading presentations of research findings in primary reports of research can also distort clinicians' understanding of the evidence (see Chapter 11.3, Dealing With Misleading Presentations of Clinical Trial Results). Panels that develop guidelines may include experts whose preferences are biased in favor of the interests of their source for research funding, honoraria, and other enticements. This is particularly problematic when adherence to guidelines becomes linked to monetary incentives (ie, pay-for-performance programs). Patients may perceive something amiss when clinicians make treatment recommendations that are too expensive, too invasive, or too new. Such patients, if unable to participate fully, may forgo these treatments after the visit, lose trust in the physician, or seek attention elsewhere.

Misinformation may also affect the patients. Distorted messages reach patients through advertisements in traditional media, lay medical or health publications, social networks, and the Internet. Patients convinced of what they see in print may feel empowered to request a prescription from their clinician for interventions that they do not need or would not want if they were adequately informed. Given time and skill constraints, patients who seek attention knowing what they want may leave physician offices with their wishes satisfied, whereas physicians are left feeling uncomfortable about the course of action chosen.[33]

Thus, physicians should spend more time considering decisions for which they suspect they and their patients have a distorted knowledge base. Strategies to calibrate the physicians' knowledge base may include the review of the evidence that supports claims of effectiveness and strong recommendations from practice guidelines using the skills taught in this book. Strategies to calibrate patients' knowledge are less clear but may include involving the patient in such evidence reviews. An alternative approach is, when they are available, to use evidence-based decision aids.

Administrative Solutions

Clinicians could consider delaying making a decision for another visit, designated for that specific purpose. This assumes that clinicians want to allot this time in their schedule for these additional focused visits.

Get Help

Another option is to refer the patient to a specialist colleague with time and expertise in shared decision making. In some centers, decision coaches (often nurses or other health care professionals) provide detailed exploration of important decisions.[34]

Use a Decision Aid

Patients considering important decisions may benefit from educational material that they can take home and review with family, friends, and advisors. They could then return with questions and potentially with their final decision. There are more than 300 such decision aids in the Cochrane Inventory found at the Cochrane Decision Aid Registry (http://decisionaid.ohri.ca/cochinvent.php). This inventory, kept by investigators at the Ottawa Health Decision Centre, describes the decision aid and its purpose and offers contact information about each tool's developer and availability. Almost 80% of these tools have not been evaluated clinically. Despite that almost 80% are reportedly available on the Internet, their dissemination and uptake in practice remain limited.

CONCLUSION

EBM highlights the extent to which medical decisions reflect underlying values and preferences (see Chapter 2, The Philosophy of Evidence-Based Medicine).

It follows that choices should be those that fully informed patients would make. Achieving that goal represents a major challenge and a fruitful area for clinical research. Clinicians should be aware of the different approaches to clinical decision making and the need to tailor the approach to the individual patient. They should understand how evidence and values and preferences fit together in the decision-making process. For now, clinicians should use the limited evidence available and consider the advice of experts who have given thought to these issues in finding the approaches that are right for them and for their patients.

References

1. Gafni A, Charles C, Whelan T. The physician-patient encounter: the physician as a perfect agent for the patient versus the informed treatment decision-making model. *Soc Sci Med.* 1998;47(3):347-354.

2. Gafni A. When does a competent patient make an irrational choice? *N Engl J Med.* 1990;323:1354.

3. Kahneman D, Tversky A. Prospect theory: an analysis of decisions under risk. *Econometrica.* 1979;47(2):263-292.

4. Gafni A, Birch S. Preferences for outcomes in economic evaluation: an economic approach to addressing economic problems. *Soc Sci Med.* 1995;40(6):767-776.

5. Heyland DK, Gafni A, Levine MA. Do potential patients prefer tissue plasminogen activator (TPA) over streptokinase (SK)? an evaluation of the risks and benefits of TPA from the patient's perspective. *J Clin Epidemiol.* 2000;53(9):888-894.

6. GUSTO Investigators. An international randomized trial comparing four thrombolytic strategies for acute myocardial infarction. *N Engl J Med.* 1993;329 (10):673-682.

7. Decision-making in the physician-patient encounter: revisiting the shared treatment decision-making model. *Soc Sci Med.* 1999;49(5):651-661.

8. Charles C, Gafni A, Whelan T. Shared decision-making in the medical encounter: what does it mean? (or it takes at least two to tango). *Soc Sci Med.* 1997;44 (5):681-692.

9. Devereaux PJ, Anderson DR, Gardner MJ, et al. Differences between perspectives of physicians and patients on anticoagulation in patients with atrial fibrillation: observational study. *BMJ.* 2001;323(7323):1218-1222.

10. Mazur DJ, Hickam DH, Mazur MD. The role of doctor's opinion in shared decision making: what does shared decision making really mean when considering invasive medical procedures? *Health Expect.* 2005;8(2):97-102.

11. Charles C, Whelan T, Gafni A. What do we mean by partnership in making decisions about treatment? *BMJ.* 1999;319(7212):780-782.

12. Gaston CM, Mitchell G. Information giving and decision-making in patients with advanced cancer: a systematic review. *Soc Sci Med.* 2005;61(10):2252-2264.

13. Levinson W, Kao A, Kuby A, Thisted RA. Not all patients want to participate in decision making: a national study of public preferences. *J Gen Intern Med.* 2005;20(6):531-535.

14. Beaver K, Bogg J, Luker KA. Decision-making role preferences and information needs: a comparison of colorectal and breast cancer. *Health Expect.* 1999;2(4):266-276.

15. Montori V, Rothman R. Weakness in numbers: the challenge of numeracy in health care. *J Gen Intern Med.* 2005;20(11):1071-1072.

16. Whelan T, Gafni A, Charles C, Levine M. Lessons learned from the decision board: a unique and evolving decision aid. *Health Expect.* 2000;3(1):69-76.

17. O'Connor AM, Stacey D, Entwistle V, et al. Decision aids for people facing health treatment or screening decisions. *Cochrane Database Syst Rev.* 2003;(2):CD001431.

18. Charles C, Gafni A, Whelan T, O'Brien MA. Treatment decision aids: conceptual issues and future directions. *Health Expect.* 2005;8(2):114-125.

19. Torrance GW. Measurement of health state utilities for economic appraisal. *J Health Econ.* 1986;5(1):1-30.

20. Puhan MA, Guyatt GH, Montori VM, et al. The standard gamble demonstrated lower reliability than the feeling thermometer. *J Clin Epidemiol.* 2005;58(5):458-465.

21. Schunemann HJ, Armstrong D, Degl'innocenti A, et al. A randomized multicenter trial to evaluate simple utility elicitation techniques in patients with gastroesophageal reflux disease. *Med Care.* 2004;42(11):1132-1142.

22. Schunemann HJ, Griffith L, Stubbing D, Goldstein R, Guyatt GH. A clinical trial to evaluate the measurement properties of 2 direct preference instruments administered with and without hypothetical marker states. *Med Decis Making.* 2003;23(2):140-149.

23. Straus SE. Individualizing treatment decisions: the likelihood of being helped or harmed. *Eval Health Prof.* 2002;25(2):210-224.

24. Zuger A. Dissatisfaction with medical practice. *N Engl J Med.* 2004;350(1):69-75.

25. Yarnall KS, Pollak KI, Ostbye T, Krause KM, Michener JL. Primary care: is there enough time for prevention? *Am J Public Health.* 2003;93(4):635-641.

26. Mechanic D, McAlpine DD, Rosenthal M. Are patients' office visits with physicians getting shorter? *N Engl J Med.* 2001;344(3):198-204.

27. Getz L, Sigurdsson JA, Hetlevik I. Is opportunistic disease prevention in the consultation ethically justifiable? *BMJ.* 2003;327(7413):498-500.

28. Kaplan SH, Gandek B, Greenfield S, Rogers W, Ware JE. Patient and visit characteristics related to physicians' participatory decision-making style: results from the Medical Outcomes Study. *Med Care.* 1995;33(12):1176-1187.

29. Gotler RS, Flocke SA, Goodwin MA, Zyzanski SJ, Murray TH, Stange KC. Facilitating participatory decision-making: what happens in real-world community practice? *Med Care.* 2000;38(12):1200-1209.

30. Edwards A, Elwyn G, Hood K, et al. Patient-based outcome results from a cluster randomized trial of shared decision making skill development and use of risk communication aids in general practice. *Fam Pract.* 2004;21(4):347-354.

31. Charles C, Gafni A, Whelan T. Self-reported use of shared decision-making among breast cancer specialists and perceived barriers and facilitators to implementing this approach. *Health Expect.* 2004;7(4):338-348.

32. Edwards A, Elwyn G, Wood F, Atwell C, Prior L, Houston H. Shared decision making and risk communication in practice: a qualitative study of GPs' experiences. *Br J Gen Pract.* 2005;55(510):6-13.

33. Mintzes B, Barer ML, Kravitz RL, et al. Influence of direct to consumer pharmaceutical advertising and patients' requests on prescribing decisions: two site cross sectional survey. *BMJ.* 2002;324(7332):278-279.

34. Woolf SH, Chan EC, Harris R, et al. Promoting informed choice: transforming health care to dispense knowledge for decision making. *Ann Intern Med.* 2005; 143(4):293-300.

MOVING FROM EVIDENCE TO ACTION: RECOMMENDATIONS ABOUT SCREENING

Alexandra Barratt, Les Irwig, Paul Glasziou,
Robert Cumming, Angela Raffle, Nicholas Hicks,
J. A. Muir Gray, and Gordon Guyatt

IN THIS CHAPTER:

Clinical Scenario

Should a 47-Year-Old Couple Undergo Colon Cancer Screening?

Finding the Evidence

Consequences of Screening

Are the Recommendations Valid?

Is There Randomized Trial Evidence That the Intervention Benefits People With Asymptomatic Disease?

Study Designs for Randomized Trials of Screening

Were the Data Identified, Selected, and Combined in an Unbiased Fashion?

What Are the Recommendations and Will They Help You in Caring for Patients?

What Are the Benefits?

What Are the Harms?

How Do Benefits and Harms Compare in Different People and With Different Screening Strategies?

What Is the Effect of Values and Preferences?

What Is the Effect of Uncertainty Associated With the Evidence?

What Is the Cost-effectiveness?

Clinical Resolution

CLINICAL SCENARIO

Should a 47-Year-Old Couple Undergo Colon Cancer Screening?

You are a primary care physician treating a 47-year-old woman and her husband of the same age. They are concerned because a friend of theirs recently received news she had colon cancer and has urged them both to undergo screening with fecal occult blood tests (FOBTs) because, she says, prevention is much better than the cure she is now undergoing.

Neither of these patients has a family history of colon cancer or a change in bowel habit. They ask whether you agree that they should be screened. You know that trials of FOBT screening have demonstrated that screening can reduce mortality from colorectal cancer (CRC), but you also recall that FOBTs can have a high false-positive rate, which then necessitates investigation by colonoscopy. You are unsure whether screening these relatively young, asymptomatic people with no risk factors for colon cancer is likely to do more good than harm. You decide to check the literature to see whether there are any guidelines or recommendations about screening for CRC that might help you respond to their question.

FINDING THE EVIDENCE

You log on and use PubMed to search MEDLINE using the terms "colorectal neoplasms AND mass screening" and limit your search to practice guidelines and English language. Your search retrieves 36 citations, including 2 recent citations that look especially promising. These are clinical guidelines by the US Preventive Services Taskforce (USPSTF)[1] and the American Gastroenterological Association

(AGA).[2] Both are available online. You obtain the full version of the USPSTF guideline, including the *systematic review* on which the recommendations are based, from their Web site,[3] in addition to the AGA guideline. A quick scan of these articles reveals that the USPSTF guideline has more about the adverse effects of screening that is of particular interest, so you first look at these guidelines.

CONSEQUENCES OF SCREENING

The best way to think about screening is as a therapeutic intervention. Doing so immediately clarifies the *evidence* required to support a policy of screening: randomized trials examining the effect of screening vs no screening on patient-important outcomes.[4-6] In this chapter, we probe specific issues introduced in Chapter 21, How to Use a Patient Management Recommendation, focusing on those that are specific to screening (Table 22.3-1).

Table 22.3-2 presents the possible consequences of screening. Some people will have true-positive results with clinically important disease (cell a); some of this group—the proportion depending on the effectiveness of treatment and the severity of the detected disease—will benefit from screening. For instance, children found on screening to have phenylketonuria will experience large, long-lasting benefits because there is effective treatment for asymptomatic disease, and it is better than waiting and treating the disease once symptoms develop. If no effective treatment for asymptomatic disease is available or knowing about the disease does not otherwise provide benefit, screening is not sensible.

Other people will have true-positive results, but their disease will be clinically irrelevant (overdetection) (cell b). These people meet pathologic criteria, but their

TABLE 22.3-1

Users' Guides for Recommendations About Screening

Are the recommendations valid?

Is there randomized trial evidence that the intervention benefits people with asymptomatic disease?

Were the data identified, selected, and combined in an unbiased fashion?

What are the recommendations and will they help you in caring for patients?

What are the benefits?

What are the harms?

How do benefits and harms compare in different people and with different screening strategies?

What is the effect of individuals' values and preferences?

What is the effect of uncertainty associated with the evidence?

What is the cost-effectiveness?

TABLE 22.3-2

Summary of Benefits and Harms of Screening by Underlying Disease State

Screening	Reference Standard Results		
Test Result	Disease or Risk Factor Present		Disease or Risk Factor Absent
Positive	True positives[a]	"True" positives (clinically irrelevant disease)[b]	False positives[c]
Negative	False negatives[d]	"False" negatives (clinically irrelevant disease)[e]	True negatives[f]

[a]Disease or risk factor that will cause symptoms in the future.
[b]Disease or risk factor asymptomatic until death (clinically irrelevant disease).
[c]False-positive results.
[d]Missed disease that will be symptomatic in the future.
[e]Missed disease that will be clinically irrelevant in the future.
[f]True-negative results.

Sensitivity = a + b / a + b + d + e; specificity = f / c + f.

disease is destined not to become clinically relevant within their lifetime. Consider, for instance, a man in whom screening reveals low-grade prostate cancer but who dies some years later from coronary artery disease before his prostate cancer becomes clinically manifest. This man has had to cope with a cancer diagnosis and may have had treatment and adverse effects from that treatment. Thus, these individuals may experience labeling, investigation, and treatment for a disease or *risk factor* that, without screening, would not have affected their lives.

Overdetection and overtreatment may turn out to be the most important downside of screening for some conditions. For example, approximately 50% of the prostate cancers found by screening in men aged 50-70 would have remained clinically silent in the men's lifetimes.[7] In breast cancer screening, detection of some, perhaps even the majority, of ductal carcinoma in situ (DCIS) may be overdetection[8]; estimates of the extent of overdetection of invasive breast cancer range widely from 2% to 30%.[9-11]

People with *false positive* results (cell c) may be adversely affected by the *risks* associated with investigation of the screen-detected abnormality, such as the complications of colonoscopy after a positive FOBT result. People with *false negative* results of clinically important disease (cell d) may experience *harm* if false reassurance results in delayed presentation or investigation of symptoms. Screened patients may feel emotional distress and anger if they discover they have disease despite having negative screening test results.

By contrast, patients with false-negative results with clinically irrelevant disease (cell e) are not harmed by their disease being missed because it was never destined to affect them. Patients with *true negative* results (cell f) may experience benefit associated with an accurate reassurance of being disease free, but they may also experience inconvenience, cost, and anxiety.

The longer the gap between possible detection and patient-important consequences, the greater the number of people who may experience overdetection (cell b). When screening for risk factors (such as high blood pressure or elevated cholesterol level), one must screen and treat very large numbers of people to prevent 1 adverse event years later.[12]

ARE THE RECOMMENDATIONS VALID?

Is There Randomized Trial Evidence That the Intervention Benefits People With Asymptomatic Disease?

Guidelines recommending screening are on strong ground if they are based on *randomized controlled trials* (*RCTs*) in which screening is compared with conventional care. In the past, many screening programs, some of them effective (such as cervical cancer screening and screening for phenylketonuria), have been implemented on the strength of observational data. When the benefits are enormous and the downsides are minimal, there is no need for randomized trials. More often, however, the benefits and risks from screening are finely balanced, and *observational studies* of screening may be misleading.

There are a number of reasons observational studies may be misleading. Survival, as measured from the time of diagnosis, may be increased not because patients live longer but because screening lengthens the time that they know they have disease (lead time *bias*). Patients whose disease is discovered by screening also may appear to do better or live longer than people whose disease presents clinically with symptoms because screening tends to detect disease that is destined to progress slowly and which therefore has a good prognosis (length time bias). Length time bias occurs when rapidly progressing disease becomes symptomatic before the next scheduled screening test and so is not detected by screening, whereas slowly progressing disease is still asymptomatic and detectable by screening at the next screening round. This adds an additional bias to studies that compare the prognosis in tumors detected by screening to those not detected by screening. These considerations dictate performing randomized trial assessment of the therapy that patients will receive before implementation of screening programs.

Study Designs for Randomized Trials of Screening

Investigators may choose one of 2 study designs to test the effect of screening. Investigators may assess the entire screening process (early detection and early intervention; see Figure 22.3-1), in which case they randomize people to be screened and treated if early abnormality is detected or not screened (and treated only if symptomatic disease occurs). Trials of mammographic screening have used this design.[13]

Alternatively, all participants may undergo screening, and those with positive results are randomized to be treated or not treated (Figure 22.3-1). If those who receive treatment do get better, then one can conclude that early treatment has provided

FIGURE 22.3-1

Designs for Randomized Controlled Trials of Screening

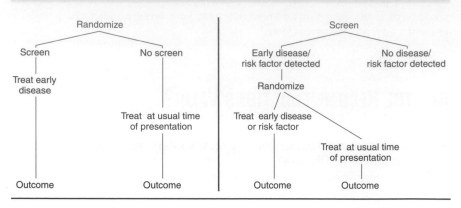

Reproduced from Barratt et al,[4] with permission from *JAMA*.

benefit. Investigators usually use this study design when screening detects not the disease itself but factors that increase the risk of disease. Tests of screening programs for hypertension and high cholesterol level have used this design.[14] The principles outlined in this chapter apply to both of the study designs (Figure 22.3-1) used in addressing screening issues.

Regardless of which design investigators use, a successful outcome of screening depends on optimal, or at least appropriate, application of testing and treatment that follows a positive screening test result.

Were the Data Identified, Selected, and Combined in an Unbiased Fashion?

As is true for all guidelines, developers must specify the inclusion criteria and exclusion criteria for the studies they choose to consider, conduct a comprehensive search, and assess the methodologic quality of the studies they include.

USING THE GUIDES

Both guides consider CRC screening using a range of tests, including FOBT. The USPSTF provides details of the search strategies used, inclusion and exclusion criteria, studies found, and the quality of evidence each study provides. The AGA guideline updates an earlier guideline and gives limited information about its *review* process. Three randomized trials of screening using FOBT were identified by both guides, providing high-quality-level evidence of clinically and statistically significant reductions in the risk of death from CRC. Both also include evidence from a range of other studies addressing issues of test accuracy and, in the guideline by the USPSTF, adverse effects of screening. The AGA guideline also provides recommendations for screening people with a familial or inherited risk of CRC.

What Are the Recommendations and Will They Help You in Caring for Patients?

Recommendations about a screening program should include evidence about benefits and risks; for example, in a "balance sheet."[15] Ideally, they should also provide information about how these benefits and risks can vary in subgroups of the population and under different screening strategies.

What Are the Benefits?

What outcomes must investigators measure to estimate the benefits of a screening program? If treatment is effective, some of those who test positive will experience a reduction in mortality or an increase in quality of life. One can estimate the benefit as an absolute risk reduction or a *relative risk reduction* (*RRR*) in adverse outcomes (see Chapter 7, Does Treatment Lower Risk? Understanding the Results). The *number of people needed to screen* (*NNS*) to prevent an adverse outcome provides another way of presenting benefit (see Chapter 7, Does Treatment Lower Risk? Understanding the Results). When the benefit is a reduction in mortality, we would like to see a reduction in both disease-specific and total mortality (ie, mortality from any and all possible causes). Because the target condition is typically only one of many causes of death, however, even important reductions in disease-specific mortality are unlikely to result in statistically significant reductions in total mortality. In some conditions for which mortality is high, it may be reasonable to expect a reduction in total mortality, as well as in disease-specific mortality. For the most part, however, we will have to be satisfied with demonstrated reductions in disease-specific mortality only, although it is reassuring if investigators present data showing no increase in total mortality.

In addition to prevention of adverse outcomes, people may also regard knowledge of the presence of an abnormality as a benefit, as in antenatal screening for Down syndrome. Another potential benefit of screening comes from the reassurance afforded by a negative test result if a person is experiencing anxiety because a family member or friend has developed the target condition or from discussion in the popular media. However, a test can increase rather than decrease a person's self-perception as being at risk. In instances in which anxiety is a result of the publicity surrounding the screening program itself, we would not view anxiety reduction as a benefit.

The USPSTF reports results from the 3 randomized trials of FOBT screening that have published outcome results. All used Hemoccult tests (Beckman Coulter, Fullerton, CA). Two European trials (1 in England and 1 in Denmark) provided biennial screening and reported RRRs of 15% and 18%, respectively.[16,17] The third trial (in Minnesota) evaluated annual and biennial screening and found RRRs of 33% and 21%, respectively, for these strategies.[18,19] A meta-analysis by Towler et al[20] (cited by the USPSTF) provides a pooled RRR of 23% from biennial screening; this estimate is adjusted for compliance, so it provides an estimate of the effect among people who actually attend for screening regularly.

What Are the Harms?

Among those who test positive, adverse consequences may include

- complications arising from investigation (screening test);
- adverse effects of treatment;
- unnecessary (over-)treatment of persons having true-positive results (clinically irrelevant disease, overdetection);
- adverse effects of labeling and early diagnosis;
- anxiety generated by the investigations and treatment; and
- costs and inconvenience incurred during investigations and treatment.

The USPSTF review observed that test accuracy data are conventionally reported for a test at a single point, whereas for a screening program, cumulative test-positive data over time are more relevant. The colonoscopy rate was about 5% in the European trials during 8 to 10 years but much higher (38% for annual screening and 28% for biennial screening) in the Minnesota trial. The Minnesota study primarily used rehydrated tests that increase the sensitivity but also increase the false-positive rate. As a result, the AGA guideline recommends using unhydrated tests, whereas the USPSTF just states the tradeoff.

For the European trials, which used unrehydrated tests in biennial screening, the false-positive rate was about 2% in the initial screening round and about 1% in subsequent rounds. Because the target condition is relatively rare (and the pretest probability is low), many of the positive results will be false positives. Of those who tested positive, only 2.2% in the Minnesota trial and 8% to 18% in the 2 European studies proved to have CRC.

Adverse effects of colonoscopy are one of the main risks of CRC screening. Data from the UK trial showed that 7 (0.5%) of 1474 people undergoing colonoscopy experienced a major complication (5 perforations, 1 hemorrhage, and 1 snare entrapment; 6 of 7 people required surgical intervention).[21] More recently, results of the first round of a demonstration pilot of screening for CRC in the United Kingdom found that 0.24% of patients were admitted for overnight observation because of bleeding or abdominal pain.[22] The USPSTF review reports data from 16 studies of the complications of colonoscopy. Estimates range from 0% to 0.7% for perforation, from 0% to 2.1% for bleeding, and from 0% to 0.06% for death.[3]

To date, there are few data published on overdetection of invasive cancer in bowel cancer screening.[21] Many people have polyps found (25% of people aged 50 years or older have polyps, some of which will be judged to need removal, depending on the size of the polyp). Part of the benefit of screening will come from removal of the small proportion of polyps that would have progressed to invasive cancer. Part of the harm of screening will come from regular colonoscopies that are recommended for people who have had polyp removal but who were destined to never develop CRC. As noted earlier among those who test negative, adverse consequences may include false reassurance and delayed presentation of later symptomatic disease. FOBT screening will detect only about 50% of the cancers that occur in a population of regularly screened people.[3] Thus, the interval cancer rate (which includes both missed cancers and cancers that develop de novo in the screening interval) is about 50%. There are also the costs, inconvenience, and anxiety generated by just having the screening test, even for those who receive a normal test result.

Balancing Benefits and Harms

Neither the USPSTF report nor the AGA guideline reports the data in a user-friendly format, such as outcomes per 10000 people aged 40, 50, and 60 years during 10 years who are screened or not screened.[23] We can, however, use the data to construct a simple balance sheet (see Table 22.3-3).[15] To start with, we need to know what the cumulative 10-year risk of death from CRC is without screening. Data on cancer mortality rates are available through a large American cancer registry (Surveillance, Epidemiology and End Results [SEER]).[24] Currently, the 10-year cumulative mortality for men aged 40, 50, and 60 years is approximately 7, 24, and 65 per 10000, respectively. For women, the rates are 5, 16, and 39 per 10000, respectively. Among people who are regularly screened, we expect the risk of death from CRC to be reduced by 23%.[20] So, with screening, the mortality rates would be approximately 5, 19, and 50 per 10000 for men. For women who are screened, the rates will be 4, 12, and 30 per 10000. We can enter these data into the top row of our balance sheet.

Using the test positivity rates reported in the European trials (2% initial round and 1% each subsequent round), we can estimate that about 6%, or 600 of 10000 people, will have a positive test result during 5 rounds and thus receive a recommendation for colonoscopy. We can add this estimate to our balance sheet (Table 22.3-3, row 2). Finally, we add estimates of the number of adverse events from colonoscopy to our balance sheet (Table 22.2-3, row 3). We could use the UK trial data, which are about midrange in the estimates provided by the USPSTF report (ie, a total adverse event rate of 0.5%). So of the 600 people having colonoscopy, we would expect 3 people to have a serious event (Table 22.3-3).

Simple and approximate, the balance sheet provides perspective on the benefits and harms of CRC screening. Unfortunately, we have no data on the risk of overdetection or on anxiety and effect on quality of life. This balance sheet tells us that screening 10000 men biennially with FOBT from age 50 years will prevent approximately 5 deaths from CRC during 10 years but will lead to about 600 colonoscopies and 3 major colonoscopy complications during the same period. The balance of benefits vs harms becomes more favorable with increasing age.

These data assume that the screening programs will deliver the same magnitude of benefit and harms as found in RCTs; this will be true only if the program is delivered to the same standard of quality as that in the trials. Otherwise, benefits will be smaller and the harms will be greater.

TABLE 22.3-3

Balance Sheet of Outcomes During 10 Years of Bowel Cancer Screening per 10 000 People Aged 40, 50, and 60 Years Who Accept or Decline Biennial Screening[a]

	40-Year-Olds		50-Year-Olds		60-Year-Olds	
	Screen (10 000)	No Screen (10 000)	Screen (10 000)	No Screen (10 000)	Screen (10 000)	No Screen (10 000)
Deaths caused by CRC						
Men	5	7	19	24	50	65
Women	4	5	12	16	30	39
Positive screening test results leading to recommendation for colonoscopy	600		600		600	
Major adverse effects of colonoscopy (eg, perforation, hemorrhage)	3		3		3	

Abbreviation: CRC, colorectal cancer.

[a]Based on data from SEER[24] and US Life Tables.[25]

How Do Benefits and Harms Compare in Different People and With Different Screening Strategies?

The USPSTF review[3] strongly recommends that CRC screening be offered to all people older than 50 years. The review discusses several screening strategies: FOBT, colonoscopy, flexible sigmoidoscopy, and double-contrast barium enema. The magnitude of benefits and harms will vary in different patients and with different screening strategies, as the following discussion reveals. The benefits of screening are experienced at some point in the future, whereas harms may be experienced at any time, including immediately after the first screening.

Risk of Disease

Assuming that the RRR is constant over a broad range of risk of disease, benefits will be greater for people at higher risk of disease. For example, mortality from CRC increases with age, and the mortality benefit achieved by screening increases accordingly (Figure 22.3-2). But the life-years lost to CRC are related both to the age at which mortality is highest and the length of life still available. Thus, the number of life-years that can be saved by CRC screening increases with age to about 80 years and then decreases again as life expectancy declines (Figure 22.3-2). Because of a greater benefit, it may be rational for a person aged 60 years to decide

FIGURE 22.3-2A

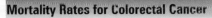

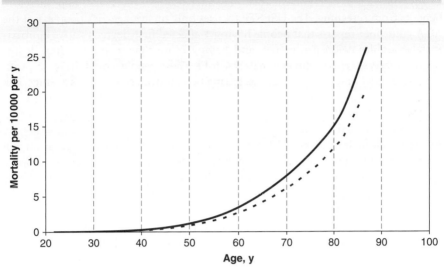

FIGURE 22.3-2B

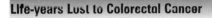

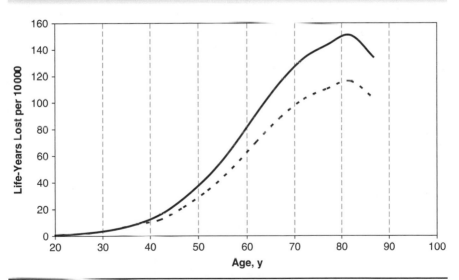

A and B, The solid lines represent disease-specific mortality from colorectal cancer and life-years lost as a result of colorectal-cancer deaths in patients who do not undergo screening. The dashed line represents results in patients who undergo screening.

Data based on SEER[24] and US Life Tables.[25]

screening is worthwhile, whereas a person aged 40 years with smaller potential benefit might decide it is not worthwhile.

Factors such as a family history may increase risk of disease and therefore benefits from screening. The USPSTF focuses only on average-risk people, but the AGA guideline[2] reports that people having 1 affected first-degree relative approximately doubles colon cancer risk and having more than 1 affected first-degree relative increases risk by approximately 4-fold. These people would derive approximately 2 and 4 times, respectively, as great a benefit from screening as average-risk people.

Screening Interval

As the screening interval gets shorter, the effectiveness of a screening program will tend to improve. For example, screening twice as often could theoretically double the relative mortality reduction obtainable by screening. In practice, however, the effect is usually much less. Cervical cancer screening, for instance, may reduce the incidence of invasive cervical cancer by 64%, 84%, and 94% if screening is conducted at 10-, 5-, and 1-year intervals, respectively.[26] The frequency of harms also will increase with more frequent screening, potentially directly in proportion to the frequency of screening. Thus, we will see diminishing marginal return as the screening interval is shortened. Ultimately, the marginal harms will outweigh the marginal benefit of further reductions in the screening interval. For example, in our balance sheet, if patients undergo screening annually, the benefit would be a little larger, but the number of colonoscopies and adverse events from colonoscopies would be approximately doubled.

Test Characteristics

If the sensitivity of a new test is greater than that of the test used in the trials and if it is detecting significant disease earlier, the benefit of screening will increase. But it may be that the new and apparently more sensitive test is detecting more cases of inconsequential disease (eg, by detecting more low-grade prostate cancers or more low-grade cervical epithelial abnormalities[27]), which will increase the potential for harm. If specificity is improved and testing produces fewer false-positive results, net benefit will increase and the test may now be useful in groups in which the old test was not as useful.[28]

What Is the Effect of Values and Preferences?

How people value the benefits and harms of screening varies. For example, couples considering fetal screening for Down syndrome may make different choices, depending on the value they place on having a child with Down syndrome vs the risk of iatrogenic abortion from amniocentesis.[29] Individuals can make the right choice for themselves only if they have access to high-quality information about the benefits and risks of screening and if they are able to weigh that information.

Patient decision aids, which provide high-quality balanced information about difficult decisions, are instruments that help patients make the best decisions for their health care.[30] They have already been widely evaluated for treatment decisions and have been found to increase knowledge and reduce decisional conflict without increasing anxiety (see Chapter 22.2, Decision Making and the Patient). Increasingly, investigators are developing patient decision aids for screening decisions, although few have yet been evaluated.[31,32] Patient decision aids are increasingly available online.[33,34]

What Is the Effect of Uncertainty Associated With the Evidence?

There is always uncertainty about the benefits and harms of screening. The 95% *confidence interval* around the estimates of magnitude of each benefit and adverse consequence provides an indication of the amount of uncertainty in each estimate. When sample size is limited, the confidence intervals will be wide and clinicians should alert potential screening participants that the magnitude of the benefit or harm could be considerably smaller or greater than the point estimate.

What Is the Cost-effectiveness?

Although clinicians will be most interested in the balance of benefits and harms for individual patients, policy makers must consider issues of cost-effectiveness analysis and local resources in their decisions (see Chapter 22.1, Economic Analysis).

The USPSTF review reports that the estimated cost-effectiveness of FOBT screening is between $10 000 and $25 000 per life-year gained among people older than 50 years (although, like the absolute size of the benefit, it will vary with risk of disease).[1] These cost-effectiveness ratios are within the range of other screening programs such as mammographic screening for women aged 50 to 69 years (estimated at $21 400 per life-year saved),[35] ultrasonographic screening for patient with carotid stenosis (incremental cost per quality adjusted life-year gained is estimated at $39 495),[36] and ultrasonographic screening for abdominal aortic aneurysm in men aged 60 to 80 years (estimated $41 550 per life-year gained).[37]

CLINICAL RESOLUTION

Neither the USPSTF report nor the AGA guideline provides age-specific mortality reductions attributable to screening; therefore, you cannot easily quantify the benefit for your patients in your practice unless you do it yourself, as described here. Returning to our opening clinical scenario, it is up to the patients before you to weigh whether the benefit of reduced risk of death from CRC is worth the potentially adverse consequences, including the inconvenience of colonoscopy and the complications arising from colonoscopy, the adverse effects of early treatment for colon cancer, adverse effects of treatment, and the anxiety generated by the investigations and treatment. You may assist them to do this by providing them with a relevant patient decision aid and then reviewing their views with them. For example, if they are not bothered by the prospect of a colonoscopy, they would probably choose screening. But if they place a high value on avoiding colonoscopy now, they may prefer to reconsider screening in a few years when, because their risk for colon cancer will be higher, the balance of benefits to harms will be more favorable than it is now.

References

1. Pignone M, Rich M, Teutsch SM, Berg AO, Lohr KN. Screening for colorectal cancer in adults at average risk: a summary of the evidence for the US Preventive Services Task Force. *Ann Intern Med.* 2002;137(2):132-141. Summary for patients in *Ann Intern Med.* 2002;137(2):138.

2. Winawer S, Fletcher R, Rex D, et al; Gastrointestinal Consortium Panel. Colorectal cancer screening and surveillance: clinical guidelines and rationale—update based on new evidence. *Gastroenterology.* 2003;124(2):544-560.

3. Agency for Healthcare Research and Quality. Screening for colorectal cancer: summary of recommendations. http://www.ahrq.gov/clinic/uspstf/uspscolo.htm. Accessed November 17, 2005.

4. Barratt A, Irwig L, Glasziou P, et al. Users' guides to the medical literature, XVII: how to use guidelines and recommendations about screening: Evidence-Based Medicine Working Group. *JAMA.* 1999;281(21):2029-2034.

5. Gray JA. *Evidence-Based Healthcare.* London, England: Churchill Livingstone; 1997.

6. Sackett DL, Haynes RB, Tugwell P. *Clinical Epidemiology: A Basic Science for Clinical Medicine.* 2nd ed. Boston, MA: Little, Brown & Company; 1991.

7. Draisma G, Boer R, Otto SJ, et al. Lead times and overdetection due to prostate-specific antigen screening: estimates from the European Randomized Study of Screening for Prostate Cancer. *J Natl Cancer Inst.* 2003;95(12):868-878.

8. Ernster VL, Ballard-Barbash R, Barlow WE, et al. Detection of ductal carcinoma in situ in women undergoing screening mammography. *J Natl Cancer Inst.* 2002;94 (20):1546-1554.

9. Paci E, Warwick J, Falini P, Duffy SW. Overdiagnosis in screening: is the increase in breast cancer incidence rates a concern? *J Med Screen.* 2004;11(1):23-27.

10. Anttila A, Koskela J, Hakama M. Programme sensitivity and effectiveness of mammography service screening in Helsinki, Finland. *J Med Screen.* 2002;9(4):153-158.

11. Zahl PH, Strand BH, Maehlen J. Incidence of breast cancer in Norway and Sweden during introduction of nationwide screening: prospective cohort study. *BMJ.* 2004;328(7445):921-924.

12. Khaw KT, Rose G. Cholesterol screening programmes: how much potential benefit? *BMJ.* 1989;299(6699):606-607.

13. Tabar L, Fagerberg G, Duffy SW, Day NE. The Swedish Two County Trial of mammographic screening for breast cancer: recent results and calculation of benefit. *J Epidemiol Commun Health.* 1989;43(2):107-114.

14. Frick MH, Elo O, Haapa K, et al. Helsinki Heart Study: primary-prevention trial with gemfibrozil in middle-aged men with dyslipidemia: safety of treatment, changes in risk factors, and incidence of coronary heart disease. *N Engl J Med.* 1987;317(20):1237-1245.

15. Eddy DM. Comparing benefits and harms: the balance sheet. *JAMA.* 1990;263 (18):2493, 2498, 2501, 2505.

16. Hardcastle JD, Chamberlain JO, Robinson MH, et al. Randomised controlled trial of faecal-occult-blood screening for colorectal cancer. *Lancet.* 1996;348(9040):1472-1477.

17. Kronborg O, Fenger C, Olsen J, Jorgensen OD, Sondergaard O. Randomised study of screening for colorectal cancer with faecal-occult-blood test. *Lancet.* 1996;348(9040):1467-1471.

18. Mandel JS, Church TR, Ederer F, Bond JH. Colorectal cancer mortality: effectiveness of biennial screening for fecal occult blood. *J Natl Cancer Inst.* 1999; 91(5):434-437.

19. Mandel JS, Church TR, Bond JH, et al. The effect of fecal occult-blood screening on the incidence of colorectal cancer. *N Engl J Med.* 2000;343(22):1603-1607.

20. Towler B, Irwig L, Glasziou P, Kewenter J, Weller D, Silagy C. A systematic review of the effects of screening for colorectal cancer using the faecal occult blood test, Hemoccult. *BMJ.* 1998;317(7158):559-565.

21. Robinson MH, Hardcastle JD, Moss SM, et al. The risks of screening: data from the Nottingham Randomised Controlled Trial of Faecal Occult Blood Screening for Colorectal Cancer. *Gut.* 1999;45(4):588-592.

22. UK Colorectal Cancer Screening Pilot Group. Results of the first round of a demonstration pilot of screening for colorectal cancer in the United Kingdom. *BMJ.* 2004;329(7458):133-137.

23. Barratt A, Howard K, Irwig L, Salkeld G, Houssami N. Model of outcomes of screening mammography: information to support informed choices. *BMJ.* 2005;330(7497):936-940.

24. National Cancer Institute. Surveillance, Epidemiology and End Results (SEER) program (http://www.seer.cancer.gov). SEER*Stat Database: Mortality—all COD, public-use with state, total U.S. (1969-2004), National Cancer Institute, DCCPS, Surveillance Research Program, Cancer Statistics Branch, released April 2005. Underlying mortality data provided by NCHS. http://www.cdc.gov/nchs. Accessed November 17, 2005.

25. Arias E. *United States Life* Tables, 2002: National *Vital Statistics Reports, Volume 53, Number 6*. Hyattsville, MD: National Center for Health Statistics; 2004.

26. International Agency for Research on Cancer; Working Group on Evaluation of Cervical Cancer Screening Programmes. Screening for squamous cervical cancer: duration of low risk after negative results of cervical cytology and its implication for screening policies. *BMJ Clin Res Ed*. 1986;293(6548):659-664.

27. Raffle AE. New tests in cervical screening. *Lancet*. 1998;351(9098):297.

28. Irwig L, Houssami N, Glasziou P, Armstrong B. How should we evaluate new screening tests for breast cancer? *BMJ*. 2006;332(7543):678-679.

29. Fletcher J, Hicks NR, Kay JD, Boyd PA. Using decision analysis to compare policies for antenatal screening for Down's syndrome. *BMJ*. 1995;311(7001):351-356.

30. O'Connor AM, Rostom A, Fiset V, et al. Decision aids for patients facing health treatment or screening decisions: systematic review. *BMJ*. 1999;319(7212):731-734.

31. Gattellari M, Ward JE. A community-based randomised controlled trial of three different educational resources for men about prostate cancer screening. *Patient Educ Couns*. 2005;57(2):168-182.

32. Pignone M, Harris R, Kinsinger L. Videotape-based decision aid for colon cancer screening: a randomized, controlled trial. *Ann Intern Med*. 2000;133(10):761-769.

33. Ottawa Health Research Institute. Patient decision aids. http://decisionaid.ohri.ca/index.html. Accessed March 4, 2008.

34. Sydney Health Decision Group. University of Sydney School of Public Health Web site. http://www.health.usyd.edu.au/.shdg/resources/decision_aids.php. Accessed March 4, 2008.

35. Salzmann P, Kerlikowske K, Phillips K. Cost-effectiveness of extending screening mammography guidelines to include women 40 to 49 years old. *Ann Intern Med*. 1997;127(11):955-965.

36. Yin D, Carpenter JP. Cost-effectiveness of screening for asymptomatic carotid stenosis. *J Vasc Surg*. 1998;27(2):245-255.

37. Frame PS, Fryback DG, Patterson C. Screening for abdominal aortic aneurysm in men ages 60 to 80 years: a cost-effectiveness analysis. *Ann Intern Med*. 1993;119(5):411-416.

GRADING
RECOMMENDATIONS

Holger J. Schünemann, Gunn E. Vist,
Roman Jaeschke, Regina Kunz,
Deborah J. Cook, and Gordon Guyatt

IN THIS CHAPTER:

CLINICAL SCENARIO

You are the primary care physician considering the possibility of warfarin use for a 76-year-old woman with congestive heart failure and chronic atrial fibrillation (AF) who had just entered your practice. The patient has received aspirin for the 10 years she has had AF. Her other medical problem is hypertension, for which she has been taking hydrochlorothiazide and metoprolol, which also control her heart rate. She does not have valvular disease, diabetes, or other comorbidities, and she does not smoke. Your assessment of the *clinical practice guideline* (see Chapter 21, How to Use a Patient Management Recommendation) and the decision analysis, together with the exploration of the patient's values, indicated that she would be best served by taking warfarin to prevent strokes (strong recommendation, based on high-quality evidence). You reflect that an increasing number of clinical practice guidelines are valid and that you are using them more and more. You decide to learn about the grading system used in the guideline. You send an e-mail to the author of the chapter describing the methods that the guideline authors used; he sends you 2 articles to help you understand how evidence is graded and recommendations are made in practice guidelines.[1,2]

THE GRADE SYSTEM FOR GRADING RECOMMENDATIONS

Treatment recommendations involve a tradeoff between likely benefits on one hand and undesirable effects (harms, burden, and costs) on the other. To place recommendations in the context of individual patients before them, clinicians need to understand the underlying *evidence* and judgments. A systematic approach to grading the strength of treatment recommendations can minimize *bias* and aid interpretation in the development and implementation of guidelines. This chapter provides a guide to readers about how guideline developers assess the quality of evidence and strength of recommendations.

The Grades of Recommendation, Assessment, Development and Evaluation (GRADE) Working Group developed a system for grading the quality of evidence and strength of recommendations.[1,2] The aims of the GRADE Working Group include developing explicit and transparent criteria for evaluating evidence and formulating recommendations while reducing confusion caused by many grading systems. Several organizations involved in guideline development, including the World Health Organization, the American College of Physicians, American College of Chest Physicians, the American Endocrine Society, the American Thoracic Society, and UpToDate, have adopted the GRADE system in its original format or with minor modifications.[3] The GRADE system entails an initial assessment of the quality of evidence, followed by judgment about the direction and strength of recommendations. Because clinicians (the most common frontline consumers of recommendations) will be most interested in the best course of action, the GRADE system presents the strength of the recommendation first, followed by the quality of the evidence. Separating the judgments regarding the quality of evidence from judgments about the strength of recommendations is a critical and defining feature of this relatively new but already widely adopted grading system.

STRENGTH OF THE RECOMMENDATION

Using GRADE, guideline developers focus on the degree of confidence in the balance between desirable effects of a treatment on the one hand and undesirable effects on the other in determining the strength of their recommendations (Table 22.4-1). Desirable effects or benefits can include beneficial health outcomes, decreased burden of treatment, and decreased resource use (usually measured as costs). Undesirable effects or downsides can include rare major adverse events, minor adverse effects, greater patient burden, and more resource consumption. Burdens are the demands of adhering to a recommendation that patients or caregivers (eg, family) may dislike, such as taking medication or inconvenient laboratory monitoring or physician visits. If desirable effects of an intervention outweigh undesirable effects, experts will recommend that clinicians offer the intervention to typical patients (Figure 22.4-1). How close the balance between desirable and undesirable effects is, and the uncertainty associated with that balance, will determine the strength of recommendations.

If guideline developers are confident that the desirable effects of adherence to a recommendation outweigh the undesirable effects or vice versa, they will make a strong recommendation (Figure 22.4-1). Such confidence usually requires high-quality evidence that provides precise estimates of both benefits and downsides and a clear balance in favor, or against, the benefits vs the downsides of an intervention. Guideline developers will typically offer a weak recommendation when low-quality evidence results in appreciable uncertainty about the magnitude of benefits or downsides or the benefits and downsides are finely balanced. Other reasons for not being confident include imprecise estimates of benefits or harms, uncertainty or variation in how different individuals value the outcomes and thus their preferences regarding management alternatives, small benefits, or situations in which benefits may not be worth the costs (including the costs of implementing the recommendation). Although the degree of confidence is a continuum and a lack of a precise threshold between a strong and a weak recommendation exists, the presence of important concerns about one or more of the above factors makes a weak recommendation more likely.

Interpreting Strong and Weak Recommendations

Clinicians are becoming increasingly aware of the importance of patient values and preferences in individualized clinical decision making (see Chapter 22.2, Decision

TABLE 22.4-1

GRADE Approach to Grading Recommendations

Grade of Recommendation[a]	Confidence in Clarity of Benefits vs Harms, Burden, and Cost
Strong recommendation, high-quality evidence	Desirable effects clearly outweigh undesirable effects or vice versa
Strong recommendation, moderate-quality evidence	Desirable effects clearly outweigh undesirable effects or vice versa
Strong recommendation, low-quality evidence	Desirable effects clearly outweigh undesirable effects or vice versa
Strong recommendation, very-low-quality evidence (very rarely applicable)	Desirable effects clearly outweigh undesirable effects or vice versa
Weak recommendation, high-quality evidence	Desirable effects closely balanced with undesirable effects
Weak recommendation, moderate-quality evidence	Desirable effects closely balanced with undesirable effects
Weak recommendation, low-quality evidence	Desirable effects closely balanced with undesirable effects
Weak recommendation, very-low-quality evidence	Desirable effects closely balanced with undesirable effects

Abbreviations: GRADE, grades of recommendation, assessment, development, and evaluation; RCT, randomized controlled trial.

[a]In addition to describing in words the quality of evidence and strength of a recommendation, letters, numbers, and symbols are frequently used.[2] GRADE suggests the following symbols for quality of evidence: high, ⊕⊕⊕⊕; ⊕⊕⊕○; low, ⊕⊕○○; very low, ⊕○○○.

Quality of Supporting Evidence	Implications
Consistent evidence from well-performed RCTs or exceptionally strong evidence from unbiased observational studies	Recommendation can apply to most patients in most circumstances. Further research is unlikely to change our confidence in the estimate of effect.
Evidence from RCTs with important limitations (inconsistent results, methodologic flaws, indirect evidence, or imprecise results) or unusually strong evidence from unbiased observational studies	Recommendation can apply to most patients in most circumstances. Further research (if performed) is likely to have an important effect on our confidence in the estimate of effect and may change the estimate.
Evidence for at least 1 critical outcome from observational studies, from RCTs with serious flaws or indirect evidence	Recommendation may change when higher-quality evidence becomes available. Further research (if performed) is likely to have an important influence on our confidence in the estimate of effect and is likely to change the estimate.
Evidence for at least 1 of the critical outcomes from unsystematic clinical observations or very indirect evidence	Recommendation may change when higher-quality evidence becomes available; any estimate of effect, for at least 1 critical outcome, is uncertain.
Consistent evidence from well-performed RCTs or exceptionally strong evidence from unbiased observational studies	The best action may differ, depending on circumstances or patients or societal values. Further research is unlikely to change our confidence in the estimate of effect.
Evidence from RCTs with important limitations (inconsistent results, methodologic flaws, indirect evidence, or imprecise results) or unusually strong evidence from unbiased observational studies	Alternative approaches likely to be better for some patients under some circumstances. Further research (if performed) is likely to have an important influence on our confidence in the estimate of effect and may change the estimate.
Evidence for at least 1 critical outcome from observational studies, from RCTs with serious flaws, or indirect evidence	Other alternatives may be equally reasonable. Further research is likely to have an important influence on our confidence in the estimate of effect and is likely to change the estimate.
Evidence for at least 1 critical outcome from unsystematic clinical observations or very indirect evidence	Other alternatives may be equally reasonable. Any estimate of effect, for at least 1 critical outcome, is uncertain.

For the strength of recommendations, GRADE suggests arrows: a strong recommendation corresponds to ↑↑ or ↓↓, a weak recommendation ↑? or ↓?. GRADE suggests the following letters and numbers: high quality, moderate quality, low quality, and very low quality correspond to A, B, C, and D, respectively, and strong and weak recommendations correspond to the 1 and 2, respectively.

FIGURE 22.4-1

Strength of Recommendations

Evaluating desirable and undesirable effects

Desirable << Undesirable effects   Desirable ?> Undesirable effects

Desirable ?< Undesirable effects   Desirable >> Undesirable effects

Formulating a recommendation

Against		**For**	
Strong	Weak	Weak	Strong
↓↓	?↓	↑?	↑↑
1	2	2	1

The figure describes the balance between important benefits and downsides related to a recommendation. The process begins by evaluating whether desirable effects outweigh undesirable effects or vice versa. Moving on to making a recommendation requires a decision: if the balance is clear, a strong recommendation for or against an action follows (↓↓ and ↑↑ denote a clear balance). If the balance is not clear, a weak recommendation for or against an action follows (?↓ and ?↑ denote a balance that is not clear). Widely differing values (the importance or preference patients assign to a certain health state) can also lead to a less clear balance of benefits vs downsides. The numbers indicate the recommended symbolic representation of strong (1) and weak (2) recommendations.

Making and the Patient). One way to interpret strong and weak recommendations is in relation to patient values and preferences. For decisions in which it is clear that benefits far outweigh downsides or downsides far outweigh benefits, almost all patients will make the same choice, and guideline developers can offer a strong recommendation.

For instance, consistent results from high-quality randomized trials suggest that aspirin (acetylsalicylic acid, or ASA) reduces the *relative risk* (*RR*) of death after myocardial infarction by approximately 25%. Depending on their age and factors such as the presence of heart failure, typical patients with myocardial infarction face risks of death in the first 30 days after infarction of between 2% and 40%.[4] We can therefore expect a 0.5% absolute reduction in risk (from 2% to 1.5%) in the lowest-risk patients and a 10% reduction (from 40% to 30%) in the highest-risk ones. Acetylsalicylic acid has minimal adverse effects and very low cost. Because the benefits clearly outweigh the risks and adverse consequences (even in the lowest-risk subgroups), administration of ASA is strongly endorsed and widely used. Using letters and numbers to express the quality of the evidence and strength of recommendations (Table 22.4-1), both recommendations would fall within the category of a strong recommendation based on high-quality evidence or GRADE 1A (1 because the benefits clearly outweigh the downsides and A because the estimate of benefit comes from high-quality randomized trials that yielded consistent results).

Thus, another way for clinicians to interpret strong recommendations is that they provide, for typical patients, a mandate for the clinician to provide a simple explanation of the intervention, along with a suggestion that the patient will benefit from its use. Further elaboration will seldom be necessary. On the other hand, when clinicians face weak recommendations, they should more carefully consider the benefits, harms, and burden in the context of the patient before them and ensure that the treatment decision is consistent with the patient's values and preferences. These situations arise when appreciable numbers of patients, because of variability in values and preferences, will make different choices.

Consider a 40-year-old man with idiopathic deep venous thrombosis (DVT) followed by treatment with adjusted-dose warfarin for 1 year to prevent recurrent DVT and pulmonary embolism.[5] Continuing to receive standard-intensity warfarin beyond 1 year will reduce his absolute risk for recurrent DVT by more than 7% per year for several years.[6] The burdens of treatment include taking warfarin daily, keeping dietary intake of vitamin K constant, monitoring the intensity of anticoagulation with blood tests, living with the increased risk of both minor and major bleeding, and, for some, experiencing those events. Patients who are averse to a recurrent DVT would consider the benefits of avoiding DVT worth the downsides of taking warfarin. Other patients are likely to consider the benefit not worth the harms and burden.

Individualization of clinical decision making in weak recommendations remains a challenge. Although clinicians should always consider patients' values and preferences, weak recommendations dictate more detailed conversations with patients to ensure that the ultimate decision is consistent with the patients' values. For patients who are interested, a decision aid that presents patients with both benefits and downsides of therapy is likely to improve knowledge, decrease decision-making conflict, and promote a decision most consistent with underlying values and preferences (see Chapter 22.2, Decision Making and the Patient).[7] For strong recommendations, the use of decision aids is inefficient.

Other ways of interpreting strong and weak recommendations relate to performance or quality indicators. Strong recommendations are candidate performance indicators. For weak recommendations, performance could be measured by monitoring whether clinicians have discussed recommended actions with patients or their surrogates or carefully documented the evaluation of benefits and downsides in the patient's medical record. Table 22.4-2 summarizes several ways that developers and consumers of guidelines can interpret strong and weak recommendations.

Factors That Influence the Strength of a Recommendation

Table 22.4-3 shows the factors that guideline panels should include in deciding on the direction and strength of a recommendation. The issues in Table 22.4-3 are relevant to each of benefits, harms, and burden from therapy.

The first row in Table 22.4-3, the quality of the evidence, is a major topic that we will describe later in this chapter. The second row indicates that guideline panels

TABLE 22.4-2

Examples of Implications of Strong and Weak Recommendations

Strong recommendation for a particular intervention

- **For clinicians:** Most individuals should receive the intervention.

- **For quality monitors:** Adherence to this recommendation according to the guideline could be used as a quality criterion or performance indicator of your practice.

- **For patients:** Most individuals in this situation would want the recommended course of action and only a small proportion would not. Formal decision aids are not likely to be needed to help individuals make decisions consistent with their values and preferences.

Weak recommendation for a particular intervention

- **For patients:** The majority of individuals in this situation would want the suggested course of action, but many would not.

- **For clinicians:** Offering the suggested action and helping individuals to make a decision could be used as a quality criterion or performance indicator. Decision aids may well be useful helping individuals making decisions consistent with their values and preferences. Examine the evidence or a summary of the evidence yourself and be prepared to discuss the factors that influence patients' decisions.

- **For quality monitors:** Consider clinicians' discussion of the pros and cons of the intervention with the patients as a quality criterion.

---

should, in general, make stronger recommendations for interventions that decrease adverse outcomes with high patient importance[8] (those to which on average patients assign greater values and preferences) than those that decrease outcomes of lesser patient importance.

For example, consider treating 5 patients with gastroesophageal reflux disease and chronic cough with a proton-pump inhibitor to enable 1 patient to have reduction in cough severity.[9] Contrast this with the requirement to treat 10 patients with acute respiratory distress syndrome with a low-tidal-volume ventilation strategy to prevent a premature death.[10] Despite the higher number needed to treat (NNT) in the acute respiratory distress syndrome patient, because patients would value prolongation of life more highly than relieving cough, if all else is equal, the latter intervention would warrant a stronger recommendation. The choice of adjusted-dose warfarin vs ASA for prevention of stroke in patients with AF illustrates a number of the factors that will influence the strength of a recommendation. A *systematic review* and *meta-analysis* found an RRR of 46% in all strokes with warfarin vs ASA.[11] This large effect supports a strong recommendation for warfarin. Furthermore, the relatively narrow 95% *confidence interval (CI)* (RRR, 29%-57%) suggests that warfarin provides an RRR of at least 29% and further supports a strong recommendation. At the same time, warfarin is associated with burdens that include keeping dietary intake of vitamin K constant, monitoring the intensity of anticoagulation with blood tests, and living with the increased risk of both minor and major bleeding. Most patients, however, are much more averse to

TABLE 22.4-3

Factors That Influence the Strength of a Recommendation

Issue	Recommended Process and Example
Quality of Evidence	
1. Quality of evidence	Strong recommendations usually require higher-quality evidence for all the critical outcomes. The lower the quality of evidence, the less likely a strong recommendation.
	Example: Many high-quality randomized trials have demonstrated the benefit of inhaled steroids in asthma, whereas only case series have examined the utility of pleurodesis in pneumothorax.
Balance of Benefits and Downsides	
2. Relative importance of the outcomes	Guideline panels should be explicit about the relative value they place on the range of relevant patient-important outcomes. If values and preferences vary widely, a strong recommendation becomes less likely.
	Example: Consider toxic chemotherapy for newly developed cancer in a young vs an elderly person. Most young, healthy people will put a high value on prolonging their lives (and thus incur suffering to do so); the elderly and infirm are likely to vary in the value they place on prolonging their lives and in the suffering they are ready to experience to do so.
3. Baseline risks of outcomes	Guideline panels should consider the baseline risk for an outcome and, if the magnitude of that risk will vary appreciably, make separate recommendations for different populations. The higher the baseline risk, the higher the magnitude of benefit and the more likely the recommendation is strong.
	Example: Some surgical patients are at low risk of postoperative DVT and pulmonary embolism, and thromboprophylaxis is questionable or unnecessary, whereas other surgical patients have considerably higher rates of DVT and pulmonary embolism that mandate thromboprophylaxis.
4. Magnitude of RR	Large relative effects will lead to a higher likelihood of a strong recommendation in favor of a treatment.
	Example: Clopidogrel vs ASA leads to a smaller stroke reduction in TIA (RRR, 8.7%) and is therefore less likely to lead to a strong recommendation than anticoagulation vs placebo in AF (RRR, 68%).
5. Absolute magnitude of the effect	Large absolute benefits are more likely to lead to strong recommendation in favor of a treatment.
	Example: In patients with a similar risk of 4% per year in stroke, administering clopidogrel vs ASA to patients with TIAs leads to a smaller absolute stroke reduction per year (0.3%) than administering warfarin vs ASA to patients with AF (2%)

(Continued)

TABLE 22.4-3

Factors That Influence the Strength of a Recommendation (*Continued*)

Issue	Recommended Process and Example
	Balance of Benefits and Downsides
6. Precision of the estimates of the effects	The greater the precision, the more likely the recommendation is strong.
	Example: ASA vs placebo in AF has a wider confidence interval than ASA for stroke prevention in patients with TIAs.
7. Costs	Consider that important benefits should come at a reasonable cost. The higher the incremental cost, all else being equal, the less likely that the recommendation in favor of an intervention is strong.
	Example: Clopidogrel has much higher cost in patients with TIA than ASA.

Abbreviations: AF, atrial fibrillation; ASA, acetylsalicylic acid; DVT, deep venous thrombosis; RR, relative risk; RRR, relative risk ratio; TIA, transient ischemic attack.

stroke than to bleeding.[12] As a result, almost all patients with high risk of stroke would choose warfarin, suggesting the appropriateness of a strong recommendation.

A patient's baseline risk of the adverse outcome (also called control event risk or rate) that treatment is expected to prevent may prove a key consideration. Consider another 65-year-old patient with AF and no other risk factors for stroke. This individual's risk for stroke in the next year is approximately 2%. Dose-adjusted warfarin can, relative to ASA, reduce the risk to approximately 1%. Some patients who are very stroke averse may consider the downsides of taking warfarin well worth it. Others are likely to consider the benefit not worth the risks and inconvenience. When, across the range of their values and preferences, fully informed patients are apt to make different choices, guideline panels should offer weak (grade 2) recommendations.

Although it is ideal for clinicians to elicit preferences and values directly from patients and for guideline panels to obtain values and preference estimates from population-based studies, such studies are often unavailable. When value or preference judgments are particularly important for the interpretation of recommendations, clinicians should look for statements of the key values guideline panelists have attributed in making recommendations. For example, providing a recommendation for use of combination chemotherapy and radiotherapy vs radiotherapy alone in unresectable, locally advanced non–small-cell lung cancer requires consideration reducing the risk for death corresponding to a mean gain in life expectancy of a few months. Harm and burden related to chemotherapy would be increased. Thus, considering the values and preferences patients would place on the small survival benefit in view of the harms and burdens, guideline panels may offer a weak recommendation because of the small gain in life expectancy. As benefits and risks become more finely balanced, or more uncertain, decisions to administer an effective therapy also become more cost sensitive. When dealing with resource allocation issues, guideline panels face challenges of limited expertise, paucity of rigorous and unbiased cost-effectiveness analyses, and wide variability of costs and ability to pay across jurisdictions. Ignoring the issue of costs is, however, becoming less and less tenable for guideline panels.[13] Clinicians becoming familiar with the GRADE system will quickly realize that the strength of the recommendation is also expressed by the wording that guideline panels use when developing recommendations. A recommendation phrased as "we recommend" or including the word "should" is a strong recommendation. In comparison, weak recommendations are phrased as "we suggest" or include the word "might" instead of "should."

How Methodologic Quality Contributes to Grades of Recommendation

The GRADE approach specifies four levels of quality (Table 22.4-4). The highest-quality evidence comes from 1 or more well-designed and well-executed *randomized controlled trial (RCT)* yielding consistent and directly applicable results. High-quality evidence can also come from well-done observational studies yielding large effects. RCTs with important limitations and well-done observational studies yielding large effects constitute the moderate-quality category. Well-done observational studies and, on occasion, RCTs with serious limitations will be rated as low-quality evidence. The very-low-quality category includes poorly controlled observational studies and unsystematic clinical observations (eg, case series or case reports). The remainder of this chapter describes the methodologic quality grading system in more detail.

TABLE 22.4-4

The GRADE System Quality of Evidence

Underlying Methodology	Quality Rating
RCTs or double-upgraded observational studies	High
Downgraded RCTs or upgraded observational studies	Moderate
Double-downgraded RCTs or observational studies	Low
Triple-downgraded RCTs, downgraded observational studies, or case series/case reports	Very low

Abbreviations: GRADE, grades of recommendation, assessment, development, and evaluation; RCT, randomized controlled trial.

Factors That Decrease the Quality of Evidence

The following limitations, listed in Table 22.4-5, may decrease the quality of evidence supporting a recommendation.

1. Limitation of methodology: Our confidence in recommendations decreases if studies have major limitations that are likely to result in a biased assessment of the treatment effect. These methodologic limitations include failure to adhere to an intention-to-treat analysis, lack of blinding with subjective outcomes highly susceptible to bias, a large loss to follow-up, or RCTs stopped early for benefit (see Chapter 6, Therapy).

   For instance, a randomized trial suggests that danaparoid sodium is of benefit in treating heparin-induced thrombocytopenia complicated by thrombosis.[14] That trial, however, was unblinded, and the key outcome trial was the clinicians' assessment of when the thromboembolism had resolved, a subjective judgment.

2. Unexplained heterogeneity of results (inconsistent results): When studies yield widely differing estimates of the treatment effect (heterogeneity or variability in results), investigators should look for explanations for that heterogeneity. For instance, drugs may have larger relative effects in sicker populations or when given in larger doses. When heterogeneity exists but investigators fail to identify a plausible explanation, the quality of evidence decreases (see Chapter 20.3, Making Sense of Variability in Study Results). For example, RCTs of pentoxifylline in patients with intermittent claudication have shown conflicting results that so far defy explanation.[15,16]

3. Indirectness of evidence (ie, the question being addressed in the guideline is quite different from the available evidence in regard to the population, intervention, comparison, or outcome): Investigators may have undertaken studies in similar but not identical populations to those under consideration for a recommendation. As an example of differences in populations, avian flu is a disease caused by influenza A (H5N1) virus and associated with a high case fatality (approximately 33% to >50% of patients die). Potential exposure to the virus raises the concern of chemoprophylaxis. Pharmacologic interventions could include the use of antivi-

TABLE 22.4-5

Factors That May Decrease the Quality of Evidence

- Limitations in the design and implementation of available randomized controlled trials, suggesting high likelihood of bias
- Inconsistency of results (including problems with subgroup analyses)
- Indirectness of evidence (indirect population, intervention, control, outcomes)
- Imprecision of results (wide confidence intervals)
- High probability of publication bias

ral neuraminidase inhibitors such as oseltamivir. Oseltamivir, however, has been used only in studies of patients with seasonal influenza with a different influenza A virus, an entirely different patient population.[17]

Differences among the population, intervention, and outcome of interest, and those included in the relevant studies, all represent other sources of indirectness. Table 22.4-6 presents examples of each.

4. Lack of precision: When studies include few patients and few events and thus have wide CIs, a guideline panel will judge the quality of the evidence lower than it otherwise would be because of resulting uncertainty in the results. For instance, a well-designed and rigorously conducted RCT addressed the use of nadroparin, a low-molecular-weight heparin, in patients with cerebral venous sinus thrombosis.[18] Of 30 treated patients, 4 had a poor outcome, as did 6 of 29 patients in the control group. The investigators' analysis[18] suggests a 7% absolute risk reduction (which, if true, would correspond to a requirement to treat approximately 14 patients to prevent a single poor outcome), but the confidence interval also included not only a 26% absolute difference in favor of treatment but a 12% difference in favor of placebo.

5. Publication bias: The quality of evidence may be reduced if investigators fail to report studies (typically those that show no effect) or outcomes (typically those that may be harmful or for which no effect was observed) or if other reasons lead to results not being reported. While such selective reporting of outcomes can be considered a form of publication bias, this is part of the assessment of limitations in the design and implementation. Unfortunately, guideline panels are still required to make guesses about the

TABLE 22.4-6

Evidence Is Weaker if Comparisons Are Indirect

Question of Interest	Source of Indirectness
Relative effectiveness of alendronate and risedronate in osteoporosis	Indirect comparison: Randomized trials have compared alendronate to placebo and risedronate to placebo, but trials comparing alendronate to risedronate are unavailable.
Oseltamivir for prophylaxis of avian flu caused by influenza A (H5N1) virus	Differences in population: Randomized trials of oseltamivir are available for seasonal influenza but not for avian flu.
Sigmoidoscopic screening for prevention of colon cancer mortality	Differences in intervention: Randomized trials of fecal occult blood screening provide indirect evidence bearing on the potential effectiveness of sigmoidoscopy.
Rosiglitazone for prevention of diabetic complications in patients at high risk of developing diabetes	Differences in outcome: A randomized trial shows delay in the development of biochemical diabetes with rosiglitazone but was underpowered to address diabetic complications.

likelihood of publication bias. A prototypical situation that should elicit suspicion of publication bias is when published evidence includes a number of small trials, all of which are industry funded.[19] For example, 14 trials of flavanoids in patients with hemorrhoids have shown apparent large benefits but enrolled a total of only 1432 patients.[20] The heavy involvement of sponsors in most of these trials raises questions of whether unpublished trials suggesting no benefit exist.

A particular body of evidence can have more than 1 of these limitations, and the greater the limitations, the lower the quality of the evidence. One could imagine a situation in which RCTs were available, but all or virtually all of these limitations would be present, and in serious form, a very low quality of evidence would result.

Factors That Increase the Quality of Evidence

Observational studies can provide moderate or strong evidence. Although well-done observational studies will generally yield low-quality evidence, there may be unusual circumstances in which guideline panels classify such evidence as moderate or even high quality (Table 22.4-7).

1. On rare occasions when methodologically strong observational studies yield large or very large and consistent estimates of the magnitude of a treatment effect, we may be confident about the results. In those situations, whereas the observational studies are likely to have provided an overestimate of the true effect, the weak study design may not explain all of the apparent benefit. Thus, despite reservations based on the observational study design, we are confident that the effect exists. Table 22.4-7 shows how the magnitude of the effect in these studies may move the assigned quality of evidence from low to moderate (if the effect is large in the absence of other methodologic limitations). For example, a meta-analysis of observational studies showed that bicycle helmets reduce the risk of head injuries in cyclists (odds ratio, 0.31; 95% CI, 0.26-0.37) by a large margin.[21] This large effect suggests a rating of moderate-quality evidence. A meta-analysis of 37 observational studies evaluating the effect of warfarin prophylaxis in cardiac valve replacement found that the RR for thromboembolism with warfarin was 0.17 (95% CI, 0.13-0.24). This large effect suggests a rating of high-quality evidence.[22]

TABLE 22.4-7

Factors That May Increase the Quality of Evidence

- Large magnitude of effect (direct evidence: relative risk (RR) >2 or RR <0.5 with no plausible confounders; very large with RR >5 or RR <0.2 and no threats to validity
- All plausible confounding would reduce a demonstrated effect
- Dose-response gradient

2. On occasion, all plausible biases from observational studies may be working to underestimate an apparent treatment effect. For example, if only sicker patients receive an experimental intervention or exposure, yet they still fare better, it is likely that the actual intervention or exposure effect is larger than the data suggest. For instance, a rigorous systematic review of observational studies including a total of 38 million patients demonstrated higher death rates in private for-profit vs private nonprofit hospitals.[23] One possible bias relates to different disease severity in patients in the 2 hospital types. It is likely, however, that patients in the nonprofit hospitals were sicker than those in the for-profit hospitals. Thus, to the extent that residual confounding existed, it would bias results against the nonprofit hospitals. The second likely bias was the possibility that higher numbers of patients with excellent private insurance coverage could lead to a hospital's having more resources and a spillover effect that would benefit those without such coverage. Because for-profit hospitals are likely to admit a larger proportion of such well-insured patients than nonprofit hospitals, the bias is once again against the nonprofit hospitals. Because the plausible biases would all diminish the demonstrated treatment effect, one might consider the evidence from these observational studies as moderate rather than low quality.

3. The presence of a dose-response gradient may also increase our confidence in the findings of observational studies and thereby enhance the assigned quality of evidence. For example, our confidence in the result of observational studies that show an increased risk of bleeding in patients who have supratherapeutic anticoagulation levels is increased by the observation that there is a dose-response gradient between higher levels of the international normalized ratio and the increased risk of bleeding.[24]

WHAT TO DO WHEN QUALITY OF EVIDENCE DIFFERS ACROSS OUTCOMES

Recommendations depend on evidence regarding a number of outcomes, and in the approach we have described above, one would establish the quality of evidence for each patient-important outcome. This presents a potential dilemma: How should one rate the overall quality of evidence if quality differs across patient-important outcomes? Consider, for instance, administration of selective digestive decontamination (SDD) in intensive care unit patients. Several meta-analyses of high-quality RCTs suggested a decrease in the incidence of infections and, likely, the mortality of patients receiving ventilation with SDD.[25-27] The quality of evidence on the effect of SDD on the emergence of bacterial antibiotic resistance, and its clinical relevance, is much less clear. One might reasonably rate the evidence about this feared potential adverse effect as low quality. Should the overall quality of evidence for use of SDD therefore be considered high, moderate, or low?

The GRADE approach suggests that guideline developers should consider whether downsides of therapy are critical to the decision regarding the optimal management strategy. If the outcome for which evidence is lower quality is indeed important and critical for decision making, then the rating of overall quality of the evidence must reflect this lower-quality evidence. If the outcome for which evidence is lower quality is important but not critical, the GRADE approach suggests an overall rating reflecting the higher-quality evidence from the critical outcomes.

PRESENTATION OF EVIDENCE AND DEVELOPING RECOMMENDATIONS USING THE GRADE APPROACH

Table 22.4-8 offers a checklist for those wanting to understand applying the GRADE approach during development and grading of recommendations.

A comprehensive way for displaying all relevant data related to a clinical question is a GRADE evidence profile (Table 22.4-9). These evidence profiles provide summaries of the information for each critical outcome that influences clinical decision making, including a detailed evaluation of the study quality by outcome and the associated effects, as well as the relative importance of outcomes that can serve as a guide for clinicians. These profiles can be used by guideline developers to develop recommendations. The column for importance relates to the values and preferences guideline developers assign to the outcomes. The example (Table 22.4-10) from the management of AF with oral anticoagulation shows how guideline developers might work through the issues that influence the quality of evidence and strength of a recommendation.

After reading these 2 articles,[1,2] you understand more about the criteria that guideline developers use to assess the quality of evidence and the balance of benefits and downsides. Resulting recommendations are more transparent to you now. Having reflected on the considerations that influence the strength of recommendations will help you to explain guidelines to your learners and use guidelines in your practice. In the future, you decide to look for clinical practice guidelines that use the GRADE system, or at least guidelines that have explicit criteria for evaluating the evidence and developing recommendations.

TABLE 22.4-8

Checklist for Developing and Grading Recommendations

Define the population, intervention and alternative, and the relevant outcomes.

Summarize the relevant evidence (relying on systematic reviews), including evidence regarding values and preferences.

If RCTs are available, start by assuming high quality; if well-done observational studies are available, assume low quality, but then check for the following:

- serious methodologic limitations (lack of blinding, allocation concealment, high loss to follow-up, stopped early)
- indirectness in population, intervention, or outcome (use of surrogates)
- inconsistency in results
- imprecision in estimates

Grade RCTs down from high to moderate, low or very low depending on limitations or observational studies, to very low.

If no RCTs are available but well-done observational studies are available (including indirectly relevant trials and well-done observational study), start by assuming low quality and then check for the following:

- large or very large treatment effect
- all plausible confounders that would diminish the effect of intervention
- dose-response gradient

Grade up to moderate or even high, depending on special strengths or weaknesses.

Studies starting at very low will not be upgraded. Observational studies with limitations will not be upgraded. Only observational studies with no threats to validity can be upgraded.

Decide on best estimates of benefits, harms, burden, and costs for relevant population.

Decide on whether the benefits are, overall, worth the harms, burden, and costs for relevant population and decide how clear and precise is this balance in the context of patients' values and preferences.

Abbreviation: RCT, randomized controlled trial.

TABLE 22.4-9

Grade Evidence Profiles

GRADE Evidence Profile

Author(s): Holger Schünemann

Date: 4/28/2006

Question: Should warfarin vs placebo or no treatment be used for patients with nonvalvular atrial fibrillation?

Patient or population: Patients with nonvalvular atrial fibrillation

Settings: Long-term outpatient management

Systematic review: Van Walraven et al[11] and Aguilar and Hart[28]

	Quality Assessment					No. of Patients		Effect (Summary of Findings)		
No. of Studies	Design	Limitations	Consistency	Directness	Other Considerations	Warfarin	Placebo or No Treatment	Relative Risk (95% CI)	Absolute Risk (95% CI)	Quality	Importance
Disabling or fatal stroke (ischemic and hemorrhagic) (neuroimaging or autopsy[a]; mean follow-up, 1.5 y)											
5	Randomized trials	No limitations[b,c]	No important inconsistency	No uncertainty	Strong association[d]	18/1154 (1.6%)	39/1159 (3.4%)	0.46 (0.27-0.81)	20/1000 (30 fewer/1000 to 10 fewer/1000)	⊕⊕⊕⊕, high, A	9[e]

	Quality Assessment					No. of Patients		Summary of Findings			
								Effect			
No. of Studies	Design	Limitations	Consistency	Directness	Other Considerations	Warfarin	Placebo or No Treatment	Relative Risk (95% CI)	Absolute Risk (95% CI)	Quality	Importance
Intracranial hemorrhage (clinical diagnosis confirmed by computed tomography or postmortem; mean follow-up, 1.5 y)											
5	Randomized trials	No limitations	No important inconsistency	No uncertainty	Imprecise or sparse data (−1)[f]	5/1154 (0.4%)	2/1159 (0.2%)	1.87 (0.51-6.82)	3/1000 (0 more/1000 to 10 more/1000)	⊕⊕⊕O, moderate, B	8
Extracranial hemorrhage (transfusion or invasive procedure requirement[g]; mean follow-up, 1.9 y)[h]											
6	Randomized trials	No limitations[b]	No important inconsistency	No uncertainty	None	85/1939 (4.4%)	52/2113 (2.6%)	1.71 (1.21-2.41)	18 more/1000 (5 more/1000 to 30 more/1000)	⊕⊕⊕⊕, high, A	7
All-cause mortality[i,j] (direct patient follow-up; mean follow-up, 1.5 y)											
5	Randomized trials	No limitations[k]	No important inconsistency	No uncertainty	None	69/1225 (5.6%)	99/1236 (8%)	0.70 (0.52-0.95)	20/1000 (40 fewer/1000 to 1 fewer/1000)	⊕⊕⊕⊕, high, A	9

(Continued)

TABLE 22.4-9

Grade Evidence Profiles (*Continued*)

No. of Studies	Quality Assessment					No. of Patients		Effect		Quality	Importance
	Design	Limitations	Consistency	Directness	Other Considerations	Warfarin	Placebo or No Treatment	Relative Risk (95% CI)	Absolute Risk (95% CI)		
Vascular death[l] (death due to stroke, heart disease, hemorrhage, and sudden death; mean follow-up, 1.5 y)											
5	Randomized trials	No limitations[k]	No important inconsistency	No uncertainty	None	43/1154 (3.7%)	51/1159 (4.4%)	0.85 (0.57-1.26)	1/1000 (3 fewer/1000 to 1 more/1000)	⊕⊕⊕⊕, high, A	9
All ischemic stroke (neuroimaging or autopsy[a,m]; mean follow-up, 1.5 y)											
5	Randomized trials	No limitations[b,n]	No important inconsistency	No uncertainty	Strong association (+1)[o]	22/1154 (1.9%)	69/1159 (6%)	0.32 (0.20-0.51)	40/1000 (60 fewer/1000 to 20 fewer/1000)	⊕⊕⊕⊕, high	7

Abbreviations: AFASAK I, the First Copenhagen Atrial Fibrillation, Aspirin, and Anticoagulation trial; ASA, acetylsalicylic acid; CAFA, the Canadian Atrial Fibrillation Anticoagulation study; CI, confidence interval; GRADE, grades of recommendation, assessment, development, and evaluation; MI, myocardial infarction; RR, relative risk; SPINAF, the Stroke Prevention in Nonrheumatic Atrial Fibrillation study; TIA, transient ischemic attack.

[a] Follow-up for this outcome was less than 100%.
[b] In 2 studies (CAFA and the SPINAF), patients and outcome assessors were blind to oral anticoagulant administration, whereas in the remaining trials, treatment was given open label, with outcomes verified by those unaware of treatment assignment.
[c] Loss to follow-up not reported in the AFASAK I trial and CAFA study; this ranged from 0% to 3% in the other studies.
[d] Strong association present: RR, 0.46.
[e] Importance is rated on a scale from 1 to 9, where 1 represents least important (not important for decision making) and 9 most important (for decision making).
[f] Only 17 events in the oral anticoagulant group and 16 events in the control group.
[g] Required transfusion of 2 or more units of red blood cells, hospitalization, or invasive procedures to control bleeding, and those that resulted in death or permanent functional impairment (eg, blindness) were included.
[h] Data from systematic review by van Walraven et al[11] (control is ASA therapy).
[i] All-cause mortality: death from any cause (vascular and nonvascular) within 30 days from onset of stroke symptoms. For this outcome, results of published data, which included about 6% of patients with previous stroke or TIA, were used.
[j] From Figure 10 of Aguilar and Hart.[28]
[k] Lack of blinding in 2 trials is of lesser concern.
[l] The diagnosis of MI was usually based on electrocardiographic changes, increase of enzyme levels, or postmortem examination. These consisted of death caused cause by stroke, heart disease, hemorrhage, and sudden deaths of unknown cause.
[m] Ischemic stroke was an identified outcome in all trials, with the ischemic nature confirmed by neuroimaging or autopsy in most cases.
[n] Methodologic quality was not downgraded because the lack of blinding in some studies did not have important effect on the results.
[o] Strong association present: RR, 0.32.

TABLE 22.4-10

Checklist and Example for Developing Recommendations[5,29]

Question: Should elderly patients with AF receive oral anticoagulation?

Patients: Patients with AF, older than 75 years and no other risk factors

Intervention: Warfarin

Outcomes: Thromboembolic disabling or fatal stroke, all-cause mortality, hemorrhage

Evidence summary:

Systematic review of 5 randomized trials including 2313 patients showed statistically significant reduction of disabling or fatal stroke (RR, 0.46; 95% CI, 0.27-0.81; NNT, 50 in 1.5 years; 95% CI, 30-100) and all-cause mortality (RR, 0.70; 95% CI, 0.52-0.95; NNT, 50; 95% CI, 25-1000).[28] An increase in intracranial and extracranial hemorrhage was not statistically significant in the RCTs included in this review, but another review and observational studies show an absolute risk increase for hemorrhage in patients receiving oral anticoagulation that corresponds to approximately 1.8% (NNH, 55).[11]

Quality of evidence:

RCTs without serious limitations provide direct and consistent evidence pointing toward large effect size. At the same time, 3 studies were unblinded, and the total number of events (stroke) was only 57 in 2313 patients. In balance, the evidence may be considered high because the unblinded studies showed similar effects compared with the blinded studies and the effect for stroke prevention is large and statistically significant.

Best estimates:

Reduction of thromboembolic stroke and all-cause mortality and increase in bleeding risk.

Judgment of benefits vs risks, burden, and cost:

Information available suggests benefits of prophylaxis, and most patients would accept oral anticoagulation, given the NNTs and NNH.

Grade of recommendation:

Quality of evidence is high for patient-important outcomes. The recommendation could be expressed as, "For elderly patients with atrial fibrillation and no history of stroke who are at high risk, we recommend oral anticoagulation (strong recommendation based on high-quality evidence)." A statement about the underlying values and preferences could follow ("This recommendation places a relatively high value on preventing thromboembolic strokes and death and a relatively low value on bleeding induced by oral anticoagulants").

Abbreviations: AF, atrial fibrillation; CI, confidence interval; NNH, number needed to harm; NNT, number needed to treat; RCT, randomized controlled trial; RR, relative risk.

References

1. Atkins D, Best D, Briss PA, et al. Grading quality of evidence and strength of recommendations. *BMJ.* 2004;328(7454):1490.

2. Schünemann HJ, Best D, Vist G, Oxman AD. Letters, numbers, symbols and words: how to communicate grades of evidence and recommendations. *CMAJ.* 2003;169(7):677-680.

3. Guyatt G, Vist G, Falck-Ytter Y, Kunz R, Magrini N, Schünemann H. An emerging consensus on grading recommendations [editorial]? *ACP J Club.* 2006;144(1):A8-A9.

4. Stevenson RRK, Wilkinson P, Roberts R, Timmis AD. Short and long term prognosis of acute myocardial infarction since introduction of thrombolysis. *BMJ.* 1993;307(6900):349-353.

5. Guyatt G, Gutterman D, Baumann M, et al. Grading strength of recommendations and quality of evidence in clinical guidelines. *Chest.* 2006;129(1):174-181.

6. Buller HR, Agnelli G, Hull RD, Hyers TM, Prins MH, Raskob GE. Antithrombotic therapy for venous thromboembolic disease: the Seventh ACCP Conference on Antithrombotic and Thrombolytic Therapy. *Chest.* 2004;126(3)(suppl):401S-428S.

7. O'Connor AM, Stacey D, Entwistle V, et al. Decision aids for people facing health treatment or screening decisions. *Cochrane Database Syst Rev.* 2003;(2):CD001431.

8. Guyatt GM, Devereaux PJ, Schünemann H, Bhandari HM. Patients at the centre: in our practice, and in our use of language. *ACP J Club.* 2004;140(1):A11-A12.

9. Chang AB, Lasserson TJ, Kiljander TO, Connor FL, Gaffney JT, Garske LA. Systematic review and meta-analysis of randomised controlled trials of gastro-oesophageal reflux interventions for chronic cough associated with gastro-oesophageal reflux. *BMJ.* 2006;332(7532):11-17.

10. Petrucci N, Iacovelli W. Ventilation with lower tidal volumes versus traditional tidal volumes in adults for acute lung injury and acute respiratory distress syndrome. *Cochrane Database Syst Rev.* 2004;(2):CD003844.

11. van Walraven C, Hart RG, Singer DE, et al. Oral anticoagulants vs aspirin in nonvalvular atrial fibrillation: an individual patient meta-analysis. *JAMA.* 2002;288(19):2441-2448.

12. Devereaux PA, Anderson DR, Gardner MJ, et al. Differences between perspectives of physicians and patients on anticoagulation in patients with atrial fibrillation: observational study. *BMJ.* 2001;323(7323):1218-1222.

13. Guyatt G, Baumann M, Pauker S, et al. Addressing resource allocation issues in recommendations from clinical practice guideline panels: suggestions from an American College of Chest Physicians task force. *Chest.* 2006;129(1):182-187.

14. Chong B, Gallus AS, Cade JF, et al. Prospective randomised open-label comparison of danaparoid with dextran 70 in the treatment of heparin-induced thrombocytopenia with thrombosis: a clinical outcome study. *Thromb Haemost.* 2001;86(5):1170-1175.

15. Hood SC, Moher D, Barber GG. Management of intermittent claudication with pentoxifylline: meta-analysis of randomized controlled trials. *CMAJ.* 1996;155(8):1053-1059.

16. Clagett GP, Sobel M, Jackson MR, Lip GY, Tangelder M, Verhaeghe R. Antithrombotic therapy in peripheral arterial occlusive disease: the Seventh ACCP Conference on Antithrombotic and Thrombolytic Therapy. *Chest.* 2004;126(3)(suppl):609S-626S.

17. Schünemann HJ, Hill S, Kakad M, et al. WHO Rapid Advice Guidelines for the pharmacological management of human infection with avian influenza A (H5N1) virus. *Lancet Infect Dis.* 2007;7(1):21-31.

18. de Bruijn S, Stam J. Stroke: randomized, placebo-controlled trial of anticoagulant treatment with low-molecular-weight heparin for cerebral sinus thrombosis. *Stroke.* 1999;30(3):484-488.

19. Bhandari M, Busse JW, Jackowski D, et al. Association between industry funding and statistically significant pro-industry findings in medical and surgical randomized trials. *CMAJ.* 2004;170(4):477-480.

20. Alonso-Coello P, Zhou Q, Martinez-Zapata MJ, et al. Meta-analysis of flavonoids for the treatment of haemorrhoids. *Br J Surg.* 2006;93(8):909-920.

21. Thompson DC, Rivara FP, Thompson R. Helmets for preventing head and facial injuries in bicyclists. *Cochrane Database Syst Rev.* 2000;(2):CD001855.

22. Cannegieter SC, Rosendaal FR, Briet E. Platelets/thromboembolism: thromboembolic and bleeding complications in patients with mechanical heart valve prostheses. *Circulation.* 1994;89(2):635-641.

23. Devereaux PJ, Choi PT, Lacchetti C, et al. A systematic review and meta-analysis of studies comparing mortality rates of private for-profit and private not-for-profit hospitals. *CMAJ.* 2002;166(11):1399-1406.

24. Levine MN, Raskob G, Beyth RJ, Kearon C, Schulman S. Hemorrhagic complications of anticoagulant treatment: the Seventh ACCP Conference on Antithrombotic and Thrombolytic Therapy. *Chest.* 2004;126(3)(suppl):287S-310S.

25. Malenka DJ, Baron JA, Johansen S, Wahrenberger JW, Ross JM. The framing effect of relative and absolute risk. *J Gen Intern Med.* 1993;8(10):543-548.

26. Heyland DK, Cook DJ, Jaeschke R, Griffith L, Lee HN, Guyatt GH. Selective decontamination of the digestive tract: an overview. *Chest.* 1994;105(4):1221-1229.

27. Kollef MH. The role of selective digestive tract decontamination on mortality and respiratory tract infections: a meta-analysis. *Chest.* 1994;105(4):1101-1108.

28. Aguilar MI, Hart R. Oral anticoagulants for preventing stroke in patients with non-valvular atrial fibrillation and no previous history of stroke or transient ischemic attacks. *Cochrane Database Syst Rev.* 2005;(3):CD001927.

29. Schünemann HJ, Jaeschke J, Cook D, et al; ATS Documents Development and Implementation Committee. An official ATS statement: grading the quality of evidence and strength of recommendations for guidelines and recommendations. *Am J Respir Crit Care Med.* 2006;174(5):605-614.

DRUG CLASS EFFECTS

Regina Kunz, Heiner C. Bucher,
Finlay A. McAlister, Anne Holbrook,
and Gordon Guyatt

IN THIS CHAPTER:

CLINICAL SCENARIO
Which Statin Is Best—Or Is There Any Difference?

As a busy primary care clinician, you care for many patients with elevated serum cholesterol levels and others with normal cholesterol levels but established atherosclerotic vascular disease, in whom statins (hydroxymethylglutaryl–coenzyme A reductase inhibitors) lower the risk of atherosclerotic vascular events. A speaker at a recent continuing medical education conference reviewed the benefits of cholesterol-lowering therapy, stressed the importance of maximal low-density lipoprotein (LDL) lowering, and commented in favor of the most potent drug. Although you approve of using statin therapy for patients with elevated cholesterol levels and for those who have "normal" lipid levels but have known atherosclerosis, you are uncertain about which of the 6 statins currently available is the best. You ask a local cardiologist and endocrinologist; one suggests pravastatin, and the other, rosuvastatin. They raise a variety of issues: efficacy in different patient populations, demonstrated benefit in *randomized controlled trials* (*RCTs*) (part of the case for pravastatin), maximal LDL lowering (the major argument for rosuvastatin, which has not been tested in RCTs to determine its effect on patient-important outcomes), safety profile, drug interactions, and pricing. Faced with competing claims, you realize that you need a framework for making your statin selection.

WHAT IS A DRUG CLASS?

Most classes of drugs include multiple substances. The interests of clinicians, manufacturers, and drug reimbursement plans may conflict around questions of whether a particular drug is as effective or more effective than others in its class.[1] In this chapter, we provide a framework for grading the body of *evidence* that confirms or contests the presence of a class effect among similar drugs.

Many drug classification systems exist; most involve a hierarchic approach, grouping drugs first by general therapeutic area, then by mechanism of action, eventually by chemical class, and then specific drug. Drugs generally belong to the same class for one of 3 reasons: their chemical structure is similar, their mechanisms of action are similar, or their pharmacologic effects on biological end points are similar (Table 22.5-1). For the purposes of this discussion, we will consider a drug class to include those drugs that share a similar chemical structure and mechanism of action.

Because of common chemical structure and mechanisms of action, the compounds of a class may plausibly confer similar pharmacologic effects and patient-

TABLE 22.5-1

Different Definitions of Drug Classes

Definition	Example
A group of drugs with similar chemical structure	Dihydropyridine calcium-channel blockers have a dihydropyridine ring.
A group of drugs with similar mechanism of action	Calcium-channel blockers block the voltage-dependent calcium channels on the surfaces of cell membranes.
A group of drugs that share a similar pharmacologic effect	Antihypertensive agents (eg, calcium-channel blockers, angiotensin-converting enzyme inhibitors, β-blockers, thiazides, angiotensin-receptor blockers) lower blood pressure.

important outcomes (class effects). Assumption of a class effect is a key medical heuristic that underlies many clinical *practice guidelines* and reimbursement practices; these practices involve extrapolation from studies involving 1 or more drugs to other drugs of the same class. If a class effect exists, one can assume that the beneficial effects are similar and choose a drug on the basis of cost, convenience, and minimizing adverse effects.

For example, experts recommend both β-blockers and angiotensin-converting enzyme (ACE) inhibitors for survivors of myocardial infarction and for patients with heart failure. In both situations, clinicians and patients are likely to be interested in the drug within each class with the least adverse effects, payers will pursue the most cost-effective drug from a class, and manufacturers will do their best to ensure that their drug is prescribed as much as possible.

ACCEPTING, OR REJECTING, A DRUG CLASS EFFECT IS CHALLENGING

Although drugs of the same class typically exhibit similar pharmacologic effects and clinical outcomes, situations occur in which researchers and clinicians assume a class effect when in truth there is none.

For example, although initial guidelines for β-blockers in heart failure recommended the class, more recent guidelines[2] have focused this recommendation to encompass only those 3 β-blockers proven in RCTs to improve outcomes in patients with heart failure (carvedilol, bisoprolol, and metoprolol) after one trial failed to demonstrate any benefit with a fourth β-blocker (bucindolol) in heart failure.[3]

β-Blockers also provide an example for the opposite situation—rejecting a class effect when in truth there is one. Certain chemical structures in some types of β-blocker produced physiologic effects called intrinsic sympathetic activity. Results of a *meta-analysis*[4] suggested that β-blockers with intrinsic sympathomimetic activity (ISA) had a favorable effect on heart rate, glucose and lipid levels, and the respiratory system but a less favorable effect on patients after myocardial infarction than non-ISA β-blockers. Subsequent trials,[5] however, failed to confirm this difference, and consideration of the entire body of evidence[6] now suggests little or no difference between β-blocker subgroups.

Ideally, a strong conclusion that a class effect exists would come from head-to-head comparisons in RCTs that demonstrate equivalent, or at least similar, influence on patient-important outcomes. Unfortunately, there are a number of reasons such evidence is usually unavailable. First, confidence intervals (CIs) around the difference between agents would generally need to be narrow to exclude an important difference favoring one or the other. Excluding such a difference requires large sample sizes and large numbers of events (see Chapter 8, Confidence Intervals). Second, drug companies and funding agencies are seldom interested in devoting the resources necessary to clearly establish a class effect. Third, when there are more than 2 drugs in a class, the challenges become even more daunting. Picture the resources required to definitively establish similar magnitude of effect in patient-important outcomes across the 6 available statins. Large amounts of money are often involved in the choice among competing drugs within a class. Consider, for instance, the gigantic worldwide market for statins. The lack of ideal evidence inflames the debate over the existence of a class effect. Nevertheless, clinicians need to make a decision in the absence of ideal evidence and, therefore, need a framework for so doing.

GRADE Provides a Framework for Assessing Class Effects

An international group of methodologists, clinicians, and biostatisticians has recently developed a structured and comprehensive approach (see Chapter 22.4, Grading Recommendations) for examining the evidence underlying choices in patient management. The grades of recommendation, assessment, development, and evaluation (GRADE) approach applies a critical appraisal of the quality of the evidence, including the study design and implementation, directness of the comparisons, precision of the point estimates, consistency of the findings, magnitude of the effect, and likelihood of reporting bias, and classifies the evidence into high, moderate, low, or very low quality (see Table 22.5-2). It also

TABLE 22.5-2

Factors That May Decrease or Raise the Quality of Evidence

Quality of Evidence	Study Designs	Criteria to Decrease the Quality Category	Criteria to Raise the Quality Category
High	Randomized trials	• Limitations of study quality resulting in high risk of bias	• Strong associations
Moderate			• Presence of a dose-response gradient
		• Imprecision	
Low	Observational studies	• Reporting bias	
		• Indirect evidence	
Very low	Any other evidence	• Inconsistency of results	

ranks the outcomes according to their clinical relevance, both for benefit and harm, and offers an explicit approach for carrying out the judgments involved. Originally developed for grading recommendations, the framework is well suited for addressing the question of whether drug effects are similar or dissimilar. For such assessments to be credible, they must occur in the context of a rigorous *systematic review* that will ensure a comprehensive and unbiased assessment of all the relevant evidence (see Chapter 19, Summarizing the Evidence).

APPLYING GRADE TO THE STATIN QUESTION: FINDING THE EVIDENCE

The key question with regard to class effect is whether the action of 2 or more drugs of similar chemical structure and similar mechanism of action confers similar pharmacologic effects and patient-important outcomes. Applied to the clinical scenario, you pose your question as, Are the beneficial effects of the various statins on patient-relevant cardiovascular outcomes, including major coronary events, revascularization, or stroke, similar enough that we can use other considerations such as adverse effects, cost per equivalent dose, and convenience when choosing the drug?

You search PubMed for a comprehensive meta-analysis, using the term "statins," restricted to the publication type "meta-analysis" and to recent publications "2003 to 2006," and identify 51 meta-analyses that were published during this period. One is a recent individual patient data (IPD) meta-analysis by the Cholesterol Treatment Trialists' Collaborators.[7] In this IPD meta-analysis, the investigators shared the original patient data from each RCT and built a single large database. In comparison to a conventional meta-analysis that uses only trial-level data, the IPD allows more precise analyses on time to event and more powerful exploration of possible differences in effect in patient subgroups.

The IPD meta-analysis that you identified in your literature search provides additional advantages. When designing the IPD meta-analysis prospectively in 1994 to include current and planned large-scale RCTs of cholesterol treatment regimens, the investigators could integrate their anticipated methodologic problems of pooling at a very early stage and could assure the collection of key variables across studies to answer questions that an individual trial cannot answer. The prospective design also deals effectively with the problem of reporting bias.

A quick look at the meta-analysis reveals that it includes only drug-placebo comparisons, whereas you would ideally like to see head-to-head comparisons between alternative statins. You, therefore, conduct another search for individual trials comparing these agents and discover 2 such RCTs: the IDEAL study[8] and the PROVE-IT trial.[9]

APPLYING GRADE TO THE STATIN QUESTION: METHODOLOGIC QUALITY AND RESULTS FROM HEAD-TO-HEAD COMPARISONS

The IPD meta-analysis included 14 large RCTs, and in addition, you have decided to focus on 2 head-to-head comparison trials. Looking back to Table 22.5-2, we see that because the evidence comes from RCTs, it holds promise to provide high-quality evidence. Still, we need to look carefully at 5 possible limitations.

First, although the report did not thoroughly evaluate the methodologic quality of the individual studies, another recent meta-analysis[10] reported a methodologic assessment of the relevant studies and confirmed their high quality.

Second, we must consider whether the studies are too small, with too few events, to yield reliable estimates. With more than 1000 patients each (assuring reasonably narrow CIs) and a follow-up of at least 2 years, we will not need to downgrade our assessment of methodologic quality as a result of imprecision.

Third, we need to address the possibility of reporting bias. Because the trials in the IPD were prospectively identified and the decision was made to ultimately examine the results together, we can exclude reporting bias as a problem. Issues that remain to be addressed include indirectness and inconsistency. When considering the head-to-head comparison trials, the issue of reporting bias remains. It is likely, however, that the very large trials that are the focus of our inquiry would appear in the published literature; thus, reporting bias does not appear a major threat.

Only 2 studies provide head-to-head comparisons (and thus show promise for passing the fourth hurdle of possible downgrading of methodologic quality). To address the final issue, that of consistency, we must examine their results. The IDEAL study, an RCT comparing high-dose atorvastatin (80 mg/d) with lower-dose simvastatin (20 mg/d, with the possibility of up-titration to 40 mg/d to achieve target LDL cholesterol level) in patients with stable coronary disease, failed to demonstrate a significant difference between the 2 drugs in reducing a major coronary event (simvastatin 10.4% vs atorvastatin 9.3%; hazard ratio, 0.89; 95% CI, 0.78-1.01),[8] although one might interpret this result as strengthening the evidence for a class effect; if the lower boundary of the CI (a reduction in hazard of 22%) represented the truth, one would conclude an important benefit of atorvastatin over simvastatin.

A second head-to-head-comparison (PROVE-IT study) that compared high-dose atorvastatin (80 mg/d) with moderate-dose pravastatin (40 mg/d) suggested that atorvastatin is superior to pravastatin in reducing relevant cardiovascular outcomes (largely angina and hospitalization) in patients with acute coronary syndrome (pravastatin 26.3% vs atorvastatin 22.4%; hazard ratio, 0.84; 95% CI, 0.74-0.95).[9] This result casts further doubt on the class effect hypothesis. A closer inspection of PROVE-IT reveals, however, that besides using different drugs, atorvastatin was administered with a more potent dose that achieved a 35% lower level of LDL cholesterol than the dose used for pravastatin. This raises another complexity of the statin issue: in this context, what exactly do we mean by a class effect?

STATIN DOSING AND LDL LEVELS

Consider a situation in which investigators found that a high dose of one member of a drug class (drug A) yielded a larger treatment effect than an inadequate dose of a second drug class member (drug B). Would this lead you to reject a class effect? Clearly, it would not; rather, one would interpret the finding as supporting a dose-response relationship. Thus, the class effect question is best framed in terms of whether more or less equivalent doses of alternative agents lead to similar effects ("equipotency" is the relevant term sometimes used for more or less equivalent doses).

This introduces the question of how one decides whether, in fact, investigators have used equivalent doses of alternative agents within a class. In the case of statins, one possibility is to define equivalent doses as those that provide the same level of LDL-level lowering. Justification for this definition originally came from cohort studies that consistently show a strong relationship between serum LDL cholesterol level and the incidence of coronary heart disease: a difference in serum cholesterol level of ~0.6 mmol/L is associated with a 54% reduction of coronary heart disease among men in their forties, a 39% *relative risk reduction (RRR)* in men in their fifties, and a 20% RRR among men in their seventies.[11] The data for women at the time were limited but indicated a similar effect.[11] If large rigorous RCTs consistently demonstrated that 2 statins produced more or less the same LDL lowering and yet the effect of cardiovascular events differed, one would have strong evidence of differences in pharmacologic effect and could thus reject the class effect hypothesis.

This is not true in the PROVE-IT RCT. Atorvastatin's greater effect on cardiovascular events seems quite plausibly explained by its greater reduction in LDL cholesterol level. Thus, PROVE-IT did not conduct the comparison we would ideally like to see to substantiate a class effect, a trial in which the investigators tested doses of similar potency to reduce LDL cholesterol level and demonstrated the same effect on cardiovascular events. Thus, PROVE-IT is consistent with a class effect, but the evidence is somewhat indirect.

Considering the limitations of our 2 direct comparisons—a CI that includes important superiority of atorvastatin in IDEAL and the difference in LDL-level lowering in PROVE-IT—so far, we have moderate-quality evidence in support of the class effect.

MORE INDIRECT EVIDENCE FOR A STATIN CLASS EFFECT

As we have pointed out, establishing a definitive statin class effect would require head-to-head RCT comparisons of all relevant drugs in doses that achieved similar reductions in LDL and demonstrated similar effects on crucial patient-relevant end points. The IPD meta-analysis included only studies with placebo, usual care, or no treatment in control groups. Therefore, we must make deductions about relative magnitude of effect on the basis of between-study comparisons (eg, assess the relative impact of atorvastatin vs simvastatin by looking at the effects of atorvastatin vs placebo and simvastatin vs placebo). The meta-analysis has further limitations: it reports only on 5 of 6 currently available statins (no trials on rosuvastatin are available), and the available trials tested only relatively low doses.

How can we use these data? A naive indirect comparison contrasts the results of individual arms between trials as if they were from a single trial. For example, one can compare patients in the simvastatin arm of a placebo-controlled trial to patients in the pravastatin arm of another placebo-controlled trial. This comparison loses the prognostic balance achieved by randomization and leaves us with a cohort study with all its limitations. Not surprisingly, both simulation studies and empirical evidence suggest that such comparisons are subject to both bias and spuriously precise estimates.[12]

A more appropriate approach compares proportional effects such as *relative risk* (*RR*), RRR, or *odds ratio* (*OR*) seen with each drug against placebo, a strategy that assumes the absence of bias in patient selection and trial performance and a consistent treatment effect across different patient subgroups and baseline risk. This latter assumption holds true in most (but not all) situations.[13] Authors have suggested a variety of statistical approaches to making the appropriate indirect comparisons.[14] All approaches, however, assume that there are no factors in patient selection, study design, or study implementation that will influence the magnitude of treatment effect.

Although these remain relatively strong assumptions, one might ask how well indirect comparisons predict the results of direct comparison in practice. It is not difficult to find instances of discrepancies between results. For instance, a systematic review of strategies to prevent *Pneumocystis carinii* pneumonia in human immunodeficiency virus–positive patients documented that the indirect comparison of trimethoprim/sulfamethoxazole vs dapsone/pyrimethamine suggested a much larger effect size from trimethoprim/sulfamethoxazole (OR, 0.37; 95% CI, 0.21-0.65) than was seen in the direct comparison (OR, 0.64; 95% CI, 0.45-0.90).[14]

A systematic, comprehensive review across a variety of medical topics reanalyzed 44 direct and indirect comparisons of the same intervention from 28 published meta-analyses of RCTs.[12] Fifteen of these 44 comparisons addressed drugs within 1 class. The investigators documented a moderate agreement between the statistical conclusions from the direct and adjusted indirect comparisons ($\kappa = 0.53$). Only 3 of the 44 comparisons found a significant discrepancy between the direct and the adjusted indirect estimate, none of which occurred with drugs of the same class. The relative efficacy of an intervention was equally likely to be overestimated and underestimated by the indirect comparison. It appears that in most, but not all, cases, results from adjusted indirect comparisons are similar to those of direct comparisons. In the GRADE approach, this uncertainty associated with indirect comparisons immediately downgrades the quality of the evidence from high to moderate.

The IPD meta-analysis showed differences in apparent treatment effects among the different statins. For example, the RR of major coronary events ranged from 0.83 (95% CI, 0.56-1.25) for pravastatin in the Gruppo Italiano per lo Studio della Sopravvivenza nell'Infarto Miocardico (GISSI) prevention study[15] to 0.63 (95% CI, 0.53-0.75) for simvastatin in the Scandinavian Simvastatin Survival Study (4S).[16] One might, of course, find differences this large or larger simply by chance. For instance, the Collaborative Group on ACE Inhibitor Trials[17] suggested that there is a class effect for ACE inhibitors in patients with symptomatic heart failure despite that the OR point estimates for mortality effects ranged from 0.14 (95% CI, 0-7.6) for perindopril (1 trial, 125 patients) to 0.78 (95% CI, 0.67-0.91) for enalapril (7 trials, 3381 patients). Our confidence in this class effect stems from the recognition that the overall OR in 32 trials involving 7105 patients was 0.77 (95% CI, 0.67-0.88), the CIs for each of the ACE inhibitors overlapped, and there was no statistical heterogeneity between trials of different agents ($P = .87$).

Varying absolute LDL cholesterol-level reduction (which ranged from –0.35 mmol/L in the GISSI[15] prevention study using 20 mg pravastatin to –1.77 mmol/L in the 4S study,[16] which used higher doses of 20-40 mg of simvastatin) can explain these differences. Indeed, the investigators' analysis suggests a strong relation between degree of LDL cholesterol-level lowering and cardiovascular end points: in the IPD meta-analysis, the RR (weighted per mmol/LDL cholesterol-level reduction) was 0.77 (95% CI, 0.74-0.80) for coronary events; it was 0.76 (95% CI, 0.73-0.80) for coronary revascularization, and it was the same for stroke and major vascular events, and there was no evidence for heterogeneity in any of the estimates ($P_{\text{heterogeneity}}$ between .9 and .3).[7]

Thus, the IPD meta-analysis provides more indirect (and thus moderate-quality) evidence in support of a class effect. Overall, we can conclude that we have moderate-quality evidence from both direct and indirect comparison suggesting a class effect for statins; that is, whatever drug one uses to produce a particular reduction in LDL level, one is likely to find a similar reduction in risk of cardiovascular events.

HAVING FOUND MODERATE-QUALITY EVIDENCE FOR A CLASS EFFECT—WHAT NEXT?

Given that it appears likely we can achieve similar reductions in patient-important outcomes with different statins, we should base the prescribing decision on risks and harms, convenience, and cost. Thus, we need to consider the evidence regarding risks associated with the different statins.

With one exception, statins seemed to be relatively safe drugs. A cohort study comparing cerivastatin with other statins found a 10-fold increase in risk for rhabdomyolysis (95% CI, 3.1-32.7) with cerivastatin; this increased to more than 1400 (95% CI, 496-4013) when patients took cerivastatin in combination with a fibrate.[18,19] As a result, cerivastatin has been withdrawn from the market.

The most common adverse effects of the statins include muscle damage (which very rarely results in rhabdomyolysis and death) and increases in liver enzymes. In the randomized direct comparisons of pravastatin vs atorvastatin,[9] the 2 drugs resulted in similar discontinuation rates because of adverse effects, in particular, myalgia, increase in creatine kinase, or rhabdomyolysis. Patients receiving atorvastatin experienced an increase in liver enzyme levels more frequently (3.3% vs 1.1%; $P < .001$) than those taking pravastatin. The results are consistent with the IDEAL study, in which investigators observed a similar frequency of myopathy or rhabdomyolysis and cancer mortality with atorvastatin and simvastatin but a more frequent increase in liver enzyme levels and a more frequent permanent discontinuation for adverse effect in patients receiving atorvastatin (9.6% vs 4.2%; $P < .001$).[8]

Observational data from the New Drug Applications and the US Food and Drug Administration Web sites, with a special focus on cerivastatin and rosuvastatin, the most recently introduced drug,[20] suggest a dose-effect relationship for adverse effects for all statins. This seems to be the case for an increase in transaminase levels and development of myopathy and proteinuria. As with most drugs, adverse effects of statins have received less attention than beneficial effects,[21,22] a situation that creates quandaries in clinical decision making that involves balancing benefits and downsides of therapy.

In summary, although there is some suggestion of increased adverse effects from atorvastatin and rosuvastatin, these differences could be a function of the doses used rather than differences in the drugs themselves, and there is thus little to choose between the available drugs in terms of adverse effects. Other considerations, such as drug interaction profile, cost (some statins now are available as cheaper generic drugs), and convenience may therefore dominate the decision.

USING THE GUIDE

Returning to our opening scenario, having used the GRADE process, you have concluded that moderate-quality evidence suggests a class effect such that it matters little what drug you use to achieve LDL-level reductions that will result in a decrease in cardiovascular events. Further, you have learned that differences in adverse effects are relatively minor. All these drugs are administered once daily, and they therefore provide similar convenience for regular use. You are left weighing the importance of choosing a statin that has evidence from RCTs showing benefit on patient-important outcomes vs others with benefit on LDL cholesterol level and presumed benefit for vascular events. Several of your colleagues restrict their statin choices this way—to simvastatin, atorvastatin, pravastatin, or fluvastatin. Others consider the length of time the drugs have been on the market; the longer the use, the less likely that evidence of unexpected rare severe toxicity will emerge. Cost is also an issue. As it turns out, your patient's drug coverage reimburses statins according to their dose potency, with approximate potency equivalents of atorvastatin 20 mg = lovastatin 80 mg = pravastatin > 80 mg = simvastatin 80 mg = fluvastatin > 80 mg = rosuvastain 5-10 mg.[21,23,24] You decide that you are comfortable with a class effect and, for this patient, can prescribe any statin readily available. For patients whose drug coverage includes substantial cost gradients, you will choose the drug that is least expensive for achieving the desired reduction in LDL level.

References

1. Skolnick AA. Drug firm suit fails to halt publication of Canadian Health Technology Report. *JAMA.* 1998;280(8):683-684.

2. Arnold JM, Liu P, Demers C, et al. Canadian Cardiovascular Society Consensus Conference Recommendations on Heart Failure 2006: diagnosis and management. *Can J Cardiol.* 2006;22(1):23-45.

3. Beta-Blocker Evaluation of Survival Trial Investigators. A trial of the beta-blocker bucindolol in patients with advanced chronic heart failure. *N Engl J Med.* 2001;344(22):1659-1667.

4. Yusuf S, Peto R, Lewis J, Collins R, Sleight P. Beta blockade during and after myocardial infarction: an overview of the randomized trials. *Prog Cardiovasc Dis.* 1985;27(5):335-371.

5. Boissel JP, Leizorovicz A, Picolet H, Peyrieux JC. Secondary prevention after high-risk acute myocardial infarction with low-dose acebutolol. *Am J Cardiol.* 1990;66(3):251-260.

6. McAlister FA, Teo KK. Antiarrhythmic therapies for the prevention of sudden cardiac death. *Drugs.* 1997;54(2):235-252.

7. Baigent C, Keech A, Kearney PM, et al. Efficacy and safety of cholesterol-lowering treatment: prospective meta-analysis of data from 90,056 participants in 14 randomised trials of statins. *Lancet.* 2005;366(9493):1267-1278.

8. Pedersen TR, Faergeman O, Kastelein JJ, et al. High-dose atorvastatin vs usual-dose simvastatin for secondary prevention after myocardial infarction: the IDEAL study: a randomized controlled trial. *JAMA.* 2005;294(19):2437-2445.

9. Cannon CP, Braunwald E, McCabe CH, et al. Intensive versus moderate lipid lowering with statins after acute coronary syndromes. *N Engl J Med.* 2004;350 (15):1495-1504.

10. Studer M, Briel M, Leimenstoll B, Glass TR, Bucher HC. Effect of different antilipidemic agents and diets on mortality: a systematic review. *Arch Intern Med.* 2005;165(7):725-730.

11. Law MR, Wald NJ, Thompson SG. By how much and how quickly does reduction in serum cholesterol concentration lower risk of ischaemic heart disease? *BMJ.* 1994;308(6925):367-372.

12. Song F, Altman DG, Glenny AM, Deeks JJ. Validity of indirect comparison for estimating efficacy of competing interventions: empirical evidence from published meta-analyses. *BMJ.* 2003;326(7387):472-476.

13. Furukawa TA, Guyatt GH, Griffith LE. Can we individualize the "number needed to treat"? an empirical study of summary effect measures in meta-analyses. *Int J Epidemiol.* 2002;31(1):72-76.

14. Bucher HC, Guyatt GH, Griffith LE, Walter SD. The results of direct and indirect treatment comparisons in meta-analysis of randomized controlled trials. *J Clin Epidemiol.* 1997;50(6):683-691.

15. GISSI Prevenzione Investigators (Gruppo Italiano per lo Studio della Sopravvivenza nell'Infarto Miocardico). Results of the low-dose (20 mg) pravastatin GISSI Prevenzione trial in 4271 patients with recent myocardial infarction: do stopped trials contribute to overall knowledge? *Ital Heart J.* 2000;1(12):810-820.

16. Randomised trial of cholesterol lowering in 4444 patients with coronary heart disease: the Scandinavian Simvastatin Survival Study (4S). *Lancet.* 1994;344 (8934):1383-1389.

17. Garg R, Yusuf S. Overview of randomized trials of angiotensin-converting enzyme inhibitors on mortality and morbidity in patients with heart failure: Collaborative Group on ACE Inhibitor Trials. *JAMA.* 1995;273(18):1450-1456.

18. Graham DJ, Staffa JA, Shatin D, et al. Incidence of hospitalized rhabdomyolysis in patients treated with lipid-lowering drugs. *JAMA.* 2004;292(21):2585-2590.

19. Chang JT, Staffa JA, Parks M, Green L. Rhabdomyolysis with HMG-CoA reductase inhibitors and gemfibrozil combination therapy. *Pharmacoepidemiol Drug Saf.* 2004;13(7):417-426.

20. Jacobson TA. Statin safety: lessons from new drug applications for marketed statins. *Am J Cardiol.* 2006;97(8A):44C-51C.

21. McKenney JM. Optimizing LDL-C lowering with statins. *Am J Ther.* 2004;11 (1):54-59.

22. Fontanarosa PB, Rennie D, DeAngelis CD. Postmarketing surveillance—lack of vigilance, lack of trust. *JAMA.* 2004;292(21):2647-2650.

23. Jones P, Kafonek S, Laurora I, Hunninghake D. Comparative dose efficacy study of atorvastatin versus simvastatin, pravastatin, lovastatin, and fluvastatin in patients with hypercholesterolemia (the CURVES study). *Am J Cardiol.* 1998; 81(5):582-587.

24. Teramoto T, Watkins C. Review of efficacy of rosuvastatin 5 mg. *Int J Clin Pract.* 2005;59(1):92-101.

PARALLEL BUT SEPARATE GOALS: EVIDENCE-BASED PRACTITIONERS AND EVIDENCE-BASED CARE

Gordon Guyatt, Maureen O. Meade, Brian Haynes,
Roman Jaeschke, Deborah J. Cook, Mark Wilson,
and Scott Richardson

IN THIS CHAPTER:

Top-quality health care implies the practice of medicine that is consistent with the best evidence (*evidence-based health care*). An intuitively appealing way to achieve *evidence-based practice* is to train clinicians who can independently find, appraise, and judiciously apply the best evidence (evidence-based experts). Indeed, our fondest hope for this book is that it will help you become an evidence-based expert. The following discussion will, however, illustrate that training evidence-based experts is not, by itself, an optimal strategy for ensuring patients receive evidence-based health care.[1]

In this chapter, we acknowledge the challenges to developing expertise in *evidence-based medicine (EBM)*. Next, we will highlight an alternative approach to providing evidence-based care, which is training clinicians who can use evidence-based summaries and recommendations, what we call *evidence-based practitioners*. We then acknowledge the limitations of this strategy and suggest a solution to these limitations. Finally, we will present some of the reasons you might wish to acquire advanced EBM skills, although these skills are not prerequisites for practicing EBM.

BECOMING AN EVIDENCE-BASED MEDICINE EXPERT IS A DAUNTING (THOUGH MANAGEABLE) TASK

The skills needed to provide an evidence-based solution to a clinical dilemma include precisely defining the problem, conducting an efficient search to locate the best evidence, critically appraising the evidence, and considering that evidence—and its implications—in the context of patients' circumstances and values. Although attaining these skills at a basic level is relatively easy, developing the expertise to allow efficient and sophisticated critical appraisal and application to the individual patient requires intensive study and frequent, occasionally time-consuming, application.

The advanced topics chapters of this book highlight the challenges of becoming an EBM expert. You must have a deep understanding of and be alert to violations of the principles of valid scientific inquiry (issues such as early stopping of randomized trials, the intention-to-treat principle, and interpreting *composite endpoints*). In addition, you must be aware of how even valid studies may mislead (note the 10 strategies to avoid being mislead in Chapter 11.3, Dealing With Misleading Presentations of Clinical Trial Results, and additional issues such as the use of *surrogate endpoints* and composite endpoints). Becoming an EBM expert is achievable and gratifying, but it is not for everyone.

BECOMING AN EVIDENCE-BASED PRACTITIONER IS EASIER

Considering the challenges of becoming an EBM expert, it comes as no surprise that most internal medicine residents at McMaster, even in a program explicitly committed to the systematic training in EBM,[2] are not interested in attaining an advanced level of EBM skills. Our trainees' responses mirror those of general practitioners in the United Kingdom who often use evidence-based summaries generated by others (72%) and evidence-based practice guidelines or protocols (84%) but who overwhelmingly (95%) believe that "learning the skills of EBM" is not the most appropriate method for "moving…to EBM."[3]

At McMaster and in other residency programs,[4] we have observed that even the trainees who are less interested in evidence-based methods develop an appreciation for and an ability to track down, recognize, and use secondary sources of preappraised evidence (evidence-based resources) that provide immediately applicable conclusions. Having mastered this more restricted set of EBM skills, these trainees can become highly competent, up-to-date practitioners who deliver evidence-based care—evidence-based practitioners.

A World of Evidence-Based Practitioners Does Not Guarantee Evidence-Based Care

Unfortunately, even the availability of evidence-based resources and recommendations and practitioners trained to use them will be insufficient to produce consistent evidence-based care. Like other physicians, evidence-based practitioners are subject to habit, local practice patterns, and product marketing (in particular, pharmaceutical industry marketing). These forces are often stronger determinants of practice than current best evidence. *Randomized controlled trials* have shown that traditional continuing education has little effect on combating these forces and changing physician behavior.[5]

Behavior Change Strategies Can Help to Achieve Evidence-Based Care

Changing specific clinical behaviors to make them consistent with the best evidence requires strategies beyond training in EBM. Complementary approaches include one-to-one conversations with an expert (academic detailing); computerized decision supports, including alerting systems and reminders[6]; preceptorships; advice from opinion leaders; and targeted audit and feedback.[7] Administrative strategies equally removed from practitioners' direct use of the medical literature include the availability of restricted drug formularies and the application of financial incentives (eg, pay for performance) and institutional guidelines. Thus, achieving evidence-based care requires a variety of strategies that focus on behavior change.

ADVANTAGES OF EVIDENCE-BASED MEDICINE EXPERTISE

We hope that the previous paragraphs have not dissuaded you from continuing to read and study this book. Powerful reasons remain for you to achieve the highest possible skill level in evidence-based practice.

First, attempts to change physician practice will sometimes be directed to objectives, such as increasing specific drug use or reducing health care costs, which have little to do with evidence-based care. Only those with advanced skills in interpreting the medical literature will be able to determine the extent to which studies of pharmaceutical interventions, or restricted drug formularies, are consistent with the best evidence. Second, a high level of EBM skills will allow you to use the original literature effectively, regardless of whether preappraised *synopses* and evidence-based recommendations are available. Third, sophisticated EBM skills facilitate taking an effective leadership role in the medical community.

If you are a medical educator, a manager, or a policy maker, take note. As we encourage medical trainees to achieve the highest possible level of EBM skills, 2 phenomena will be necessary to ensure high levels of evidence-based health care: (1) the widespread availability of comprehensive, preappraised, evidence-based summaries and recommendations; and (2) the widespread implementation of strategies demonstrated to alter clinicians' behavior toward evidence-based practice.

References

1. Guyatt G, Meade M, Jaeschke R, Cook D, Haynes R. Practitioners of evidence-based care: not all clinicians need to appraise evidence from scratch but all clinicians need some EBM skills [editorial]. *BMJ*. 2000;320(7240):954-955.

2. Evidence-Based Medicine Working Group. Evidence-based medicine: a new approach to teaching the practice of medicine. *JAMA*. 1992;268(17):2420-2425.

3. McColl A, Smith H, White P, Field J. General practitioners' perceptions of the route to evidence based medicine: a questionnaire survey. *BMJ*. 1998;316(16):361-365.

4. Akl E, Izuchukwu I, El-Dika S, Fritsche L, Kunz R, Schunemann H. Integrating an evidence-based medicine rotation into an internal medicine residency program. *Acad Med*. 2004;79(9):897-904.

5. Grimshaw J, McAuley LM, Bero LA, et al. Systematic reviews of the effectiveness of quality improvement strategies and programmes. *Qual Saf Health Care*. 2003;12(4):298-303.

6. Garg A, Adhikari N, McDonald H, et al. Effects of computerized clinical decision support systems on practitioner performance and patient outcomes: a systematic review. *JAMA*. 2005;293(10):1223-1238.

7. Grimshaw J, Eccles M, Tetroe J. Implementing clinical guidelines: current evidence and future implications. *J Contin Educ Health Prof*. 2004;24(suppl 1):S31-S37.

ADVANCED TOPICS IN MOVING
FROM EVIDENCE TO ACTION

CHANGING BEHAVIOR TO APPLY BEST EVIDENCE IN PRACTICE

Deborah J. Cook, Richard J. Wall, Robbie Foy,
Elie A. Akl, Gordon Guyatt,
Holger J. Schünemann, Lee Green,
and J. Randall Curtis

IN THIS CHAPTER:

6. Create a Data Collection System

7. Decide How to Report Results to Your Target Audience

8. Select and Introduce Behavior Change Strategies

9. Reevaluate Performance and Modify Behavior as Necessary

10. Conclusion and the Final Step (or "Move On to the Next Project!")

CLINICAL SCENARIO

Can We Increase the Use of Heparin Thromboprophylaxis in General Surgical Patients on the Perioperative Consultation Service?

Hospital accreditation looms ahead, and at your monthly general internal medicine divisional meeting, your chief reports a request from the chair of medicine. Each division is asked to define one "best practice strategy," document the extent to which practice is consistent with this strategy, and demonstrate improvement in the next year. Your division chief asks for ideas, and a number of suggestions follow. You propose to evaluate whether your division is using heparin to prevent venous thromboembolism (VTE) on the surgical wards as part of your perioperative service and outline the rationale for your proposal, as well as how you will achieve this goal.

Members of your general internal medicine division consult on about 70% of the general surgical patients as part of the perioperative consultation service. You describe a recent patient whom you were asked to see in consultation for treatment of a deep vein thrombosis (DVT) by a general surgeon. She was 6 days status posthemicolectomy, and you recall that thromboprophylaxis had been neglected throughout her hospital stay. Three of your colleagues refer to similar patients they have treated, acknowledging that your hospital may have a problem with suboptimal attention to this preventive strategy. You remind your colleagues that the American College of Chest Physicians' Antithrombotic and Thrombolytic Guidelines are current, comprehensive, and *evidence* based, citing heparin thromboprophylaxis as a grade A recommendation (indicating high-quality evidence) for surgical patients according to numerous high-quality *randomized controlled trials* (*RCTs*).[1] You know that the Agency for Healthcare Research and Quality rated thromboprophylaxis as the number 1 patient safety intervention for hospitalized patients.[2] Your chief captures the consensus of the discussion that ensues and gives you the mandate to develop your idea further, then brief the division at your next meeting.

Ten Steps to Change Behavior to Implement Evidence in Practice

There are substantial gaps between best *evidence* and its application in practice. Glasziou and Haynes[3] estimated that as few as 20% of effective interventions may actually reach patients. Changing clinician behavior to ensure implementation of best evidence in practice is challenging. In this chapter, we do not outline how to critically appraise a specific type of study. Instead, we outline 10 steps to achieve this goal (Table 22.7-1). Our approach is pragmatic, based not only on the published evidence but also on our own experience.

1. Start With a Manageable Problem and Specify an Achievable Goal

The goal of a project to change clinician behavior and implement best evidence can be summarized using the patient/intervention/comparison/outcome (PICO) format (see Chapter 3, What Is the Question?). In this case, one can frame the question as follows: for clinicians caring for hospitalized surgical patients (population), do behavior change strategies (intervention), compared with no active implementation (comparison), increase the use of appropriate heparin thromboprophylaxis (outcome)? Many problems are framed in quality improvement literature as so-called indicator conditions, a term used to reflect a state, diagnosis, disease, or symptom for which there is sound evidence about a beneficial intervention that is targeted for improvement. The indicator condition in this case is general surgery.

Several features exemplify a worthwhile quality improvement project.[4] Ideally, the practice problem must be important (eg, high prevalence, high morbidity), and the measurement target must be valid (measuring what it is supposed to measure),

TABLE 22.7-1

Ten Steps to Changing Behavior to Implement Evidence in Practice

1. Start with a manageable problem and specify an achievable goal.
2. Key ingredients: teamwork and leadership.
3. Do an environmental scan.
4. Develop a formal proposal.
5. Understand current behavior.
6. Create a data collection system.
7. Decide how to report results to your target audience.
8. Select and introduce behavior change strategies.
9. Reevaluate performance and modify behavior as necessary.
10. Conclusion and the final step (or "move on to the next project!").

reliable (yield the same result when assessed by different raters or yield the same result when it has not changed and is rated again by the same rater or over time), responsive (able to detect change when change has truly occurred), feasible (easy to obtain), and interpretable (easy to understand).

In the current example, a meta-analysis of dozens of RCTs has demonstrated that heparin thromboprophylaxis lowers rates of DVT, fatal pulmonary embolism, and mortality.[5] Note that the improvement outcome on which you focus in this case is not the clinical outcome measure—rates of VTE—but rather a process measure, rates of administration of thromboprophylaxis. Table 22.7-2 presents the relative merits of choosing process vs clinical outcome measures as the target of a quality improvement project.

When high-quality (ideally, RCT) evidence exists that an intervention improves patient-important outcomes, the target for quality improvement should be changing

TABLE 22.7-2

Advantages and Disadvantages of Process and Outcome Measures for Quality Improvement Projects

	Process Measure (Quality of Care)	Outcome Measure (Morbidity, Mortality)
Do patients care about this?	Less understandable to patients	Yes; if patient-important outcomes are measured
Do providers care about this?	Yes; it relates directly to what providers are doing	Yes; however, informed providers are appropriately wary of confounding and of the limitations of risk adjustment models
Obtain from routinely collected data?	Usually	Sometimes, additional data are needed that are not routinely collected
Interpretable for feedback and quality improvement?	Provides clear feedback about what providers are actually doing	Difficult for providers to definitively know where to target efforts because outcomes are usually affected by several different processes
Directly measures prevention?	Yes	No
Need for risk adjustment?	No; however, need to clearly define eligible patients	Yes; need different models for each outcome
Time needed for measurement?	Less	More
Sample size requirements?	Smaller	Larger

Reproduced from Curtis et al,[6] with permission from Critical Care Medicine.

process measures (eg, thromboprophylaxis), rather than patient outcome measures (eg, VTE). There are many determinants that influence clinical outcomes, and treatment effects are typically modest (on the order of 25% relative risk reductions). Therefore, large RCTs are required to demonstrate the differences in clinical outcomes between intervention and control. In quality improvement projects, we are trying to demonstrate the difference between partial and more complete implementation of a therapy; thus, focusing on patient outcomes in such contexts is very inefficient. Moreover, when one improves the administration of effective therapy, one may not observe improved outcomes if the population one is treating has become more ill—that is, has a worse prognosis—over time. Overall, monitoring of clinical outcome measures is mandatory only in restricted situations in which the relevant process measures have not been tested in RCTs and found to improve patient outcomes.

Many quality improvement projects use a before-after study design. However, this approach does not guard against *bias*, and the strength of inference is necessarily weaker with this design than RCTs. Time series designs and controlled time series designs, although stronger, can never ensure that the results actually reflect the true effect of the quality improvement intervention. Thus, interventions studied using these designs may appear effective when in fact characteristics of the population and changes in other aspects of care are responsible for improved outcomes.

> For instance, investigators documented reduction in adverse cardiovascular outcomes of coronary artery bypass surgery after a rather dramatic quality improvement maneuver: publishing hospitals' and surgeons' results in the newspaper. The authors concluded that, "Quality improvement programs based on similar principles for other procedures and conditions should be undertaken." A subsequent investigation demonstrated, however, that parallel improvements in outcome occurred in jurisdictions that did not implement this quality improvement strategy.[7]

The converse is also true. Clinicians who have implemented a quality improvement project that suggests no improvement in patient-important outcome may be unnecessarily disappointed because the intervention actually was effective, but the patients enrolled in the "after" phase of the study had poorer prognosis than those in the "before" phase.

BACK TO THE CLINICAL SCENARIO

Having decided that a process measure is your focus, you must define the process explicitly. Because heparin (either unfractionated heparin or low-molecular-weight heparin) is more effective than mechanical prophylaxis (antiembolic stockings or pneumatic compression devices), you define best practice as heparin thromboprophylaxis and consider mechanical approaches only when patients have heparin contraindications (have current or recent bleeding, are at serious risk of bleeding, or have severe thrombocytopenia or coagulopathy).

2. Key Ingredients: Teamwork and Leadership

Although implementing best evidence in practice is up to each clinician, changing behavior institution-wide requires collaborative teamwork and interdisciplinary leadership. A local consensus process is needed, at least on the quality improvement team (and ideally, more broadly across key stakeholders in the institution), before a project is begun. If a well-functioning quality improvement committee already exists, members may comprise a ready-made project team. Alternatively, a newly formed group can synergize to implement best evidence in practice. Including someone with biostatistical skills in the early planning stages will help to ensure your design and data collection are appropriate and ultimately make your analyses more straightforward.

As for any project, it is important to know your colleagues well. Do they have the requisite skills, interests, and ability to follow through? Can they work productively in a multidisciplinary team and lead change? A team leader can emerge or be appointed. Leadership is an activity, not a title. Ideally, all team members on a quality improvement team are "change agents." Ten leadership attributes of team members that help to effect such change (otherwise known as black belt change agents) are suggested by the Six Sigma method[8] (Table 22.7-3). Six Sigma is a well-known approach to quality improvement, popularized in the United States, that aims to define, measure, analyze, improve, and control the vital few processes that matter most, to tie quality improvement directly to bottom-line results.[9] However, not everyone in the team can be such a superhero, which is why good planning and purposeful leadership are necessary throughout the venture.

BACK TO THE CLINICAL SCENARIO

After rounds the next day, you meet with the medicine nurse manager. She suggests that case management rounds could be a useful weekly venue to focus on effective thromboprophylaxis. You then meet with the pharmacy director, along with 2 pharmacy interns just starting clinical placement on the surgical wards. They envision exciting opportunities for their department, asking whether you could supervise aspects of this project as part of a pharmacy internship program.

The pharmacy director brings special expertise to this project. As an MBA graduate familiar with the Six Sigma approach to quality improvement, she urges you to you research to first define the problem. She suggests further expanding your team, which is currently composed of you, the pharmacy director, nurse manager, 2 pharmacy interns, and chief resident. You plan to invite a respected open-minded senior surgeon to join you, who is a local opinion leader and likely to galvanize your team, model behavior change, and address colleagues' questions that may arise. You pledge to propose this as a unique collaboration to the general medicine and general surgery chiefs as a joint quality improvement project for purposes of accreditation. You also plan to contact one of the local university biostatisticians to help plan the design and analysis.

TABLE 22.7-3

Leadership Attributes of Black Belt Change Agents

1. Work well independently and in groups
2. Remain calm under pressure
3. Anticipate problems and act immediately
4. Respect colleagues and are respected by them
5. Inspire others
6. Delegate tasks to others and coordinate efforts
7. Understand abilities and limitations of colleagues
8. Show genuine concern for others for what they need and want
9. Accept criticism well
10. Want improvement

Reproduced from Blue.[9] Copyright © 2002, with permission of the McGraw-Hill Companies.

3. Do an Environmental Scan

Without preliminary data on the quality of care in current practice, it is difficult to know whether any behavior change strategy is required. Doing an environmental scan is a crucial initial step.[10]

Clinical or administrative databases can be a useful source of data to examine current practice, but they often require sophisticated biostatistical analyses. Retrospective chart *reviews* are a familiar way to examine current practice but often fail to distinguish between drugs prescribed and drugs actually administered on the ward. Direct prospective observational studies are less likely to be limited by poor documentation in medical records but can be time consuming and costly to conduct. Surveys of reported practice patterns provide an alternative strategy for environmental scans and may provide evidence about practices that are difficult to measure, such as use of antiembolic stockings, which may not be recorded well in charts. Nevertheless, self-administered surveys can also complement observational studies of actual practice with information about knowledge, attitudes, and beliefs that can provide important insights into barriers to changing behavior (Table 22.7-4).

BACK TO THE CLINICAL SCENARIO

Knowing that surveys of self-reported practice do not always reflect actual practice and knowing that some of your colleagues believe that your thromboprophylaxis rates are fine, you decide against a survey. You suspect that poor documentation of contraindications to heparin prophylaxis in medical charts will limit the utility of a retrospective chart review. When the pharmacists show you the hospital's drug-prescribing database, you find that reasons for nonprescription of heparin are not itemized, precluding its use for assessment of prescribing appropriateness.

Given these issues, your modest budget, and tight timeline, you invite the chief medical resident to collaborate on a single-center prospective observational study of thromboprophylaxis for perioperative surgical consultations for her quality improvement project mandated by the internal medicine residency program.

Learning how much time the 2 pharmacy interns and chief resident have available causes you to scale down your initial plans for a prospective audit. You plan to include consecutive patients admitted to your hospital's 5 surgical wards for the next 3 months who are 16 years or older and who are hospitalized for 24 hours or longer. At baseline, you will collect demographic and VTE risk factor data. Daily, one of the pharmacy interns will document whether the following is used: anticoagulant VTE prophylaxis (unfractionated heparin or low-molecular-weight heparin) or therapeutic anticoagulation (intravenous heparin or oral warfarin). For patients not receiving heparin, you will record whether this was an error of omission or because of a heparin contraindication and whether mechanical approaches were used instead.

Streamlining the data collection forms, creating an operations manual including definitions, and pretesting the methods lead to initial delays. Finally, during the first month of satisfactory data collection, you document prophylaxis practice in more than 1000 patient-days on the surgical wards. A quick review of the data shows that only about 50% of patient-days involve heparin thromboprophylaxis. Empowered by your documentation of a problem and excited about the prospects of this initiative but daunted by its scope, you realize that you need to better define the limits of the project. You pledge to enlist the help of your collaborators thus far and of other interested colleagues after drafting a proposal for circulation and feedback. You meet with the chiefs of general medicine and surgery; they are pleased at your plan for a joint venture focusing on perioperative medicine and give you permission to take the lead.

TABLE 22.7-4

Attributes of Surveys and Observational Studies for Environmental Scanning for Quality Improvement Projects

Attributes	Surveys	Observational Studies
Practice information	Stated practice	Actual practice
Other information	Knowledge, attitudes, beliefs, preferences	Inferences about these issues are limited
Cost	Usually less costly	Usually more costly

4. Develop a Formal Proposal

A written proposal for a quality improvement project symbolizes commitment, helps stimulate ideas among colleagues, and forces you to be specific. A proposal should outline the project rationale (including results of your environmental scan), key roles and activities, contributors, a timeline, and projected costs (Table 22.7-5).[6] This is also a good time to flag (at least to yourselves) some uncertainties that might lead to an appropriate modification of your initial plan. For instance, if you find, to your surprise, that the perioperative general surgical consultation patients have a very high rate of thromboprophylaxis, you may target a different population such as bed-bound inpatients on the medical wards or revisit some of your colleagues' ideas, including use of prophylaxis against atheroembolism.

You should also invite critical feedback at this stage and reconsider whether the benefits of your efforts to change practice will realistically be repaid by important improvements in patient-important outcomes, cost savings, or other benefits to the organization.[11] The goal here is important and underlines the case for investing more in quality improvement; indeed, the gains to society are potentially much greater from investing more resources in efforts to get interventions of known effectiveness into routine practice than much primary research that produces marginal gains in effectiveness and population impact.[12]

BACK TO THE CLINICAL SCENARIO

Your initial draft proposal covers all the items in Table 22.7-5 except the final one. Because you have no personal experience creating a formal business plan, you stop short of creating such a document but subsequently discuss this with an entrepreneurial colleague. She convinces you of the merits of a business plan to outline expenses, request resources, and predict potential savings to the hospital. You ask for her help drafting one.

TABLE 22.7-5

Quality Improvement Proposal for Heparin Thromboprophylaxis in Surgical Patients

1. State the objective of the project.
2. Summarize the current local, national, or global burden of illness.
3. Outline clinical complications and resource implications.
4. Describe the primary outcome.
5. List potential collaborators and their tasks.
6. Draft a timeline and work schedule.
7. Itemize personnel and nonpersonnel costs.
8. Create a business plan.

Adapted from Curtis et al.[6]

5. Understand Current Behavior

Developing strategies to overcome barriers to behavior change requires understanding existing practice. Although each practice setting is unique in terms of the clinicians and the local organizational culture, there are some generalizable principles. Common barriers include clinician habit, lack of awareness of (or resistance to) new information, reliance on physiologic outcomes rather than patient-important outcomes when interpreting evidence, and low-outcome expectancy among clinicians who question whether the benefits observed in the research setting will be realized in the practice setting.[13] Using some form of explicit framework, such as identifying barriers at the levels of individual clinicians, clinical teams, the organization, or wider environment, may ensure that you do not miss any critical factors in your planning.[14]

To understand current practice, informal interviews or group discussions with relevant colleagues can be illuminating and are often sufficient, if thoughtfully conducted and interpreted. A stakeholder analysis is a more structured approach to seek understanding of stakeholder interests, behavior, relationships, and plans through a comprehensive series of interviews. This analysis generates information about stakeholders' levels of influence, support, and resources that might bear on a quality improvement project. Formal qualitative research involving focus groups and in-depth interviews are more powerful for empirically generating insights to elucidate the range of barriers in implementing best practice and their relative importance to specific groups.[15] Often, qualitative studies are beyond the scope and skills of quality improvement teams, but when they are possible to conduct, the results can be very fruitful.

In summary, understanding current behaviors requires reflecting on existing practice, diagnosing possible causes of suboptimal performance, and interpreting their origin and influences. Once one achieves this understanding, one can identify interventions that may improve practice and select among those that are likely to be effective.

BACK TO THE CLINICAL SCENARIO

You realize that to change behavior, you need to first understand it. Because you do not have the time or training to conduct a formal qualitative study, you elucidate perceived barriers to thromboprophylaxis informally at your next division meeting. You make an appointment to attend one of the surgical department meetings to copresent the project with your surgical collaborator. You also discuss the issue of heparin errors of omission at morning report with the senior house staff who conduct surgical consultations with your group. According to these meetings, you generate a list of possible barriers to heparin thromboprophylaxis.

To help you to identify which barriers to address in the quality improvement project, you set up one-on-one 30-minute meetings with 3 internal medicine colleagues who, at your initial divisional meeting, acknowledged that you might have a problem. You also meet with one of the senior bedside nurses on the surgical ward. You ask for their candid views about the most important barriers to heparin thromboprophylaxis from the long list of possible causes you generated. One of them reminds you of the "80/20 rule" based on the ideas of the Italian economist Vilefredo Pareto. In the 1890s, he enunciated what is now known as the 80/20 principle, from the original observation that 80% of the wealth in Italy was owned by 20% of the people. This 80/20 rule of thumb expresses the fact that 80% of the results are determined by only about 20% of the causes. Your colleagues' views agree with this principle. They believe that errors of omission regarding heparin thromboprophylaxis have little to do with unfamiliarity with RCT evidence (although this might not be true for house staff); such errors are more likely as a result of forgetting to initiate heparin or failing to reinstitute heparin after transient contraindications disappear. Therefore, you focus on 2 barriers: forgetting to write the order (for attending physicians) and lack of knowledge about the importance of VTE prophylaxis (for house staff). Beginning to think ahead to how to address these barriers, your colleagues volunteer that more than basic education for the house staff is needed. They request prompts and reminders at the point of care and information about how they are doing over time. They also suggest a more active role for the hospital pharmacists and bedside nurses.

Although you have not yet decided on the final implementation strategies, you have some time because some of your skeptical colleagues will ask to see data first to document just how much of a problem your division has with heparin thromboprophylaxis on the perioperative consultation service. Indeed, ongoing data collection for the baseline measurements is the agenda item for your next team meeting.

6. Create a Data Collection System

Without accurate baseline data on how evidence is applied currently, it is not possible to document whether practice improves after a behavior change strategy. A 1-month utilization review provides insights about a suitable long-term data collection system. For example, you could choose a different denominator, such as general surgical ward patients who are on the perioperative consultation service, admitted for 72 hours or longer instead of 24 hours or longer (summarizing N consecutive admissions over period X) or choose another all-or-nothing metric (declaring success if at least 90% of hospital-days involve heparin and failure otherwise).[16] Another option is to record only the denominator of patient-days and missed opportunities for thromboprophylaxis, which could involve more interpretation but less data collection.

If the methods you used in your environmental scan were sufficiently rigorous, this scan may also serve to complete your baseline data collection. However, data from initial environment scans are often insufficient for a reliable baseline measure. Deciding how often to collect data is inevitably influenced by tradeoffs. Frequent data collection will improve precision of the estimates but require more time and effort. Infrequent data collection may be more feasible but increases the chance of sampling error (a common problem with the popular rapid cycle "plan-do-study-act" approaches to quality).

Deciding who will perform the measurement may depend on what you are measuring and when. Explicitly incorporating data collection into someone's job description can ensure that it is done properly. Likewise, identifying someone specifically devoted to projects of this sort can be immensely helpful. Regardless of who collects the data, training in data collection methods and pilot studies to test interrater or intrarater reliability of key data abstraction are useful. If resources permit, periodic data audits can help to ensure data integrity and allow positive feedback (or constructive criticism and remediation, as necessary). Ideally, the individual collecting the data should be blinded to whether the behavior change intervention has been applied. However, in quality improvement projects, this is often not feasible. Therefore, it is important to take steps to ensure that the data collection procedures minimize the potential for bias being introduced by the data collector who may have an investment in showing that the quality improvement project was successful. This is possible by having the data collectors blinded to the goals of the project.

BACK TO THE CLINICAL SCENARIO

You call another meeting with the project team to discuss completion of the baseline data collection. Having worked out a manageable data collection system for the first month of the environmental scan, you still consider viable alternatives that might gain efficiency without sacrificing accuracy. Ultimately, however, you do not not find any compelling reasons to change methods. You plan data collection for a total of 3 months. You decide that the primary outcome will be the proportion of hospital ward days during which heparin thromboprophylaxis is appropriately administered.

One pharmacy intern offers to collect the remaining data during the second and third months, whereas the other pharmacy intern offers to create a simple database and enter the data. You ask the second pharmacist to retrospectively conduct a reliability check on 5% of the charts from the first month. They raise the possibility that prescribing patterns of clinicians may improve because of the presence of one of the pharmacy interns who are also working as ward pharmacists, prompting optimal prescribing during this baseline data collection period. To avoid potentially biasing baseline data, the pharmacy director changes the pharmacy interns' schedules so that they do not have clinical responsibilities on the surgical wards during their baseline data collection. You also decide that the interns will become part of the behavior change intervention in the future to address one of the key barriers to optimal thromboprophylaxis.

7. Decide How to Report Results to Your Target Audience

Informative, transparent, and timely reporting of results is crucial to a quality improvement project's success. The objectives of data reporting are to document performance, motivate behavior change when performance warrants improvement, and give positive feedback when performance is excellent. To demonstrate and sustain improvements, results must be interpretable and actionable. Obscure feedback reports are impotent and may cause projects to lose momentum.[6]

When deciding how to report results, you should consider the project goals, the background of the target audience, and local familiarity with existing data reports. Before disseminating reports, pilot the presentation formats and solicit suggestions about interpretability from your target audience. Possible formats include figures, tables, text, and combinations thereof. Each has advantages and disadvantages. Graphs and figures (eg, run charts; see Figure 22.7-1), instrument panels,[17] and report cards) can visually display data over time but may require more expertise to create. Tables can be easily assembled, hold large amounts of information in a small space, and have explanatory legends. Tables simplify data presentation but are less useful for showing data over time. Text is a familiar vehicle for communication but may take more space and be less inviting to read than tables. Showing both past and present performance is helpful.

Determining when to report results will depend partly on (1) how often the target is measured, (2) for whom the report is intended, and (3) the purpose of the reports (whether the reports are "for their information," to keep them in the loop administratively, or whether the reports are instrumental audits; in other words, whether they are actually part of your behavior change strategy). For administrators, you can negotiate the frequency and content of reports; in some situations, a

FIGURE 22.7-1

Thromboprophylaxis Quality Improvement Project (for Your Next General Internal Medicine Division Business Meeting)

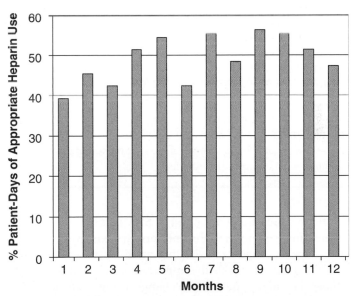

final report of the findings is sufficient. For project team reports, the frequency and level of detail should be sufficient to help optimize the execution of the project. For changing clinician behavior, daily reports of target outcomes could be infeasible; moreover, if data are reported too often, clinicians may stop attending to the information, and it may lose its impact as a prompt for behavior change. Weekly or monthly reports may be suitable initially. The final choice of feedback timing and frequency requires a practical balance between sustaining improvement gains and acknowledging the limits of your local system.[18] Finally, the frequency and content of reporting often change over the course of the project according to early successes and failures and the reality that all quality improvement teams want to do the least amount of work possible for the maximum benefit of the project.

BACK TO THE CLINICAL SCENARIO

When the 3-month data collection is over, you ask your biostatistical colleague to help with the analysis and reporting. Fortunately, because you involved her early in the project, she is familiar with your plans, methods, and progress.

You could choose to express the median percentage of hospital-days of heparin thromboprophylaxis per week. During 3216 patient-days in the hospital, you find that the proportion of surgical ward days during which heparin thromboprophylaxis was appropriately administered during this 3-month period was 49.6% (median; interquartile range, 0-87.3).

At your team meeting, you outline 3 target audiences for your results and decide to develop 3 unique templates for each of these audiences. First, you prepare a detailed working table for your next project team meeting (Table 22.7-6); you plan to meet monthly to review these tables (which will contain data as current as possible, given the inevitable delay required for data entry and analysis). Second, you write the key findings in text format, summarizing the first 3 months; henceforth, you plan similar monthly e-mail dissemination to your medical and surgical colleagues, providing or using the perioperative consultation service (Table 22.7-7). This is a key part of your behavior change strategy. Third, you create a simple run chart format to display anonymized group monthly results, which you plan to take to each monthly general medical and surgical division meeting as part of your behavior change strategy (Figure 22.7-1). You plan to ask the recipients of each of these templates for feedback on the usefulness of the format of results.

8. Select and Introduce Behavior Change Strategies

After documenting suboptimal thromboprophylaxis, your next step is to implement behavior change strategies that are likely to improve the situation. Although it makes sense to tackle the important barriers, it is also important to prioritize those potentially amenable to change, using strategies of documented

TABLE 22.7-6

Tabular Summary of Heparin Thromboprophylaxis Quality Improvement Project: Initial 3-Month Data Before Launching Behavior Change Strategies (for Your Next Project Team Meeting)[a]

Proportion of Hospital Days With	Month 1 (36 Patients, 1083 Days)	Month 2 (35 Patients, 1124 Days)	Month 3 (37 Patients, 1009 Days)	Overall (108 Patients, 3216 Days)
Heparin prophylaxis[b]	51 (0-100)	56 (20-100)	43 (13-100)	49.6 (0-87)
Prophylactic or therapeutic anticoagulation	69 (0-100)	80 (29-100)	73 (31-100)	75 (36-100)
Mechanical prophylaxis only	0 (0-23)	20 (0-85)	10 (0-70)	14 (9-56)
Error of omission, no heparin prophylaxis	20 (0-54)	17 (0-36)	24 (0-52)	19 (0-45)

[a]Values are given as median (interquartile range). The types of thromboprophylaxis in months 1, 2, and 3 are shown. Mechanical prophylaxis refers to either antiembolic stockings or pneumatic compression devices. Errors of omission considered if heparin omitted without a contraindication to heparin (current or potential bleeding, coagulopathy [international normalized ratio, > 2.0; partial thromboplastin time, > 60 seconds], thrombocytopenia [platelets, $< 75 \times 10^9$/L], known or suspected heparin-induced thrombocytopenia, disseminated intravascular coagulation).
[b]Denominator excludes days on which patient received therapeutic anticoagulation.

TABLE 22.7-7

Text Summary of Heparin Thromboprophylaxis Quality Improvement Project: Initial 3-Month Data (to Be Modified for Monthly E-mail Dissemination to General Medical and Surgical Colleagues)

Dear Colleagues,

With a mandate from the Divisions of General Internal Medicine and General Surgery, the Joint Collaboration Heparin CQI Team has been busy documenting our adherence to this evidence-based intervention. To keep you up to date, we plan to send you e-mails periodically.

Our chief medical resident and 2 pharmacy interns recorded heparin use for more than 3000 patient-days in our hospital during a recent 3-month period. We considered thromboprophylaxis with either unfractionated heparin or low-molecular-weight heparin or therapeutic anticoagulation with intravenous heparin or oral warfarin. Each day, for patients not receiving heparin, we classified whether this was an error of omission or because of one of several predefined heparin contraindications. The median proportion of patient-days during which heparin thromboprophylaxis was appropriately administered was only 49%. This indicates that we have room for improvement!

We are now embarking on the next step this CQI project to better understand our prophylaxis patterns; we will then try to overcome any barriers that exist.

Thanks for your support and interest. All offers of assistance or critique are welcome.

Sincerely,

The Heparin QI Project Team

effectiveness. Strategies may encompass professional interventions (eg, continuing medical education, audit, feedback), financial interventions, organizational interventions (eg, expanded role of nurses in the usual setting, explicit nurse practitioner positions), or regulatory interventions (eg, professional credentialing).[19]

You refer to the Cochrane Effective Practice and Organization of Care Review Group, which published a summary of 41 *systematic reviews* of hundreds of original studies testing the effects of different behavior change strategies on clinician behavior and patient outcomes.[20] This review has suggested that active strategies are more likely to be effective at changing behavior than relatively passive strategies (such as distribution of printed educational materials). However, this has been challenged by a more recent review of 235 studies of guideline dissemination and implementation strategies.[21] When used alone, the average absolute effect size of most interventions was very small, approximately 9% (or 0.09). Effect size is the difference in mean scores between the treatment and control groups divided by the standard deviation of the scores in the control group (or the pooled standard deviation of the treatment and control groups, or the pooled standard deviation of the change score) (see Chapter 10.5, Measuring Patients' Experience). A rule of thumb to help interpret the magnitude of the effect sizes is as follows: values in the range of 0.2 represent a small effect, values in the range of 0.5 represent a moderate effect, and values in the range of 0.8 represent a large effect.[22] Translating this average absolute effect size of 0.09 into the relevant natural units in this case is about 2 patient-days.

Unexpectedly, you learn that distributing educational materials appeared to be as effective as audit and feedback. However, effects were larger and more consistent for manual or computerized prompts and reminders aimed at clinicians than either educational material or audit and feedback. Previous reviews also suggested that combinations of quality improvement interventions (multifaceted interventions) are more likely to overcome multiple barriers to improved care. Yet, the recently updated review[21] found no clear pattern with respect to the effectiveness of the number of strategies. One possible explanation is that multiple and more complex strategies are preferentially used in settings in which tougher barriers exist to optimal patient care.

Most interventions are effective under some circumstances, but none are effective under all circumstances. Ideally, implementation strategies should be based on identified needs and barriers, thereby tailoring the behavior change strategies to the setting and making more efficient use of scarce resources. Although this approach is intuitively attractive, little empirical evidence exists on how best to do this and on which approach to choose in different settings. Furthermore, the costs of some interventions—such as the time and expense of computer decision support systems for centers without clinical information systems—may outweigh any potential benefits or anticipated cost savings (see Chapter 9.6, Clinical Decision Support Systems).[11]

BACK TO THE CLINICAL SCENARIO

You convene your project group weekly to report on problems, progress, and assignments from the last meeting. You circulated 2 systematic reviews, one on strategies for changing physician behavior in general using guidelines[21] and another on strategies evaluated to improve thromboprophylaxis specifically.[23] You find this evidence on changing behavior challenging to digest. From both systematic reviews, you conclude that most interventions appear to effect some positive change, although the magnitude is generally small and the effects are inconsistent. Your group acknowledges the need to choose implementation strategies that are simple, readily available, relatively inexpensive, well accepted, and easily applied, thereby enhancing the feasibility of your project.

You realize that a working environment that facilitates change is a powerful facilitator to apply best evidence in practice and that lack of supporting health care infrastructure can compromise the efforts. To obtain a more scholarly perspective, you review a relevant multicenter qualitative study designed to understand the environmental factors perceived to increase β-blocker use for patients with myocardial infarction.[24] The investigators used semistructured interviews with clinicians, quality management staff, and administrators to identify 6 factors that were found to increase β-blocker use (Table 22.7-8). You reflect on which of these environmental influences might encourage heparin thromboprophylaxis in your hospital. Running through the list, you are certain about your goals. You have not just administrative support from the chair of medicine and the chief of general internal medicine but also an administrative directive. You are certain that your colleagues are happy that it is your turn to take the lead in fulfilling your division's quality improvement mandate. You have carefully crafted data collection and reporting systems and now are planning the behavior change strategies.

The nurse manager suggests preprinted physician orders for thromboprophy-laxis, pointing out how helpful they have been in achieving therapeutic anticoagu-lation at your institution. However, you lament that taking the process through the forms committee for approval would take about 9 months, delaying your evalua-tion of their effect. You are concerned about the time required to properly implement patient-mediated interventions to change clinician prescribing but plan to ask the Community Liaison Department if they have the interest in developing such a program, given public concern about thrombosis and the recent Society for Hospital Medicine–led Coalition to Prevent Deep-Vein Thrombosis naming March DVT Awareness month (http://www.preventdvt.org).

Given your lack of experience in changing behavior institution-wide, you turn to a useful background article to read about evidence implementation associated with the American College of Chest Physicians Antithrombotic and Thrombolytic guidelines.[25] You are particularly interested in a report of a survey of thrombosis experts on the acceptability, feasibility, and cost of various behavior change interventions designed to improve thromboprophylaxis (Table 22.7-9).

Because you do not have a computer-order entry at your hospital, you are not able to use computer decision supports to change behavior. You decide on a multifaceted approach tailored to your teaching institution, targeting different clinicians and including (1) residents (educational meetings in the form of teaching sessions and daily verbal reminders from ward pharmacists), (2) bedside nurses (with periodic educational in-services and an explicit request for them to incorporate in daily rounds, reminders to physicians about heparin thromboprophylaxis), and (3) staff physicians involved in perioperative consultation (with monthly audit and feedback to general internists and general surgeons by e-mail, monthly discussion at division meetings, and quarterly public display of run charts). The 2 pharmacy interns have scheduled their surgical ward rotation next so they can provide verbal reminders to the team, leveraging the sentinel effect to improve the performance of those being evaluated to help induce optimal practice. The chief resident offers to present the results during case management rounds each Friday when the nurse manager reviews each patient's medication profile. You will e-mail the department of medicine's attending physicians weekly to ensure that they are aware of the project. Knowing the power of a narrative and case-based learning, you prepare a case summary illustrating thromboprophylaxis errors of omission for an upcoming grand rounds presentation, during which you will describe your project. Now, you refine the goal of your quality improvement project as follows: for clinicians caring for hospitalized surgical patients on the perioperative consultation service (population), does a multimethod behavior change strategy including educational meetings, reminders, and audit and feedback (intervention) compared with no active implementation (comparison) increase the use of appropriate heparin thromboprophylaxis (outcome)?

During the 6 months of behavior-change interventions, you document that the proportion of days during which heparin thromboprophylaxis is administered increases steadily to 90% (interquartile range, 50%-100%). Concomitantly, the proportion of patient-days during which heparin was not administered decreased. Because, given the observational design, you cannot be certain which of the several behavior change strategies you introduced were responsible (or even whether concomitant events independent of your efforts were, at least in part, responsible) and because your hospital is a teaching institution, you decide to continue the educational components of your project. However, you decrease the intensity of reminders on the wards and decrease the audit and feedback to every quarter.

9. Reevaluate Performance and Modify Behavior as Necessary

After implementation of a behavior change strategy that is even somewhat successful, it is difficult to know whether performance will be sustained unless you formally reevaluate the target outcome. Throughout this process, it is important to

TABLE 22.7-8

Environmental Factors That Increase Application of β-Blockers Post–Myocardial Infarction

1. Setting goals
2. Administrative support
3. Clinician support
4. Design and implementation of improvement initiatives
5. Use of data
6. Contextual factors (eg, turnover of senior administrative and clinical staff)

Reproduced from Bradley et al,[24] with permission from *JAMA*.

keep the data collection methods and analysis simple, streamlining this aspect of the project over time. For example, when a project starts, data are often manually collected, whereas later, methods may become more automated. One downside of changing data collection methods is that this may change results, independent of whether practice actually changed. Computerized clinical information systems may sustain the target behavior more easily over time, although such an approach could be prohibitively costly in centers without clinical information systems. Although it is advisable to keep familiar report formats over time, it is also helpful to report temporal trends in a visually compelling way if these are being used to maintain behavior change.

TABLE 22.7-9

Survey Results of the American College of Chest Physicians' Consensus Conference on Antithrombotic Therapy: Participant Behavior Change Interventions

Domains[a]	Dissemination of Educational Material	Educational Meetings	Educational Outreach Visits	Computer Reminders	Patient-Mediated Interventions	Audit and Feedback
Feasibility	5.8 (1.0)	5.4 (1.2)	4.3 (1.5)	4.1 (1.8)	4.1 (1.5)	3.5 (1.5)
Acceptability	5.8 (1.0)	5.7 (1.1)	4.3 (1.4)	4.7 (1.5)	4.7 (1.4)	3.6 (1.5)
Cost	4.6 (1.1)	4.1 (1.5)	3.0 (1.4)	3.7 (1.8)	4.1 (1.3)	3.1 (1.4)

[a]Scores are on a 1 to 7 scale in which higher scores indicate greater feasibility and acceptability but lower cost. Mean and median were similar, and therefore only mean values (standard deviation) are shown.
Reproduced from Schunemann et al,[25] with permission from *CHEST*.

BACK TO THE CLINICAL SCENARIO

During the ensuing 3 months, monitoring shows that the initial favorable trend has reversed. The proportion of days during which heparin thromboprophylaxis is administered has decreased to 80% (interquartile range, 45%-95%). You decide to refocus attention on recapturing and sustaining the initial improvement by intensifying verbal reminders; you revert to weekly audit and feedback. Gratifyingly, the next evaluation demonstrates higher thromboprophylaxis rates.

The hospital administration decides to use the success of this project as a model hospital-wide and begins this project in the medical wards. Excited at this prospect, you are aware that few interventions to change professional practice work across all contexts because individual practice circumstances and the knowledge, attitudes, and beliefs of clinicians also influence individual and group behavior. While celebrating with your team over dinner, you reflect on the trials and tribulations of your project. You debate ways to sustain your success with less effort. You explore ways to adapt and streamline your approach for other settings. You further discuss how you will share your lessons learned with colleagues in the hospital to optimize inpatient care.

10. Conclusion and the Final Step (or "Move On to the Next Project!")

When guided by a proposal and several steps as outlined here, another view of a quality improvement project is that it is one comprehensive mixed-methods study. Mixed methods are often used to study service delivery and organization by combining several study designs (eg, surveys, interviews, observations, evaluation of change). Regardless of the scope, synergistic collaborative teamwork, interdisciplinary leadership, and careful measurement, evaluation and planning are crucial to change behavior institution-wide and successfully implement best evidence in practice.

What about the tenth step? It is to advance to the next quality improvement project to implement best evidence in practice!

References

1. Geerts WH, Pineo GF, Heit JA, et al. Prevention of venous thromboembolism: the Seventh ACCP Conference on Antithrombotic and Thrombolytic Therapy. *Chest.* 2004;126(3)(suppl):338S-400S.

2. AHCPR Evidence Report/Technology Assessment. *Prevention of Venous Thromboembolism After Injury.* Rockville, MD: AHCPR; 2003.

3. Glasziou P, Haynes B. The paths from research to improved health outcomes. *Evidence Based Nurs.* 2005;8(2):36-38.

4. Brook RH, McGlynn EA, Cleary PD. Quality of health care, part 2: measuring quality of care. *N Engl J Med.* 1996;335(13):966-970.

5. Collins R, Scrimgeour A, Yusuf S, Peto R. Reduction in fatal pulmonary embolism and venous thrombosis by perioperative administration of subcutaneous heparin: overview of results of randomized trials in general, orthopedic, and urologic surgery. *N Engl J Med.* 1988;318(18):1162-1173.

6. Curtis JR, Cook DJ, Wall RJ, et al. Intensive care unit quality improvement: a "how-to" guide for the interdisciplinary team. *Crit Care Med.* 2006;34(1):211-218.

7. Ghali WA, Ash AS, Hall RE, Moskowitz MA. Statewide quality improvement initiatives and mortality after cardiac surgery. *JAMA.* 1997;277(5):379-382.

8. Blue G. *Six Sigma for Managers*. New York, NY: McGraw-Hill; 2002:88.

9. Blue G. *Six Sigma for Managers*. New York, NY: McGraw-Hill; 2002:19.

10. Cook DJ, Montori VM, McMullin JP, Finfer SR, Rocker GM. Improving patients' safety locally: changing clinician behaviour. *Lancet.* 2004;363(9416):1224-1230.

11. Mason J, Freemantle N, Nazareth I, Eccles M, Haines A, Drummond M. When is it cost-effective to change the behavior of health professionals? *JAMA.* 2001;286(23): 2988-2992.

12. Woolf SH, Johnson RE. The break-even point: when medical advances are less important than improving the fidelity with which they are delivered. *Ann Fam Med.* 2005;3(6):545-552.

13. Cabana MD, Rand CS, Powe NR, et al. Why don't physicians follow clinical practice guidelines? a framework for improvement. *JAMA.* 1999;282(15):1458-1465.

14. Fretheim A, Oxman AD, Flottorp S. Improving prescribing of antihypertensive and cholesterol-lowering drugs: a method for identifying and addressing barriers to change. *BMC Health Serv Res.* 2004;4(1):23.

15. Cook DJ, Meade MO, Hand LE, McMullin JP. Toward understanding evidence uptake: semirecumbency for pneumonia prevention. *Crit Care Med.* 2002;30(7): 1472-1477.

16. Nolan T, Berwick DM. All-or-none measurement raises the bar on performance. *JAMA.* 2006;295(10):1168-1170.

17. Dodek PM, Heyland DK, Rocker GM, Cook DJ. Translating family satisfaction data into quality improvement. *Crit Care Med.* 2004;32(9):1922-1927.

18. Wall RJ, Ely EW, Elasy TA, et al. Using real time process measurements to reduce catheter related bloodstream infections in the intensive care unit. *Qual Saf Health Care.* 2005;14(4):295-302.

19. Grol R. Personal paper: beliefs and evidence in changing clinical practice. *BMJ.* 1997;315(7105):418-421.

20. Grimshaw JM, Shirran L, Thomas R, et al. Changing provider behavior: an overview of systematic reviews of interventions. *Med Care.* 2001;39(8)(suppl 2):II2-45.

21. Grimshaw JM, Thomas RE, MacLennan G, et al. Effectiveness and efficiency of guideline dissemination and implementation strategies. *Health Technol Assess.* 2004;8(6):iii-iv, 1-72.

22. Cohen J. *Statistical Power Analysis in the Behavioral Sciences*. Hillsdale, NJ: Erlbaum; 1988.

23. Tooher R, Middleton P, Pham C, et al. A systematic review of strategies to improve prophylaxis for venous thromboembolism in hospitals. *Ann Surg.* 2005;241(3):397-415.

24. Bradley EH, Holmboe ES, Mattera JA, Roumanis SA, Radford MJ, Krumholz HM. A qualitative study of increasing beta-blocker use after myocardial infarction: why do some hospitals succeed? *JAMA.* 2001;285(20):2604-2611.

25. Schunemann HJ, Cook D, Grimshaw J, et al. Antithrombotic and thrombolytic therapy: from evidence to application: the Seventh ACCP Conference on Antithrombotic and Thrombolytic Therapy. *Chest.* 2004;126(3)(suppl):688S-696S.

TEACHERS' GUIDES TO THE USERS' GUIDES

Peter C. Wyer, Deborah J. Cook,
W. Scott Richardson, Mahmoud Elbarbary,
and Mark Wilson

IN THIS CHAPTER:

SCENARIOS

SCENARIO 1

You are an attending physician in your hospital's intensive care unit (ICU) in which most patients are mechanically ventilated. An agency nurse expresses surprise that they are all positioned at 45 degrees backrest elevation.

SCENARIO 2

You are on ward attending duty in general medicine. A resident is preparing to lead a brief discussion on evaluation and management of deep venous thrombosis (DVT) in tomorrow's morning report. She plans to build the presentation around the case of a patient with cancer who has recently been admitted to the service. Several issues about diagnosis and initial DVT therapy have arisen during work rounds.

SCENARIO 3

You are the faculty advisor for journal club in your program. The resident who is assigned to lead this month's session attended the patient with cancer from scenario 2 in the emergency department and proposes to review the literature on the choice of low-molecular-weight vs unfractionated heparin as initial DVT therapy.

These 3 scenarios raise issues related to teaching *evidence-based medicine* (*EBM*). Readers of the *Users' Guides* who are engaged in clinical teaching have doubtless already begun to ponder how to incorporate its concepts into their teaching. In this chapter, we provide some suggestions.

Evidence-Based Medicine and Clinical Teaching: More Than Just Journal Club

How might learning and teaching EBM differ from learning and teaching any other complex set of skills? EBM is not yet fully incorporated into many curricula for clinical training and continuing education. Practitioners not familiar with EBM may believe that demands on them to learn the new approach are an unwanted intrusion. As a result, teachers may face considerable challenges in communicating the relevance of EBM to day-to-day practice.

Our 3 scenarios illustrate different aspects of these challenges. In the first scenario, time pressure and custom may result in a response on the part of the director such as, "Our ICU director believes that head elevation is preferable for ventilated patients, and so we have incorporated it into daily practice." Similarly, in the slightly less time-pressed context of the second scenario, the resident may be tempted to limit the presentation to pronouncements from sources such as standard textbooks and narrative reviews. The third presents a setting in which EBM concepts are likely to be perceived as pertinent. The challenge here is to persuasively link the content of the exercise to the process of making clinical decisions. In the following section, we offer suggestions for incorporating EBM teaching into these and other settings.

Interactive teaching approaches, generally more effective than conventional didactic approaches to teaching and updating clinical skills,[1,2] are particularly well suited to teaching EBM.[2] Table 22.8-1 summarizes interactive techniques not unique to EBM but highly relevant to its teaching.[3]

Modes of Teaching

Straus et al[3] and Richardson[6] describe 3 modes of teaching EBM that may help incorporate EBM into routine clinical teaching (Table 22.8-2).

The opening 3 scenarios correspond to the above 3 modes. When role modeling, the teacher demonstrates the use of clinical evidence as a routine aspect of clinical practice and decision making. During integrated teaching of EBM, the teacher adds clinical evidence to the mixture of knowledge taught about a clinical topic, weaving it in where it fits naturally. Direct teaching of specific EBM skills involves communicating about specific ways to seek, appraise, or use evidence in clinical decision making. We will refer to these modes throughout the rest of this chapter.

Matching Content and Context: Evidence-Based Teaching Scripts

Learning is more effective and more likely to lead to change in behavior when it takes place in the context in which it will be applied.[7,8] It is particularly important

TABLE 22.8-1

Interactive and Self-learning Techniques for Teaching Evidence-Based Medicine (EBM)

Individual	Educational prescription[a]
	Identify patient-important problems calling for EBM skills
Smaller group	Role playing
	Team learning interludes[b]
	Establish roles and guidelines as appropriate
	• Timekeeper
	• Chalkboard scribe
	• Discourage distracting conversations
	• Use time-outs to discuss process and refocus discussion
	Interjected teaching tips
	Poll group members on key questions and practice decisions before giving suggested answers
	Avoid answering questions before involving group
Larger group presentations	Team learning interludes[b]
	Buzz group interludes[c]
	Poll audience on key questions and practice decisions before giving suggested answers
	Avoid answering questions before involving group

[a]Encourage the learner to take on an assignment that requires use of EBM skills to complete.
[b]Team learning involves breaking a larger group into a set of smaller groups and assigning them 1 or more identical or related tasks, followed by sharing of solutions between the groups.[4,5]
[c]Buzz groups may be seen as a variant of the team learning technique in which the smaller groups consist of only 2 or 3 individuals.

to center as much of the teaching of EBM in clinical teaching settings as possible.[6,9] This requires the teacher to be skilled in each of the 3 teaching modes.

The clinical teacher will find it advantageous to present the content of our *Users' Guides* in small, discrete segments woven into discussions of clinical problems. These constitute a type of teaching script that Irby,[10] Schmidt et al,[11] and Wyer et al[12] have described: well-prepared, structured, interactive presentations of key concepts. Later in this chapter, we will provide examples of short instructional segments that may be incorporated into such scripts. We encourage clinical teachers, as they read through this book, to ponder the development of their own scripts incorporating EBM skills and concepts and consider where they might apply these scripts.

Learner Needs and Interests

An effective teaching script encompasses content adapted to the teaching venue, time period, and competing demands, as well as the learners' previous knowledge, readiness,

TABLE 22.8-2

Modes of Teaching

Mode	Description	Goal	Example Venues	Example Content
Role modeling	Demonstrating the incorporation of *evidence* into patient care decisions	Communicating clinical decisions and recommendations to health care team members or patients	Work rounds, sign-out rounds, clinical precepting	Summary of a study relevant to the care of an active patient or results of a related quick literature search in course of a work rounds sign-out
Integrated teaching	Combining consideration of relevant clinical evidence with clinical teaching	Teaching clinical skills, principles of assessment, and disease-oriented management	Morning report, clinical topic sessions, morbidity and mortality case reviews, quality improvement meetings	Interactive discussion of relevant study or *synopsis* during extended case discussion
Direct skills teaching	Teaching in which EBM skills constitute the direct subject	Enhancing learners' independent capacity to bring EBM skills to bear on their decisions	Journal club, EBM carve-outs[a] within integrated teaching sessions	Systematic examination of process of solving a problem using EBM skills

Abbreviation: EBM, evidence-based medicine.

[a]Pertinent evidence summaries may be used as the pretext for relevant explanatory digressions. For example, reference to the performance of a diagnostic test, as demonstrated in a cited study, may be supplemented by a quick explanation of the interpretation of *likelihood ratios*.

and inclination to absorb new content. Irby[13] posited that the ability to modify and adapt a teaching script to learner needs and knowledge level while being attentive to the needs posed by the patient problem at hand is the hallmark of a master clinical teacher.

A medical student just beginning clinical rotations is likely to be preoccupied with connecting knowledge of disease to patients. A senior resident doing a rotation in his or her specialty will be ready to contemplate specific diagnostic and therapeutic choices and the evidence available to inform those choices (see Chapter 3, What Is the Question? and Chapter 4, Finding the Evidence).

Learners emerging from undergraduate training may have been exposed to the skills of EBM in the form of prerequisites or obligatory courses. Their knowledge base in this area may equal or exceed their mastery of traditional clinical skills. Therefore, teachers may elect to minimize emphasis on EBM skills per se in favor of their application to the clinical decisions at hand (integrated mode). When previous exposure to EBM skills is minimal, teachers may, when teaching in the direct skills teaching mode, elect to include brief demonstrations as outlined below.

The degree of incorporation of EBM within a teaching program or practice environment may shape learner priorities. When EBM is not routinely modeled and is quite new to the learner, the most fruitful initial focus may be the basics of asking questions and choosing appropriate online resources to answer them (see Chapter 3, What Is the Question? and Chapter 4, Finding the Evidence). On the other hand, in a graduate medical education environment in which EBM has matured and is commonly modeled by the clinical faculty, entry-level residents might be primarily interested in the process of routine incorporation of clinical evidence in decision making. The teaching focus in this context would be how to interpret the results of studies of therapy and diagnosis and apply those results to their patient care.[14]

The gifted clinical teacher will ensure that all learners achieve skills adequate to routinely access and consider relevant preappraised resources for decision making while they also guide a smaller number of learners who are motivated to deepen their appraisal skills and contribute to the development of resources for EBM in their specialties (see Chapter 22.6, Parallel but Separate Goals: Evidence-Based Practitioners and Evidence-Based Care).[15]

Verbal and Written Synopses

A verbal and written synopsis of critically appraised articles can provide a summary of key evidence for consideration in practice. Several days after such critical appraisal teaching sessions, both learners and teachers may experience difficulty formulating such synopses. We believe that both students and teachers are likely to benefit from practicing this skill, particularly at the end of formal teaching sessions.

Figure 22.8-1 summarizes 3 key components to a verbal study synopsis: context, content, and comments. The context includes the clinical question leading to access of the study and the problem it is addressing (framed according to population, intervention or exposure, and outcome). The content includes an executive summary of the 3 classical steps in a critical appraisal exercise: the validity, the results, and the applicabiliy. Comments at the end can be used to underscore key features of the article, such as a recent, classic, or controversial contribution, its exceptional quality, or its relevance given the burden of illness it addresses.

Teachers can emphasize specific context points (eg, the direct relevance of the population enrolled in the study to the patient at hand) or content issues (eg, underscoring the results in terms of the magnitude of influence on the patient-important outcomes about which the patient was most concerned) to suit the audience. They can also engage learners by highlighting the landmark nature of the article or its potential to change practice.

The benefits of a verbal study synopsis are that it is a paperless exercise that can be done anywhere at any time with anyone. Teachers can request a study synopsis after a critical appraisal exercise (unannounced or advertised before-hand). Learners may want to write out their study synopsis first. It is also instructive to ask for a verbal study synopsis several hours or several days after a critical appraisal exercise. With a little practice, students and teachers can call forth study synopses during rounds or in a clinic setting, thereby role-modeling

FIGURE 22.8-1

Verbal Synopsis

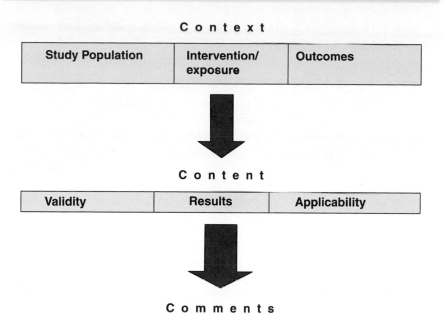

C o n t e x t

Study Population	Intervention/ exposure	Outcomes

C o n t e n t

Validity	Results	Applicability

C o m m e n t s

Unique Feature	Bottom Line

EBM, and with increasing experience, the portfolio of study synopses grows. The following examples illustrate the use of synopses in practice. The first 2 correspond to synopses used by one of us (D.J.C.) in a critical care setting. The third is drawn from the clinical example used to frame the chapter on therapy in this book (see Chapter 6, Therapy).

Example 1
Context. ICU nurse regarding recently admitted mechanically ventilated patient: "I am surprised to find that Mrs Richards has been placed at 45 degrees from the horizontal. Someone mentioned this is to prevent pneumonia." Underlying questions: In critically ill patients, what is the effect of semirecumbent positioning on the incidence of pneumonia?
Content. ICU attending physician: "This is an inexpensive approach tested in a *randomized controlled trial* that showed that patients placed at 45 degrees from the horizontal have a lower rate of ventilator-associated pneumonia (VAP) than patients in the supine position.[16] Given that Mrs Richards has no contraindications to semirecumbency, let us reposition her (results apply to this patient)."

Example 2

Context. ICU resident: "Mr Jones is 1 day post–abdominal aortic aneurysm surgery. His blood pressure and urine output are on the low side, with episodes of hypotension. We gave him 1 L of albumin and 1.5 L of normal saline. Should we give him only colloids today?" Underlying question: In critically ill patients with hypotension, what is the effect of colloids vs crystalloids on mortality?

Content and Comments. ICU attending physician: "There's a longstanding debate about whether we should use colloids or crystalloids for fluid resuscitation. The most recent meta-analysis is the eighth on this topic. Reviewers searched comprehensively for and included all randomized controlled trials (RCTs) comparing albumin with any crystalloid reporting death rates.[17] Quality of the original RCTs—that is, their validity—was poor to moderately good. The overall odds ratio (OR) was 1.1 (95% confidence interval [CI], 0.95-1.28), and all subgroups such as trauma (1.1), burns (1.8), and hypoalbuminemia (1.6) show a trend toward increased mortality with albumin. A 7000-patient RCT subsequently found no mortality difference (relative risk, 0.99) in patients resuscitated with albumin vs crystalloid.[18] No subgroups showed benefit, and head-injured patients had increased mortality with albumin. It is hard to justify using albumin, given the lack of benefit and higher costs compared with crystalloids (the results have direct applicability to this decision)."

Example 3

Context. Mr Smith has stable angina, peptic ulcer disease, and a recent history of gastrointestinal bleeding while receiving aspirin. You are Mr Smith's primary care physician and discussing the choice of antiplatelet agent with his gastroenterologist, who is a member of your group and is inclined to switch his medication to clopidogrel.

Underlying question: In patients with indication for aspirin to prevent atheroembolic events and a history of gastrointestinal bleeding, what is the effect of clopidogrel vs continued ASA and a proton-pump inhibitor on gastrointestinal bleeding?

Content and Comments. Primary care practitioner: An RCT (very useful and relevant) of 320 patients who bled while taking aspirin for cardiovascular reasons suggests that adding a proton-pump inhibitor to aspirin is safer than switching from aspirin to clopidogrel.[19,20] It was a randomized, concealed, and well-blinded trial, with 99% 12-month follow-up and with analysis adhering to the intention-to-treat principle—thus, high validity. Those receiving aspirin with esomeprazole had 0.6% recurrent bleeding, and those receiving clopidogrel had 8% recurrent bleeding, for a number needed to treat of 13. Mortality and other important outcomes either showed trends in favor of aspirin and esomeprazole or were similar between groups. "We should consider continuing to give patients like Mr Smith, who are likely to benefit from antiplatelet therapy but who have bled while receiving aspirin, aspirin combined with a proton-pump inhibitor."

Verbal synopses constitute one format that teachers and learners may use to summarize their own appraisals of clinical evidence. Synopses can also be written and stored as paper-, Web-, or personal-digital-assistant-based summaries for sharing and future use. In this case, they are a form of critically appraised topics, or CATs (see below), and take on a broader range of utility and application.

Critically Appraised Topics

CATs are customized summaries of clinical evidence relevant to specific clinical problems. Sauve et al,[21] working under the guidance of David Sackett, originally developed CATs as a vehicle for honing the critical appraisal skills of medical residents and fellows. CATs may be used to facilitate teaching of EBM.[22,23] The content and design of a CAT are perhaps best determined to meet the needs envisioned by its creator.

One can use CATs in each of the 3 modes we identified in Table 22.8-2. In the role-modeling mode, the teacher may distribute a CAT that he or she has previously completed as a means of reinforcing a verbal synopsis of evidence at the bedside. In the integrated teaching mode, the teacher may draw on CATs as a means of interjecting clinical evidence into venues otherwise dominated by traditional case discussions. Finally, CATs may constitute a powerful vehicle for direct teaching of EBM skills using examples that are salient to one's specialty and setting. The teacher may also use CATs as a vehicle for improving a learner's ability to carry out a complex educational prescription.

Teachers may find online aids for creating and accessing CATs useful (http://www.cebm.net/downloads.asp). The following scenario illustrates the use of a CAT that one of us (P.C.W.) frequently uses in the course of supervising residents in the emergency department.

> In the emergency department, a resident describes a 55-year-old male smoker with chest pain. His pain woke him up from sleep, lasted for more than 15 minutes, and was still present when the paramedics arrived but was relieved shortly after they administered sublingual nitroglycerin. The pain was right sided, radiating to the ipsilateral trapezius area, and was not accompanied by other symptoms. There is no history of similar pain or exercise-related symptoms. The resident emphasizes the response to nitroglycerin, stating that this increases the likelihood that the pain represents coronary ischemia. You give her a verbal synopsis of a study that refutes such an inference.[24] You have found it difficult to locate this study quickly and have verified that it is not included in the ACP Journal Club database of synopses. You have taken the time to do your own CAT summary of the article, which you proceed to call up and print out as a means of reinforcing your modeling of *evidence-based practice*. This takes less than 1 minute. Table 22.8-3 is a modified version of the original CAT summary stored on a password-protected site (http://ebem.org/jcb/journalclubbank.html).

The format of Table 22.8-3 reflects a structured electronic entry based on an earlier version of the *Users' Guides* to studies of diagnostic tests. It is customized to fit the intended needs of its creator. When P.C.W. uses this in the course of

TABLE 22.8-3

Example Critically Appraised Topic

Title: Chest Pain Relief by Nitroglycerin Does Not Predict Active Coronary Artery Disease

Citation: *Ann Intern Med.* 2003;139(12):979-986

Authors: Henrikson CA, Howell EE, Bush DE, Miles JS, Meininger GR

Reviewer: Peter Wyer (pwyer@att.net), New York Presbyterian Hospital

Entry date: Wed Jan 28 10:27:58 2004

Search strategy: Ovid nitroglycerin (keyword + exp MeSH) AND exp "Sens and Spec" 13 hits during 2003, including index citation

Summary of study: MEDLINE abstract reproduced here.

Diagnosis Questions

1. Are the results valid?

Was there an independent, blind comparison with a reference standard?

A positive nitroglycerin (NTG) test was a greater than 50% decrease in pain at 5 minutes, evaluated before any reference standards were applied. A positive reference standard for acute coronary artery disease (CAD) was any of (*a*) elevated troponin level, (*b*) positive stress test results, (*c*) at least 70% stenosis on catheterization, or (*d*) clinical assessment by attending physician and confirmed by a blinded cardiologist. Blinding of the first 3 reference standard options (*a-c*) to NTG response was not stated. A 4-month follow-up was achieved in 85% of patients. Clinical follow-up during 4 months was used as the sole reference standard for 122 patients, of whom 43 (9% of the study population) were excluded from the analysis because the reference assessment was indeterminate.

Did the patient sample include an appropriate spectrum of patients to whom the test will be applied?

All patients admitted to a single center through the emergency department to rule out myocardial infarction were included from February to June 2001. Seventeen percent were evaluated without stress or catheterization. Overall, 34% had positive CAD results by reference standard.

Did the results of the test being evaluated influence the decision to perform the reference standard?

Response to NTG was known to physicians and could have contributed to the decision to do definitive testing. Resulting *bias* could be in either direction, depending on the clinicians' interpretation of the NTG response.

Were the test's methods described clearly enough to permit replication?

Yes. The 10-point pain scale pre- and post-NTG required 50% reduction in pain.

2. What are the results?

What are the LRs for the test results?

Positive LR response, 0.84 (0.64-1.1)

Negative LR response, 1.1 (0.95-1.3)

Confidence intervals were calculated using the online statistics calculator: http://statpages.org/ctab2x2.html

Comments: This single-center study demonstrates that the response to NTG among patients suspected of having CAD should not be interpreted as having diagnostic significance.

precepting, he usually does so in the course of role modeling or using integrated modes. It sometimes leads to a discussion of interpretation of likelihood ratios (direct skills teaching mode).

TEACHING CONTENT FROM THE *USERS' GUIDES*

The *Users' Guides* is replete with demonstrations and illustrations suitable for incorporation into teaching scripts or worksheets and other adjuncts to teaching. Indeed, in many cases, the text reflects approaches that were originally developed as interactive teaching scripts. Recently, an independent series of EBM teaching tips has presented some of these examples in their original interactive form (http://www.cmaj.ca/cgi/collection/evidence_based_medicine_series).[12] The resulting teachers' and learners' versions interface with the *Users' Guides* Interactive Web site (http://www.jamaevidence.com) in the form of online interactive versions of the tips, equipping teachers of EBM with an array of concepts and interactive tools useful in a broad range of settings.

The teaching tips installments present an assortment of teaching approaches to a commonly encountered issue in using the medical literature to solve patient problems. These approaches vary by level of EBM expertise and by the time required for their use. Abbreviated approaches are most suitable when one is teaching in the role-modeling or integrated mode. More extended and detailed demonstrations, involving some simple calculations, are appropriate for occasions that call for direct skills teaching. Clinically oriented learners appreciate bite-sized aliquots of EBM skills teaching selected as directly relevant to clinical problems at hand. Some will be inclined to seek knowledge beyond that required by the immediate circumstance, and seasoned teachers are prepared with extended scripts that meet such needs.

Teaching Materials From the *Users' Guides*

For purposes of direct teaching of EBM skills, you will find many examples in the *Users' Guides*. For example, as an adjunct to skills teaching regarding asking answerable questions, the teacher might convert the framework illustrated in Table 3-1 (see Chapter 3, What Is the Question?) into a worksheet such as that illustrated in Table 22.8-4. Many variations on this table are possible to accommodate the

TABLE 22.8-4

Worksheet for Formulating a Clinical Question
Patients
Interventions and Comparisons
Outcomes

needs and goals of different situations. For example, depending on the context, intended uses, and learning goals, one might add rows conforming to the designation of the clinical question type and the preferred study design. In a setting in which these domains are pertinent, the teacher might augment this even further by asking the learners to specify their preferred choice of online resource for doing a search for articles, syntheses, or synopses meeting these specifications (see Chapter 4, Finding the Evidence).

Similarly, creating worksheets for individual study and skills-based seminars from the *Users' Guides* chapters on critical appraisal of questions of therapy, harm, diagnosis, prognosis, and others is straightforward. As an example, one can convert Table 6-1 (see Chapter 6, Therapy) into the worksheet shown in Table 22.8-5. An online version exists for all worksheets for harm, diagnosis, prognosis,

TABLE 22.8-5

Worksheet for a Critical Review of an Article on Therapy

Guide	Comments
I. Are the results valid?	
Did intervention and control groups start with a similar prognosis?	
1. Were patients randomized?	
2. Was randomization concealed?	
3. Were patients in the study groups similar with respect to known prognostic factors?	
Was prognostic balance maintained as the study progressed?	
4. To what extent was the study blinded?	
Were the groups prognostically balanced at the study's completion?	
5. Was follow-up complete?	
6. Were patients analyzed in the groups to which they were randomized?	
7. Was the trial stopped early?	
II. What are the results?	
1. How large was the treatment effect?	
2. How precise was the treatment effect?	
III. How can I apply the results to my patient care?	
1. Were the study patients similar to my patient?	
2. Were all patient-important outcomes considered?	
3. Are the likely benefits worth the potential harms and costs?	

systematic reviews, and others at the *Users' Guides* Interactive Web site (http://www.JAMAevidence.com).

Teachers may modify these worksheets to fit the circumstances. For example, the applicability questions from the worksheet for studies of diagnostic test performance are appropriate for the corresponding section of a worksheet for appraisal of a meta-analysis of such studies. Similarly, in the rare case that a case control study constitutes the best available evidence relating to a question of therapy, the applicability questions from the therapy worksheet (Table 22.8-5) are most appropriate.

Finally, the worksheets illustrated in Tables 22.8-4 and 22.8-5 might be appropriate for use in an extended direct skills teaching session involving an adaptation of a team-learning interactive exercise with learner subgroups working on similar designated tasks.[4,5]

A Directory of Teaching Tips From the *Users' Guides*

The first step in developing a teaching tip is to detect the need for it. Table 22.8-6 summarizes criteria that you may use to determine when you need such a tool.

When 1 or more of the foregoing criteria are met, you are likely to find it useful to review how the *Users' Guides* and, if they have addressed it, how the EBM teaching tips publications have handled the issue.

Table 22.8-7 provides a roadmap of selected content segments across the *Users' Guides* that will guide readers in identifying potential teaching tips. Table 22.8-8 provides links to the teaching tips segments corresponding to some of these items.

Demonstrations

The following scenes with comments illustrate how you might use the concepts, approaches, and materials identified above in specific teaching settings.

TABLE 22.8-6

Criteria for Detecting the Need for a Teaching Tip

Criterion	Example
1. Frequency	A particular issue comes up often and predictably in a certain context
2. Clinical importance	A particular concept is crucial to the understanding of study quality and clinical effect
3. Stumbling blocks	Learners characteristically get stuck on specific concepts or repeatedly make the same errors
4. Visual aids	Simple graphic illustrations or calculations can help learners overcome the stumbling blocks

SCENE 1

You are an attending physician in a hospital emergency department. At sign-out, you present to your colleagues a 60-year-old man presenting with a 4-day history of left leg pain that began a week after a transcontinental plane trip. The clinical examination is noncontributory except for mild tenderness in the left calf muscle, with no swelling or inflammation; laboratory values, including coagulation profile, were normal. You have ordered Doppler compression ultrasonography. A member of the incoming team asks whether the patient has started receiving heparin treatment for a presumptive diagnosis of DVT. You reply, "A well-conducted cohort study enrolling patients with suspected DVT in 2 emergency departments demonstrated that a few clinical criteria allow a reliable stratification of patients into risk categories using a protocol that included serial ultrasonography and venography as the reference standard.[26] I accessed their decision aid using an online Web link (http://www.mssm.edu/medicine/general-medicine/ebm/#cpr) and determined that this patient's risk of DVT is about 50% but would be only about 5% if the ultrasonographic result is normal. My judgment is that the risks of premature initiation of heparin outweigh any risk of waiting for the result before initiating therapy."

TABLE 22.8-7

Teachers' Roadmap of Potential Teaching Tips in the *Users' Guides*[a]

Content Issue	*Users' Guides* Chapter	Figure/ Table(s)	Learner Stumbling Block
Connecting study designs to specific questions, once asked	Chapter 3, What Is the Question	Figures 3-2 to 3-6	Understanding study designs other than RCTs for questions other than therapy
Sources of bias and ways of reducing bias in studies addressing questions of therapy (randomized trials) and harm (observational studies)	Chapter 5, Why Study Results Mislead: Bias and Random Error	Table 5-3	Understanding categories of bias and the link between bias reduction strategies in randomized trials and observational studies
When does loss to follow-up seriously threaten validity?	Chapter 6, Therapy	Table 6-3	An antidote to old guide, still around, that suggests loss to follow-up only a problem if >20%

TABLE 22.8-7

Teachers' Roadmap of Potential Teaching Tips in the *Users' Guides*[a] *(Continued)*

Content Issue	*Users' Guides* Chapter	Figure/ Table(s)	Learner Stumbling Block
Relative vs absolute risk[b]	Chapter 7, Does Treatment Lower Risks? Understanding the Results	Figure 7-1	Understanding effect of baseline risk on absolute risk reduction
Baseline risk and number needed to treat[b]	Chapter 7	Figure 7-3	Understanding how number needed to treat varies with baseline risk when relative risk reductions is constant
Confidence intervals and study size[b]	Chapter 8, Confidence Intervals	Tables 8-1 to 8-2	Understanding how confidence intervals vary with study size
Clinical interpretation of confidence intervals[b]	Chapter 8	Figure 8-1	Understanding how treatment thresholds determine whether a result is definitive
Bias and *random error*	Chapter 9.1, An Illustration of Bias and Random Error	Figure 9.1-1	Understanding bias as systematic error, independent of study size
Why is early stopping for benefit a problem?	Chapter 9.3, Randomized Trials Stopped Early for Benefit	Figure 9.3-1	Apparent credibility of point estimates and confidence intervals from trials stopped early for benefit
Intention to treat	Chapter 9.4, The Principle of Intention to Treat (and Montori and Guyatt[25])	Figures 9.4-1 to 9.4-3	Understanding how postrandomization exclusions may undermine randomization
P values and hypothesis testing[b]	Chapter 10.1, Hypothesis Testing	Figure 10.1-1	Understanding the limitations of *P* values as yes/ no answers to effectiveness
Odds	Chapter 10.2, Understanding the Results: More About Odds Ratios	Figure 10.2-3	Understanding odds and when odds are close to risk

(Continued)

TABLE 22.8-7

Teachers' Roadmap of Potential Teaching Tips in the *Users' Guides*[a] *(Continued)*

Content Issue	Users' Guides Chapter	Figure/Table(s)	Learner Stumbling Block
Regression	Chapter 13.1, Correlation and Regression	Figures 13.1-2, 13.1-4, and 13.1-5	Regression analysis intimidating to most clinicians
Thresholds in diagnostic decision making	Chapter 14, The Process of Diagnosis	Figure 14.2	Determinants of diagnostic and therapeutic thresholds
Spectrum and bias in studies of diagnostic tests[b]	Chapter 17.1, Spectrum Bias	Figures 17.1-1 to 17.1-3	Understanding why lack of clinical uncertainty in a study population introduces systematic error in performance estimates of diagnostic tests
Measuring agreement[b]	Chapter 17.3, Measuring Agreement Beyond Chance	Figure 17.3-1	Understanding how chance contributes to measured agreement
Calculating κ[b]	Chapter 17.3	Figures 17.3-2 to 17.3-4 and Table 17.3-2	Understanding how chance agreement is influenced by prevalence
Appraising prediction rules	Chapter 17.4, Clinical Prediction Rules	Figure 17.4-2 and Table 17.4-1	Understanding the difference among derivation, clinical validation, and impact analysis
Publication bias	Chapter 20.1, Reporting Bias	Figures 20.1-1 and 20.1-2A and B	Understanding the nature of publication bias
Fixed- and random-effect models	Chapter 20.2, Fixed-Effect and Random-Effect Models	Figures 20.2 1 and 20.2-2	Understanding how fixed- and random-effect models influence pooled estimates in meta-analyses
Assessing variability in trial results[b]	Chapter 20.3, Making Sense of Variability in Study Results	Figures 20.3-1 to 20.3-3	Understanding what factors contribute to heterogeneity

Abbreviation: RCT, randomized controlled trial.

[a]In each case, the cited figures and immediately associated text may be adapted into an interactive teaching tip.
[b]Topics have been dealt with in the Evidence-Based Medicine Teaching Tips series (Table 22.8-8). A continuation of this series is scheduled to be published in the January 2008 issue of the *Journal of General Internal Medicine* and will address understanding odds ratios, likelihood ratios, and adjustment for confounders, as well as other topics.

TABLE 22.8-8

Links to *Canadian Medical Association Journal* (*CMAJ*) EBM Teaching Tips Installments by Topic

Topic	Description	Citation	Web link
Relative and absolute risk, number needed to treat	Understanding the relationship between measures of association	*CMAJ.* 2004;171(4): online 1–online 8; appendix to *CMAJ.* 2004;171:353-358	http://www.cmaj.ca/cgi/data/171/4/353/DC1/1
Confidence intervals and *P* values	Clinical interpretation of confidence intervals and the limitations of *P* values	*CMAJ.* 2004;171: online 1–online 12; appendix to *CMAJ.* 2004;171:611-615	http://www.cmaj.ca/cgi/data/171/6/611/DC1/1
κ	Understanding and calculating agreement above chance	*CMAJ.* 2004;171: online 1–online 9; appendix to *CMAJ.* 2004;171:1369-1373	http://www.cmaj.ca/cgi/data/171/11/1369/DC1/1
Heterogeneity	Assessment of variation in trial results and when it is acceptable to pool results	*CMAJ.* 2005;172: online 1–online 8; appendix to *CMAJ.* 2004;171:1369-1373	http://www.cmaj.ca/cgi/data/172/5/661/DC1/1
Spectrum bias	Lack of diagnostic uncertainty as source of systematic error in estimates of test performance	*CMAJ.* 2005;173: online 1–online 7; appendix to *CMAJ.* 2005;173:385-390	http://www.cmaj.ca/cgi/data/173/4/385/DC1/1

Comment. This scene illustrates role modeling of EBM through the use of a verbal study synopsis in the context of routine clinical communication. If this is a question that comes up frequently in your practice, you might choose to develop a CAT corresponding to the related articles[26,27] as a means of summarizing and transmitting this evidence at the same time as modeling evidence-based care. Should your interaction unmask interest on the part of members of the care team in relevant critical appraisal, you could use the relevant *Users' Guides* chapter (see Chapter 17.4, Clinical Prediction Rules).

SCENE 2

You are the incoming emergency attending physician who has assumed the care of the patient described in scene 1 above. A senior resident has taken the time to visit the online prediction rule calculator to which your colleague referred and noticed that the study does not address the actual performance of Doppler compression ultrasonography. The resident suggests that this is a crucial piece of evidence pertaining to the decision at hand. She is particularly keen to develop EBM skills, and you offer her an educational prescription of finding a relevant study to fill this knowledge gap. You take 3 minutes to develop the question with her into the PICO (patient/problem, intervention, comparison, outcome) form, using a formatted handout that you have posted on your Web site (Table 22.8-4). You also quickly discuss the best relevant study design and choice of an appropriate resource (see Chapter 4, Finding the Evidence).

Comment. You have shifted from the role-modeling mode to the direct EBM skills teaching mode by virtue of an educational prescription. This is an ideal outcome of such role modeling, particularly with a learner who is motivated to go beyond—or even challenge—the reasoning and conclusions of their preceptors. Such prescriptions may lead to subsequent teaching sessions involving a larger group of learners. Such sessions might conform to either an integrated mode, such as morning report, or an extended direct EBM skills teaching session such as a journal club.

SCENE 3

The patient introduced in scene 1 had an ultrasonographic result that revealed complete occlusion of the left common femoral vein. The patient was admitted to the hospital for initiation of anticoagulant therapy. You are the ward attending physician and preceptor for morning report, which customarily includes a 30-minute teaching session conducted by one of the senior residents and focused on one of the active patients. The resident has selected this patient as the subject and discusses the content of the didactic session with you. You suggest that she look through the relevant sections of UpToDate (http://www.utdol.com), available through your library's online collections, and consider incorporating 1 or 2 brief summaries of original clinical research evidence included in those sections and pertinent to key issues of the case at hand. Later that day, she reports that she has chosen the accuracy of the clinical diagnosis of DVT after a brief summary of the pathophysiology of venous thrombosis. She notes that the UpToDate sections deal with all of these questions. In discussing her choices, you are aware of the tendency for enthusiastic young teachers to bite off much more than either they or their learners can chew and digest. You suggest to her that the diagnostic issue and the choice of antithrombotic agent particularly lend themselves to concise evidence summaries and suggest that she prepare brief CATs to back up her discussion. She agrees, and, noting that several medical students will be present, proposes to bring copies of a recent installment in the *Journal of the American Medical Association* Rational Clinical Examination series on the clinical diagnosis of DVT as handouts.[28]

Comment. In recommending UpToDate to the resident in a setting that allows incorporation of clinical evidence into a clinical and disease-oriented teaching session, you have selected a type of resource particularly appropriate to the integrated teaching mode. You may also have refined the resident's appreciation of the resource itself. Clinicians who are not well versed in the precepts of EBM frequently use UpToDate primarily as a convenient source of background information and overlook its value as a source of integrated clinical evidence (see Chapter 4, Finding the Evidence). The resident, in turn, has taken your prompt a step farther in extending the integrated approach to address the likely learning needs of the medical students. We suggest that, among categories of resources, systems and synopses are particularly appropriate to modeling and integrated teaching, whereas summaries and studies are ideal for direct teaching of EBM skills (see Chapter 4, Finding the Evidence).

SCENE 4

The emergency medicine resident who looked after the patient with DVT in the emergency department is responsible for organizing the journal club this month; you are the faculty preceptor. He would like to focus on the issue of low-molecular-weight vs unfractionated heparin as initial treatment. He reports that the UpToDate section summarizes several meta-analyses and individual studies addressing this question. You suggest that a systematic review would seem to be appropriate in a situation in which substantial research has been published. He returns to report that he has found a review in the *Cochrane Database of Systematic Reviews*,[29] which includes more recent studies than those included in the evidence summarized in UpToDate. You discuss the potential downside of using a Cochrane review, which can be complex and intimidating to clinicians. Your resident remains enthusiastic and stresses that a previous journal club session dealt with a systematic review published in a conventional biomedical journal and addressed how a systematic review is different from a narrative review. When planning the session, the resident elects to start with a brief presentation of the patient and to use a PICO table derived from Table 3-1 (see Chapter 3, What Is the Question?) and Table 22.8-4 and a critical appraisal worksheet derived from Table 19-2 (see Chapter 19, Summarizing the Evidence) to facilitate successive phases of the exercise. For the new session, the resident decides to include a brief discussion on assessing heterogeneity of studies and study results. You recommend that he consider the relevant chapter of the *Users' Guides* (see Chapter 20.3, Making Sense of Variability in Study Results) and also the related installment in the *CMAJ* teaching tips series.[30,31]

The interactive group session goes well, aided by the vigilant assistance of a resident timekeeper appointed by the session leader. To consolidate the educational experience, you have the resident who led the session give a 60-second verbal synopsis summarizing the *Cochrane Review*, starting with a summary of the patient's problem and framed to simulate a potential incorporation of its content and conclusions into bedside communication. You have several other participants attempt to improve on the resident's attempt. The presenting resident subsequently composes a CAT that you review before its posting on the resident Web site.

Comment. The combination of a compelling issue arising from patient care, a motivated learner, and a teaching assignment requiring active consideration of critical appraisal skills provides circumstances conducive to direct EBM skills teaching. Journal club is easily adapted to an EBM format but may fail if links to clinical practice and problem solving are not built into the exercise.[32] Building the exercise around a question that arose while taking care of an actual patient goes a long way toward ensuring clinical relevance. Including the development of a CAT summary as part of the exercise and posting the resulting CATs in a location accessible at the point of care creates something enduring from the exercise. In this case, the teacher went a step farther by having the resident participants rehearse the process of actively incorporating the evidence into practice using the verbal study synopsis approach. In addition to sharpening the conceptual grasp of the exercise, use of the verbal synopsis in this way helps set the stage for an additional bridge between the journal club exercise and clinical care.

One of us (M.E.) tries to solve the relevance challenge by bringing primary literature to the point of patient care. He calls it CAT on the Fly and finds that residents are able to do an abbreviated written summary of an article, after determining its clinical relevance, in as short a time as 20 minutes. The approach reflects a conscious decision on the part of the preceptor to sacrifice some of the rigor and depth of the review in exchange for increased perception of clinical relevance of such exercises.

FULFILLING EXTERNAL MANDATES

In recent years, regulatory mandates for graduate medical education have incorporated components of the standard EBM skill domains "ask, acquire, appraise, and apply." For instance, the Canadian Royal College of Physicians and Surgeons' CanMEDS program[33] and the Outcomes Project[34] of its US counterpart, the Accreditation Council for Graduate Medical Education (ACGME), both provide for assessment of EBM component skills within a competency-based framework. The Outcomes Project includes competency in EBM as one aspect of what is defined as practice-based learning and improvement.[35] Carrying through EBM to the point of implementation and incorporation into practice is an explicit aspect of EBM teaching[36] and of the *Users' Guides* (see Chapter 22.6, Parallel but Separate Goals: Evidence-Based Practitioners and Evidence-Based Care, and Chapter 22.7, Changing Behavior to Apply Best Evidence in Practice). The ACGME practice-based learning mandate makes this even more explicit, requiring that EBM skills and competency be assimilated as aspects of improvement learning.[35]

Teaching strategies and approaches to assessment of graduate EBM competency as defined within CanMEDS and by the ACGME are evolving. The use of resident learner portfolios as means of documenting and tracking resident activity in this area is one favored approach.[37,38] Preceptors and program directors may draw on familiarity with the contents of the *Users' Guides* to inform and assess all aspects of such activity.

Review of portfolio entries may, in turn, present the teacher with useful opportunities for direct EBM skills teaching. Here, the teacher gains a direct glimpse of a resident-learner's ability to apply EBM to the raw material of clinical practice and may fruitfully choose to focus on aspects of defining and analyzing answerable questions and searching for answers by using appropriate resources. The components of a resident portfolio entry may be seen as the equivalent to a CAT and might include a summary of the patient presentation, documentation of a search, an evidence summary, and a plan of action that addresses not only the patient in question but also similar future patients. The latter might be as straightforward as a plan to post the CAT online for quick reference in conjunction with the next encounter with a similar patient. Both resident learner and faculty preceptor may make use of relevant chapters of the *Users' Guides* for the purpose of preparing and reviewing portfolio entries. Such reviews hold the potential for valuable opportunities for direct EBM skills teaching and integrated teaching of EBM and general clinical practice.

Evaluating Teaching and Assessing Learner Skills

The development of tools for skill assessment and evaluation of EBM teaching efforts constitute a frontier area in the development of EBM.[39] Particularly pertinent to our discussion in this chapter, the lack of such tools is an important reason that only very weak evidence supports the suggestions and recommendations we have made.

A paucity of validated outcome measures constitutes a major limitation of education research in EBM.[40,41] Reviews of studies evaluating the teaching of EBM and critical appraisal report heavy reliance on self-assessment and other unvalidated measures.[42,43] Nevertheless, several assessment tools have undergone psychometric evaluation.[44-46] Of these, 2 have been reported in detail. Fritsche et al[44] developed a 15-item multiple-choice questionnaire that largely tests knowledge of and ability to calculate and interpret outcomes measures in studies of therapy and diagnosis. Ramos et al[45] adopted a more open-ended approach using clinical scenarios with related short-answer questions aimed at assessment of problem-solving ability, particularly in the context of questions of therapy. Promising as these developments are, a comprehensive approach to evaluating EBM skills, teaching skills, and effectiveness of different EBM learning/teaching approaches is called for and will require the development of psychometrically sound evaluation tools.[47]

FURTHER READING

We have provided examples that illustrate how concepts and derived materials drawn from the *Users' Guides* may be brought to bear on a variety of settings and contexts for the purpose of stimulating the learning of EBM skills. Much literature is directly and indirectly relevant to our offering. We mention a few that have caught our attention.

The concept of the 3 modes of teaching EBM was introduced and articulated in a chapter in another EBM text.[3] Approaches to teaching EBM have been heavily influenced by problem-based learning and by related concepts pertaining to small-group learning settings. The ABC of Learning and Teaching Medicine series published in *BMJ* offers a convenient set of articles on these and related topics and is available free at http://www.bmj.com/cgi/search?&titleabstract=%22ABC+of+learning+and+teaching+in+medicine%22&&journalcode=bmj&&hits=20. Likewise, adult learning theory and related concepts have potential bearing on the concepts we have elaborated here,[48] as do writings on the development of expertise.[49-51]

In this chapter, we addressed undergraduate and graduate medical training settings. Direct teaching of EBM skills to practitioners who have finished formal clinical training poses its own challenges and frequently requires an even more explicit negotiation of learning and teaching goals. EBM workshops, continuing medical education programs, and the integration of article reviews as items in division meetings can be useful in this regard but are beyond the scope of our discussion.[52]

References

1. Davis D. Impact of formal continuing medical education: do conferences, workshops, rounds, and other traditional continuing education activities change physician behavior or health care outcomes? *JAMA.* 1999;282(9):867-874.

2. Ghali WA, Saitz R, Eskew AH, Gupta M, Quan H, Hershman WY. Successful teaching in evidence-based medicine. *Med Educ.* 2000;34(1):18-22.

3. Straus SE, Richardson WS, Glasziou P, Haynes RB, eds. Teaching methods. In: *Evidence-Based Medicine: How to Practice and Teach EBM.* 3rd ed. Edinburgh, Scotland: Elsevier/Churchill Livingstone; 2005:199-245.

4. Haidet P, O'Malley KJ, Richards B. An initial experience with "team learning" in medical education. *Acad Med.* 2002;77(1):40-44.

5. Hunt DP, Haidet P, Coverdale JH, Richards B. The effect of using team learning in an evidence-based medicine course for medical students. *Teach Learn Med.* 2003;15(2):131-139.

6. Richardson WS. Teaching evidence-based practice on foot [editorial]. *ACP J Club.* 2005;143(2):A10-A12.

7. Norman GR, Eva KW, Schmidt HG. Implications of psychology-type theories for full curriculum interventions. *Med Educ.* 2005;39(3):243-249.

8. Norman GR, Schmidt HG. Effectiveness of problem-based learning curricula: theory, practice and paper darts. *Med Educ.* 2000;34(9):721-728.

9. Coomarasamy A, Khan KS. What is the evidence that postgraduate teaching in evidence based medicine changes anything? a systematic review. *BMJ.* 2004; 329(7473):1017-1021.

10. Irby DM. How attending physicians make instructional decisions when conducting teaching rounds. *Acad Med.* 1992;67(10):630-638.

11. Schmidt HG, Norman GR, Boshuizen HP. A cognitive perspective on medical expertise: theory and implication. *Acad Med.* 1990;65(10):611-621.

12. Wyer PC, Keitz S, Hatala R, et al. Tips for learning and teaching evidence-based medicine: introduction to the series. *CMAJ.* 2004;171(4):347-348.

13. Irby DM. What clinical teachers in medicine need to know. *Acad Med.* 1994;69 (5):333-342.

14. Weingart S, Wyer P, eds. *Emergency Medicine Decision Making: Critical Choices in Chaotic Environments.* New York, NY: McGraw-Hill Co; 2006.

15. Guyatt GH, Meade MO, Jaeschke RZ, Cook DJ, Haynes RB. Practitioners of evidence based care: not all clinicians need to appraise evidence from scratch but all need some skills [editorial]. *BMJ.* 2000;320(7240):954-955.

16. Drakulovic MB, Torres A, Bauer TT, Nicolas JM, Nogué S, Ferrer M. Supine body position as a risk factor for nosocomial pneumonia in mechanically ventilated patients: a randomised trial. *Lancet.* 1999;354(9193):1835-1836.

17. Wilkes MM, Navickis RJ. Patient survival after human albumin administration: a meta-analysis of randomized, controlled trials. *Ann Intern Med.* 2001;135(3):149-164.

18. SAFE Study Investigators. A comparison of albumin and saline for fluid resuscitation in the intensive care unit. *N Engl J Med.* 2004;350(22):2247-2256.

19. Chan FK, Peterson WL. Aspirin plus esomeprazole reduced recurrent ulcer bleeding more than clopidogrel in high-risk patients. *ACP J Club.* 2005;143(1):9.

20. Chan FK, Ching JY, Hung LC, et al. Clopidogrel versus aspirin and esomeprazole to prevent recurrent ulcer bleeding. *N Engl J Med.* 2005;352(3):238-244.

21. Sauve S, Lee HN, Meade MO, et al. The critically appraised topic: a practical approach to learning critical appraisal. *Ann R Coll Phys Surg Can.* 1995;28(7):396-398.

22. Sackett DL, Straus SE. Finding and applying evidence during clinical rounds: the "evidence cart." *JAMA.* 1998;280(15):1336-1338.

23. Wyer PC. The critically appraised topic: closing the evidence-transfer gap. *Ann Emerg Med.* 1997;30(5):639-640.

24. Henrikson CA, Howell EE, Bush DE, et al. Chest pain relief by nitroglycerin does not predict active coronary artery disease. *Ann Intern Med.* 2003;139(12):979-986.

25. Montori VM, Guyatt GH. Intention-to-treat principle. *CMAJ.* 2001;165(10):1339-1341.

26. Anderson DR, Wells PS, Stiell I, et al. Thrombosis in the emergency department: use of a clinical diagnosis model to safely avoid the need for urgent radiological investigation. *Arch Intern Med.* 1999;159(5):477-482.

27. Wells PS, Hirsh J, Anderson DR, et al. Accuracy of clinical assessment of deep-vein thrombosis. *Lancet.* 1995;345(5):1326-1330.

28. Khan NA, Rahim SA, Anand SS, Simel DL, Panju A. Does the clinical examination predict lower extremity peripheral arterial disease? *JAMA.* 2006;295(5):536-546.

29. van Dongen CJJ, van den Belt AGM, Prins NH, Lensing AWA. Fixed dose subcutaneous low molecular weight heparins versus adjusted dose unfractionated heparin for venous thromboembolism. *Cochrane Database Syst Rev.* 2004;(4):CD001100.

30. Hatala R, Keitz S, Wyer P, Guyatt G, for the Evidence-Based Medicine Teaching Tips Working Group X. Tips for learners of evidence-based medicine, 4: assessing heterogeneity of primary studies in systematic reviews and whether to combine their results. *CMAJ.* 2005;172(5):661-665.

31. Hatala R, Keitz S, Wyer P, Guyatt G, for the Evidence-Based Medicine Teaching Tips Working Group X. Tips for teachers of evidence-based medicine, 4: assessing heterogeneity of primary studies in systematic reviews and whether to combine their results. *CMAJ.* 2005;172(5):online 1-online 8.

32. Phillips RS, Glasziou P. What makes evidence-based journal clubs succeed [editorial]? *ACP J Club.* 2004;140(3):A11-A12.

33. Societal Needs Working Group X. CanMEDS 2000 project: skills for the new millennium. *Ann R Coll Phys Surg Can.* 1996;29(4):206-216.

34. Batalden P, Leach D, Swing S, Dreyfus H, Dreyfus S. General competencies and accreditation in graduate medical education. *Health Aff (Millwood).* 2002;21(5):103-111.

35. Headrick LA. Two kinds of knowledge to achieve better care. *J Gen Intern Med.* 2000;15(9):675-676.

36. Straus SE, Richardson WS, Glasziou P, Haynes RB, eds. *Evidence-Based Medicine: How to Practice and Teach EBM.* 3rd ed. Edinburgh, Scotland: Elsevier Churchill Livingstone; 2005.

37. Mathers NJ, Challis MC, Howe AC, Field NJ. Portfolios in continuing medical education: effective and efficient? *Med Educ.* 1999;33(7):521-530.

38. Lynch DC, Swing SR, Horowitz SD, Holt K, Messer JV. Assessing practice-based learning and improvement. *Teach Learn Med.* 2004;16(1):85-92.

39. Straus SE, Green ML, Bell DS, et al. Evaluating the teaching of evidence based medicine: conceptual framework. *BMJ.* 2004;329(7473):1029-1032.

40. Hatala R, Guyatt G. Evaluating the teaching of evidence-based medicine. *JAMA.* 2002;288(9):1110-1112.

41. Dobbie AE, Schneider FD, Anderson AD, Littlefield J. What evidence supports teaching evidence-based medicine? *Acad Med.* 2000;75(12):1184-1185.

42. Shaneyfelt TM, Baum K, Bell DS, et al. Evaluating evidence-based medicine competence: a systematic review of instruments [abstract]. *J Gen Intern Med.* 2005;20(1)(suppl 1):155.

43. Green ML. Graduate medical education training in clinical epidemiology, critical appraisal, and evidence-based medicine: a critical review of curricula. *Acad Med.* 1999;74(6):686-694.

44. Fritsche L, Greenhalgh T, Falck-Ytter Y, Neumayer HH, Kunz R. Do short courses in evidence based medicine improve knowledge and skills? validation of Berlin questionnaire and before and after study of courses in evidence based medicine. *BMJ.* 2002;325(7376):1338-1341.

45. Ramos KD, Schafer S, Tracz SM. Validation of the Fresno test of competence in evidence based medicine. *BMJ.* 2003;326(7384):319-321.

46. Taylor R, Reeves B, Mears R, et al. Development and validation of a questionnaire to evaluate the effectiveness of evidence-based practice teaching. *Med Educ.* 2001;35(6):544-547.

47. Norman G. Commentary: a conceptual framework may be of limited value. *BMJ.* 2004;329(7473):1032.

48. Bransford JD, Brown AL, Cocking RR, eds. *How People Learn: Brain, Mind, Experience and School.* Washington, DC: National Academy Press; 2000.

49. Ericsson KA, ed. *The Road to Excellence: The Acquisition of Expert Performance in the Arts and Sciences, Sports and Games.* Mahwah, NJ: Erlbaum; 1996.

50. Ericsson KA. Deliberate practice and the acquisition and maintenance of expert performance in medicine and related domains. *Acad Med.* 2004;79(10)(suppl):S70-S81.

51. Ananthakrishnan N. Microteaching as a vehicle of teacher training: its advantages and disadvantages. *J Postgrad Med.* 1993;39(3):142-143.

52. Leipzig RM, Wallace EZ, Smith LG, Sullivant J, Dunn K, McGinn T. Teaching evidence-based medicine: a regional dissemination model. *Teach Learn Med.* 2003;15(3):204-209.

GLOSSARY

Term	Definition
Absolute Difference	The absolute difference in rates of good or harmful outcomes between experimental groups (experimental group risk, or EGR) and control groups (control group risk, or CGR), calculated as the risk in the control group minus the risk in the experimental group (CGR – EGR). For instance, if the rate of adverse events is 20% in the control group and 10% in the treatment group, the absolute difference is 20% – 10% = 10%.
Absolute Risk (or Baseline Risk or Control Event Rate [CER])	The risk of an event (eg, if 10 of 100 patients have an event, the absolute risk is 10% expressed as a percentage, or 0.10 expressed as a proportion).
Absolute Risk Increase (ARI)	The absolute difference in risk of harmful outcomes between experimental groups (experimental group risk, or EGR) and control groups (control group risk, or CGR), calculated as risk of harmful outcome in experimental group minus rate of harmful outcome in control group (EGR – CGR). Typically used to describe a harmful exposure or intervention (eg, if the rate of adverse outcomes is 20% in treatment and 10% in control, the absolute risk increase would be 10% expressed as a percentage and 0.10 expressed as a proportion). See also absolute risk reduction; number needed to harm.
Absolute Risk Reduction (ARR) or Risk Difference	The absolute difference (risk difference) in risks of harmful outcomes between experimental groups (experimental group risk, or EGR) and control groups (control group risk, or CGR), calculated as the risk of harmful outcome in the control group minus the risk of harmful outcome in the experimental group (CGR – EGR). Typically used to describe a beneficial exposure or intervention (eg, if 20% of patients in the control group have an adverse event, as do 10% among treated patients, the ARR or risk difference would be 10% expressed as a percentage or 0.10 expressed as a proportion).
Academic Detailing (or Educational Outreach Visits)	A strategy for changing clinician behavior. Use of a trained person who meets with professionals in their practice settings to provide information with the intent of changing their practice. The pharmaceutical industry frequently uses this strategy, to which the term *detailing* is applied. Academic detailing is such an interaction initiated by an academic group or institution rather than the pharmaceutical industry.

Term	Definition
Adherence (or Compliance)	Extent to which patients carry out health care recommendations, or the extent to which health care providers carry out the diagnostic tests, monitoring equipment, interventional requirements, and other technical specifications that define optimal patient management.
Adjusted Analysis	An adjusted analysis takes into account differences in prognostic factors (or baseline characteristics) between groups that may influence the outcome. For instance, when comparing an experimental and control intervention, if the experimental group is on average older, and thus at higher risk of an adverse outcome than the control group, the analysis adjusted for age will show a larger treatment effect than the unadjusted analysis.
Alerting (or Alerting Systems)	A strategy for changing clinician behavior. A type of computer decision support system that alerts the clinician to a circumstance that might require clinical action (eg, a system that highlights out-of-range laboratory values).
Algorithm	An explicit description of an ordered sequence of steps with branching logic that can be applied under specific clinical circumstances. The logic of an algorithm is: if a, then do x; if b, then do y; etc.
Allocation Concealment (or Concealment)	Randomization is concealed if the person who is making the decision about enrolling a patient is unaware of whether the next patient enrolled will be entered in the intervention or control group (using techniques such as central randomization or sequentially numbered opaque sealed envelopes). If randomization is not concealed, patients with differing prognosis may be differentially recruited to treatment or control groups. Of particular concern, patients with better prognoses may tend to be preferentially enrolled in the active treatment arm, resulting in exaggeration of the apparent benefit of the intervention (or even the false conclusion that the intervention is efficacious).
α Level	The probability of erroneously concluding there is a difference between comparison groups when there is in fact no difference (type I error). Typically, investigators decide on the chance of a false-positive result they are willing to accept when they plan the sample size for a study (eg, investigators often set α level at .05).
Audit and Feedback	A strategy for changing clinician behavior. Any written or verbal summary of clinician performance (eg, based on chart review or observation of clinical practice) during a period of time. The summary may also include recommendations to improve practice.

Term	Definition
Background Questions	These clinical questions are about physiology, pathology, epidemiology, and general management and are often asked by clinicians in training. The answers to background questions are often best found in textbooks or narrative review articles.
Base Case	In an economic evaluation, the base case is the best estimates of each of the key variables that bear on the costs and effects of the alternative management strategies.
Baseline Characteristics	Factors that describe study participants at the beginning of the study (eg, age, sex, disease severity); in comparison studies, it is important that these characteristics be initially similar between groups; if not balanced or if the imbalance is not statistically adjusted, these characteristics can cause confounding and can bias study results.
Baseline Risk (or Baseline Event Rate or Control Event Rate [CER])	The proportion or percentage of study participants in the control group in whom an adverse outcome is observed.
Bayesian Diagnostic Reasoning	The essence of bayesian reasoning is that one starts with a prior probability or probability distribution and incorporates new information to arrive at a posterior probability or probability distribution. The approach to diagnosis presented in this book assumes that diagnosticians are intuitive bayesian thinkers and move from pretest to posttest probabilities as information accumulates.
Before-After Design (or One-Group Pretest-Posttest Design)	Study in which the investigators compare the status of a group of study participants before and after the implementation of an intervention.
Bias (or Systematic Error)	Systematic deviation from the underlying truth because of a feature of the design or conduct of a research study (for example, overestimation of a treatment effect because of failure to randomize). Sometimes, authors label specific types of bias in a variety of contexts. 1. Channeling Effect or Channeling Bias: Tendency of clinicians to prescribe treatment according to a patient's prognosis. As a result of the behavior, in observational studies, treated patients are more or less likely to be high-risk patients than untreated patients, leading to biased estimate of treatment effect. 2. Data Completeness Bias: Using a computer decision support system (CDSS) to log episodes in the intervention group and using a manual system in the non-CDSS control group can create variation in the completeness of data. 3. Detection Bias (or Surveillance Bias): Tendency to look more carefully for an outcome in one of the comparison groups.

(Continued)

Term	Definition
Bias (or Systematic Error) (*Continued*)	4. Differential Verification Bias: When test results influence the choice of the reference standard (eg, test-positive patients undergo an invasive test to establish the diagnosis, whereas test-negative patients undergo long-term follow-up without application of the invasive test) the assessment of test properties may be biased.
	5. Expectation Bias: In data collection, an interviewer has information that influences his or her expectation of finding the exposure or outcome. In clinical practice, a clinician's assessment may be influenced by previous knowledge of the presence or absence of a disorder.
	6. Incorporation Bias: Occurs when investigators use a reference standard that incorporates a diagnostic test that is the subject of investigation. The result is a bias toward making the test appear more powerful in differentiating target positive from target negative than it actually is.
	7. Interviewer Bias: Greater probing by an interviewer of some participants than others, contingent on particular features of the participants.
	8. Lead Time Bias: Occurs when outcomes such as survival, as measured from the time of diagnosis, may be increased not because patients live longer, but because screening lengthens the time that they know they have disease.
	9. Length Time Bias: Occurs when patients whose disease is discovered by screening also may appear to do better or live longer than people whose disease presents clinically with symptoms because screening tends to detect disease that is destined to progress slowly and that therefore has a good prognosis.
	10. Observer Bias: Occurs when an observer's observations differ systematically according to participant characteristics (eg, making systematically different observations in treatment and control groups).
	11. Partial Verification Bias: Occurs when only a selected sample of patients who underwent the index test is verified by the reference standard, and that sample is dependent on the results of the test. For example, patients with suspected coronary artery disease whose exercise test results are positive may be more likely to undergo coronary angiography (the reference standard) than those whose exercise test results are negative.
	12. Publication Bias: Occurs when the publication of research depends on the direction of the study results and whether they are statistically significant.
	(Continued)

Term	Definition
Bias (or Systematic Error) (*Continued*)	13. Recall Bias: Occurs when patients who experience an adverse outcome have a different likelihood of recalling an exposure than patients who do not experience the adverse outcome, independent of the true extent of exposure. 14. Referral Bias: Occurs when characteristics of patients differ between one setting (such as primary care) and another setting that includes only referred patients (such as secondary or tertiary care). 15. Reporting Bias (or selective outcome reporting bias): The inclination of authors to differentially report research results according to the magnitude, direction, or statistical significance of the results. 16. Social Desirability Bias: Occurs when participants answer according to social norms or socially desirable behavior rather than what is actually the case (for instance, underreporting alcohol consumption). 17. Spectrum Bias: Ideally, diagnostic test properties will be assessed in a population in which the spectrum of disease in the target-positive patients includes all those in whom clinicians might be uncertain about the diagnosis, and the target-negative patients include all those with conditions easily confused with the target condition. Spectrum bias may occur when the accuracy of a diagnostic test is assessed in a population that differs from this ideal. Examples of spectrum bias would include a situation in which a substantial proportion of the target-positive population have advanced disease and target-negative participants are normal or asymptomatic. Such situations typically occur in diagnostic case-control studies (for instance, comparing those with advanced disease to normal individuals). Such studies are liable to yield an overly sanguine estimate of the usefulness of the test. 18. Surveillance Bias. See Detection Bias. 19. Verification Bias. See Differential Verification Bias. 20. Workup Bias. See Differential Verification Bias.
Binary Outcome	See Dichotomous Outcome.
Blind (or Blinded or Masked)	Patients, clinicians, data collectors, outcome adjudicators, or data analysts unaware of which patients have been assigned to the experimental or control group. In the case of diagnostic tests, those interpreting the test results are unaware of the result of the reference standard or vice versa.
Boolean Operators (or Logical Operators)	Words used when searching electronic databases. These operators are AND, OR, and NOT and are used to combine terms (AND/OR) or exclude terms (NOT) from the search strategy.

Term	Definition
Bootstrap Technique	A statistical technique for estimating parameters such as standard errors and confidence intervals based on resampling from an observed data set with replacement from the original sample.
Case-Control Study	A study designed to determine the association between an exposure and outcome in which patients are sampled by outcome. Those with the outcome (cases) are compared with those without the outcome (controls) with respect to exposure to the suspected harmful agent.
Case Series	A report of a study of a collection of patients treated in a similar manner, without a control group. For example, a clinician might describe the characteristics of an outcome for 25 consecutive patients with diabetes who received education for prevention of foot ulcers.
Case Study	In qualitative research, an exploration of a case defined by some boundaries or contemporary phenomena usually within a real-life context.
Categorical Variable	A categorical variable may be nominal or ordinal. Categorical variables can be defined according to attributes without any associated order (eg, medical admission, elective surgery, or emergency surgery); these are called nominal variables. A categorical variable can also be defined according to attributes that are ordered (eg, height such as high, medium, or low); these are called ordinal variables.
Chance-Corrected Agreement	The proportion of possible agreement achieved beyond that which one would expect by chance alone, often measured by the φ statistic.
Chance-Independent Agreement	The proportion of possible agreement achieved that is independent of chance and unaffected by the distribution of ratings, as measured by the φ statistic.
Channeling Effect or Channeling Bias	See Bias.
Checklist Effect	The improvement seen in medical decision making because of more complete and structured data collection (eg, clinicians fill out a detailed form, so their decisions improve).
χ^2 Test	A nonparametric test of statistical significance used to compare the distribution of categorical outcomes in 2 or more groups, the null hypothesis of which is that the underlying distributions are identical.
Class Effect (or Drug Class Effect)	When similar effects are produced by most or all members of a class of drugs (eg, β-blockers or calcium antagonists).
Clinical Decision Rules (or Decision Rules, Clinical Prediction Rules, or Prediction Rules)	A guide for practice that is generated by initially examining, and ultimately combining, a number of variables to predict the likelihood of a current diagnosis or a future event. Sometimes, if the likelihood is sufficiently high or low, the rule generates a suggested course of action.

Term	Definition
Clinical Decision Support System	A strategy for changing clinician behavior. An information system used to integrate clinical and patient information and provide support for decision-making in patient care. See also Computer Decision Support System.
Clinical Practice Guidelines (or Guidelines or Practice Guidelines)	A strategy for changing clinician behavior. Systematically developed statements or recommendations to assist practitioner and patient decisions about appropriate health care for specific clinical circumstances.
Cluster Analysis	A statistical procedure in which the unit of analysis matches the unit of randomization, which is something other than the patient or participant (eg, school, clinic).
Cluster Assignment (or Cluster Randomization)	The assignment of groups (eg, schools, clinics) rather than individuals to intervention and control groups. This approach is often used when assignment by individuals is likely to result in contamination (eg, if adolescents within a school are assigned to receive or not receive a new sex education program, it is likely that they will share the information they learn with one another; instead, if the unit of assignment is schools, entire schools are assigned to receive or not receive the new sex education program). Cluster assignment is typically randomized, but it is possible (though not advisable) to assign clusters to treatment or control by other methods.
Cochrane Q	A common test for heterogeneity that assumes the null hypothesis that all the apparent variability between individual study results is due to chance. Cochrane Q generates a probability, presented as a P value, based on a χ^2 distribution, that between-study differences in results equal to or greater than those observed are likely to occur simply by chance.
Cohort	A group of persons with a common characteristic or set of characteristics. Typically, the group is followed for a specified period to determine the incidence of a disorder or complications of an established disorder (prognosis).
Cohort Study (or Longitudinal Study or Prospective Study)	This is an investigation in which a cohort of individuals who do not have evidence of an outcome of interest but who are exposed to the putative cause is compared with a concurrent cohort of individuals who are also free of the outcome but not exposed to the putative cause. Both cohorts are then followed forward in time to compare the incidence of the outcome of interest. When used to study the effectiveness of an intervention, it is an investigation in which a cohort of individuals who receive the intervention is compared with a concurrent cohort who does not receive the intervention, wherein both cohorts are followed forward to compare the incidence of the outcome of interest. Cohort studies can be conducted retrospectively in the sense that someone other than the investigator has followed patients, and the investigator obtains the data base and then examines the association between exposure and outcome.

Term	Definition
Cointerventions	Interventions other than intervention under study that affect the outcome of interest and that may be differentially applied to intervention and control groups and thus potentially bias the result of a study.
Comorbidity	Disease(s) or conditions that coexist in study participants in addition to the index condition that is the subject of the study.
Compliance (or Adherence)	See Adherence.
Composite Endpoint (or Composite Outcome)	When investigators measure the effect of treatment on an aggregate of endpoints of various importance, this is a composite endpoint. Inferences from composite endpoints are strongest in the rare situations in which (1) the component endpoints are of similar patient importance, (2) the endpoints that are more important occur with at least similar frequency to those that are less important, and (3) strong biologic rationale supports results that, across component endpoints, show similar relative risks with sufficiently narrow confidence intervals.
Computer Decision Support System (CDSS)	A strategy for changing clinician behavior. Computer-based information systems used to integrate clinical and patient information and provide support for decision making in patient care. In clinical decision support systems that are computer based, detailed individual patient data are entered into a computer program and are sorted and matched to programs or algorithms in a computerized database, resulting in the generation of patient-specific assessments or recommendations. CDSSs can have the following purposes: alerting, reminding, critiquing, interpreting, predicting, diagnosing, and suggesting. See also Clinical Decision Support System.
Concealment (or Allocation Concealment)	See Allocation Concealment.
Concepts	The basic building blocks of theory.
Conceptual Framework	An organization of interrelated ideas or concepts that provides a system of relationships between those ideas or concepts.
Conditional Probabilities	The probability of a particular state, given another state (ie, the probability of A, given B).
Confidence Interval (CI)	Range of values within which it is probable that the true value of a parameter (eg, a mean, a relative risk) lies.
Conflict of Interest	A conflict of interest exists when investigators, authors, institutions, reviewers, or editors have financial or nonfinancial relationships with other persons or organizations (such as study sponsors), or personal investments in research projects or the outcomes of projects, that may inappropriately influence their interpretation or actions. Conflicts of interest can lead to biased design, conduct, analysis, and interpretation of study results.

Term	Definition
Confounder (or Confounding Variable or Confounding)	A factor that is associated with the outcome of interest and is differentially distributed in patients exposed and unexposed to the outcome of interest.
Consecutive Sample (or Sequential Sample)	A sample in which all potentially eligible patients treated throughout a period are enrolled.
Consequentialist (or Utilitarian)	A consequentialist or utilitarian view of distributive justice contends that, even in individual decision making, the clinician should take a broad social view, favoring actions that provide the greatest good to the greatest number. In this broader view, the effect on others of allocating resources to a particular patient's care would bear on the decision. This is an alternative to the deontologic view.
Construct Validity	In measurement theory, a construct is a theoretically derived notion of the domain(s) we wish to measure. An understanding of the construct will lead to expectations about how an instrument should behave if it is valid. Construct validity therefore involves comparisons between the instrument being evaluated and other measures (eg, characteristics of patients or other scores) and the logical relationships that should exist between them.
Contamination	Occurs when participants in either the experimental or control group receive the intervention intended for the other arm of the study.
Continuous Variable (or Interval Data)	A variable that can theoretically take any value and in practice can take a large number of values with small differences between them (eg, height). Continuous variables are also sometimes called interval data.
Control Event Rate (CER) (or Baseline Risk or Baseline Event Rate)	See Baseline Risk.
Control Group	A group that does not receive the experimental intervention. In many studies, the control group receives either usual care or a placebo.
Controlled Time Series Design (or Controlled Interrupted Time Series)	Data are collected at several times both before and after the intervention in the intervention group and at the same times in a control group. Data collected before the intervention allow the underlying trend and cyclical (seasonal) effects to be estimated. Data collected after the intervention allow the intervention effect to be estimated while accounting for underlying secular trends. Use of a control group addresses the greatest threat to the validity of a time series design, which is the occurrence of another event at the same time as the intervention, both of which may be associated with the outcome.
Correlation	The magnitude of the relationship between 2 variables.
Correlation Coefficient	A numeric expression of the magnitude and direction of the relationship between 2 variables, which can take values from −1.0 (perfect negative relationship) to 0 (no relationship) to 1.0 (perfect positive relationship).

Term	Definition
Cost Analysis	An economic analysis in which only costs of various alternatives are compared. This comparison informs only the resource-use half of the decision (the other half being the expected outcomes).
Cost-Benefit Analysis	An economic analysis in which both the costs and the consequences (including increases in the length and quality of life) are expressed in monetary terms.
Cost-Effectiveness Acceptability Curve	The cost-effectiveness acceptability is plotted on a graph that relates the maximum one is willing to pay for a particular treatment alternative (eg, how many dollars one is willing to pay to gain 1 life-year) on the x-axis to the probability that a treatment alternative is cost-effective compared with all other treatment alternatives on the y-axis. The curves are generated from uncertainty around the point estimates of costs and effects in trial-based economic evaluations or uncertainty around values for variables used in decision analytic models. As one is willing to pay more for health outcomes, treatment alternatives that initially might be considered unattractive (eg, a high cost per life-year saved) will have a higher probability of becoming more cost-effective. Cost-effectiveness acceptability curves are a convenient method of presenting the effect of uncertainty on economic evaluation results on a single figure instead of through the use of numerous tables and figures of sensitivity analyses.
Cost-Effectiveness Analysis	An economic analysis in which the consequences are expressed in natural units (eg, cost per life saved or cost per bleeding event averted). Sometimes, cost-utility analysis is classified as a subcategory of cost-effectiveness analysis.
Cost-Effectiveness Efficiency Frontier	The cost and effectiveness results of each treatment alternative from an economic evaluation can be graphed on a figure known as the cost-effectiveness plane. The cost-effectiveness plane plots cost on the vertical axis (ie, positive infinity at the top and negative infinity and the bottom) and effects such as life-years on the horizontal axis (ie, negative infinity at the far left and positive infinity at the far right). One treatment alternative such as usual care is plotted at the origin (ie, 0, 0) and all other treatment alternatives are plotted relative to the treatment at the origin. Treatment alternatives are considered dominated if they have both higher costs and lower effectiveness relative to any other. Line segments can be drawn connecting the nondominated treatment alternatives, and the combination of line segments that join these nondominated treatment alternatives is referred to as the cost-effectiveness efficiency frontier. Constructed in this way, any treatment alternative that lies above the cost-effectiveness efficiency frontier is considered to be inefficient (dominated) by a treatment alternative or combination of alternatives on the efficiency frontier.

Term	Definition
Cost-Minimization Analysis	An economic analysis conducted in situations in which the consequences of the alternatives are identical and the only issue is their relative costs.
Cost-to-Charge Ratio	Where there is a systematic deviation between costs and charges, an economic analysis may adjust charges using a cost-to-charge ratio to approximate real costs.
Cost-Utility Analysis	A type of economic analysis in which the consequences are expressed in terms of life-years adjusted by peoples' preferences. Typically, one considers the incremental cost per incremental gain in quality-adjusted life-years (QALYs).
Cox Regression Model	A regression technique that allows adjustment for known differences in baseline characteristics or time-dependent characteristics between 2 groups applied to survival data.
Credibility (or Trustworthiness)	In qualitative research, a term used instead of validity to reflect whether the investigators engaged thoroughly and sensitively with the material and whether the investigators' interpretations are credible. Signs of credibility can be found not only in the procedural descriptions of methodology but also through an assessment of the coherence and depth of the findings reported.
Criterion Standard (or Gold Standard or Reference Standard)	A method having established or widely accepted accuracy for determining a diagnosis that provides a standard to which a new screening or diagnostic test can be compared. The method need not be a single or simple procedure but could include patient follow-up to observe the evolution of their condition or the consensus of an adjudication committee about their outcome.
Critical Theory	A qualitative research tradition focused on understanding the nature of power relationships and related constructs, often with the intention of helping to remedy systemic injustices in society.
Critiquing (or Critiquing System)	A strategy for changing clinician behavior. A decision support approach in which the computer evaluates a clinician's decision and generates an appropriateness rating or an alternative suggestion.
Cronbach α Coefficient	Cronbach α is an index of reliability, homogeneity, or internal consistency of items on a measurement instrument. The Cronbach α increases with the magnitude of the interitem correlation and with the number of items.
Cross-Sectional Study	The observation of a defined population at a single point in time or during a specific interval. Exposure and outcome are determined simultaneously.
Data Completeness Bias	See Bias.

Term	Definition
Data Dredging	Searching a data set for differences between groups on particular outcomes, or in subgroups of patients, without explicit a priori hypotheses.
Decision Aid	A tool that endeavors to present patients with the benefits and harms of alternative courses of action in a manner that is quantitative, comprehensive, and understandable.
Decision Analysis	A systematic approach to decision making under conditions of uncertainty. It involves identifying all available alternatives and estimating the probabilities of potential outcomes associated with each alternative, valuing each outcome, and, on the basis of the probabilities and values, arriving at a quantitative estimate of the relative merit of each alternative.
Decision Rules (or Clinical Decision Rules)	See Clinical Decision Rules.
Decision Tree	Most clinical decision analyses are built as decision trees; articles usually will include 1 or more diagrams showing the structure of the decision tree used for the analysis.
Degrees of Freedom	A technical term in a statistical analysis that has to do with the power of the analysis. The more degrees of freedom, the more powerful the analysis. The degrees of freedom typically refers to the number of observations in a sample minus the number of unknown parameters estimated for the model. It reflects a sort of adjusted sample size, with the adjustment based on the number of unknowns that need to be estimated in a model. For example, in a 2-sample t test the degrees of freedom is n1 + n2 − 1 − 1, because there are n1 + n2 subjects altogether and 1 mean estimated in one group and 1 mean in another, giving n1 + n2 − 2.
Deontologic	A deontologic approach to distributive justice holds that the clinician's only responsibility should be to best meet the needs of the individual under his or her care. This is an alternative to the consequentialist or utilitarian view.
Dependent Variable (or Outcome Variable or Target Variable)	The target variable of interest. The variable that is hypothesized to depend on or be caused by another variable, the independent variable.
Detection Bias (or Surveillance Bias)	See Bias.
Determinants of Outcome	The factors most strongly determining whether or not a target event will occur.
Dichotomous Outcome (or Binary Outcome)	A categorical variable that can take one of 2 discrete values rather than an incremental value on a continuum (eg, pregnant or not pregnant, dead or alive).

Term	Definition
Differential Diagnosis (or Active Alternatives)	The set of diagnoses that can plausibly explain a patient's presentation.
Differential Verification Bias	See Bias.
Direct Observation	See Field Observation.
Directness	A key element to consider when grading the quality of evidence for a health care recommendation. Evidence is direct to the extent that study participants, interventions, and outcome measures are similar to those of interest.
Discriminant Analysis	A statistical technique similar to logistic regression analysis that identifies variables that are associated with the presence or absence of a particular categorical (nominal) outcome.
Disease-Specific Health-Related Quality of Life	See Health-Related Quality of Life.
Document Analysis	In qualitative research, this is one of 3 basic data collection methods. It involves the interpretive review of written material.
Dominate	In economic evaluation, if the intervention of interest is both more effective and less costly than the control strategy, it is said to dominate the alternative.
Dose-Response Gradient (or Dose Dependence)	Exists when the risk of an outcome changes in the anticipated direction as the quantity or the duration of exposure to the putative harmful or beneficial agent increases.
Downstream Costs	Costs due to resources consumed in the future and associated with clinical events in the future that are attributable to the intervention.
Drug Class Effects (or Class Effects)	See Class Effects.
Ecologic Study	Ecologic studies examine relationships between groups of individuals with exposure to a putative risk factor and an outcome. Exposures are measured at the population, community, or group level rather than at the individual level. Ecologic studies can provide information about an association; however, they are prone to bias: the ecologic fallacy. The ecologic fallacy holds that relationships observed for groups necessarily hold for individuals (eg, if countries with more dietary fat have higher rates of breast cancer, then women who eat fatty foods must be more likely to get breast cancer). These inferences may be correct but are only weakly supported by the aggregate data.
Economic Analysis (or Economic Evaluation)	A set of formal, quantitative methods used to compare 2 or more treatments, programs, or strategies with respect to their resource use and their expected outcomes.

Term	Definition
Educational Meetings (or Interactive Workshops)	A strategy for changing clinician behavior. Participation of professionals in workshops that include interaction and discussion.
Educational Outreach Visits (or Academic Detailing)	See Academic Detailing.
Effect Size	The difference in outcomes between the intervention and control groups divided by some measure of variability, typically the standard deviation.
Efficiency	Technical efficiency is the relationship between inputs (costs) and outputs (in health, quality-adjusted life-years [QALYs]). Interventions that provide more QALYs for the same or fewer resources are more efficient. Technical efficiency is assessed using cost minimization, cost-effectiveness, and cost-utility analysis. Allocative efficiency recognizes that health is not the only goal that society wishes to pursue, so competing goals must be weighted and then related to costs. This is typically done through cost-benefit analysis.
Efficiency Frontier	When the cost and effectiveness results of an economic evaluation are graphed on a cost-effectiveness plane along with incremental cost-effectiveness ratios, the resultant line segments are referred to as the efficiency frontier. Any strategy that has a base-case cost-effectiveness that is above the efficiency frontier would be considered dominated.
Endpoint	Event or outcome that leads to completion or termination of follow-up of an individual in a study (eg, death or major morbidity).
Equivalence Studies (or Equivalence Trial or Noninferiority Trials)	Trials that estimate treatment effects that exclude any patient-important superiority of interventions under evaluation are equivalence trials. Equivalence trials require a priori definition of the smallest difference in outcomes between these interventions that patients would consider large enough to justify a preference for the superior intervention (given the intervention's harms and burdens). The confidence interval for the estimated treatment effect at the end of the trial should exclude that difference for the authors to claim equivalence (ie, the confidence limits should be closer to zero than the minimal patient-important difference). This level of precision often requires investigators to enroll large number of patients with large number of events. Equivalence trials are helpful when investigators want to see whether a cheaper, safer, simpler (or increasingly often, better method to generate income for the sponsor) intervention is neither better nor worse (in terms of efficacy) than a current intervention. Claims of equivalence are frequent when results are not significant, but one must be alert to whether the confidence intervals exclude differences between the interventions that are as large as or larger than those patients would consider important. If they do not, the trial is indeterminate rather than yielding equivalence.

Term	Definition
Ethnography (or Ethnographic Study)	In qualitative research, an approach to inquiry that focuses on the culture or subculture of a group of people to try to understand the world view of those under study.
Evidence	A broad definition of evidence is any empirical observation, whether systematically collected or not. The unsystematic observations of the individual clinician constitute one source of evidence. Physiologic experiments constitute another source. Clinical research evidence refers to systematic observation of clinical events and is the focus of this book.
Evidence-Based Experts	Clinicians who can, in a sophisticated manner, independently find, appraise, and judiciously apply the best evidence to patient care.
Evidence-Based Health Care (EBHC)	The conscientious, explicit, and judicious use of current best evidence in making decisions about the care of individual patients. Evidence-based clinical practice requires integration of individual clinical expertise and patient preferences with the best available external clinical evidence from systematic research and consideration of available resources.
Evidence-Based Medicine (EBM)	EBM can be considered a subcategory of evidence-based health care, which also includes other branches of health care practice such as evidence-based nursing or evidence-based physiotherapy. EBM subcategories include evidence-based surgery and evidence-based cardiology. See also Evidence-Based Health Care.
Evidence-Based Policy Making	Policy making is evidence based when practice policies (eg, use of resources by clinicians), service policies (eg, resource allocation, pattern of services), and governance policies (eg, organizational and financial structures) are based on research evidence of benefit or cost-benefit.
Evidence-Based Practice (EBP)	EBP is clinical practice in which patient management decisions are consistent with the principles of evidence-based health care. This means that decisions will be, first of all, consistent with the best evidence about the benefits and downsides of the alternative management strategies. Second, decisions will be consistent with the values and preferences of the individual patient.
Evidence-Based Practitioners	Clinicians who can differentiate evidence-based summaries and recommendations from those that are not evidence-based and understand results sufficiently well to apply them judiciously in clinical care, ensuring decisions are consistent with patients' values and preferences.

Term	Definition
Exclusion Criteria	The characteristics that render potential participants ineligible to participate in a study or that render studies ineligible for inclusion in a systematic review.
Expectation Bias	See Bias.
Experimental Therapy (or Experimental Treatment or Experimental Intervention)	A therapeutic alternative to standard or control therapy, which is often a new intervention or different dose of a standard drug.
Exposure	A condition to which patients are exposed (either a potentially harmful intervention or a potentially beneficial one) that may affect their health.
External Validity (or Generalizability)	The degree to which the results of a study can be generalized to settings or samples other than the ones studied.
Face Validity	The extent to which a measurement instrument appears to measure what it is intended to measure.
Fail-Safe N	The minimum number of undetected studies with negative results that would be needed to change the conclusions of a meta-analysis. A small fail-safe N suggests that the conclusion of the meta-analysis may be susceptible to publication bias.
False Negative	Those who have the target disorder, but the test incorrectly identifies them as not having it.
False Positive	Those who do not have the target disorder, but the test incorrectly identifies them as having it.
Feedback Effect	The improvement seen in medical decision because of performance evaluation and feedback.
Feeling Thermometer	A feeling thermometer is a visual analogue scale presented as a thermometer, typically with markings from 0 to 100, with 0 representing death and 100 full health. Respondents use the thermometer to indicate their utility rating of their health state or of a hypothetical health state.
Field Observation	In qualitative research, this is one of 3 basic data collection methods. It involves investigators witnessing and recording events as they occur. There are 3 approaches to field observation. With direct observation, investigators record detailed field notes from the milieu they are studying. In nonparticipant observation, the researcher participates relatively little in the interactions he or she is studying. In participant observation, the researcher assumes a role in the social setting beyond that of a researcher (eg, clinician, committee member).

Term	Definition
Fixed-Effects Models	A model to generate a summary estimate of the magnitude of effect in a meta-analysis that restricts inferences to the set of studies included in the meta-analysis and assumes that a single true value underlies all of the primary study results. The assumption is that if all studies were infinitely large, they would yield identical estimates of effect; thus, observed estimates of effect differ from one another only because of random error. This model takes only within-study variation into account and not between-study variation.
Focus Group	See Interview.
Follow-up (or Complete Follow-up)	The extent to which investigators are aware of the outcome in every patient who participated in a study. If follow-up is complete, the outcome is known for all study participants.
Foreground Questions	These clinical questions are more commonly asked by seasoned clinicians. They are questions asked when browsing the literature (eg, what important new information should I know to optimally treat my patients?) or when problem solving (eg, defining specific questions raised in caring for patients, and then consulting the literature to resolve these problems).
Funnel Plot	A graphic technique for assessing the possibility of publication bias in a systematic review. The effect measure is typically plotted on the horizontal axis and a measure of the random error associated with each study on the vertical axis. In the absence of publication bias, because of sampling variability, the graph should have the shape of a funnel. If there is bias against the publication of null results or results showing an adverse effect of the intervention, one quadrant of the funnel plot will be partially or completely missing.
Generalizability (or External Validity)	See External Validity.
Generic Health-Related Quality of Life	See Health-Related Quality of Life.
Gold Standard (or Reference Standard or Criterion Standard)	See Criterion Standard.
Grounded Theory	In qualitative research, an approach to collecting and analyzing data with the aim of developing a theory grounded in real-world observations.
Harm	Adverse consequences of exposure to an intervention.
Hawthorne Effect	The tendency for human performance to improve when participants are aware that their behavior is being observed.

Term	Definition
Hazard Ratio	The weighted relative risk of an outcome (eg, death) during the entire study period; often reported in the context of survival analysis.
Health Costs (or Health Care Costs)	Health care resources that are consumed. These reflect the inability to use the same resources for other worthwhile purposes (opportunity costs).
Health Outcomes	All possible changes in health status that may occur for a defined population or that may be associated with exposure to an intervention. These include changes in the length and quality of life, major morbid events, and mortality.
Health Profile	A type of data collection tool, intended for use in the entire population (including the healthy, the very sick, and patients with any sort of health problem), that attempts to measure all important aspects of health-related quality of life (HRQL).
Health-Related Quality of Life (HRQL)	1. Health-Related Quality of Life: Measurements of how people are feeling, or the value they place on their health state. Such measurements can be disease specific or generic. 2. Disease-Specific Health-Related Quality of Life: Disease-specific HRQL measures evaluate the full range of patients' problems and experiences relevant to a specific condition or disease. 3. Generic Health-Related Quality of Life: Generic HRQL measures contain items covering all relevant areas of HRQL. They are designed for administration to people with any kind of underlying health problem (or no problem at all). Generic HRQL measures allow comparisons across diseases or conditions.
Health State	The health condition of an individual or group during a specified interval (commonly assessed at a particular point).
Heterogeneity	Differences among individual studies included in a systematic review, typically referring to study results; the terms can also be applied to other study characteristics.
Hierarchic Regression	Hierarchic regression examines the relation between independent variables or predictor variables (eg, age, sex, disease severity) and a dependent variable (or outcome variable) (eg, death, exercise capacity). Hierarchic regression differs from standard regression in that one predictor is a subcategory of another predictor. The lower-level predictor is nested within the higher-level predictor. For instance, in a regression predicting likelihood of withdrawal of life support in intensive care units (ICUs) participating in an international study, city is nested within country and ICU is nested within city.

Term	Definition
Hierarchy of Evidence	A system of classifying and organizing types of evidence, typically for questions of treatment and prevention. Clinicians should look for the evidence from the highest position in the hierarchy.
Historiography	A qualitative research methodology concerned with understanding both historical events and approaches to the writing of historical narratives.
I^2 Statistic	The I^2 statistic is a test of heterogeneity. I^2 can be calculated from Cochrane Q (the most commonly used heterogeneity statistic) according to the formula: $I^2 = 100\% \times$ (Cochrane Q − degrees of freedom) / Cochran Q. Any negative values of I^2 are considered equal to 0, so that the range of I^2 values is between 0% and 100%.
Incidence	Number of new cases of disease occurring during a specified period, expressed as a proportion of the number of people at risk during that time.
Inclusion Criteria	The characteristics that define the population eligible for a study or that define the studies that will be eligible for inclusion in a systematic review.
Incorporation Bias	See Bias.
Incremental Cost-Effectiveness Ratio	The price at which additional units of benefit can be obtained.
Independent Association	When a variable is associated with an outcome after adjusting for multiple other potential prognostic factors (often after regression analysis), the association is an Independent association.
Independent Variable	The variable that is believed to cause, influence, or at least be associated with the dependent variable.
Indicator Condition	A clinical situation (eg, disease, symptom, injury, or health state) that occurs reasonably frequently and for which there is sound evidence that high-quality care is beneficial. Indicator conditions can be used to evaluate quality of care by comparing the care provided (as assessed through chart review or observation) to that which is recommended.
Indirect Costs and Benefits	The effect of alternative patient management strategies on the productivity of the patient and others involved in the patient's care.
Individual Patient Data Meta-analysis	A meta-analysis in which individual patient data from each primary study are used to create pooled estimates. Such an approach can facilitate more accurate intention-to-treat analyses and informed subgroup analyses.
Informational Redundancy	In qualitative research, the point in the analysis at which new data fail to generate new themes and new information. This is considered an appropriate stopping point for data collection in most methods and an appropriate stopping point for analysis in some methods.

Term	Definition
Informed Consent	A participant's expression (verbal or written) of willingness, after full disclosure of the risks, benefits, and other implications, to participate in a study.
Intention-to-Treat Principle	Analyzing participant outcomes according to the group to which they were randomized, even if participants in that group did not receive the planned intervention. This principle preserves the power of randomization, thus ensuring that important known and unknown factors that influence outcomes are likely to be equally distributed across comparison groups. We do not use the term *intention-to-treat analysis* because of ambiguity created by patients lost to follow-up, which can cause exactly the same sort of bias as failure to adhere to the intention-to-treat principle.
Internal Validity	Whether a study provides valid results depends on whether it was designed and conducted well enough that the study findings accurately represent the direction and magnitude of the underlying true effect (ie, studies that have higher internal validity have a lower likelihood of bias/systematic error).
Interrater Reliability	The extent to which 2 or more raters are able to consistently differentiate subjects with higher and lower values on an underlying trait (typically measured with an intraclass correlation).
Interrupted Time Series Design (or Time Series Design)	See Time Series Design.
Interval Data (or Continuous Variable)	See Continuous Variable.
Intervention Effect (or Treatment Effect)	See Treatment Effect.
Interview	In qualitative research, this is one of 3 basic data collection methods. It involves an interviewer asking questions to engage participants in dialogue to allow interpretation of experiences and events in the participants' own terms. The 2 most common interviews are semistructured, detailed interviews of individuals or discussion-based interviews of several people, called focus groups. In quantitative research, a method of collecting data in which an interviewer obtains information from a participant through conversation.
Interviewer Bias	See Bias.
Intraclass Correlation Coefficient	This is a measure of reproducibility that compares variance between patients to the total variance, including both between- and within-patient variance.
Intrarater Reliability	The extent to which a rater is able to consistently differentiate participants with higher and lower values of an underlying trait on repeated ratings over time (typically measured with an intraclass correlation).

Term	Definition
Inverse Rule of 3s	A rough rule of thumb, called the inverse rule of 3s, tells us the following: If an event occurs, on average, once every x days, we need to observe 3x days to be 95% confident of observing at least 1 event.
Investigator Triangulation	See Triangulation.
Judgmental Sampling (or Purposive Sampling or Purposeful Sampling)	See Purposive Sampling.
Kaplan-Meier Curve (or Survival Curve)	See Survival Curve.
κ Statistic (or Weighted κ or κ Value)	A measure of the extent to which observers achieve agreement beyond the level expected to occur by chance alone.
Law of Multiplicative Probabilities	The law of multiplicative probabilities for independent events (where one event in no way influences the other) tells us that the probability of 10 consecutive heads in 10 coin flips can be found by multiplying the probability of a single head (1/2) 10 times over; that is, 1/2, 1/2, 1/2, and so on.
Leading Hypothesis (or Working Diagnosis)	See Working diagnosis.
Lead Time Bias	See Bias.
Length Time Bias	See Bias.
Levels of Evidence	A hierarchy of research evidence to inform practice, usually ranging from strongest to weakest.
Likelihood Ratio (LR)	For a screening or diagnostic test (including clinical signs or symptoms), the LR expresses the relative likelihood that a given test would be expected in a patient with, as opposed to one without, a disorder of interest. An LR of 1 means that the posttest probability is identical to the pretest probability. As LRs increase above 1, the posttest probability progressively increases in relation to the pretest probability. As LRs decrease below 1, the posttest probability progressively decreases in relation to the pretest probability. An LR is calculated as the proportion of target positive with a particular test result (which, with a single cut point, would be either a positive or negative result) divided by the proportion of target negative with same test result.
Likert Scales	Scales, typically with 3 to 9 possible values, that include extremes of attitudes or feelings (such as from totally disagree to totally agree) that respondents mark to indicate their rating.
Linear Regression	The term used for a regression analysis when the dependent variable or target variable is a continuous variable and the relationship between the dependent variable and independent variable is thought to be linear.

Term	Definition
Local Consensus Process	A strategy for changing clinician behavior. Inclusion of participating clinicians in discussions to create agreement with a suggested approach to change provider practice.
Local Opinion Leaders (or Opinion Leaders)	A strategy for changing clinician behavior. These persons are clinician peers who are recognized by their colleagues as model caregivers or who are viewed as having particular content expertise.
Logical Operators (or Boolean Operators)	See Boolean Operators.
Logistic Regression	A regression analysis in which the dependent variable is binary.
Longitudinal Study (or Cohort Study or Prospective Study)	See Cohort Study.
Lost to Follow-up	Patients whose status on the outcome or endpoint of interest is unknown.
Markov Model (or Multistate Transition Model)	Markov models are tools used in decision analyses. Named after a 19th-century Russian mathematician, Markov models are the basis of software programs that model what might happen to a cohort of patients during a series of cycles (eg, periods of 1 year). The model allows for the possibility that patients might move from one health state to another. For instance, one patient may have a mild stroke in one 3-month cycle, continue with minimal functional limitation for a number of cycles, have a gastrointestinal bleeding episode in a subsequent cycle, and finally experience a major stroke. Ideally, data from randomized trials will determine the probability of moving from one state to another during any cycle under competing management options.
Masked (or Blind or Blinded)	See Blind.
Matching	A deliberate process to make the intervention group and comparison group comparable with respect to factors (or confounders) that are extraneous to the purpose of the investigation but that might interfere with the interpretation of the study's findings. For example, in case-control studies, individual cases may be matched with controls on the basis of comparable age, sex, or other clinical features.
Median Survival	Length of time that half the study population survives.
Medical Subject Headings (MeSH)	The National Library of Medicine's controlled vocabulary used for indexing articles for MEDLINE/PubMed. MeSH terminology provides a consistent way to retrieve information that may use different terminologies for the same concepts.

Term	Definition
Member Checking	In qualitative research, this involves sharing draft study findings with the participants to inquire whether their viewpoints were faithfully interpreted and to ascertain whether the account makes sense to participants.
Meta-analysis	A statistical technique for quantitatively combining the results of multiple studies measuring the same outcome into a single pooled or summary estimate.
Meta-Regression Analysis	When summarizing patient or design characteristics at the individual trial level, meta-analysts risk failing to detect genuine relationships between these characteristics and the size of treatment effect. Further, the risk of obtaining a spurious explanation for variable treatment effects is high when the number of trials is small and many patient and design characteristics differ. Meta-regression techniques can be used to explore whether patient characteristics (eg, younger or older patients) or design characteristics (eg, studies of low or high quality) are related to the size of the treatment effect.
Meta-Synthesis	A procedure for combining qualitative research on a specific topic in which researchers compare and analyze the texts of individual studies and develop new interpretations.
Minimal Important Difference	The smallest difference in a patient-important outcome that patients perceive as beneficial and that would mandate, in the absence of troublesome adverse effects and excessive cost, a change in the patient's health care management.
Mixed-Methods Study	A study that combines data collection approaches, sometimes both qualitative and quantitative, into the study methodology and is commonly used in the study of service delivery and organization. Some mixed-methods studies combine study designs (eg, investigators may embed qualitative or quantitative process evaluations alongside quantitative evaluative designs to increase understanding of factors influencing a phenomenon). Some mixed-methods studies include a single overarching research design but use mixed-methods for data collection (eg, surveys, interviews, observation, and analysis of documentary material).
Model	The term *model* is often used to describe statistical regression analyses involving more than 1 independent variable and 1 dependent variable. This is a multivariable or multiple regression (or multivariate) analysis.
Multifaceted Interventions	Use of multiple strategies to change clinician behavior. Multiple strategies may include a combination that includes 2 or more of the following: audit and feedback, reminders, local consensus processes, patient-mediated interventions, or computer decision support systems.

Term	Definition
Multistate Transition Model	See Markov Model.
Multivariate Regression Analysis (or Multivariable Analysis or Multivariable Regression Equation)	A type of regression that provides a mathematical model that attempts to explain or predict the dependent variable (or outcome variable or target variable) by simultaneously considering 2 or more independent variables (or predictor variables).
n-of-1 Randomized Controlled Trial (or n-of-1 RCT)	An experiment designed to determine the effect of an intervention or exposure on a single study participant. In one n-of-1 design, the patient undergoes pairs of treatment periods organized so that 1 period involves the use of the experimental treatment and 1 period involves the use of an alternate treatment or placebo. The patient and clinician are blinded if possible, and outcomes are monitored. Treatment periods are replicated until the clinician and patient are convinced that the treatments are definitely different or definitely not different.
Narrative Review	A review article (such as a typical book chapter) that is not conducted using methods to minimize bias (in contrast to a systematic review).
Natural History	As distinct from prognosis, natural history refers to the possible consequences and outcomes of a disease or condition and the frequency with which they can be expected to occur when the disease condition is untreated.
Negative Predictive Value (NPV)	See Predictive Value.
Negative Study (or Negative Trial)	Studies in which the authors have concluded that the comparison groups do not differ statistically in the variables of interest. Research results that fail to support the researchers' hypotheses.
Neural Network	The application of nonlinear statistics to pattern-recognition problems. Neural networks can be used to develop clinical prediction rules. The technique identifies those predictors most strongly associated with the outcome of interest that belong in a clinical prediction rule and those that can be omitted from the rule without loss of predictive power.
Nomogram	Graphic scale facilitating calculation of a probability. The most-used nomogram in the EBM world is one developed by Fagan to move from a pretest probability, through a likelihood ratio, to a posttest probability.
Nonadherent	Patients are nonadherent if they are not exposed to the full course of a study intervention (eg, most commonly, they do not take the prescribed dose or duration of a drug or they do not participate fully in the study program).

Term	Definition
Noninferiority Trial (or Equivalence Trial)	Trials that estimate treatment effects that exclude any patient-important superiority of the control intervention under evaluation are noninferiority trials. Noninferiority trials require a previous definition of the smallest difference in outcomes between the interventions that patients would consider large enough in favor of the control group to justify a preference for the control intervention. The confidence interval for the estimated treatment effect at the end of the trial should exclude that difference in favor of the control group for the authors to claim noninferiority (ie, the upper limit of the confidence interval should be closer to zero than the minimal patient important difference). This level of precision requires fewer patients and events than an equivalence trial. Noninferiority trials are helpful when investigators want to see whether a cheaper, safer, simpler intervention is better than or the same (is not worse in terms of efficacy) as what is done currently.
Nonparticipant Observation	See Field Observation.
Null Hypothesis	In the hypothesis-testing framework, this is the starting hypothesis that the statistical test is designed to consider and possibly reject, which contends that there is no relationship between the variables under study.
Null Result	A nonsignificant result; no statistically significant difference between groups.
Number Needed to Harm (NNH)	The number of patients who, if they received the experimental intervention, would lead to 1 additional patient being harmed during a specific period. It is the inverse of the absolute risk increase (ARI), expressed as a percentage (100/ARI).
Number Needed to Screen (NNS)	The number of patients who would need to be screened to prevent 1 adverse event.
Number Needed to Treat (NNT)	The number of patients who need to be treated during a specific period to achieve 1 additional good outcome. When NNT is discussed, it is important to specify the intervention, its duration, and the desirable outcome. It is the inverse of the absolute risk reduction (ARR), expressed as a percentage (100/ARR).
Observational Study (or Observational Study Design)	An observational study can be used to describe many designs that are not randomized trials (eg, cohort studies or case-control studies that have a goal of establishing causation, studies of prognosis, studies of diagnostic tests, and qualitative studies). The term is most often used in the context of cohort studies and case-control studies in which patient or caregiver preference, or happenstance, determines whether a person is exposed to an intervention or putative harmful agent or behavior (in contrast to the exposure's being under the control of the investigator, as in a randomized trial).

Term	Definition
Observer Bias	See Bias.
Odds	The ratio of events to nonevents; the ratio of the number of study participants experiencing the outcome of interest to the number of study participants not experiencing the outcome of interest.
Odds Ratio (OR) (or Relative Odds)	A ratio of the odds of an event in an exposed group to the odds of the same event in a group that is not exposed.
Odds Reduction	The odds reduction expresses, for odds, what relative risk reduction expresses for risks. Just as the relative risk reduction is 1 − relative risk, the odds reduction is 1 − relative odds (the relative odds and odds ratio being synonymous). Thus, if a treatment results in an odds ratio of 0.6 for a particular outcome, the treatment reduces the odds for that outcome by 0.4.
One-Group Pretest-Posttest Design (or Before-After Design)	See Before-After Design.
Open-Ended Questions	Questions that offer no specific structure for the respondents' answers and allow the respondents to answer in their own words.
Opinion Leaders (or Local Opinion Leaders)	See Local Opinion Leaders.
Opportunity Costs	The value of (health or other) benefits forgone in alternative uses when a resource is used.
Outcome Variable (or Dependent Variable or Target Variable)	The target variable of interest. The variable that is hypothesized to depend on or be caused by another variable (the independent variable).
Partial Verification Bias	See Bias.
Participant Observation	See Field Observation.
Patient-Important Outcomes	Outcomes that patients value directly. This is in contrast to surrogate, substitute, or physiologic outcomes that clinicians may consider important. One way of thinking about a patient-important outcome is that, were it to be the only thing that changed, patients would be willing to undergo a treatment with associated risk, cost, or inconvenience. This would be true of treatments that ameliorated symptoms or prevented morbidity or mortality. It would not be true of treatments that lowered blood pressure, improved cardiac output, improved bone density, or the like, without improving the quality or increasing the length of life.
Patient-Mediated Interventions	A strategy for changing clinician behavior. Any intervention aimed at changing the performance of health care professionals through interactions with, or information provided by or to, patients.

Term	Definition
Patient Preferences	The relative value that patients place on various health states. Preferences are determined by values, beliefs, and attitudes that patients bring to bear in considering what they will gain—or lose—as a result of a management decision. Explicit enumeration and balancing of benefits and risks that is central to evidence-based clinical practice brings the underlying value judgments involved in making management decisions into bold relief.
Per-Protocol Analysis	An analysis restricted to patients who adhered to their assigned treatment in a randomized trial (omitting patients who dropped out of the study or for other reasons did not actually receive the planned intervention). This analysis can provide a misleading estimate of effect because all patients randomized are no longer included, raising concerns about whether important unknown factors that influence outcome are equally distributed across comparison groups.
Phase I Studies	Studies often conducted in normal volunteers that investigate a drug's physiologic effect and evaluate whether it manifests unacceptable early toxicity.
Phase II Studies	Initial studies on patients that provide preliminary evidence of possible drug effectiveness.
Phase III Studies	Randomized controlled trials designed to test the magnitude of benefit and harm of a drug.
Phase IV Studies (or Postmarketing Surveillance Studies)	Studies conducted after the effectiveness of a drug has been established and the drug marketed, typically to establish the frequency of uncommon or unanticipated toxic effects.
Phenomenology	In qualitative research, an approach to inquiry that emphasizes the complexity of human experience and the need to understand the experience holistically as it is actually lived.
φ (Or φ Statistic)	A measure of chance-independent agreement.
PICO (or Patient, Intervention, Comparison, Outcome)	A method for answering clinical questions.
Placebo	A biologically inert substance (typically a pill or capsule) that is as similar as possible to the active intervention. Placebos are sometimes given to participants in the control arm of a drug trial to help ensure that the study is blinded.
Placebo Effect	The effect of an intervention independent of its biologic effect.
Point Estimate	The single value that best represents the value of the population parameter.
Pooled Estimate	A statistical summary measure representing the best estimate of a parameter that applies to all the studies that contribute to addressing a similar question (such as a pooled relative risk and 95% confidence intervals from a set of randomized trials).

Term	Definition
Positive Predictive Value (PPV)	See Predictive Value.
Positive Study (or Positive Trial)	A study with results that show a difference that investigators interpret as beyond the play of chance.
Posttest Odds	The odds of the target condition being present after the results of a diagnostic test are available.
Posttest Probability	The probability of the target condition being present after the results of a diagnostic test are available.
Power	The ability of a study to reject a null hypothesis when it is false (and should be rejected). Power is linked to the adequacy of the sample size: if a sample size is too small, the study will have insufficient power to detect differences between groups.
Practice Guidelines (or Clinical Practice Guidelines or Guidelines)	See Clinical Practice Guidelines.
Prediction Rules (or Clinical Prediction Rules)	See Clinical Prediction Rules.
Predictive Value	Two categories: Positive predictive value—the proportion of people with a positive test result who have the disease; negative predictive value—the proportion of people with a negative test result and who are free of disease.
Preferences	See Values and Preferences.
Pretest Odds	The odds of the target condition being present before the results of a diagnostic test are available.
Pretest Probability	The probability of the target condition being present before the results of a diagnostic test are available.
Prevalence	Proportion of persons affected with a particular disease at a specified time. Prevalence rates obtained from high-quality studies can inform pretest probabilities.
Prevent (Prevention)	A preventive maneuver is an action that decreases the risk of a future event or the threatened onset of disease. Primary prevention is designed to stop a condition from developing. Secondary prevention is designed to stop or slow progression of a disease or disorder when patients have a disease and are at risk for developing something related to their current disease. Often, secondary prevention is indistinguishable from treatment. An example of primary prevention is vaccination for pertussis. An example of secondary prevention is administration of an antiosteoporosis intervention to women with low bone density and evidence of a vertebral fracture to prevent subsequent fractures. An example of tertiary prevention is a rehabilitation program for patients experiencing the adverse effects associated with a myocardial infarction.

Term	Definition
Primary Studies	Studies that collect original data. Primary studies are differentiated from synopses that summarize the results of individual primary studies and they are different from systematic reviews that summarize the results of a number of primary studies.
Probability	Quantitative estimate of the likelihood of a condition existing (as in diagnosis) or of subsequent events (such as in an intervention study).
Prognosis	The possible consequences and outcomes of a disease and the frequency with which they can be expected to occur.
Prognostic Factors	Patient or participant characteristics that confer increased or decreased risk of a positive or adverse outcome.
Prognostic Study	A study that enrolls patients at a point in time and follows them forward to determine the frequency and timing of subsequent events.
Prospective Study (or Cohort Study or Longitudinal Study)	See Cohort Study.
Publication Bias	See Bias.
Purposive Sampling (or Purposeful Sampling or Judgmental Sampling)	In qualitative research, a type of nonprobability sampling in which theory or personal judgment guides the selection of study participants. Depending on the topic, examples include maximum variation sampling to document range or diversity; extreme case sampling, in which one selects cases that are opposite in some way; typical or representative case sampling to describe what is common in terms of the phenomenon of interest; critical sampling to make a point dramatically; and criterion sampling, in which all cases that meet some predetermined criteria of importance are studied.
P Value (or P)	The probability that results as extreme as or more extreme than those observed would occur if the null hypothesis were true and the experiment were repeated over and over. $P < .05$ means that there is a less than 1 in 20 probability that, on repeated performance of the experiment, the results as extreme as or more extreme than those observed would occur if the null hypothesis were true.
Qualitative Research	Qualitative research focuses on social and interpreted, rather than quantifiable, phenomena and aims to discover, interpret, and describe rather than to test and evaluate. Qualitative research makes inductive, descriptive inferences to theory concerning social experiences or settings, whereas quantitative research makes causal or correlational inferences to populations. Qualitative research is not a single method but a family of analytic approaches that rely on the description and interpretation of qualitative data. Specific methods include, for example, grounded theory, ethnography, phenomenology, case study, critical theory, and historiography.

Term	Definition
Quality-Adjusted Life-Year (QALY)	A unit of measure for survival that accounts for the effects of suboptimal health status and the resulting limitations in quality of life. For example, if a patient lives for 10 years and his or her quality of life is decreased by 50% because of chronic lung disease, survival would be equivalent to 5 QALYs.
Quality Improvement	An approach to defining, measuring, improving, and controlling practices to maintain or improve the appropriateness of health care services.
Quality of Care	The extent to which health care meets technical and humanistic standards of optimal care.
Quantitative Research	The investigation of phenomena that lend themselves to test well-specified hypotheses through precise measurement and quantification of predetermined variables that yield numbers suitable for statistical analysis.
Random	Governed by a formal chance process in which the occurrence of previous events is of no value in predicting future events. For example, the probability of assigning a participant to one of 2 specified groups is 50%.
Random Allocation (or Randomization)	See Randomization.
Random-Effects Model	A model used to give a summary estimate of the magnitude of effect in a meta-analysis that assumes that the studies included are a random sample of a population of studies addressing the question posed in the meta-analysis. Each study estimates a different underlying true effect, and the distribution of these effects is assumed to be normal around a mean value. Because a random-effects model takes into account both within-study and between-study variability, the confidence interval around the point estimate is, when there is appreciable variability in results across studies, wider than it could be if a fixed-effects model were used.
Random Error (or Chance)	We can never know with certainty the true value of an intervention effect because of random error. It is inherent in all measurement. The observations that are made in a study are only a sample of all possible observations that could be made from the population of relevant patients. Thus, the average value of any sample of observations is subject to some variation from the true value for that entire population. When the level of random error associated with a measurement is high, the measurement is less precise and we are less certain about the value of that measurement.
Randomization (or Random Allocation)	Allocation of participants to groups by chance, usually done with the aid of a table of random numbers. Not to be confused with systematic allocation or quasi-randomization (eg, on even and odd days of the month) or other allocation methods at the discretion of the investigator.

Term	Definition
Randomized Controlled Trial (RCT) (or Randomized Trial)	Experiment in which individuals are randomly allocated to receive or not receive an experimental diagnostic, preventive, therapeutic, or palliative procedure and then followed to determine the effect of the intervention.
Randomized Trial (or Randomized Controlled Trial)	See Randomized Controlled Trial.
Random Sample	A sample derived by selecting sampling units (eg, individual patients) such that each unit has an independent and fixed (generally equal) chance of selection. Whether a given unit is selected is determined by chance; for example, by a table of randomly ordered numbers.
Recall Bias	See Bias.
Receiver Operating Characteristic Curve (or ROC Curve)	A figure depicting the power of a diagnostic test. The ROC curve presents the test's true-positive rate (ie, sensitivity) on the horizontal axis and the false-positive rate (ie, 1 – specificity) on the vertical axis for different cut points dividing a positive from a negative test. An ROC curve for a perfect test has an area under the curve of 1.0, whereas a test that performs no better than chance has an area under the curve of only 0.5.
Recursive Partitioning Analysis	A technique for determining the optimal way of using a set of predictor variables to estimate the likelihood of an individual's experiencing a particular outcome. The technique repeatedly divides the population (eg, old vs young; among young and old) according to status on variables that discriminate between those who will have the outcome of interest and those who will not.
Reference Standard (or Gold Standard or Criterion Standard)	See Criterion Standard.
Referral Bias	See Bias.
Reflexivity	In qualitative research using field observation, whichever of the 3 approaches used, the observer will always have some effect on what is being observed, small or large. This interaction of the observer with what is observed is called reflexivity. Whether it plays a positive or negative role in accessing social truths, the researcher must acknowledge and investigate reflexivity and account for it in data interpretation.
Regression (or Regression Analysis)	A technique that uses predictor or independent variables to build a statistical model that predicts an individual patient's status with respect to a dependent variable or target variable.

Term	Definition
Relative Diagnostic Odds Ratio	The diagnostic odds ratio is a single value that provides one way of representing the power of the diagnostic test. It is applicable when we have a single cut point for a test and classify tests results as positive and negative. The diagnostic odds ratio is calculated as the product of the true positive and true negative divided by the product of the false positives and false negatives. The relative diagnostic odds ratio is the ratio of one diagnostic odds ratio to another.
Relative Odds	See Odds Ratio. Just as relative risk and risk ratio are synonymous, relative odds and odds ratio are synonymous.
Relative Risk (RR) (or Risk Ratio)	Ratio of the risk of an event among an exposed population to the risk among the unexposed.
Relative Risk Increase (RRI)	The proportional increase in risk of harmful outcomes between experimental and control participants. It is calculated by dividing the risk of a harmful outcome in the experimental group (experimental group risk, or EGR) minus the risk of a harmful outcome in the control group (control group risk, or CGR) by the risk of a harmful outcome in the control group ([EGR − CGR]/ CGR). Typically used with a harmful exposure.
Relative Risk Reduction (RRR)	The proportional reduction in risk of harmful outcomes between experimental and control participants. It is calculated by dividing the risk of harmful outcome in the control group (control group risk, or CGR) minus the risk of a harmful outcome in the experimental group (experimental group risk, or EGR) by the risk of a harmful outcome in the control group ([CGR − EGR]/ CGR). Used with a beneficial exposure or intervention. See also relative risk; risk; treatment effect.
Reliability	Reliability is used as a technical statistical term that refers to a measurement instrument's ability to differentiate between subjects, patients, or participants in some underlying trait. Reliability increases as the variability between subjects increases and decreases as the variability within subjects (over time, or over raters) increases. Reliability is typically expressed as an intraclass correlation coefficient with between-subject variability in the numerator and total variability (between-subject and within-subject) in the denominator.
Reminding (or Reminders or Reminder Systems)	A strategy for changing clinician behavior. Manual or computerized reminders to prompt behavior change.
Reporting Bias (or Selective Outcome Reporting Bias)	See Bias.
Residual Confounding	Unknown, unmeasured, or suboptimally measured prognostic factors that remain unbalanced between groups after full covariable adjustment by statistical techniques. The remaining imbalance will lead to a biased assessment of the effect of any putatively causal exposure.

Term	Definition
Responsiveness	The sensitivity or ability of an instrument to detect change over time.
Review	A general term for articles that summarize the results of more than 1 primary study. See also Systematic Review.
Risk	A measure of the association between exposure and outcome (including incidence, adverse effects, or toxicity).
Risk Factors	Risk factors are patient characteristics associated with the development of a disease in the first place. Prognostic factors are patient characteristics that confer increased or decreased risk of a positive or adverse outcome from a given disease.
Risk Ratio (or Relative Risk)	See Relative Risk.
Screening	Services designed to detect people at high risk of experiencing a condition associated with a modifiable adverse outcome, offered to persons who have neither symptoms of nor risk factors for a target condition.
Secondary Journal	A secondary journal does not publish original research but rather includes synopses of published research studies that meet prespecified criteria of both clinical relevance and methodologic quality.
Secular Trends	Changes in the probability of events with time, independent of known predictors of outcome.
Semistructured Interview	In qualitative research, the interviewer asks a number of specific questions, but additional questions or probes are used at the discretion of the interviewer.
Sensitivity	The proportion of people with a positive test result among those with the target condition.
Sensitivity Analysis	Any test of the stability of the conclusions of a health care evaluation over a range of probability estimates, value judgments, and assumptions about the structure of the decisions to be made. This may involve the repeated evaluation of a decision model in which one or more of the parameters of interest are varied.
Sentinel Effect	The tendency for human performance to improve when participants are aware that their behavior is being evaluated; in contrast to the Hawthorne effect, which refers to behavior change as a result of being observed but not evaluated.
Sequential Sample (or Consecutive Sample)	See Consecutive Sample.
Sign	Any abnormality indicative of disease, discoverable by the clinician at an examination of the patient. It is an objective aspect of a disease.

Term	Definition
Signal-to-Noise Ratio	Signal refers to the target of the measurement; noise, to random error that obscures the signal. When one is trying to discriminate among people at a single point in time (who is better off, who is worse off) the signal comes from differences in scores between patients. The noise comes from variability or differences in score within patients over time. The greater the noise, the more difficult it is to detect the signal. When one is trying to evaluate change over time, the signal comes from the difference in scores in patients whose status has improved or deteriorated. The noise comes from the variability in scores in patients whose status has not changed.
Sign Test	A nonparametric test for comparing 2 paired groups according to the relative ranking of values between the pairs.
Silo Effect	One of the main reasons for considering narrower viewpoints in conducting an economic analysis is to assess the effect of change on the main budget holders because budgets may need to be adjusted before a new intervention can be adopted (the silo effect).
Simple Regression (or Univariate Regression)	See Univariable Regression.
Social Desirability Bias	See Bias.
Specificity	The proportion of people who are truly free of a designated disorder who are so identified by the test. The test may consist of, or include, clinical observations.
Spectrum Bias	See Bias.
Stakeholder Analysis	A strategy that seeks to increase understanding of stakeholder behavior, plans, relationships, and interests and seeks to generate information about stakeholders' levels of influence, support, and resources.
Standard Error	The standard deviation of an estimate of a population parameter. The standard error of the mean is the standard deviation of the estimate of the population mean value.
Standard Gamble	A direct preference or utility measure that effectively asks respondents to rate their quality of life on a scale from 0 to 1.0, where 0 is death and 1.0 is full health. Respondents choose between a specified time x in their current health state and a gamble in which they have probability P (anywhere from 0 to .99) of full health for time x, and a probability $1 - P$ of immediate death.
Statistical Significance	A term indicating that the results obtained in an analysis of study data are unlikely to have occurred by chance and the null hypothesis is rejected. When statistically significant, the probability of the observed results, given the null hypothesis, falls below a specified level of probability (most often $P < .05$).

Term	Definition
Stopped Early Trials (Truncated Trials)	Truncated randomized controlled trials (RCTs) are trials stopped early because of apparent harm because the investigators have concluded that they will not be able to demonstrate a treatment effect (futility), or because of apparent benefit. Believing the treatment from RCTs stopped early for benefit will be misleading if the decision to stop the trial resulted from catching the apparent benefit of treatment at a random high.
Stopping Rules	These are methodologic and statistical guides that inform decisions to stop trials early. They can incorporate issues such as the planned sample size, planned and conducted interim analyses, presence and type of data monitoring including independent research oversight, statistical boundaries, and statistical adjustments for interim analyses and stopping.
Structured Abstract	A brief summary of the key elements of an article following pre-specified headings. For example, the *ACP Journal Club* therapy abstracts include major headings of question, methods, setting, patients, intervention, main results, and conclusion. More highly structured abstracts include sub-headings. For example, *ACP Journal Club* therapy abstracts methods sections include design, allocation, blinding, and follow-up period.
Subgroup Analysis	The separate analysis of data for subgroups of patients, such as those at different stages of their illness, those with different comorbid conditions, or those of different ages.
Substitute Outcomes or Endpoints (or Surrogate Outcomes or Endpoints)	See Surrogate Endpoints.
Surrogate Outcomes or Endpoints (or Substitute Outcomes or Endpoints)	Outcomes that are not in themselves important to patients but are associated with outcomes that are important to patients (eg, bone density for fracture, cholesterol for myocardial infarction, and blood pressure for stroke). These outcomes would not influence patient behavior if they were the only outcomes that would change with an intervention.
Surveillance Bias	See Bias.
Survey	Observational study that focuses on obtaining information about activities, beliefs, preferences, knowledge, or attitudes from respondents through interviewer-administered or self-administered methods.
Survival Analysis	A statistical procedure used to compare the proportion of patients in each group who experience an outcome or endpoint at various intervals throughout the duration of the study (eg, death).
Survival Curve (or Kaplan-Meier Curve)	A curve that starts at 100% of the study population and shows the percentage of the population still surviving (or free of disease or some other outcome) at successive times for as long as information is available.

Term	Definition
Symptom	Any phenomenon or departure from the normal in function, appearance, or sensation reported by the patient and suggestive or indicative of disease.
Syndrome	A collection of signs or symptoms or physiologic abnormalities.
Synopsis	Brief summary that encapsulates the key methodologic details and results of a single study or systematic review.
Systematic Error (or Bias)	See Bias.
Systematic Review	The identification, selection, appraisal, and summary of primary studies addressing a focused clinical question using methods to reduce the likelihood of bias.
Systems	Systems include practice guidelines, clinical pathways, or evidence-based textbook summaries that integrate evidence-based information about specific clinical problems and provide regular updates to guide the care of individual patients.
Target Condition	In diagnostic test studies, the condition the investigators or clinicians are particularly interested in identifying (such as tuberculosis, lung cancer, or iron-deficiency anemia).
Target Outcome (or Target Endpoints or Target Events)	In intervention studies, the condition the investigators or clinicians are particularly interested in identifying and in which it is anticipated the intervention will decrease (such as myocardial infarction, stroke, or death) or increase (such as ulcer healing).
Target-Negative	In diagnostic test studies, patients who do not have the target condition.
Target-Positive	In diagnostic test studies, patients who have the target condition.
Target Variable (or Dependent Variable or Outcome Variable)	See Dependent Variable.
Test Threshold (or No-Test Test Threshold)	The probability below which the clinician decides a diagnosis warrants no further consideration.
Theoretical Saturation	In qualitative research, this is the point in the analysis at which themes are well organized into a coherent theory or conceptual framework. This is considered an appropriate stopping point for data analysis, especially in grounded theory methods.
Theory	Theory consists of concepts and their relationships.
Theory Triangulation	See Triangulation.
Threshold NNT (or Threshold NNH)	Maximum number needed to treat (NNT) or number needed to harm (NNH) accepted as justifying the benefits and harms of therapy.

Term	Definition
Time Series Design (or Interrupted Time Series Design)	In this study design, data are collected at several points both before and after the intervention. Data collected before the intervention allow the underlying trend and cyclical (seasonal) effects to be estimated. Data collected after the intervention allow the intervention effect to be estimated while accounting for underlying secular trends. The time series design monitors the occurrence of outcomes or end points during a number of cycles and determines whether the pattern changes coincident with the intervention.
Treatment Effect (or Intervention Effect)	The results of comparative clinical studies can be expressed using various intervention effect measures. Examples are absolute risk reduction (ARR), relative risk reduction (RRR), odds ratio (OR), number needed to treat (NNT), and effect size. The appropriateness of using these to express an intervention effect and whether probabilities, means, or medians are used to calculate them depend on the type of outcome variable used to measure health outcomes. For example, ARR, RRR, and NNT are used for dichotomous variables, and effect sizes are normally used for continuous variables.
Treatment Target	The manifestation of illness (a symptom, sign, or physiologic abnormality) toward which a treatment is directed.
Treatment Threshold (or Therapeutic Threshold)	Probability above which a clinician would consider a diagnosis confirmed and would stop testing and initiate treatment.
Trial of Therapy	In a trial of therapy, the physician offers the patient an intervention, reviews the effect of the intervention on that patient at some subsequent time, and, depending on the effect, recommends either continuation or discontinuation of the intervention.
Triangulation	In qualitative research, an analytic approach in which key findings are corroborated using multiple sources of information. There are different types of triangulation. Investigator triangulation requires more than 1 investigator to collect and analyze the raw data, such that the findings emerge through consensus among a team of investigators. Theory triangulation is a process whereby emergent findings are corroborated with existing social science theories.
Trim-and-Fill Method	When publication bias is suspected in a systematic review, investigators may attempt to estimate the true intervention effect by removing, or trimming, small positive-result studies that do not have a negative-result study counterpart and then calculating a supposed true effect from the resulting symmetric funnel plot. The investigators then replace the positive-result studies they have removed and add hypothetical studies that mirror these positive-result studies to create a symmetric funnel plot that retains the new pooled effect estimate. This method allows the calculation of an adjusted confidence interval and an estimate of the number of missing trials.

Term	Definition
True Negative	Those whom the test correctly identifies as not having the target disorder.
True Positive	Those whom the test correctly identifies as having the target disorder.
Truncated Trials (Stopped Early Trials)	See Stopped Early Trials.
Trustworthiness (or Credibility)	See Credibility.
t Test	A parametric statistical test that examines the difference between the means of 2 groups of values.
Type I Error	An error created by rejecting the null hypothesis when it is true (ie, investigators conclude that a relationship exists between variables when it does not).
Type II Error	An error created by accepting the null hypothesis when it is false (ie, investigators conclude that no relationship exists between variables when, in fact, a relationship does exist).
Unblinded (or Unmasked)	Patients, clinicians, those monitoring outcomes, judicial assessors of outcomes, data analysts, and manuscript authors are aware of whether patients have been assigned to the experimental or control group.
Unit of Allocation	The unit or focus used for assignment to comparison groups (eg, individuals or clusters such as schools, health care teams, hospital wards, outpatient practices).
Unit of Analysis	The unit or focus of the analysis; although it is most often the individual study participant, in a study that uses cluster allocation, the unit of analysis is the cluster (eg, school, clinic).
Unit of Analysis Error	When investigators use any sort of cluster randomization (randomize by physician instead of patient, practice instead of physician or patient, or village instead of participant) and analyze as if they have randomized according to patient or participant, they have made a unit of analysis error. The appropriate analysis acknowledges the cluster randomization and takes into account the extent to which outcomes differ between clusters independent of treatment effect.
Univariate Regression (or Univariable Regression or Simple Regression)	Regression when there is only 1 independent variable under evaluation with respect to a dependent variable.
Unmasked (or Unblinded)	See Unblinded.
Up-Front Costs	Costs incurred to "produce" the treatment such as the physician's time, nurse's time, and materials.
Utilitarian (or Consequentialist)	See Consequentialist.

Term	Definition
Utilization Review	An organized procedure to review admissions; duration of stay; and professional, pharmacologic, or programmatic services provided and to evaluate the need for those services and promote their most efficient use.
Validity (or Credibility)	In health status measurement terms, validity is the extent to which an instrument measures what it is intended to measure. In critical appraisal terms, validity reflects the extent to which the study results are likely to be subject to systematic error and thus be more or less likely to reflect the truth. See also Credibility.
Values and Preferences	When used generically, as in "values and preferences," we refer to the collection of goals, expectations, predispositions, and beliefs that individuals have for certain decisions and their potential outcomes. The incorporation of patient values and preferences in decision making is central to evidence-based medicine. These terms also carry specific meaning in other settings. Measurement tools that require a choice under conditions of uncertainty to indirectly measure preference for an outcome in health economics (such as the standard gamble) quantify preferences. Measurement tools that evaluate the outcome on a scale with defined favorable and unfavorable ends (eg, visual analog scales, feeling thermometers) quantify values.
Variance	The technical term for the statistical estimate of the variability in results.
Verification Bias	See Differential Verification Bias.
Visual Analogue Scale	A scaling procedure consisting of a straight line anchored on each end with words or phrases that represent the extremes of some phenomenon (eg, "worst pain I have ever had" to "absolutely no pain"). Respondents are asked to make a mark on the line at the point that corresponds to their experience of the phenomenon.
Washout Period	In a crossover or n-of-1 trial, the period required for the treatment to cease to act once it has been discontinued.
Working Diagnosis (or Leading Hypothesis)	The clinician's single best explanation for the patient's clinical problem(s).
Workup Bias	See Differential Verification Bias.

INDEX

A

Abdominal aortic aneurysm (AAA),
452-453
Abdominojugular reflux, 422
Absolute risk reduction (ARR), 76,
88-89, 105, 202, 292, 669
vs RR, 90-91
Accreditation Council for Graduate
Medical Education
(ACGME), 763
ACE inhibitors
(See Angiotensin-converting enzyme
inhibitors)
Acetaminophen, 408
Acetylsalicylic acid (ASA), 684
ACGME
(See Accreditation Council for Gradu-
ate Medical Education)
Acid reflux, 404
ACP Journal Club, 34, 40, 68, 304-305,
524
Acquired brain injury, 513, 514
Acute airflow limitation, 456, 458-459
Acute appendicitis, 453, 454
Acute cholecystitis, 453, 455-456
Acute coronary syndrome, 404, 497
Acute diarrhea, 416
Acute dyspnea, 441, 443
Acute myeloid leukemia
Chemotherapy for, 155, 156
Acute myocardial infarction, 453, 456,
457-458
Acute pulmonary embolism, 471,
472-474
Acute respiratory distress syndrome,
234
Acute rhinosinusitis, 307
Acyclovir, 13

Adherence in patients, 75
Nonadherence, 75
Adopting new interventions
Caution in, 311
Adverse drug reactions, 342
AGA
(See American Gastroenterological
Association)
Age, 278-279
Agency for Healthcare Policy and
Research
(See US Agency for Healthcare
Research and Quality)
Aggressive therapy, 511
AIDS, 326
AIDS-related morbidity and mortality,
326
Albumin, 303-304
Albuminuria, 318
Alcohol abuse, 456, 459
Alendronate, 557, 558, 585
American Endocrine Society, 680
American Gastroenterological Associa-
tion (AGA), 664-665, 668,
670
American Heart Association, 572
American Thoracic Society, 680
Amitriptyline, 187, 306
Amlodipine
vs Irbesartan in Diabetic Nephropathy
Trial, 244
Anchor-based methods, 262-263
Angiotensin-converting enzyme (ACE)
inhibitors, 100, 103-104,
238, 305, 306, 308, 319, 328,
330-331, 705
ACE inhibitor–based vs
diuretic-based antihyperten-
sive therapy, 584, 585
Heart failure, patients with, 325

B

C

N

Q

R

S

W

X

Y

Z